# Doing Business in West Africa 2009-2010

## Comparative & In-Depth Macro-economic Analyses of 48 Sub-Saharan Africa Economies during the Past Ten Years with Particular Focus on West Africa

By

Tony Okoromadu

:Graffiti:

Published by Graffiti Media 2010

Graffiti Media
United Kingdom

frontdesk@graffiticoncept.com
www.graffiticoncept.com



ISBN 978-0-9564526-0-3

Printed in Great Britain by Lightning Source Ltd., Pitfield, Milton Keynes



The purpose of the book is to provide critical information for corporations, governments, organisations and persons with business, development or other pertinent interest in Africa. It is not a substitute for sound advice and necessary due diligence as each case may warrant. Its publishers and author may not be held responsible for decisions made on the basis of its contents. These contents should serve for reference only, and they will be found immensely useful in obtaining a picture and idea of the economic trends in Sub-Saharan Africa. What the book does is provide a map of the terrain, but the user decides how to navigate it.

All the information and data applied in the book are available in the public domain, and acknowledgement of source has been made at every turn.

The accuracy of the data and analyses in this work cannot be guaranteed, even though they have been arrived at with rigour, and intense stress tests have been applied for checks and balances. As such, neither Graffiti Media nor Tony Okoromadu may be held liable for decisions or actions taken in reliance on the information in this document.

Queries and observations may be sent by email to: frontdesk@graffiticoncept.com.

With thanks:

A number of persons have helped on this project, with their suggestions, support and encouragement. They are not all mentioned individually here, but only so that I might avoid the risk of inadvertently leaving someone out. Close friends have been of almost indispensable help, and I will be forever grateful to them. We must mention one in particular though, Gbenro Adegbola, who was frequently there with a word and support, from the project's inception to its completion. As well as David White, Lynda Chalker and Pascal G Dozie, who came in at critical moments and actually never refused me their help and advice. The people at the Netherhall Educational Association were a constant source of encouragement and energy. And everyone at Africa Matters was graciously ever ready whenever I knocked on their door: thank you, Roger Martin and Beccy Stendall, and the staff there whom I never met, but whose efficiency I am testimony to. I must mention our bank, HSBC, and its indefatigable staff at our branch, whom I - alas - may not identify more closely, for understandable reasons. They didn't realise just how much morale-boosting support they gave me through their cheerfully-rendered services.

That said, standing tall at the top of that list of silent collaborators are my very loving family, blood and adopted, who never wavered in their optimism and confidence in my work: mum and late dad; Chinyere, Michael & Funmi, Jenny & Winston, and Chioma; Ike, Ngozi and Afam. I should also say a big thank you to Uncle Chris and Aunt Chizo. Oh, and I musn't leave out Ella, Nneka, Tony Jr. and Tianna: the most delightful nephew and nieces you could ever have. God bless and keep you all.

# Contents

Contents *iii*
Indicators & Sources *vi*
Foreword *ix*

**Introduction** *1*

**Part I: Continent Overview** *5*

**1. Sub-Saharan Africa, Its Regions, Its Countries** *7*

1.1 Sub-Saharan Africa *8*
1.2 Central Africa *10*
1.3 East Africa *11*
1.4 Southern Africa & Sudan *12*
1.5 West Africa *13*

**2. Size, Populations, Ages, Economic Vigour** *15*

2.1a Land Mass of the Regions *16*
2.1b Land Mass in SSA: Top 10 *17*
2.2a Population of the Regions *18*
2.2b Share of Population in SSA: Top 10 *19*
2.3a Population Age Profiles of the Regions: %s *20*
2.3b Population Age Profiles of the Regions: numbers *21*
2.4a Population Age Density of the Regions *22*
2.4b Population Density in the Countries: Top 10 *23*
2.5a Urban Population in the Regions: % and numbers *24*
2.5b Urban Population in SSA: %. Top 10 *25*
2.6a Rural Population in the Regions: % and numbers *26*
2.6b Rural Population in SSA: %. Top 10 *27*
2.7 GDP in Sub-Saharan Africa's Regions ($PPP) *28*

**3. The Size of Foreign Direct Investment** *29*

3.1 FDI Outcome in the World's Development Groups *30*
3.2 FDI Outcome in the Developing Economies *31*
3.3 FDI Outcome in the 5 Continents *32*
3.4 FDI Outcome in Sub-Saharan Africa *33*
3.5 Share of FDI & Share of Population in S.S. Africa *34*
3.6 Share of FDI & Share of Population in West Africa *35*

**4. Tricky Relations** *37*

4.1 Tricky Relations: Foreign Aid & Quality of Life *38*
4.2 Tricky Relations: Foreign Aid & Economic Growth *40*
4.3 Tricky Relations: Foreign Aid & Child Mortality *42*
4.4 Tricky Relations: Foreign Aid & Life Expectancy *44*
4.5 Tricky Relations: Foreign Aid & Emigration *46*
4.6 Tricky Relations: Economic Growth & Qlty of life *48*
4.7 Tricky Relations: Population & Economic Growth *50*

**Part II: The Analyses** *53*

**1. West Africa & Its Countries** *55*

Prelims *57*
Charts *58*
Tables *59*
1.1 Land Mass: The Large 5 *60*
1.2 Population: The Swarming 5 *61*
1.3 Population Age Profiles: 2005-2010 *62*
1.4 Population Density: 2005-2010 *64*
1.5 Urban Population: 2005-2010 *66*
1.6 Rural Population: 2005-2010 *67*
1.7 GDP: The Top 5 *68*
1.8 Economic Vigour *69*
1.9 Female % of the Labour Force *70*
Leaders & Stragglers *71*

**2. Quality of Life** *73*

Prelims *75*
Charts *76*
Tables *77*
2.1 Human Development Ranking *78*
2.2 Life Expectancy *82*
2.3 Child Mortality (Under-5 year olds) *84*
2.4 Babies Immunization: Measles *86*
2.5 Babies Immunization: Tuberculosis *88*
2.6 Population with Access to Safe Water *90*
2.7 Population with Access to Sanitation *91*
2.8 Phones per Population (Fixed & Mobiles) *92*
2.9 Number of Mobile Phone Users *94*
2.10 Literacy *95*
2.11 Number of Internet Users *96*
2.12 Personal Computers per Population *98*
2.13 Net Migration *100*
Leaders & Stragglers *101*
Wrap-up: Quality of Life *103*

**3. Economic Strength** *105*

Prelims *107*
Charts *110*
Tables *111*
3.1 Nigeria GDP in Sub-Saharan Africa ($PPP) *112*
3.2 Nigeria GDP in West Africa ($PPP) *113*

## Contents


3.3 GDP per Person ($PPP) 114
3.4 Growth in GDP per Person 116
3.5 GNI per Person ($PPP) 118
3.6 Growth in GNI per Person 120
3.7 Real GDP Growth 122
3.8 Real Non-Oil GDP Growth 124
3.9 Inflation 126
3.10 Movement of Consumer Prices 128
3.11 Exchange Rate Stability 130
Leaders & Stragglers 132
Wrap-up: Economic Strength 133

**4. Economic Productivity 135**

Prelims 137
Charts 141
Tables 143
4.1 Country "Productivity Index" 144
4.2 Country Economy "Development Status" 148
4.3 Productivity in Agriculture as % of GDP 150
4.4 Productivity in Agriculture as $PPP per Person 152
4.5 Growth in Agriculture Productivity 154
4.6 Productivity in Industry as % of GDP 156
4.7 Productivity in Industry as $PPP per Person 158
4.8 Growth in Industry Productivity 160
4.9 *Manufacturing* and *Other Industry* Productivity 162
4.10 Growth in *Man.* and *Other Industry* Productivity 164
4.11 Build-up in *Man.* and *Other Industry* Productivity 166
4.12 Productivity in Services as % of GDP 168
4.13 Productivity in Services as $PPP per Person 170
4.14 Growth in Services Productivity 172
4.15 Build-up in Productivity in the 3 Sectors 174
Leaders & Stragglers 176
Wrap-up: Economic Productivity 177

**5. Govt. Earnings & Spending 179**

Prelims 181
Charts 183
Tables 184
5.1 Fiscal Deficit & Surplus as % of GDP 186
5.2 Fiscal Deficit & Surplus per Person ($PPP) 188
5.3 Govt. Earnings as % of GDP 190
5.4 Govt. Earnings per Person ($PPP) 192
5.5 Govt. Earnings & Spending as % of GDP 194
5.6 Govt. Earnings & Spending per Person ($PPP) 195
5.7 Growth in Govt. Earnings per Person 196
5.8 Build-up in Govt. Earnings & Spending 198
5.9 Current Account Balance as % of GDP 200
5.10 Debt Service as % of GNI 202
5.11 Build-up in Debt Service and GNI 204
Leaders & Stragglers 205
Wrap-up: Govt. Earnings & Spending 207

**6. Spending on Health 209**

Prelims 211
Charts 212
Tables 213
6.1 Total Spending (Govt. & Private) on Health as % of GDP 214
6.2 Total Spending (Govt. & Private) on Health per Person, $PPP 216
6.3 Build-up of Govt. & Private Spending on Health 219
6.4 Govt. Spending on Health as % of Total Govt. Spending 220
6.5 Out-of-Pocket Spending on Health as % of Total Health Spending 222
6.6 Out-of-Pocket Spending on Health as Part of Total Spending on Health per Person, $PPP 224
6.7 Out-of-Pocket as % of Private Spending on Health 226
6.8 *Out-of-Pocket & Other Private* Spending on Health per Person 228
6.9 *Out-of-Pocket*, *Other Private* and *Govt.* Portions of Total Spending on Health per Person 230
Leaders & Stragglers 232
Wrap-up: Spending on Health 233

**7. Purchasing Power 235**

Prelims 237
Charts 238
Tables 239
7.1 Government Consumption as % of GDP 240
7.2 Household Consumption as % of GDP 241
7.3 Government Consumption per Person ($PPP) 242
7.4 Household Consumption per Person ($PPP) 243
7.5 Consumption from 1999 to 2007 244
7.6 Growth in Government Consumption per Person 246
7.7 Growth in Household Consumption per Person 247
7.8 Build-up of Consumption from 1999 to 2007 248
Leaders & Stragglers 249
Wrap-up: Purchasing Power 251

**8. Self-Reliance 253**

Prelims 255
Charts 257
Tables 258
8.1 Exports & Imports of Goods & Services 260
8.2 Growth in Goods Exports and Imports 264
8.3 Growth in services Exports and Imports 266
8.4 Imports Dependence in Merchandise 268
8.5 Imports Dependence in Services 270
8.6 Composition of Goods Exports and Imports 272
8.7 Foreign Reserves (months of imports) 274
8.8 Foreign Debt (as % of GDP) 276
8.9 Foreign Debt (as $PPP per Person) 278

## Contents


8.10 Service of Foreign Debt (as % of exports) 280
8.11 Growth of Income & Growth of Debt 282
8.12 Aid Dependency (as % of GDP) 284
8.13 Aid Dependency (as $PPP per person) 286
Leaders & Stragglers 288
Wrap-up: Self-Reliance 289

**9. Investor Confidence 291**

Prelims 293
Charts 294
Tables 295
9.1 FDI as % of GDP 296
9.2 FDI per Person 298
9.3 Growth in FDI per Person 300
9.4 FDI as % of Total Capital Investment 302
9.5 Total Capital Investment as % of GDP 304
9.6 Total Capital Investment per Person 306
9.7 Growth in Total Capital Investment per Person 308
9.8 Private Component of TCI as % of GDP 310
9.9 Private Component of TCI as Investment per Person 312
9.10 Growth of Private (& Public) Component of TCI 314
9.11 Domestic Credit to the Private Sector as % of GDP 316
9.12 Domestic Credit to the Private Sector in $PPP 318
9.13 Growth in Domestic Credit to the Private Sector 320
Leaders & Stragglers 322
Wrap-up: Investor Confidence 323

**10. Regulatory Environment 325**

Prelims 327
Charts 329
Tables 330
10.1 Ease of Starting a Business: Rank 332
10.2 Ease of Dealing with Construction Permits: Rank 334
10.3 Ease of Employing Workers: Rank 336
10.4 Ease of Registering Property: Rank 339
10.5 Ease of Getting Credit: Rank 342
10.6 Extent of Investor Protection: Rank 343
10.7 Ease of Paying Taxes: Rank 346
10.8 Ease of External Trade: Rank 350
10.9 Ease of Enforcing Contracts: Rank 354
10.10 Ease of Closing a Business: Rank 357
10.11 Ease of Doing Business: Rank 359
Leaders & Stragglers 360
Wrap-up: Regulatory Environment 361

**11. Business Friendliness 363**

Prelims 365
Charts 367
Tables 368
11.1 Index of Economic Freedoms: Rank 369
11.2 Personal Income Tax Rate: 2008 372
11.3 Corporate Tax Rate: 2008 373
11.4 Voice and Accountability: Rank 374
11.5 Political Stability: Rank 376
11.6 Government Effectiveness: Rank 378
11.7 Regulatory Quality: Rank 380
11.8 Rule of Law: Rank 382
11.9 Control of Corruption: Rank 384
Leaders & Stragglers 386
Wrap-up: Business Friendliness 387

**12. The Final Ratings 389**

Prelims 391
Tables 392
12.1 Dba Ranking by Rank 393
12.2 Dba Ranking by Rating 394
12.3 Dba Ranking by Country 395
12.4 Dba Ranking by Sub-Region 396

**Part III: Appendices 397**

**A. Dba Index & Rankings & Ratings 399**

A1 Dba 401

**B. performance tables 403**

B1 performance tables - region overview 405
B2 performance tables - quality of life 408
B3 performance tables - economic strength 411
B4 performance tables - economic productivity 416
B5 performance tables - govt. earnings & spending 423
B6 performance tables - spending on health 428
B7 performance tables - purchasing power 432
B8 performance tables - self-reliance 435
B9 performance tables - investor confidence 447
B10 performance tables - regulatory environment 454
B11 performance tables - business friendliness 459
B12 performance tables - the final (end-chapter) ratings 463

# Indicators & Sources

## 1. West Africa & its Countries

Land mass
Population
Population age profile: percentages
Population age profiles: numbers
Population density
Urban population: percentages
Urban population: numbers
Urban population: growth rates
Rural population: percentages
Rural population: numbers
Rural population: growth rates
GDP, $PPP
Productivity index
Population: % of Sub-Saharan Africa
GDP: % of Sub-Saharan GDP
Female % of labour force

## 2. Quality of Life

Human development ranking
Life expectancy
Under-5 child mortality
% of 1-yr olds immunized against measles
% of 1-yr olds immunized against tuberculosis
% of Population with access to safe water
% of Population with access to sanitation
Phones per population (fixed & mobiles)
Mobile phones per population
Total adult literacy rate
Number of internet users
Personal computers per population
Net migration

## 3. Economic Strength

GDP contribution of Nigeria in Sub-Saharan Africa
GDP contribution of Nigeria in West Africa
GDP per person, $PPP
Growth in GDP per person
GNI per person, $PPP
Growth in GNI per person
Real GDP growth
Real non-oil GDP growth
Inflation
Movement of consumer prices
Exchange rate stability
Movement of real exchange rate

## 4. Economic Productivity

Country "productivity index"
Country economy "development status": GDP breakdown into the 3 sectors
Productivity in agriculture as % of GDP
Productivity in agriculture as $PPP per person
Growth in agriculture productivity
Productivity in industry as % of GDP
Productivity in industry as $PPP per person
Growth in industry productivity
Productivity in industry as $US per person
Breakdown of industry productivity into manufacturing and other industry productivity: %
Growth in $US industry productivity
Growth in $US manufacturing productivity
Growth in $US other industry productivity
Build-up of manufacturing productivity
Build-up of other industry productivity
Productivity in services as % of GDP
Productivity in services as $PPP per person
Growth in services productivity
Build-up of Agriculture productivity
Build-up of Industry productivity
Build-up of Services productivity

## 5. Govt. Earnings & Spending

Fiscal deficit/surplus, % of GDP
Fiscal deficit/surplus as $PPP per person
Govt. earnings as % of GDP
Govt. earnings as $PPP per person
Govt. spending as % of GDP
Govt. spending as $PPP per person
Growth in govt. earnings per person
Build-up in govt. earnings
Build-up in govt. spending
Current account balance as % of GDP
Debt service as % of GNI
Build-up in debt service
Build-up in GNI

## 6. Spending on Health

Total spending on health as % of GDP
Govt. spending on health as % of GDP
Private spending on health as % of GDP
Total spending on health as $PPP per person
Govt. spending on health as $PPP per person
Private spending on health as $PPP per person
Build-up of govt. spending on health
Build-up of private spending on health
Govt. spending on health as % of total govt. spending
Out-of-pocket spending on health as % of total health spending
Out-of-pocket spending on health as part of total spending on health per person, $PPP
Out-of-pocket spending on health as % of private health spending

## 7. Purchasing Power

Govt. consumption as % of GDP
Household consumption as % of GDP
Govt. consumption as $PPP per person
Household consumption as $PPP per person
Growth of govt. consumption per person
Growth of household consumption per person
Build-up of govt. consumption per person
Build-up of household consumption per person

## 8. Self-Reliance

Total exports per person of population
Total imports per person of population
Goods and services exports, %
Goods and services imxports, %
Total exports as % of GDP
Total imports as % of GDP
Growth in goods exports per person
Growth in goods imports per person
Build-up of goods exports per person
Build-up of goods imports per person
Growth in services exports per person
Growth in services imports per person
Build-up of services exports per person
Build-up of services imports per person
Net goods exports per person
Net services exports per person
Composition of goods exports and imports
Composition of services exports and imports
Foreign reserves as months of imports
Foreign debt as % of GDP
Foreign debt as $PPP per person
Service of foreign debt as % of exports
Growth rate of debt
Growth rate of income
Build-up of debt
Build-up of income
Foreign aid as % of GDP
Foreign aid as $PPP per person

## 9. Investor Confidence

FDI as % of GDP
FDI as $US per person
Growth in FDI per person
FDI as % of total capital investment
Total capital investment as % of GDP
Total capital investment as $US per person
Growth in total capital investment per person
Private component of TCI as % of GDP
Public component of TCI as % of GDP
Private component of TCI as $PPP per person
Public component of TCI as $PPP per person
Growth of private component of TCI
Growth of public component of TCI
Build-up of private component of TCI
Build-up of public component of TCI
Domestic credit to the private sector as % of GDP
Domestic credit to the private sector in $PPP
Growth in domestic credit to the private sector

# Indicators & Sources

## 10. Regulatory Environment

Ease of starting a business: rank
Ease of starting a business: no. of days
Ease of starting a business: no. of procedures
Ease of dealing with construction permits: rank
Ease of dealing with construction permits: no. of days
Ease of dealing with construction permits: no. of procedures
Ease of employing workers: rank
Ease of employing workers: ease of hiring
Ease of employing workers: flexibility of hours
Ease of employing workers: ease of firing
Ease of employing workers: cost of firing
Ease of registering property: rank
Ease of registering property: no. of procedures
Ease of registering property: no. of days
Ease of registering property: cost
Ease of getting credit: rank
Extent of investor protection: rank
Extent of investor protection: disclosure index
Extent of investor protection: liability index
Extent of investor protection: shareholder suits index
Ease of paying taxes: rank
Ease of paying taxes: no. of payments
Ease of paying taxes: time required
Ease of paying taxes: % tax on profits
Ease of paying taxes: % labour tax and contributions
Ease of paying taxes: other taxes
Ease of paying taxes: total tax rate
Ease of external trade: rank
Ease of external trade: cost to export one container
Ease of external trade: cost to import one container
Ease of external trade: no. of documents needed to export
Ease of external trade: no. of documents needed to import
Ease of external trade: no. of days for export
Ease of external trade: no. of days for import
Ease of enforcing contracts: rank
Ease of enforcing contracts: no. of procedures
Ease of enforcing contracts: time in days
Ease of enforcing contracts: cost
Ease of closing a business: rank
Ease of closing a business: recovery rate
Ease of doing business: rank

## 11. Business Friendliness

Index of economic freedoms: rank
Personal income tax rate
Corporate tax rate
Voice and accountability: rank
Political stability: rank
Govt. effectiveness: rank
Regulatory quality: rank
Rule of law: rank
Control of corruption: rank

Shown in red are the indicators that go towards the Dba Index, Rankings and Ratings. Introduced and explained in both the book's introduction and its appendices.

## Sources:

African Development Bank AfDB
The Heritage Foundation/The Wall Street Journal
International Bank for Reconstruction and Development IBRD
International Finance Corporation IFC
International Monetary Fund IMF
International Telecommunication Union ITU
United Nations Children's Fund UNICEF
United Nations Conference on Trade and Development UNCTAD
United Nations Development Programme UNDP
United Nations Population Division UNPD
The World Bank
World Health Organisation WHO
World Trade Organisation WTO

# Foreword

The past decade has seen a sea change in the way in which Africa is viewed by the international business community. Negative images, many of them based on inaccurate or out of date information, are steadily being replaced, albeit sometimes rather slowly, with a more balanced picture. With that has come a growing recognition that today Africa, more perhaps than any other landmass in the world, is *the* continent of real opportunity.

Nevertheless, Africa still poses many challenges for international companies and investors. Not least of these is the continuing problem of accurate data. Statistics are improving, but in many African countries there remains a dearth of proper economic data. Even where these exist, there is no proper interpretation to provide the international investor with guidance. Yet without accurate advice the political and economic landscape of a country can look confusing and forbidding. The potential for commercial and political risk grows, and with it comes a disinclination to invest. Other regions look safer havens.

If African nations are to achieve poverty reduction and rise to become middle income countries or better, they cannot afford to see the inward investment momentum of the past ten years slacken. The arrival of *Doing Business in West Africa* is therefore timely. It both sheds light on the commercial realities of an important region of the continent and provides a guiding hand to investors.

Drawing on verified sources of information covering the past ten years, Tony Okoromadu has added value to these with a lively, colourful and insightful interpretation. His novel approach both sets today's statistics in a recognisable context and clearly improves the landscape for decision-making. International investors and African governments alike should welcome this as an important contribution to the economic growth of the continent.

**Lynda, Baroness Chalker of Wallasey**

**March 2010**

Baroness Chalker was a member of the British Government for eighteen years, serving as Minister for Europe for nearly 4 years, Minister for Africa for nearly 12 and as Minister for Overseas Development for 8 years. She holds the joint record for length of continuous government service in the United Kingdom during the 20th century. She is now involved in a wide number of projects and initiatives focusing on Africa, and serves on the boards of several multinational companies and NGOs. She also founded and chairs the independent consultancy, Africa Matters Limited, which provides advice and assistance to companies with investment and business activities in Africa.

# Introduction

***Doing Business in West Africa (DBWA) 2009-2010*** is compiled for the organisation that conducts business, or has interests, in Sub-Saharan Africa; whatever the sector those activities or concerns fall into. It will prove an immensely useful tool for all economic, business, development, administrative, government and even political roles in the continent. It is geared towards a range of sectors: corporate, multinationals, governments, diplomatic missions, multilateral organisations, development agencies, universities and research institutions, think-tanks.

Possibly the first thing noticed about this volume is its vivid colours and exciting appearance. That is deliberate. A pivotal plank on which the project was built is that it had to be invigorating and inviting to read. It had to win the first challenge, which is to pull the observer inwards - quickly - and to keep them there. In this light, of particular consequence are the incisive and pithy commentaries that accompany the analyses outcomes on every page.

The second pivotal support was this: that the project's aesthetics and engagement with the reader must not compromise its depth, exhaustiveness and thoroughness. That its contents, side-by-side with their engaging presentation, must be of the highest and most rigourous academic and analytical standards. We are confident the book works well on both counts, firmly supported and kept confidently upright by those two pivots.

## Welcome to the Region

The book opens with Part I, which is an introduction to Sub-Saharan Africa, after placing it in the context of other continents of the world, and in the context of the economic and geographical groupings of the world's economies. Some knotty issues are also briefly explored there, as they affect the continent's 48 economies. Issues like the effect of population growth, the experiences with foreign aid and economic development, the effect of economic growth on quality of life, and so on. That sub-chapter is called *"Tricky Relations"* and what it does is compile and compare data on the various connections and then draw conclusions from the emerging picture.

## 200 Indicators, 660+ Tables, 200+ Charts, 48 Countries, 8 to 10 Years

DBWA 2009-2010 is quite possibly the most comprehensive and in-depth body of country analyses ever attempted for Sub-Saharan Africa.

It employs data from the multilateral development agencies like the World Bank, IMF, UNDP, UNCTAD, etc., and analyses this across several hundreds of macro and socio-economic indicators. In the end it produces a body of work that is a comparative dissection and examination of the trends within these country-economies during the past 8 to 10 years. The sources of data employed are always identified at every turn.

Perhaps the most striking feature of this work is the way it presents and analyses the myriad economic sectors and activities; the way it employs specific and seemingly complex barometers and indicators, and yet makes certain that the procedures and import of their findings are as easily understood by the reader as is feasibly possible. As explained in the earlier paragraphs, this was a condition set early on as a must-be.

Too often, economic concepts and analyses are presented as complex material understandable only by the tutored, and in formats that are only easily comprehended by experts. While it may be true that several areas in the broad subject of economics and finance might indeed be intricate and labyrinthine, it need not be so for those basic aspects necessary to get a useful picture or idea of a country's progress or decline.

Rather than use one year's performance as basis for assessment, blocks of 4-year moving averages are used almost everywhere, instead. For this 2009-2010 volume, they begin at 1999 and continue till the latest years for which data is available. Where the data is yet provisional (usually 2008 to 2010) this is indicated appropriately. It is considered that these moving averages should produce a more accurate and balanced reading of country performance.

Whatever the case, the eventual outcomes provide reliable enough grounds on which to assess a particular country's comparative strengths and weaknesses in the short to medium term.

## West Africa

West Africa is given prominence such that, while all 48 countries are assessed as they performed across each indicator and across the 8 to 10 years period, the countries of West Africa are singled out in each chapter and their respective positions across the moving average block-phases of the period since 1999, is illustrated by ladder-tables. And so, one ladder shows the country's position on the West Africa scale during the first period (usually 1999-2002), and then contrasts this against a second West Africa ladder for the next period (usually 2003-2006), and for a third where data is available (2007-2010).

## Nigeria

Much of this sub-continent's trajectory is tracked from the perspective of its largest economy - Nigeria. In many cases, the country's trajectory over the past 10 years is traced and illustrated with charts that timeline its progress from 1999. For every indicator, Nigeria's performance and position in Africa and West Africa is highlighted. The "running commentary" that trails through every chapter is a guided tour telling West Africa's story from the Nigeria perspective.

Nigeria being an oil-driven economy, a second set of ladders, this time for Africa's major oil exporters, compares the countries' positions across the same 8 to 10 years, also using moving average block-phases (1999-2002, 2003-2006, 2007-2010; or similar).

## Per-Capita Calibration

As much as possible, the indices and quantities used have been expressed in ratios, usually percentages of GDP and per person bases; reason being that applying solely absolute size could easily be misleading.

For example, ranking countries according to the total volume of foreign investment might well bring out the countries with the largest FDI portfolios, but it would say little about whether these countries are matching their potential, or about what scope there might still be for growth; until the same FDI is expressed as investment per person of population, or as a percentage of country GDP.

The same is perhaps even more easily seen in the evaluation of country output, GDP. Absolute size does matter (large economies have the advantages of their huge resources outlays being readily available) but only to a point; because it speaks much more about the respective economy and its efficiency and potential, when that GDP is expressed in per person terms.

Both senses (per population and as percentage GDP) are used throughout the book and help provide a more balanced and representative conclusion.

## Purchasing Power Parity Dollars

Wherever possible, monetary value has been expressed in $PPP. This is the format most favoured in economic evaluations when cross-country comparisons are to be made.

$PPP represents a (theoretical) monetary currency that has the same value everywhere, because it weeds out the effects of price movements and so on, across borders. Thus, one PPP dollar would have exactly the same value in every country. In other words, one PPP dollar in the Republic of Congo would purchase the exact same quantities of goods as it would in Sierra Leone and South Africa.

More on this is explained in the introduction to chapter 3, Economic Strength.

## Thorough, but Friendly

DBWA 2009-2010 is at once a very exhaustive treatise on economic performance in Sub-Saharan Africa's 48 countries, as it is also - hopefully - a pleasant and engaging document to follow. Great effort has been made to ensure that its contents are immediately comprehensible to as wide a spectrum of reader-backgrounds as possible, without at any level compromising its depth and thoroughness.

## 11 Chapters, with Closing Analysis and Submissions

The 200 indices employed are spread across 11 divisions, which intend to - as closely as possible - represent broad brackets into which the spectrum of macro-economic, business and socio-economic activity in a country-economy may be divided:

- General Size
- Quality of life
- Economic strength
- Economic productivity
- Government earning and spending
- Spending on Health
- Purchasing power
- Self-reliance
- Investor confidence
- Regulatory environment
- Business friendliness

Each chapter opens with a *"Prelims"* section, which essentially is a primer for the concepts and measures that are employed there.

The scrupulous data-crunching of the myriad indices follows in the sub-chapters and the outcomes are every time illustrated in an engaging and stimulating way.

The major implications and deductions from the charts and trends that emerge, are explained with pithy yet incisive running commentaries, as it were. But these deductions are by no means exhaustive: closer and closer scrutiny will almost always throw up yet more inferences.

We do not expect that every step will come easy to the reader, but the chapter presentation is such that anybody with a fundamental appreciation of broad economic concepts should feel carried along through every stage. Every chapter has a very strong user-friendly feel to it.

The chapters close with two one-page summation sections: *Leaders & Stragglers*, and *Wrap-up*.

***Leaders & Stragglers***. This section involves the evaluation and ranking of country performance across some indicators considered to be more "critical" among the indices involved in the said chapter. It leads to the rankings table at each chapter's end.

(At the book's end, the countries are again evaluated and ranked, this time according to their performance across all of these "critical" indices through every sector examined in the book. The result is the 2009/2010 Dba [dee-be-ay] Ranking of country performance for the latest 8 to 10 years leading up to the publication reference year; in this case, 2009-2010.)

***Wrap-up***. It takes a closing and broad look back at the chapter and traces the overall performance of Nigeria by comparing it with the best overall performing country from West Africa. It does so by comparing both countries' outcomes across all the major indicators in that section.

## The Dba Index ™

The *Dba [dee-bee-ay] Index*, as a measure, is explained in Appendix A. It is evaluated using the 56 indicators classed as "critical" among the 200 involved in the overall analyses in this volume. These 56 are identified in their respective chapters by the Dba sign rendered in white inside a small red rectangular box. Dba is a yearly rating and ranking (beginning with 2009-2010) of Sub-Saharan Africa economies; it will serve as a credible annual comparative evaluation of African country performance.

## Complete Country Tables

Appendix B presents 264 tables that show the rankings of all 48 countries as they scored across both the Dba and non-Dba indicators, through the 8 to 10 year periods.

## Final Word

This survey is not a critique. It does not aim to render praise or apportion blame. Nor does it seek to provide remedies. What it does is provide a snapshot of the continent's economies as they stood during the preceding 10 years. In so doing, it will provide decision makers with a platform on which to plan the future by reviewing the past. It offers an unambiguous illustration of status quo: a clear and concise depiction of the state of affairs in that country during the study period.

*DBWA 2009-2010* will be immensely valuable to corporations, institutions, governments, development agencies, and other organisations and establishments with functions and business anywhere in Africa. DBWA will be produced annually with updated data and analyses.

The *Dba Rankings* and *Ratings* of African economies performance will also be produced yearly. We envisage that these rankings - starting with this first set presented here - will immediately become a reference point wherever Sub-Saharan Africa economies are discussed or examined, and will provide practitioners in myriad sectors in that continent with a benchmark tool to measure the comparative fortunes of its countries over the years. Dba (Index, Rating and Ranking) is a comprehensive and credible evaluation of the business and investment climates that exist in the countries of the continent. Its constituent socio-economic indicators and their individual weightings will be reviewed every year as appropriate.

### Please Note

When mention is made of "Africa" in this compilation, it almost always means Sub-Saharan Africa, unless otherwise stated or otherwise obvious from the context.

The IMF tends to include Sudan, Djibouti and Mauritania in "Middle East and Central Asia". While the World Bank includes all three in Sub-Saharan Africa. We have followed the bank's classification here.

Sub-Saharan Africa aggregate data often do not include Zimbabwe and Somalia, because of the volatile and out-of-sync situations there.

Dba Index, Dba Ranking and Dba Rating are protected by relevant and extant patent, copyright and trademark laws.

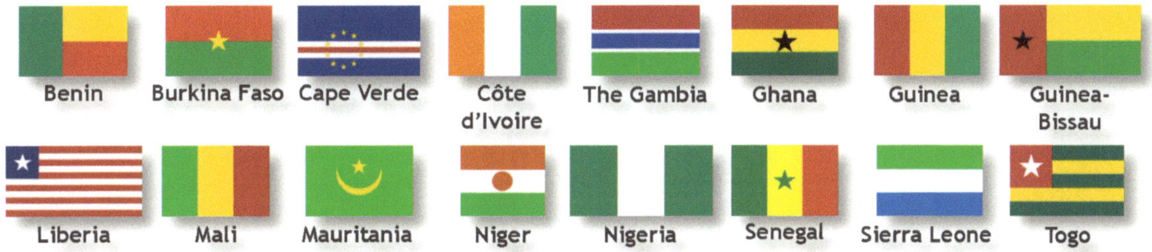

# Part I:

# Continent Overview

# 1. Sub-Saharan Africa, Its Regions, Its Countries

# 1.1 Sub-Saharan Africa

- Central Africa
- East Africa
- Southern Africa
- Sudan
- West Africa

| | Country | Years since Independence 2009 | Population 2007 (millions) | Population Density 2005-2010 (pers/ sq.km.) | GDP 2007 ($US, millions) | GDP per Person 2007 ($US) | Region |
|---|---|---|---|---|---|---|---|
| 1 | Angola | 34 | 16 | 14 | 59,263 | 3,629 | Central Africa |
| 2 | Benin | 49 | 8 | 82 | 5,554 | 707 | West Africa |
| 3 | Botswana | 43 | 2 | 3 | 12,339 | 7,005 | Southern Africa |
| 4 | Burkina Faso | 49 | 14 | 55 | 6,769 | 493 | West Africa |
| 5 | Burundi | 47 | 8 | 313 | 975 | 125 | East Africa |
| 6 | Cameroon | 49 | 19 | 39 | 20,433 | 1,084 | Central Africa |
| 7 | Cape Verde | 34 | 1 | 134 | 1,513 | 3,080 | West Africa |
| 8 | Central African Rep. | 49 | 4 | 7 | 1,700 | 398 | Central Africa |
| 9 | Chad | 49 | 10 | 9 | 7,018 | 739 | Central Africa |
| 10 | Comoros | 34 | 1 | 381 | 466 | 729 | East Africa |
| 11 | Congo, Dem. Rep. | 49 | 61 | 27 | 10,013 | 164 | Central Africa |
| 12 | Congo, Rep. | 49 | 4 | 12 | 7,657 | 2,159 | Central Africa |
| 13 | Côte d'Ivoire | 49 | 20 | 61 | 19,824 | 983 | West Africa |
| 14 | Djibouti | 32 | 1 | 37 | 848 | 1,108 | East Africa |
| 15 | Equatorial Guinea | 41 | 1 | 18 | 12,576 | 10,437 | Central Africa |
| 16 | Eritrea | 16 | 5 | 42 | 1,316 | 271 | East Africa |
| 17 | Ethiopia | n/a | 77 | 77 | 19,535 | 253 | East Africa |
| 18 | Gabon | 49 | 1 | 5 | 11,571 | 8,076 | Central Africa |
| 19 | Gambia, The | 44 | 2 | 153 | 651 | 410 | West Africa |
| 20 | Ghana | 52 | 22 | 99 | 15,014 | 683 | West Africa |
| 21 | Guinea | 51 | 10 | 39 | 4,157 | 417 | West Africa |
| 22 | Guinea-Bissau | 36 | 2 | 48 | 382 | 225 | West Africa |
| 23 | Kenya | 46 | 35 | 66 | 27,102 | 782 | East Africa |
| 24 | Lesotho | 43 | 2 | 66 | 1,672 | 694 | Southern Africa |
| 25 | Liberia | 162 | 4 | 35 | 745 | 199 | West Africa |
| 26 | Madagascar | 49 | 20 | 34 | 7,343 | 373 | East Africa |
| 27 | Malawi | 45 | 13 | 120 | 3,586 | 268 | East Africa |
| 28 | Mali | 49 | 13 | 10 | 7,156 | 548 | West Africa |
| 29 | Mauritania | 49 | 3 | 3 | 2,819 | 952 | West Africa |
| 30 | Mauritius | 41 | 1 | 621 | 6,927 | 5,494 | East Africa |
| 31 | Mozambique | 34 | 20 | 27 | 8,102 | 398 | East Africa |
| 32 | Namibia | 19 | 2 | 3 | 8,831 | 4,355 | Southern Africa |
| 33 | Niger | 49 | 13 | 11 | 4,252 | 318 | West Africa |
| 34 | Nigeria | 49 | 144 | 162 | 165,921 | 1,153 | West Africa |
| 35 | Rwanda | 47 | 9 | 377 | 3,412 | 363 | East Africa |
| 36 | São Tomé & Príncipe | 34 | 0.2 | 165 | 145 | 923 | Central Africa |
| 37 | Senegal | 49 | 12 | 64 | 11,300 | 924 | West Africa |
| 38 | Seychelles | 33 | 0.1 | 191 | 912 | 10,728 | East Africa |
| 39 | Sierra Leone | 48 | 6 | 82 | 1,664 | 290 | West Africa |
| 40 | Somalia | 49 | n/a | n/a | n/a | n/a | East Africa |
| 41 | South Africa | 78 | 48 | 40 | 283,381 | 5,922 | Southern Africa |
| 42 | Sudan | 53 | 37 | 16 | 46,531 | 1,252 | North Africa |
| 43 | Swaziland | 41 | 1 | 66 | 2,946 | 2,892 | Southern Africa |
| 44 | Tanzania | 45 | 39 | 44 | 16,691 | 428 | East Africa |
| 45 | Togo | 49 | 7 | 118 | 2,503 | 387 | West Africa |
| 46 | Uganda | 47 | 31 | 131 | 11,916 | 385 | East Africa |
| 47 | Zambia | 45 | 12 | 16 | 11,411 | 990 | East Africa |
| 48 | Zimbabwe | 29 | 12 | 35 | 3,583 | 305 | East Africa |

# 1.2 Central Africa

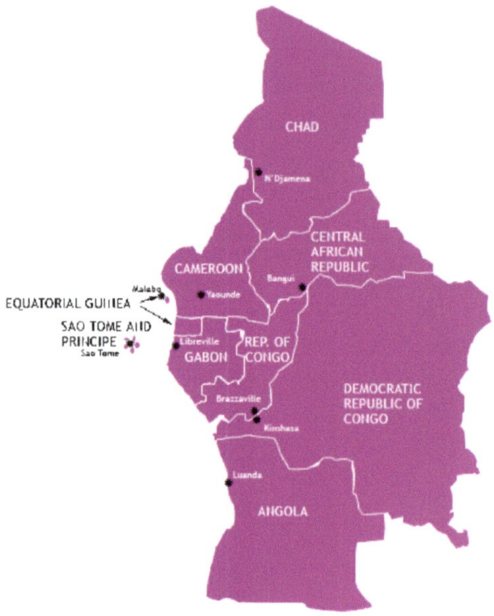

Primary Data: IMF

| | Country | Population 2007 (millions) | Average GDP per Person 2004-07 ($US) | Average Annual Real GDP Growth 2004-07 (%) | Average Annual Inflation Rate 2004-07 (%) | National Currency | Exchange Rate 2009 (currency oer $US) | Exchange Rate Stability relative to rest of S-S Africa during 2004-09 (0=least stable; 10=most stable) | Official Language |
|---|---|---|---|---|---|---|---|---|---|
| 1 | •Angola | 16 | 2,447 | 17.7 | 23.0 | Kwanza | 79 | 8.7 | Portuguese |
| 2 | •Cameroon | 19 | 976 | 3.1 | 2.1 | Central African CFA Franc | 478 | 6.9 | English, French |
| 3 | •Central African Rep. | 4.3 | 349 | 2.7 | 2.1 | Central African CFA Franc | 478 | 5.6 | French, Sangho |
| 4 | •Chad | 9.5 | 643 | 10.5 | -0.2 | Central African CFA Franc | 478 | 4.7 | French, Arabic |
| 5 | •Congo, Dem. Rep. | 61 | 139 | 6.6 | 13.8 | Congolese Franc | 784 | 0.4 | French |
| 6 | •Congo, Rep. | 3.5 | 1,913 | 4.0 | 3.3 | Central African CFA Franc | 478 | 4.9 | French |
| 7 | •Equatorial Guinea | 1.2 | 7,650 | 17.6 | 4.3 | Central African CFA Franc | 480 | 7.8 | Spanish, French |
| 8 | •Gabon | 1.4 | 6,664 | 2.7 | 1.3 | Central African CFA Franc | 478 | 6.7 | French |
| 9 | •São Tomé & Príncipe | 0.2 | 800 | 6.2 | 17.9 | Dobra | 16,336 | 0.7 | Portuguese |

# 1.3 East Africa

Primary Data: IMF

| | Country | Population 2007 (millions) | Average GDP per Person 2004-07 ($US) | Average Annual Real GDP Growth 2004-07 (%) | Average Annual Inflation Rate 2004-07 (%) | National Currency | Exchange Rate 2009 (currency oer $US) | Exchange Rate Stability relative to rest of S-S Africa during 2004-09 (0=least stable; 10=most stable) | Official Language |
|---|---|---|---|---|---|---|---|---|---|
| 1 | Burundi | 8 | 111 | 3.6 | 8.1 | Burundian Franc | 1,208 | 3.8 | Kirundi, French |
| 2 | Comoros | 1 | 653 | 1.4 | 3.8 | Comorian Franc | 358 | 6 | Arabic, French |
| 3 | Djibouti | 0.8 | 1,010 | 4.0 | 3.7 | Djiboutian Franc | 178 | 9.8 | French, Arabic |
| 4 | Eritrea | 4.9 | 260 | 1.1 | 15.5 | Nafka | 15 | 9.1 | Tigrinya, Arabic, English |
| 5 | Ethiopia | 77 | 191 | 11.4 | 10.9 | Birr | 10 | 3.3 | Amharic |
| 6 | Kenya | 34.7 | 624 | 6.0 | 11.5 | Kenyan Shilling | 80 | 6.2 | English, Kiswahili |
| 7 | Madagascar | 19.7 | 293 | 5.3 | 13.4 | Ariary | 1,972 | 4 | French, Malagasy |
| 8 | Malawi | 13.4 | 232 | 6.0 | 12.2 | Malawian Kwacha | 141 | 2.4 | English, Nyanja |
| 9 | Mauritius | 1.3 | 5,124 | 3.8 | 6.9 | Mauritian Rupee | 29 | 8.2 | English, French |
| 10 | Mozambique | 20.3 | 348 | 8.0 | 10.1 | Metical | 27,037 | 4.2 | Portuguese |
| 11 | Rwanda | 9.4 | 290 | 6.9 | 9.7 | Rwandan Franc | 574 | 9.6 | Rwanda, French, English |
| 12 | Seychelles | 0.1 | 10,755 | 5.0 | 2.0 | Seychellois Rupee | 14 | 0 | English, French |
| 13 | Somalia | n/a | n/a | n/a | n/a | Somali Shilling | n/a | n/a | Somali |
| 14 | Tanzania | 39.0 | 383 | 7.3 | 5.7 | Tanzanian Shilling | 1,325 | 3.6 | Kiswahili, Kiunguju, English |
| 15 | Uganda | 30.9 | 331 | 8.1 | 6.6 | Ugandan Shilling | 1,905 | 8.9 | English |
| 16 | Zambia | 11.5 | 754 | 5.8 | 14.0 | Zambian Kwacha | 5,182 | 2.2 | English |
| 17 | Zimbabwe | 11.7 | 322 | -5.2 | 10.6 | Zimbabwean Dollar | n/a | n/a | English |

# 1.4 Southern Africa & Sudan

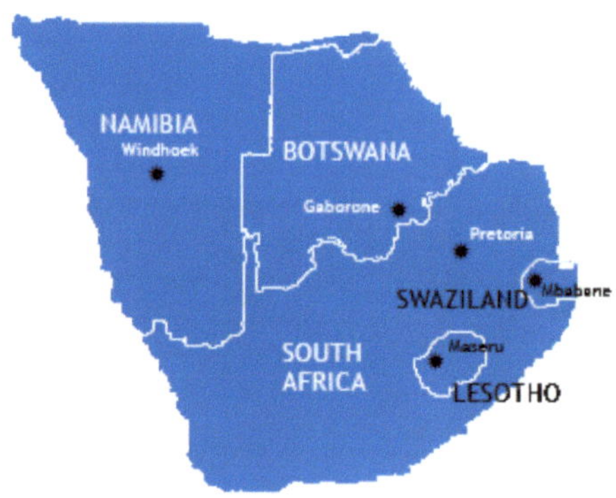


Primary Data: IMF

| | Country | Population 2007 (millions) | Average GDP per Person 2004-07 ($US) | Average Annual Real GDP Growth 2004-07 (%) | Average Annual Inflation Rate 2004-07 (%) | National Currency | Exchange Rate 2009 (currency oer $US) | Exchange Rate Stability relative to rest of S-S Africa during 2004-09 (0=least stable; 10=most stable) | Official Language |
|---|---|---|---|---|---|---|---|---|---|
| 1 | • Sudan | 37 | 916 | 8.2 | 8.0 | Sudanese Pound | 2 | 3.1 | Arabic |
| 1 | • Botswana | 1.8 | 6,331 | 4.3 | 8.6 | Pula | 7 | 1.1 | Setswana, English |
| 2 | • Lesotho | 2.4 | 624 | 4.6 | 5.6 | Loti | 9 | 1.8 | Sesotho, English |
| 3 | • Namibia | 2 | 3,841 | 6.8 | 4.5 | Namibian Dollar | 9 | 1.6 | English |
| 4 | • South Africa | 47.9 | 5,299 | 5.1 | 4.1 | Rand | 8 | 2 | English and 10 others |
| 5 | • Swaziland | 1.0 | 2,608 | 2.7 | 5.4 | Lilangeni | 9 | 1.3 | English, siSwati |

# 1.5 West Africa

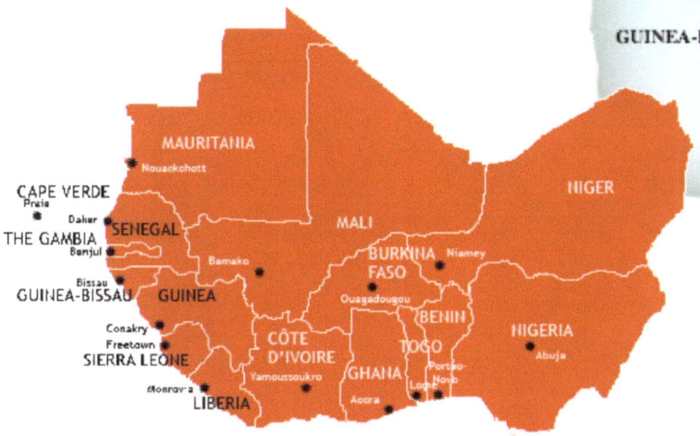


Primary Data: IMF

| | Country | Population 2007 (millions) | Average GDP per Person ($US) | Average Annual Real GDP Growth 2004-07 (%) | Average Annual Inflation Rate 2004-07 (%) | National Currency | Exchange Rate 2009 (currency oer $US) | Exchange Rate Stability relative to rest of S-S Africa during 2004-09 (0=least stable; 10=most stable) | Official Language |
|---|---|---|---|---|---|---|---|---|---|
| 1 | • Benin | 8 | 622 | 3.6 | 2.8 | West African CFA Franc | 501 | 8 | French |
| 2 | • Burkina Faso | 14 | 433 | 5.2 | 2.0 | West African CFA Franc | 490 | 7.6 | French |
| 3 | • Cape Verde | 0.5 | 2,399 | 7.3 | 1.9 | Escudo | 80 | 4.4 | Portuguese |
| 4 | • Côte d'Ivoire | 20.2 | 893 | 1.4 | 2.4 | West African CFA Franc | 477 | 5.8 | French |
| 5 | • Gambia, The | 2 | 329 | 6.3 | 6.7 | Dalasi | 27 | 2.7 | English |
| 6 | • Ghana | 22.0 | 557 | 5.9 | 12.2 | Cedi | 14,617 | 0.9 | English |
| 7 | • Guinea | 10.0 | 360 | 2.4 | 26.6 | Guinean Franc | 4,997 | 0.2 | French |
| 8 | • Guinea-Bissau | 1.7 | 198 | 2.2 | 2.4 | West African CFA Franc | 484 | 7.3 | Portuguese |
| 9 | • Liberia | 3.8 | 165 | 6.3 | 7.9 | Liberian Dollar | n/a | n/a | English |
| 10 | • Mali | 13.1 | 469 | 4.2 | 1.6 | West African CFA Franc | 478 | 5.3 | French |
| 11 | • Mauritania | 3.0 | 771 | 5.8 | 9.0 | Ouguiya | 247 | 9.3 | Arabic |
| 12 | • Niger | 13.4 | 277 | 4.2 | 2.1 | West African CFA Franc | 478 | 5.1 | French |
| 13 | • Nigeria | 143.9 | 918 | 7.3 | 11.6 | Naira | 152 | 2.9 | English |
| 14 | • Senegal | 12.2 | 791 | 4.7 | 2.5 | West African CFA Franc | 480 | 6.4 | French |
| 15 | • Sierra Leone | 5.7 | 244 | 7.1 | 11.9 | Leone | 3,150 | 8.4 | English |
| 16 | • Togo | 6.5 | 352 | 2.4 | 2.6 | West African CFA Franc | 484 | 7.1 | French |

# 2. Size, Populations, Ages, Economic Vigour

# 2.1a Land Mass of the Regions

*their surface areas*

| | Country | sq. km. |
|---|---|---|
| 1 | Sudan | 2,505,810 |
| 2 | Congo, DR | 2,344,860 |
| 3 | Chad | 1,284,000 |
| 4 | Niger | 1,267,000 |
| 5 | Angola | 1,246,700 |
| 6 | Mali | 1,240,190 |
| 7 | South Africa | 1,219,090 |
| 8 | Ethiopia | 1,104,300 |
| 9 | Mauritania | 1,025,520 |
| 10 | Tanzania | 945,090 |
| 11 | Nigeria | 923,770 |
| 12 | Namibia | 824,290 |
| 13 | Mozambique | 801,590 |
| 14 | Zambia | 752,610 |
| 15 | Somalia | 637,660 |
| 16 | Central African Rep. | 622,980 |
| 17 | Madagascar | 587,040 |
| 18 | Botswana | 581,730 |
| 19 | Kenya | 580,370 |
| 20 | Cameroon | 475,440 |
| 21 | Zimbabwe | 390,760 |
| 22 | Congo, Rep. | 342,000 |
| 23 | Côte d'Ivoire | 322,460 |
| 24 | Burkina Faso | 274,000 |
| 25 | Gabon | 267,670 |
| 26 | Guinea | 245,860 |
| 27 | Uganda | 241,040 |
| 28 | Ghana | 238,540 |
| 29 | Senegal | 196,720 |
| 30 | Malawi | 118,480 |

**Central Africa**
**6,612,660 sq.km.**

**East Africa**
**6,335,440 sq.km.**

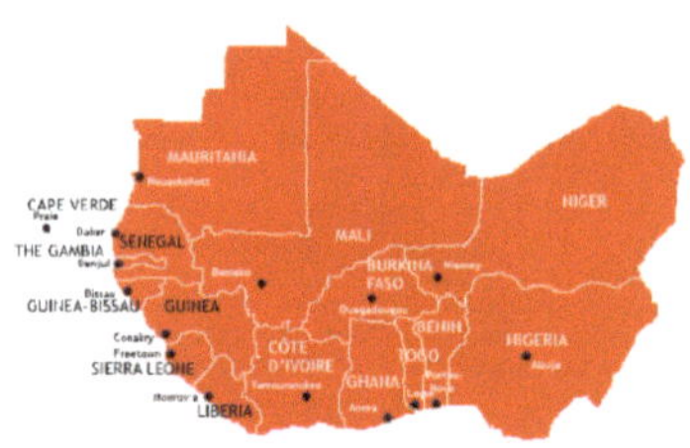


**West Africa**
**6,138,030 sq.km.**

**Southern Africa**
**2,672,820 sq.km.**

**Sudan**
**2,505,810 sq.km.**

# 2.1b Land Mass in SSA: Top 10

*the large 10 in SSA*

1. **Sudan**
2,505,810 sq.km.
10%

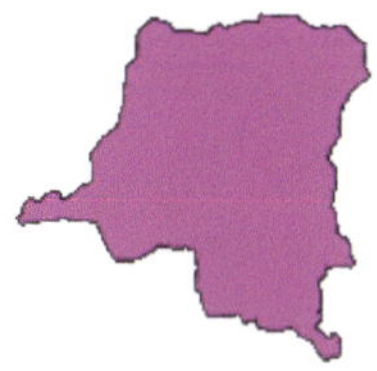

2. **Congo, Dem. Rep.**
2,344,860 sq.km.
10%

3. **Chad**
1,284,000 sq.km
5%

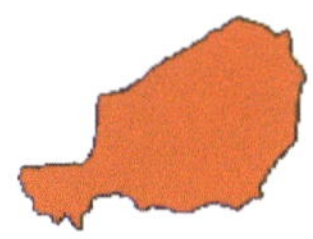

4. **Niger**
1,267,000 sq.km
5%

5. **Angola**
1,246,700 sq.km.
5%

6. **Mali**
1,240,190 sq.km.
5%

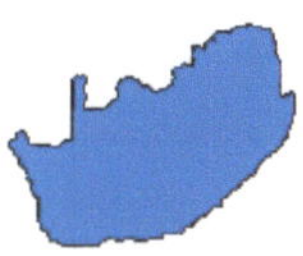

7. **South Africa**
1,219,090 sq.km.
5%

8. **Ethiopia**
1,104,300 sq.km.
4.5%

9. **Mauritania**
1,025,520 sq.km.
4%

10. **Tanzania**
945,090 sq.km.
4%

- Central Africa
- East Africa
- Southern Africa
- North Africa
- West Africa

| | Country | sq. km. |
|---|---|---|
| 31 | Eritrea | 117,600 |
| 32 | Benin | 112,620 |
| 33 | Liberia | 117,370 |
| 34 | Sierra Leone | 71,740 |
| 35 | Togo | 56,790 |
| 36 | Guinea-Bissau | 36,120 |
| 37 | Lesotho | 30,350 |
| 38 | Equatorial Guinea | 28,050 |
| 39 | Burundi | 27,830 |
| 40 | Rwanda | 26,340 |
| 41 | Djibouti | 23,200 |
| 42 | Swaziland | 17,360 |
| 43 | Gambia | 11,300 |
| 44 | Cape Verde | 4,030 |
| 45 | Comoros | 2,230 |
| 46 | Mauritius | 2,040 |
| 47 | Sao Tome and Principe | 960 |
| 48 | Seychelles | 460 |

# 2.2a Population of the Regions

*their populations*

| | Country | 2009 |
|---|---|---|
| 1 | Nigeria | 151,874,000 |
| 2 | Ehiopia | 81,238,000 |
| 3 | Congo, DR | 64,772,000 |
| 4 | South Africa | 48,812,000 |
| 5 | Tanzania | 40,538,000 |
| 6 | Sudan | 39,117,000 |
| 7 | Kenya | 35,884,000 |
| 8 | Uganda | 33,195,000 |
| 9 | Ghana | 23,108,000 |
| 10 | Mozambique | 21,456,000 |
| 11 | Cameroon | 19,926,000 |
| 12 | Côte d'Ivoire | 19,317,000 |
| 13 | Madagascar | 17,894,000 |
| 14 | Angola | 17,312,000 |
| 15 | Burkina Faso | 14,365,000 |
| 16 | Niger | 14,191,000 |
| 17 | Malawi | 13,931,000 |
| 18 | Mali | 13,667,000 |
| 19 | Senegal | 12,820,000 |
| 20 | Zambia | 12,749,000 |
| 21 | Guinea | 10,564,000 |
| 22 | Chad | 9,973,000 |
| 23 | Rwanda | 9,792,000 |
| 24 | Benin | 8,334,000 |
| 25 | Burundi | 8,108,000 |
| 26 | Togo | 6,793,000 |
| 27 | Sierra Leone | 6,040,000 |
| 28 | Eritrea | 4,973,000 |
| 29 | Central African Rep. | 4,442,000 |
| 30 | Liberia | 4,134,000 |

2009 IMF estimates

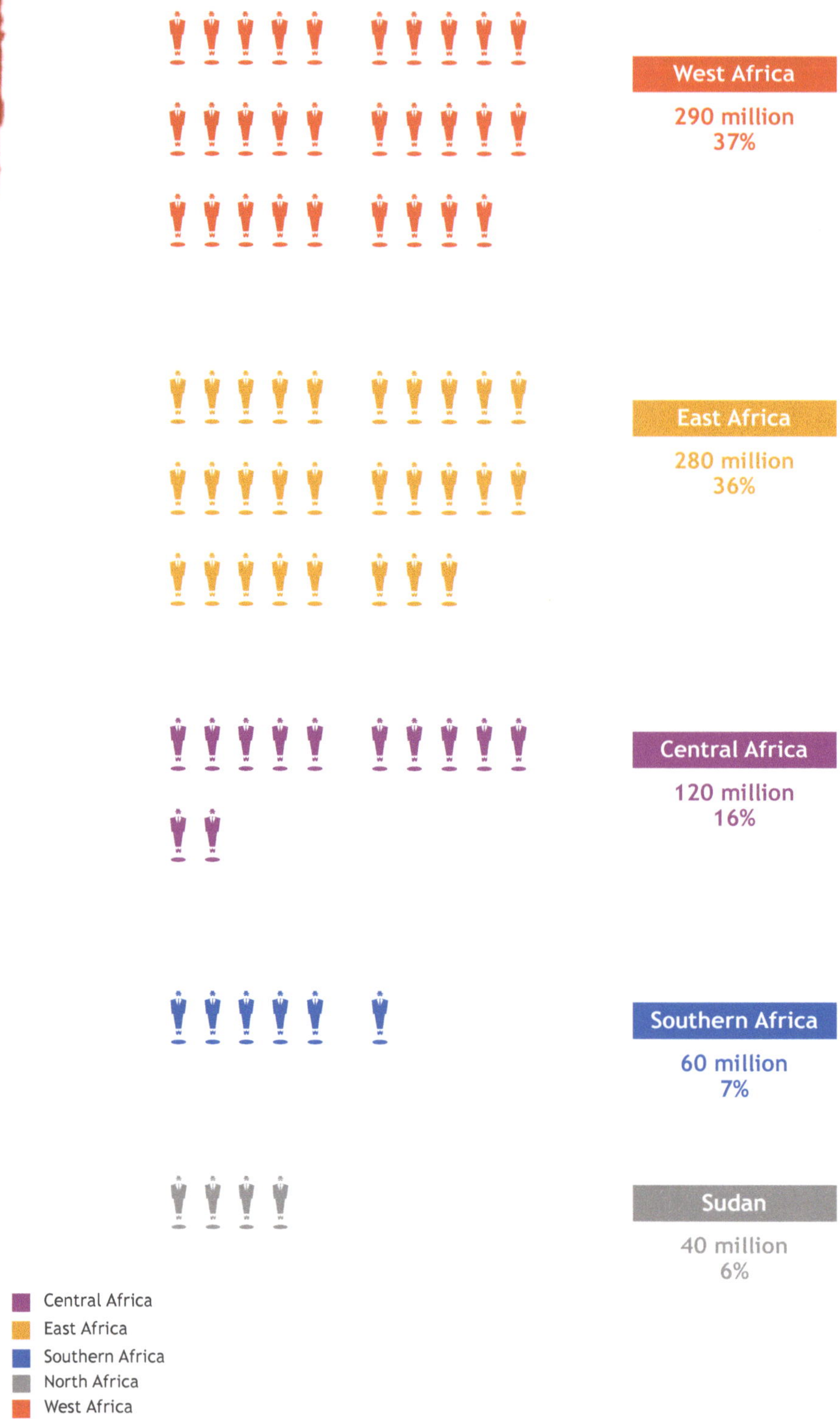

# 2.2b Share of Population in SSA: Top 10

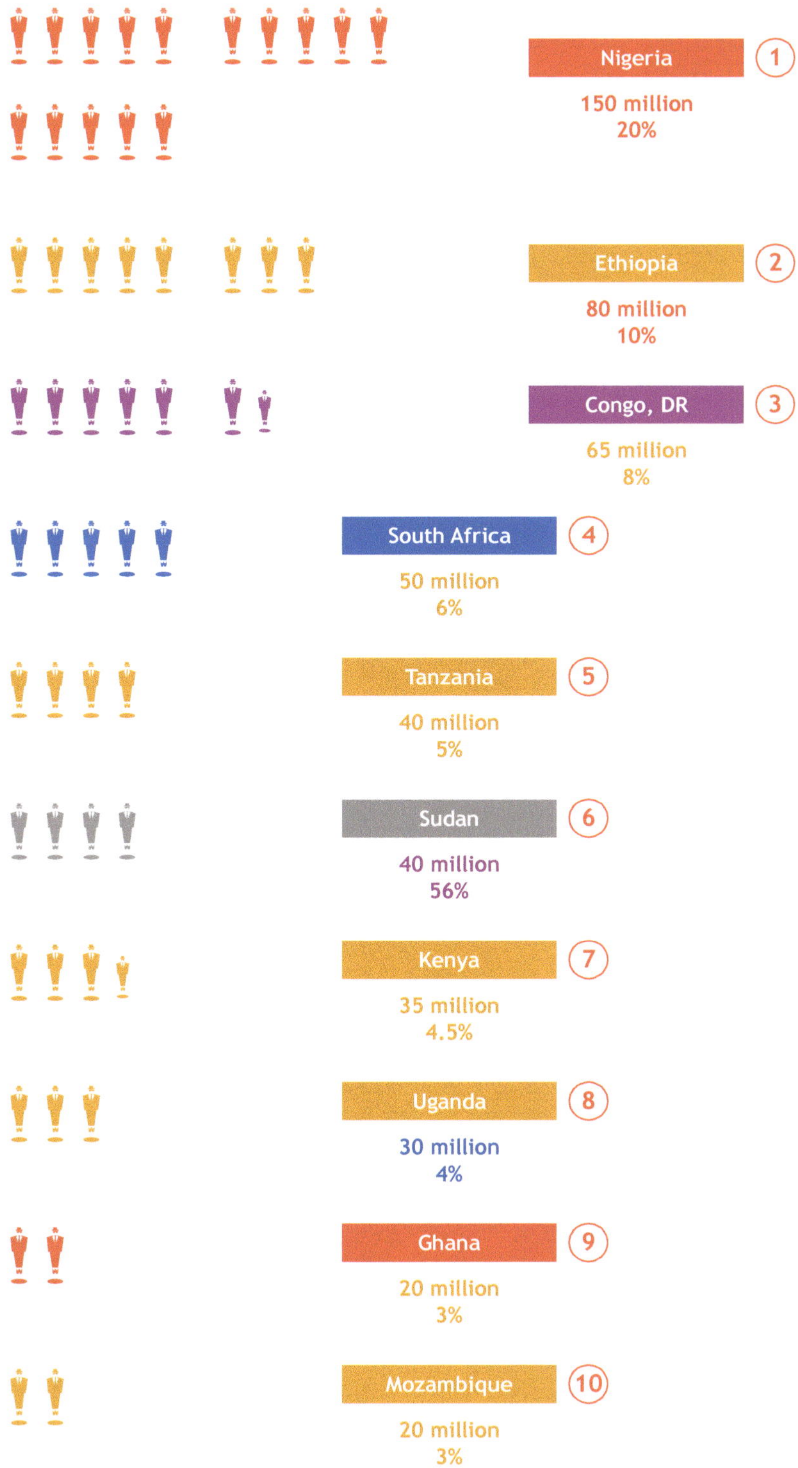


*the swarming 10 in SSA*

- Central Africa
- East Africa
- Southern Africa
- North Africa
- West Africa

| | Country | 2009 |
|---|---|---|
| 31 | Congo, Rep. | 3,756,000 |
| 32 | Mauritania | 3,105,000 |
| 33 | Lesotho | 2,496,000 |
| 34 | Namibia | 2,100,000 |
| 35 | Guinea-Bissau | 1,767,000 |
| 36 | Gambia | 1,672,000 |
| 37 | Botswana | 1,530,000 |
| 38 | Gabon | 1,475,000 |
| 39 | Mauritius | 1,281,000 |
| 40 | Equatorial Guinea | 1,276,000 |
| 41 | Swaziland | 1,195,000 |
| 42 | Djibouti | 804,000 |
| 43 | Comoros | 666,000 |
| 44 | Cape Verde | 513,000 |
| 45 | Sao Tome and Principe | 171,000 |
| 46 | Seychelles | 83,000 |
| 47 | Somalia | n/a |
| 48 | Zimbabwe | n/a |

# 2.3a Population Age Profiles of the Regions: %s

*their ages*

UNPD estimates for 2005-10

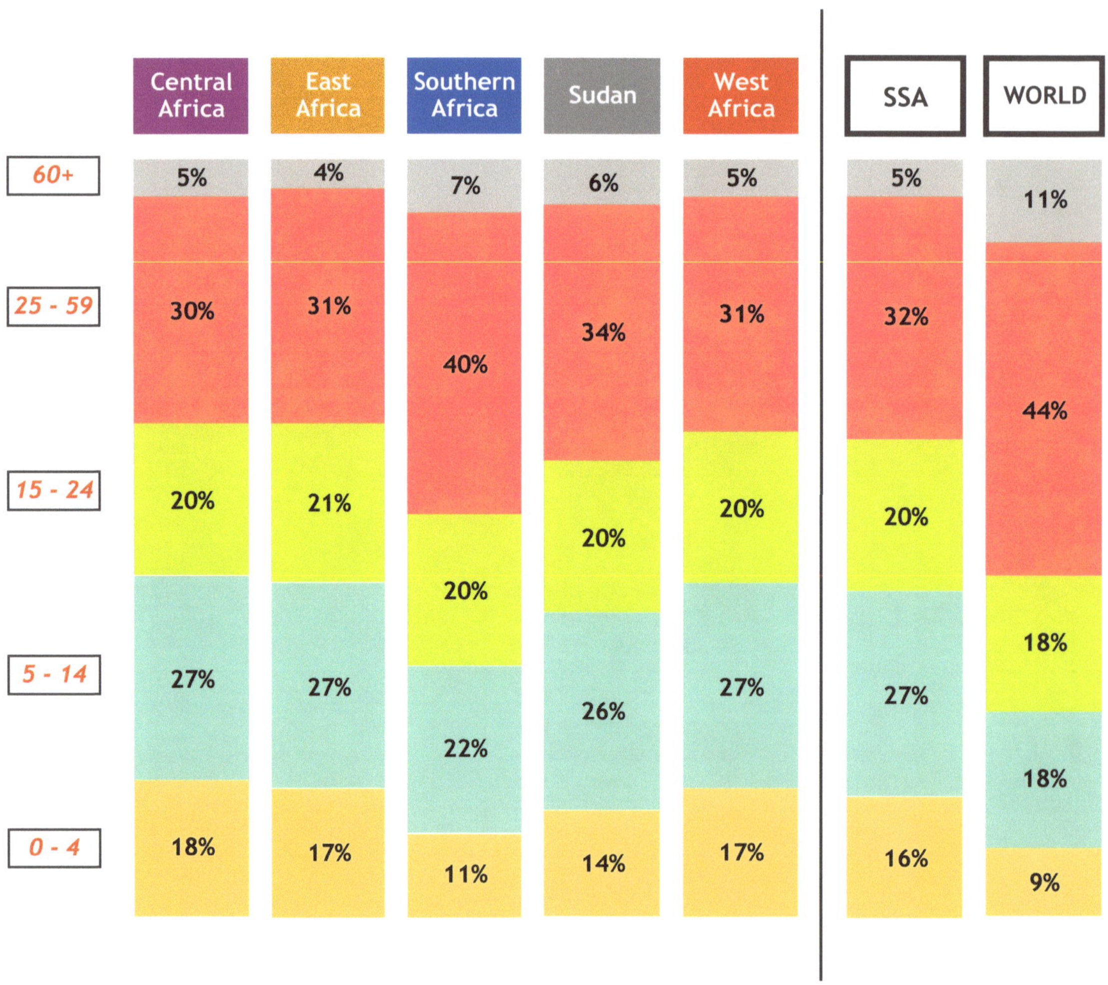

# 2.3b Population Age Profiles of the Regions: numbers

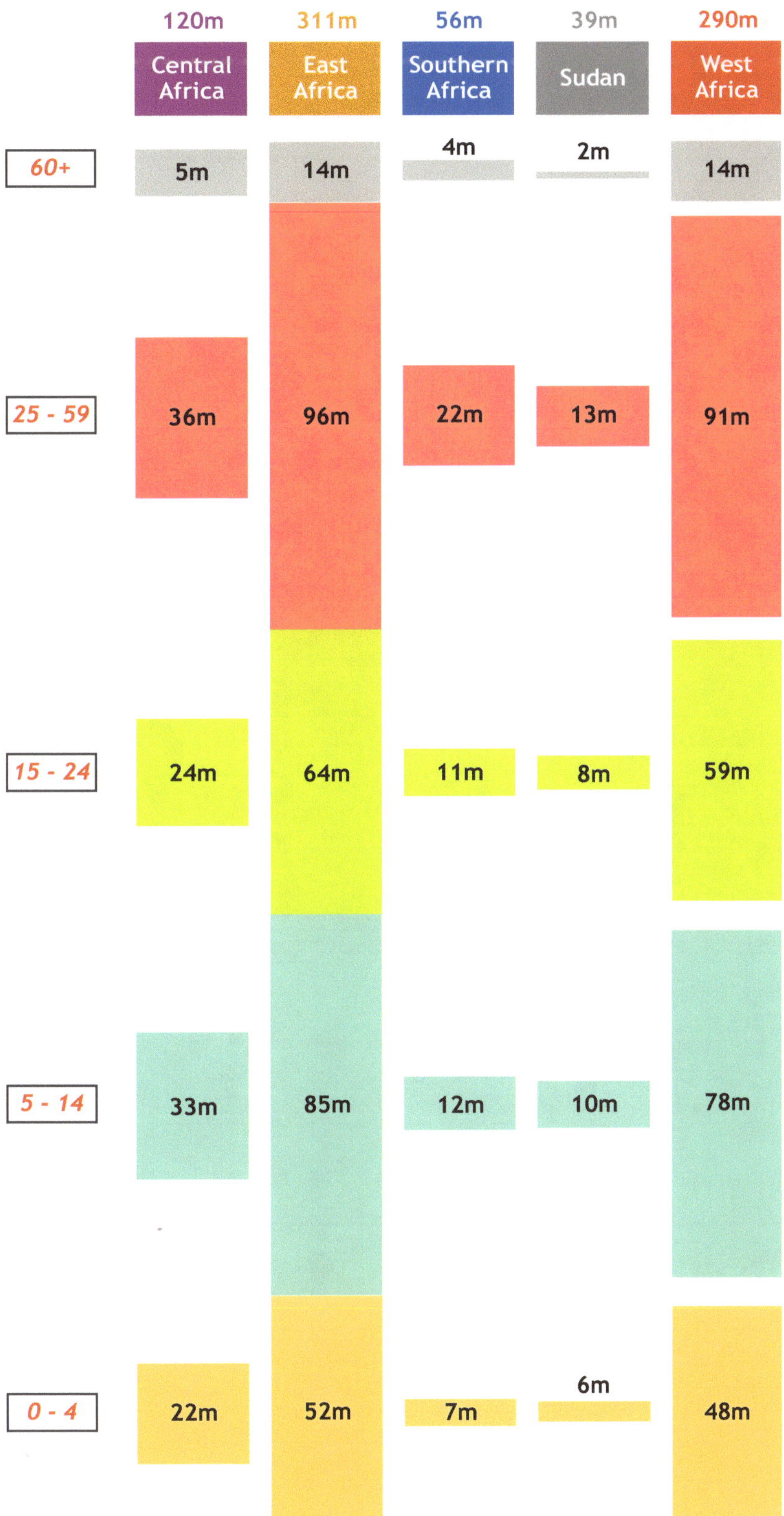


*the numbers, this time*

UNPD estimates for 2005-10

Total figure for East Africa differs from that in section 2.2 because the IMF estimates there exclude Somalia and Zimbabwe.

# 2.4a Population Density of the Regions

*their people per square kilometre*

| # | Country | 2005-10 |
|---|---|---|
| 1 | Mauritius | 621 |
| 2 | Comoros | 381 |
| 3 | Rwanda | 377 |
| 4 | Burundi | 313 |
| 5 | Seychelles | 191 |
| 6 | Sao Tome & Principe | 165 |
| 7 | Nigeria | 162 |
| 8 | Gambia | 153 |
| 9 | Cape Verde | 134 |
| 10 | Uganda | 131 |
| 11 | Malawi | 120 |
| 12 | Togo | 118 |
| 13 | Ghana | 99 |
| 14 | Sierra Leone | 82 |
| 15 | Benin | 82 |
| 16 | Ethiopia | 77 |
| 17 | Lesotho | 66 |
| 18 | Swaziland | 66 |
| 19 | Kenya | 66 |
| 20 | Senegal | 64 |
| 21 | Côte d'Ivoire | 61 |
| 22 | Burkina Faso | 55 |
| 23 | Guinea-Bissau | 48 |
| 24 | Tanzania | 44 |
| 25 | Eritrea | 42 |
| 26 | South Africa | 40 |
| 27 | Cameroon | 39 |
| 28 | Guinea | 39 |
| 29 | Djibouti | 37 |
| 30 | Liberia | 35 |

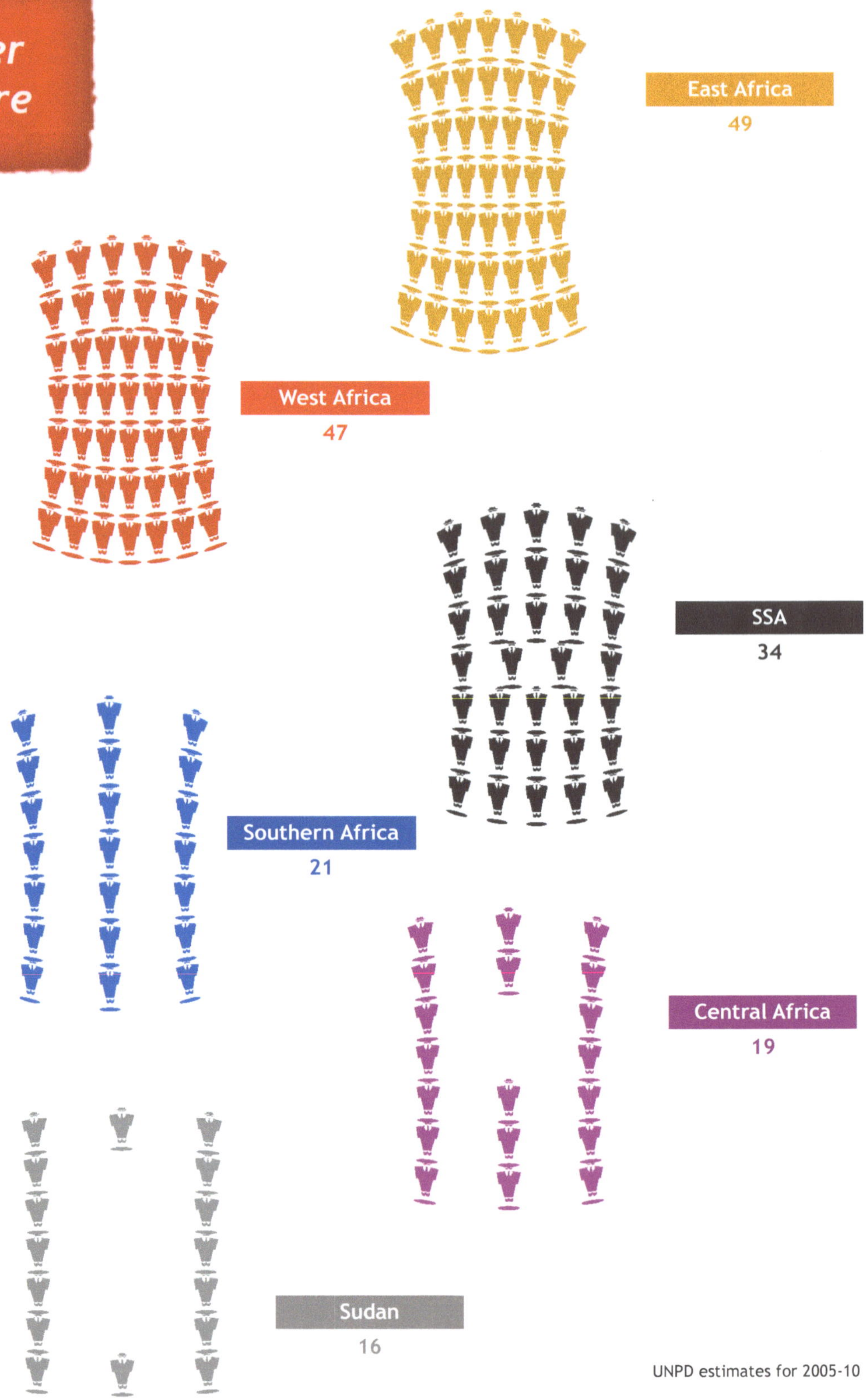


UNPD estimates for 2005-10

# 2.4b Population Density in the Countries: Top 10

*the packed 10 in SSA*

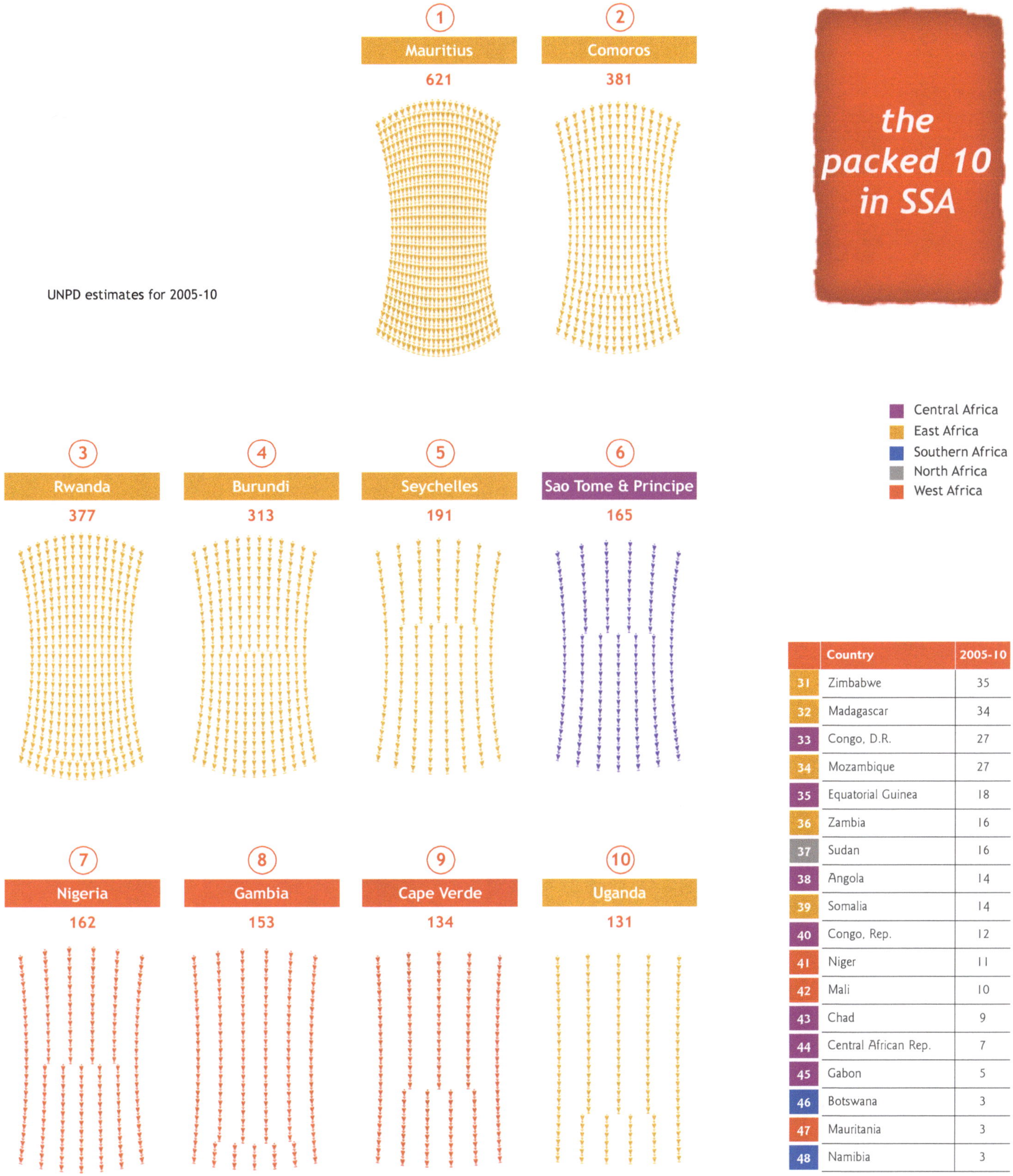


UNPD estimates for 2005-10

| | Country | 2005-10 |
|---|---|---|
| 31 | Zimbabwe | 35 |
| 32 | Madagascar | 34 |
| 33 | Congo, D.R. | 27 |
| 34 | Mozambique | 27 |
| 35 | Equatorial Guinea | 18 |
| 36 | Zambia | 16 |
| 37 | Sudan | 16 |
| 38 | Angola | 14 |
| 39 | Somalia | 14 |
| 40 | Congo, Rep. | 12 |
| 41 | Niger | 11 |
| 42 | Mali | 10 |
| 43 | Chad | 9 |
| 44 | Central African Rep. | 7 |
| 45 | Gabon | 5 |
| 46 | Botswana | 3 |
| 47 | Mauritania | 3 |
| 48 | Namibia | 3 |

# 2.5a Urban Population in the Regions: % and numbers

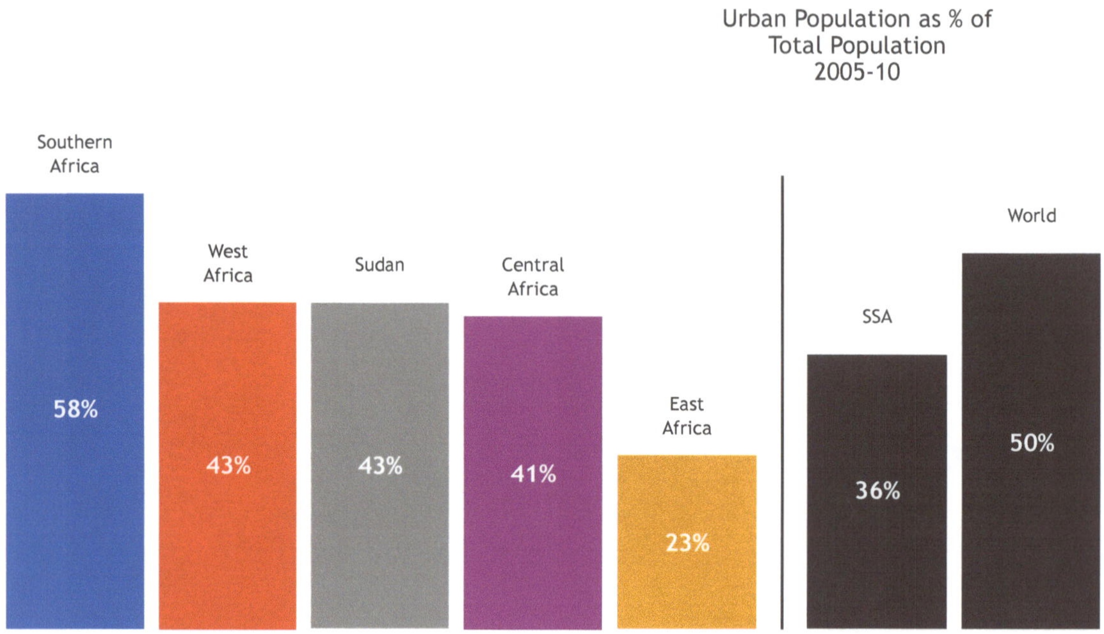


## *the city slickers within*

# 2.5b Urban Population in SSA: %. Top 10

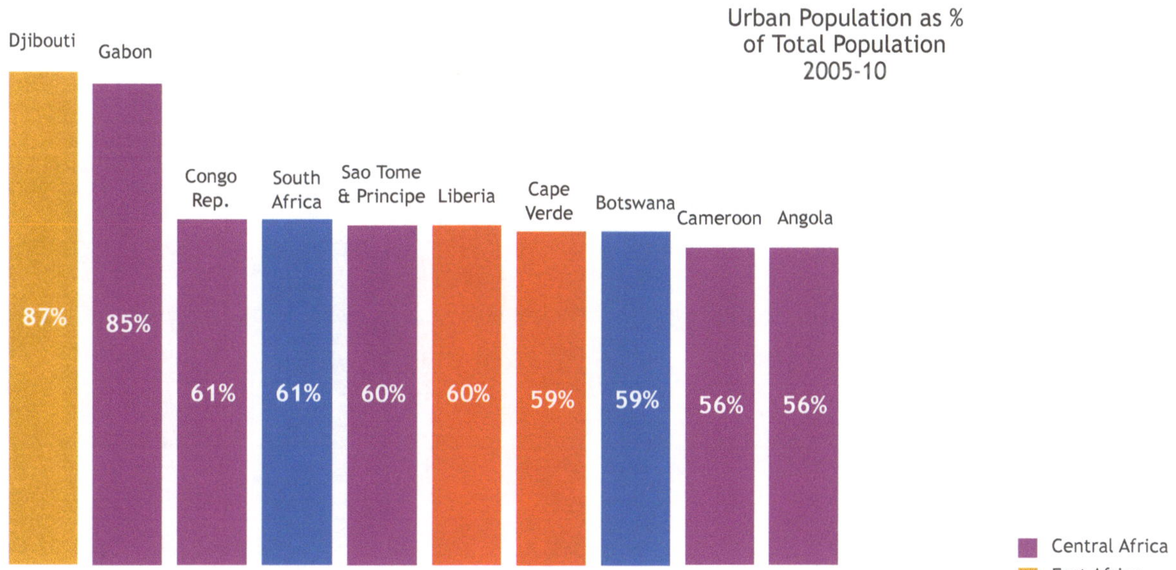


**city slicking**

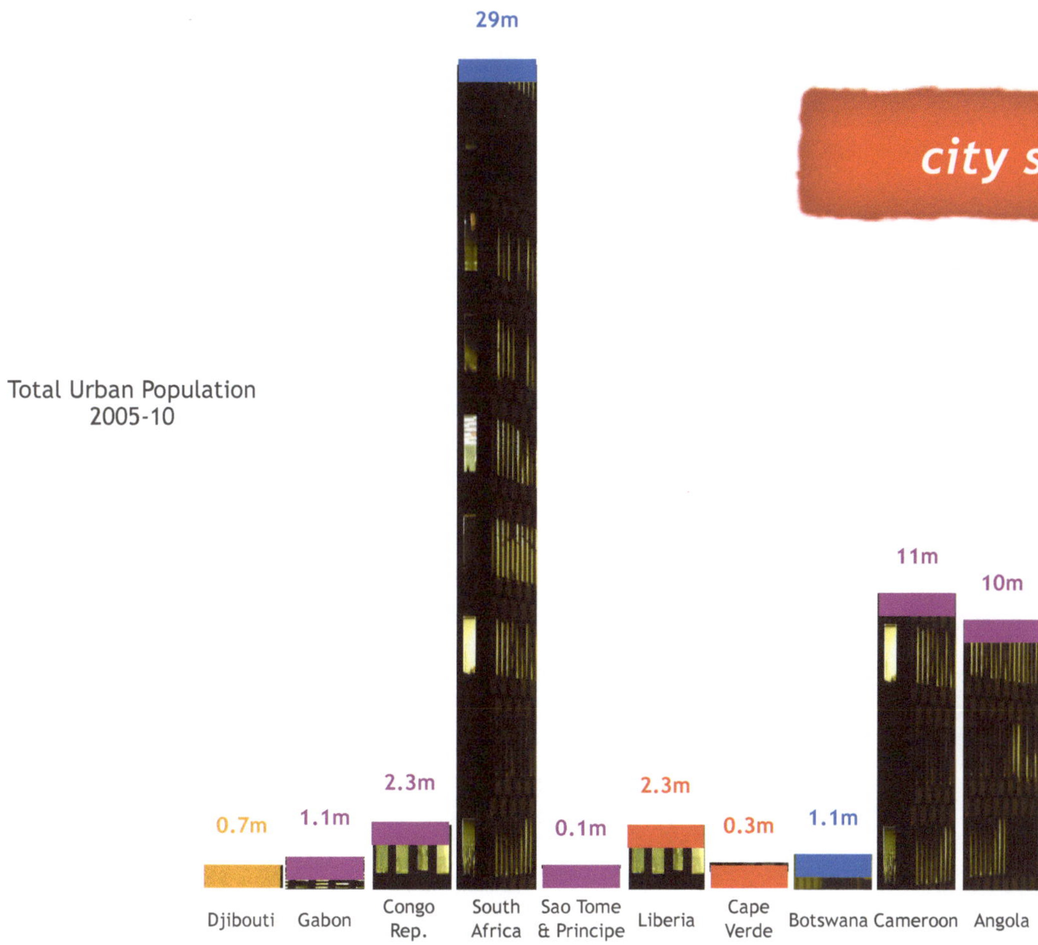


UNPD estimates

# 2.6a Rural Population in the Regions: % and numbers

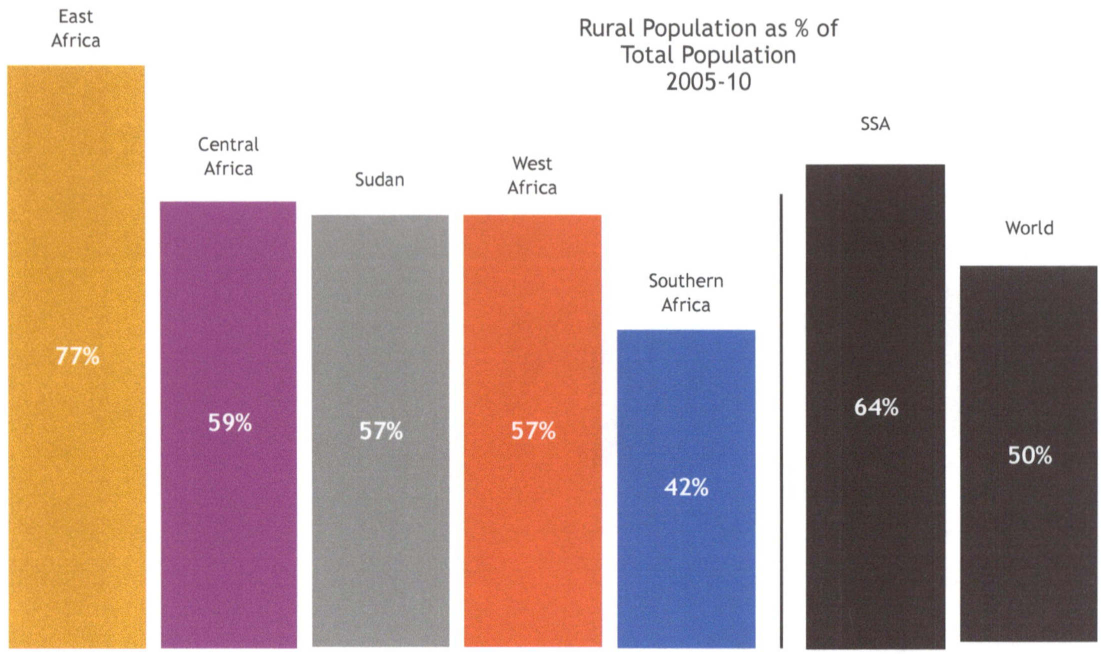


**_the country folk within_**

# 2.6b Rural Population in SSA: %. Top 10

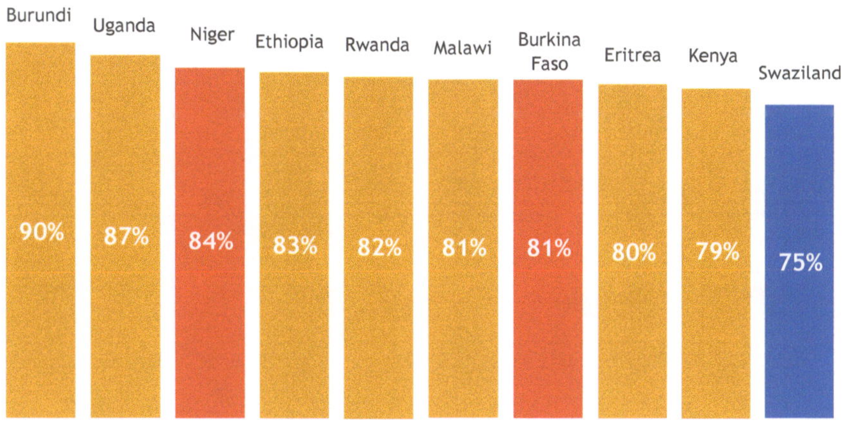


Rural Population as % of Total Population 2005-10

Central Africa
East Africa
Southern Africa
North Africa
West Africa

*us, country folk*

Total Rural Population 2005-10

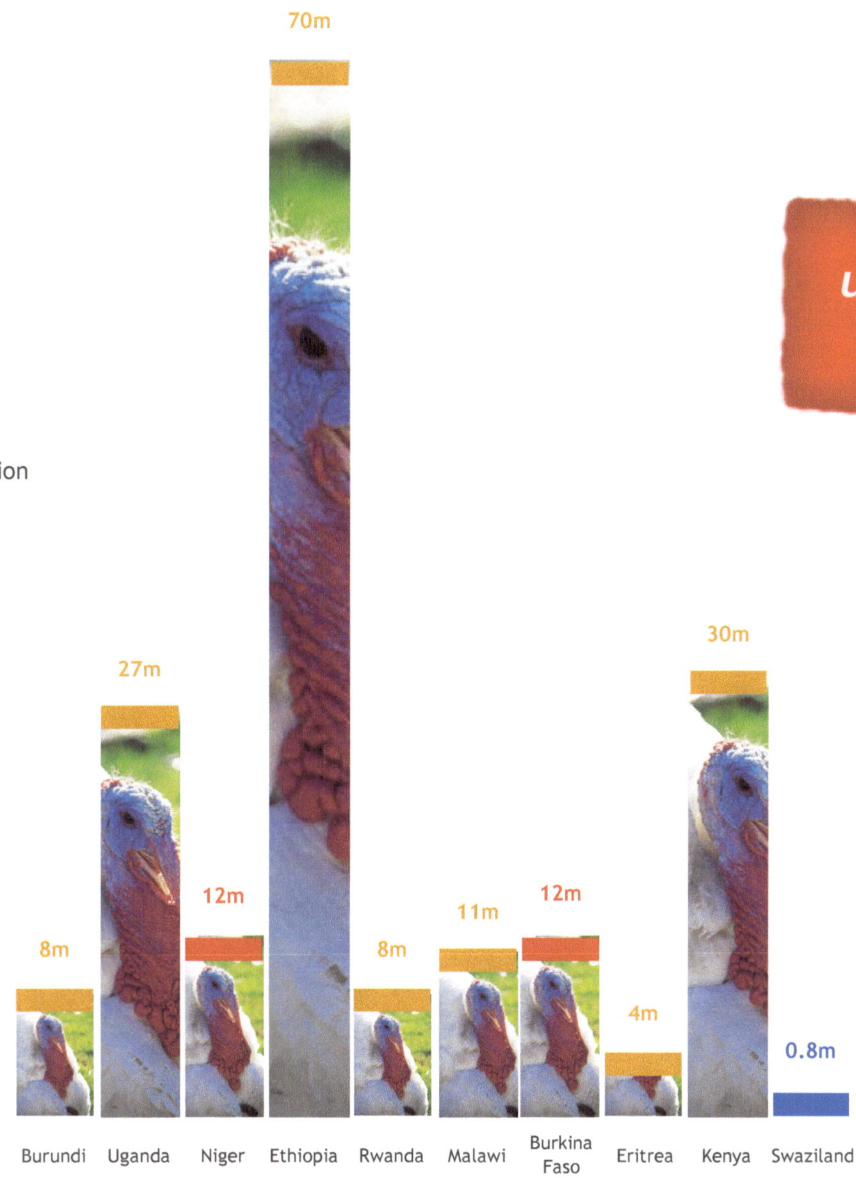


UNPD estimates

# 2.7 GDP in Sub-Saharan Africa's Regions ($PPP)

GDP of Sub-Saharan Africa during 1999/2002

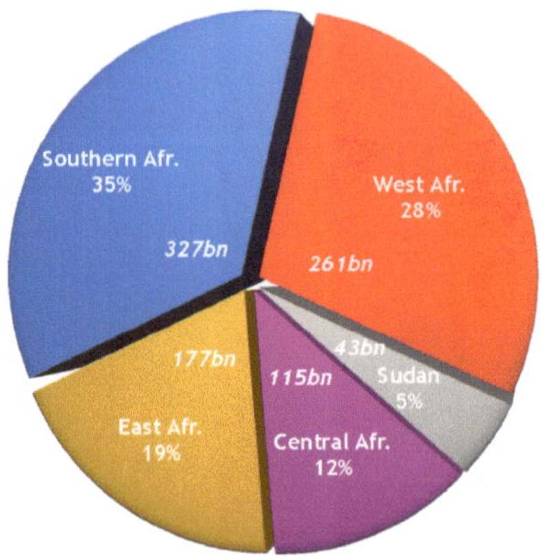


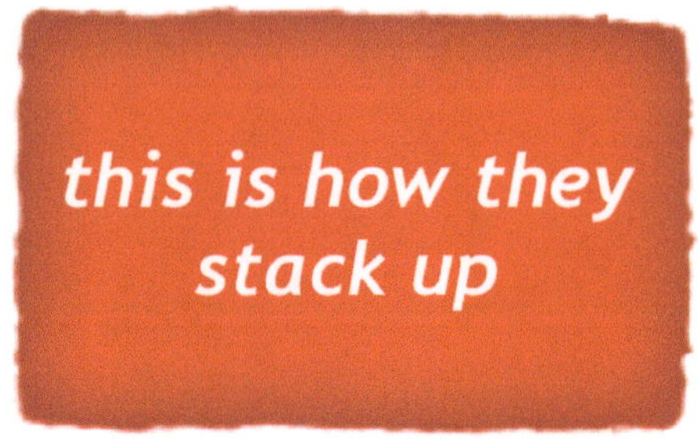


GDP of Sub-Saharan Africa during 2003/06

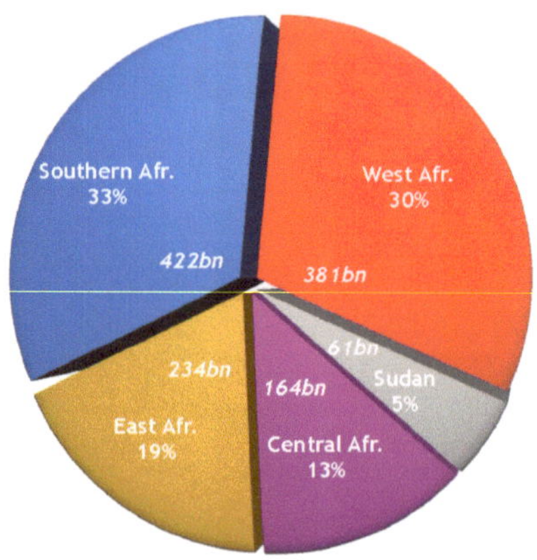


Contribution to the continent's GDP in 2009

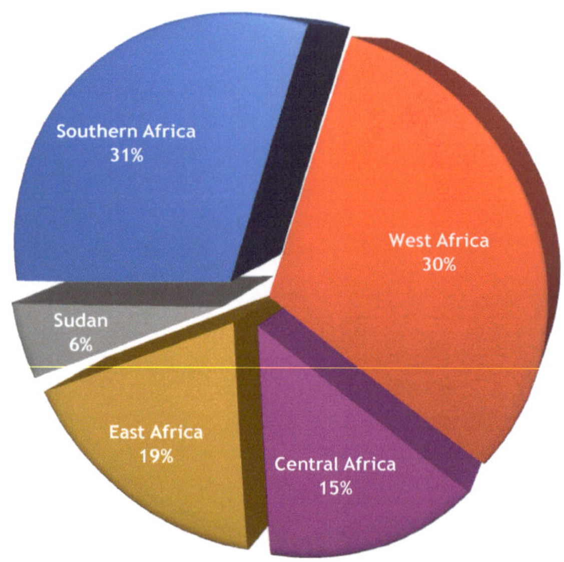


GDP of Sub-Saharan Africa during 2007/10

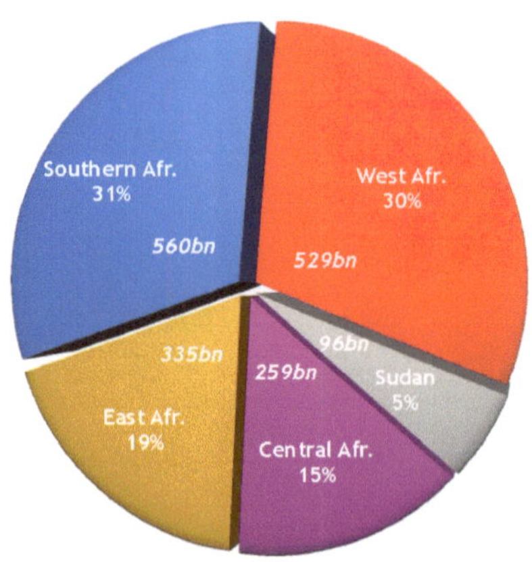


| 2009 | GDP $PPP billions | GDP per Person $PPP |
|---|---|---|
| Southern Africa | 574 | 10,229 |
| West Africa | 552 | 1,890 |
| East Africa | 345 | 1,219 |
| Central Africa | 272 | 2,208 |
| Sudan | 102 | 2,597 |

Primary data: IMF

# 3. The Size of Foreign Direct Investment

# 3.1 FDI Outcome in the World's Development Groups

FDI share in the world's economies ($US): 2007

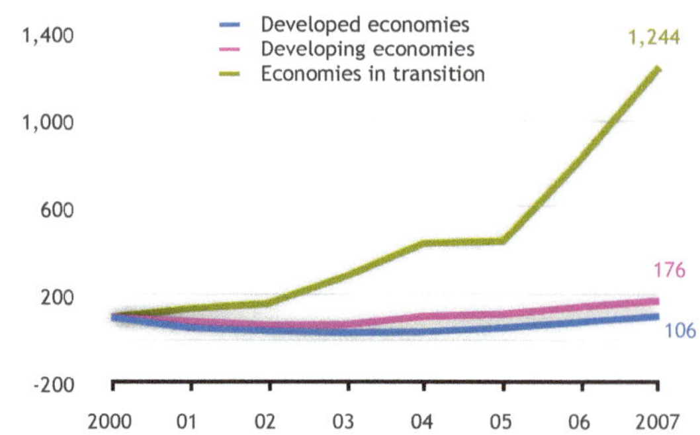


Build-up of FDI per person in the world's economies from 2000 to 2007: 2000=100

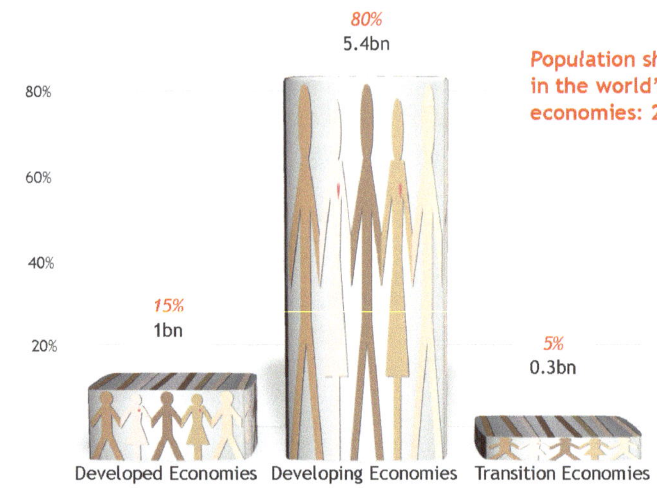


Population share in the world's economies: 2007

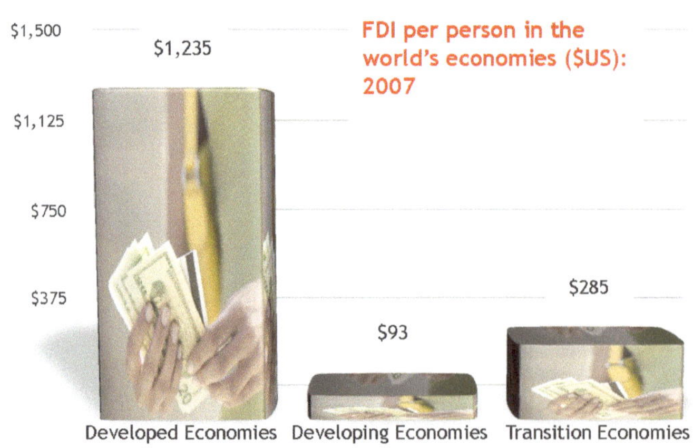


FDI per person in the world's economies ($US): 2007

- Not a surprising picture, perhaps. Most of the world's foreign investment by far, went to the developed nations. And the smallest effectively (when measured per person of population) ended up in the developing economies of the world.
- Partly because these developing economies have the largest population (5-and-a-half times the developed world's) and partly because they attracted a too small share of the world's FDI.
- The transition economies (mainly in eastern Europe and parts of south-east Asia) were a favourite destination between 2000 and 2007, with investment per person taking off and leaving both the developed and developing countries in its wake. Even though the latter two groups built on their year 2000 levels, albeit only marginally so.

Primary Data: UNCTAD

# 3.2 FDI Outcome in the Developing Economies

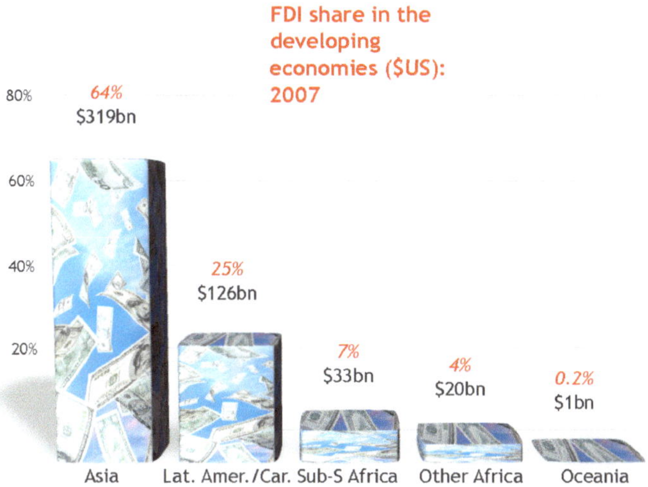


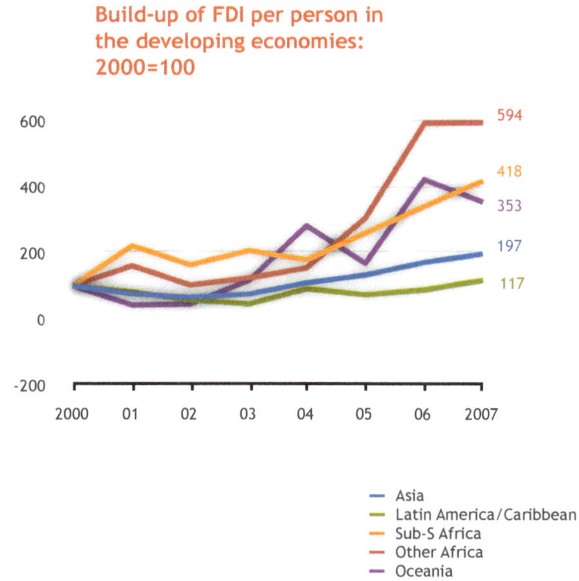


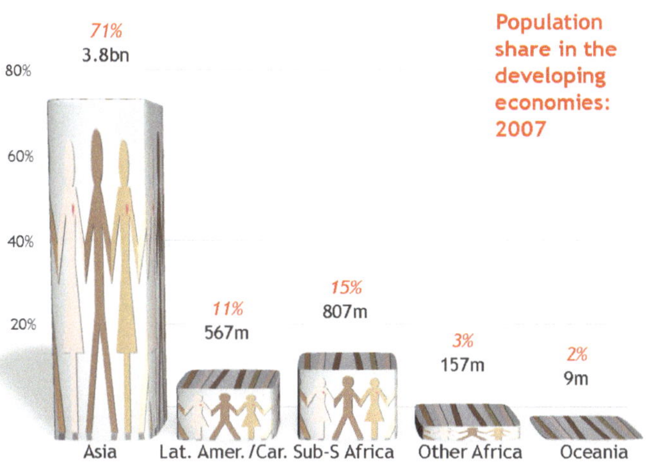


- Among the developing economies, Asian countries attracted the most FDI by a distance. But they also hold the highest number of residents, leaving them with only a moderate investment per person.
- That figure was still high, though, compared to the Sub-Saharan Africa level.
- Only Latin America/Caribbean & Other Africa attracted a share of developing world FDI larger than their shares of its population.
- Sub-Saharan Africa had the smallest FDI per inhabitant.
- Africa was gaining ground, though, building up on foreign investment faster than the rest of the developing world.

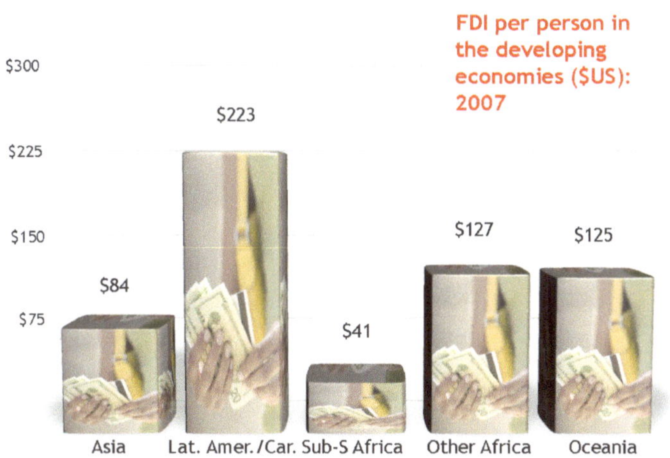


Primary Data: UNCTAD

# 3.3 FDI Outcome in the 5 Continents

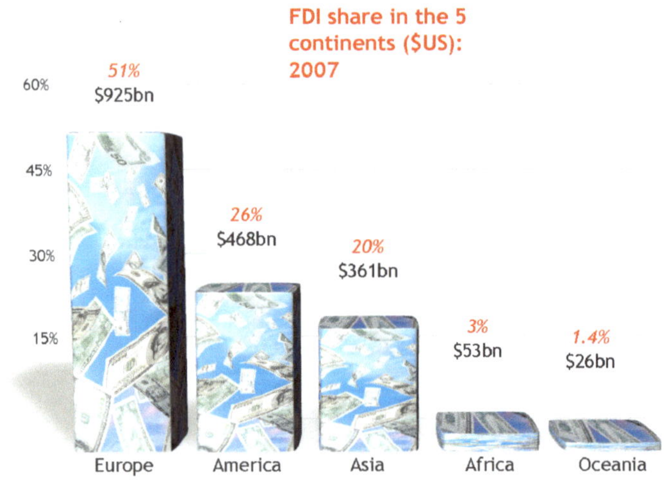


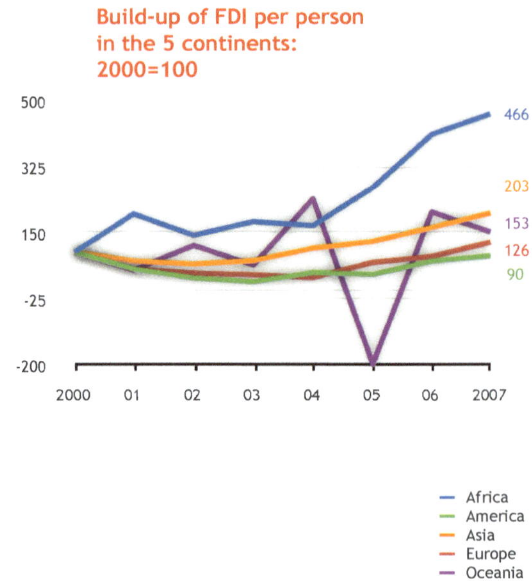


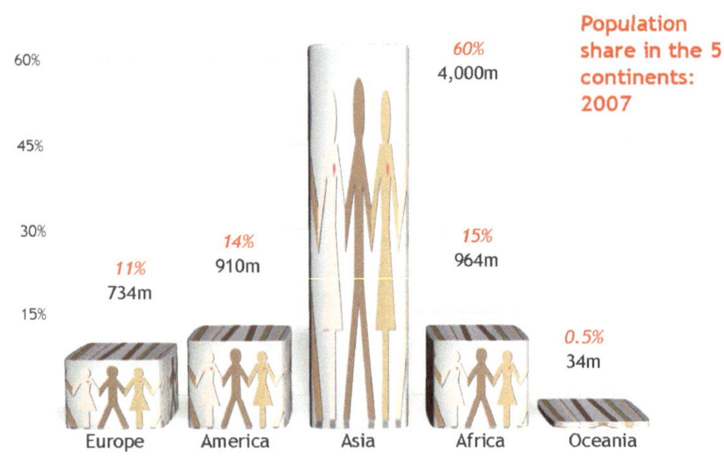


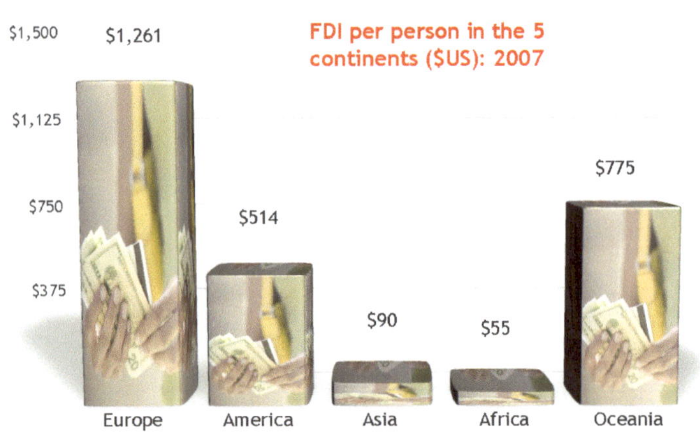


- Asia is the most populous of the 5 continents, commanding the third largest volume of foreign direct investment; behind Europe and both Americas.
- Africa is the 2nd most populous, behind Asia and ahead of America, Europe and Oceania. It cornered the least investment per person.
- That situation seems on course to change, though: Africa was building up FDI per population faster than the rest of the world, since the year 2000.

Primary Data: UNCTAD

# 3.4 FDI Outcome in Sub-Saharan Africa

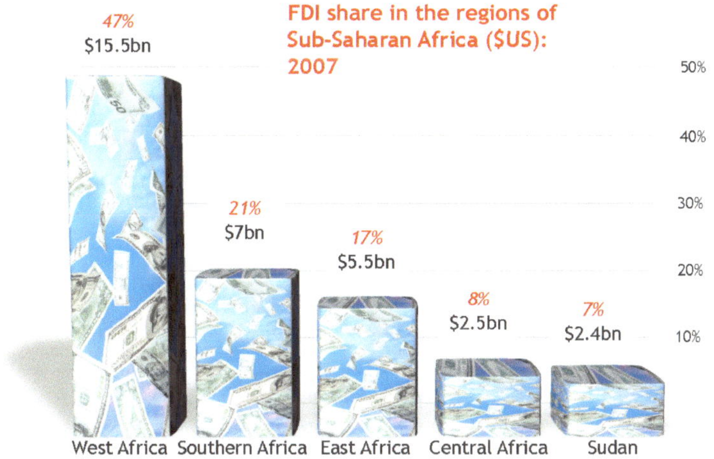


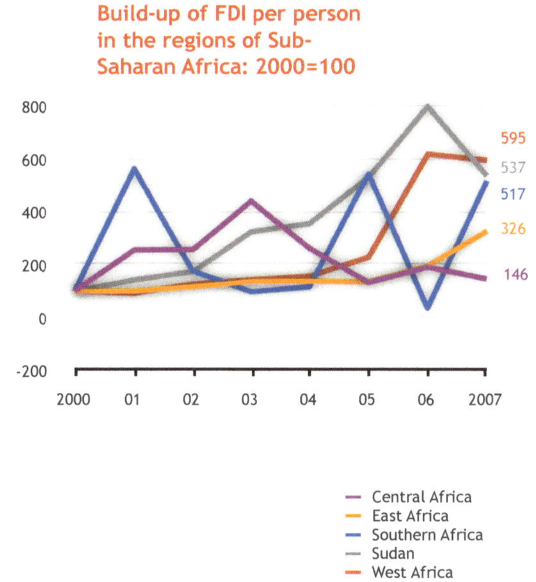


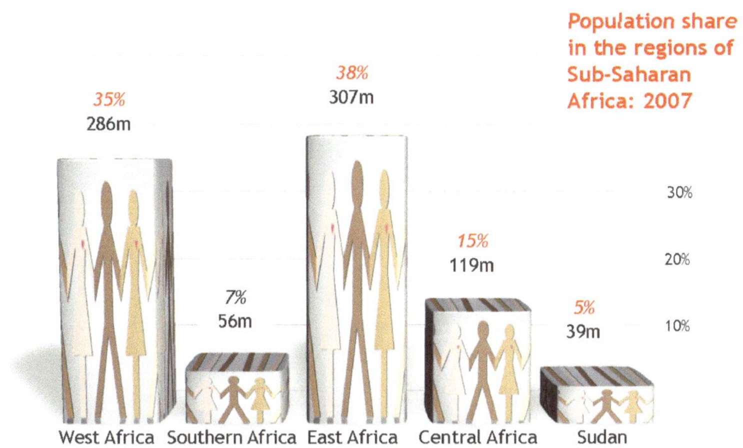


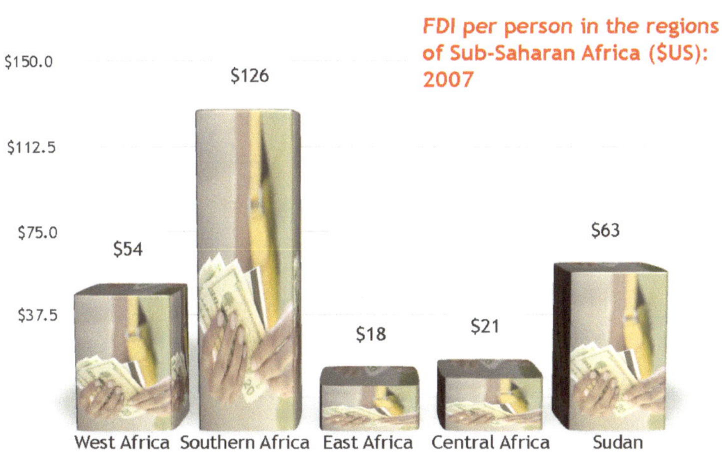


- Within Sub-Saharan Africa itself, West Africa was the final destination of most FDI, 47% of total. The next region was Southern Africa, with 21%, less than half West Africa's.

- Nevertheless, Southern Africa still ends up with the highest investment per resident, because its population is much smaller than West Africa's. Indeed, it had the highest FDI per person in the continent.

- Southern Africa was followed by Sudan in 2nd place, and West Africa in 3rd. Then Central Africa and East Africa in 4th and 5th place, respectively.

- In terms of levels of investment since the year 2000, West Africa was doing best, as at 2007. But it had been surpassed for many years by Sudan, until 2007. Southern Africa had varied haphazardly and Central Africa - of the 5 regions - had performed worst.

# 3.5 Share of FDI & Share of Population in S.S. Africa

**03-06**

| Share of FDI ▲ / Share of Population ▶ | bottom tier of population | middle tier of population | top tier of population |
|---|---|---|---|
| TOP TIER FDI: ranks 1 - 16 | Equat. Guinea<br>Botswana<br>Mauritania<br>Namibia | Chad<br>Zambia<br>Congo, Rep. | Nigeria<br>Sudan<br>South Africa<br>Angola<br>Ethiopia<br>Tanzania<br>Uganda<br>Cameroon<br>Côte d'Ivoire |
| MIDDLE TIER FDI: ranks 17 - 32 | Gabon<br>Seychelles<br>Cape Verde<br>Djibouti<br>Lesotho<br>Mauritius | Mali<br>Senegal<br>Guinea<br>Togo<br>Malawi<br>Benin<br>Sierra Leone | Ghana<br>Mozambique<br>Madagascar |
| BOTTOM TIER FDI: ranks 33 - 48 | Gambia<br>Sao Tome & Prin.<br>Guinea-Bissau<br>Comoros<br>Swaziland<br>Liberia | Somalia<br>Niger<br>Central Afr. Rep.<br>Rwanda<br>Eritrea<br>Burundi | Kenya<br>Zimbabwe<br>Burkina Faso<br>Congo, Dem. R. |

Central Africa
East Africa
Southern Africa
North Africa
West Africa

Primary Data: UNCTAD

| | % Share: 03-06 | FDI | Popn. |
|---|---|---|---|
| 1 | Nigeria | 31.6 | 18.4 |
| 2 | Sudan | 11.8 | 4.8 |
| 3 | South Africa | 10.4 | 6.3 |
| 4 | Equatorial Guinea | 9.0 | 0.1 |
| 5 | Angola | 4.9 | 2.1 |
| 6 | Chad | 3.4 | 1.3 |
| 7 | Ethiopia | 2.5 | 10.3 |
| 8 | Tanzania | 2.3 | 5.0 |
| 9 | Zambia | 2.3 | 1.5 |
| 10 | Botswana | 2.1 | 0.2 |
| 11 | Mauritania | 2.0 | 0.4 |
| 12 | Congo, Rep. | 1.9 | 0.5 |
| 13 | Uganda | 1.7 | 3.8 |
| 14 | Cameroon | 1.7 | 2.3 |
| 15 | Namibia | 1.5 | 0.3 |
| 16 | Côte d'Ivoire | 1.5 | 2.4 |

| | % Share: 03-06 | FDI | Popn. |
|---|---|---|---|
| 17 | Ghana | 1.4 | 2.9 |
| 18 | Mozambique | 1.1 | 2.7 |
| 19 | Gabon | 1.0 | 0.2 |
| 20 | Madagascar | 0.8 | 2.4 |
| 21 | Mali | 0.7 | 1.5 |
| 22 | Senegal | 0.5 | 1.5 |
| 23 | Guinea | 0.5 | 1.2 |
| 24 | Seychelles | 0.4 | 0.0 |
| 25 | Cape Verde | 0.4 | 0.1 |
| 26 | Djibouti | 0.4 | 0.1 |
| 27 | Togo | 0.3 | 0.8 |
| 28 | Lesotho | 0.3 | 0.3 |
| 29 | Malawi | 0.3 | 1.7 |
| 30 | Mauritius | 0.3 | 0.2 |
| 31 | Benin | 0.3 | 1.1 |
| 32 | Sierra Leone | 0.3 | 0.7 |

| | % Share: 03-06 | FDI | Popn. |
|---|---|---|---|
| 33 | Kenya | 0.3 | 4.6 |
| 34 | Gambia, The | 0.2 | 0.2 |
| 35 | Zimbabwe | 0.2 | 1.7 |
| 36 | Somalia | 0.2 | 1.1 |
| 37 | Niger | 0.2 | 1.7 |
| 38 | Burkina Faso | 0.2 | 1.8 |
| 39 | Central African Rep. | 0.1 | 0.5 |
| 40 | Sao Tome & Principe | 0.1 | 0.0 |
| 41 | Rwanda | 0.1 | 1.2 |
| 42 | Guinea-Bissau | 0.0 | 0.2 |
| 43 | Eritrea | 0.0 | 0.6 |
| 44 | Comoros | 0.0 | 0.1 |
| 45 | Burundi | 0.0 | 1.0 |
| 46 | Swaziland | 0.0 | 0.1 |
| 47 | Congo, Dem. Rep. | 0.0 | 7.6 |
| 48 | Liberia | -1.3 | 0.4 |

| | FDI per Person ($US) | 2007 |
|---|---|---|
| 1 | Equatorial Guinea | 3,402 |
| 2 | Seychelles | 2,861 |
| 3 | Namibia | 336 |
| 4 | Cape Verde | 334 |
| 5 | Mauritius | 269 |
| 6 | Botswana | 263 |
| 7 | Djibouti | 235 |
| 8 | Sao Tome & Principe | 224 |
| 9 | Gabon | 202 |
| 10 | South Africa | 117 |
| 11 | Congo, Rep. | 93 |
| 12 | Nigeria | 84 |
| 13 | Zambia | 83 |
| 14 | Sudan | 63 |
| 15 | Chad | 56 |
| 16 | Lesotho | 53 |
| 17 | Madagascar | 51 |
| 18 | Mauritania | 49 |
| 19 | Burkina Faso | 41 |
| 20 | Gambia, The | 37 |
| 21 | Ghana | 36 |
| 22 | Swaziland | 33 |
| 23 | Mali | 29 |
| 24 | Côte d'Ivoire | 22 |
| 25 | Mozambique | 20 |
| 26 | Kenya | 19 |
| 27 | Somalia | 16 |
| 28 | Cameroon | 15 |
| 29 | Tanzania | 15 |
| 30 | Sierra Leone | 14 |
| 31 | Uganda | 12 |
| 32 | Guinea | 12 |
| 33 | Congo, Dem. Rep. | 11 |
| 34 | Liberia | 11 |
| 35 | Togo | 10 |
| 36 | Rwanda | 7 |
| 37 | Senegal | 6 |
| 38 | Central African Rep. | 6 |
| 39 | Benin | 5 |
| 40 | Zimbabwe | 5 |
| 41 | Guinea-Bissau | 4 |
| 42 | Malawi | 4 |
| 43 | Ethiopia | 3 |
| 44 | Niger | 2 |
| 45 | Comoros | 1 |
| 46 | Burundi | 0 |
| 47 | Eritrea | -1 |
| 48 | Angola | -88 |

# 3.6 Share of FDI & Share of Population in West Africa

**this is how it worked out**

**2003 - 2006:**

- Nigeria, expectedly, gulped the greatest part of the foreign direct investment in West Africa.
- Only 4 countries of the 16 cornered a larger share of West Africa's foreign direct investment than their share of its population size: Nigeria, Mauritania, Cape Verde, and - marginally - The Gambia.

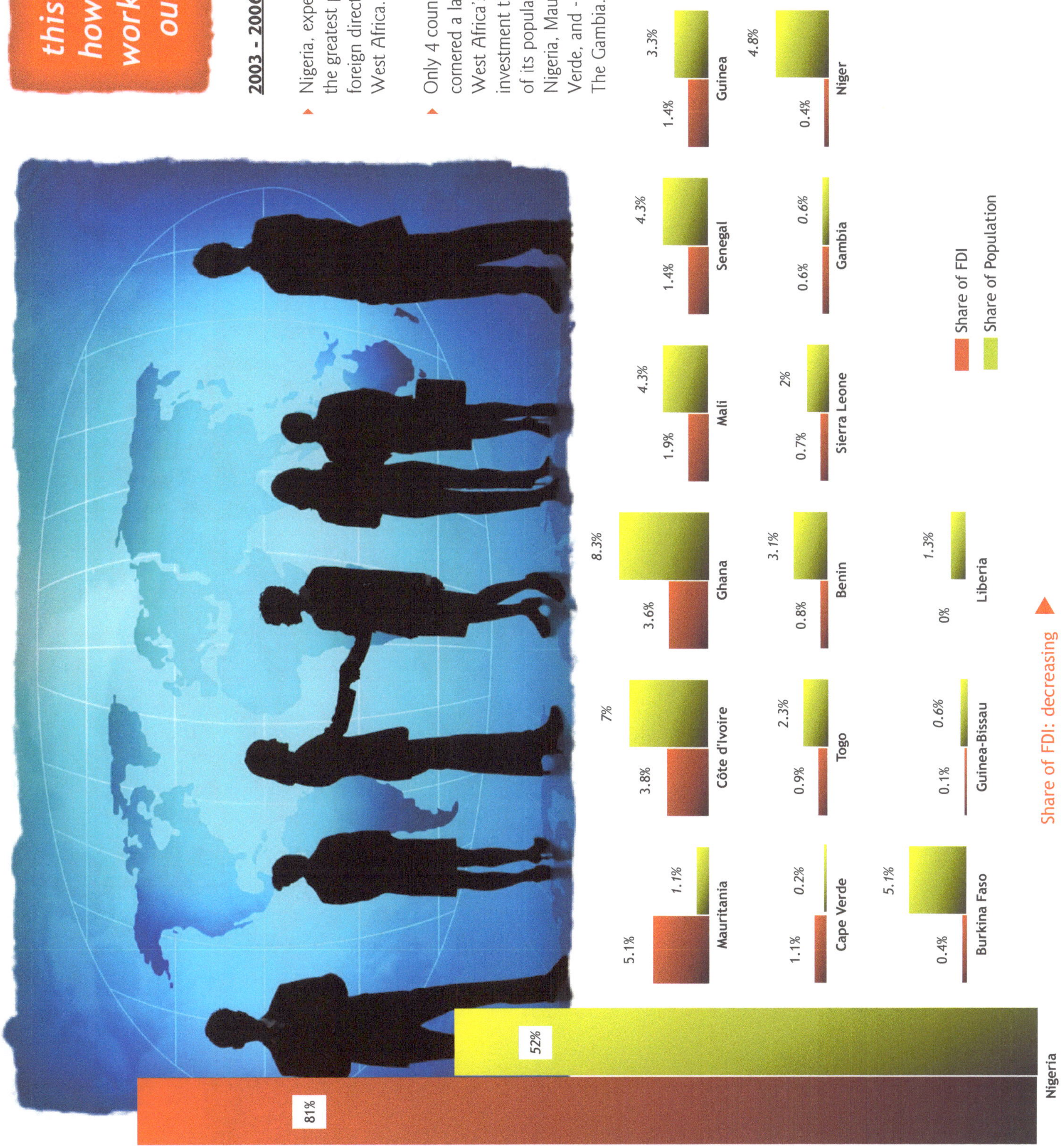

# 4. Tricky Relations

# 4.1 Tricky Relations: Foreign Aid & Quality of Life

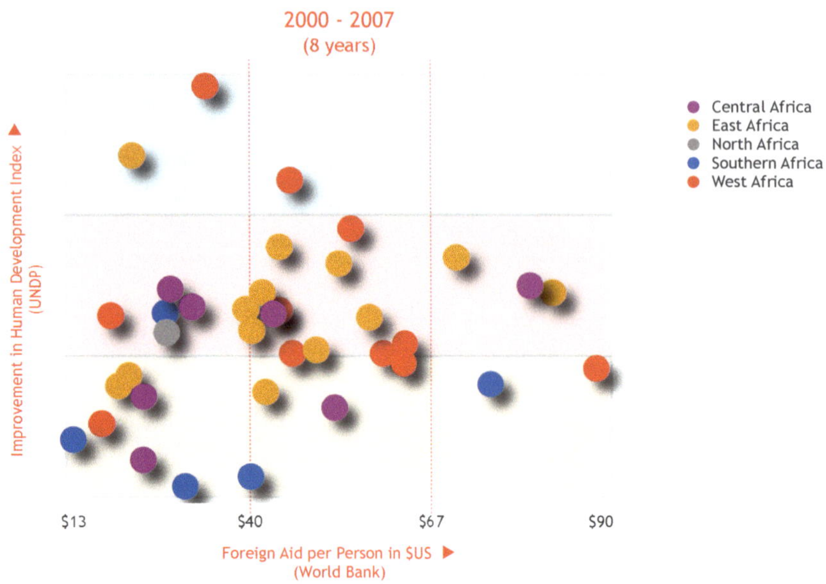


% distribution:

| A 5% | D 3% | G 0% | 8% |
|---|---|---|---|
| B 16% | E 27% | H 8% | 51% |
| C 19% | F 17% | I 5% | 41% |
| 40% | 47% | 13% | |

A: low aid, high improvement in quality of life
B: low aid, medium improvement in quality of life
C: low aid, low improvement in quality of life

D: medium aid, high improvement in quality of life
E: medium aid, medium improvement in quality of life
F: medium aid, low improvement in quality of life

G: high aid, high improvement in quality of life
H: high aid, medium improvement in quality of life
I: high aid, low improvement in quality of life

**A**
1. Niger
2. Ethiopia

2

**D**
1. Burkina Faso

1

**G**

0

**B**
1. Chad
2. Congo, D.R.
3. Burundi
4. Botswana
5. Nigeria
6. Sudan

6

**E**
1. Mali
2. Tanzania
3. Rwanda
4. Uganda
5. Benin
6. Equat. Guinea
7. Eritrea
8. Madagascar
9. Guinea-Bissau
10. Comoros

10

**H**
1. Mozambique
2. Congo, Rep.
3. Zambia

3

**C**
1. Mauritius
2. Kenya
3. Gabon
4. Côte d'Ivoire
5. South Africa
6. Central Afr. R.
7. Swaziland

7

**F**
1. Senegal
2. Ghana
3. Liberia
4. Malawi
5. Cameroon
6. Lesotho

6

**I**
1. Mauritania
2. Namibia

2

| | Country | Improvemt in Qlty of Life (%) | Aid per Pers. (US$) |
|---|---|---|---|
| 1 | Niger | 3.92 | 33 |
| 2 | Ethiopia | 3.13 | 22 |
| 3 | Burkina Faso | 2.85 | 45 |
| 4 | Mali | 2.3 | 54 |
| 5 | Tanzania | 2.09 | 43 |
| 6 | Mozambique | 1.97 | 69 |
| 7 | Rwanda | 1.9 | 52 |
| 8 | Congo, Rep. | 1.65 | 80 |
| 9 | Chad | 1.61 | 27 |
| 10 | Uganda | 1.57 | 41 |
| 11 | Zambia | 1.57 | 83 |
| 12 | Congo, Dem. Rep. | 1.41 | 31 |
| 13 | Burundi | 1.38 | 38 |
| 14 | Benin | 1.37 | 43 |
| 15 | Botswana | 1.34 | 27 |
| 16 | Equatorial Guinea | 1.33 | 42 |
| 17 | Nigeria | 1.31 | 19 |
| 18 | Eritrea | 1.29 | 57 |
| 19 | Madagascar | 1.14 | 39 |
| 20 | Sudan | 1.12 | 27 |
| 21 | Guinea-Bissau | 0.99 | 62 |
| 22 | Comoros | 0.92 | 49 |
| 23 | Ghana | 0.88 | 45 |
| 24 | Senegal | 0.88 | 59 |
| 25 | Liberia | 0.77 | 62 |
| 26 | Mauritania | 0.71 | 90 |
| 27 | Cape Verde | 0.71 | 270 |
| 28 | Mauritius | 0.63 | 21 |
| 29 | Namibia | 0.53 | 74 |
| 30 | Kenya | 0.51 | 20 |
| 31 | Malawi | 0.44 | 41 |
| 32 | Gabon | 0.39 | 24 |
| 33 | Cameroon | 0.26 | 51 |
| 34 | Côte d'Ivoire | 0.08 | 17 |
| 35 | Seychelles | 0.06 | 137 |
| 36 | South Africa | -0.1 | 13 |
| 37 | Central African Rep. | -0.33 | 23 |
| 38 | Lesotho | -0.52 | 39 |
| 39 | Swaziland | -0.63 | 30 |

## 4. Tricky Relations

- Data on foreign aid here is as provided by the World Bank. Improvement in quality of life is as assessed by the United Nations Development Programme (UNDP) through its Human Development Index. 39 Sub-Saharan Africa countries had enough data to compare the two indices, but 2 countries had unusually high foreign aid per person, which flew way beyond the other countries, so they were left out of the chart-comparison here, leaving 37 countries. Those two countries are Cape Verde, with $270 per capita, and Seychelles, with $137. They would both have fallen within the "low improvement in quality of life" sector.

- It should be borne in mind that low improvement in quality of life does not necessarily translate into low quality of life. The progress made during these 8 years (2000-2007) might very well be smaller in country Y compared to country Z, but country Y's level of quality of life might very well be vastly superior to Z's, even though the leap in level across the 8 years is smaller. (Indeed, the leap might be smaller precisely because there isn't much more room to improve from the subsisting level. Hence South Africa and Mauritius fall into the bottom quality of life improvement group. Nonetheless, for the majority of African economies, the improvement levels shown would still be an appropriate reflection of the existing levels of quality of life.)

- It turns out that there isn't an obvious pattern to the foreign aid received and the ensuing level of quality of life. Most countries ended up in the average levels: 47% received medium aid, and 51% turned up with medium improvements in quality of life. The scattered dots show the absence of any clearly defined pattern.

- However, it can be seen that of the 3 countries with the best improvement in quality of life, 2 are from West Africa (Niger, followed by Burkina Faso) and 1 from East Africa (Ethiopia). It is also interesting to note that Niger received less aid than Burkina Faso, but outdid it in quality of life improvement, as did Ethiopia as well.

- In the medium segment of quality of life improvement, a West African country also comes out tops: Mali, and it received average foreign aid amounts.

- Mauritania received the most aid ($90) but didn't make much progress in quality of life.

- Even though most of Southern Africa fell into the bottom quality of life improvement category, as explained above, they still had high absolute levels of quality of life. Nonetheless, South Africa, Lesotho and Swaziland, actually recorded deterioration in quality of life, albeit to small extents.

- ***Hence, no apparent relationship between foreign aid and improvement in quality of life. There must be other stronger factors at play.***

# 4.2 Tricky Relations: Foreign Aid & Economic Growth

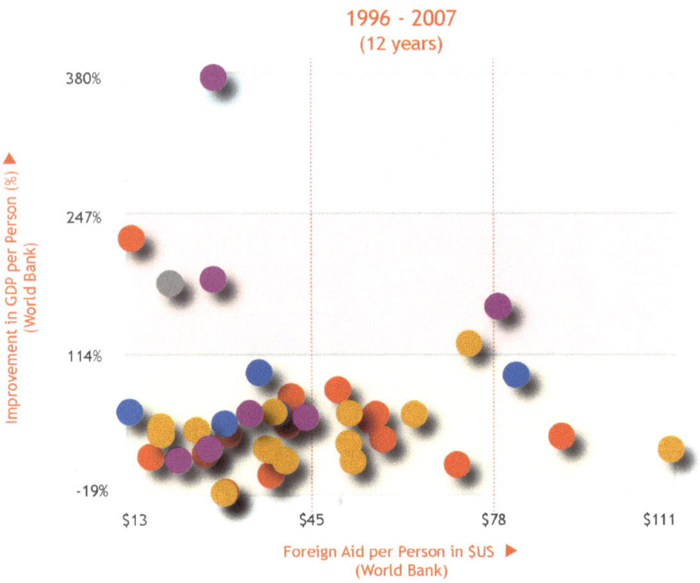


% distribution:

| | | | |
|---|---|---|---|
| A 2% | D 0% | G 0% | 2% |
| B 7% | E 2% | H 2% | 11% |
| C 58% | F 22% | I 7% | 87% |
| 67% | 24% | 9% | |

A: low aid, high economic growth
B: low aid, medium economic growth
C: low aid, low economic growth

D: medium aid, high economic growth
E: medium aid, medium economic growth
F: medium aid, low economic growth

G: high aid, high economic growth
H: high aid, medium economic growth
I: high aid, low economic growth

**A**
1. Angola

1

**D**

0

**G**

0

**B**
1. Nigeria
2. Chad
3. Sudan

3

**E**
1. Zambia

1

**H**
1. Congo, Rep.

1

**C**
1. Botswana
2. Burkina Faso
3. Benin
4. South Africa
5. Tanzania
6. Lesotho
7. Gabon
8. Cameroon
9. Swaziland
10. Ghana
11. Ethiopia
12. Mauritius
13. Niger
14. Kenya
15. Uganda
16. Central Afr. R.
17. Madagascar
18. Côte d'Ivoire
19. Togo
20. Congo, D.R.
21. Malawi
22. Gambia
23. Guinea
24. Burundi

24

**F**
1. Mali
2. Comoros
3. Mozambique
4. Senegal
5. Liberia
6. Sierra Leone
7. Eritrea
8. Rwanda
9. Guinea-Bissau

9

**I**
1. Namibia
2. Mauritania
3. Djibouti

3

| | Country | Improvement in GDP/pers | Aid/pers. |
|---|---|---|---|
| | | (%) | (US$) |
| 1 | Angola | 379 | 28 |
| 2 | Nigeria | 225 | 13 |
| 3 | Chad | 186 | 28 |
| 4 | Sudan | 182 | 20 |
| 5 | Congo, Rep. | 160 | 80 |
| 6 | Zambia | 124 | 74 |
| 7 | Cape Verde | 102 | 278 |
| 8 | Botswana | 96 | 36 |
| 9 | Namibia | 94 | 83 |
| 10 | Mali | 80 | 50 |
| 11 | Burkina Faso | 73 | 42 |
| 12 | Benin | 60 | 41 |
| 13 | South Africa | 59 | 13 |
| 14 | Tanzania | 58 | 39 |
| 15 | Comoros | 57 | 52 |
| 16 | Lesotho | 57 | 39 |
| 17 | Gabon | 57 | 34 |
| 18 | Mozambique | 56 | 64 |
| 19 | Senegal | 56 | 57 |
| 20 | Cameroon | 54 | 45 |
| 21 | Seychelles | 52 | 170 |
| 22 | Liberia | 50 | 56 |
| 23 | Swaziland | 47 | 30 |
| 24 | Ghana | 46 | 41 |
| 25 | Ethiopia | 45 | 18 |
| 26 | Mauritius | 41 | 25 |
| 27 | Niger | 38 | 30 |
| 28 | Kenya | 37 | 18 |
| 29 | Mauritania | 35 | 91 |
| 30 | Sierra Leone | 33 | 59 |
| 31 | Eritrea | 28 | 52 |
| 32 | Uganda | 23 | 37 |
| 33 | Central African Rep. | 23 | 27 |
| 34 | Djibouti | 23 | 111 |
| 35 | Madagascar | 22 | 38 |
| 36 | Côte d'Ivoire | 18 | 26 |
| 37 | Togo | 16 | 16 |
| 38 | Congo, Dem. Rep. | 12 | 21 |
| 39 | Malawi | 12 | 41 |
| 40 | Rwanda | 11 | 53 |
| 41 | Guinea-Bissau | 8 | 72 |
| 42 | Gambia, The | -2 | 38 |
| 43 | Guinea | -18 | 30 |
| 44 | Burundi | -19 | 30 |

## 4. Tricky Relations

- This time, the comparison is possible for a period as long as 12 years: the average foreign aid per capita during 1996-2007 is compared with the change in GDP per capita during the same years. That change is evaluated by taking the moving 3-year average at the period's start and comparing it with the closing moving 3-year average at its end.

- 44 countries in total, but two are dropped from the chart because of their extreme aid-per-person figures. They are Cape Verde ($278) and the Seychelles ($170). They would both have fallen into the low economic growth segment, hardly altering the conclusion.

- The majority of countries by far (87%) ended up in the low economic growth group. Even making allowances for the large economies among them (few, like South Africa) that may not be able - and may not need - to grow as rapidly as counterpart smaller economies, the outcome nevertheless strongly suggests that foreign aid has borne little connection to economic outcomes.

- The economies that grew fastest, ending up in the top two rows, were mainly oil exporters: Angola in the top row, then Nigeria, Chad, Sudan, and Republic of the Congo. Zambia is the only non-oil economy among them. Of these six, the leading four received less foreign aid than most of the continent.

- Indeed, the highest aid recipient on the chart is Djibouti, and that doesn't seem to have affected its rate of economic growth during the 12 year period.

- It doesn't seem that there are geographical peculiarities, either: the bottom row is awash with countries from all corners of the region.

- ***Tricky relations? Perhaps. But it does seem that volume of foreign aid received does not affect the pace of economic change.***

# 4.3 Tricky Relations: Foreign Aid & Child Mortality

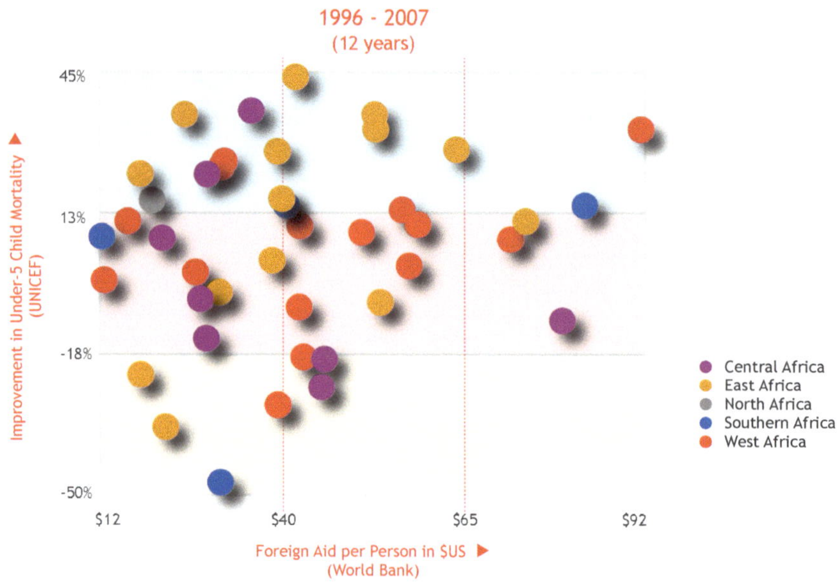


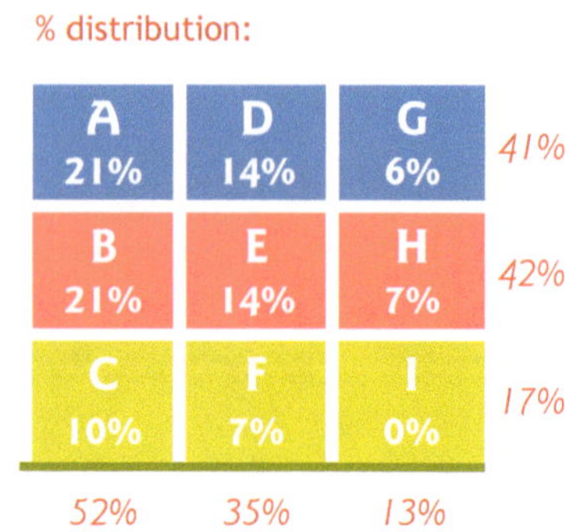


A: low aid, best improvement in child mortality
B: low aid, average improvement in child mortality
C: low aid, least improvement in child mortality

D: medium aid, best improvement in child mortality
E: medium aid, average improvement in child mortality
F: medium aid, least improvement in child mortality

G: high aid, best improvement in child mortality
H: high aid, average improvement in child mortality
I: high aid, least improvement in child mortality

**A**

1. Gabon
2. Mauritius
3. Madagascar
4. Niger
5. Guinea
6. Ethiopia
7. Angola
8. Tanzania
9. Sudan

9

**D**

1. Malawi
2. Eritrea
3. Comoros
4. Mozambique
5. Lesotho
6. Liberia

6

**G**

1. Mauritania
2. Namibia

2

**B**

1. Togo
2. South Africa
3. Congo, D.R.
4. Uganda
5. Côte d'Ivoire
6. Nigeria
7. Burundi
8. Central Afr. R.
9. Chad

9

**E**

1. Sierra Leone
2. Benin
3. Mali
4. Senegal
5. Rwanda
6. Ghana

6

**H**

1. Zambia
2. Guinea-Bissau
3. Congo, Rep.

3

**C**

1. Kenya
2. Gambia
3. Zimbabwe
4. Swaziland

4

**F**

1. Burkina Faso
2. Equat. Guinea
3. Cameroon

3

**I**

0

| | Country | Improvement in U-5 Mortalty | Aid/pers. |
|---|---|---|---|
| | | (%) | ($US) |
| 1 | • Cape Verde | 54 | 278 |
| 2 | • Malawi | 45 | 41 |
| 3 | • Gabon | 37 | 34 |
| 4 | • Mauritius | 36 | 25 |
| 5 | • Eritrea | 36 | 52 |
| 6 | • Comoros | 33 | 52 |
| 7 | • Mauritania | 33 | 91 |
| 8 | • Seychelles | 29 | 170 |
| 9 | • Mozambique | 28 | 64 |
| 10 | • Madagascar | 28 | 38 |
| 11 | • Niger | 26 | 30 |
| 12 | • Guinea | 24 | 30 |
| 13 | • Ethiopia | 23 | 18 |
| 14 | • Angola | 23 | 28 |
| 15 | • Tanzania | 17 | 39 |
| 16 | • Djibouti | 17 | 111 |
| 17 | • Sudan | 17 | 20 |
| 18 | • Lesotho | 16 | 39 |
| 19 | • Namibia | 16 | 83 |
| 20 | • Liberia | 15 | 56 |
| 21 | • Zambia | 12 | 74 |
| 22 | • Togo | 12 | 16 |
| 23 | • Sierra Leone | 11 | 59 |
| 24 | • Benin | 11 | 41 |
| 25 | • Mali | 9 | 50 |
| 26 | • South Africa | 8 | 13 |
| 27 | • Congo, Dem. Rep. | 8 | 21 |
| 28 | • Guinea-Bissau | 8 | 72 |
| 29 | • Uganda | 3 | 37 |
| 30 | • Senegal | 2 | 57 |
| 31 | • Côte d'Ivoire | 0 | 26 |
| 32 | • Nigeria | -2 | 13 |
| 33 | • Burundi | -4 | 30 |
| 34 | • Central African Rep. | -6 | 27 |
| 35 | • Rwanda | -7 | 53 |
| 36 | • Ghana | -8 | 41 |
| 37 | • Congo, Rep. | -11 | 80 |
| 38 | • Chad | -15 | 28 |
| 39 | • Burkina Faso | -19 | 42 |
| 40 | • Equatorial Guinea | -20 | 45 |
| 41 | • Kenya | -23 | 18 |
| 42 | • Cameroon | -26 | 45 |
| 43 | • Gambia, The | -30 | 38 |
| 44 | • Sao Tome & Principe | -33 | 231 |
| 45 | • Zimbabwe | -35 | 22 |
| 46 | • Swaziland | -48 | 30 |
| 47 | • Botswana | -93 | 36 |

- Data is available this time for all 48 countries except Somalia. Under-5 child mortality, here provided by UNICEF, refers to the number of children out of 1,000 who die before their 5th birthday. We measured improvement by comparing the opening 3-yr moving average (1996-1998) of the mortality figure, to the closing 3-yr moving average (2005-2007).

- Within those 47 countries, 5 fell around the chart extremes and were left out of it for better analysis. Four of them had extreme aid per person figures: Cape Verde ($278), Sao Tome & Principe ($231), the Seychelles ($170) and Djibouti ($111). All of them, except Sao Tome & Principe, would have landed in the top row of improvement in child mortality, as can be gleaned from the table at left. Botswana is the 5th country removed, this time for the extremity of its mortality deterioration, 93%.

- It turns out that there might indeed be a trend towards a bigger improvement in mortality figures with the increase of foreign aid. The countries which suffered the worst improvement were generally those which had received less aid. As aid increased, the mortality situation seemed to improve alongside it.

- It can be noted, though, that among the least aid recipients were to be found some countries that nonetheless posted the best improvements in under-5 mortality: Gabon and Mauritius, particularly, among 7 others. The most improvement was notched by Malawi, and it received less than the average aid per capita on the continent.

- ***Still, there seems to be a trend towards improvement in mortality figures with the increase of foreign aid. Perhaps these specific aid tranches were aimed directly at health targets.***

# 4.4 Tricky Relations: Foreign Aid & Life Expectancy

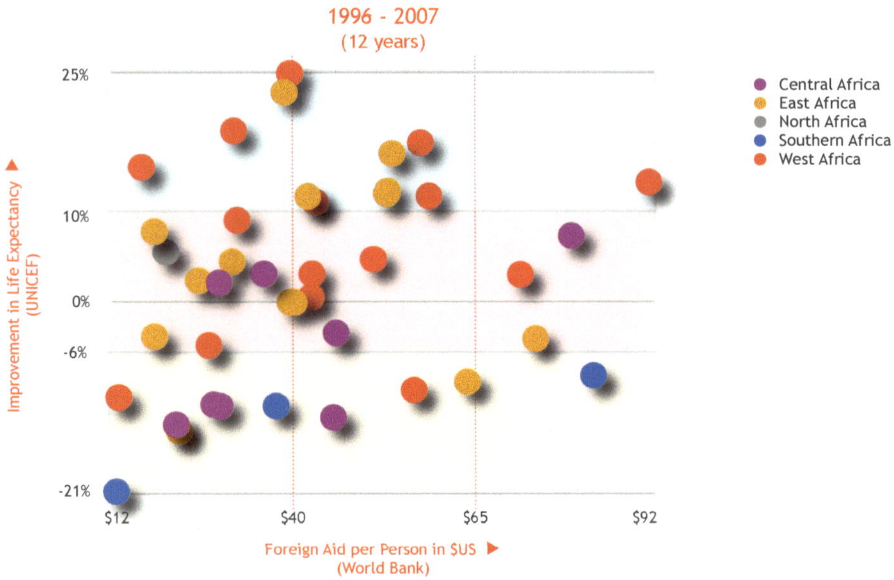


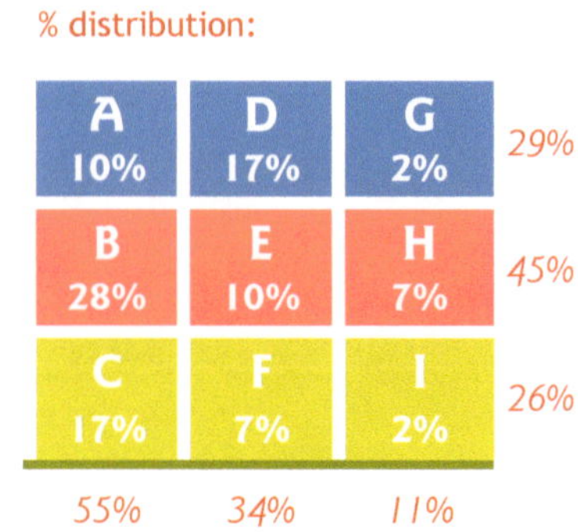


A: low aid, best improvement in life expectancy
B: low aid, average improvement in life expectancy
C: low aid, least improvement in life expectancy

D: medium aid, best improvement in life expectancy
E: medium aid, average improvement in life expectancy
F: medium aid, least improvement in life expectancy

G: high aid, best improvement in life expectancy
H: high aid, average improvement in life expectancy
I: high aid, least improvement in life expectancy

**A**

1. Gambia
2. Uganda
3. Guinea
4. Togo

4

**D**

1. Senegal
2. Rwanda
3. Comoros
4. Eritrea
5. Sierra Leone
6. Malawi
7. Burkina Faso

7

**G**

1. Mauritania

1

**B**

1. Niger
2. Ethiopia
3. Sudan
4. Burundi
5. Gabon
6. Mauritius
7. Chad
8. Tanzania
9. Madagascar
10. Kenya
11. Côte d'Ivoire

11

**E**

1. Mali
2. Benin
3. Ghana
4. Equat. Guinea

4

**H**

1. Congo, Rep.
2. Guinea-Bissau
3. Zambia

3

**C**

1. Nigeria
2. Central Afr. R.
3. Botswana
4. Angola
5. Congo, D.R.
6. Zimbabwe
7. South Africa

7

**F**

1. Mozambique
2. Liberia
3. Cameroon

3

**I**

1. Namibia

1

| | Country | Improvmt in Life Exp. | Aid per Pers. |
|---|---|---|---|
| | | (%) | ($US) |
| 1 | Gambia, The | 25 | 38 |
| 2 | Uganda | 23 | 37 |
| 3 | Guinea | 18.7 | 30 |
| 4 | Senegal | 17.4 | 57 |
| 5 | Rwanda | 16.2 | 53 |
| 6 | Togo | 14.8 | 16 |
| 7 | Mauritania | 13.1 | 91 |
| 8 | Comoros | 12.1 | 52 |
| 9 | Eritrea | 11.8 | 52 |
| 10 | Malawi | 11.6 | 41 |
| 11 | Sierra Leone | 11.6 | 59 |
| 12 | Burkina Faso | 10.9 | 42 |
| 13 | Niger | 9 | 30 |
| 14 | Ethiopia | 7.7 | 18 |
| 15 | Congo, Rep. | 7.3 | 80 |
| 16 | Djibouti | 7.3 | 111 |
| 17 | Cape Verde | 5.9 | 278 |
| 18 | Sudan | 5.5 | 20 |
| 19 | Mali | 4.7 | 50 |
| 20 | Burundi | 4.4 | 30 |
| 21 | Gabon | 3.1 | 34 |
| 22 | Benin | 3.1 | 41 |
| 23 | Guinea-Bissau | 3 | 72 |
| 24 | Mauritius | 2.3 | 25 |
| 25 | Chad | 2.1 | 28 |
| 26 | Ghana | 0.6 | 41 |
| 27 | Tanzania | 0 | 39 |
| 28 | Madagascar | 0 | 38 |
| 29 | Sao Tome & Principe | -2 | 231 |
| 30 | Equatorial Guinea | -3.4 | 45 |
| 31 | Kenya | -3.8 | 18 |
| 32 | Zambia | -4 | 74 |
| 33 | Côte d'Ivoire | -4.7 | 26 |
| 34 | Namibia | -8 | 83 |
| 35 | Mozambique | -8.7 | 64 |
| 36 | Liberia | -9.6 | 56 |
| 37 | Nigeria | -10.4 | 13 |
| 38 | Central African Rep. | -11.2 | 27 |
| 39 | Angola | -11.3 | 28 |
| 40 | Botswana | -11.3 | 36 |
| 41 | Cameroon | -12.6 | 45 |
| 42 | Congo, Dem. Rep. | -13.4 | 21 |
| 43 | Zimbabwe | -14.1 | 22 |
| 44 | South Africa | -20.7 | 13 |
| 45 | Lesotho | -31.8 | 39 |
| 46 | Swaziland | -38.5 | 30 |

- Data was available this time for all 48 countries except Somalia and the Seychelles. Cape Verde ($278), Sao Tome & Principe ($231) and Djibouti ($111) were removed from the chart, for extremity of aid data. Cape Verde and Djibouti reported improvement in life expectancy (Cape Verde: 6%, Djibouti: 7.3%) and would have qualified for the middle row of average improvement. Sao Tome & Principe, however, reported a deterioration (-2%) but would still have qualified in the middle row. Their absence doesn't alter the chart outcome much.

- On the contrary, the other two countries omitted from the chart might have done. Lesotho and Swaziland had the worst performance by far, clocking -32% and -39%, respectively. Southern Africa had the worst life expectancy deterioration figures: South Africa (-21%), Lesotho (-32%) and Swaziland (-39%) had the worst drops.

- Of the countries that received average aid, a greater number ended up in the top improvement bracket, than ended up in the bottom. It was almost the same for those that received the highest aid. Unlike those that received the least aid (more of them ended up at bottom than did at the top). Small bias towards concluding that more aid brought better advancement in life expectancy, but probably valid, nonetheless.

- West Africa made more progress in life expectancy than any other region, squeezing 7 of its 16 countries into the top row. No Central African country made top row. All Southern Africa fell into the bottom row; they were hardest hit by the pace of deterioration in life expectancy.

- ***Close call, but aid seems to have helped life expectancy outcomes.***

# 4.5 Tricky Relations: Foreign Aid & Emigration

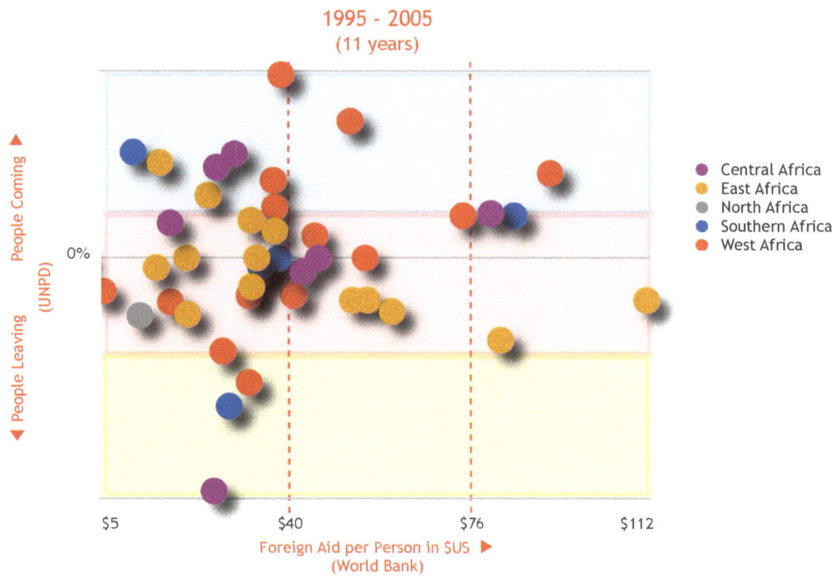


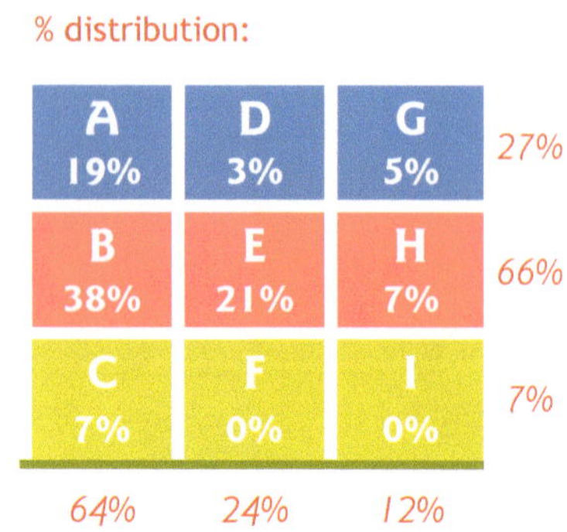


A: low aid, best migration situation
B: low aid, average migration situation
C: low aid, worst migration situation

D: medium aid, best migration situation
E: medium aid, average migration situation
F: medium aid, worst migration situation

G: high aid, best migration situation
H: high aid, average migration situation
I: high aid, worst migration situation

**A**

1. South Africa
2. Angola
3. Kenya
4. Chad
5. Burkina Faso
6. Burundi
7. Ghana

7

**D**

1. Sierra Leone

1

**G**

1. Mauritania
2. Congo, Rep.

2

**B**

1. Uganda
2. Congo, D.R.
3. Malawi
4. Lesotho
5. Madagascar
6. Mauritius
7. Botswana
8. Ethiopia
9. Gambia
10. Tanzania
11. Nigeria
12. Guinea
13. Togo
14. Zimbabwe
15. Sudan
16. Niger

16

**E**

1. Guinea-Bissau
2. Mali
3. Senegal
4. Equat. Guinea
5. Gabon
6. Liberia
7. Rwanda
8. Comoros
9. Mozambique

9

**H**

1. Namibia
2. Djibouti
3. Zambia

3

**C**

1. Côte d'Ivoire
2. Swaziland
3. Central Afr. R.

3

**F**

0

**I**

0

| | Country | Improvemt in Migration | Aid per Pers. |
|---|---|---|---|
| | | (%) | ($US) |
| 1 | • Eritrea | 2400 | 56 |
| 2 | • Benin | 433 | 40 |
| 3 | • Sierra Leone | 323 | 54 |
| 4 | • South Africa | 250 | 12 |
| 5 | • Angola | 246 | 31 |
| 6 | • Kenya | 225 | 17 |
| 7 | • Chad | 214 | 28 |
| 8 | • Mauritania | 200 | 93 |
| 9 | • Burkina Faso | 183 | 39 |
| 10 | • Burundi | 148 | 26 |
| 11 | • Ghana | 120 | 39 |
| 12 | • Congo, Rep. | 106 | 81 |
| 13 | • Namibia | 100 | 86 |
| 14 | • Guinea-Bissau | 100 | 76 |
| 15 | • Uganda | 89 | 34 |
| 16 | • Congo, Dem. Rep. | 83 | 19 |
| 17 | • Malawi | 65 | 39 |
| 18 | • Mali | 53 | 47 |
| 19 | • Equatorial Guinea | 0 | 48 |
| 20 | • Sao Tome & Principe | 0 | 279 |
| 21 | • Madagascar | 0 | 36 |
| 22 | • Mauritius | 0 | 22 |
| 23 | • Lesotho | 0 | 40 |
| 24 | • Senegal | 0 | 57 |
| 25 | • Botswana | -20 | 36 |
| 26 | • Ethiopia | -24 | 16 |
| 27 | • Gabon | -33 | 44 |
| 28 | • Gambia, The | -33 | 37 |
| 29 | • Cape Verde | -50 | 273 |
| 30 | • Tanzania | -68 | 35 |
| 31 | • Nigeria | -79 | 6 |
| 32 | • Liberia | -89 | 43 |
| 33 | • Guinea | -89 | 34 |
| 34 | • Rwanda | -100 | 57 |
| 35 | • Comoros | -100 | 54 |
| 36 | • Djibouti | -100 | 111 |
| 37 | • Togo | -104 | 19 |
| 38 | • Mozambique | -127 | 62 |
| 39 | • Zimbabwe | -133 | 22 |

| | Country | Improvemt in Migration | Aid per Pers. |
|---|---|---|---|
| | | (%) | ($US) |
| 40 | • Sudan | -136 | 13 |
| 41 | • Zambia | -194 | 83 |
| 42 | • Niger | -220 | 29 |
| 43 | • Côte d'Ivoire | -294 | 34 |
| 44 | • Swaziland | -350 | 30 |
| 45 | • Central African Rep. | -550 | 27 |

- Aid per person is as assessed by the World Bank, and migration numbers are provided by the United Nations Population Division (UNPD) and computed every five years. For this comparison, change in net migration is computed for the period 1995 - 2005 by evaluating the percentage change in net migration figures for 1995 - 2000 and 2000 - 2005. A positive percentage would indicate a net movement of people into the country (immigration) and a negative percentage would indicate a net exodus of people (emigration) for the period.

- 45 countries with data available this time, and 3 removed from the chart for their extremity: Sao Tome & Principe ($279) and Cape Verde ($273) for their aid per capita, and Eritrea for its extreme net positive migration change (2,400%); most likely the return of its peoples after the long war years.

- At first glance, it appears that an increase in foreign aid brings with it a higher possibility that populations would return rather than leave. Countries completely disappear from the lowest band of the chart as aid increases, meaning immigrant rather than emigrant populations.

- Most of the 26 countries with small aid per person end up having average migration numbers (16 of them; mostly below zero, meaning emigration), the next highest is the batch of high returnees (7 countries), followed lastly by those with exiting populations (3 countries).

- No country with average aid per capita has high emigration numbers, and most end up in the average migration band.

- More of the 5 countries with high aid per capita turned out to encourage returnees rather than emigrants.

- ***Perhaps, in the end, foreign aid does influence migration figures by discouraging populations from leaving. Caution should be exercised with that conclusion, though. The relationship between both factors may not be a direct one.***

# 4.6 Tricky Relations: Economic Growth & Qlty of Life

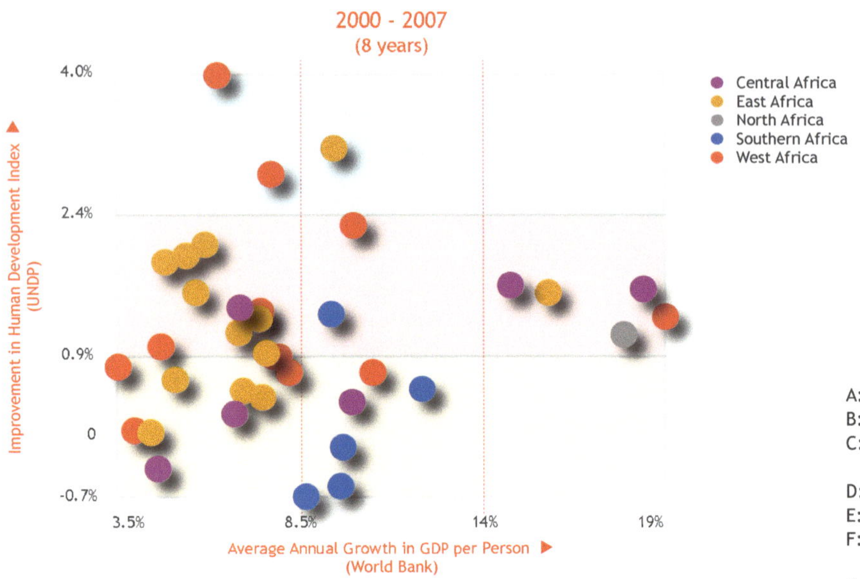


% distribution:

| | | | |
|---|---|---|---|
| A 5% | D 3% | G 0% | 8% |
| B 27% | E 5% | H 14% | 46% |
| C 30% | F 16% | I 0% | 46% |
| 62% | 24% | 14% | |

A: low econ. growth, high improvement in quality of life
B: low econ. growth, medium improvement in quality of life
C: low econ. growth, low improvement in quality of life

D: medium econ. growth, high improvement in quality of life
E: medium econ. growth, medium improvement in quality of life
F: medium econ. growth, low improvement in quality of life

G: high econ. growth, high improvement in quality of life
H: high econ. growth, medium improvement in quality of life
I: high econ. growth, low improvement in quality of life

**A**

1. Niger
2. Burkina Faso

2

**D**

1. Ethiopia

1

**G**

0

**B**

1. Tanzania
2. Mozambique
3. Rwanda
4. Uganda
5. Congo, D.R.
6. Benin
7. Eritrea
8. Madagascar
9. Guinea-Bissau
10. Comoros

10

**E**

1. Mali
2. Botswana

2

**H**

1. Congo, Rep.
2. Chad
3. Zambia
4. Nigeria
5. Sudan

5

**C**

1. Ghana
2. Senegal
3. Liberia
4. Mauritania
5. Mauritius
6. Kenya
7. Malawi
8. Cameroon
9. Côte d'Ivoire
10. Seychelles
11. Central Afr. R.

11

**F**

1. Cape Verde
2. Namibia
3. Gabon
4. South Africa
5. Lesotho
6. Swaziland

6

**I**

0

| | Country | Improvemt in Qlty of Life | Growth in GDP/pers |
|---|---|---|---|
| | | (%) | (%) |
| 1 | Niger | 3.92 | 6.4 |
| 2 | Ethiopia | 3.13 | 9.7 |
| 3 | Burkina Faso | 2.85 | 7.9 |
| 4 | Mali | 2.3 | 10.2 |
| 5 | Tanzania | 2.09 | 6.0 |
| 6 | Mozambique | 1.97 | 5.5 |
| 7 | Rwanda | 1.9 | 4.9 |
| 8 | Congo, Rep. | 1.65 | 14.6 |
| 9 | Chad | 1.61 | 18.4 |
| 10 | Uganda | 1.57 | 5.8 |
| 11 | Zambia | 1.57 | 15.7 |
| 12 | Congo, Dem. Rep. | 1.41 | 7.0 |
| 13 | Burundi | 1.38 | 0.4 |
| 14 | Benin | 1.37 | 7.6 |
| 15 | Botswana | 1.34 | 9.6 |
| 16 | Equatorial Guinea | 1.33 | 36.8 |
| 17 | Nigeria | 1.31 | 19.0 |
| 18 | Eritrea | 1.29 | 7.6 |
| 19 | Madagascar | 1.14 | 7.0 |
| 20 | Sudan | 1.12 | 17.8 |
| 21 | Guinea-Bissau | 0.99 | 4.8 |
| 22 | Comoros | 0.92 | 7.8 |
| 23 | Ghana | 0.88 | 8.1 |
| 24 | Senegal | 0.88 | 8.0 |
| 25 | Liberia | 0.77 | 3.6 |
| 26 | Cape Verde | 0.71 | 10.7 |
| 27 | Mauritania | 0.71 | 8.4 |
| 28 | Mauritius | 0.63 | 5.2 |
| 29 | Namibia | 0.53 | 12.1 |
| 30 | Kenya | 0.51 | 7.1 |
| 31 | Malawi | 0.44 | 7.7 |
| 32 | Gabon | 0.39 | 10.2 |
| 33 | Cameroon | 0.26 | 6.9 |
| 34 | Côte d'Ivoire | 0.08 | 4.1 |
| 35 | Seychelles | 0.06 | 4.5 |
| 36 | South Africa | -0.1 | 9.9 |
| 37 | Central African Rep. | -0.33 | 4.7 |
| 38 | Lesotho | -0.52 | 9.8 |
| 39 | Swaziland | -0.63 | 8.9 |

# 4. Tricky Relations

- Intuitive wisdom would expect that these two components would share a simple relationship: quality of life moving up as economic growth improved or took root. But the resulting picture doesn't fit that structure.

- It might also be that 8 years are too few for such an analysis, but they were the best the data could afford for the majority of countries. A quite feasible explanation for the non-relationship might be a simple one: that the benefits of economic growth have not been well harnessed to translate into better educational and health infrastructure in the main, which would have had a direct and even immediate impact on the population's living conditions.

- Equatorial Guinea and Burundi are left out of the chart on account of extreme values of GDP growth rates, 37% and 0.4% respectively. They both ended up in the middle band of life improvement.

- There are some interesting observations from the chart, though. 4 of the 5 countries posting the fastest rate of economic growth in those 8 years are oil exporters; only Zambia isn't. And they all return medium quality of life improvements; none of them does worse - or better - than that.

- All 5 Southern African countries post medium growth rates of GDP, but only 1 makes reasonable progress in quality of life. Most countries of West and East Africa show bottom-third rates of GDP growth, but 2 of those countries (Niger & Burkina Faso, West Africa) nevertheless report very high (top 3) improvements in quality of life over the period. Ethiopia is the only other African country that revealed high quality of life improvements.

- As for trends - if at all there are any - of the 23 countries posting low economic growth, most (11) return the lowest life improvements, followed by the medium improvements (10).

- By the time focus shifts a step higher to the mid-level economic growth countries - 9 of them in total - most (6) still return poor life improvement, followed by the middle improvement band (2).

- As said already, the 5 fastest-growing economies manage only average improvements in the quality of their populations' life conditions.

- ***No visible direct relationship between economic growth rate and quality of life in Africa. A striking disconnect.***

# 4.7 Tricky Relations: Population & Economic Growth

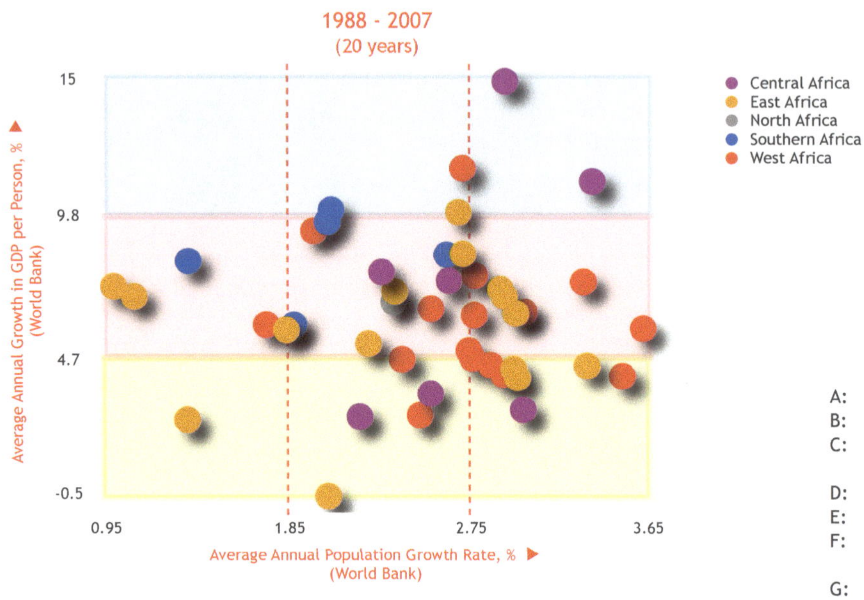


% distribution:

| | | | |
|---|---|---|---|
| A 0% | D 7% | G 5% | 12% |
| B 12% | E 25% | H 20% | 57% |
| C 2% | F 11% | I 18% | 31% |
| 14% | 43% | 43% | |

A: low population growth, high GDP/pers growth
B: low population growth, medium GDP/pers growth
C: low population growth, low GDP/pers growth

D: medium population growth, high GDP/pers growth
E: medium population growth, medium GDP/pers growth
F: medium population growth, low GDP/pers growth

G: high population growth, high GDP/pers growth
H: high population growth, medium GDP/pers growth
I: high population growth, low GDP/pers growth

**A**

0

**D**

1. Nigeria
2. Botswana
3. Zambia

3

**G**

1. Angola
2. Chad

2

**B**

1. Lesotho
2. Mauritius
3. Seychelles
4. Sierra Leone
5. Rwanda

5

**E**

1. Swaziland
2. Cape Verde
3. Malawi
4. Namibia
5. Congo, Rep.
6. Gabon
7. Mozambique
8. Sudan
9. Ghana
10. South Africa
11. Comoros

11

**H**

1. Mali
2. Benin
3. Kenya
4. Tanzania
5. Burkina Faso
6. Madagascar
7. Mauritania
8. Gambia
9. Senegal

9

**C**

1. Zimbabwe

1

**F**

1. Guinea-Bissau
2. Cameroon
3. Liberia
4. Central Afr. R.
5. Burundi

5

**I**

1. Guinea
2. Togo
3. Uganda
4. Ethiopia
5. Côte d'Ivoire
6. Niger
7. Djibouti
8. Congo, D.R.

8

| | Country | Growth in GDP/pers | Growth in Population |
|---|---|---|---|
| | | (%) | (%) |
| 1 | • Angola | 14.8 | 2.9 |
| 2 | • Nigeria | 11.6 | 2.7 |
| 3 | • Chad | 11.2 | 3.4 |
| 4 | • Botswana | 10.1 | 2.1 |
| 5 | • Zambia | 10.0 | 2.7 |
| 6 | • Swaziland | 9.7 | 2.1 |
| 7 | • Cape Verde | 9.4 | 2.0 |
| 8 | • Malawi | 8.5 | 2.7 |
| 9 | • Namibia | 8.5 | 2.6 |
| 10 | • Lesotho | 8.3 | 1.4 |
| 11 | • Congo, Rep. | 7.9 | 2.3 |
| 12 | • Mali | 7.7 | 2.8 |
| 13 | • Gabon | 7.6 | 2.7 |
| 14 | • Benin | 7.5 | 3.3 |
| 15 | • Mauritius | 7.3 | 1.0 |
| 16 | • Kenya | 7.2 | 2.9 |
| 17 | • Mozambique | 7.2 | 2.4 |
| 18 | • Tanzania | 7.0 | 2.9 |
| 19 | • Seychelles | 7.0 | 1.1 |
| 20 | • Sudan | 6.8 | 2.4 |
| 21 | • Ghana | 6.5 | 2.6 |
| 22 | • Burkina Faso | 6.4 | 3.0 |
| 23 | • Madagascar | 6.4 | 3.0 |
| 24 | • Mauritania | 6.3 | 2.8 |
| 25 | • South Africa | 6.0 | 1.9 |
| 26 | • Sierra Leone | 6.0 | 1.8 |
| 27 | • Gambia, The | 5.8 | 3.6 |
| 28 | • Rwanda | 5.8 | 1.9 |
| 29 | • Comoros | 5.3 | 2.3 |
| 30 | • Senegal | 5.0 | 2.8 |
| 31 | • Guinea | 4.7 | 2.8 |
| 32 | • Guinea-Bissau | 4.7 | 2.4 |
| 33 | • Togo | 4.5 | 2.9 |
| 34 | • Uganda | 4.5 | 3.3 |
| 35 | • Ethiopia | 4.4 | 3.0 |
| 36 | • Côte d'Ivoire | 4.2 | 2.9 |
| 37 | • Niger | 4.1 | 3.5 |
| 38 | • Djibouti | 4.0 | 3.0 |
| 39 | • Cameroon | 3.5 | 2.6 |

| | Country | Growth in GDP/pers | Growth in Population |
|---|---|---|---|
| | | (%) | (%) |
| 40 | • Congo, Dem. Rep. | 2.9 | 3.0 |
| 41 | • Liberia | 2.7 | 2.5 |
| 42 | • Central African Rep. | 2.6 | 2.2 |
| 43 | • Zimbabwe | 2.5 | 1.4 |
| 44 | • Burundi | -0.3 | 2.1 |

## 4. Tricky Relations

Movement of *Population, GDP* and *GDP/pers* in Sub-Saharan Africa across 20 Years from 1987 to 2007: 1987=100

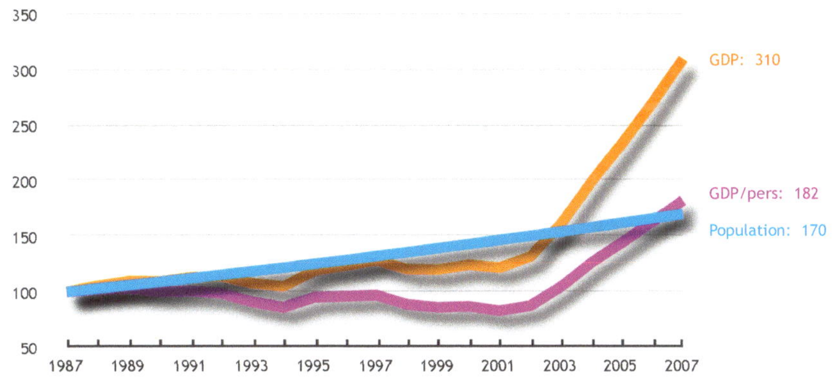


- Comparing growth of population to growth of GDP would help address the query of population being a spur or an impediment to economic development, or being entirely extraneous to it. Perhaps it will not provide a definitive answer, but compiling and comparing such data could only help elucidate any relationship, where present.

- In that regard, it might be more appropriate to compare growth of population not with growth of GDP, but with growth of GDP-per-Person. GDP growth could only be regarded as adequate if it outstrips the nation's rate of population growth. In other words, the country might indeed grow GDP, but unless this GDP is adequate for its growing number of residents, it should still be regarded as a decline in economic performance.

- Equatorial Guinea was left out of the chart because of its extreme GDP per Person growth rate: 30%. Its population growth rate (3.2%) would have placed it in sector G, high population growth accompanied by high GDP per person growth.

- As it is, the continent is just about equal in number of countries with medium and high population growth rate (43% both ways). There were only 6 countries with low population growth.

- None of those 6 attains high GDP growth; they mainly do medium, save for Zimbabwe which returns a low GDP per person growth rate.

- Of the 19 countries (43% of total) that fall into the medium population growth category, more than half attain medium GDP rates or better: 14 (32% ot total).

- And of the 19 that fall into the high population growth category, 11 (25% of total) do medium GDP growth rates or better.

- During the nineties, GDP struggled to keep up with the rate of population growth on the continent as a whole. It began to pick up around 2001. By 2005, it was soaring away, outdoing population in build-up. GDP per person took longer to catch up with population estimates, but had in turn begun to outdo it by 2006.

- ***Seems too close to call, regarding the demerits or otherwise of the effects of fast growing populations on GDP build-up. It does look certain, though, that slow growing populations across the past 20 years in Africa have not gained much of an advantage in cranking out their GDP.***

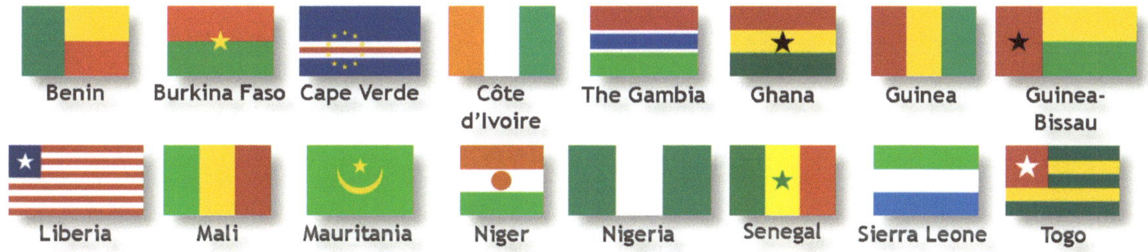

# Part II:

# The Analyses

# 1. West Africa & Its Countries

*placing them in context*

1.1 Land Mass: The Large 5
1.2 Population: The Swarming 5
1.3 Population Age Profiles: 2005-2010
1.4 Population Density: 2005-2010
1.5 Urban Population: 2005-2010
1.6 Rural Population: 2005-2010
1.7 GDP: The Top 5
1.8 Economic Vigour
1.9 Female % of the Labour Force
Leaders & Stragglers

# Prelims

West Africa is the most populous region of Sub-Saharan Africa, with 37% of overall population, followed by East Africa on 36%. It isn't the largest of the regions in surface area, though, but 2nd largest, behind Central Africa. In terms of people density, it comes second (47 pers/sq km) after East Africa (49 pers/sq km). And so on.

This opening chapter attempts to present the sub-region in the context of of its constituent countries. Where possible, West Africa is also placed in the context of the other sub-regions of the continent also.

The result should be a commencement to the rest of the book's body of analyses on a convenient footing.

For this introductory chapter, various start-off indices are used, most of which do not require much elaboration.

- **Land mass (in square kilometres)**
- **Population**
- **The age profiles of the population**
- **Population density**
- **Urban population**
- **Rural population**
- **GDP**
- **Economic Vigour**
- **Percentage of females in the labour force**

"Economic Vigour" is an attempt to quantify the efficiency of a country's economy in broad terms. We define it as the percentage share of the continent's GDP compared to the percentage share of its population. In other words, we ask the question: has the country contributed a larger share to the continent's output (GDP) than its share of the continent's population might warrant? Does the country supply a larger percentage of GDP to the continent than the percentage of the continent's population it contains?

Productivity Index, which quantifies this vigour, is obtained by dividing a country's share of GDP by its share of population.

The chapter closes with a broad evaluation of the countries' basic strengths in population size and GDP output, illustrated in the Leaders & Stragglers section. This provides a ranking of 41 Sub-Saharan African countries for which most of the 200 indicators in this study were available.

Subsequent chapters will provide a closing section called "Wrap-up", where Nigeria will be benchmarked against the best performing West African country in that chapter of the economy under consideration, according to the key indicators employed in the chapter.

**Sources of Primary Data:** IMF, World Bank, UNPD

# Charts

Population Age Profiles: 2005-2010

Population Density: 2005-2010

Urban Populations in the Countries of West Africa during 2005 - 2010

Urban % of the Populations in the Countries of West Africa during 2005 - 2010

Growth Rate of the Urban Populations in the Countries of West Africa during 2005 - 2010

Rural Populations in the Countries of West Africa during 2005 - 2010

Rural % of the Populations in the Countries of West Africa during 2005 - 2010

Growth Rate of the Rural Populations in the Countries of West Africa during 2005 - 2010

GDP in Countries of West Africa (Top 5) in 2009

Productivity Index in the Countries of West Africa in 2009

Female % of the Labour Force in Countries of West Africa in 2006

# Tables

Land Mass of the Countries of West Africa

Population of the Countries of West Africa in 2009

Productivity Index of the Countries of West Africa during 2009

**General-Size Rankings: 2009**

# 1.1 Land Mass: The Large 5

**Niger**

**1,267,000 sq.km.**

**Mali**

**1,240,190 sq.km.**

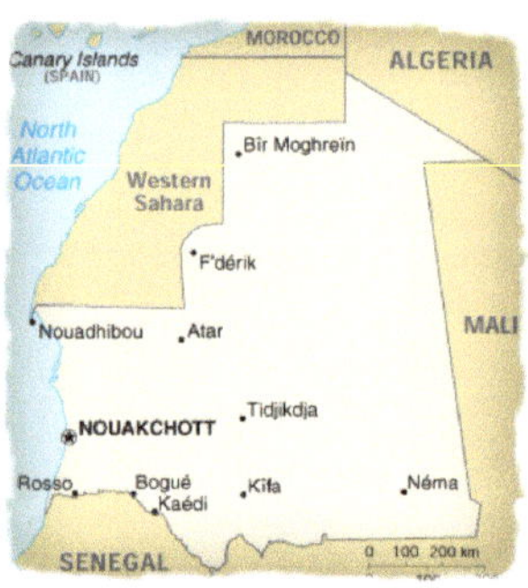


**Mauritania**

**1,025,520 sq.km.**

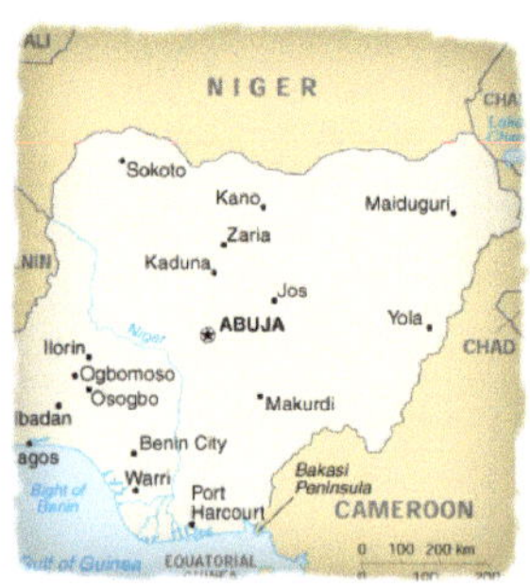


**Nigeria**

**923,770 sq.km.**

**Côte d'Ivoire**

**322,460 sq.km.**

| | | Land Mass (sq.km) |
|---|---|---|
| 6 | Burkina Faso | 274,000 |
| 7 | Guinea | 245,860 |
| 8 | Ghana | 238,540 |
| 9 | Senegal | 196,720 |
| 10 | Benin | 112,620 |
| 11 | Liberia | 111,370 |
| 12 | Sierra Leone | 71,740 |
| 13 | Togo | 56,790 |
| 14 | Guinea-Bissau | 36,120 |
| 15 | Gambia, The | 11,300 |
| 16 | Cape Verde | 4,030 |

# 1.2 Population: The Swarming 5

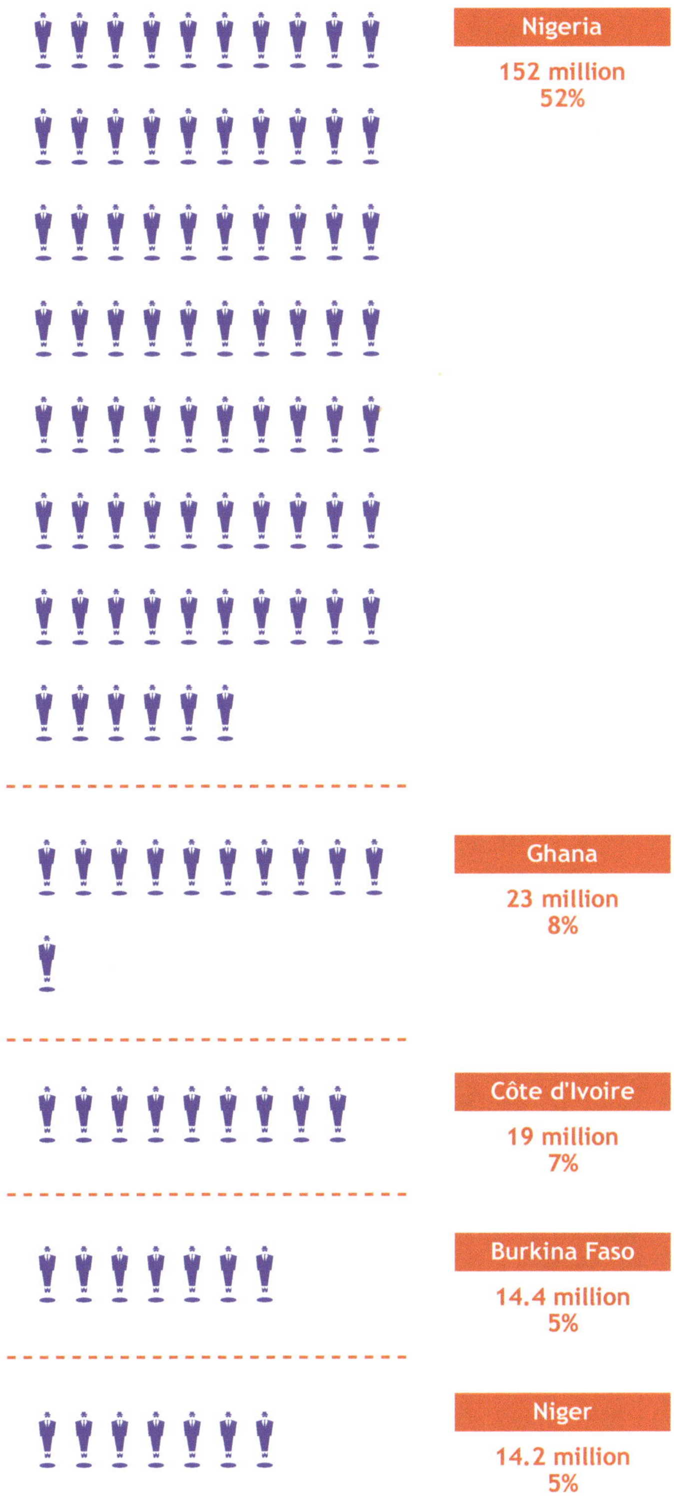


2009 IMF estimates

| | 2009 | Population (millions) | % of West Africa |
|---|---|---|---|
| 6 | Mali | 13.6 | 4.7% |
| 7 | Senegal | 13 | 4.4% |
| 8 | Guinea | 11 | 3.6% |
| 9 | Benin | 8 | 2.9% |
| 10 | Togo | 7 | 2.3% |
| 11 | Sierra Leone | 6 | 2.1% |
| 12 | Liberia | 4 | 1.4% |
| 13 | Mauritania | 3 | 1.1% |
| 14 | Guinea-Bissau | 1.8 | 0.6% |
| 15 | Gambia, The | 1.7 | 0.6% |
| 16 | Cape Verde | 0.5 | 0.2% |

1 in 2 West Africans is Nigerian. The country isn't the largest of the 16, but it holds more than half of the sub-region's population.

# 1.3 Population Age Profiles: 2005-2010

Everywhere, near 90% of the population are younger than 60; & about 60% are younger than 25.

Again, the numbers for Nigeria in every age band completely eclipse the rest of West Africa.

UNPD estimates

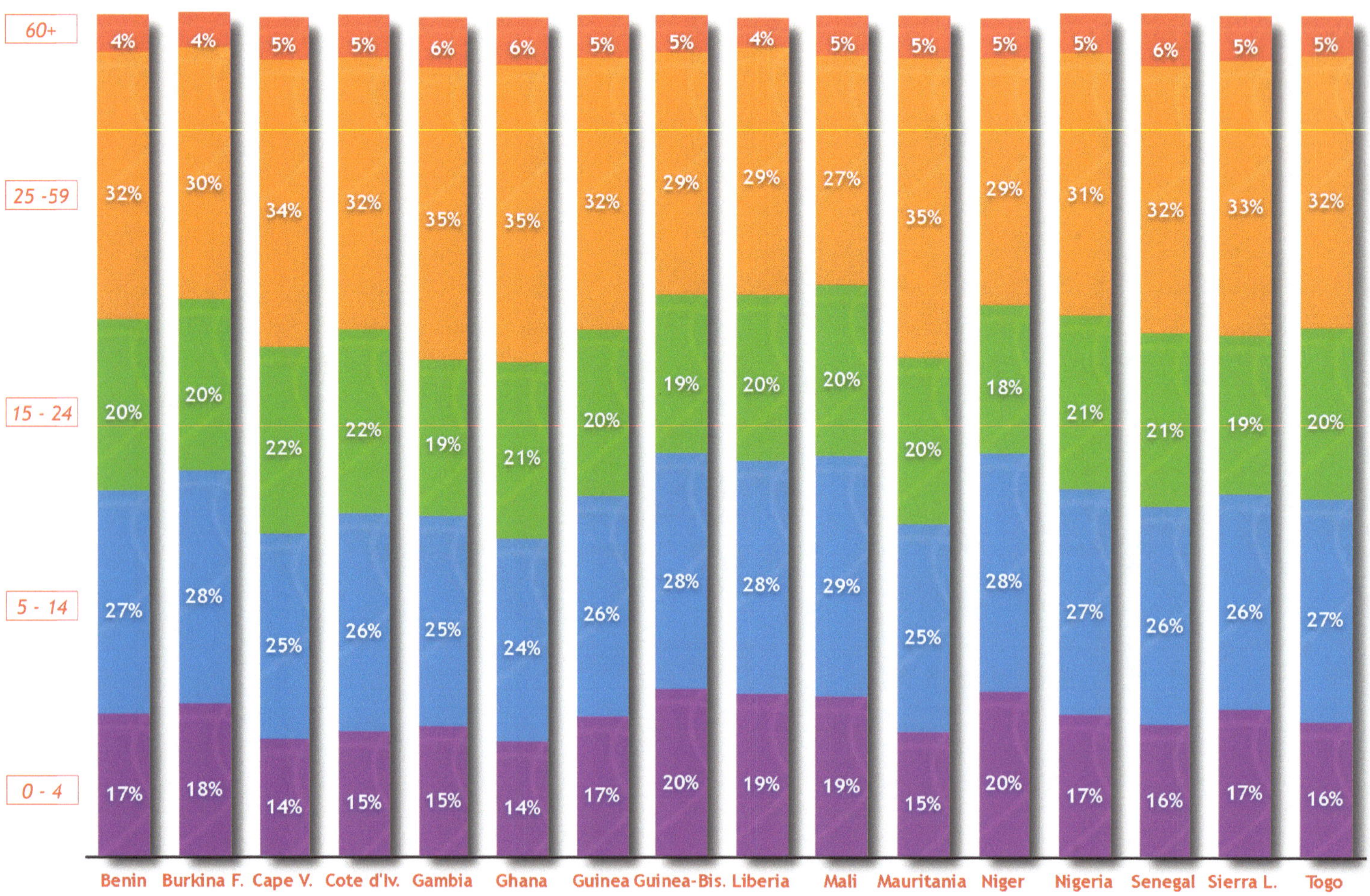


| Age | Benin | Burkina F. | Cape V. | Cote d'Iv. | Gambia | Ghana | Guinea | Guinea-Bis. | Liberia | Mali | Mauritania | Niger | Nigeria | Senegal | Sierra L. | Togo |
|---|---|---|---|---|---|---|---|---|---|---|---|---|---|---|---|---|
| 60+ | 4% | 4% | 5% | 5% | 6% | 6% | 5% | 5% | 4% | 5% | 5% | 5% | 5% | 6% | 5% | 5% |
| 25 -59 | 32% | 30% | 34% | 32% | 35% | 35% | 32% | 29% | 29% | 27% | 35% | 29% | 31% | 32% | 33% | 32% |
| 15 - 24 | 20% | 20% | 22% | 22% | 19% | 21% | 20% | 19% | 20% | 20% | 20% | 18% | 21% | 21% | 19% | 20% |
| 5 - 14 | 27% | 28% | 25% | 26% | 25% | 24% | 26% | 28% | 28% | 29% | 25% | 28% | 27% | 26% | 26% | 27% |
| 0 - 4 | 17% | 18% | 14% | 15% | 15% | 14% | 17% | 20% | 19% | 19% | 15% | 20% | 17% | 16% | 17% | 16% |

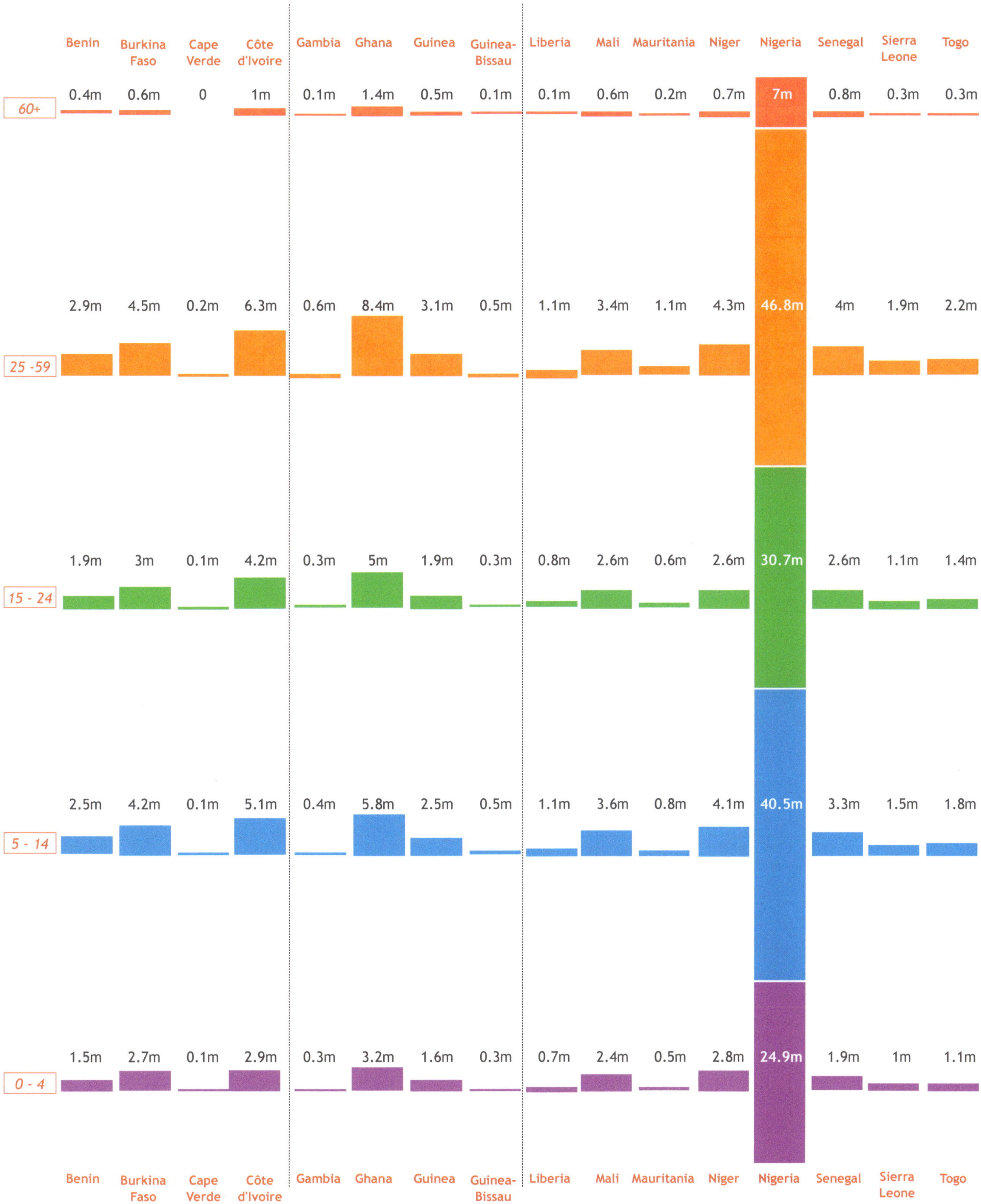
Benin
Burkina Faso
Cape Verde
Côte d'Ivoire
Gambia
Ghana
Guinea
Guinea-Bissau
Liberia
Mali
Mauritania
Niger
Nigeria
Senegal
Sierra Leone
Togo
60+
0.4m 0.6m 0 1m 0.1m 1.4m 0.5m 0.1m 0.1m 0.6m 0.2m 0.7m 7m 0.8m 0.3m 0.3m
25 -59
2.9m 4.5m 0.2m 6.3m 0.6m 8.4m 3.1m 0.5m 1.1m 3.4m 1.1m 4.3m 46.8m 4m 1.9m 2.2m
15 - 24
1.9m 3m 0.1m 4.2m 0.3m 5m 1.9m 0.3m 0.8m 2.6m 0.6m 2.6m 30.7m 2.6m 1.1m 1.4m
5 - 14
2.5m 4.2m 0.1m 5.1m 0.4m 5.8m 2.5m 0.5m 1.1m 3.6m 0.8m 4.1m 40.5m 3.3m 1.5m 1.8m
0 - 4
1.5m 2.7m 0.1m 2.9m 0.3m 3.2m 1.6m 0.3m 0.7m 2.4m 0.5m 2.8m 24.9m 1.9m 1m 1.1m
Benin
Burkina Faso
Cape Verde
Côte d'Ivoire
Gambia
Ghana
Guinea
Guinea-Bissau
Liberia
Mali
Mauritania
Niger
Nigeria
Senegal
Sierra Leone
Togo

# 1.4 Population Density: 2005-2010

Mauritania, Mali & Niger are the 3 most sparsely populated countries. Indeed, consideably less dense than the Sub-Saharan Africa average.

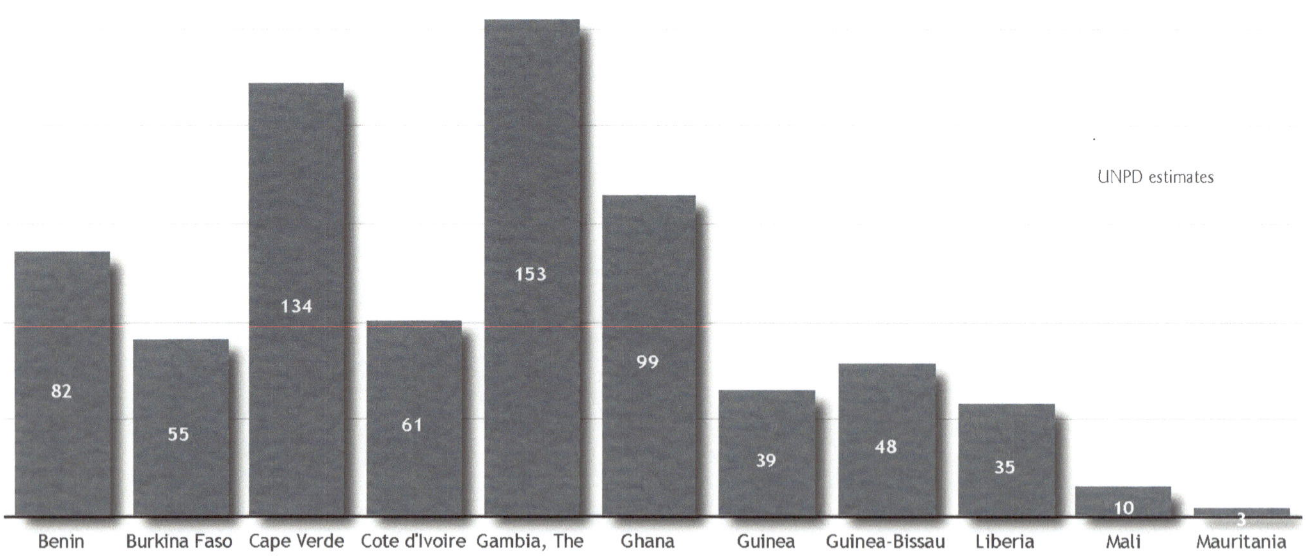

Nigeria, Gambia & Cape Verde are the 3 most densely populated. Only East Africa holds more people per square kilometre than West Africa.

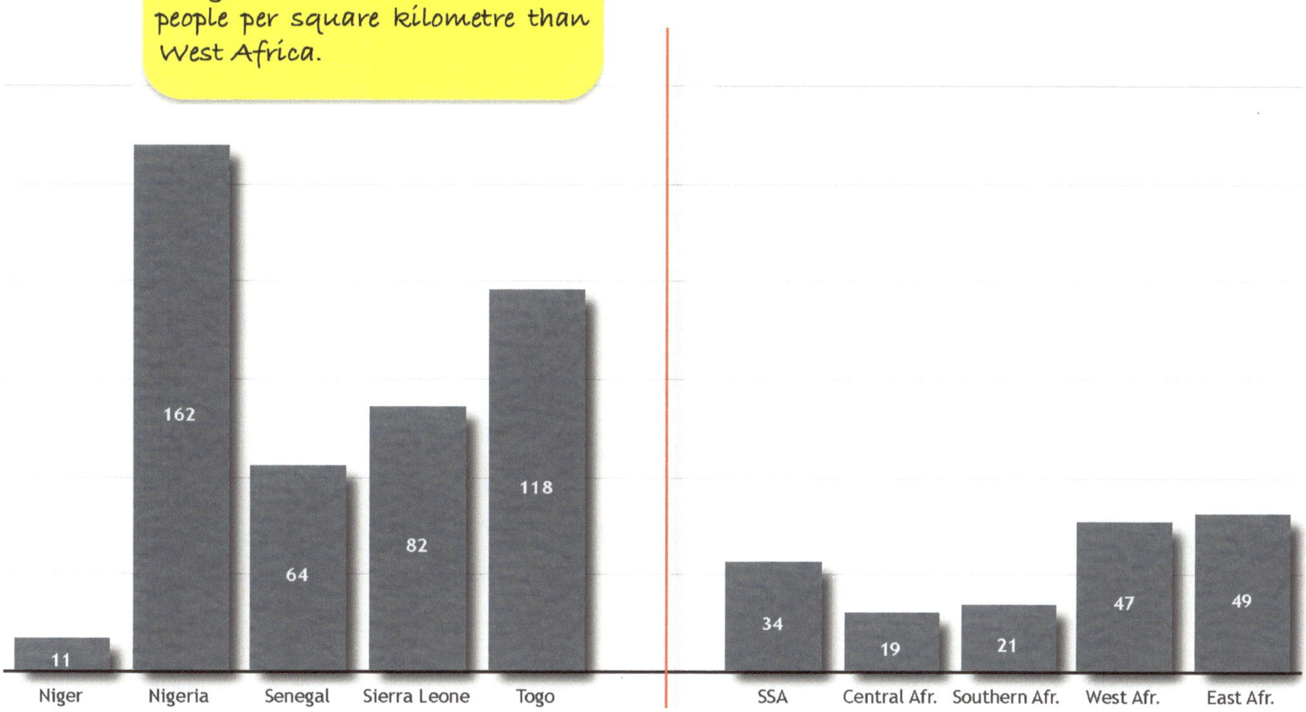

# 1.5 Urban Population: 2005-2010

Urban population is growing fastest in Liberia, Burkina Faso & Mali. But the most urban dwellers are in Nigeria, Ghana & Côte d'Ivoire.

Urban Populations in the Countries of West Africa during 2005 - 2010. (millions)

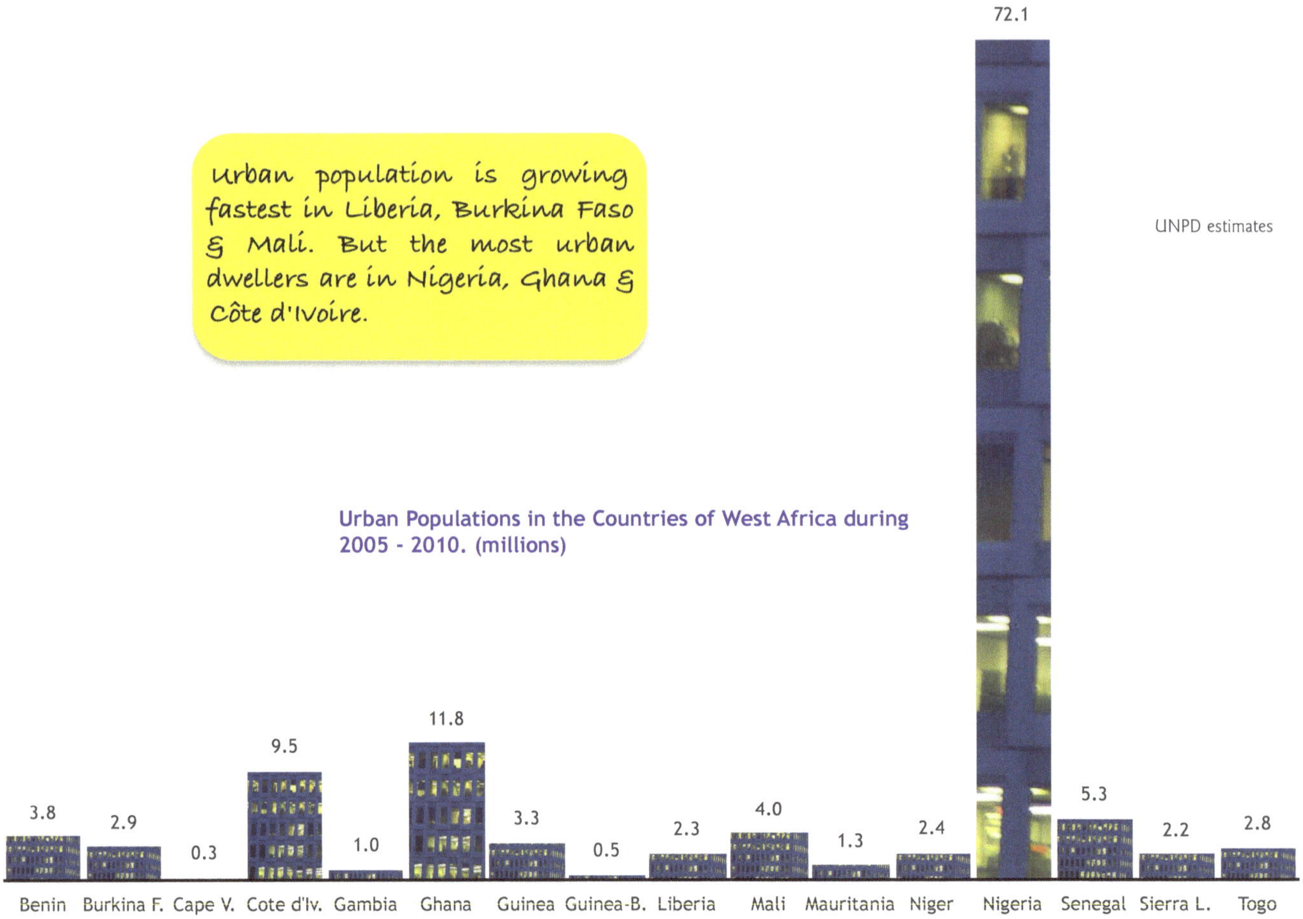


Urban % of the Populations in the Countries of West Africa during 2005 - 2010.

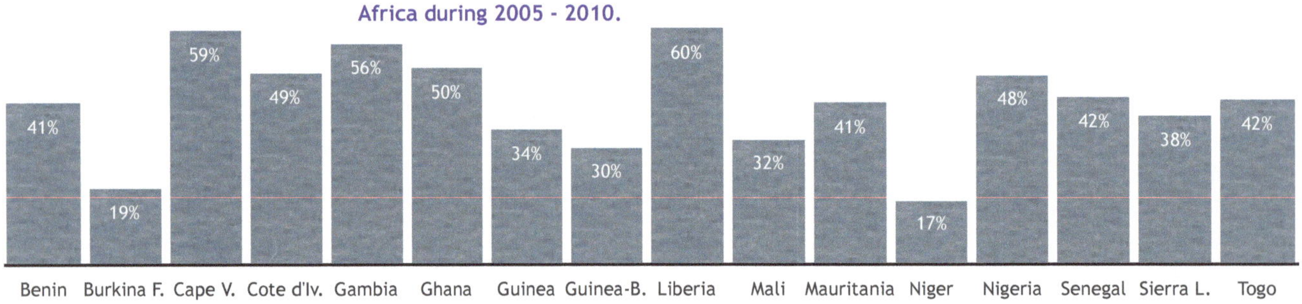


Growth Rate of the Urban Populations in the Countries of West Africa during 2005 - 2010.

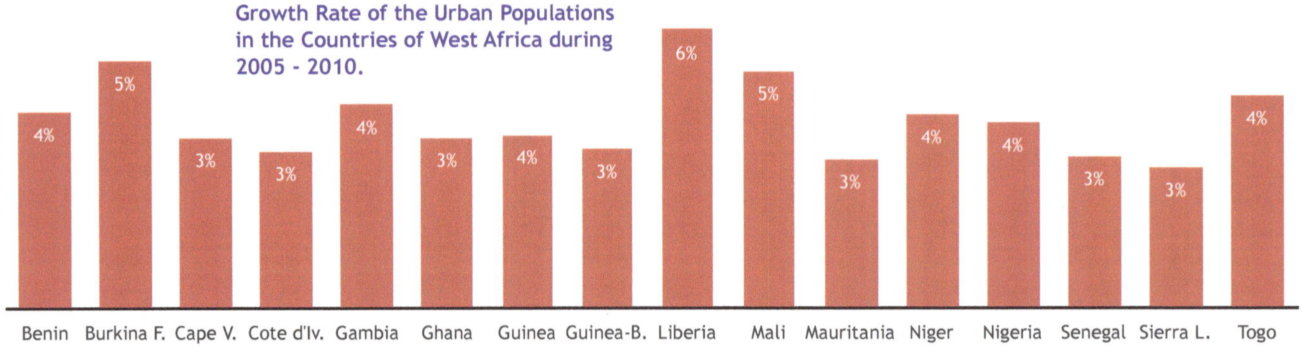

# 1.6 Rural Population: 2005-2010

Rural populations are growing everywhere, but slower than urban growth. Again, Nigeria, Ghana & Côte d'Ivoire hold the most rural dwellers.

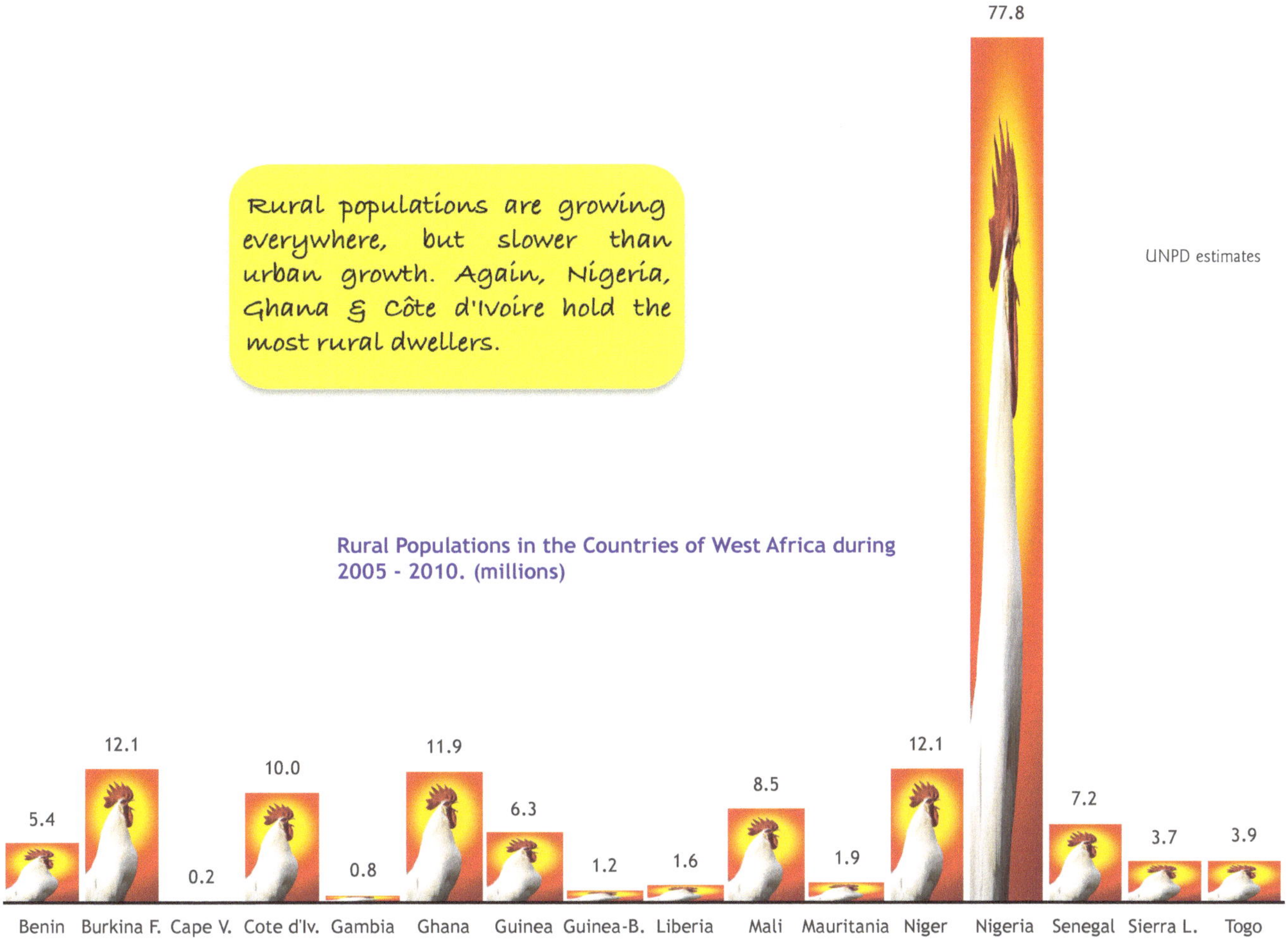


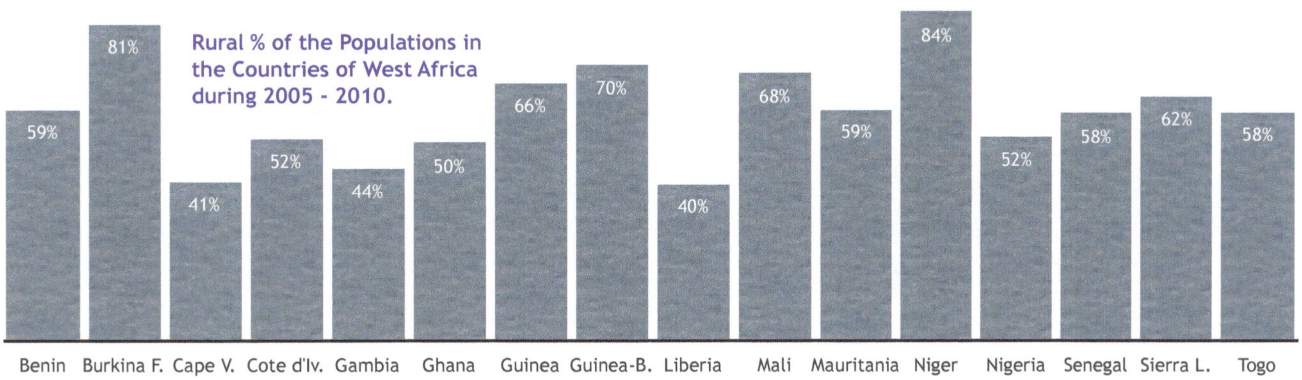


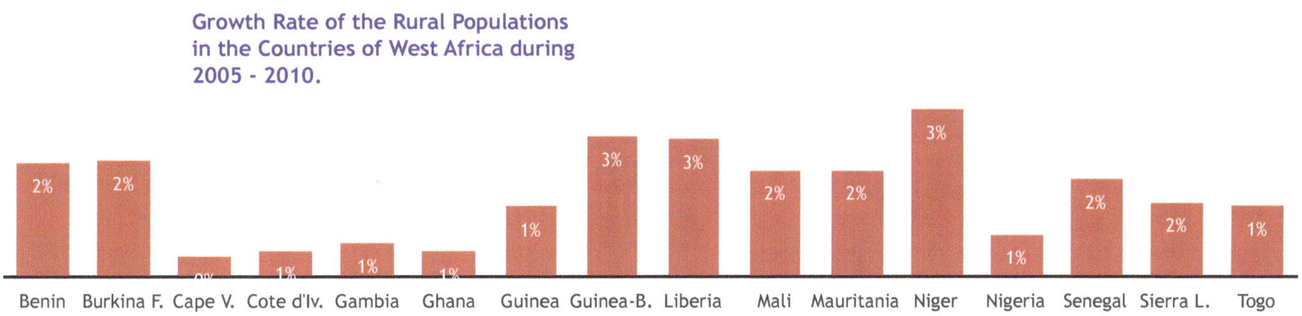

# 1.7 GDP: The Top 5

| | 2009 | GDP ($PPP bn) |
|---|---|---|
| 6 | Mali | 15.3 |
| 7 | Benin | 14.0 |
| 8 | Guinea | 12.3 |
| 9 | Niger | 10.1 |
| 10 | Mauritania | 7.0 |
| 11 | Togo | 5.8 |
| 12 | Sierra Leone | 4.7 |
| 13 | Gambia, The | 2.5 |
| 14 | Cape Verde | 1.9 |
| 15 | Liberia | 1.7 |
| 16 | Guinea-Bissau | 0.9 |

As with population, so with GDP; Nigeria, Ghana and Côte d'Ivoire provide the bulk. Nigeria's GDP is nearly twice that of the rest of West Africa.

IMF estimates

# 1.8 Economic Vigour

Productivity Index of the Countries of West Africa during 2009

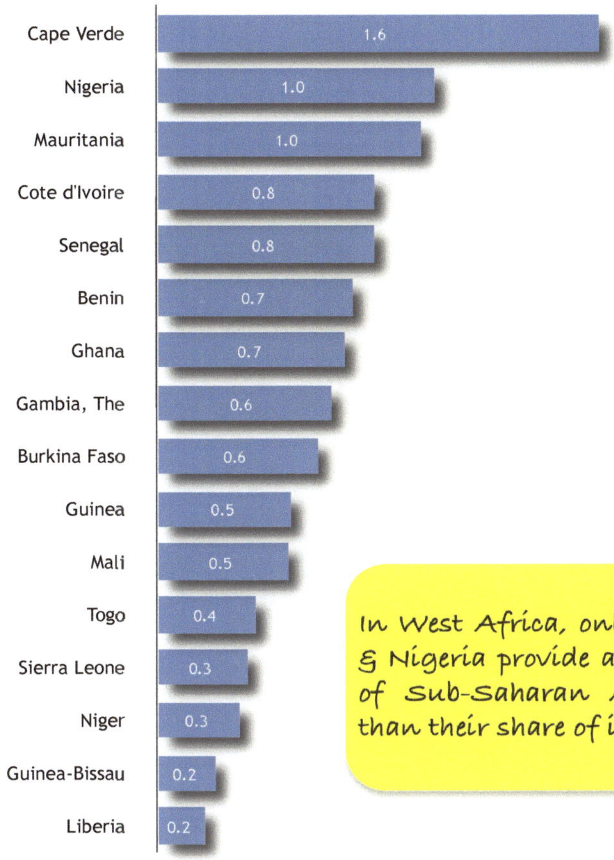


| | 2009 | % of SSA Population | % of SSA GDP |
|---|---|---|---|
| 1 | Cape Verde | 0.06 | 0.10 |
| 2 | Nigeria | 19.15 | 19.47 |
| 3 | Mauritania | 0.39 | 0.38 |
| 4 | Côte d'Ivoire | 2.44 | 1.96 |
| 5 | Senegal | 1.62 | 1.29 |
| 6 | Benin | 1.05 | 0.76 |
| 7 | Ghana | 2.91 | 2.03 |
| 8 | Gambia, The | 0.21 | 0.13 |
| 9 | Burkina Faso | 1.81 | 1.07 |
| 10 | Guinea | 1.33 | 0.66 |
| 11 | Mali | 1.72 | 0.83 |
| 12 | Togo | 0.86 | 0.31 |
| 13 | Sierra Leone | 0.76 | 0.25 |
| 14 | Niger | 1.79 | 0.55 |
| 15 | Guinea-Bissau | 0.22 | 0.05 |
| 16 | Liberia | 0.52 | 0.09 |

In West Africa, only Cape Verde & Nigeria provide a greater share of Sub-Saharan Africa's GDP than their share of its population.

Primary data: IMF

## 1.9 Female % of Labour Force

2006: World Bank

## Leaders & Stragglers

# first impressions

This ranking is only an introductory one, basing its outcome on two criteria: relative size of population and relative size of GDP.

But it is of significance, as size of population might point to potential size of market. Size of GDP might point to size of wealth.

The ensuing end-of-chapter tables in the rest of the book will provide the more robust and comprehensive diverse bases for consequent sector rankings.

### General-Size Rankings: 2009

| Rank | Country | Rank | Country | Rank | Country |
|---|---|---|---|---|---|
| 1 | Nigeria | 11 | Burkina Faso | 23 | Mauritius |
| 2 | South Africa | 12 | Zambia | | Namibia |
| 3 | Ethiopia | 13 | Mali | | Sierra Leone |
| 4 | Kenya | 14 | Chad | 24 | Burundi |
| | Tanzania | | Malawi | | Eritrea |
| 5 | Angola | 15 | Niger | 25 | Central Afr. Rep. |
| | Congo, Dem. Rep. | 16 | Botswana | 26 | Lesotho |
| | Ghana | 17 | Guinea | 27 | Swaziland |
| 6 | Cameroon | 18 | Benin | 28 | Gambia |
| | Uganda | 19 | Gabon | 29 | Guinea-Bissau |
| 7 | Côte d' Ivoire | 20 | Congo, Rep. | 30 | Cape Verde |
| 8 | Mozambique | 21 | Rwanda | 31 | Comoros |
| 9 | Madagascar | 22 | Equatorial Guinea | | Seychelles |
| 10 | Senegal | | Togo | | |
| | TOP | | MIDDLE | | BOTTOM |

Primary Data: IMF

Central Africa
East Africa
Southern Africa
West Africa

## 1. West Africa & Its Countries

# 2. Quality of Life

*last things first*

2.1 Human Development Ranking
2.2 Life Expectancy
2.3 Child Mortality
2.4 Immunization against Measles
2.5 Immunization against Tuberculosis
2.6 Access to Safe Water
2.7 Access to Sanitation
2.8 Telephones
2.9 Mobile Phone Users
2.10 Literacy
2.11 Internet Users
2.12 Personal Computers
2.13 Net Migration
Leaders & Stragglers
Wrap-up

Usually, the condition of an economy's people is discussed at the end, preceded by chapters that describe the (technical) macro-economic characters of the group of countries and then lead from there on to the standards of living as outcomes of that character. We have opted to place quality of life early on here, simply to reiterate the point that an economy exists for the people and not the other way round. That is, management of an economy has one sole defining reason: to improve the welfare of its constituent population. It is on that (overriding) basis that performance may be assessed.

Various indices have been employed here to assess the standard of living of the population and the quality of life that this represents.

**Human Development Ranking**: based on the "human development index" as evaluated by the United Nations Development Program. It is the most widely respected evaluation of the quality of life in the different countries of the world and is an amalgamation of various parameters to rate and compare the standards of living across countries.

**Life Expectancy at Birth**: the number of years newborn children would live if subject to the mortality risks prevailing for the cross-section of population at that time of their birth.

**Child Mortality (Under-5):** the probability of dying between birth and exactly five years of age, based on actual recorded number of deaths. It is usually expressed per 1,000 live births.

**Babies Immunization: Measles** percentage of 1-year old children who have been immunized against measles.

**Babies Immunization: Tuberculosis** percentage of 1-year old children who have been immunized against tuberculosis.

**Population with Access to Safe Water:** percentage of population with access to clean water: i.e. "population using improved drinking water sources". Improved water sources include household connections, public standpipes, boreholes, protected dug wells, protected springs, and rainwater collections - UNICEF/WHO

**Population with Access to Sanitation:** percentage of population using adequate sanitation facilities; adequate sanitation includes connection to public sewers, connection to septic systems, and [efficient] latrine systems - UNICEF/WHO

**Phones per Population (Fixed & Mobile)**: the number of phone lines (fixed and mobile) per 100 inhabitants.

**Number of Mobile Phone Users:** the number of mobile phone lines per 100 inhabitants.

**Number of Internet Users:** out of every 1,000 persons.

**Personal Computers per Population:** out of every 1,000 persons.

**Migration:** net migration: the number of immigrants less the number of emigrants.

**Sources of Primary Data:** UNDP, UNICEF, AfDB, ITU, UNPD

# Charts


2.1 Quality of Life Ranking in West Africa among 46 Sub-Saharan Africa Countries during 2003-2005

2.2 Human Development Index Rankings of West African Countries among 46 Sub-Saharan Africa Countries during 2003-2005

2.3 Life Expectancy at Birth in West Africa during 2003-2006

2.4 Life Expectancy at Birth in Nigeria and Sub-Saharan Africa from 1999 to 2007

2.5 Under-5 Child Mortality in West Africa during 2003-06

2.6 Under-5 Child Mortality in Nigeria and Sub-Saharan Africa from 1999 to 2007

2.7 % of 1-yr olds Immunized against Measles in West Africa during 2003-06

2.8 % of 1-yr olds Immunized against Measles in Nigeria and Sub-Saharan Africa from 1997 to 2007

2.9 % of 1-yr olds Immunized against Tuberculosis in West Africa during 2003-06

2.10 % of 1-yr olds Immunized against Tuberculosis in Nigeria and Sub-Saharan Africa from 1997 to 2007

2.11 % of Population with Access to Safe Water in West Africa during 2004-06

2.12 % of Population with Access to Sanitation in West Africa during 2004-06

2.13 Phones (fixed & mobile) for every 100 Persons of Population in West Africa during 2000 & 2007

2.14 Mobile Phones for every 100 Persons of Population in West Africa during 2000 & 2007

2.15 Total Adult Literacy Rate (%) in West Africa during 2000 & 2007

2.16 Internet Users out of every 1,000 Persons of Population in West Africa during 2000 & 2007

2.17 Number of Personal Computers for every 1,000 Persons of Population in West Africa during 2001 & 2006

2.18 Net Migration out of every one million Persons of Population in West Africa during 2000-05

- **Wrap-up**

# Tables

*1999-2002; 2003-2006:*
- *self-comparison to preceding period;*
- *performance in S-Saharan Africa;*
- *performance in West Africa;*
- *performance among oil-exporters;*

*for:*

Human Development Ranking*

Life Expectancy

Child Mortality

Babies Immunization: Measles

Babies Immunization: Tuberculosis

*1990; 2004-2006:*
- *self-comparison to preceding period;*
- *performance in S-Saharan Africa;*
- *performance in West Africa;*
- *performance among oil-exporters;*

*for:*

Population with Access to Safe Water

Population with Access to Sanitation

*2000; 2007:*
- *self-comparison to preceding period;*
- *performance in S-Saharan Africa;*
- *performance in West Africa;*
- *performance among oil-exporters;*

*for:*

Phones per Population (Fixed & Mobiles)

Number of Mobile Phone Users

Literacy

Number of Internet Users

Personal Computers per Population**

Net Migration per Population***

- Human Development Index in Sub-Saharan Africa during 2003-05: Rankings
- Life Expectancy in Sub-Saharan Africa during 2003-06: Rankings
- Under-5 Child Mortality in Sub-Saharan Africa during 2003-06: Rankings
- Phones (Fixed & Mobiles) per Population in Sub-Saharan Africa during 2007: Rankings
- Internet Users per Population in Sub-Saharan Africa during 2007: Rankings
- Personal Computers per Population in Sub-Saharan Africa during 2006: Rankings
- **Quality of Life Rankings: 2003-07**

* 1999-2002; 2003-2005

** 2001; 2006

*** 2000-2005

# 2.1 Human Development Ranking

*smile, their beloved country*

| | 99-02 | 03-05 |
|---|---|---|
| Self-comparison to Preceding Period | | ▼ |
| Performance in Sub-Saharan Africa | ▼ | ▼ |
| Performance in West Africa | ▲ | ▲ |
| | Cape Verde | Cape Verde |
| | Ghana | Ghana |
| | Togo | Togo |
| | **Nigeria** | Mauritania |
| | Mauritania | Gambia, The |
| | Senegal | Senegal |
| | Gambia, The | **Nigeria** |
| | Côte d'Ivoire | Guinea |
| | Benin | Benin |
| | Guinea | Côte d'Ivoire |
| | Guinea-Bissau | Guinea-Bissau |
| | Mali | Mali |
| | Burkina Faso | Burkina Faso |
| | Niger | Niger |
| | Sierra Leone | Sierra Leone |
| Performance among Oil-Exporters | ▼ | ▼ |
| | Equatorial Guinea | Gabon |
| | Gabon | Equatorial Guinea |
| | Cameroon | Congo, Rep. |
| | Congo, Rep. | Sudan |
| | Sudan | Cameroon |
| | **Nigeria** | **Nigeria** |
| | Côte d'Ivoire | Angola |
| | Angola | Côte d'Ivoire |
| | Chad | Chad |

2.1

Quality of Life Ranking in West Africa among 46 Sub-Saharan Africa Countries during 2003-2005 (1=best, 46=worst)

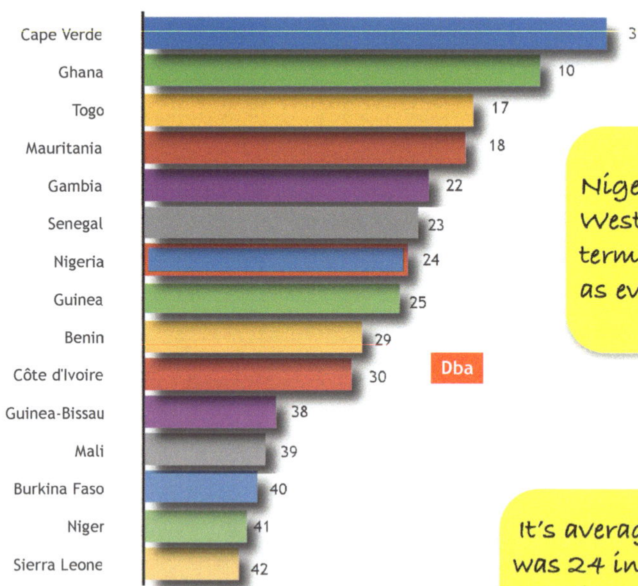


Dba

Nigeria placed 7th in 16-nation West Africa during 2003-05 in terms of "human development", as evaluated by the UNDP.

It's average rank for those years was 24 in Sub-Saharan Africa, out of 46. Cape Verde was best in West Africa, and 3rd best on the continent.

Primary Data: UNDP

| | |
|---|---|
| ▲ | improved *or* better than average |
| ▼ | worsened *or* worse than average |
| ◁▷ | no change *or* average |

2.2

Human Development Index Rankings of West African Countries among 46 Sub-Saharan Africa Countries during 1999 to 2006

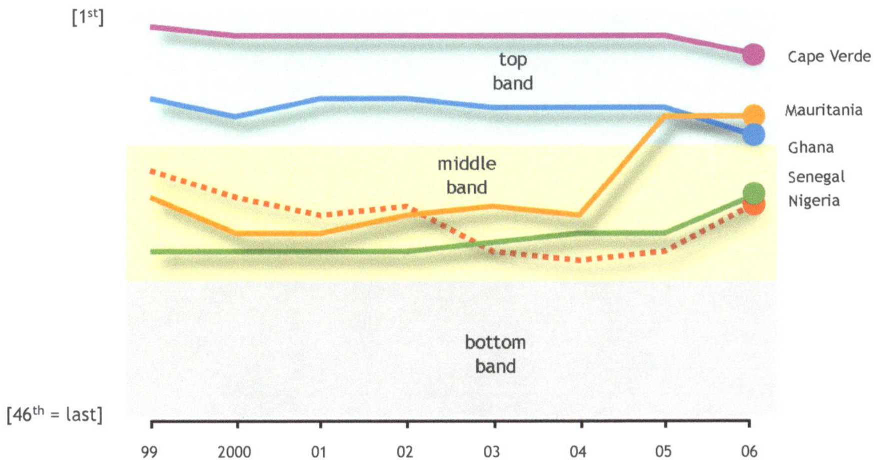


Nigeria's position might have been stronger if the country hadn't returned worse Human Development indices for 03-05 than the preceding 99-02 period.

It fell back within Sub-Saharan Africa and West Africa as well. Among the oil economies it stayed worse than average.

Cape Verde and Ghana were the only countries of West Africa to consistently stay in the top band of SSA performance throughout the 8 years of 99-06.

2.2

Human Development Index Rankings of West African Countries among 46 Sub-Saharan Africa Countries during 1999 to 2006

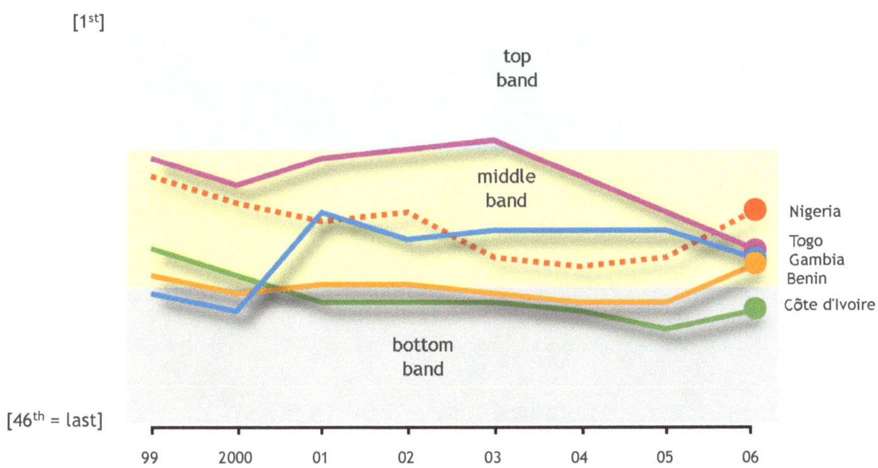


Mauritania joined the top band in 2005, and Togo was there for a brief stay in 2003 but dived back down alarmingly thereafter.

Nigeria remained firmly in the SSA middle band. Senegal and Gambia overtook it after 2003, but Gambia fell behind again after 2005.

Primary Data: UNDP

**2.2**

Human Development Index Rankings of West African Countries among 46 Sub-Saharan Africa Countries during 1999 to 2006

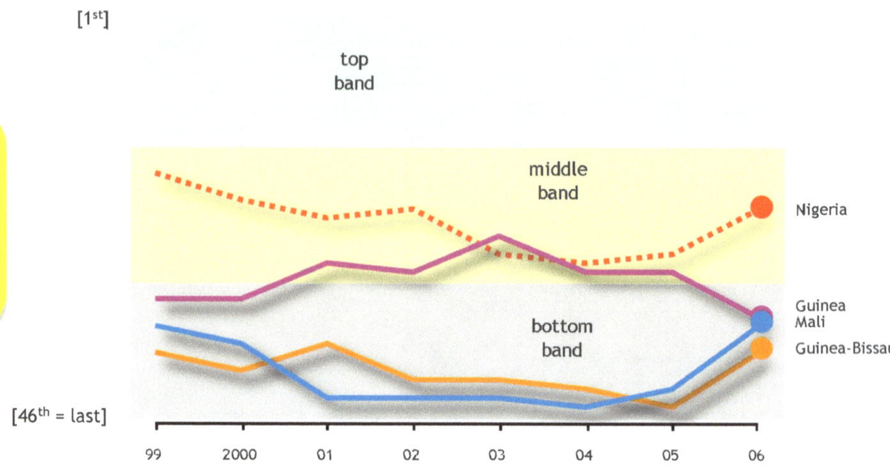


As such, the best living conditions in West Africa during 1999-2006 were to be found in Cape Verde and Ghana.

Besides those two, and Mauritania and Senegal, the rest of West Africa performed at a lower level than Nigeria throughout 1999-2006.

**2.2**

Human Development Index Rankings of West African Countries among 46 Sub-Saharan Africa Countries during 1999 to 2006

By 2006, Sierra Leone was 45th (2nd from the bottom) in SSA. Burkina Faso & Niger were 40th and 41st respectively.

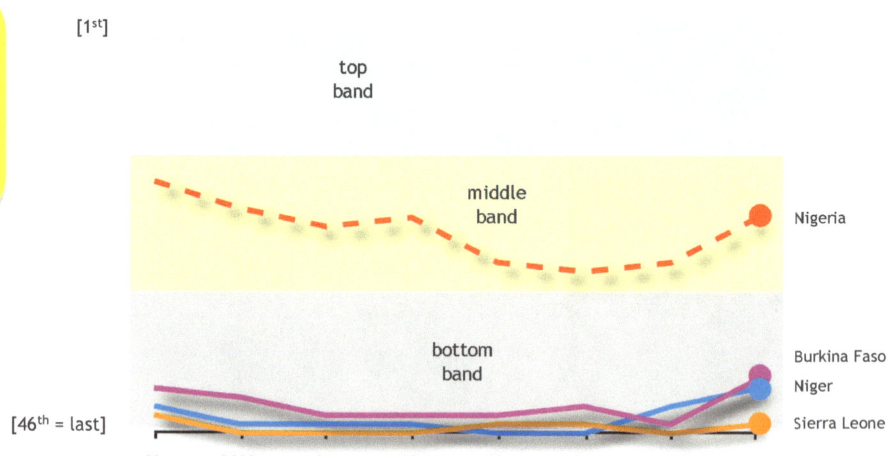


Primary Data: UNDP

Seychelles had the best index in Africa, followed by Mauritius, Cape Verde, South Africa and Gabon in the top-5 bracket. War-ravaged Sierra Leone was bottom.

In West Africa, 2 countries made the top band: Cape Verde & Ghana; 7 made middle; and 5 made bottom.

Human Development Index in Sub-Saharan Africa during 2003-05: Rankings

| Rank | Country |
|---|---|
| 1 | Seychelles |
| 2 | Mauritius |
| 3 | Cape Verde |
| 4 | South Africa |
| 5 | Gabon |
| 6 | Equatorial Guinea |
| 7 | Namibia |
| 8 | Botswana |
| 9 | Comoros |
| 10 | Ghana |
| 11 | Congo, Rep. |
| 12 | Madagascar |
| 13 | Swaziland |
| 14 | Cameroon |

TOP

| Rank | Country |
|---|---|
| 15 | Lesotho |
| 16 | Togo |
| | Uganda |
| 17 | Kenya |
| 18 | Gambia, The |
| 19 | Senegal |
| 20 | Eritrea |
| | Nigeria |
| 21 | Guinea |
| 22 | Rwanda |
| 23 | Angola |
| 24 | Tanzania |
| 25 | Benin |
| 26 | Côte d' Ivoire |
| 27 | Malawi |
| 28 | Zambia |

MIDDLE

| Rank | Country |
|---|---|
| 29 | Congo, Dem. Rep. |
| 30 | Burundi |
| 31 | Mozambique |
| 32 | Ethiopia |
| 33 | Central Afr. Rep. |
| | Chad |
| 34 | Guinea-Bissau |
| 35 | Mali |
| 36 | Burkina Faso |
| 37 | Niger |
| 38 | Sierra Leone |

BOTTOM

Primary Data: UNDP

# 2.2 Life Expectancy

**running on extra-time?**

| | 99-02 | 03-06 |
|---|---|---|
| Self-comparison to Preceding Period | | ▼ |
| Performance in Sub-Saharan Africa | ▲ | ▼ |

**Performance in West Africa**

| ▲ (99-02) | ▼ (03-06) |
|---|---|
| Cape Verde | Cape Verde |
| Ghana | Ghana |
| Senegal | Senegal |
| Benin | Gambia, The |
| Mauritania | Mauritania |
| Mali | Togo |
| **Nigeria** | Benin |
| Togo | Guinea |
| Gambia, The | Mali |
| Guinea | Burkina Faso |
| Liberia | Niger |
| Niger | **Nigeria** |
| Burkina Faso | Côte d'Ivoire |
| Côte d'Ivoire | Guinea-Bissau |
| Guinea-Bissau | Liberia |
| Sierra Leone | Sierra Leone |

2.3

Life Expectancy at Birth in West Africa during 2003-2006

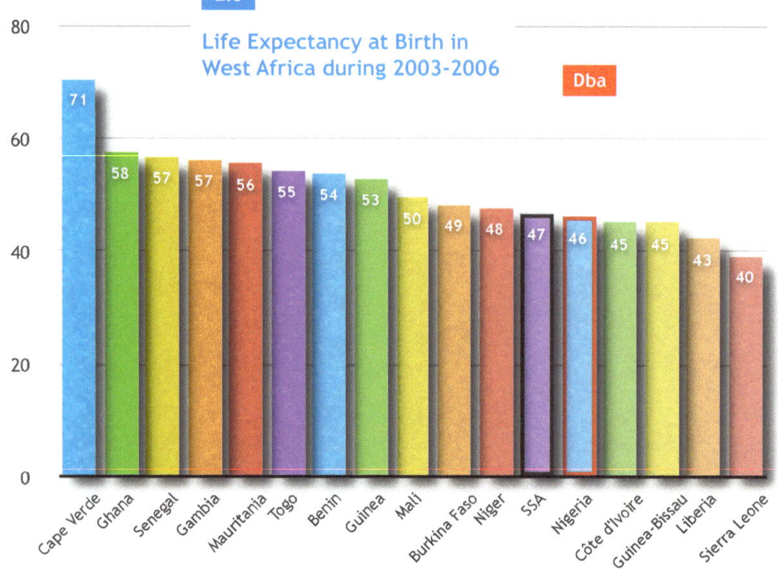


Primary Data: UNICEF

**Performance among Oil-Exporters**

| ▲ (99-02) | ▼ (03-06) |
|---|---|
| Sudan | Sudan |
| Gabon | Gabon |
| **Nigeria** | Congo, Rep. |
| Cameroon | Cameroon |
| Equatorial Guinea | Equatorial Guinea |
| Congo, Rep. | **Nigeria** |
| Chad | Chad |
| Côte d'Ivoire | Côte d'Ivoire |
| Angola | Angola |

If born in Nigeria, you were likely to live shorter than you would being born in 11 countries of West Afr., and just a shade shorter if born elsewhere in Africa.

You were likely to live longest in Cape Verde, followed by Ghana, within West Africa.

| | |
|---|---|
| ▲ | improved *or* better than average |
| ▼ | worsened *or* worse than average |
| ◁▷ | no change *or* average |

You might expect to live longer in Nigeria, though, if you were born before 2003.

After that point, chances of a long life fell behind most of West Africa and Sub-Saharan Africa, and also behind most of the oil countries.

2.4

Life Expectancy at Birth in Nigeria and Sub-Saharan Africa from 1999 to 2007

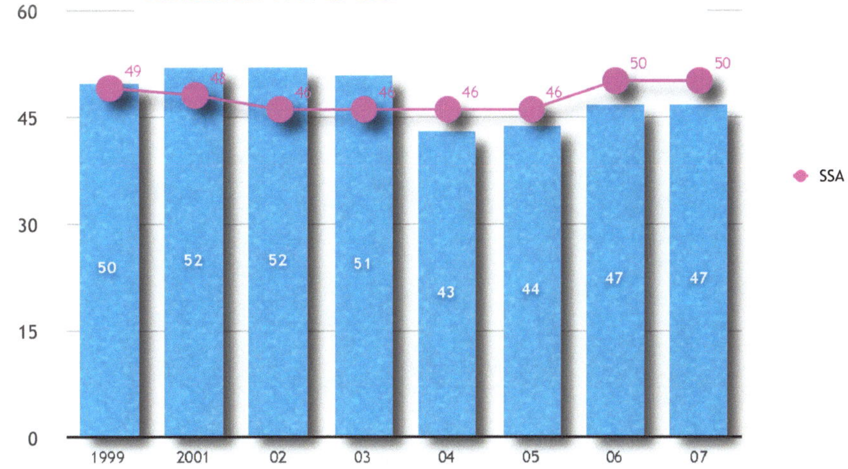


Life Expectancy in Sub-Saharan Africa during 2003-06: Rankings

| Rank | Country |
|---|---|
| 1 | Mauritius |
| 2 | Cape Verde |
| 3 | Comoros |
| 4 | Ghana |
| 5 | Senegal |
| 6 | Gambia, The |
| 7 | Madagascar |
| 8 | Gabon |
| 9 | Eritrea |
| | Togo |

HIGHEST

| Rank | Country |
|---|---|
| 19 | Burundi |
| 20 | Congo, Dem. Rep. |
| 21 | Rwanda |
| 22 | Angola |
| | Malawi |
| | Mozambique |
| 23 | Central Afr. Rep. |
| 24 | Botswana |
| | Sierra Leone |
| 25 | Zambia |
| 26 | Lesotho |
| 27 | Swaziland |
| N/A | Seychelles |

BOTTOM

| Rank | Country |
|---|---|
| 10 | Benin |
| 11 | Guinea |
| 12 | Congo, Rep. |
| 13 | Mali |
| 14 | Burkina Faso |
| | Ethiopia |
| | Kenya |
| | Niger |
| | Uganda |
| 15 | Cameroon |
| | Namibia |
| | South Africa |
| | Tanzania |
| 16 | Equatorial Guinea |
| | **Nigeria** |
| 17 | Chad |
| 18 | Côte d' Ivoire |
| | Guinea-Bissau |

MIDDLE

Primary Data: UNICEF

# 2.3 Child Mortality (Under-5 year olds)

*infant survival*

| | 99-02 | 03-06 |
|---|---|---|
| Self-comparison to Preceding Period | | ▼ |
| Performance in Sub-Saharan Africa | ▼ | ▼ |
| Performance in West Africa | ▼ | ▼ |

Primary Data: UNICEF

| 99-02 | 03-06 |
|---|---|
| Cape Verde | Cape Verde |
| Ghana | Ghana |
| Gambia, The | Gambia, The |
| Senegal | Senegal |
| Togo | Togo |
| Benin | Mauritania |
| Guinea | Benin |
| Côte d'Ivoire | Guinea |
| Mauritania | Côte d'Ivoire |
| **Nigeria** | **Nigeria** |
| Burkina Faso | Burkina Faso |
| Guinea-Bissau | Guinea-Bissau |
| Mali | Mali |
| Liberia | Liberia |
| Niger | Niger |
| Sierra Leone | Sierra Leone |

2.5

Under-5 Child Mortality in West Africa during 2003-06

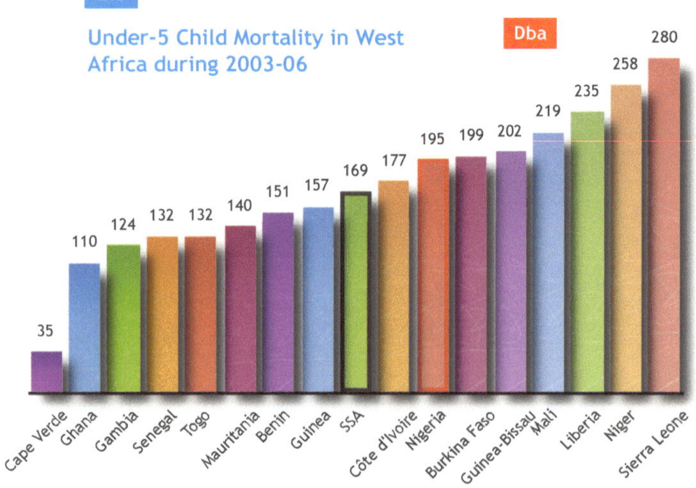


| Performance among Oil-Exporters | ▼ | ▼ |
|---|---|---|
| | Sudan | Sudan |
| | Congo, Rep. | Gabon |
| | Gabon | Congo, Rep. |
| | Equatorial Guinea | Cameroon |
| | Cameroon | Côte d'Ivoire |
| | Côte d'Ivoire | Equatorial Guinea |
| | **Nigeria** | **Nigeria** |
| | Chad | Chad |
| | Angola | Angola |

| | |
|---|---|
| ▲ | improved *or* better than average |
| ▼ | worsened *or* worse than average |
| ◁▷ | no change *or* average |

Effective increase in child mortality in Nigeria across 99/07, although numbers began to dip; slightly first in 04, but consistently from then on to 07.

However, it still stayed worse than the Africa average during that 8-yr period of 99-07.

**2.6**

**Under-5 Child Mortality in Nigeria and Sub-Saharan Africa from 1999 to 2007**

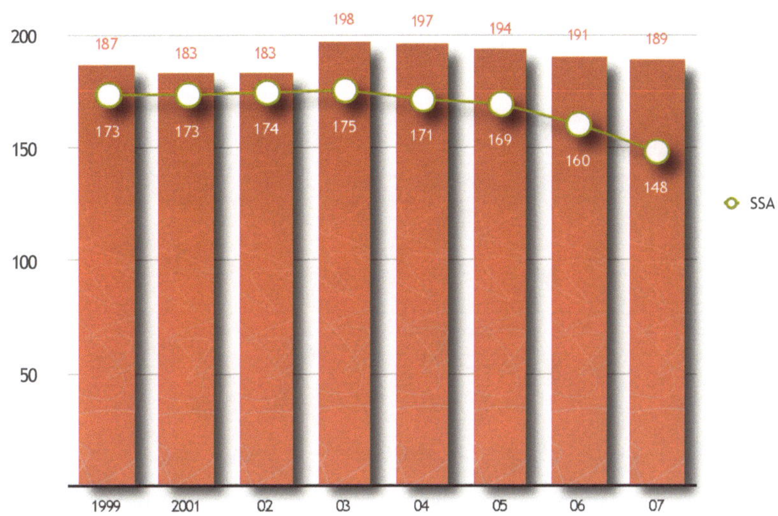


Primary Data: UNICEF

**Under-5 Child Mortality in Sub-Saharan Africa during 2003-06: Rankings**

| Rank | Country | Rank | Country | Rank | Country |
|---|---|---|---|---|---|
| 1 | Seychelles | 14 | Gambia, The | 27 | Central Afr. Rep. |
| 2 | Mauritius | 15 | Senegal | 28 | Burundi |
| 3 | Cape Verde | | Togo | 29 | Equatorial Guinea |
| 4 | Namibia | 16 | Tanzania | 30 | Rwanda |
| 5 | South Africa | 17 | Uganda | 31 | Nigeria |
| 6 | Comoros | 18 | Mozambique | 32 | Burkina Faso |
| 7 | Eritrea | 19 | Malawi | 33 | Guinea-Bissau |
| 8 | Gabon | 20 | Benin | 34 | Chad |
| 9 | Lesotho | 21 | Cameroon | 35 | Congo, Dem. Rep. |
| 10 | Ghana | 22 | Ethiopia | 36 | Mali |
| 11 | Congo, Rep. | 23 | Guinea | 37 | Niger |
| 12 | Botswana | 24 | Swaziland | 38 | Angola |
| 13 | Kenya | 25 | Côte d' Ivoire | 39 | Sierra Leone |
| | Madagascar | 26 | Zambia | | |
| | BEST | | AVERAGE | | BOTTOM |

The best child care obtained in the Seychelles.

Central Africa
East Africa
Southern Africa
West Africa

# 2.4 Babies Immunization: Measles

***got my jabs; did you get yours?***

| | 99-02 | 03-06 |
|---|---|---|
| Self-comparison to Preceding Period | | ▲ |
| Performance in Sub-Saharan Africa | ▼ | ▼ |
| Performance in West Africa | ▼ | ▼ |
| | Gambia, The | Gambia, The |
| | Benin | Benin |
| | Ghana | Ghana |
| | Cape Verde | Burkina Faso |
| | Mauritania | Mali |
| | Côte d'Ivoire | Liberia |
| | Liberia | Guinea-Bissau |
| | Togo | Togo |
| | Senegal | Senegal |
| | Guinea | Sierra Leone |
| | Burkina Faso | Niger |
| | Mali | Cape Verde |
| | Sierra Leone | Mauritania |
| | Niger | Guinea |
| | Guinea-Bissau | Côte d'Ivoire |
| | **Nigeria** | **Nigeria** |
| Performance among Oil-Exporters | ▼ | ▼ |
| | Sudan | Cameroon |
| | Angola | Sudan |
| | Côte d'Ivoire | Congo, Rep. |
| | Cameroon | Côte d'Ivoire |
| | Equatorial Guinea | Gabon |
| | Chad | Angola |
| | Gabon | Equatorial Guinea |
| | **Nigeria** | **Nigeria** |
| | Congo, Rep. | Chad |

Primary Data: UNICEF

**2.7**

% of 1-yr olds Immunized against Measles in West Africa during 2003-06

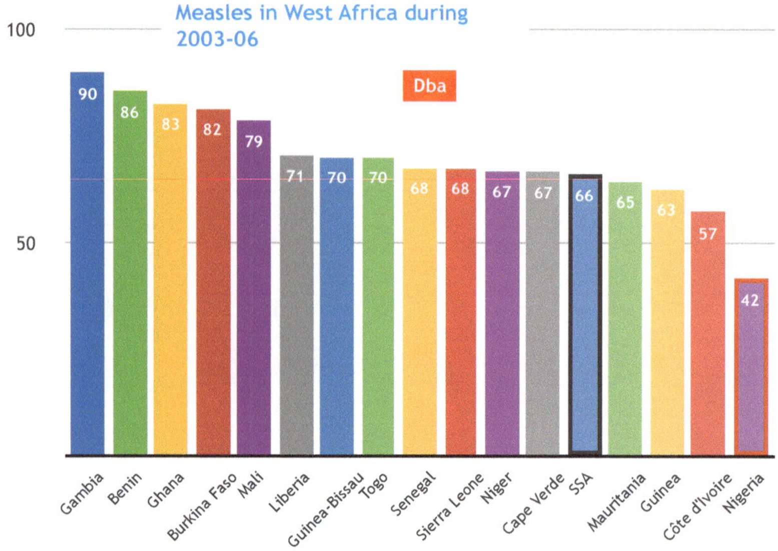


| | |
|---|---|
| ▲ | improved *or* better than average |
| ▼ | worsened *or* worse than average |
| ◁▷ | no change *or* average |

Only 42% of 1-yr olds in Nigeria got their measles inoculation during 2003-2006.

The average in Africa was 66%, and Nigeria's was the worst index within West Africa.

**2.8**

% of 1-yr olds Immunized against Measles in Nigeria and Sub-Saharan Africa from 1997 to 2007

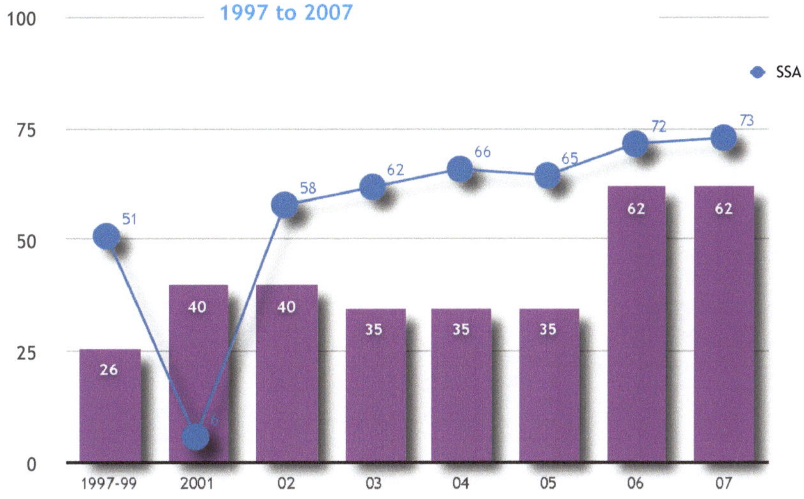


Primary Data: UNICEF

Nigeria made a concerted positive climb in 2006, which was sustained during 2007. But it still lagged behind most of Africa.

% of 1-yr olds Immunized against Measles in Sub-Saharan Africa during 2003-06: Rankings

| Rank | Country |
|---|---|
| 1 | Seychelles |
| 2 | Mauritius |
| 3 | Tanzania |
| 4 | Botswana |
| 5 | Gambia, The |
| 6 | Rwanda |
| 7 | Uganda |
| 8 | Eritrea |
| 9 | Benin |
| 10 | Zambia |
| 11 | Ghana |
| | South Africa |
| 12 | Burkina Faso |
| 13 | Malawi |

TOP

| Rank | Country |
|---|---|
| 14 | Mali |
| 15 | Lesotho |
| 16 | Mozambique |
| 17 | Burundi |
| 18 | Kenya |
| 19 | Comoros |
| 20 | Guinea-Bissau |
| | Swaziland |
| | Togo |
| 21 | Namibia |
| 22 | Senegal |
| | Sierra Leone |
| 23 | Niger |
| 24 | Cape Verde |
| 25 | Cameroon |
| 26 | Congo, Dem. Rep. |

MIDDLE

| Rank | Country |
|---|---|
| 27 | Guinea |
| 28 | Ethiopia |
| 29 | Congo, Rep. |
| 30 | Madagascar |
| 31 | Côte d' Ivoire |
| 32 | Gabon |
| 33 | Angola |
| 34 | Equatorial Guinea |
| 35 | Nigeria |
| 36 | Chad |
| 37 | Central Afr. Rep. |

BOTTOM

Central Africa
East Africa
Southern Africa
West Africa

# 2.5 Babies Immunization: Tuberculosis

*don't leave it late*

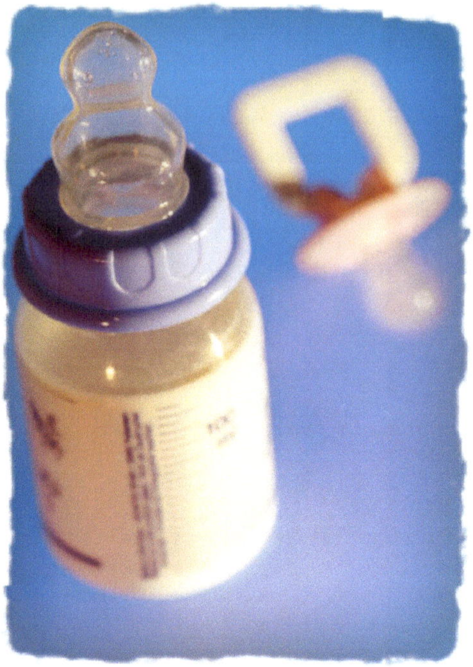

| | 99-02 | 03-06 |
|---|---|---|
| Self-comparison to Preceding Period | | ▲ |
| Performance in Sub-Saharan Africa | ▼ | ▼ |
| Performance in West Africa | ▼ | ▼ |
| | Gambia, The | Benin |
| | Benin | Gambia, The |
| | Ghana | Ghana |
| | Cape Verde | Burkina Faso |
| | Senegal | Togo |
| | Mauritania | Senegal |
| | Togo | Mauritania |
| | Mali | Sierra Leone |
| | Côte d'Ivoire | Guinea-Bissau |
| | Guinea | Guinea |
| | Burkina Faso | Cape Verde |
| | Sierra Leone | Mali |
| | Liberia | Niger |
| | Guinea-Bissau | Liberia |
| | **Nigeria** | Côte d'Ivoire |
| | Niger | **Nigeria** |
| Performance among Oil-Exporters | ▼ | ▼ |
| | Gabon | Gabon |
| | Côte d'Ivoire | Cameroon |
| | Angola | Congo, Rep. |
| | Cameroon | Equatorial Guinea |
| | Equatorial Guinea | Angola |
| | Sudan | Côte d'Ivoire |
| | Chad | Sudan |
| | Congo, Rep. | **Nigeria** |
| | **Nigeria** | Chad |

Primary Data: UNICEF

2.9

% of 1-yr olds Immunized against Tuberculosis in West Africa during 2003-06

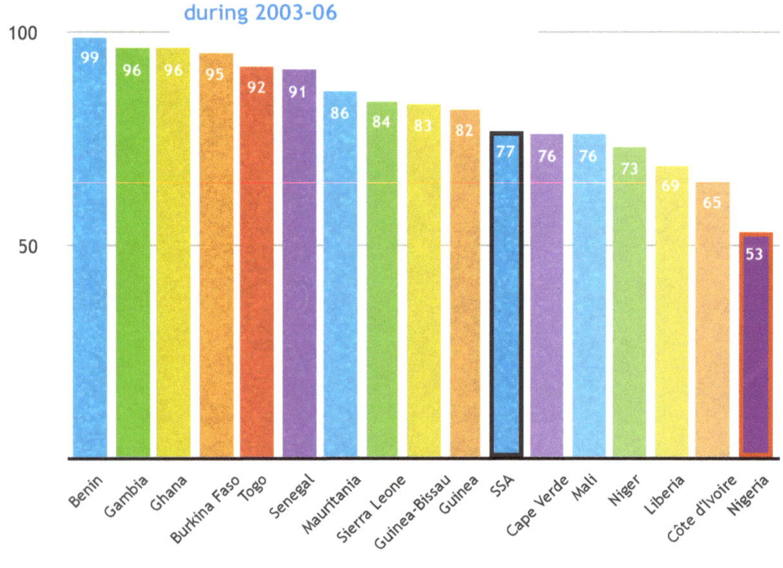


| | |
|---|---|
| ▲ | improved *or* better than average |
| ▼ | worsened *or* worse than average |
| ◁▷ | no change *or* average |

2.10

% of 1-yr olds Immunized against Tuberculosis in Nigeria and Sub-Saharan Africa from 1997 to 2007

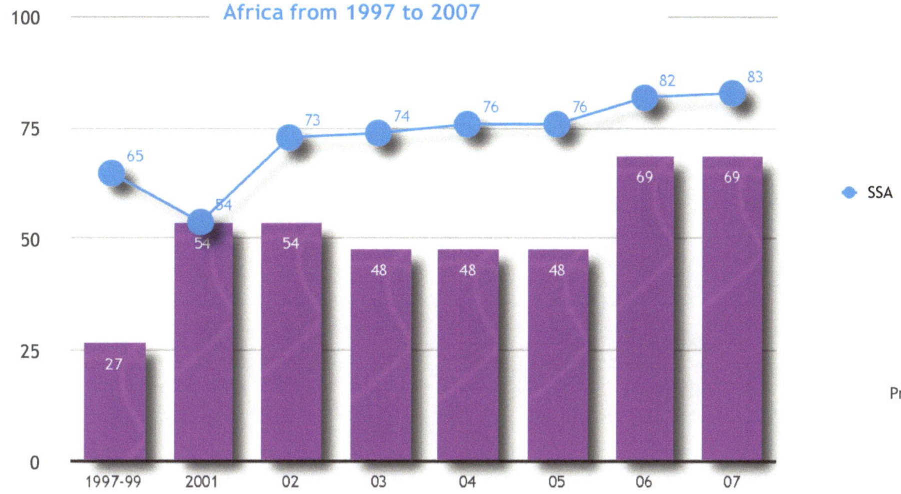


Primary Data: UNICEF

A story not dissimilar to that of measles inoculation, with the same poor trend up to 2005 and sharp improvement thereafter.

Again, most of Africa did better throughout 1999-2007.

# 2.6 Population with Access to Safe Water

**some water runs through it**

| | 1990 | 04-06 |
|---|---|---|
| Self-comparison to Preceding Period | | ▲ |
| Performance in Sub-Saharan Africa | ▼ | ▼ |
| Performance in West Africa | ◁▷ | ▼ |
| | Côte d'Ivoire | Côte d'Ivoire |
| | Senegal | Gambia, The |
| | Benin | Cape Verde |
| | Ghana | Senegal |
| | Togo | Ghana |
| | **Nigeria** | Benin |
| | Guinea | Liberia |
| | Niger | Burkina Faso |
| | Burkina Faso | Guinea-Bissau |
| | Mauritania | Sierra Leone |
| | Mali | Mauritania |
| | | Togo |
| | | **Nigeria** |
| | | Guinea |
| | | Mali |
| | | Niger |
| Performance among Oil-Exporters | ▼ | ▼ |
| | Côte d'Ivoire | Gabon |
| | Sudan | Côte d'Ivoire |
| | Cameroon | Sudan |
| | **Nigeria** | Cameroon |
| | Angola | Congo, Rep. |
| | Chad | Angola |
| | | **Nigeria** |
| | | Equatorial Guinea |
| | | Chad |

Primary Data: AfDB

2.11

% of Population with Access to Safe Water in West Africa during 2004-06

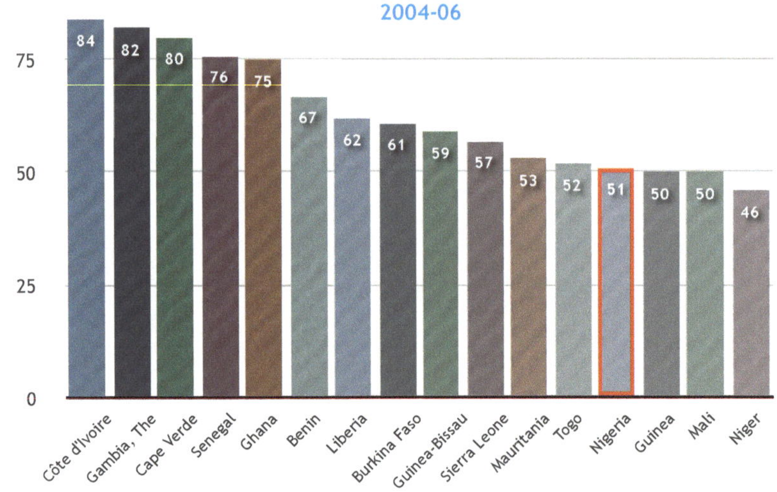


Nigerians' access to potable water improved during 04-06, compared to 1990 levels.

But they were worse off than most other West Africans, Africans, and residents of companion oil economies.

| | |
|---|---|
| ▲ | improved *or* better than average |
| ▼ | worsened *or* worse than average |
| ◁▷ | no change *or* average |

# 2.7 Population with Access to Sanitation

## but it's being sorted

| | 1990 | 04-06 |
|---|---|---|
| Self-comparison to Preceding Period | | ▲ |
| Performance in Sub-Saharan Africa | ▲ | ▲ |
| Performance in West Africa | ▲ | ▲ |
| | **Nigeria** | Senegal |
| | Liberia | Gambia, The |
| | Togo | Mali |
| | Mali | **Nigeria** |
| | Senegal | Cape Verde |
| | Mauritania | Sierra Leone |
| | Côte d'Ivoire | Côte d'Ivoire |
| | Ghana | Guinea-Bissau |
| | Guinea | Togo |
| | Benin | Mauritania |
| | Burkina Faso | Benin |
| | Niger | Liberia |
| | | Ghana |
| | | Guinea |
| | | Burkina Faso |
| | | Niger |
| Performance among Oil-Exporters | ▲ | ▲ |
| | Cameroon | Equatorial Guinea |
| | **Nigeria** | Cameroon |
| | Sudan | **Nigeria** |
| | Angola | Côte d'Ivoire |
| | Côte d'Ivoire | Gabon |
| | Chad | Sudan |
| | | Angola |
| | | Congo, Rep. |
| | | Chad |

Primary Data: AfDB

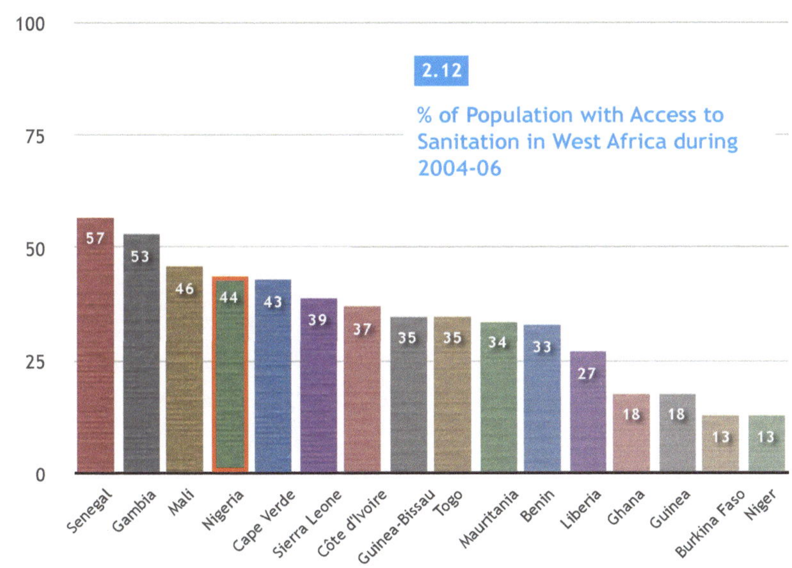


2.12

% of Population with Access to Sanitation in West Africa during 2004-06

This time, Nigeria stays among the top ranks within the entire continent, oil economies inclusive.

| | |
|---|---|
| ▲ | improved *or* better than average |
| ▼ | worsened *or* worse than average |
| ◁▷ | no change *or* average |

# 2.8 Phones per Population (Fixed & Mobiles)

*interconnected*

Primary Data: ITU

| | 2000 | 2007 |
|---|---|---|
| Self-comparison to Preceding Period | | ▲ |
| Performance in Sub-Saharan Africa | ▼ | ▲ |

**Performance in West Africa**

| 2000 ▼ | 2007 ▲ |
|---|---|
| Cape Verde | Cape Verde |
| Côte d'Ivoire | Gambia, The |
| Senegal | **Nigeria** |
| Gambia, The | Senegal |
| Togo | Ghana |
| Ghana | Côte d'Ivoire |
| Benin | Togo |
| Mauritania | Benin |
| Guinea-Bissau | Mauritania |
| Guinea | Burkina Faso |
| Burkina Faso | Mali |
| Sierra Leone | Guinea |
| **Nigeria** | Guinea-Bissau |
| Mali | Niger |
| Liberia | |
| Niger | |

| | |
|---|---|
| ▲ | improved *or* better than average |
| ▼ | worsened *or* worse than average |
| ◁▷ | no change *or* average |

**2.13**

Phones (fixed & mobile) for every 100 Persons of Population in West Africa during 2000 & 2007

*Telecommunications: Nigeria made the greatest leap across 2000 & 2007 levels, within West Africa.*

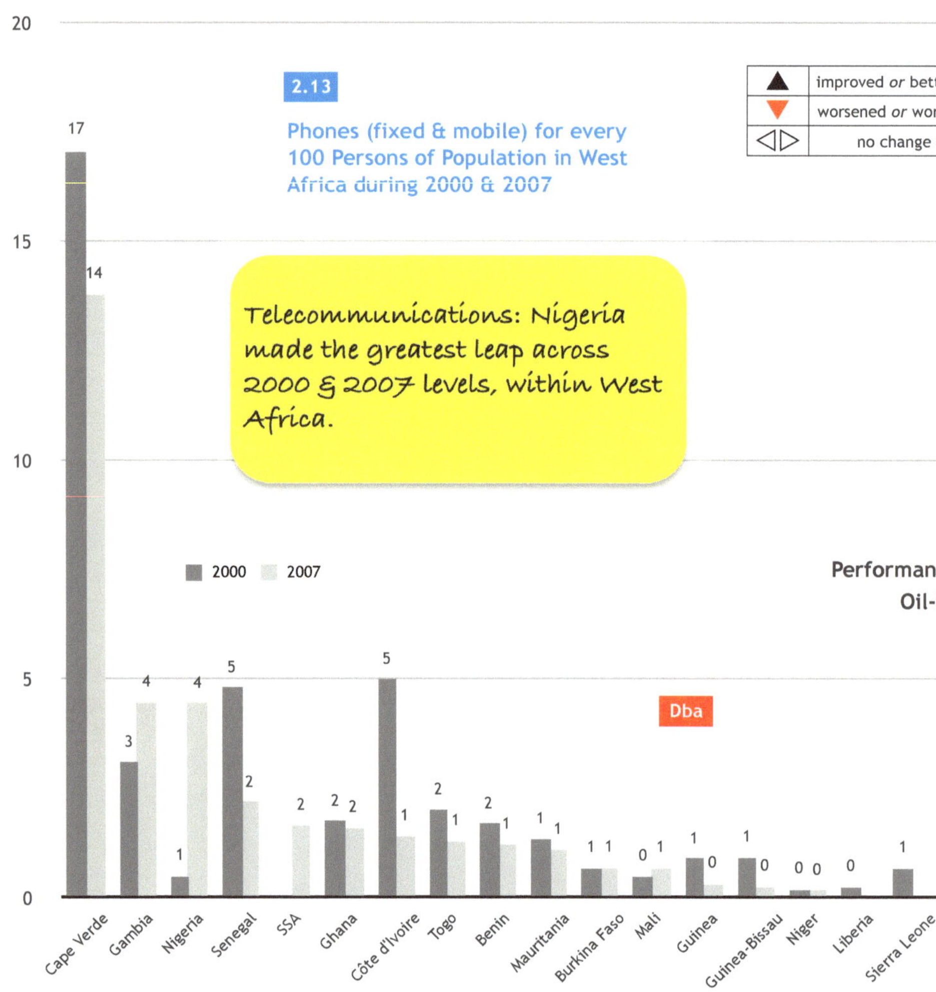


**Performance among Oil-Exporters**

| 2000 ▼ | 2007 ▲ |
|---|---|
| Gabon | **Nigeria** |
| Côte d'Ivoire | Gabon |
| Congo, Rep. | Equatorial Guinea |
| Equatorial Guinea | Côte d'Ivoire |
| Sudan | Sudan |
| Cameroon | Cameroon |
| Angola | Angola |
| **Nigeria** | Congo, Rep. |
| Chad | Chad |

Phones (Fixed & Mobiles) per Population in Sub-Saharan Africa during 2007: Rankings

| Rank | Country | Rank | Country | Rank | Country |
|---|---|---|---|---|---|
| 1 | Mauritius | 15 | Ghana | 29 | Tanzania |
| 2 | Seychelles | 16 | Côte d' Ivoire | 30 | Uganda |
| 3 | Cape Verde | 17 | Togo | 31 | Burundi |
| 4 | South Africa | 18 | Malawi | 32 | Congo, Rep. |
| 5 | Botswana | 19 | Benin | 33 | Guinea |
| 6 | Namibia | 20 | Ethiopia | 34 | Mozambique |
| 7 | Gambia, The | 21 | Eritrea | 35 | Central Afr. Rep. |
| 8 | Nigeria | 22 | Cameroon | 36 | Guinea-Bissau |
| 9 | Swaziland | 23 | Zambia | 37 | Rwanda |
| 10 | Lesotho | 24 | Kenya | 38 | Niger |
| 11 | Gabon | 25 | Burkina Faso | 39 | Chad |
| 12 | Comoros | 26 | Mali | 40 | Congo, Dem. Rep. |
| 13 | Senegal | 27 | Madagascar | N/A | Sierra Leone |
| 14 | Equatorial Guinea | 28 | Angola | | |
| TOP | | MIDDLE | | BOTTOM | |

Central Africa
East Africa
Southern Africa
West Africa

Primary Data: ITU

It climbed swiftly within the rest of Africa, too; and it topped the oil exporters group.

Nigeria was 8th best among 40 African countries as at 2007. In West Africa, Cape Verde and Gambia edged ahead of it.

# 2.9 Number of Mobile Phone Users

**she's got a new phone**

| | 2000 | 2007 |
|---|---|---|
| Self-comparison to Preceding Period | | ▲ |
| Performance in Sub-Saharan Africa | ▼ | ▲ |
| Performance in West Africa | ▼ | ▲ |
| | Cape Verde | Gambia, The |
| | Côte d'Ivoire | Mauritania |
| | Senegal | Côte d'Ivoire |
| | Togo | Senegal |
| | Benin | Ghana |
| | Ghana | Cape Verde |
| | Mauritania | **Nigeria** |
| | Guinea | Benin |
| | Gambia, The | Mali |
| | Sierra Leone | Togo |
| | Burkina Faso | Guinea-Bissau |
| | Mali | Liberia |
| | Liberia | Sierra Leone |
| | **Nigeria** | Burkina Faso |
| | Niger | Niger |
| | | Guinea |
| Performance among Oil-Exporters | ▼ | ◁▷ |
| | Gabon | Gabon |
| | Côte d'Ivoire | Equatorial Guinea |
| | Congo, Rep. | Côte d'Ivoire |
| | Equatorial Guinea | Congo, Rep. |
| | Cameroon | **Nigeria** |
| | Angola | Cameroon |
| | Chad | Angola |
| | Sudan | Sudan |
| | **Nigeria** | Chad |

| | |
|---|---|
| ▲ | improved *or* better than average |
| ▼ | worsened *or* worse than average |
| ◁▷ | no change *or* average |

Concerning mobile phones specifically, by 2007 Nigeria had the 7th highest density of 16 West African countries.

But there was still ground to be gained within the oil exporters group. Back in 2001, mobile phone occurrence in Nigeria was negligible.

**2.14**

Mobile Phones for every 100 Persons of Population in West Africa during 2000 & 2007

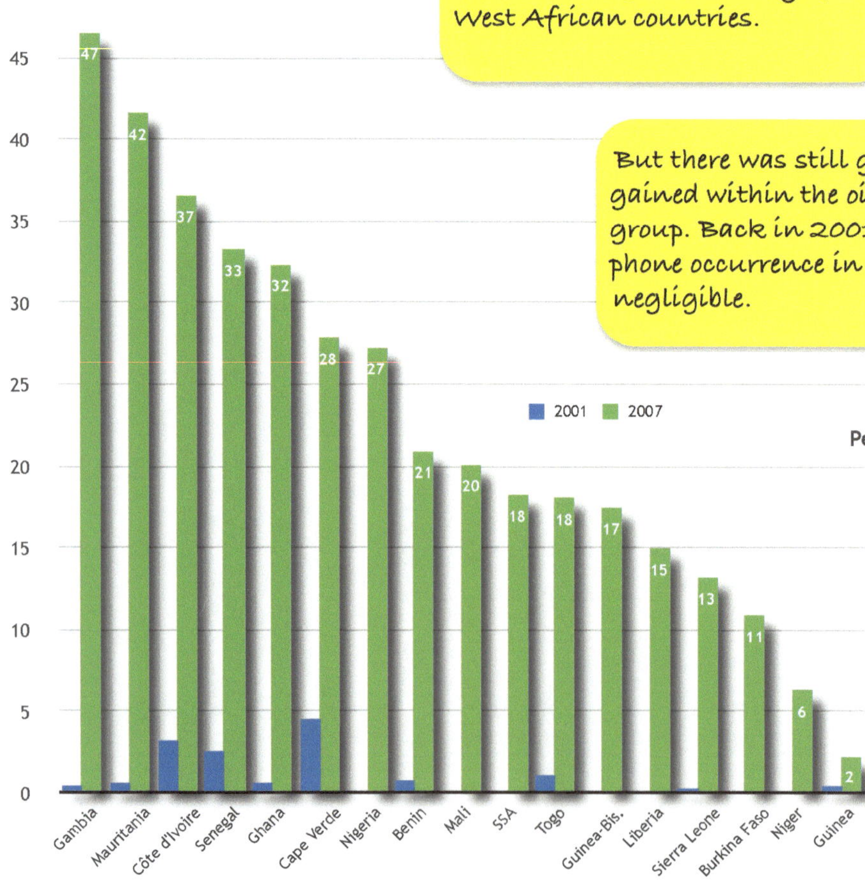


Primary Data: ITU

# 2.10 Literacy

**that's his favourite book**

| | 2000 | 2007 |
|---|---|---|
| Self-comparison to Preceding Period | | ▲ |
| Performance in Sub-Saharan Africa | ▲ | ▲ |
| Performance in West Africa | ▲ | ▲ |
| | Cape Verde | Cape Verde |
| | Ghana | Ghana |
| | **Nigeria** | **Nigeria** |
| | Togo | Togo |
| | Liberia | Liberia |
| | Côte d'Ivoire | Côte d'Ivoire |
| | Mauritania | Guinea-Bissau |
| | Guinea-Bissau | Benin |
| | Benin | Gambia, The |
| | Senegal | Senegal |
| | Gambia, The | Mauritania |
| | Mali | Mali |
| | Burkina Faso | Burkina Faso |
| | Niger | Niger |
| Performance among Oil-Exporters | ◁▷ | ◁▷ |
| | Equatorial Guinea | Equatorial Guinea |
| | Congo, Rep. | Congo, Rep. |
| | Cameroon | Cameroon |
| | **Nigeria** | **Nigeria** |
| | Sudan | Sudan |
| | Côte d'Ivoire | Côte d'Ivoire |
| | Chad | Chad |

| | |
|---|---|
| ▲ | improved *or* better than average |
| ▼ | worsened *or* worse than average |
| ◁▷ | no change *or* average |

Primary Data: AfDB

3rd best literacy levels in West Afr., bettered by only Cape Verde & Ghana. Average in the oil group, where the table stayed the same for 2007 as for 2000.

2.15

Total Adult Literacy Rate (%) in West Africa during 2000 & 2007

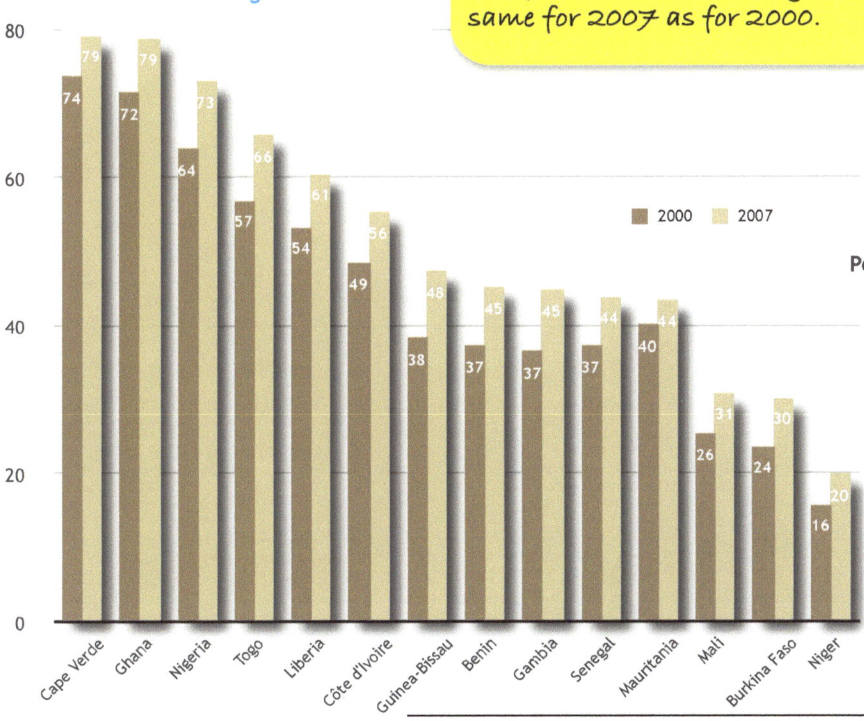

# 2.11 Number of Internet Users

*just e-mail it*

| | 2000 | 2007 |
|---|---|---|
| Self-comparison to Preceding Period | | ▲ |
| Performance in Sub-Saharan Africa | ▼ | ▲ |

**Performance in West Africa**

| 2000 ▼ | 2007 ▲ |
|---|---|
| Togo | **Nigeria** |
| Cape Verde | Senegal |
| Gambia, The | Cape Verde |
| Senegal | Gambia, The |
| Côte d'Ivoire | Togo |
| Guinea-Bissau | Ghana |
| Benin | Guinea-Bissau |
| Mauritania | Benin |
| Ghana | Côte d'Ivoire |
| Mali | Mauritania |
| Guinea | Mali |
| Sierra Leone | Burkina Faso |
| Burkina Faso | Guinea |
| **Nigeria** | Niger |
| Niger | Sierra Leone |
| Liberia | |

Primary Data: ITU

| | |
|---|---|
| ▲ | improved *or* better than average |
| ▼ | worsened *or* worse than average |
| ◁▷ | no change *or* average |

**Performance among Oil-Exporters**

| 2000 ▼ | 2007 ▲ |
|---|---|
| Gabon | **Nigeria** |
| Cameroon | Gabon |
| Côte d'Ivoire | Sudan |
| Equatorial Guinea | Cameroon |
| Angola | Congo, Rep. |
| Sudan | Côte d'Ivoire |
| **Nigeria** | Equatorial Guinea |
| Chad | Angola |
| Congo, Rep. | Chad |

2.16

Internet Users out of every 1,000 Persons of Population in West Africa during 2000 & 2007

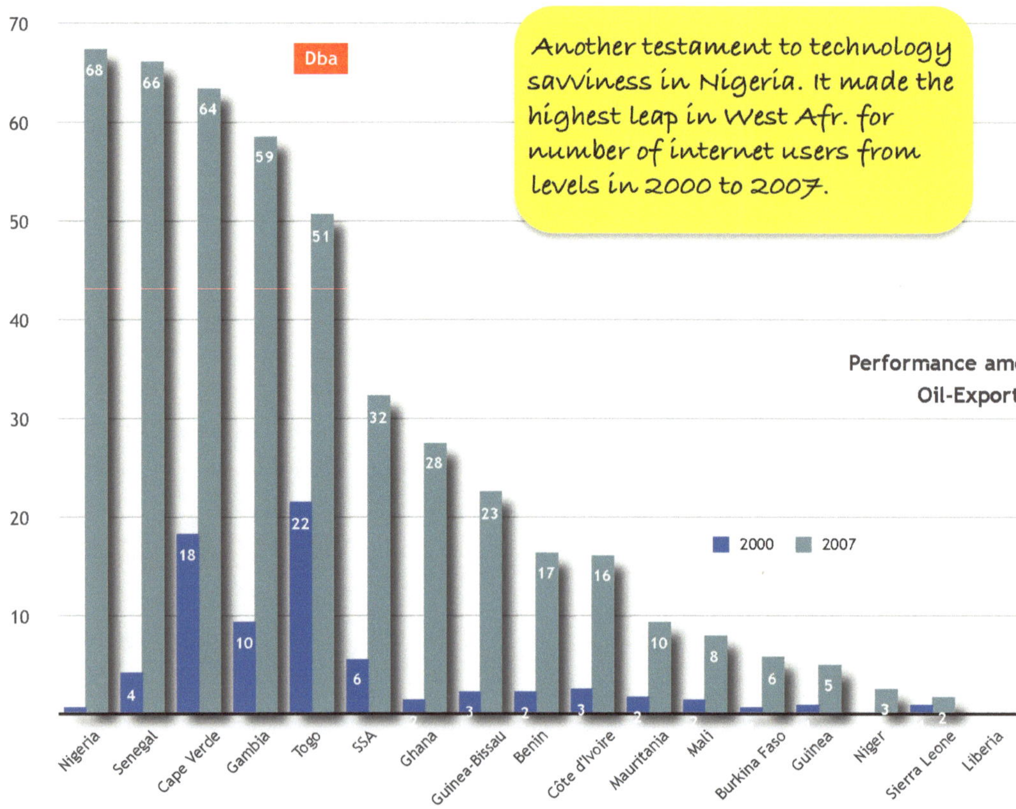


*Another testament to technology savviness in Nigeria. It made the highest leap in West Afr. for number of internet users from levels in 2000 to 2007.*

Tony Okoromadu

### Internet Users per Population in Sub-Saharan Africa during 2007: Rankings

| Rank | Country |
|---|---|
| 1 | Seychelles |
| 2 | Mauritius |
| 3 | South Africa |
| 4 | Kenya |
| 5 | Nigeria |
| 6 | Senegal |
| 7 | Uganda |
| 8 | Cape Verde |
| 9 | Gambia, The |
| 10 | Gabon |
| 11 | Togo |
| 12 | Namibia |
| 13 | Botswana |

TOP

| Rank | Country |
|---|---|
| 14 | Zambia |
| 15 | Swaziland |
| 16 | Lesotho |
| 17 | Ghana |
| 18 | Comoros |
| 19 | Guinea-Bissau |
| 20 | Cameroon |
| 21 | Eritrea |
| 22 | Congo, Rep. |
| 23 | Benin |
| 24 | Côte d' Ivoire |
| 25 | Equatorial Guinea |
| 26 | Rwanda |

MIDDLE

| Rank | Country |
|---|---|
| 27 | Malawi |
|  | Tanzania |
| 28 | Mozambique |
| 29 | Mali |
| 30 | Burundi |
| 31 | Angola |
|  | Chad |
| 32 | Burkina Faso |
| 33 | Madagascar |
| 34 | Guinea |
| 35 | Congo, Dem. Rep. |
| 36 | Ethiopia |
| 37 | Central Afr. Rep. |
| 38 | Niger |
| 39 | Sierra Leone |

BOTTOM

Primary Data: ITU

Central Africa
East Africa
Southern Africa
West Africa

It also made the biggest climb within the oil group, jumping from 7th to top place among the 9 countries.

In Africa, it was 5th out of 41 countries, bettered only by Seychelles, Mauritius, South Africa and Kenya.

# 2.12 Personal Computers per Population

***they know their gigabytes***

| | 2001 | 2006 |
|---|---|---|
| Self-comparison to Preceding Period | | ▲ |
| Performance in Sub-Saharan Africa | ▼ | ▼ |
| Performance in West Africa | ▲ | ▲ |

| 2001 | 2006 |
|---|---|
| Cape Verde | Cape Verde |
| Togo | Togo |
| Senegal | Mauritania |
| Gambia, The | Senegal |
| Mauritania | Gambia, The |
| Côte d'Ivoire | Côte d'Ivoire |
| **Nigeria** | **Nigeria** |
| Guinea | Benin |
| Ghana | Ghana |
| Guinea-Bissau | Guinea |
| Benin | Mali |
| Burkina Faso | Burkina Faso |
| Mali | Guinea-Bissau |
| Niger | Niger |

| Performance among Oil-Exporters | |
|---|---|
| 2001 | 2006 |
| ▲ | ▼ |
| Gabon | Sudan |
| Côte d'Ivoire | Gabon |
| **Nigeria** | Equatorial Guinea |
| Equatorial Guinea | Côte d'Ivoire |
| Cameroon | Cameroon |
| Congo, Rep. | **Nigeria** |
| Sudan | Angola |
| Chad | Congo, Rep. |
| Angola | Chad |

| | |
|---|---|
| ▲ | improved *or* better than average |
| ▼ | worsened *or* worse than average |
| ◁▷ | no change *or* average |

However, people owned fewer computers in Nigeria than in most of the continent; but just above the average number in West Africa.

Perhaps, taken in conjunction with no. of internet users, this suggests there is yet a yawning market gap in personal computers to be serviced.

**2.17**

Number of Personal Computers for every 1,000 Persons of Population in West Africa during 2001 & 2006

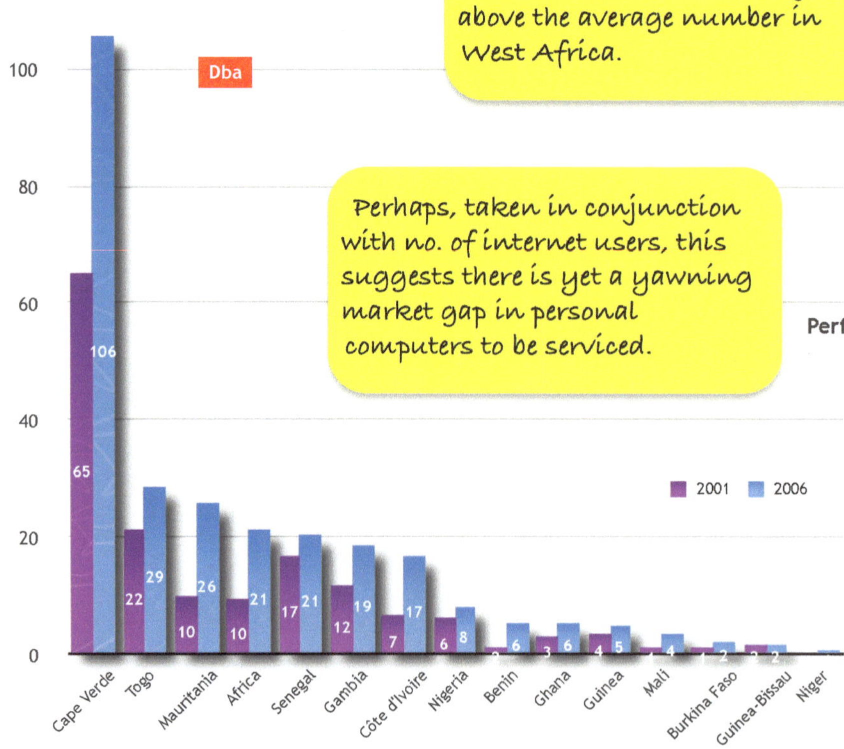


Primary Data: AfDB

### Personal Computers per Population in Sub-Saharan Africa during 2006: Rankings

| Rank | Country | Rank | Country | Rank | Country |
|---|---|---|---|---|---|
| 1 | Seychelles | 13 | Côte d' Ivoire | 25 | Madagascar |
| 2 | Mauritius | 14 | Uganda | 26 | Congo, Rep. |
| 3 | Namibia | 15 | Kenya | 27 | Guinea |
| 4 | Cape Verde | | Mozambique | 28 | Mali |
| 5 | South Africa | 16 | Zambia | 29 | Ethiopia |
| 6 | Botswana | 17 | Cameroon | 30 | Central Afr. Rep. |
| 7 | Swaziland | 18 | Tanzania | 31 | Burkina Faso |
| 8 | Gabon | 19 | **Nigeria** | 32 | Rwanda |
| 9 | Togo | 20 | Angola | 33 | Guinea-Bissau |
| 10 | Senegal | | Burundi | | Malawi |
| 11 | Gambia, The | 21 | Comoros | 34 | Chad |
| 12 | Equatorial Guinea | 22 | Eritrea | 35 | Lesotho |
| | | 23 | Benin | | Niger |
| | | 24 | Ghana | 36 | Congo, Dem. Rep. |
| | | | | N/A | Sierra Leone |
| **TOP** | | **MIDDLE** | | **BOTTOM** | |

Primary Data: AfDB

Central Africa
East Africa
Southern Africa
West Africa

In Africa, unlike the top band for internet users, Nigeria falls in the middle band for incidence of personal computers.

Again, a possible pointer to the market that is still available for computers there.

# 2.13 Net Migration

**their bags are packed, they're ready to go**

**2000-2005**

Self-comparison to Preceding Period

Performance in Sub-Saharan Africa: ◁▷

Performance in West Africa: ▼

- Sierra Leone
- Gambia, The
- Benin
- Mauritania
- Burkina Faso
- Guinea-Bissau
- Ghana
- Togo
- **Nigeria**
- Niger
- Senegal
- Cape Verde
- Mali
- Côte d'Ivoire
- Liberia
- Guinea

Primary Data: UNPD

300 persons in every million left Nigeria during 2000-2005. The same as the Africa average, but just below average for West Africa.

The highest no. of emigrants went out of Guinea & the highest no. of immigrants went to Sierra Leone, quite likely returnees after the cessation of civil war.

Performance among Oil-Exporters: ▼

- Chad
- Angola
- Gabon
- Cameroon
- Equatorial Guinea
- **Nigeria**
- Congo, Rep.
- Sudan
- Côte d'Ivoire

**2.18**

Net Migration out of every one million Persons of Population in West Africa during 2000-05

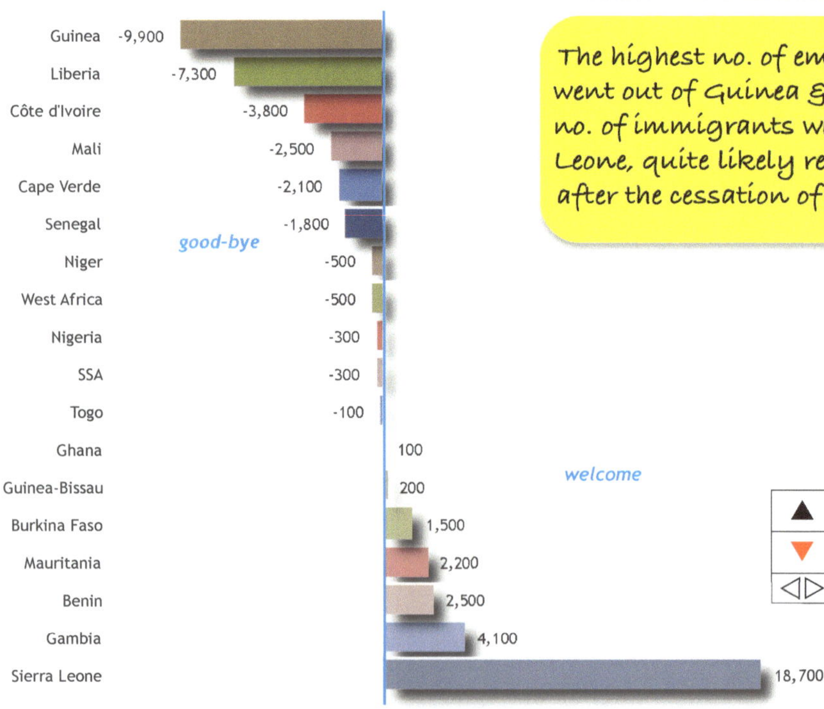


| | |
|---|---|
| ▲ | better = less people leaving *or* more people coming in |
| ▼ | worse = more people leaving *or* less people coming in |
| ◁▷ | no change *or* average |

# Leaders & Stragglers

**and they lived happily ever after**

## Quality of Life Rankings: 2003-07

| Rank | Country |
|---|---|
| 1 | Mauritius |
| 2 | Seychelles |
| 3 | Cape Verde |
| 4 | South Africa |
| 5 | Gambia, The |
| 6 | Namibia |
| 7 | Botswana |
| 8 | Gabon |
| 9 | Comoros |
| 10 | Senegal |
| 11 | Ghana |
| 12 | Togo |
| 13 | Uganda |
| 14 | Kenya |

TOP

| Rank | Country |
|---|---|
| 15 | Eritrea |
| 16 | Swaziland |
| 17 | Benin |
| 18 | Tanzania |
| 19 | Lesotho |
| 20 | Cameroon |
| 21 | **Nigeria** |
| 22 | Equatorial Guinea |
| 23 | Congo, Rep. |
| 24 | Madagascar |
| 25 | Zambia |
| 26 | Côte d' Ivoire |
| 27 | Malawi |
| 28 | Mozambique |

MIDDLE

| Rank | Country |
|---|---|
| 29 | Guinea |
| 30 | Rwanda |
| 31 | Burundi |
| 32 | Mali |
| 33 | Ethiopia |
| 34 | Burkina Faso |
| 35 | Guinea-Bissau |
| 36 | Angola |
| 37 | Niger |
| 38 | Congo, Dem. Rep. |
| 39 | Chad |
| 40 | Central Afr. Rep. |
| 41 | Sierra Leone |

BOTTOM

Central Africa
East Africa
Southern Africa
West Africa

Bang in the middle of Africa, Nigeria wasn't the best place to live during 2003-2007, but it was far from being the worst.

Within West Africa, it stood firmly in the very centre: 8th out of 15 listed countries; 7 better than it, and 7 worse.

Mauritius, Seychelles, Cape Verde, South Africa and Gambia were best in Africa.

# Wrap-up: Quality of Life

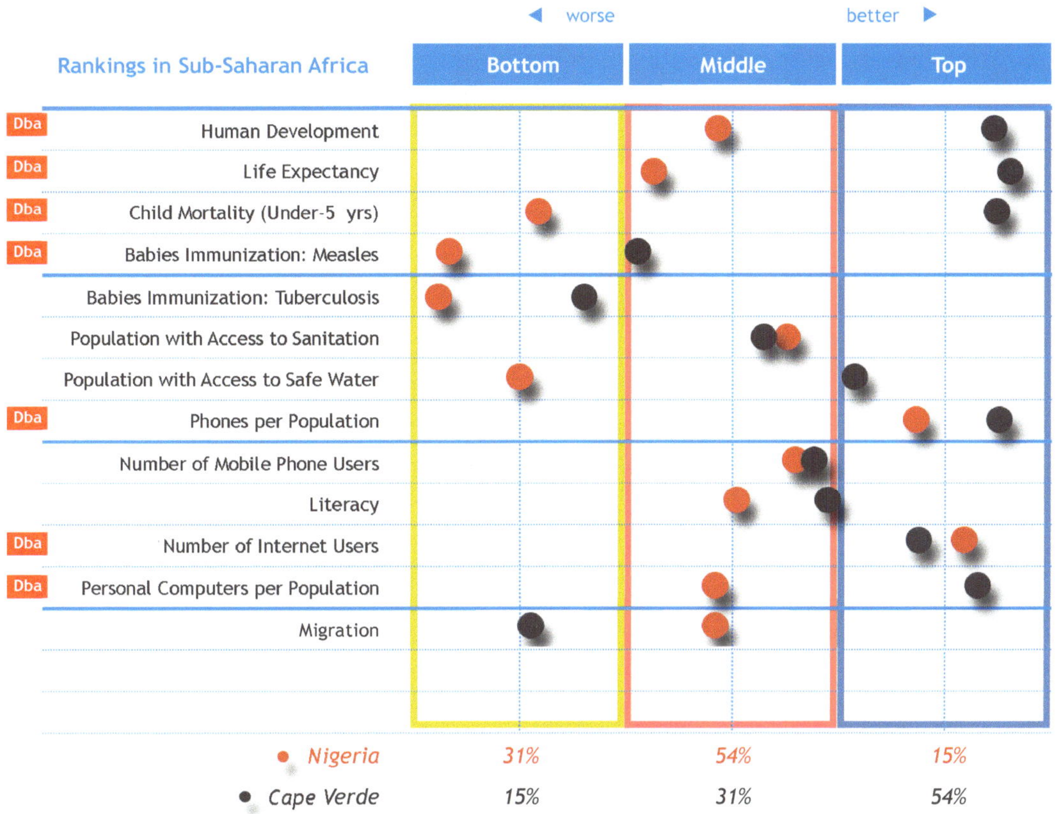


- The best West Africa performance was Cape Verde's; 3rd place in the Africa rankings. Nigeria was almost bang in the middle, at 21st position.
- Of the 13 socio-economic indicators, Nigeria had 31% falling into the bottom-third category in Africa, with the highest proportion qualifying for only average (middle-band) performance; 54%.
- In contrast, Cape Verde had most of its indicators performance, 54%, qualifying for top-third; followed by 31% in the middle-third. The smallest portion of its indicators, 15%, fell into the bottom third of Sub-Saharan Africa.
- The particularly bad Nigeria report-card belongs to babies' immunization, population's access to safe water, and child mortality. All of them health issues.
- Whereas its best showing came from one sector only: information & communication technology. Cape Verde's best came in almost all "life issues": life expectancy, child mortality, access to safe water, and human development in general. Even though they had a strong score-card in technology sectors, too.

# 3. Economic Strength

built to last

3.1 Nigeria GDP in Sub-Saharan Africa

3.2 Nigeria GDP in West Africa

3.3 GDP per Person

3.4 Growth in GDP per Person

3.5 GNI per Person

3.6 Growth in GNI per Person

3.7 Real GDP Growth

3.8 Real Non-Oil GDP Growth

3.9 Inflation

3.10 Movement of Consumer Prices

3.11 Exchange Rate Stability

Leaders & Stragglers

Wrap-up

## GDP

The muscle power of an economy is usually expressed as Gross Domestic Product (GDP), which is a measure of a country's economic activity and resulting output. It comprises the total of all economic activity in the country, across all sectors of activity. The United States is the world's largest economy since it has the highest output (GDP) year after year.

## GDP per person

However, a country might have a large GDP but also an accompanying large population. So, in strict terms, the muscle power of the economy would more accurately expressed in per capita (per person of population) bases. GDP per capita would indicate the capacity of an economy to optimally make use of its factors of production, chief of which is population (labour). Then again, a high GDP per person will not necessarily indicate a success in production; some countries are endowed with natural resources that will continuously swell their GDP and could mask existing and gravely damaging inefficiencies. Usually, though, this can be discerned and accurately distinguished from genuine efficiency in the economy.

## Purchasing Power Parity (PPP)

For more accurate country comparisons, GDP is often expressed in "Purchasing Power Parity" dollars, because this allows for a more realistic and representative comparison of economic output between countries. It puts the countries on a common platform, by cancelling out domestic financial and social peculiarities affecting the US dollar in these different environments, and using a "common currency", $PPP, instead. One PPP dollar would theoretically have the same power in each country, because it would purchase the same basket of goods in every economy. Unlike comparisons at market exchange rates, PPP reflects the real purchasing power of each country's residents and allows for more balanced comparisons across borders.

## Gross National Income

(formerly known as GNP, gross national product.) GNI is more a measure of a country's (and population's) wealth. It comprises the total of incomes earned by the country's residents both from home and from abroad, and indicates the capacity of an economy to provide for the needs of its residents.

## GNI per Person

GNI per Person in mature economies tends to grow at a slower rate than in semi-developed or developing economies. However, the GNI per person in mature economies is much higher. Usually, a strong and viable economy would have a growing GNI per capita adequate to maintain or increase consumption levels. Nevertheless, GNI does not necessarily reflect the purchasing power of the citizens; issues like distribution of wealth, gap between rich and poor (and even corruption) come into play.

## Growth Rates

In an efficient economy, GDP and GNI will grow continually, but it is interesting to note that economies will not grow indefinitely. Economic recessions will occur in cycles and redress balances. Statistically, they tend to occur every ten years or so. GDP and GNI will grow slower in developed economies (because these have exploited most of the production avenues open to them) than in developing ones (where new avenues are easier to come by). But developed world GNI will still be larger in size. The challenge for developing economies is to grow GDP as quickly (i.e. efficiently maximising resources) and sustainably as possible.

## Real Growth Rates

The important factor, however, is not merely the absolute GDP or GDP Growth, but the GDP per person and its annual growth. If GDP is not growing faster than population the economy is actually in a recession. And so, Real GDP Growth is what is usually evaluated. Assessing real growth also allows taking into account the erosion of value that inflation brings.

## Inflation

This is the rate at which the costs of goods and services increase in an economy, essentially due to demand outstripping supply. This would usually reflect the ability of the country to manage all economic sectors efficiently so that demand for goods does not overwhelm the available supply, meaning growth of demand will be a profit incentive that draws out a corresponding increase in production; rather than the opposite which would mean producers holding consumers to ransom by not investing more money to produce more goods since there isn't a profit imperative for them to do so.

However, some inflation need not be a bad thing. It helps to ensure that there is a continuous demand for goods. The opposite, (deflation: shrinking disposable income, too many goods) does not encourage increased output and thus further investment, leading thereby to an economic downturn. Because, among other things, it will lead to increased unemployment, as industries would shed staff since production levels will keep falling, due to the lack of a market incentive to produce more. However, inflation must be well controlled otherwise it spirals and leads to, for example, further problems of exchange rates and disincentives for saving, leading to insufficient funds for investment, etc.

The target for inflation is usually low single digits, that is, about 1% to 3%.

## Movement of Consumer Prices

This shows the trend in the cost of a select basket of the same goods as it is affected by the inflation rate in the country from year to year. Countries with the highest inflation rates (usually a bad sign) end up with identical goods costing more there than in another country with lower inflation rates. If cost of living is continuously rising, it makes planning more challenging, and renders the economy unattractive.

## Exchange Rate Swings

This is the fluctuation in the national currency's exchange rate with – usually – the US dollar. Ordinarily, a low value for a nation's currency aids exports (because buyers find their foreign currencies going a longer distance in the markets of the exporting country in terms of purchasing power, since they find the goods affordable) and hence these "low" values hold a certain attraction. Nevertheless, beyond a certain point, it may actually make production (and, hence, economic growth) difficult, especially where raw materials input are largely imported from abroad: the low-value local currency is unable to pay for the raw materials required.

It must be noted, though, that the main challenge may not necessarily be to keep the currency's value constant. Sometimes, especially in developing economies, circumstances might advise a devaluing. However, a one-time big-drop devaluation that occurs and holds the new exchange rate for several years, might be more desirable than the same big-drop devaluation occurring in fits and starts across the same number of years. Uncertainty is usually disdained by business.

(Note: Economy growth rates shown here are those pre-dating the worst period of the persisting global financial crisis and recession. And new rates are still constantly being revised and released by the various multilateral agencies. Nevertheless, the comparative conclusions drawn here remain appropriate, since the crisis is not limited to a particular geography or sector within Sub-Saharan Africa.)

**Sources of Primary Data:** IMF, World Bank

# Charts

3.1 GDP contribution of Nigeria in Sub-Saharan Africa during 1999/02, 2003/06, 2007/10
3.2 GDP contribution of Nigeria in Sub-Saharan Africa from 1999 to 2010
3.3 GDP contribution of Nigeria in West Africa during 1999/02, 2003/06, 2007/10
3.4 GDP contribution of Nigeria in West Africa from 1999 to 2010
3.5 GDP per Person in West Africa during 2003/06 ($PPP)
3.6 GDP per Person in Nigeria and Sub-Saharan Africa during 2003/06 ($PPP)
3.7 Growth in GDP per Person in West Africa during 2003-06
3.8 Growth in GDP per Person in Nigeria and Sub-Saharan Africa during 2003/06
3.9 GNI per Person in West Africa during 2003/06
3.10 GNI per Person in Nigeria and Sub-Saharan Africa from 1999 to 2006
3.11 Growth in GNI per Person in West Africa during 2003/06
3.12 Growth in GNI per Person in Nigeria and Sub-Saharan Africa from 2000 to 2006
3.13 Real GDP Growth in West Africa during 2003/06
3.14 Real GDP Growth in Nigeria and Sub-Saharan Africa from 1999 to 2006
3.15 Real Non-Oil GDP Growth in West Africa during 2003/06
3.16 Real Non-Oil GDP Growth in Nigeria and Sub-Saharan Africa from 1997 to 2008
3.17 Inflation in West Africa during 2003/06
3.18 Inflation in Nigeria and Sub-Saharan Africa from 1999 to 2010
3.19 Consumer Price Movement in Nigeria, Benin, Burkina Faso, Cape Verde, Côte d'Ivoire and Sub-Saharan Africa from 2000 to 2010: 2000=100
3.20 Consumer Price Movement in Nigeria, Gambia, Ghana, Guinea, Guinea-Bissau and Sub-Saharan Africa from 2000 to 2010: 2000=100
3.21 Consumer Price Movement in Nigeria, Liberia, Mali, Mauritania, Niger and Sub-Saharan Africa from 2000 to 2010: 2000=100
3.22 Consumer Price Movement in Nigeria, Senegal, Sierra Leone, Togo and Sub-Saharan Africa from 2000 to 2010: 2000=100

- **Wrap-up**

# Tables

*1999-2002; 2003-2006; 2007-2010:*
- *self-comparison to preceding period;*
- *performance in S-Saharan Africa;*
- *performance in West Africa;*
- *performance among oil-exporters;*

*for:*

GDP per Person ($PPP)

Growth in GDP per Person

Real GDP Growth

Real Non-Oil GDP Growth*

Inflation

*1999-2002; 2003-2006:*
- *self-comparison to preceding period;*
- *performance in S-Saharan Africa;*
- *performance in West Africa;*
- *performance among oil-exporters;*

*for:*

GNI per Person ($PPP)

Growth in GNI per Person

*2000-2007; 2003-2010:*
- *self-comparison to preceding period;*
- *performance in S-Saharan Africa;*
- *performance in West Africa;*
- *performance among oil-exporters;*

*for:*

Exchange Rate Stability


- GDP per Person of Population ($PPP) in Sub-Saharan Africa during 2003-06: Rankings
- Growth in GDP per Person of Population in Sub-Saharan Africa during 2003-06: Rankings
- GNI per Person of Population ($PPP) in Sub-Saharan Africa during 2003-06: Rankings
- Growth in GNI per Person of Population in Sub-Saharan Africa during 2003-06: Rankings
- Real GDP Growth in Sub-Saharan Africa during 2003-06: Rankings
- Consumer Price Movement in West Africa in 2007 and 2010: 2000=100
- Inflation in Sub-Saharan Africa during 2003-06: Rankings
- Exchange Rate Stability in Sub-Saharan Africa during 2003-06: Rankings
- Movement of Real Exchange Rates in West Africa in 2007, 2010: 2000=100
- **Economic Strength Rankings: 2003-06**


* only for the oil-exporters

# 3.1 Nigeria GDP in Sub-Saharan Africa ($PPP)

*this is how it stacks up*

Besides growing in absolute size since 1999, Nigeria's GDP has also grown as a proportion of the continent's. From 15% in 1999 to 19% in 2007.

That proportion is expected to hit close to 20% of Sub-Saharan Africa GDP by 2010.

**3.1**

GDP contribution of Nigeria in Sub-Saharan Africa during 1999/02, 2003/06, 2007/10

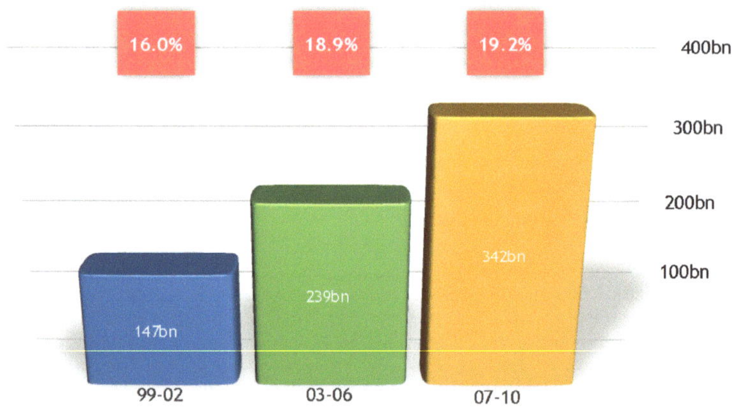


**3.2**

GDP contribution of Nigeria in Sub-Saharan Africa from 1999 to 2010

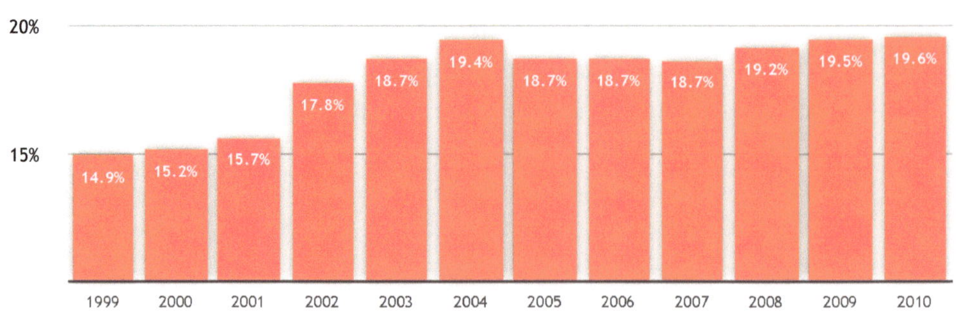

# 3.2 Nigeria GDP in West Africa ($PPP)

*and this is how this stacks up*

3.3

GDP contribution of Nigeria in West Africa during 1999/02, 2003/06, 2007/10

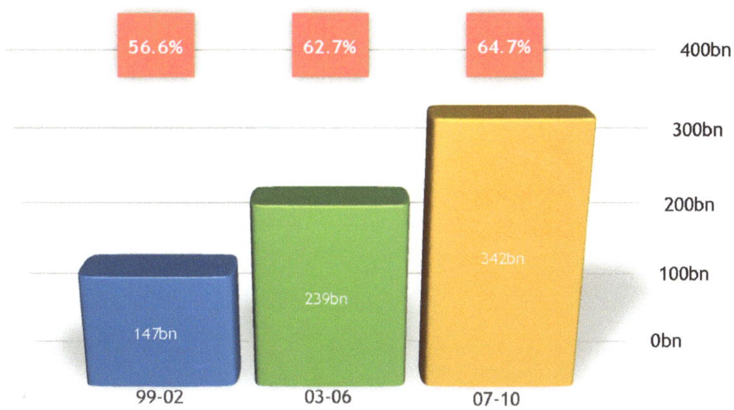


As expected, Nigeria's is the largest economy in West Africa. It has cornered more and more of the sub-region's output over the past ten years: 55% in 2000, to 65% by 2010.

3.4

GDP contribution of Nigeria in West Africa from 1999 to 2010

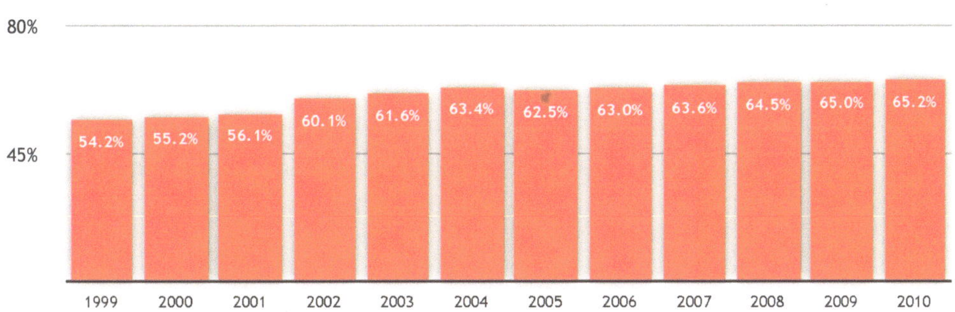

# 3.3 GDP per Person ($PPP)

## what she's bringing to the party

| | 99-02 | 03-06 | 07-10 |
|---|---|---|---|
| Self-comparison to Preceding Period | | ▲ | ▲ |
| Performance in Sub-Saharan Africa | ▼ | ▲ | ▲ |
| Performance in West Africa | ▲ | ▲ | ▲ |

| 99-02 | 03-06 | 07-10 |
|---|---|---|
| Cape Verde | Cape Verde | Cape Verde |
| Côte d'Ivoire | **Nigeria** | **Nigeria** |
| Mauritania | Mauritania | Mauritania |
| Senegal | Côte d'Ivoire | Côte d'Ivoire |
| **Nigeria** | Senegal | Senegal |
| Benin | Benin | Benin |
| Ghana | Ghana | Ghana |
| Gambia, The | Gambia, The | Gambia, The |
| Guinea | Burkina Faso | Burkina Faso |
| Burkina Faso | Guinea | Guinea |
| Mali | Mali | Mali |
| Togo | Togo | Togo |
| Niger | Niger | Sierra Leone |
| Guinea-Bissau | Sierra Leone | Niger |
| Liberia | Guinea-Bissau | Guinea-Bissau |
| Sierra Leone | Liberia | Liberia |

Despite its very large population, Nigeria scores quite high in output per inhabitant, in West Africa. Before 2003, it had posted only weak reports.

| | 99-02 | 03-06 | 07-10 |
|---|---|---|---|
| Performance among Oil-Exporters | ▼ | ▼ | ▼ |
| | Gabon | Gabon | Gabon |
| | Equatorial Guinea | Equatorial Guinea | Equatorial Guinea |
| | Congo, Rep. | Angola | Angola |
| | Angola | Congo, Rep. | Congo, Rep. |
| | Cameroon | Cameroon | Sudan |
| | Côte d'Ivoire | **Nigeria** | **Nigeria** |
| | Sudan | Sudan | Cameroon |
| | **Nigeria** | Côte d'Ivoire | Côte d'Ivoire |
| | Chad | Chad | Chad |

That improved performance is tainted, though, when Nigeria is compared to fellow oil-sustained economies. It performs below average.

Primary Data: IMF

| | |
|---|---|
| ▲ | improved *or* better than average |
| ▼ | worsened *or* worse than average |
| ◁▷ | no change *or* average |

## 3. Economic Strength

3.5

GDP per Person in West Africa during 2003/06 ($PPP)

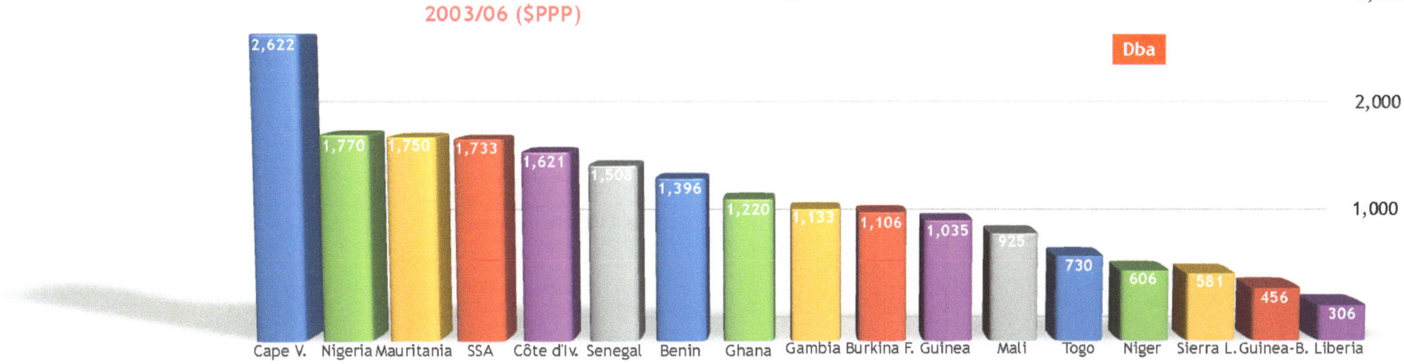


3.6

GDP per Person in Nigeria and Sub-Saharan Africa during 2003/06 ($PPP)

On the continent level, Nigeria stays just above average, coming from behind in 2000 to surpass continental performance by 2003.

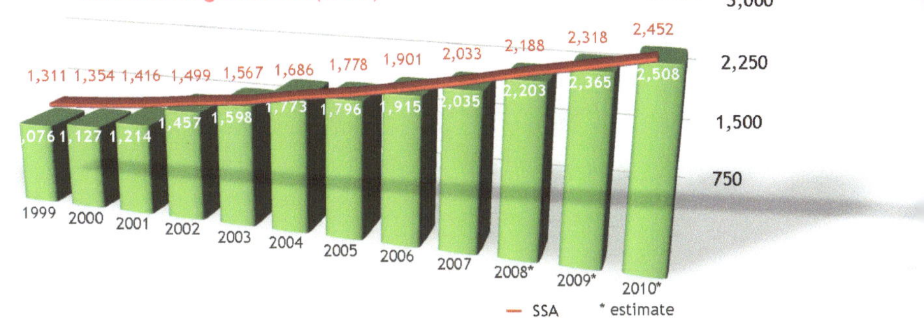


Primary Data: IMF

It does just enough to stay above water from then onwards, finishing in 13th place, out of 41 countries. Close shave.

GDP per Person of Population ($PPP) in Sub-Saharan Africa during 2003-06: Rankings

| Rank | Country | Rank | Country | Rank | Country |
|---|---|---|---|---|---|
| 1 | Seychelles | 15 | Senegal | 29 | Uganda |
| 2 | Botswana | 16 | Chad | 30 | Eritrea |
| 3 | Gabon | 17 | Kenya | 31 | Rwanda |
| 4 | Equatorial Guinea | 18 | Benin | 32 | Togo |
| 5 | Mauritius | 19 | Ghana | 33 | Mozambique |
| 6 | South Africa | 20 | Zambia | 34 | Malawi |
| 7 | Namibia | 21 | Gambia, The | 35 | Central Afr. Rep. |
| 8 | Swaziland | 22 | Lesotho | 36 | Ethiopia |
| 9 | Angola | 23 | Burkina Faso | 37 | Niger |
| 10 | Congo, Rep. | 24 | Comoros | 38 | Sierra Leone |
| 11 | Cape Verde | 25 | Tanzania | 39 | Guinea-Bissau |
| 12 | Cameroon | 26 | Guinea | 40 | Burundi |
| 13 | **Nigeria** | 27 | Mali | 41 | Congo, Dem. Rep. |
| 14 | Côte d' Ivoire | 28 | Madagascar | | |
| TOP | | MIDDLE | | BOTTOM | |

Central Africa
East Africa
Southern Africa
West Africa

# 3.4 Growth in GDP per Person

## loaded on vitamins

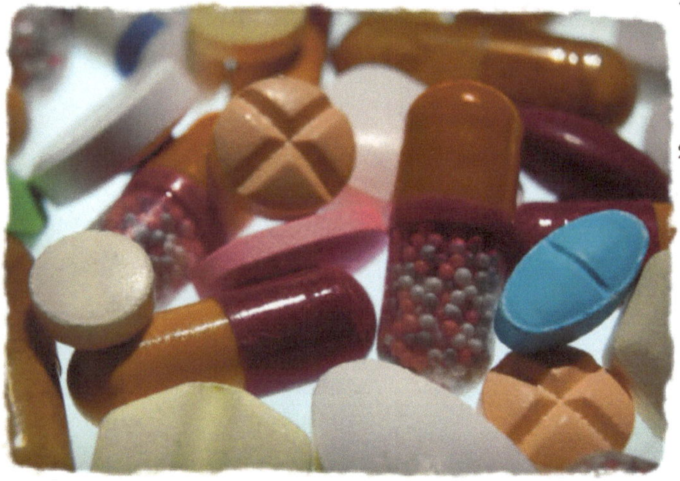

Growth rate of GDP per Person for Nigeria was falling across the 2000 to 2007 years. It did worse in 2003/07, and is projected to do relatively worse again in 2007/10.

Still, a first-rate showing in West Africa, which may suggest that the other countries faced similar climates and challenges. Or that they failed to pull their weight effectively.

A tottering performance among oil-exporters. Nigeria dropped in position during 03/06; it had done significantly better in 1999/02. But it is expected to pick up in 2007/10.

| | 00-02 | 03-06 | 07-10 |
|---|---|---|---|
| Self-comparison to Preceding Period | | ▼ | ▼ |
| Performance in Sub-Saharan Africa | ▲ | ▲ | ▲ |
| Performance in West Africa | ▲ | ▲ | ▲ |
| | Sierra Leone | Sierra Leone | Liberia |
| | **Nigeria** | Mauritania | Cape Verde |
| | Cape Verde | **Nigeria** | **Nigeria** |
| | Mali | Cape Verde | Ghana |
| | Ghana | Gambia, The | Sierra Leone |
| | Benin | Ghana | Gambia, The |
| | Burkina Faso | Mali | Senegal |
| | Guinea | Burkina Faso | Burkina Faso |
| | Liberia | Togo | Mauritania |
| | Senegal | Senegal | Côte d'Ivoire |
| | Niger | Niger | Benin |
| | Gambia, The | Benin | Mali |
| | Mauritania | Guinea-Bissau | Guinea |
| | Côte d'Ivoire | Côte d'Ivoire | Niger |
| | Togo | Guinea | Togo |
| | Guinea-Bissau | Liberia | Guinea-Bissau |
| Performance among Oil-Exporters | ▲ | ◁▷ | ▲ |
| | Equatorial Guinea | Chad | Angola |
| | **Nigeria** | Equatorial Guinea | Sudan |
| | Sudan | Angola | Equatorial Guinea |
| | Angola | Sudan | **Nigeria** |
| | Chad | **Nigeria** | Congo, Rep. |
| | Congo, Rep. | Congo, Rep. | Gabon |
| | Cameroon | Cameroon | Côte d'Ivoire |
| | Gabon | Gabon | Cameroon |
| | Côte d'Ivoire | Côte d'Ivoire | Chad |

Primary Data: IMF

| | |
|---|---|
| ▲ | improved *or* better than average |
| ▼ | worsened *or* worse than average |
| ◁▷ | no change *or* average |

3.7

Growth in GDP per Person in West Africa during 2003-06 (%)

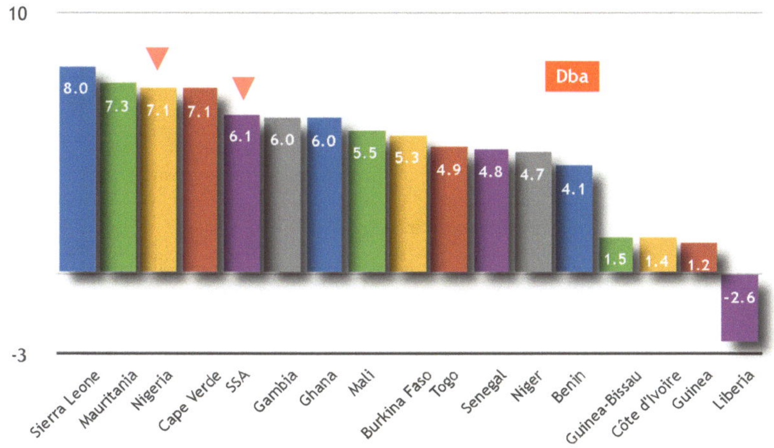


3.8

Growth in GDP per Person in Nigeria and Sub-Saharan Africa during 2003/06 (%)

Primary Data: IMF

2000 to 2004 saw Nigeria growing its output per person by several notches faster than the rest of Africa.

But, even though that rate would not afterwards fall as spectacularly as in 2005, it has struggled since then to keep up with the Africa average.

Growth in GDP per Person of Population in Sub-Saharan Africa during 2003-06: Rankings

| Rank | Country | Rank | Country | Rank | Country |
|---|---|---|---|---|---|
| 1 | Chad | 15 | Malawi | 29 | Swaziland |
| 2 | Equatorial Guinea | 16 | Congo, Dem. Rep. | 30 | Lesotho |
| 3 | Angola | 17 | Gambia, The | 31 | Benin |
| 4 | Madagascar | 18 | Ghana | 32 | Burundi |
| 5 | Ethiopia | 19 | Zambia | 33 | Cameroon |
| 6 | Botswana | 20 | Mauritius | 34 | Comoros |
| 7 | Sierra Leone | 21 | Mali | 35 | Gabon |
| 8 | Mozambique | 22 | Congo, Rep. | 36 | Central Afr. Rep. |
| 9 | Tanzania | 23 | Burkina Faso | 37 | Guinea-Bissau |
| 10 | Nigeria | 24 | Kenya | 38 | Côte d' Ivoire |
| 11 | Cape Verde | 25 | Togo | 39 | Guinea |
| 12 | South Africa | 26 | Senegal | 40 | Seychelles |
| 13 | Namibia | 27 | Uganda | 41 | Eritrea |
| 14 | Rwanda | 28 | Niger | | |
| HIGHEST | | MIDDLE | | BOTTOM | |

Central Africa
East Africa
Southern Africa
West Africa

# 3.5 GNI per Person ($PPP)

## she's earned it

GNI per capita: Nigeria improved in 03/06, compared to 99/02. but that rally wasn't strong enough to lift it above average in the continent.

That it was good enough for an upper West Africa performance might again point to a dismal showing across the entire sub-region...

...It could also be that there were systemic challenges peculiar to West Africa & absent in the rest of the continent. More likely the former, though.

Something gravely amiss with Nigeria's GNI, as the oil-exporters' table confirms:

Nigeria isn't squeezing what it can from domestic economic output and earnings from investments, etc., outside its borders.

| | 99-02 | 03-06 |
|---|---|---|
| Self-comparison to Preceding Period | | ▲ |
| Performance in Sub-Saharan Africa | ▼ | ▼ |
| Performance in West Africa | ▲ | ▲ |

| 99-02 | 03-06 |
|---|---|
| Cape Verde | Cape Verde |
| Côte d'Ivoire | Mauritania |
| Mauritania | Côte d'Ivoire |
| Senegal | Senegal |
| **Nigeria** | **Nigeria** |
| Benin | Benin |
| Guinea | Ghana |
| Ghana | Guinea |
| Gambia, The | Burkina Faso |
| Burkina Faso | Gambia, The |
| Mali | Mali |
| Togo | Togo |
| Niger | Niger |
| Guinea-Bissau | Sierra Leone |
| Sierra Leone | Guinea-Bissau |
| Liberia | Liberia |

| | 99-02 | 03-06 |
|---|---|---|
| Performance among Oil-Exporters | ▼ | ▼ |

| 99-02 | 03-06 |
|---|---|
| Gabon | Equatorial Guinea |
| Equatorial Guinea | Gabon |
| Angola | Angola |
| Congo, Rep. | Congo, Rep. |
| Cameroon | Cameroon |
| Côte d'Ivoire | Sudan |
| Sudan | Côte d'Ivoire |
| **Nigeria** | **Nigeria** |
| Chad | Chad |

Primary Data: World Bank

| | |
|---|---|
| ▲ | improved *or* better than average |
| ▼ | worsened *or* worse than average |
| ◁▷ | no change *or* average |

# 3. Economic Strength

3.9

GNI per Person in West Africa during 2003/06 ($PPP)

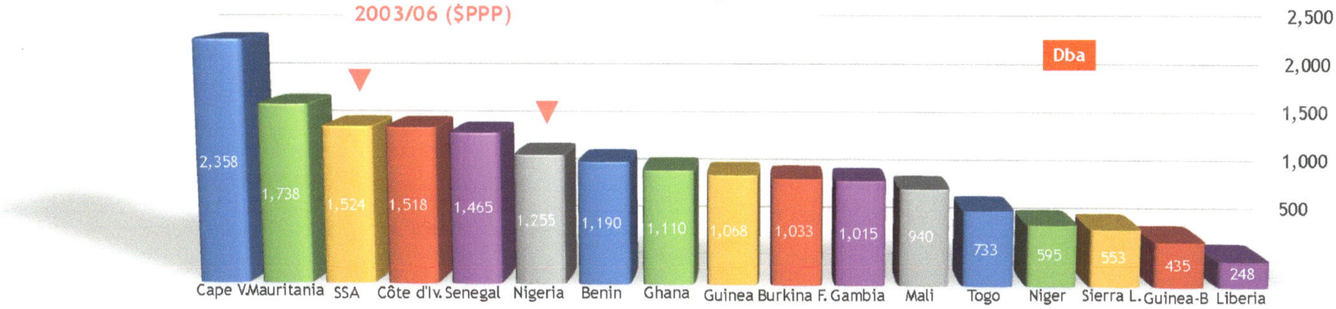


3.10

GNI per Person in Nigeria and Sub-Saharan Africa from 1999 to 2006 ($PPP)

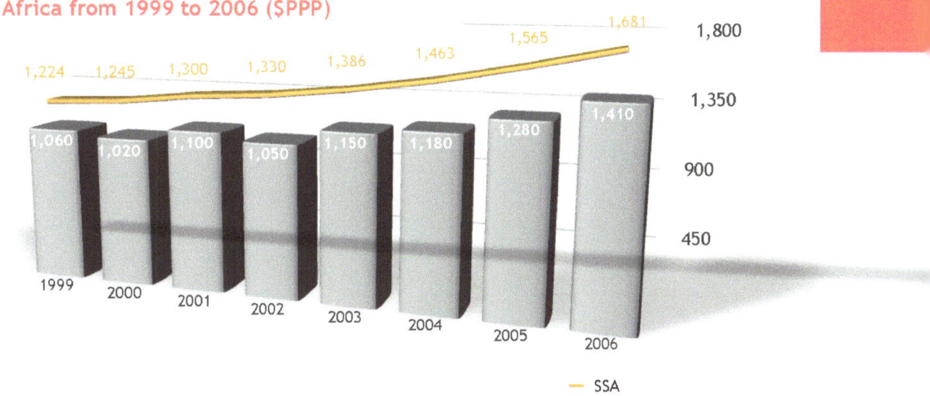


The rest of Africa left Nigeria in their wake throughout 1999-2006.

GNI per Person of Population ($PPP) in Sub-Saharan Africa during 2003-06: Rankings

| Rank | Country | Rank | Country | Rank | Country |
|---|---|---|---|---|---|
| 1 | Seychelles | 15 | Senegal | 28 | Madagascar |
| 2 | Equatorial Guinea | 16 | Kenya | 29 | Togo |
| 3 | Gabon | 17 | **Nigeria** | 30 | Eritrea |
| 4 | Botswana | 18 | Benin | 31 | Rwanda |
| 5 | Mauritius | 19 | Ghana | 32 | Central Afr. Rep. |
| 6 | South Africa | 20 | Chad | 33 | Malawi |
| 7 | Namibia | | Comoros | 34 | Mozambique |
| 8 | Swaziland | 21 | Guinea | 35 | Niger |
| 9 | Angola | 22 | Zambia | 36 | Sierra Leone |
| 10 | Cape Verde | 23 | Burkina Faso | 37 | Ethiopia |
| 11 | Congo, Rep. | 24 | Gambia, The | 38 | Guinea-Bissau |
| 12 | Cameroon | 25 | Mali | 39 | Burundi |
| 13 | Lesotho | 26 | Tanzania | 40 | Congo, Dem. Rep. |
| 14 | Côte d' Ivoire | 27 | Uganda | | |
| | HIGHEST | | MIDDLE | | BOTTOM |

To place the outcomes in perspective, Seychelles posted $13,500, Senegal $1,500, Nigeria $1,300, and Madagascar $800. The continent average was $1,500.

Primary Data: World Bank

Central Africa
East Africa
Southern Africa
West Africa

# 3.6 Growth in GNI per Person

*but is she growing it?*

A seemingly desperate attempt by Nigeria to make up for lost ground in GNI per inhabitant.

& It pulls it off, somewhat: it jumps several notches during 2003/06, within West Africa, among the oil-exporters, and within the entire continent, too.

| | 00-02 | 03-06 |
|---|---|---|
| Self-comparison to Preceding Period | | ▲ |
| Performance in Sub-Saharan Africa | ▼ | ▲ |

**Performance in West Africa**

| 00-02 ▼ | 03-06 ▲ |
|---|---|
| Sierra Leone | **Nigeria** |
| Liberia | Ghana |
| Cape Verde | Sierra Leone |
| Mauritania | Gambia, The |
| Guinea | Burkina Faso |
| Benin | Cape Verde |
| Ghana | Mali |
| Mali | Mauritania |
| Burkina Faso | Senegal |
| Senegal | Niger |
| Niger | Guinea |
| Gambia, The | Benin |
| Togo | Togo |
| Guinea-Bissau | Guinea-Bissau |
| **Nigeria** | Côte d'Ivoire |
| Côte d'Ivoire | Liberia |

**Performance among Oil-Exporters**

| 00-02 ▼ | 03-06 ◁▷ |
|---|---|
| Equatorial Guinea | Equatorial Guinea |
| Angola | Angola |
| Sudan | Sudan |
| Congo, Rep. | Chad |
| Chad | **Nigeria** |
| Cameroon | Congo, Rep. |
| Gabon | Cameroon |
| **Nigeria** | Côte d'Ivoire |
| Côte d'Ivoire | Gabon |

Primary Data: World Bank

| | |
|---|---|
| ▲ | improved *or* better than average |
| ▼ | worsened *or* worse than average |
| ◁▷ | no change *or* average |

3.11

Growth in GNI per Person in West Africa during 2003/06 (%)

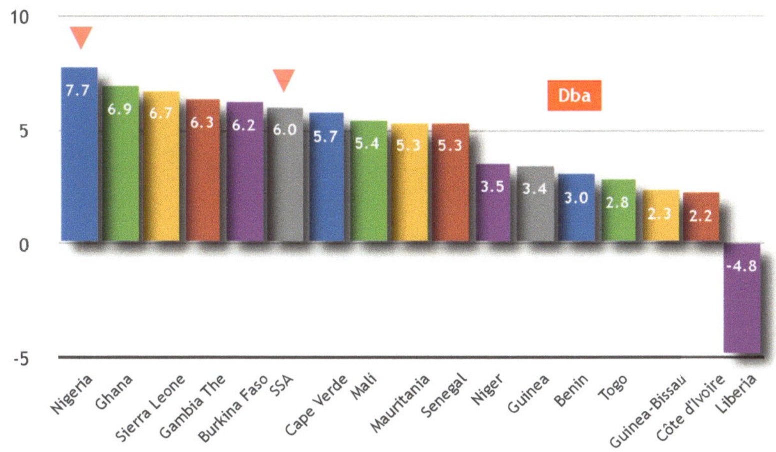


3.12

Growth in GNI per Person in Nigeria and Sub-Saharan Africa from 2000 to 2006 (%)

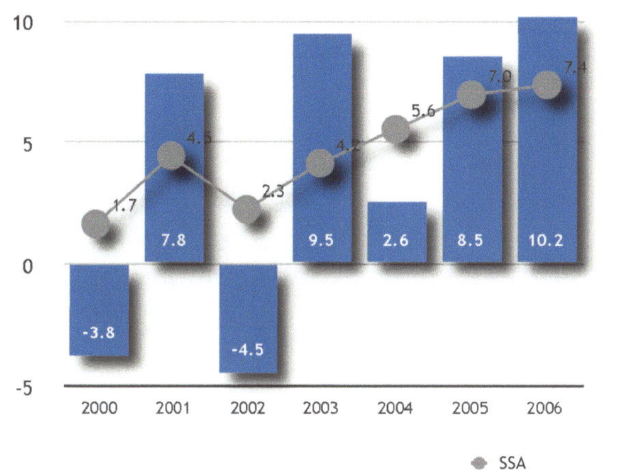


Primary Data: World Bank

*But there still was an unsteady showing: fits and starts rather than consistency.*

Growth in GNI per Person of Population in Sub-Saharan Africa during 2003-06: Rankings

| Rank | Country | Rank | Country | Rank | Country |
|---|---|---|---|---|---|
| 1 | Equatorial Guinea | 15 | Mauritius | 29 | Swaziland |
| 2 | Angola | 16 | Burkina Faso | 30 | Niger |
| 3 | Chad | 17 | Mozambique | 31 | Guinea |
| 4 | Botswana | 18 | Malawi | 32 | Seychelles |
| 5 | Nigeria | 19 | Cape Verde | 33 | Benin |
| 6 | Ethiopia | 20 | Mali | 34 | Togo |
| 7 | Lesotho | 21 | Kenya | 35 | Comoros |
| 8 | Ghana | 22 | Namibia | 36 | Guinea-Bissau |
| 9 | Sierra Leone | 23 | Congo, Rep. | 37 | Côte d' Ivoire |
| 10 | Tanzania | 24 | Senegal | 38 | Central Afr. Rep. |
| 11 | Congo, Dem. Rep. | 25 | Cameroon | 39 | Burundi |
| 12 | Madagascar | 26 | Uganda | 40 | Eritrea |
| 13 | South Africa | 27 | Rwanda | 41 | Gabon |
| 14 | Gambia, The | 28 | Zambia | | |
| TOP | | MIDDLE | | BOTTOM | |

Central Africa
East Africa
Southern Africa
West Africa

# 3.7 Real GDP Growth

**bull's-eye!**

When stripped of adornments, growth in core GDP was mixed news for Nigeria. 03/06 was worse than 99/02. And 07/10 is likely to fare, in turn, worse than 03/06.

yet in inter-country comparisons, Nigeria comes out better than most in West Africa and in the entire Africa, as well.

Nonetheless, oil-exporters put up a better struggle: Nigeria still does better than average, but it is outranked by 2 more countries in 03/06 and 07/10, than was the case previous to 03/06.

| | 99-02 | 03-06 | 07-10 |
|---|---|---|---|
| Self-comparison to Preceding Period | | ▼ | ▼ |
| Performance in Sub-Saharan Africa | ▲ | ▲ | ▲ |
| Performance in West Africa | ▲ | ▲ | ▲ |
| | Liberia | **Nigeria** | Liberia |
| | Sierra Leone | Sierra Leone | **Nigeria** |
| | **Nigeria** | Mauritania | Cape Verde |
| | Cape Verde | Gambia, The | Ghana |
| | Benin | Cape Verde | Sierra Leone |
| | Burkina Faso | Burkina Faso | Gambia, The |
| | Ghana | Ghana | Senegal |
| | Mali | Mali | Benin |
| | Guinea | Senegal | Burkina Faso |
| | Senegal | Niger | Mauritania |
| | Gambia, The | Benin | Mali |
| | Mauritania | Togo | Niger |
| | Niger | Guinea | Guinea |
| | Guinea-Bissau | Guinea-Bissau | Côte d'Ivoire |
| | Togo | Côte d'Ivoire | Togo |
| | Côte d'Ivoire | Liberia | Guinea-Bissau |

Primary Data: IMF

| | 99-02 | 03-06 | 07-10 |
|---|---|---|---|
| Performance among Oil-Exporters | ▲ | ▲ | ▲ |
| | Equatorial Guinea | Chad | Angola |
| | **Nigeria** | Angola | Sudan |
| | Angola | Equatorial Guinea | Equatorial Guinea |
| | Sudan | **Nigeria** | **Nigeria** |
| | Chad | Sudan | Congo, Rep. |
| | Cameroon | Congo, Rep. | Cameroon |
| | Congo, Rep. | Cameroon | Gabon |
| | Côte d'Ivoire | Gabon | Côte d'Ivoire |
| | Gabon | Côte d'Ivoire | Chad |

| | |
|---|---|
| ▲ | improved *or* better than average |
| ▼ | worsened *or* worse than average |
| ◁▷ | no change *or* average |

## 3. Economic Strength

3.13

Real GDP Growth in West Africa during 2003/06 (%)

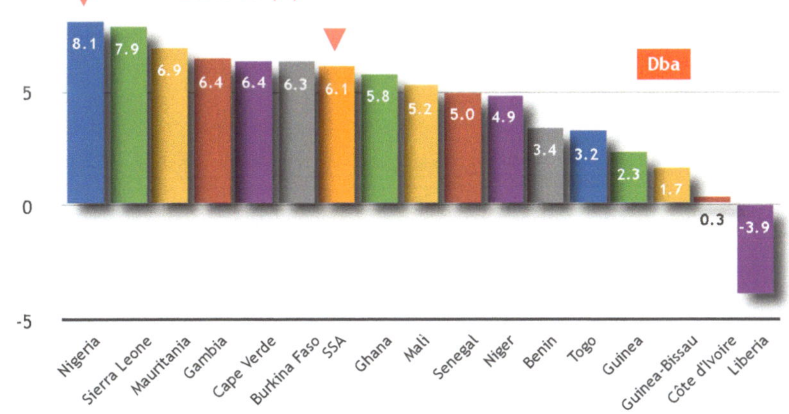


The years from 2005 to 2007 are beginning to look like bogey years for Nigeria...

...Performance again dropped during that 3-year period, even though 2008-2010 is expected to witness a bounce-back, relative to the rest of the continent.

3.14

Real GDP Growth in Nigeria and Sub-Saharan Africa from 1999 to 2006 (%)

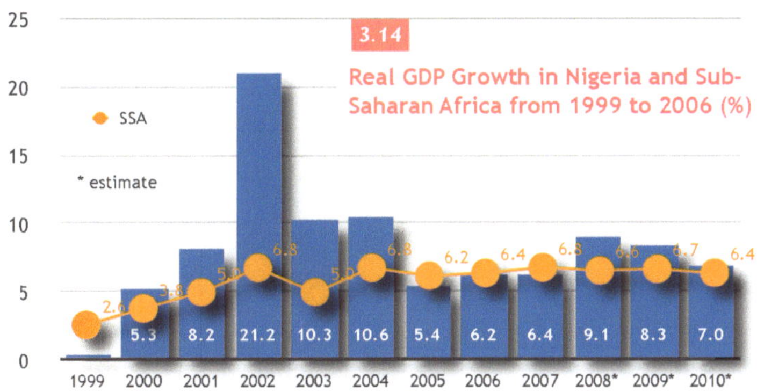


Primary Data: IMF

Real GDP Growth in Sub-Saharan Africa during 2003-06: Rankings

| Rank | Country | Rank | Country | Rank | Country |
|---|---|---|---|---|---|
| 1 | Chad | 15 | Zambia | 29 | Benin |
| 2 | Angola | 16 | Uganda | 30 | Cameroon |
| 3 | Equatorial Guinea | 17 | Mali | 31 | Togo |
| 4 | **Nigeria** | 18 | Botswana | 32 | Swaziland |
| 5 | Sierra Leone | 19 | Senegal | 33 | Burundi |
| 6 | Mozambique | 20 | Niger | 34 | Guinea |
| 7 | Ethiopia | 21 | Malawi | 35 | Gabon |
| 8 | Tanzania | 22 | Kenya | 36 | Comoros |
| 9 | Congo, Dem. Rep. | 23 | Namibia | 37 | Guinea-Bissau |
| 10 | Madagascar | 24 | South Africa | 38 | Côte d' Ivoire |
| 11 | Gambia, The | 25 | Congo, Rep. | 39 | Eritrea |
| 12 | Cape Verde | 26 | Rwanda | 40 | Central Afr. Rep. |
| 13 | Burkina Faso | 27 | Lesotho | 41 | Seychelles |
| 14 | Ghana | 28 | Mauritius | | |
| TOP | | MIDDLE | | BOTTOM | |

Central Africa
East Africa
Southern Africa
West Africa

# 3.8 Real Non-Oil GDP Growth

Expectedly, this area is more critical for the oil economies than it is for the rest. Nigeria does worse in 03/06 than previous, and just about stays at the same level for 07/08.

Among oil-exporters, it is outflanked by Equatorial Guinea in 99/02, and then also by Angola in 03/06 and 07/08. But it still keeps its head above average.

| | 97-02 | 03-06 | 07-08 |
|---|---|---|---|
| Self-comparison to Preceding Period | | ▼ | ◁▷ |
| Performance among Oil-Exporters | ▲ | ▲ | ▲ |
| | Equatorial Guinea | Equatorial Guinea | Equatorial Guinea |
| | **Nigeria** | Angola | Angola |
| | Angola | **Nigeria** | **Nigeria** |
| | Cameroon | Chad | Chad |
| | Chad | Congo, Rep. | Congo, Rep. |
| | Congo, Rep. | Cameroon | Cameroon |
| | Gabon | Gabon | Gabon |
| | Côte d'Ivoire | Côte d'Ivoire | Côte d'Ivoire |
| | Sudan | Sudan | Sudan |

| | |
|---|---|
| ▲ | improved *or* better than average |
| ▼ | worsened *or* worse than average |
| ◁▷ | no change *or* average |

Primary Data: IMF

*how fragile is that economy?*

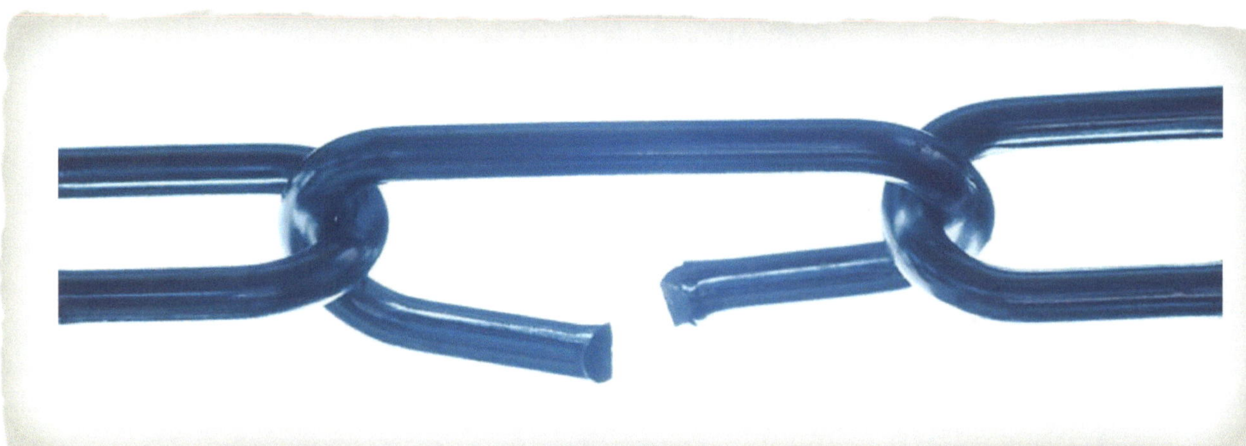

3.15

Real Non-Oil GDP Growth in West Africa during 2003/06

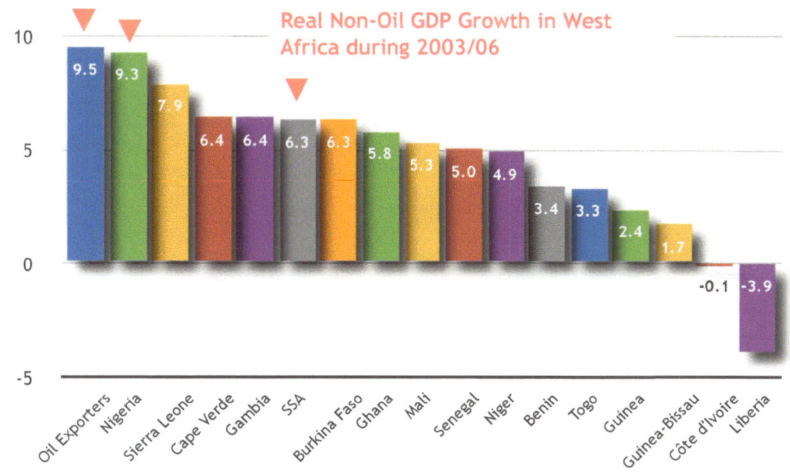


Again, the bogey years of 2005-2007. And 2008 is expected to be a further decline from 2007.

3.16

Real Non-Oil GDP Growth in Nigeria and Sub-Saharan Africa from 1997 to 2008

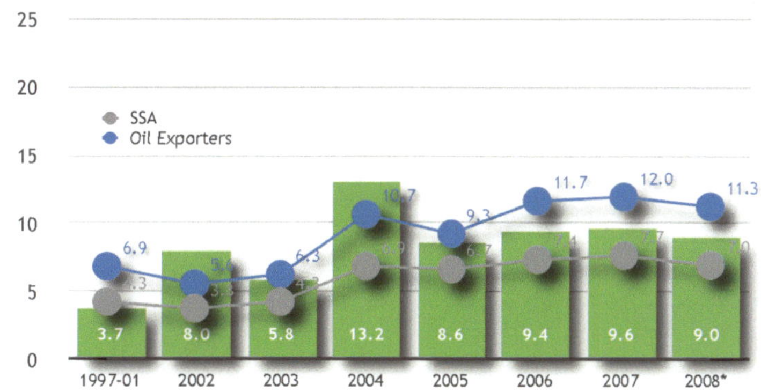


* estimate Primary Data: IMF

Nigeria does better than most of Africa, but worse than the oil-exporters, who - alas - are the crucial measurement standard.

# 3.9 Inflation

## cash overload

Poor showing. Incremental improvements only expected during 2007/10.

Below par in Africa from 2003 to 2010. Below par in West Africa from 1999 to 2010. Below par among oil economies from 1999 to 2010.

| | 99-02 | 03-06 | 07-10 |
|---|---|---|---|
| Self-comparison to Preceding Period | | ▼ | ▲ |
| Performance in Sub-Saharan Africa | ▲ | ▼ | ▼ |
| Performance in West Africa | ▼ | ▼ | ▼ |
| | Burkina Faso | Guinea-Bissau | Niger |
| | Senegal | Mali | Benin |
| | Niger | Senegal | Mali |
| | Cape Verde | Cape Verde | Burkina Faso |
| | Mali | Niger | Côte d'Ivoire |
| | Togo | Togo | Guinea-Bissau |
| | Côte d'Ivoire | Burkina Faso | Cape Verde |
| | Benin | Côte d'Ivoire | Togo |
| | Guinea-Bissau | Benin | Senegal |
| | Gambia, The | Liberia | Gambia, The |
| | Guinea | Mauritania | Mauritania |
| | Mauritania | Gambia, The | **Nigeria** |
| | Sierra Leone | Sierra Leone | Ghana |
| | Liberia | **Nigeria** | Liberia |
| | **Nigeria** | Ghana | Sierra Leone |
| | Ghana | Guinea | Guinea |
| Performance among Oil-Exporters | ▼ | ▼ | ▼ |
| | Gabon | Gabon | Chad |
| | Congo, Rep. | Cameroon | Cameroon |
| | Côte d'Ivoire | Chad | Côte d'Ivoire |
| | Cameroon | Côte d'Ivoire | Congo, Rep. |
| | Chad | Congo, Rep. | Gabon |
| | Equatorial Guinea | Equatorial Guinea | Equatorial Guinea |
| | Sudan | Sudan | Sudan |
| | **Nigeria** | **Nigeria** | **Nigeria** |
| | Angola | Angola | Angola |

Primary Data: IMF

| | |
|---|---|
| ▲ | improved *or* better than average |
| ▼ | worsened *or* worse than average |
| ◁▷ | no change *or* average |

# 3. Economic Strength

3.17

Inflation in West Africa during 2003/06 (%)

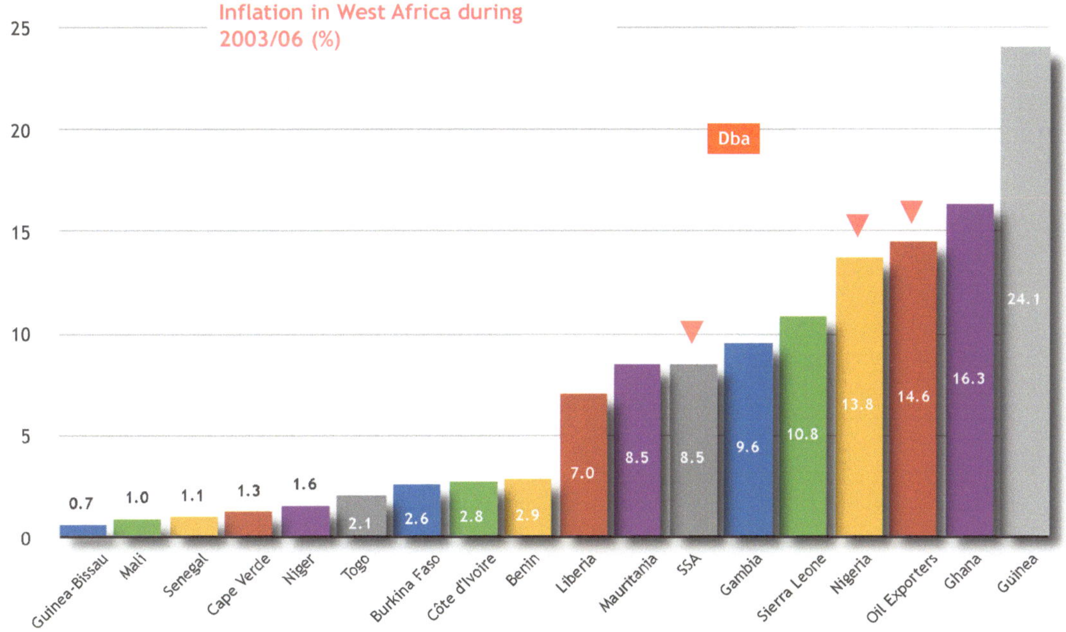


The oil exporters crashed their inflation rates from 20% in 2003 to 6% in 2007 [a 14% drop]. Nigeria's slowed more gradually from 14% to 6% [an 8% drop].

2008 to 2010 may see Nigeria faring worse than the rest of Africa again, with a rising inflation rate.

Primary Data: IMF

3.18

Inflation in Nigeria and Sub-Saharan Africa from 1999 to 2010

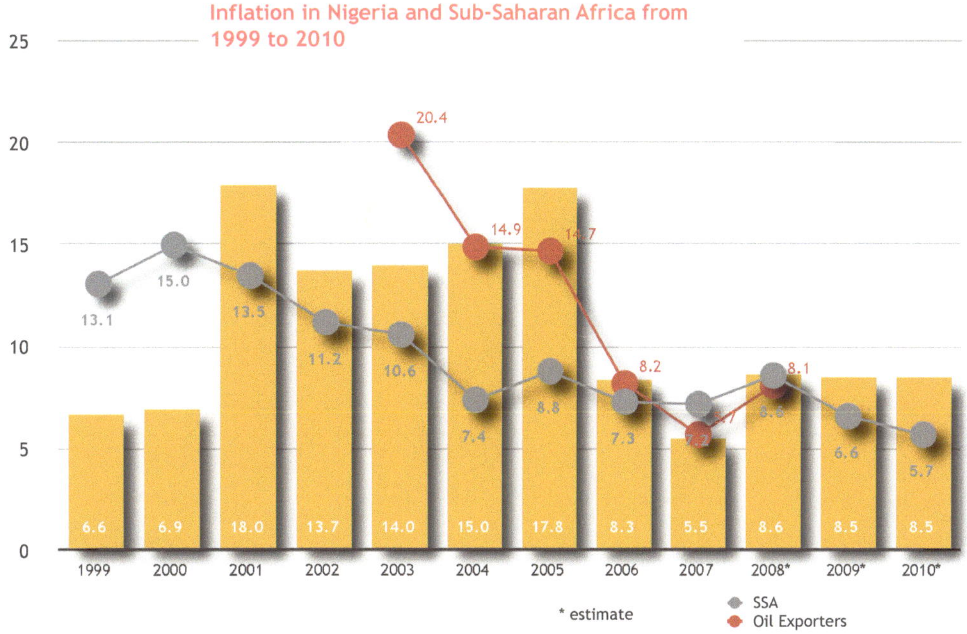

# 3.10 Movement of Consumer Prices

## *we'll be needing a larger bag*

Primary Data: IMF
Figures for 2008-10 are estimates

An item costing 100 currency units everywhere in 2000, by 2007 would cost: 240 in Nigeria and 120 in Benin, 300 in Ghana, and 170 in Mauritania.

**3.19**

**Consumer Price Movement in Nigeria, Benin, Burkina Faso, Cape Verde, Côte d'Ivoire and Sub-Saharan Africa from 2000 to 2010: 2000=100**

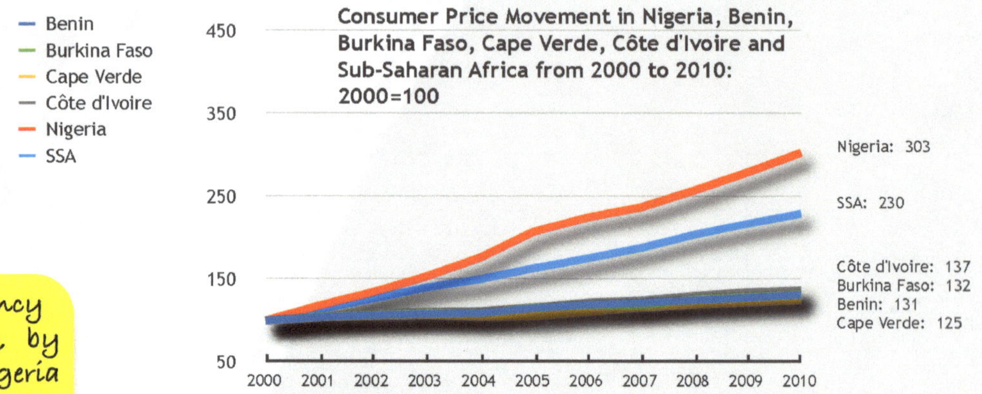


**3.20**

**Consumer Price Movement in Nigeria, Gambia, Ghana, Guinea, Guinea-Bissau and Sub-Saharan Africa from 2000 to 2010: 2000=100**

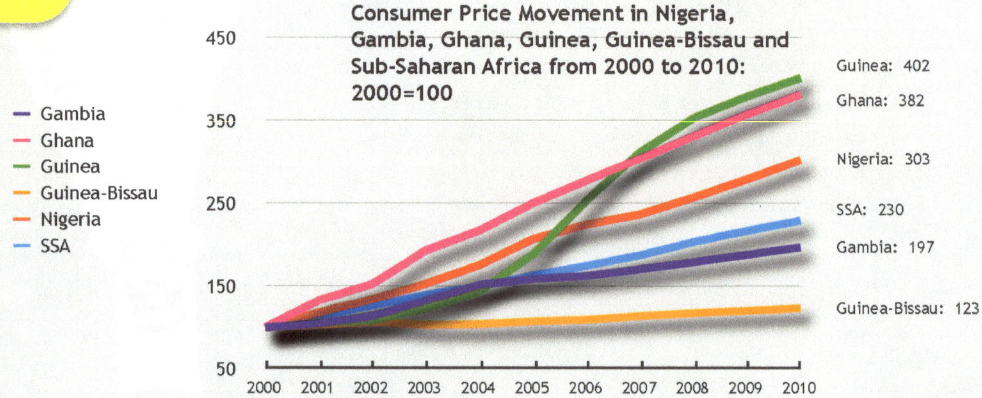


**3.21**

**Consumer Price Movement in Nigeria, Liberia, Mali, Mauritania, Niger and Sub-Saharan Africa from 2000 to 2010: 2000=100**

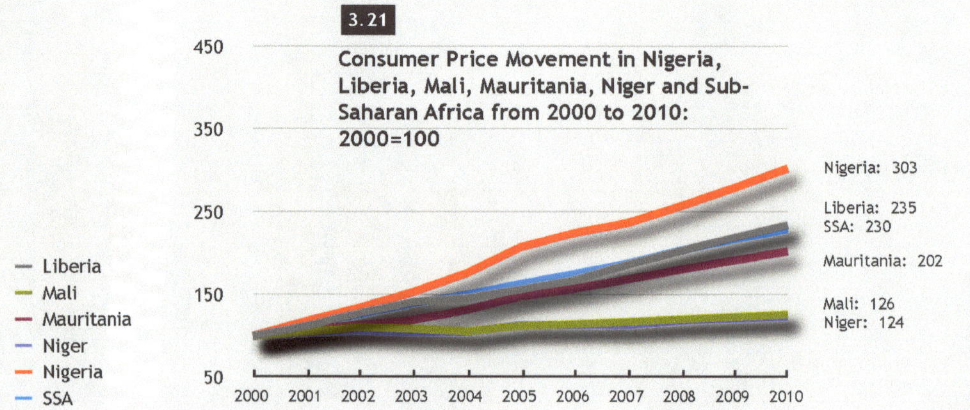

### Consumer Price Movement in West Africa in 2007 and 2010: 2000=100

| | 2000 | 2007 | 2010 |
|---|---|---|---|
| Benin | 100 | 122 | 131 |
| Burkina Faso | 100 | 118 | 132 |
| Cape Verde | 100 | 116 | 125 |
| Côte d'Ivoire | 100 | 125 | 137 |
| Gambia, The | 100 | 171 | 197 |
| Ghana | 100 | 305 | 382 |
| Guinea | 100 | 313 | 402 |
| Guinea-Bissau | 100 | 113 | 123 |
| Liberia | 100 | 187 | 235 |
| Mali | 100 | 117 | 126 |
| Mauritania | 100 | 169 | 202 |
| Niger | 100 | 114 | 124 |
| Nigeria | 100 | 237 | 303 |
| Senegal | 100 | 116 | 127 |
| Sierra Leone | 100 | 166 | 221 |
| Togo | 100 | 117 | 131 |
| SSA | 100 | 188 | 230 |

3.22

### Consumer Price Movement in Nigeria, Senegal, Sierra Leone, Togo and Sub-Saharan Africa from 2000 to 2010: 2000=100

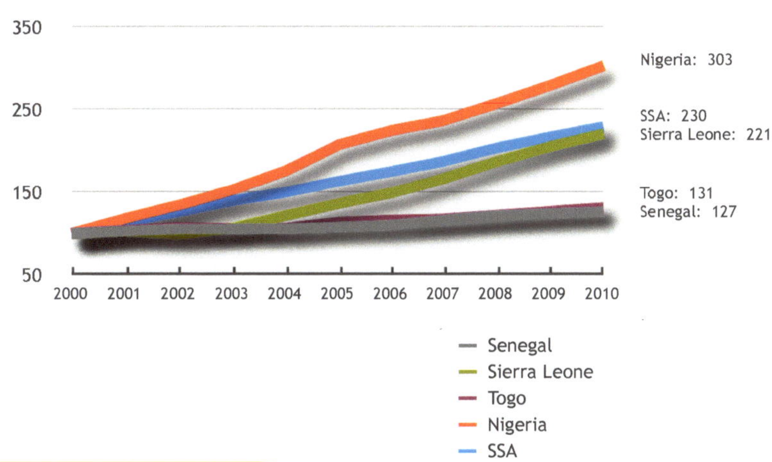


By 2010, the cost would have risen to 230 currency units as continental average, but 300 units in Nigeria.

Primary Data: IMF

### Inflation in Sub-Saharan Africa during 2003-06: Rankings

| Rank | Country | Rank | Country | Rank | Country |
|---|---|---|---|---|---|
| 1 | Gabon | 15 | Congo, Rep. | 29 | Madagascar |
| 2 | Guinea-Bissau | 16 | Comoros | 30 | Ethiopia |
| 3 | Mali | 17 | South Africa | 31 | Sierra Leone |
| 4 | Senegal | 18 | Namibia | 32 | Mozambique |
| 5 | Cape Verde | 19 | Mauritius | 33 | Kenya |
| 6 | Niger | 20 | Tanzania | 34 | Malawi |
| 7 | Seychelles | 21 | Swaziland | 35 | Congo, Dem. Rep. |
| 8 | Cameroon | 22 | Equatorial Guinea | 36 | Nigeria |
| 9 | Togo | 23 | Lesotho | 37 | Ghana |
| 10 | Chad | 24 | Uganda | 38 | Zambia |
| 11 | Burkina Faso | 25 | Burundi | 39 | Eritrea |
| 12 | Côte d' Ivoire | 26 | Botswana | 40 | Guinea |
| 13 | Benin | 27 | Rwanda | 41 | Angola |
| 14 | Central Afr. Rep. | 28 | Gambia, The | | |
| BEST | | AVERAGE | | BOTTOM | |

Central Africa
East Africa
Southern Africa
West Africa

# 3.11 Exchange Rate Stability

## *turbulence*

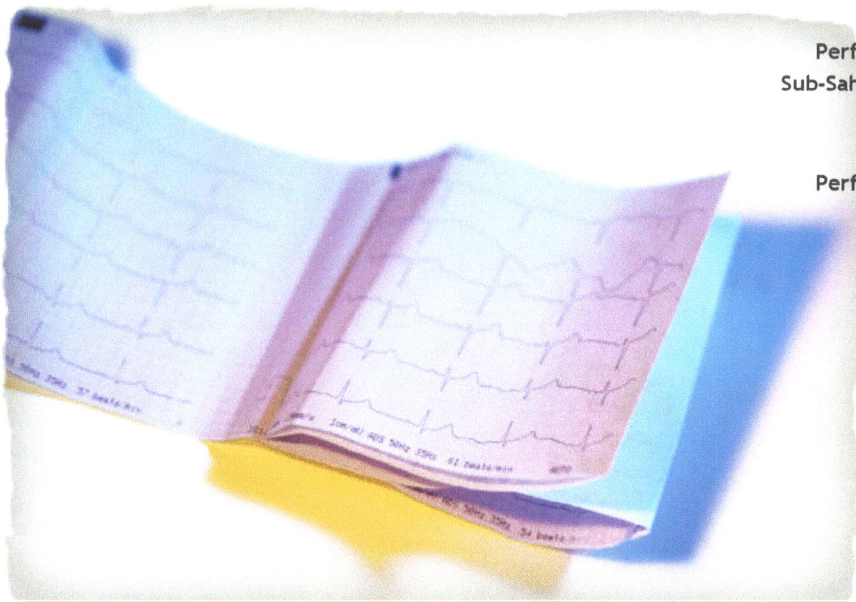

| | 00-07 | 03-10 |
|---|---|---|
| Self-comparison to Preceding Period | | ▼ |
| Performance in Sub-Saharan Africa | ▼ | ▼ |
| Performance in West Africa | ▼ | ▼ |
| | Senegal | Benin |
| | Benin | Mali |
| | Mali | Guinea-Bissau |
| | Côte d'Ivoire | Senegal |
| | Cape Verde | Côte d'Ivoire |
| | Niger | Niger |
| | Burkina Faso | Burkina Faso |
| | Guinea-Bissau | Togo |
| | Togo | Cape Verde |
| | Liberia | Liberia |
| | Sierra Leone | Gambia, The |
| | Mauritania | Sierra Leone |
| | Gambia, The | Mauritania |
| | **Nigeria** | **Nigeria** |
| | Guinea | Ghana |
| | Ghana | Guinea |

Primary Data: IMF

A rougher ride for the Nigerian Naira than for the currencies of 13 of the 15 other West African States, for the 8 years between 2000 and 2007.

| | 00-07 | 03-10 |
|---|---|---|
| Performance among Oil-Exporters | ▼ | ▼ |
| | Cameroon | Cameroon |
| | Côte d'Ivoire | Côte d'Ivoire |
| | Gabon | Gabon |
| | Congo, Rep. | Congo, Rep. |
| | Chad | Chad |
| | Sudan | Sudan |
| | Equatorial Guinea | Equatorial Guinea |
| | **Nigeria** | **Nigeria** |
| | Angola | Angola |

The same story expected for the 8 years from 2003 to 2010.

Within the oil-exporters league, only Angola did worse.

| | |
|---|---|
| ▲ | improved *or* better than average |
| ▼ | worsened *or* worse than average |
| ◁▷ | no change *or* average |

3.23

## Exchange Rate Stability in West Africa during 2003/06

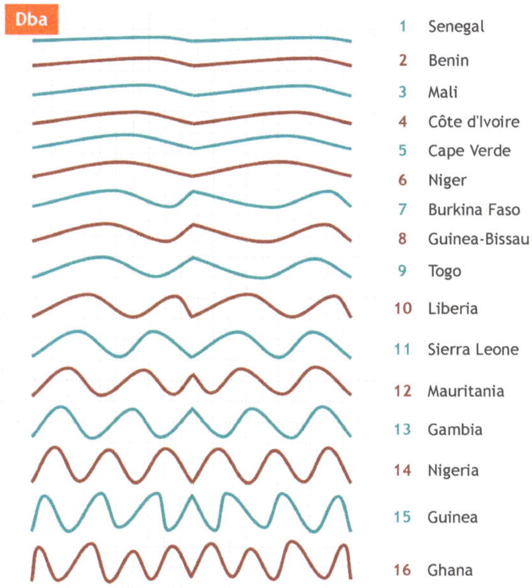


3.24

## Movement of Real Exchange Rate in Nigeria, Ghana and Senegal from 2000 to 2010: 2000=100

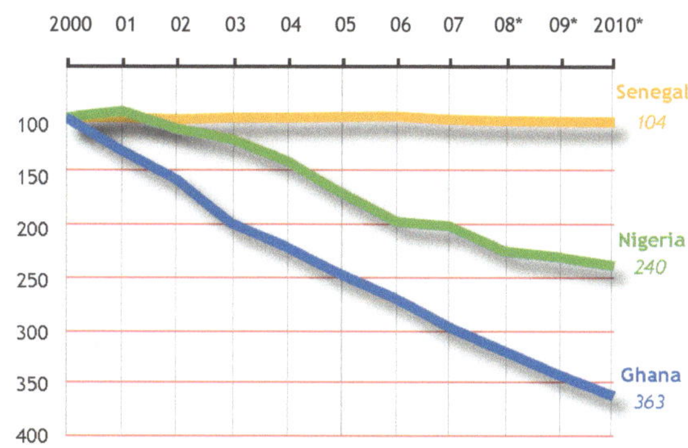


* estimate

Primary Data: IMF

From 100 currency units to one dollar everywhere in 2000, by 2007 it was 98 units in Benin, 181 in Gambia, 171 in Mauritania, 298 in Ghana.

In Nigeria it was 203 in 2007. Further declines to follow from then on to 2010.

Central Africa
East Africa
Southern Africa
West Africa

## Exchange Rate Stability in Sub-Saharan Africa during 2003-06: Rankings

| Rank | Country | Rank | Country | Rank | Country |
|---|---|---|---|---|---|
| 1 | Cameroon | 15 | Gabon | 29 | Sierra Leone |
| 2 | Senegal | 16 | Lesotho | 30 | Rwanda |
| 3 | Benin | 17 | Uganda | 31 | Equatorial Guinea |
| 4 | Mali | 18 | Namibia | 32 | Madagascar |
| 5 | Côte d' Ivoire | 19 | South Africa | 33 | Gambia |
| 6 | Cape Verde | 20 | Kenya | 34 | Nigeria |
| 7 | Niger | 21 | Swaziland | 35 | Eritrea |
| 8 | Burkina Faso | 22 | Ethiopia | 36 | Zambia |
| 9 | Guinea-Bissau | 23 | Tanzania | 37 | Guinea |
| 10 | Central Afr. Rep. | 24 | Congo, Rep. | 38 | Ghana |
| 11 | Comoros | 25 | Botswana | 39 | Malawi |
| 12 | Seychelles | 26 | Mozambique | 40 | Congo, Dem. Rep. |
| 13 | Togo | 27 | Chad | 41 | Angola |
| 14 | Mauritius | 28 | Burundi | | |
| BEST | | MIDDLE | | BOTTOM | |

## Movement of Real Exchange Rates in West Africa in 2007, 2010: 2000=100

| | 2000 | 2007 | 2010 |
|---|---|---|---|
| Benin | 100 | 98 | 101 |
| Burkina Faso | 100 | 105 | 112 |
| Cape Verde | 100 | 99 | 105 |
| Côte d'Ivoire | 100 | 105 | 109 |
| Gambia, The | 100 | 181 | 198 |
| Ghana | 100 | 298 | 363 |
| Guinea | 100 | 258 | 300 |
| Guinea-Bissau | 100 | 92 | 95 |
| Liberia | 100 | 119 | 120 |
| Mali | 100 | 99 | 103 |
| Mauritania | 100 | 171 | 171 |
| Niger | 100 | 99 | 103 |
| Nigeria | 100 | 203 | 240 |
| Senegal | 100 | 102 | 104 |
| Sierra Leone | 100 | 144 | 176 |
| Togo | 100 | 91 | 91 |

Stormy waters indeed for the Naira in Africa. 34th out of 41.

# Leaders & Stragglers

## *fit and nimble*

Overall, Nigeria fits in the top third in terms of economic strength displayed between 2003 and 2006.

Some smaller countries though, like Burkina Faso and Senegal, exhibited niftier muscles.

### Economic Strength Rankings: 2003-06

| Rank | Country | Rank | Country | Rank | Country |
|---|---|---|---|---|---|
| 1 | Equatorial Guinea | 15 | Congo, Rep. | 29 | Niger |
| 2 | Cape Verde | 16 | Gabon | 30 | Uganda |
| 3 | Chad | 17 | Seychelles | 31 | Togo |
| 4 | Botswana | 18 | Lesotho | 32 | Comoros |
| 5 | South Africa | 19 | Madagascar | 33 | Zambia |
| 6 | Senegal | 20 | Ethiopia | 34 | Rwanda |
| 7 | Mauritius | 21 | Benin | 35 | Congo, Dem. Rep. |
| 8 | Angola | 22 | Swaziland | 36 | Malawi |
| 9 | Namibia | 23 | Gambia | 37 | Guinea-Bissau |
| 10 | Burkina Faso | 24 | Kenya | 38 | Central Afr. Rep. |
| 11 | Mali | 25 | Ghana | 39 | Guinea |
| 12 | Nigeria | 26 | Sierra Leone | 40 | Burundi |
| 13 | Cameroon | 27 | Mozambique | 41 | Eritrea |
| 14 | Tanzania | 28 | Côte d' Ivoire | | |
| TOP | | MIDDLE | | BOTTOM | |

Central Africa
East Africa
Southern Africa
West Africa

# Wrap-up: Economic Strength

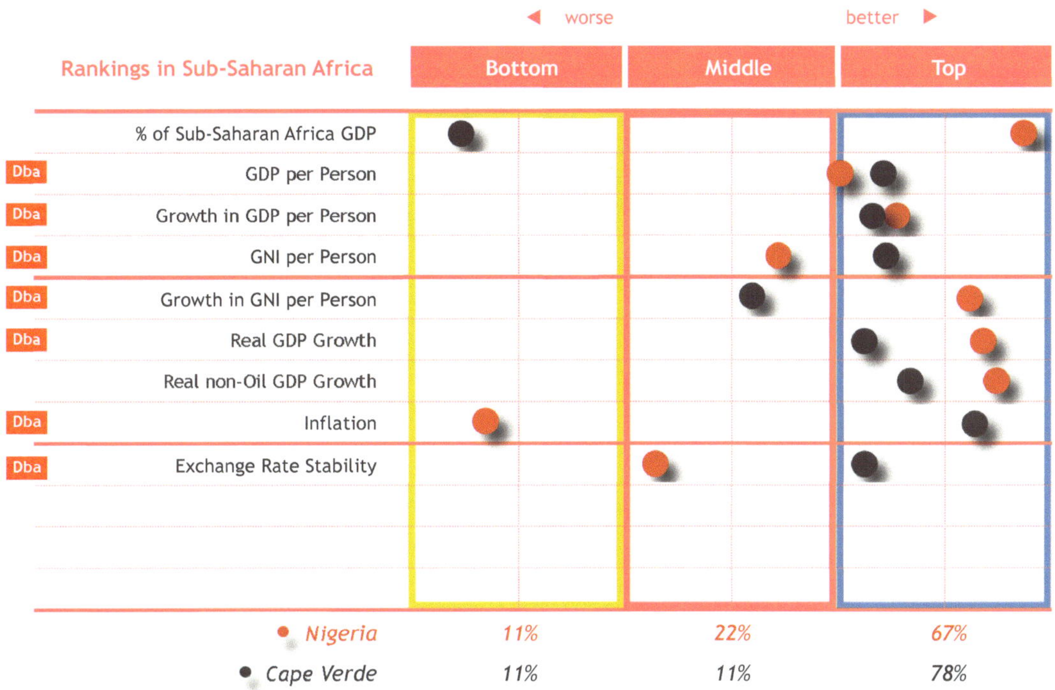


- Again, Cape Verde was the strongest economy in West Africa and 2nd strongest on the continent. Nigeria was 5th in West Africa and 12th on the continent.
- Nigeria clearly supplies a bigger chunk of the continent's economy than Cape Verde does, by a distance.
- Earnings per population (GDP, GNI) has Cape Verde better off, but it is close. However, Nigeria was growing both these (GDP & GNI) faster.
- Nigeria also grew Real GDP and non-Oil GDP faster, too. Even though non-Oil GDP isn't relevant in Cape Verde's case.
- So, it would seem a sturdy display by Nigeria on the whole. Except that Inflation and Exchange Rate Stability of the Naira did it in, and both those indicators are critical to the rankings (Dba).

# 4. Economic Productivity

*efficiency counts for much*

4.1 Country "Productivity Index"

4.2 Country Economy "Development Status"

4.3 Productivity in Agriculture as % of GDP

4.4 Productivity in Agriculture as $PPP per Person

4.5 Growth in Agriculture Productivity

4.6 Productivity in Industry as % of GDP

4.7 Productivity in Industry as $PPP per Person

4.8 Growth in Industry Productivity

4.9 *Manufacturing & Other Industry* Productivity

4.10 Growth in *Manufacturing & Other Industry* Productivity

4.11 Build-up in *Manufacturing & Other Industry* Productivity

4.12 Productivity in Services as % of GDP

4.13 Productivity in Services as $PPP per Person

4.14 Growth in Services Productivity

4.15 Build-up in Productivity in the 3 Sectors

Leaders & Stragglers

Wrap-up

The whole spectrum of economic activity is divided into 3 broad groups - **Agriculture, Industry, Services** - for ease and convenience of not just tabulation, but also categorisation of economic activities according to their nature and interconnection. This aids greatly at the point of analysing, structuring and understanding systems of different countries and groupings that would otherwise be perplexingly disparate.

The convention used for this demarcation is the International Standard Industrial Classification of All Economic Activities (ISIC), as moderated and maintained by the United Nations. It is presently structured into major groupings as follows below. The more detailed breakdown is shown at the end of this introduction.

### Agriculture (A - B)

A - Agriculture, hunting and forestry
B – Fishing

### Industry (C - F)

C - Mining and quarrying
D - Manufacturing
E - Electricity, gas and water supply
F – Construction

### Services (G - Q)

G - Wholesale and retail trade; repair of motor vehicles, motorcycles and personal and household goods
H - Hotels and restaurants
I - Transport, storage and communications
J - Financial intermediation
K - Real estate, renting and business activities
L - Public administration and defence; compulsory social security
M - Education
N - Health and social work
O - Other community, social and personal service activities
P - Activities of private households as employers and undifferentiated production activities of private households
Q - Extraterritorial organisations and bodies

By separating economic activity into sectors like these, it becomes possible to calibrate the quality of economic development and growth within and across countries.

## Productivity (or Value Added)

The contribution of each of the three sectors (agriculture, industry, services) to the overall economy is assessed by evaluating their "Value Added": simply the value of production output less the cost of input, roughly meaning "profit" or "net output".

Productivity can be measured in money terms (the monetary value of net output) or as percentages of the total value of economic output, GDP. Expressing productivity as money per person of population - rather than as just the size of the net output alone - gives a better indication of efficiency in the sectors. Expressing it as a percentage of GDP will bring to light the sectors on which an economy relies most strongly.

## "Productivity Index"

This is our further attempt to calibrate the working efficiency with which the countries exploited their comparative endowments of population size. It rates the countries by comparing their share of the continent's total population with their share in the continent's GDP output. A country that produced a larger ratio of the continent's GDP than its ratio of the continent's population, would have an index greater than 1. While, "under-performing" by producing a smaller percentage of GDP than percentage of population size, would return an index less than 1.

## Economic "Advancement"

Underdeveloped economies have larger agricultural sectors (relative to industry and services) and so a large "Productivity in Agriculture" component to their GDP. Mid-stage economies tend to have a predominant Industry component; while more mature economies have Services as the largest input into GDP. (For this reason, some economists hold that Japan should not be classified as an advanced economy, seeing that it's industrial sector outstretches the services one.)
This is not to imply, though, that African economies with predominant services sectors are "mature"; there are, of course, other major socio-economic (and even, political) factors that play a role. But these countries may be said to be the more developed of the economies in their bracket.

## Growth in Productivity

Growth in Productivity is also more accurately evaluated as growth in the productivity- per-person of population indices.

## Industry Productivity split into *Manufacturing* and *Other Industry*

For better evaluation and further precision, Industry sector of economic activity is often divided into two areas: **manufacturing** (as contained in D in the demarcation above) and **other industry** (groups C, E and F). Isolating manufacturing from other segments helps to evaluate the health of the "real sector", as it is called: generally, an increase in manufacturing activity, and consequently, output of manufactures, would indicate a healthy economy where manufacturing activity is continuous because there is a market for the products, meaning consumer spending is healthy, indicating suitable aggregate demand. And so, the trend in manufacturing activity, separated from the rest of the industry segment, often points to the state of the whole economy. Just as it also gives a rough indication of capacity utilisation in factories, as well as of their efficiency of production.

In economies heavily dependent on commodities (segment C "mining and quarrying") such as the oil exporters and exporters of precious metals, activity in that "other industry" sector can mask a deterioration in manufacturing output, if Industry Activity is not separated into the two groups. Trade in commodities is often easy and lucrative. Easy, because of the straightforward process involved (essentially extraction from the earth, and direct sale afterwards, without further industrial or manufacturing procedures going into the final product); and lucrative because of the existence of cartels such as OPEC in the oil sector. But these factors also make such commodities susceptible to perilous swings in the international market. Consequently, an economy that relies overwhelmingly on productivity in the "Other Industry" segment is more vulnerable to peaks and troughs and more likely to suffer systemic damage at the first signs of a downturn, since they are not diversified enough and cannot cushion those blows.

## Build-up of Productivity

By tying all these sectors down to a common start-point (e.g. 100 units for the year 2000), and tracing their build-up using the actual growth rates as ensued during the consequent years, a picture of the various trajectories can be clearly seen and also extrapolated. The level and quality of activity is well illustrated by these paths, and comparisons can also be made between the different segments of economic output. For example, with the Industry Sector, the trajectory of productivity between the Manufacturing and Other Industry segments would show how much development is taking place across those spheres of activity. The gap between the two groups at a particular year would indicate the disparity (or otherwise) in quality of output and activity in those areas. Detailed structure and explanatory notes follow.

**Sources of Primary Data:** AfDB, IMF, World Bank

### International Standard Industrial Classification of all Economic Activities ISIC Rev.3.1

(As published by the United Nations.
Note: the numbers are category codes and not serial numbers.)

**A - Agriculture, hunting and forestry**

01 Agriculture, hunting and related service activities
02 Forestry, logging and related service activities

**B - Fishing**

05 Fishing, aquaculture and service activities incidental to fishing

**C - Mining and quarrying**

10 Mining of coal and lignite; extraction of peat
11 Extraction of crude petroleum and natural gas; service activities incidental to oil and gas extraction, excluding surveying
12 Mining of uranium and thorium ores
13 Mining of metal ores
14 Other mining and quarrying

**D - Manufacturing**

15 Manufacture of food products and beverages
16 Manufacture of tobacco products
17 Manufacture of textiles
18 Manufacture of wearing apparel; dressing and dyeing of fur
19 Tanning and dressing of leather; manufacture of luggage, handbags, saddlery, harness and footwear
20 Manufacture of wood and of products of wood and cork, except furniture; manufacture of articles of straw and plaiting materials
21 Manufacture of paper and paper products
22 Publishing, printing and reproduction of recorded media
23 Manufacture of coke, refined petroleum products and nuclear fuel
24 Manufacture of chemicals and chemical products
25 Manufacture of rubber and plastics products
26 Manufacture of other non-metallic mineral products
27 Manufacture of basic metals
28 Manufacture of fabricated metal products, except machinery and equipment
29 Manufacture of machinery and equipment n.e.c.
30 Manufacture of office, accounting and computing machinery
31 Manufacture of electrical machinery and apparatus n.e.c.
32 Manufacture of radio, television and communication equipment and apparatus
33 Manufacture of medical, precision and optical instruments, watches and clocks
34 Manufacture of motor vehicles, trailers and semi-trailers
35 Manufacture of other transport equipment
36 Manufacture of furniture; manufacturing n.e.c.
37 Recycling

**E - Electricity, gas and water supply**

40 Electricity, gas, steam and hot water supply
41 Collection, purification and distribution of water

**F - Construction**

45 Construction

**G Wholesale and retail trade; repair of motor vehicles, motorcycles and personal and household goods**

50 Sale, maintenance and repair of motor vehicles and motorcycles; retail sale of automotive fuel
51 Wholesale trade and commission trade, except of motor vehicles and motorcycles
52 Retail trade, except of motor vehicles and motorcycles; repair of personal and household goods

**H Hotels and restaurants**

55 Hotels and restaurants

**I - Transport, storage and communications**

60 Land transport; transport via pipelines
61 Water transport
62 Air transport
63 Supporting and auxiliary transport activities; activities of travel agencies
64 Post and telecommunications

**J - Financial intermediation**

65 Financial intermediation, except insurance and pension funding
66 Insurance and pension funding, except compulsory social security
67 Activities auxiliary to financial intermediation

**K - Real estate, renting and business activities**

70 Real estate activities
71 Renting of machinery and equipment without operator and of personal and household goods
72 Computer and related activities
73 Research and development
74 Other business activities

**L - Public administration and defence; compulsory social security**

75 Public administration and defence; compulsory social security

**M - Education**

80 Education

**N - Health and social work**

85 Health and social work

**O - Other community, social and personal service activities**

90 Sewage and refuse disposal, sanitation and similar activities
91 Activities of membership organizations n.e.c.
92 Recreational, cultural and sporting activities
93 Other service activities

**P - Activities of private households as employers and undifferentiated production activities of private households**

95 Activities of private households as employers of domestic staff
96 Undifferentiated goods-producing activities of private households for own use
97 Undifferentiated service-producing activities of private households for own use

**Q - Extraterritorial organizations and bodies**

99 Extraterritorial organizations and bodies

# Charts


4.1 Country "Productivity Index" in West Africa during 2003/06

4.2 Country "Productivity Index" in West Africa during 2007/2010

4.3 Country "Productivity Index" in Nigeria from 1999 to 2010

4.4 Country "Productivity Index" and corresponding country share of continent population in West Africa during 2003/06

4.5 Breakdown of Country GDP into the 3 Sectors in West Africa during 2003/06

4.6 Breakdown of GDP into the 3 Sectors in Nigeria from 1999 to 2006

4.7 Breakdown of GDP into the 3 Sectors in Sub-Saharan Africa from 1999 to 2006

4.8 Productivity in Agriculture as % of GDP in West Africa during 2003/06

4.9 Productivity in Agriculture as % of GDP in Nigeria and Sub-Saharan Africa from 1999 to 2006

4.10 Productivity in Agriculture per Person of Population in West Africa during 2003/06 ($PPP)

4.11 Productivity in Agriculture per Person of Population in Nigeria and Sub-Saharan Africa from 1999 to 2006 ($PPP)

4.12 Growth in Agriculture Productivity in West Africa during 2003/06

4.13 Growth in Agriculture Productivity in Nigeria and Sub-Saharan Africa from 1999 to 2006

4.14 Productivity in Industry as % of GDP in West Africa during 2003/06

4.15 Productivity in Industry as % of GDP in Nigeria and Sub-Saharan Africa from 1999 to 2006

4.16 Productivity in Industry per Person of Population in West Africa during 2003/06 ($PPP)

4.17 Productivity in Industry per Person of Population in Nigeria and Sub-Saharan Africa from 1999 to 2006 ($PPP)

4.18 Growth in Industry Productivity in West Africa during 2003/06

4.19 Growth in Industry Productivity in Nigeria and Sub-Saharan Africa from 1999 to 2006

4.20 Productivity in Industry per Person of Population in West Africa during 2003/06 ($US)

4.21 % Breakdown of Industry Productivity per Person into *Manufacturing* and *Other Industry* in West Africa during 2003/06

4.22 Productivity in Industry per Person of Population in Nigeria from 1999 to 2006 ($US)

4.23 % Breakdown of Industry Productivity per Person into *Manufacturing* and *Other Industry* in Nigeria from 1999 to 2006

4.24 Growth in $US Industry Productivity in West Africa during 2003/06

4.25 Growth in $US *Manufacturing* and *Other Industry* Productivity in West Africa during 2003/06

4.26 Growth in $US Industry Productivity in Nigeria from 1999 to 2006

4.27 Growth in $US *Manufacturing* and *Other Industry* Productivity in Nigeria from 1999 to 2006

4.28 Build-up of *Manufacturing* and *Other Industry* Productivity from 2000 to 2006: Nigeria, Benin, Burkina Faso. 2000=100

4.29 Build-up of *Manufacturing* and *Other Industry* Productivity from 2000 to 2006: Nigeria, Cape Verde, Côte d'Ivoire. 2000=100

4.30 Build-up of *Manufacturing* and *Other Industry* Productivity from 2000 to 2006: Nigeria, Gambia, Ghana. 2000=100

4.31 Build-up of *Manufacturing* and *Other Industry* Productivity from 2000 to 2006: Nigeria, Guinea, Guinea-Bissau. 2000=100

4.32 Build-up of *Manufacturing* and *Other Industry* Productivity from 2000 to 2006: Nigeria, Mali, Mauritania. 2000=100

4.33 Build-up of *Manufacturing* and *Other Industry* Productivity from 2000 to 2006: Nigeria, Niger, Senegal. 2000=100

4.34 Build-up of *Manufacturing* and *Other Industry* Productivity from 2000 to 2006: Nigeria, Sierra Leone, Togo. 2000=100

4.35 Productivity in Services as % of GDP in West Africa during 2003/06

4.36 Productivity in Services as % of GDP in Nigeria and Sub-Saharan Africa from 1999 to 2006

4.37 Productivity in Services per Person of Population in West Africa during 2003/06 ($PPP)

4.38 Productivity in Services per Person of Population in Nigeria and Sub-Saharan Africa from 1999 to 2006 ($PPP)

4.39 Growth in Services Productivity in West Africa during 2003/06

4.40 Growth in Services Productivity in Nigeria and Sub-Saharan Africa from 1999 to 2006

4.41 Build-up of Agriculture Productivity in Nigeria and Sub-Saharan Africa from 2000 to 2006. 2000=100

4.42 Build-up of Industry Productivity in Nigeria and Sub-Saharan Africa from 2000 to 2006. 2000=100

4.43 Build-up of Services Productivity in Nigeria and Sub-Saharan Africa from 2000 to 2006.

4.44 Build-up of Productivity in Agriculture, Industry and Services in Nigeria from 2000 to 2006. 2000=100

4.45 Build-up of Productivity in Agriculture, Industry and Services in Sub-Saharan Africa from 2000 to 2006. 2000=100

- **Wrap-up**

# Tables

*1999-2002; 2003-2006; 2007-2010:*
- *self-comparison to preceding period;*
- *performance in S-Saharan Africa;*
- *performance in West Africa;*
- *performance among oil-exporters;*

*for:*

Country Productivity Index

*1999-2002; 2003-2006:*
- *self-comparison to preceding period;*
- *performance in S-Saharan Africa;*
- *performance in West Africa;*
- *performance among oil-exporters;*

*for:*

Productivity in Agriculture as % of GDP

Productivity in Agriculture as $PPP per Person

Growth in Agriculture Productivity

Productivity in Industry as % of GDP

Productivity in Industry as $PPP per Person

Growth in Industry Productivity

Productivity in Services as % of GDP

Productivity in Services as $PPP per Person

Growth in Services Productivity

- Productivity in Agriculture as $PPP per Person in Sub-Saharan Africa during 2003-06: Rankings
- Growth in Agriculture Productivity in Sub-Saharan Africa during 2003-06: Rankings
- Productivity in Industry as $PPP per Person in Sub-Saharan Africa during 2003-06: Rankings
- Growth in Industry Productivity in Sub-Saharan Africa during 2003-06: Rankings
- Gap between *Manufacturing* and *Other Industry* Productivity levels: 2000=100
- Productivity in Services as $PPP per Person in Sub-Saharan Africa during 2003-06: Rankings
- Growth in Services Productivity in Sub-Saharan Africa during 2003-06: Rankings
- **Economic Productivity Rankings: 2003-06**

# 4.1 Country "Productivity Index"

## *lifting above their weight*

| | 99-02 | 03-06 | 07-10 |
|---|---|---|---|
| Self-comparison to Preceding Period | | ▲ | ▼ |
| Performance in Sub-Saharan Africa | ▼ | ▲ | ▲ |
| Performance in West Africa | ▲ | ▲ | ▲ |
| | Cape Verde | Cape Verde | Cape Verde |
| | Côte d'Ivoire | **Nigeria** | **Nigeria** |
| | Mauritania | Mauritania | Mauritania |
| | Senegal | Côte d'Ivoire | Côte d'Ivoire |
| | **Nigeria** | Senegal | Senegal |
| | Benin | Benin | Benin |
| | Ghana | Ghana | Ghana |
| | Gambia, The | Gambia, The | Gambia, The |
| | Guinea | Burkina Faso | Burkina Faso |
| | Burkina Faso | Guinea | Guinea |
| | Mali | Mali | Mali |
| | Togo | Togo | Togo |
| | Niger | Niger | Sierra Leone |
| | Guinea-Bissau | Sierra Leone | Niger |
| | Liberia | Guinea-Bissau | Guinea-Bissau |
| | Sierra Leone | Liberia | Liberia |

Primary Data: IMF

| | 99-02 | 03-06 | 07-10 |
|---|---|---|---|
| Performance among Oil-Exporters | ▼ | ▼ | ▼ |
| | Gabon | Gabon | Gabon |
| | Equatorial Guinea | Equatorial Guinea | Equatorial Guinea |
| | Congo, Rep. | Angola | Angola |
| | Angola | Congo, Rep. | Congo, Rep. |
| | Cameroon | Cameroon | Sudan |
| | Côte d'Ivoire | **Nigeria** | **Nigeria** |
| | Sudan | Sudan | Cameroon |
| | **Nigeria** | Côte d'Ivoire | Côte d'Ivoire |
| | Chad | Chad | Chad |

Although Nigeria is poised to do worse in 2007-2010, it was squeezing out more from its population potential than most of West Africa. But not better than the majority of oil exporters.

| | |
|---|---|
| ▲ | improved *or* better than average |
| ▼ | worsened *or* worse than average |
| ◁▷ | no change *or* average |

## 4. Economic Productivity

4.1

Dba

### Country "Productivity Index" in West Africa during 2003/06

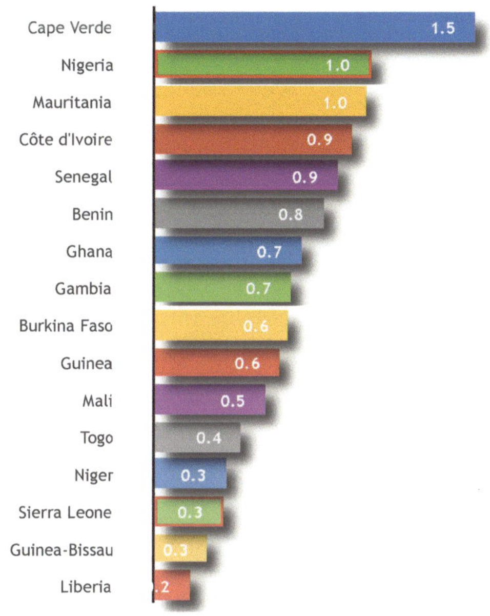


4.2

### Country "Productivity Index" in West Africa during 2007/2010

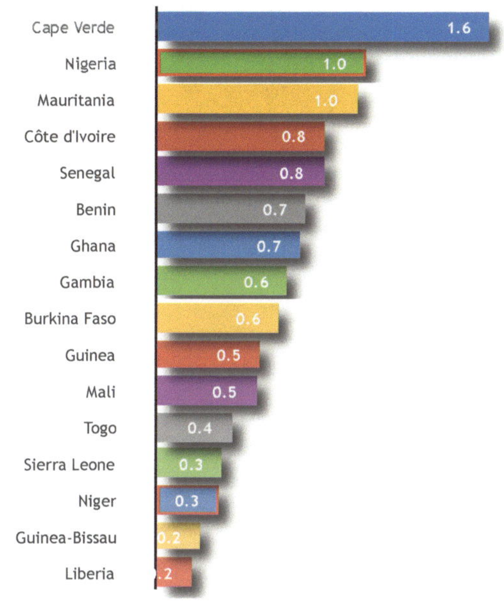


West Africa stayed much the same across 03/06 and 07/10 in terms of country economy efficiency, save for Niger and Sierra Leone, who jostled for 3rd from bottom.

4.3

### Country "Productivity Index" in Nigeria from 1999 to 2010

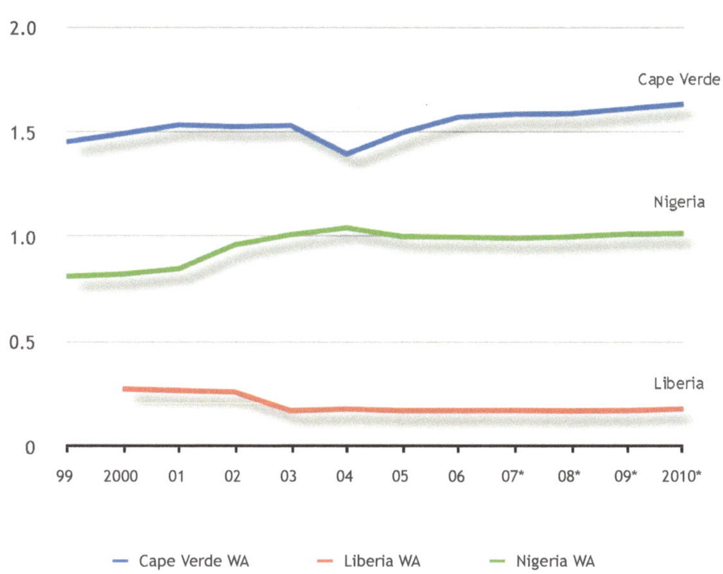


* estimate

Compared to West Africa's best performer, Cape Verde, Nigeria's "efficiency trajectory" was not dissimilar. A generally steady upward gradient.

Primary Data: IMF

## 4. Economic Productivity

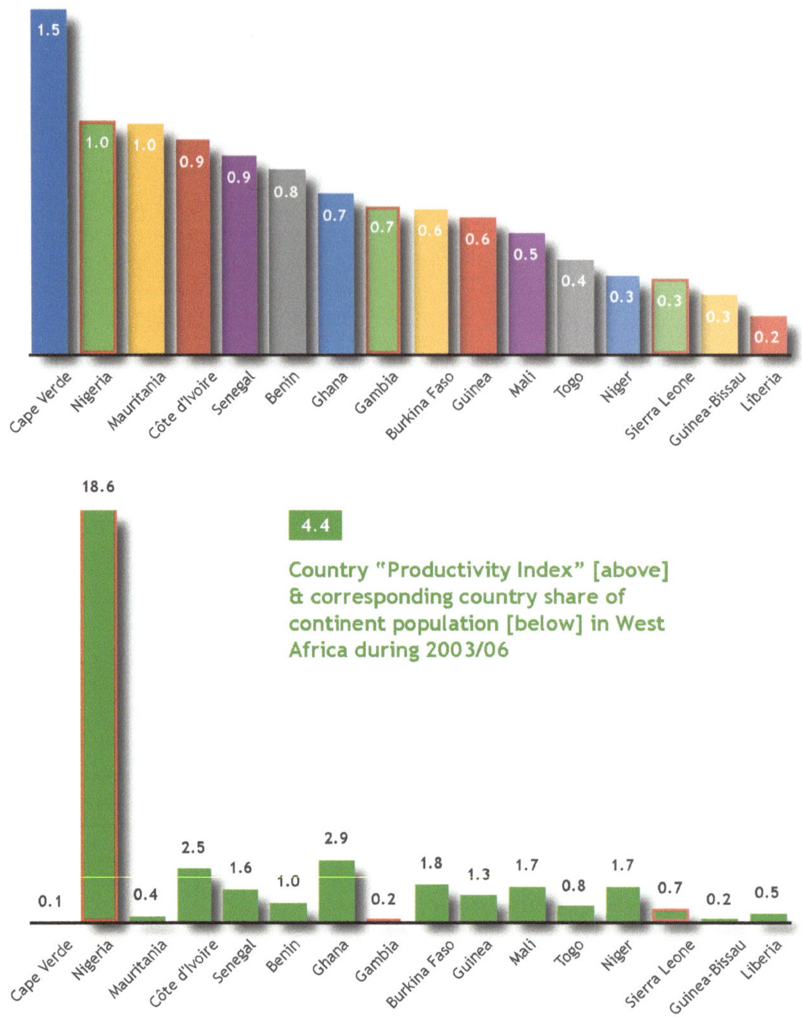


**4.4**

Country "Productivity Index" [above] & corresponding country share of continent population [below] in West Africa during 2003/06

Primary Data: IMF

Cape Verde's outstanding performance is illustrated here. With 0.06% of Sub-Saharan Africa's population, it supplied 0.09% of its GDP; 1.5 times.

Nigeria had 18.6% of the population and supplied 18.9% of the GDP. Giving it a productivity index of 1.

Going by its small share of population, Mauritania comes out looking particularly well.

# 4. Economic Productivity

### Country Productivity Index in Sub-Saharan Africa during 2003-06: Rankings

| Rank | Country | Rank | Country | Rank | Country |
|---|---|---|---|---|---|
| 1 | Seychelles | 15 | Senegal | 29 | Uganda |
| 2 | Botswana | 16 | Chad | 30 | Eritrea |
| 3 | Gabon | 17 | Kenya | 31 | Rwanda |
| 4 | Equatorial Guinea | 18 | Benin | 32 | Togo |
| 5 | Mauritius | 19 | Ghana | 33 | Mozambique |
| 6 | South Africa | 20 | Zambia | 34 | Malawi |
| 7 | Namibia | 21 | Gambia, The | 35 | Central Afr. Rep. |
| 8 | Swaziland | 22 | Lesotho | 36 | Niger |
| 9 | Angola | 23 | Burkina Faso | 37 | Ethiopia |
| 10 | Congo, Rep. | 24 | Comoros | 38 | Sierra Leone |
| 11 | Cape Verde | 25 | Tanzania | 39 | Guinea-Bissau |
| 12 | Cameroon | 26 | Guinea | 40 | Burundi |
| 13 | **Nigeria** | 27 | Mali | 41 | Congo, Dem. Rep. |
| 14 | Côte d' Ivoire | 28 | Madagascar | | |
| | **TOP** | | **MIDDLE** | | **BOTTOM** |

Central Africa
East Africa
Southern Africa
West Africa

> Nigeria just about makes it into the top segment. The best performer in West Africa, Cape Verde, was 11th in Africa. The Seychelles top the group.

# 4.2 Country Economy "Development Status"

## *eggs in one basket*

4.5

Breakdown of Country GDP into the 3 Sectors in West Africa during 2003/06

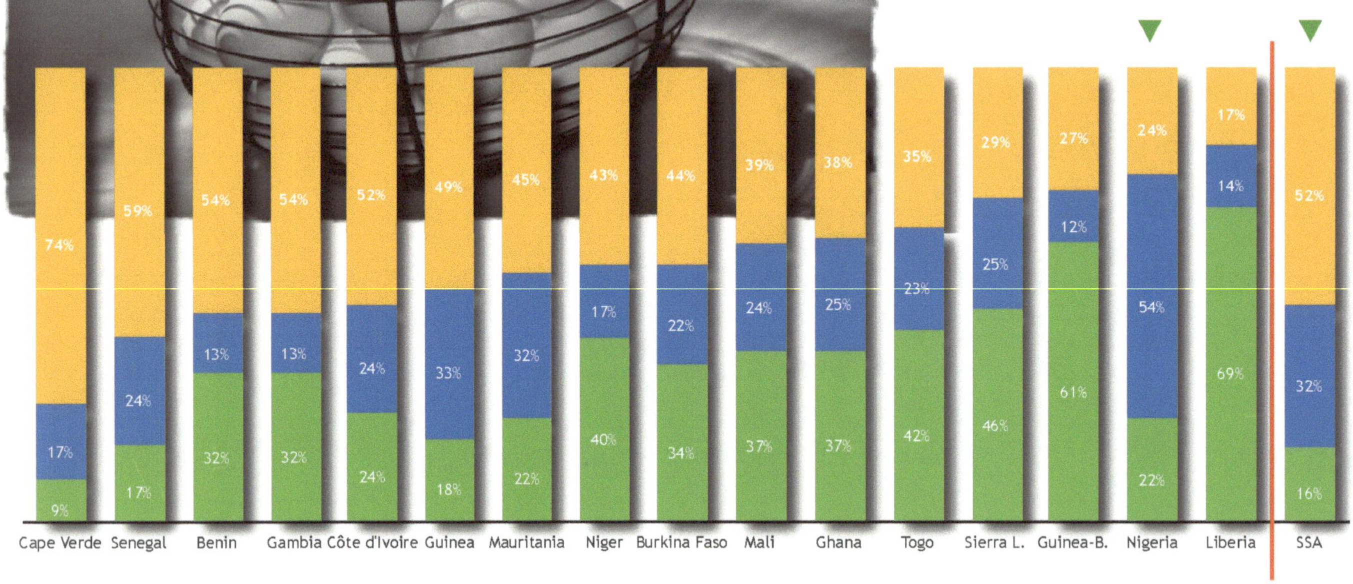


Primary Data: World Bank

Arranged in decreasing size of their services sector. Nigeria is 2nd from bottom in West Africa; suggesting that it is likely the least "developed" economy in the region.

At 24% of GDP, its services sector is less than half the Africa average.

In Africa, the services sector grew across 1999/2006, largely at the expense of agriculture, which dropped by 4%. Industry generally hovered around 30%.

Nigeria does have the largest industry sector, which is due largely to its dominating oil industry. Its agriculture sector, at 22% of GDP, is slightly larger than the Africa average.

For Nigeria, the industry sector ballooned up till 2005. Services and agriculture shrank; services by 8% and agriculture by 14%.

**4.6**

Breakdown of GDP into the 3 Sectors in Nigeria from 1999 to 2006

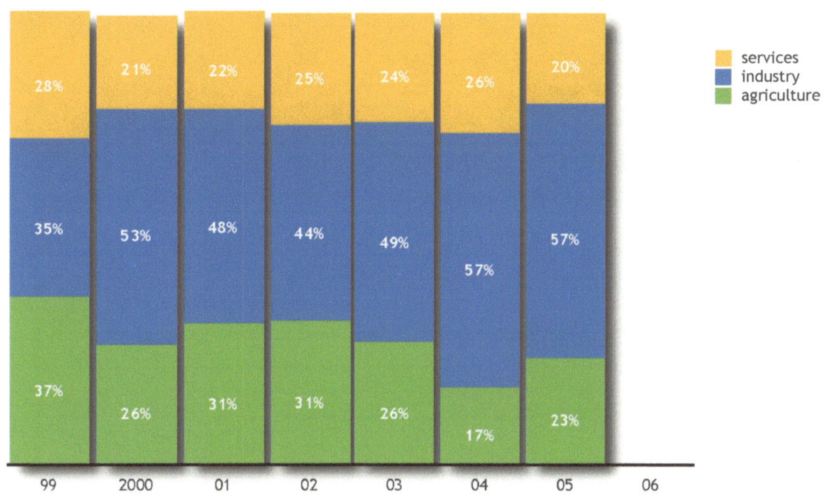


**4.7**

Breakdown of GDP into the 3 Sectors in Sub-Saharan Africa from 1999 to 2006

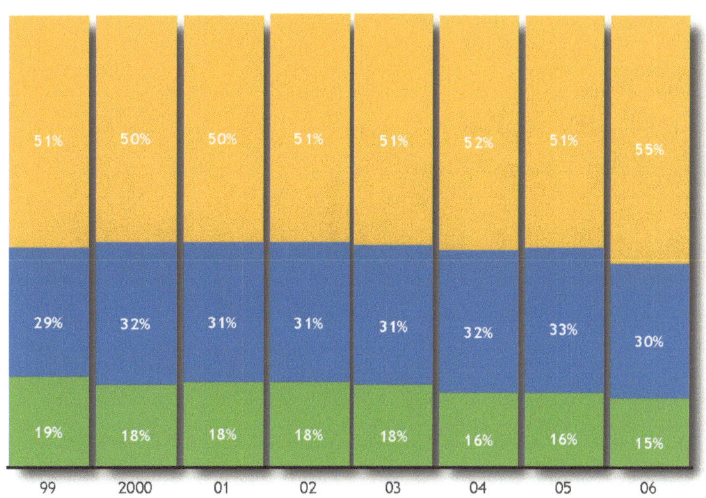

# 4.3 Productivity in Agriculture as % of GDP

**looks like a good harvest**

Primary Data: World Bank

| | 99-02 | 03-06 |
|---|---|---|
| Self-comparison to Preceding Period | | ▼ |
| Performance in Sub-Saharan Africa | ▲ | ▲ |
| Performance in West Africa | ▼ | ▼ |
| | Liberia | Liberia |
| | Guinea-Bissau | Guinea-Bissau |
| | Sierra Leone | Sierra Leone |
| | Mali | Togo |
| | Niger | Niger |
| | Togo | Ghana |
| | Benin | Mali |
| | Ghana | Gambia, The |
| | Gambia, The | Benin |
| | Burkina Faso | Burkina Faso |
| | **Nigeria** | Côte d'Ivoire |
| | Mauritania | Mauritania |
| | Côte d'Ivoire | **Nigeria** |
| | Guinea | Guinea |
| | Senegal | Senegal |
| | Cape Verde | Cape Verde |
| Performance among Oil-Exporters | ▲ | ▲ |
| | Sudan | Sudan |
| | Chad | Chad |
| | **Nigeria** | Côte d'Ivoire |
| | Côte d'Ivoire | **Nigeria** |
| | Cameroon | Cameroon |
| | Equatorial Guinea | Angola |
| | Angola | Gabon |
| | Gabon | Congo, Rep. |
| | Congo, Rep. | Equatorial Guinea |

4.8

Productivity in Agriculture as % of GDP in West Africa during 2003/06

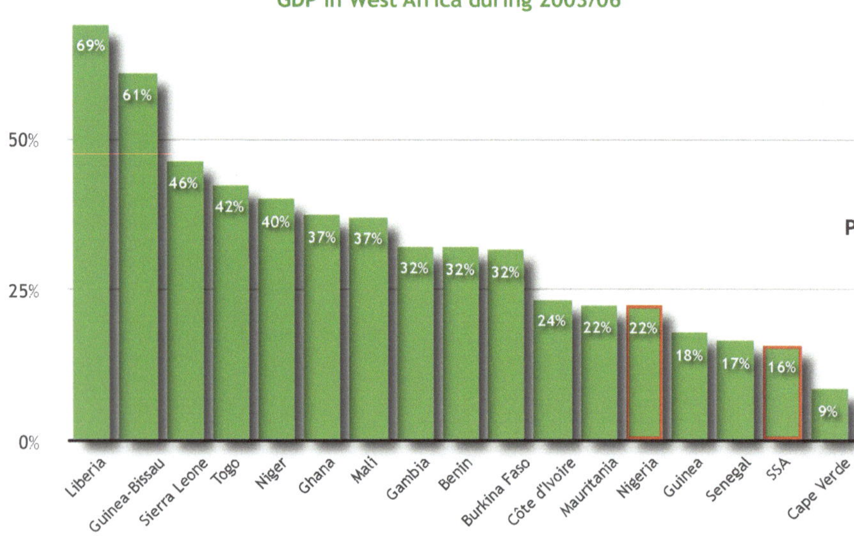


| | |
|---|---|
| ▲ | improved *or* better than average |
| ▼ | worsened *or* worse than average |
| ◁▷ | no change *or* average |

4.9

Productivity in Agriculture as % of GDP in Nigeria and Sub-Saharan Africa from 1999 to 2006

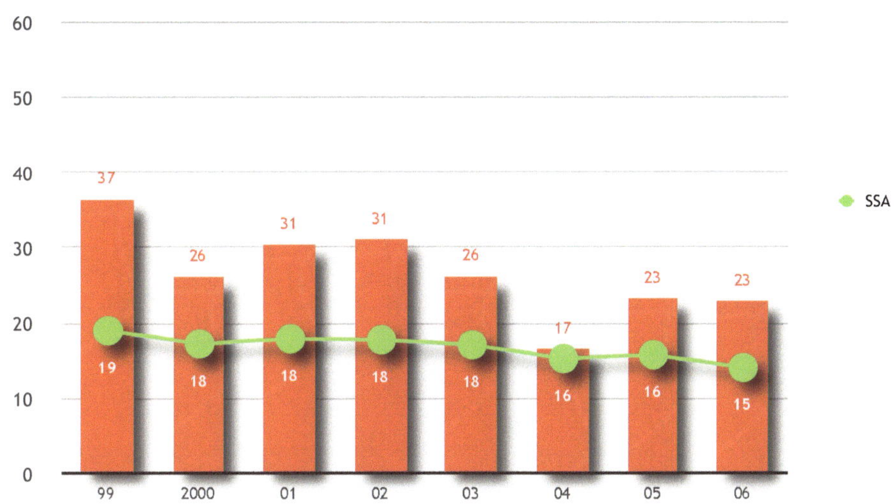


It could be argued that agriculture's part in Africa's GDP output hovered healthily between 15% and 20%. While Nigeria's swung wildly between 23% and 37%.

Agriculture is not a big player in Nigeria's GDP. 03/06 is incontrovertibly worse than 99/02. Yet, better than the Africa average.

Agriculture's share of Sub-Saharan Africa's GDP also slips downwards from 1992 through 2006, a straight fall of 4%. But Nigeria's was a fall of 14%.

# 4.4 Productivity in Agriculture as $PPP per Person

**more grains to their elbows**

Primary Data: World Bank, IMF

|  | 99-02 | 03-06 |
|---|---|---|
| Self-comparison to Preceding Period |  | ▲ |
| Performance in Sub-Saharan Africa | ▲ | ▲ |
| Performance in West Africa | ▲ | ▲ |
|  | Benin | Ghana |
|  | Mauritania | Benin |
|  | Côte d'Ivoire | **Nigeria** |
|  | **Nigeria** | Mauritania |
|  | Ghana | Côte d'Ivoire |
|  | Gambia, The | Gambia, The |
|  | Mali | Burkina Faso |
|  | Burkina Faso | Mali |
|  | Liberia | Togo |
|  | Guinea-Bissau | Guinea-Bissau |
|  | Togo | Sierra Leone |
|  | Senegal | Senegal |
|  | Guinea | Niger |
|  | Niger | Cape Verde |
|  | Cape Verde | Liberia |
|  | Sierra Leone | Guinea |
| Performance among Oil-Exporters | ▼ | ◁▷ |
|  | Gabon | Gabon |
|  | Sudan | Sudan |
|  | Equatorial Guinea | Equatorial Guinea |
|  | Cameroon | Cameroon |
|  | Chad | **Nigeria** |
|  | Côte d'Ivoire | Côte d'Ivoire |
|  | **Nigeria** | Chad |
|  | Angola | Angola |
|  | Congo, Rep. | Congo, Rep. |

But, quantify productivity as money generated per person of population, and Nigeria improves significantly.

Top-half finishes in West Africa during both 99/02 and 03/06, even though within the oil exporters fraternity it doesn't excel. Average there in 03/06.

| | |
|---|---|
| ▲ | improved *or* better than average |
| ▼ | worsened *or* worse than average |
| ◁▷ | no change *or* average |

## 4. Economic Productivity

4.10

Productivity in Agriculture per Person of Population in West Africa during 2003/06 ($PPP)

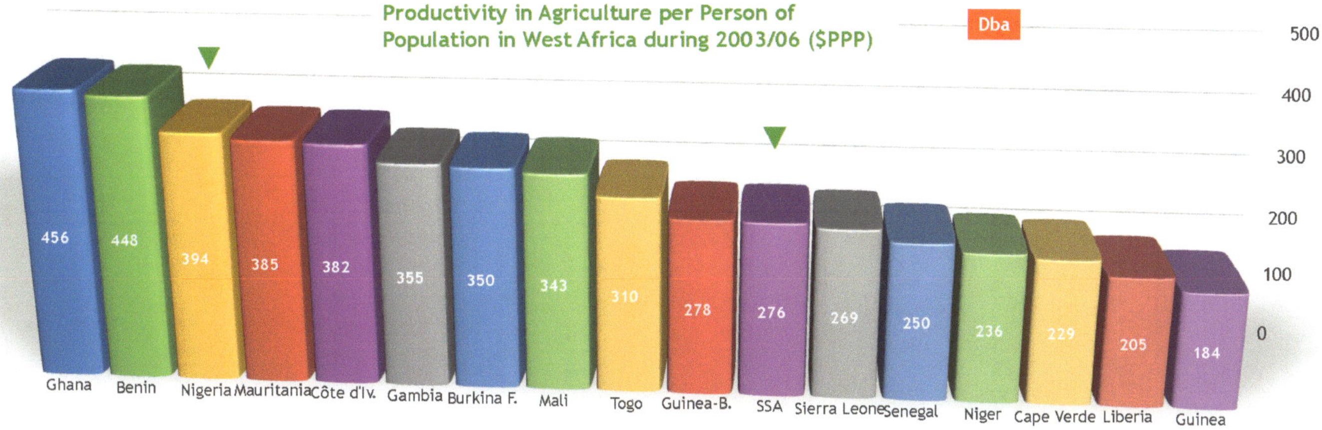


4.11

Productivity in Agriculture per Person of Population in Nigeria and Sub-Saharan Africa from 1999 to 2006 ($PPP)

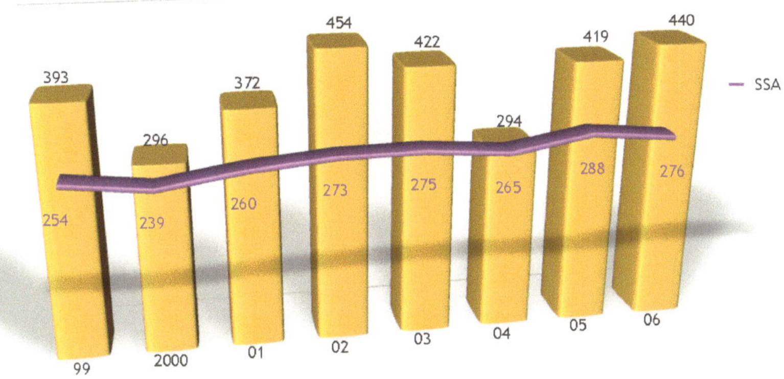


Here again, Nigeria outperforms most of Africa, just about finding room in the top band.

Productivity in Agriculture as $PPP per Person in Sub-Saharan Africa during 2003-06: Rankings

| Rank | Country | Rank | Country | Rank | Country |
|---|---|---|---|---|---|
| 1 | Gabon | 15 | Central Afr. Rep. | 29 | Zambia |
| 2 | Mauritius | 16 | Chad | 30 | Senegal |
| 3 | Comoros | 17 | Gambia, The | 31 | South Africa |
| 4 | Swaziland | 18 | Burkina Faso | 32 | Niger |
| 5 | Namibia | 19 | Mali | 33 | Malawi |
| 6 | Tanzania | 20 | Angola | 34 | Cape Verde |
| 7 | Ghana | 21 | Rwanda | 35 | Mozambique |
| 8 | Benin | 22 | Togo | 36 | Lesotho |
| 9 | Seychelles | 23 | Botswana | 37 | Guinea |
| 10 | Equatorial Guinea | 24 | Ethiopia | 38 | Congo, Rep. |
| 11 | Cameroon | 25 | Guinea-Bissau | 39 | Eritrea |
| 12 | Kenya | 26 | Uganda | 40 | Congo, Dem. Rep. |
| 13 | **Nigeria** | 27 | Sierra Leone | 41 | Burundi |
| 14 | Côte d' Ivoire | 28 | Madagascar | | |
| TOP | | MIDDLE | | BOTTOM | |

Central Africa
East Africa
Southern Africa
West Africa

# 4.5 Growth in Agriculture Productivity

## something to crow about

The bad news, though, is that the Nigeria agriculture sector wasn't growing robustly. It slowed significantly from 99/02 to 03/06. Bottom half of West Africa.

That malaise was shared by other oil exporters, who - except for Angola - actually fared worse. This highlights the much feared neglect of non-oil sectors.

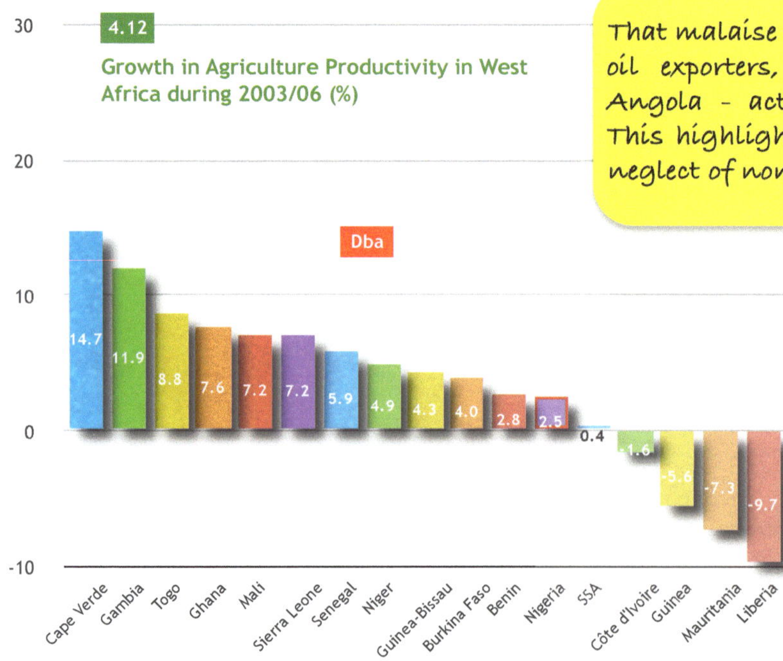


4.12 Growth in Agriculture Productivity in West Africa during 2003/06 (%)

Primary Data: World Bank, IMF

| | 99-02 | 03-06 |
|---|---|---|
| Self-comparison to Preceding Period | | ▼ |
| Performance in Sub-Saharan Africa | ▲ | ▲ |
| Performance in West Africa | ▲ | ▼ |
| | Liberia | Cape Verde |
| | Nigeria | Gambia, The |
| | Gambia, The | Togo |
| | Ghana | Ghana |
| | Sierra Leone | Mali |
| | Burkina Faso | Sierra Leone |
| | Togo | Senegal |
| | Guinea | Niger |
| | Benin | Guinea-Bissau |
| | Côte d'Ivoire | Burkina Faso |
| | Niger | Benin |
| | Senegal | Nigeria |
| | Mauritania | Côte d'Ivoire |
| | Mali | Guinea |
| | Cape Verde | Mauritania |
| | Guinea-Bissau | Liberia |
| Performance among Oil-Exporters | ▲ | ▲ |
| | Nigeria | Angola |
| | Chad | Nigeria |
| | Sudan | Sudan |
| | Côte d'Ivoire | Cameroon |
| | Cameroon | Côte d'Ivoire |
| | Angola | Gabon |
| | Gabon | Congo, Rep. |
| | Equatorial Guinea | Chad |
| | Congo, Rep. | Equatorial Guinea |

| | |
|---|---|
| ▲ | improved *or* better than average |
| ▼ | worsened *or* worse than average |
| ◁▷ | no change *or* average |

4.13

**Growth in Agriculture Productivity in Nigeria and Sub-Saharan Africa from 1999 to 2006 (%)**

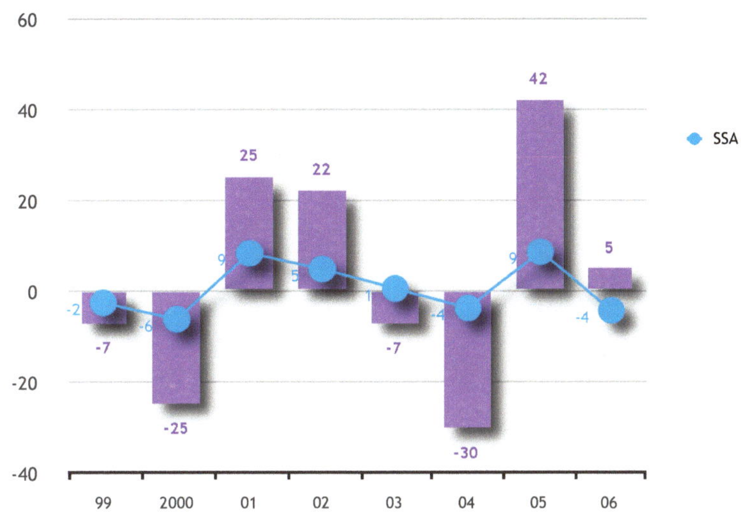


Angola, oil producer though it is, led the charge ahead of the rest of the continent. The only oil economy in the top segment.

All the other oil exporters made bottom, save for Nigeria, who just made into the middle band.

**Growth in Agriculture Productivity in Sub-Saharan Africa during 2003-06: Rankings**

| Rank | Country | Rank | Country | Rank | Country |
|---|---|---|---|---|---|
| 1 | Angola | 15 | Uganda | 29 | Seychelles |
| 2 | Cape Verde | 16 | Senegal | 30 | Comoros |
| 3 | Ethiopia | 17 | Zambia | 31 | Cameroon |
| 4 | Gambia, The | 18 | Niger | 32 | Mauritius |
| 5 | Eritrea | 19 | Guinea | 33 | Burundi |
| 6 | Togo | 20 | Lesotho | 34 | Swaziland |
| 7 | Mozambique | 21 | Burkina Faso | 35 | Côte d' Ivoire |
| 8 | Tanzania | 22 | Malawi | 36 | Gabon |
| 9 | Ghana | 23 | Congo, Dem. Rep. | 37 | South Africa |
| 10 | Mali | 24 | Botswana | 38 | Congo, Rep. |
| 11 | Sierra Leone | 25 | Kenya | 39 | Chad |
| 12 | Namibia | 26 | Benin | 40 | Guinea-Bissau |
| 13 | Madagascar | 27 | **Nigeria** | 41 | Equatorial Guinea |
| 14 | Rwanda | 28 | Central Afr. Rep. | | |
| | **TOP** | | **MIDDLE** | | **BOTTOM** |

Central Africa
East Africa
Southern Africa
West Africa

# 4.6 Productivity in Industry as % of GDP

## churning them out...

| | 99-02 | 03-06 |
|---|---|---|
| Self-comparison to Preceding Period | | ▲ |
| Performance in Sub-Saharan Africa | ▲ | ▲ |
| Performance in West Africa | ▲ | ▲ |

| 99-02 | 03-06 |
|---|---|
| Nigeria | Nigeria |
| Guinea | Guinea |
| Mauritania | Mauritania |
| Sierra Leone | Sierra Leone |
| Ghana | Ghana |
| Senegal | Senegal |
| Côte d'Ivoire | Côte d'Ivoire |
| Mali | Mali |
| Burkina Faso | Burkina Faso |
| Togo | Togo |
| Niger | Niger |
| Cape Verde | Cape Verde |
| Benin | Benin |
| Gambia, The | Gambia, The |
| Guinea-Bissau | Guinea-Bissau |
| Liberia | Liberia |

Primary Data: World Bank

Industry is the largest of the Nigeria sectors, at 55% of GDP. Considerably larger than the Africa average (32%).

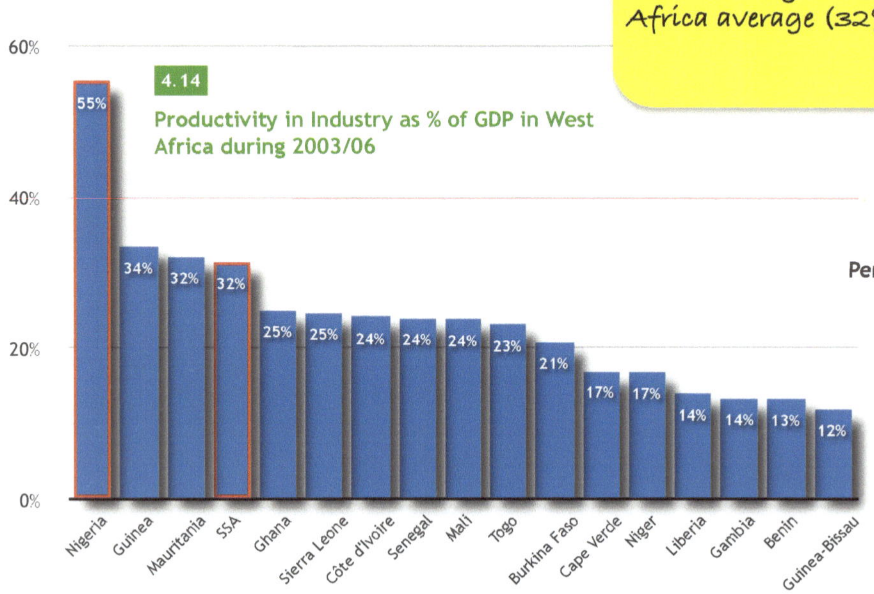


4.14 Productivity in Industry as % of GDP in West Africa during 2003/06

| | 99-02 | 03-06 |
|---|---|---|
| Performance among Oil-Exporters | ◁▷ | ◁▷ |
| | Equatorial Guinea | Equatorial Guinea |
| | Angola | Angola |
| | Congo, Rep. | Congo, Rep. |
| | Gabon | Gabon |
| | Nigeria | Nigeria |
| | Cameroon | Chad |
| | Côte d'Ivoire | Cameroon |
| | Sudan | Sudan |
| | Chad | Côte d'Ivoire |

| | |
|---|---|
| ▲ | improved *or* better than average |
| ▼ | worsened *or* worse than average |
| ◁▷ | no change *or* average |

4.15

Productivity in Industry as % of GDP in Nigeria and Sub-Saharan Africa from 1999 to 2006

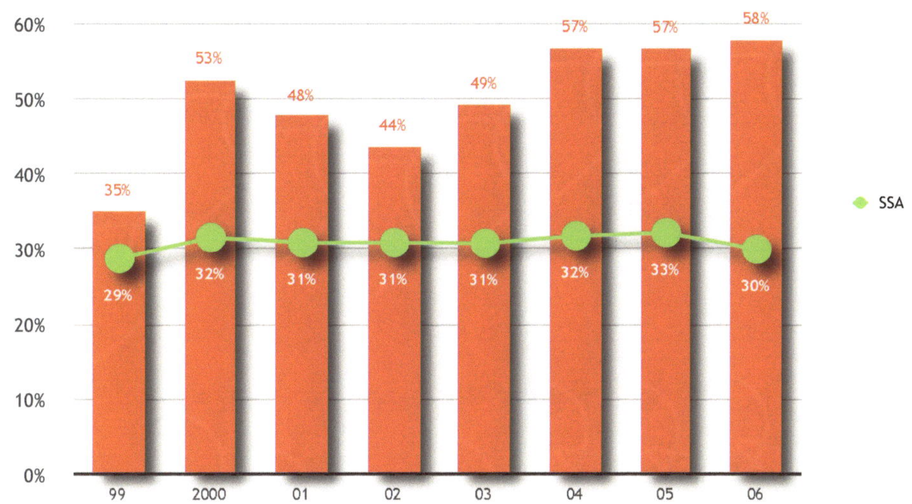


This time, Africa hovers around 30% industry in its GDP. Nigeria grew industry from 35% of GDP in 1999 to 58% in 2006.

Yet, Nigeria was only average among the oil countries. Suggesting either that the other economies are more heavily tilted towards industry, or are able to achieve more efficient output.

This may be a positive trend, or it may not. That would depend on how much of this growth was driven by the relatively easy trade in oil exports ...

... rather than an increasing capacity utilisation in its manufacturing sector.

Examined in chapter 4.9 - 4.11 below.

# 4.7 Productivity in Industry as $PPP per Person

***... and churning this out...***

Primary Data: World Bank, IMF

| | 99-02 | 03-06 |
|---|---|---|
| Self-comparison to Preceding Period | | ▲ |
| Performance in Sub-Saharan Africa | ▲ | ▲ |
| Performance in West Africa | ▲ | ▲ |

| 99-02 | 03-06 |
|---|---|
| **Nigeria** | **Nigeria** |
| Mauritania | Mauritania |
| Côte d'Ivoire | Cape Verde |
| Cape Verde | Côte d'Ivoire |
| Senegal | Senegal |
| Guinea | Guinea |
| Ghana | Ghana |
| Burkina Faso | Burkina Faso |
| Mali | Mali |
| Benin | Benin |
| Gambia, The | Togo |
| Togo | Gambia, The |
| Sierra Leone | Sierra Leone |
| Niger | Niger |
| Guinea-Bissau | Guinea-Bissau |
| Liberia | Liberia |

Almost the same trend in Industry productivity output per person, as for industry productivity % GDP. Top of West Africa; better than most Africa; average among oil exporters.

| Performance among Oil-Exporters | 99-02 | 03-06 |
|---|---|---|
| | ▼ | ◁▷ |
| | Gabon | Equatorial Guinea |
| | Equatorial Guinea | Gabon |
| | Congo, Rep. | Angola |
| | Angola | Congo, Rep. |
| | Cameroon | **Nigeria** |
| | **Nigeria** | Chad |
| | Côte d'Ivoire | Cameroon |
| | Sudan | Sudan |
| | Chad | Côte d'Ivoire |

| | |
|---|---|
| ▲ | improved *or* better than average |
| ▼ | worsened *or* worse than average |
| ◁▷ | no change *or* average |

# 4. Economic Productivity

4.16

Productivity in Industry per Person of Population in West Africa during 2003/06 ($PPP)

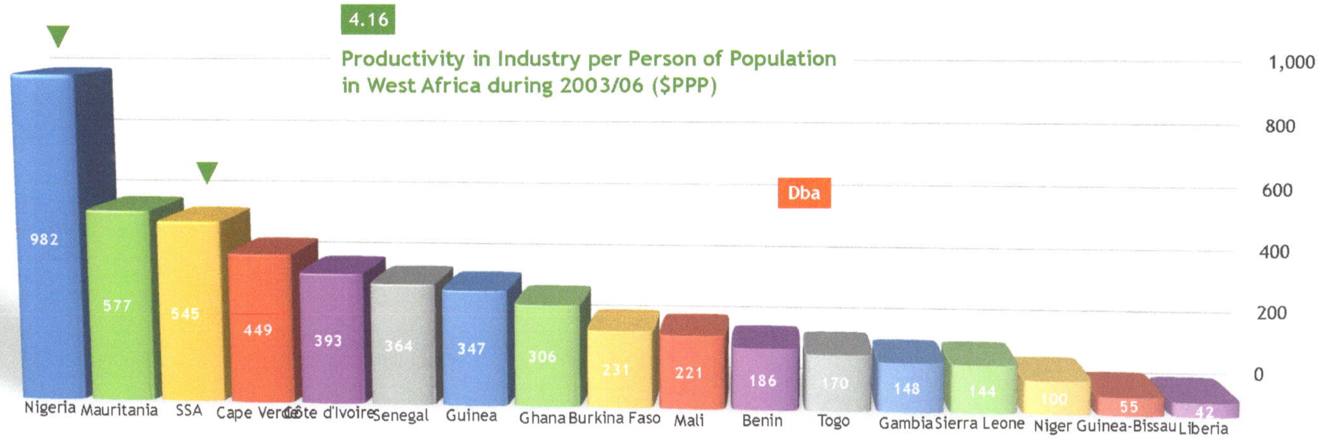


4.17

Productivity in Industry per Person of Population in Nigeria and Sub-Saharan Africa from 1999 to 2006 ($PPP)

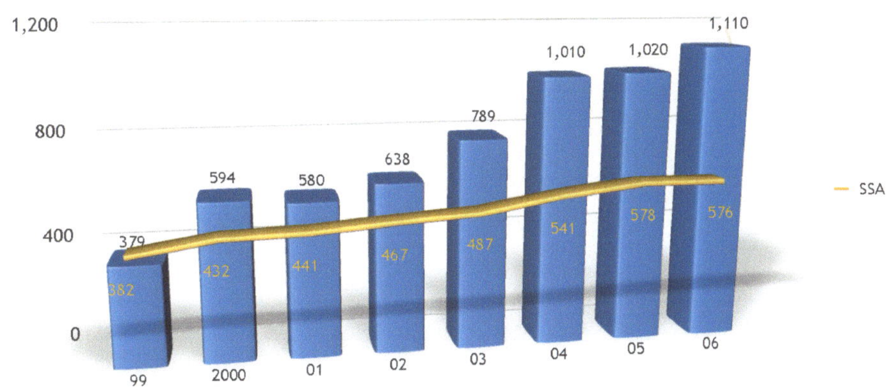


In West Africa, only Mauritania and Nigeria produced more industry output per person than the rest of Africa.

Here again, as it was for industry in % GDP, Nigeria grew industry output per person rapidly from 99 to 2006. But no celebrating until we've checked its manufacturing sector out.

Productivity in Industry as $PPP per Person in Sub-Saharan Africa during 2003-06: Rankings

| Rank | Country | Rank | Country | Rank | Country |
|---|---|---|---|---|---|
| 1 | Equatorial Guinea | 15 | Cape Verde | 29 | Uganda |
| 2 | Gabon | 16 | Côte d' Ivoire | 30 | Rwanda |
| 3 | Botswana | 17 | Senegal | 31 | Gambia, The |
| 4 | Seychelles | 18 | Guinea | 32 | Sierra Leone |
| 5 | Mauritius | 19 | Zambia | 33 | Madagascar |
| 6 | Angola | 20 | Ghana | 34 | Comoros |
| 7 | South Africa | 21 | Kenya | 35 | Malawi |
| 8 | Congo, Rep. | 22 | Burkina Faso | 36 | Niger |
| 9 | Swaziland | 23 | Mali | 37 | Central Afr. Rep. |
| 10 | Namibia | 24 | Eritrea | 38 | Ethiopia |
| 11 | Nigeria | 25 | Benin | 39 | Congo, Dem. Rep. |
| 12 | Chad | 26 | Mozambique | 40 | Burundi |
| 13 | Cameroon | 27 | Tanzania | 41 | Guinea-Bissau |
| 14 | Lesotho | 28 | Togo | | |
| **TOP** | | **MIDDLE** | | **BOTTOM** | |

Central Africa
East Africa
Southern Africa
West Africa

# 4.8 Growth in Industry Productivity

## ... but how fast?

However, many West Africans also grew industry output per person fairly rapidly. Half the sub-region did better than the Africa average.

| | 99-02 | 03-06 |
|---|---|---|
| Self-comparison to Preceding Period | | ▼ |
| Performance in Sub-Saharan Africa | ▲ | ▲ |
| Performance in West Africa | ▲ | ▲ |
| | Mali | Mauritania |
| | **Nigeria** | Liberia |
| | Sierra Leone | **Nigeria** |
| | Burkina Faso | Togo |
| | Cape Verde | Cape Verde |
| | Senegal | Sierra Leone |
| | Benin | Burkina Faso |
| | Gambia, The | Ghana |
| | Ghana | Côte d'Ivoire |
| | Guinea | Guinea |
| | Mauritania | Niger |
| | Niger | Benin |
| | Togo | Senegal |
| | Côte d'Ivoire | Mali |
| | Guinea-Bissau | Gambia, The |
| Primary Data: World Bank, IMF | Liberia | Guinea-Bissau |
| Performance among Oil-Exporters | ▲ | ▲ |
| | Equatorial Guinea | Chad |
| | **Nigeria** | Sudan |
| | Sudan | **Nigeria** |
| | Congo, Rep. | Equatorial Guinea |
| | Angola | Angola |
| | Chad | Congo, Rep. |
| | Cameroon | Gabon |
| | Gabon | Côte d'Ivoire |
| | Côte d'Ivoire | Cameroon |

4.18 Growth in Industry Productivity in West Africa during 2003/06 (%)

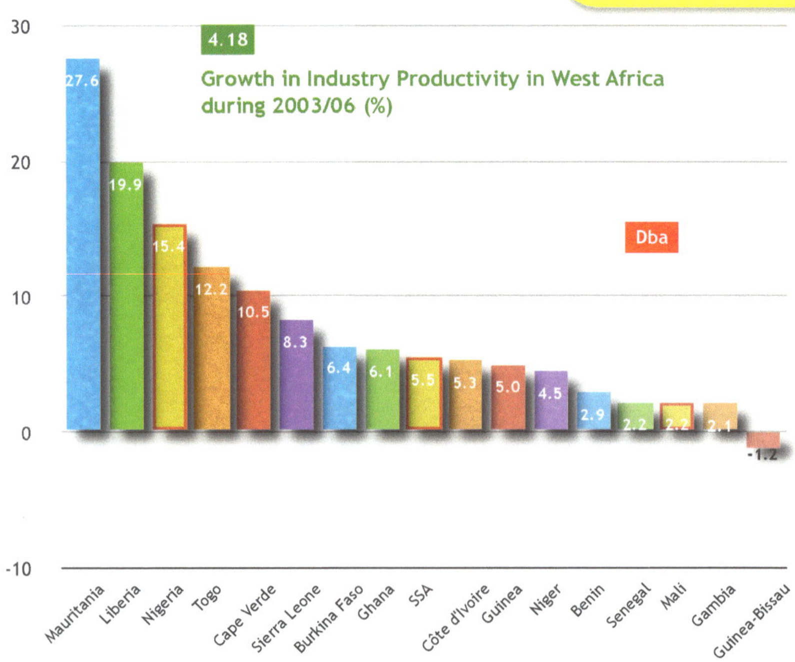


| | |
|---|---|
| ▲ | improved *or* better than average |
| ▼ | worsened *or* worse than average |
| ◁▷ | no change *or* average |

Nigeria's industry output grew fastest during 2000: 57%. It thereafter put the brakes on; only attempting another spike in 2004; but this time at 28%, half the previous pace.

Three of the four fastest growing industry sectors in Africa belonged to oil economies.

4.19

Growth in Industry Productivity in Nigeria and Sub-Saharan Africa from 1999 to 2006 (%)

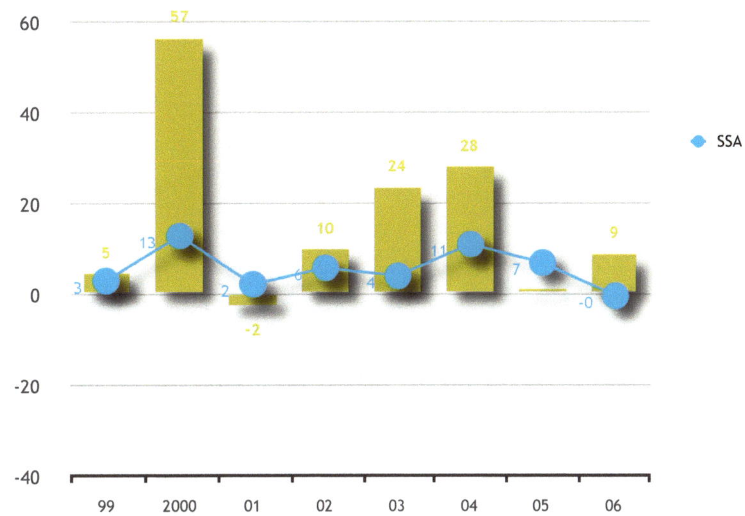


Growth in Industry Productivity in Sub-Saharan Africa during 2003-06: Rankings

| Rank | Country | Rank | Country | Rank | Country |
|---|---|---|---|---|---|
| 1 | Chad | 15 | Ethiopia | 29 | Swaziland |
| 2 | Nigeria | 16 | Botswana | 30 | Cameroon |
| 3 | Congo, Dem. Rep. | 17 | Kenya | 31 | Comoros |
| 4 | Equatorial Guinea | 18 | Gabon | 32 | Benin |
| 5 | Togo | 19 | Burkina Faso | 33 | Senegal |
| 6 | Zambia | 20 | Rwanda | 34 | Mauritius |
| 7 | Angola | 21 | Ghana | 35 | Mali |
| 8 | Madagascar | 22 | Namibia | 36 | Gambia, The |
| 9 | Mozambique | 23 | Côte d' Ivoire | 37 | Central Afr. Rep. |
| 10 | Cape Verde | 24 | Guinea | 38 | Uganda |
| 11 | Malawi | 25 | Lesotho | 39 | Guinea-Bissau |
| 12 | Congo, Rep. | 26 | Burundi | 40 | Seychelles |
| 13 | Tanzania | 27 | South Africa | 41 | Eritrea |
| 14 | Sierra Leone | 28 | Niger | | |
| TOP | | MIDDLE | | BOTTOM | |

Central Africa
East Africa
Southern Africa
West Africa

# 4.9 *Manufacturing* and *Other Industry* Productivity

*we've got to know which is which*

Primary Data: AfDB, World Bank

Crunch time.

Nigeria's high industry productivity turns out to comprise mostly of non-manufacturing activities.

As suspected, oil activity would consitute a huge chunk (part of the 92% "other industry").

In Nigeria, manufacturing accounted for only 8% of industry output: the smallest among West Africans.

The only other oil exporter in West Africa, Côte d'Ivoire, had manufacturing at 71% of its Industry sector output.

The proportions hardly changed in Nigeria during 1999-2006. Manufacturing continued to constitute about 8% of industry output throughout.

The rest would be made up largely of oil industry activity.

# 4. Economic Productivity

**4.20**

Productivity in Industry per Person of Population in West Africa during 2003/06 ($US)

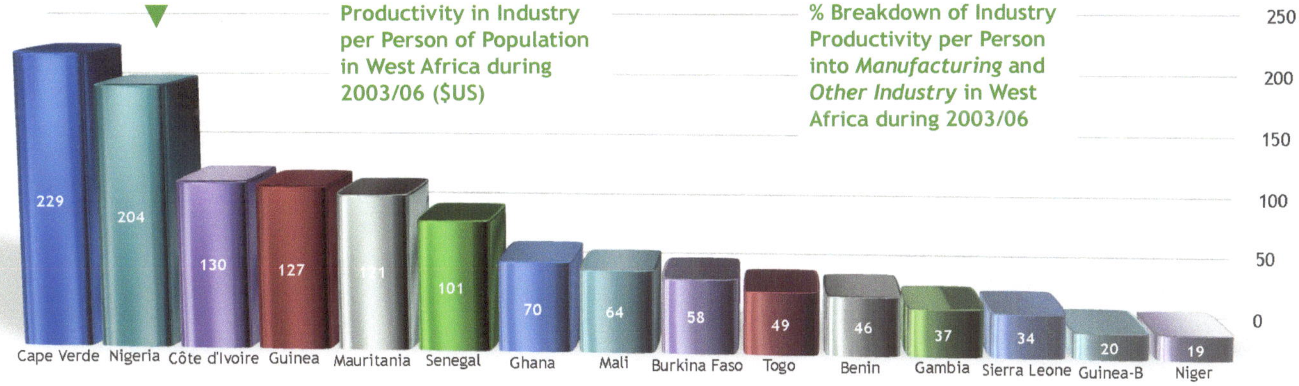


**4.21**

% Breakdown of Industry Productivity per Person into *Manufacturing* and *Other Industry* in West Africa during 2003/06

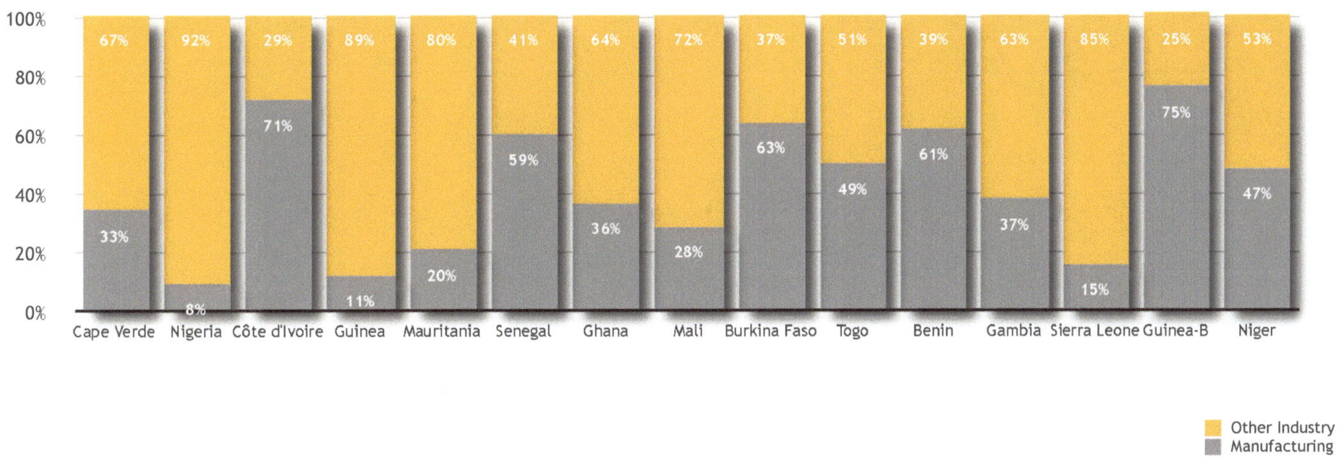


**4.22**

Productivity in Industry per Person of Population in Nigeria from 1999 to 2006 ($US)

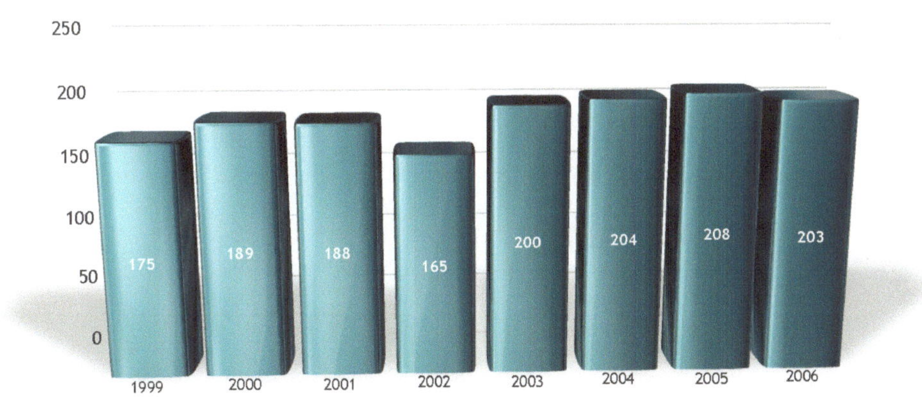


**4.23**

% Breakdown of Industry Productivity per Person into *Manufacturing* and *Other Industry* in Nigeria from 1999 to 2006

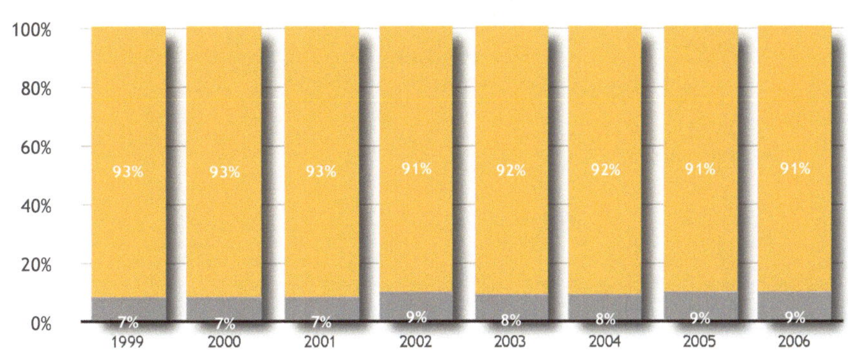

# 4.10 Growth in *Man.* and *Other Industry* Productivity

**4.26**

Growth in $US Industry Productivity in Nigeria from 1999 to 2006 (%)

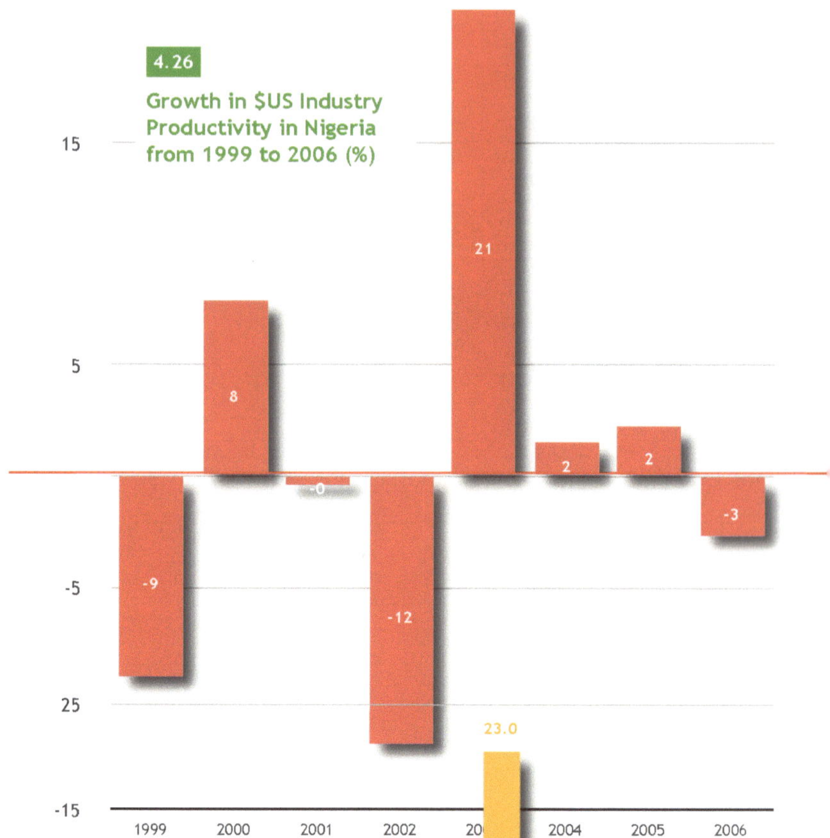


**4.27**

Growth in $US *Manufacturing* and *Other Industry* Productivity in Nigeria from 1999 to 2006 (%)

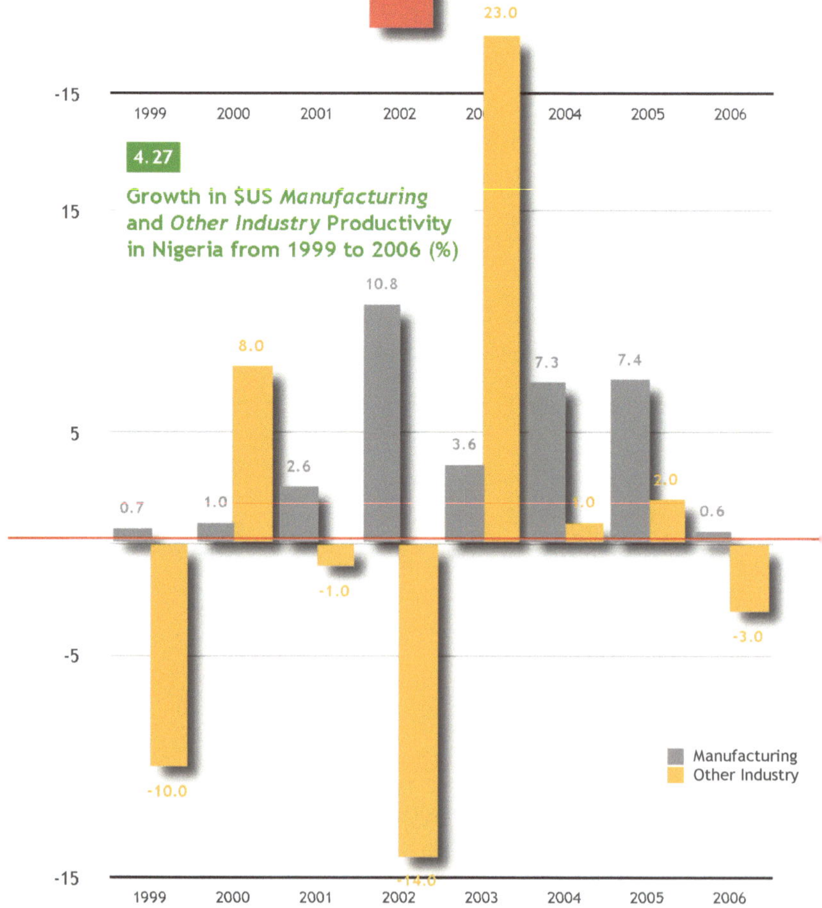


Primary Data: AfDB, World Bank

**and we've got to tell what's going where**

Nigeria's "Other Industry" grew in fits and starts. Whereas, manufacturing began to grow from 1999, then slowed during 2003. A good climb in 2004-05, but sharp drop in 2006.

4.24

Growth in $US Industry Productivity in West Africa during 2003/06 (%)

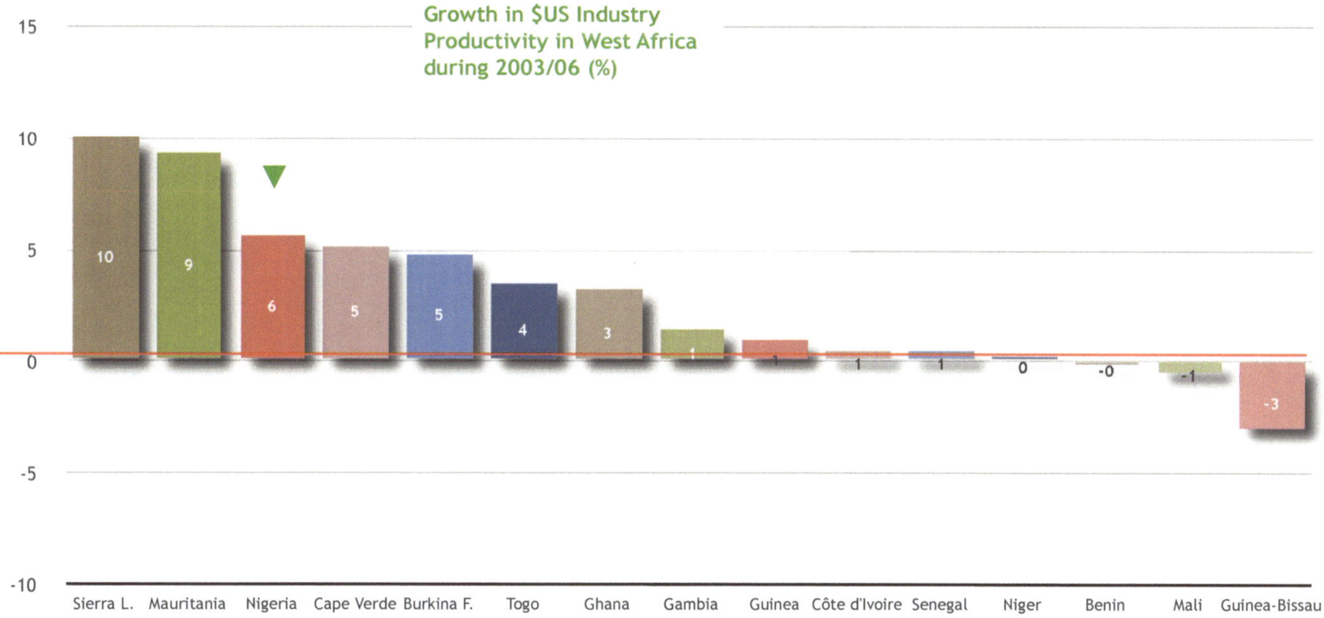


4.25

Growth in $US *Manufacturing* and *Other Industry* Productivity in West Africa during 2003/06 (%)

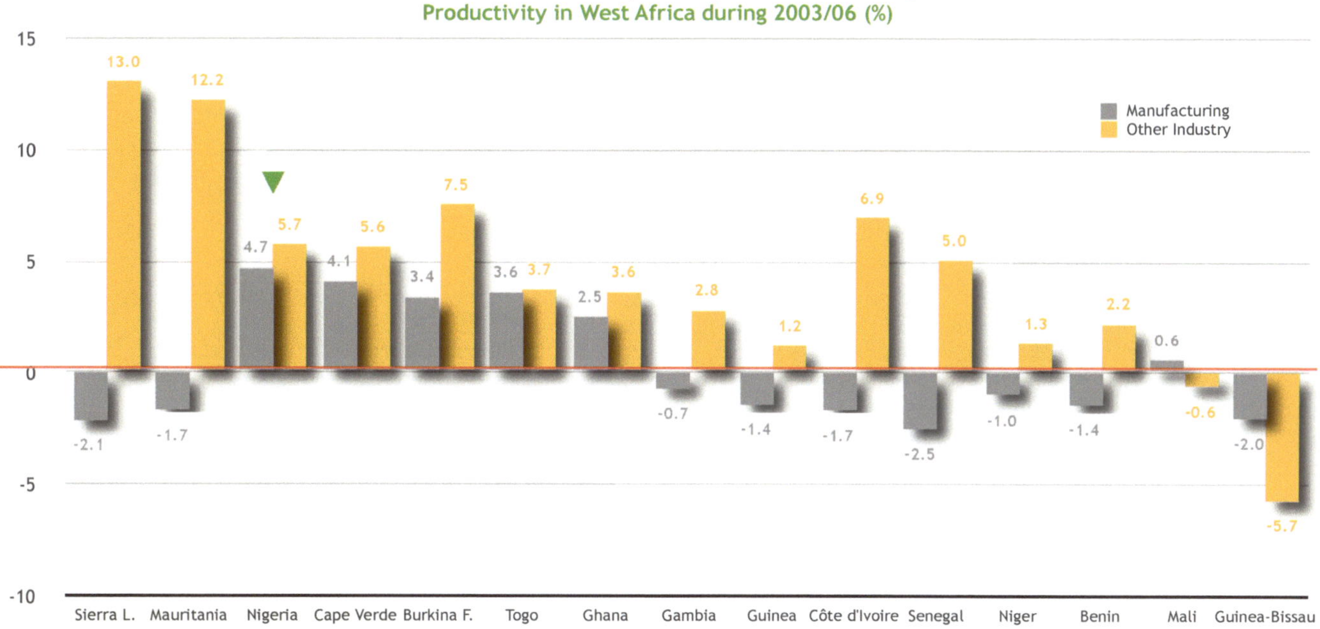


Growth patterns within the industry sector yield a similar story: high growth in general, and faster growth for "other industry" (read "oil"), at 5.7%, than for manufacturing, 4.7%.

# 4.11 Build-up in *Man.* and *Other Industry* Productivity

**or is it all just talk, talk?**

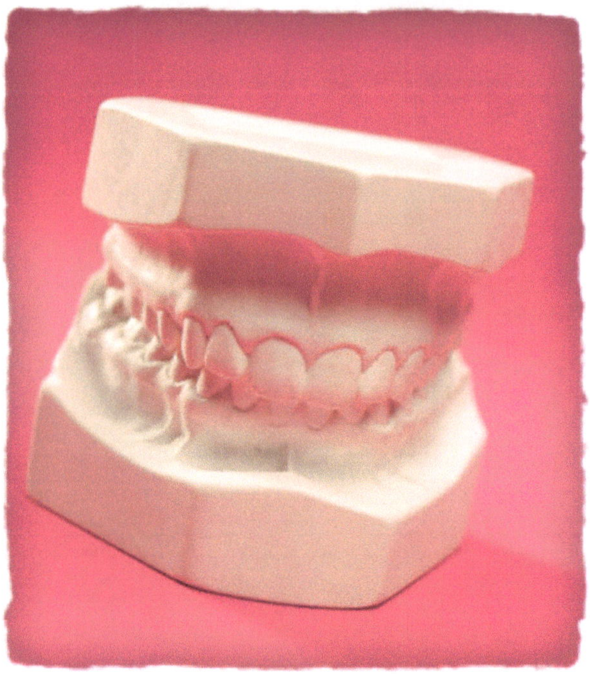

Gap between *Manufacturing* and *Other Industry* Productivity levels: 2000=100

| | West Africa | 2006 |
|---|---|---|
| 1 | Burkina Faso | 2.7 |
| 2 | Ghana | 3.9 |
| 3 | Guinea | 10.1 |
| 4 | Niger | 11.3 |
| 5 | Benin | 17.6 |
| 6 | Guinea-Bissau | 18.3 |
| 7 | Cape Verde | 18.4 |
| 8 | Togo | 21.0 |
| 9 | Gambia | 22.6 |
| 10 | Nigeria | 31.3 |
| 11 | Senegal | 33.1 |
| 12 | Mali | 50.4 |
| 13 | Côte d'Ivoire | 52.1 |
| 14 | Sierra Leone | 56.0 |
| 15 | Mauritania | 88.2 |
| 16 | Liberia | n/a |

| | oil exporters | 2006 |
|---|---|---|
| 1 | Angola | 14.2 |
| 2 | Gabon | 16.7 |
| 3 | Cameroon | 21.4 |
| 4 | Nigeria | 31.3 |
| 5 | Côte d'Ivoire | 52.1 |
| 6 | Congo, Rep. | 78.6 |
| 7 | Equatorial Guinea | 118.6 |
| 8 | Sudan | 157.3 |
| 9 | Chad | 1203.2 |

Primary Data: AfDB, World Bank

This section demonstrates the travel trajectories of industry sector growth, in its manufacturing and "other industry" components.

Burkina Faso made the best job of keeping both components moving apace. Mauritania made the worst of it. As at 2006, its industry sector components were 88 percentage points apart.

**4.28**

full lines: manufacturing
dotted lines: other industry

Build-up of *Manufacturing* and *Other Industry* Productivity from 2000 to 2006: Nigeria, Benin, Burkina Faso. 2000=100

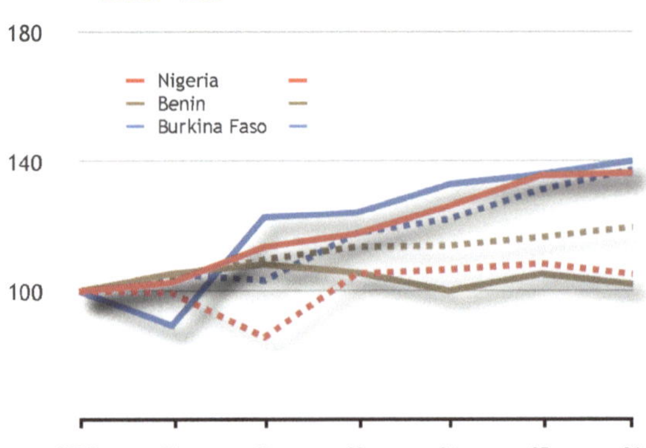


**4.29**

full lines: manufacturing
dotted lines: other industry

Build-up of *Manufacturing* and *Other Industry* Productivity from 2000 to 2006: Nigeria, Cape Verde, Côte d'Ivoire. 2000=100

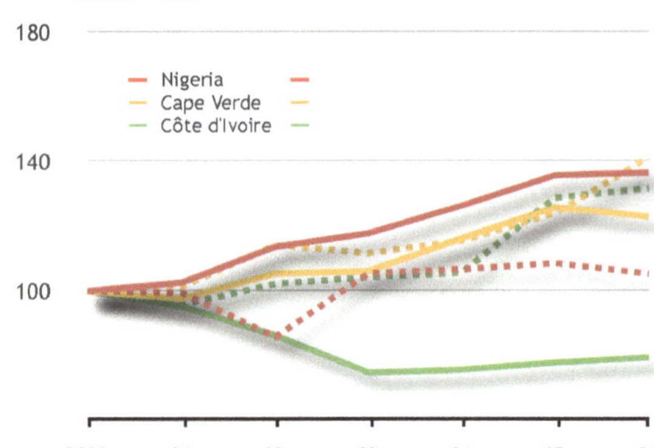

# 4. Economic Productivity

4.30

**Build-up of *Manufacturing* and *Other Industry* Productivity from 2000 to 2006: Nigeria, Gambia, Ghana. 2000=100**

full lines: manufacturing
dotted lines: other industry

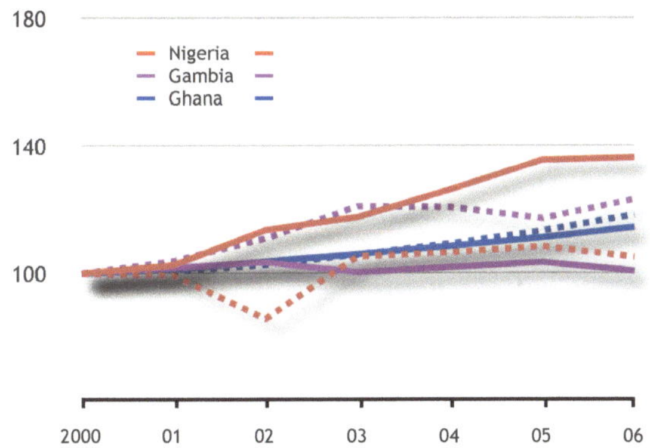


4.31

**Build-up of *Manufacturing* and *Other Industry* Productivity from 2000 to 2006: Nigeria, Guinea, Guinea-Bissau. 2000=100**

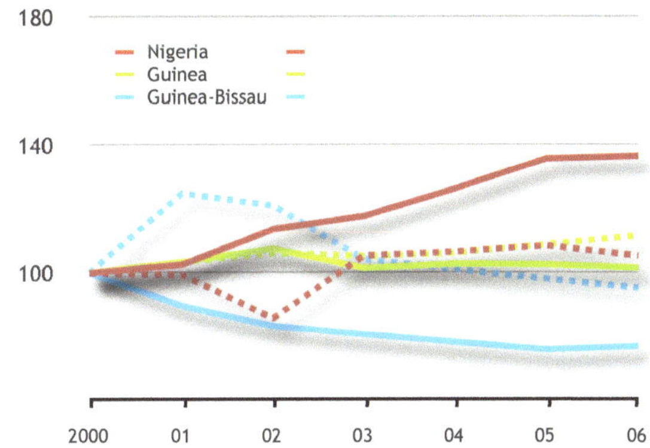


4.32

**Build-up of *Manufacturing* and *Other Industry* Productivity from 2000 to 2006: Nigeria, Mali, Mauritania. 2000=100**

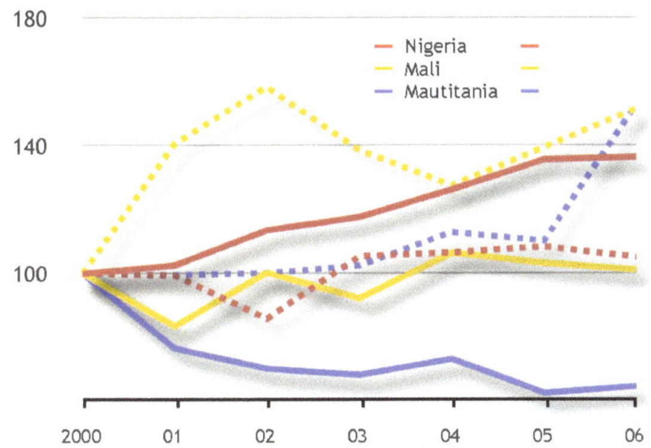


4.33

**Build-up of *Manufacturing* and *Other Industry* Productivity from 2000 to 2006: Nigeria, Niger, Senegal. 2000=100**

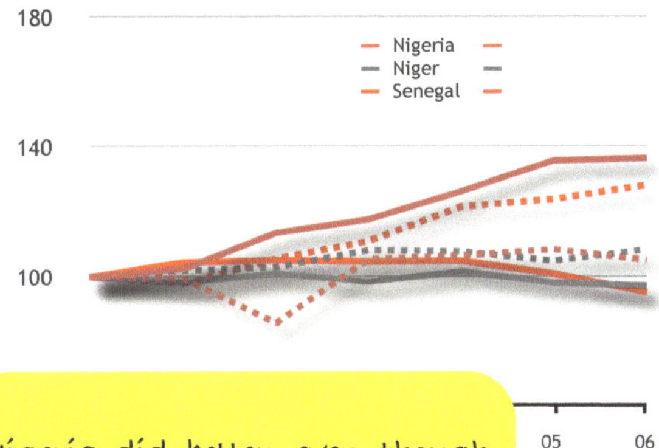


Nigeria did better, even though, at 31 percentage points, its gap is one of the worse ones in West Africa.

4.34

**Build-up of *Manufacturing* and *Other Industry* Productivity from 2000 to 2006: Nigeria, Sierra Leone, Togo. 2000=100**

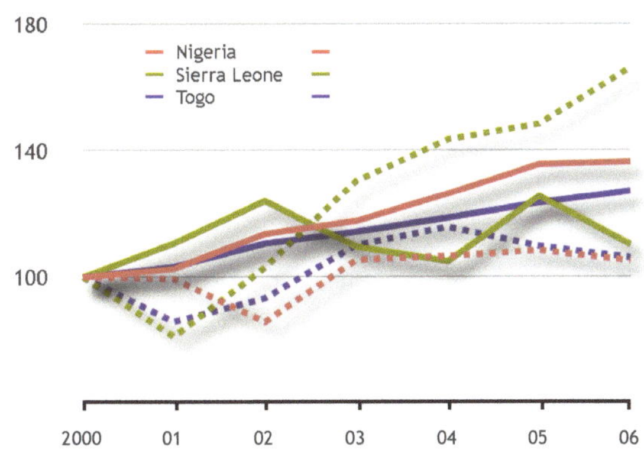


But, among the oil exporters, it was something of a triumph (finishing in the top half): Chad closed the group with a 1,203 percentage points gap!

A starker neglect of manufacturing for the easy but precarious attention to oil exports, is hardly conceivable.

# 4.12 Productivity in Services as % of GDP

**it's lunch break, that's why**

Primary Data: World Bank

| | 99-02 | 03-06 |
|---|---|---|
| Self-comparison to Preceding Period | | ▼ |
| Performance in Sub-Saharan Africa | ▼ | ▼ |
| Performance in West Africa | ▼ | ▼ |

**Performance in West Africa**

| 99-02 | 03-06 |
|---|---|
| Cape Verde | Cape Verde |
| Senegal | Senegal |
| Gambia, The | Benin |
| Côte d'Ivoire | Gambia, The |
| Benin | Côte d'Ivoire |
| Guinea | Guinea |
| Togo | Mauritania |
| Mauritania | Niger |
| Niger | Burkina Faso |
| Burkina Faso | Mali |
| Ghana | Ghana |
| Mali | Togo |
| Guinea-Bissau | Sierra Leone |
| **Nigeria** | Guinea-Bissau |
| Sierra Leone | **Nigeria** |
| Liberia | Liberia |

**Performance among Oil-Exporters**

| 99-02 | 03-06 |
|---|---|
| ▼ | ▼ |
| Côte d'Ivoire | Côte d'Ivoire |
| Chad | Cameroon |
| Cameroon | Sudan |
| Gabon | Gabon |
| Sudan | Chad |
| Congo, Rep. | Congo, Rep. |
| **Nigeria** | Angola |
| Angola | **Nigeria** |
| Equatorial Guinea | Equatorial Guinea |

4.35

Productivity in Services as % of GDP in West Africa during 2003/06

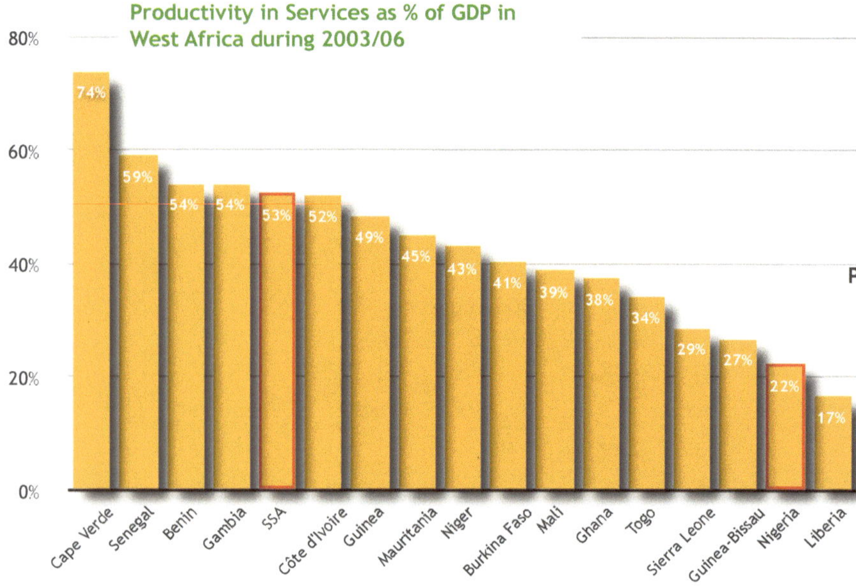


| | |
|---|---|
| ▲ | improved *or* better than average |
| ▼ | worsened *or* worse than average |
| ◁▷ | no change *or* average |

4.36

Productivity in Services as % of GDP in Nigeria and Sub-Saharan Africa from 1999 to 2006

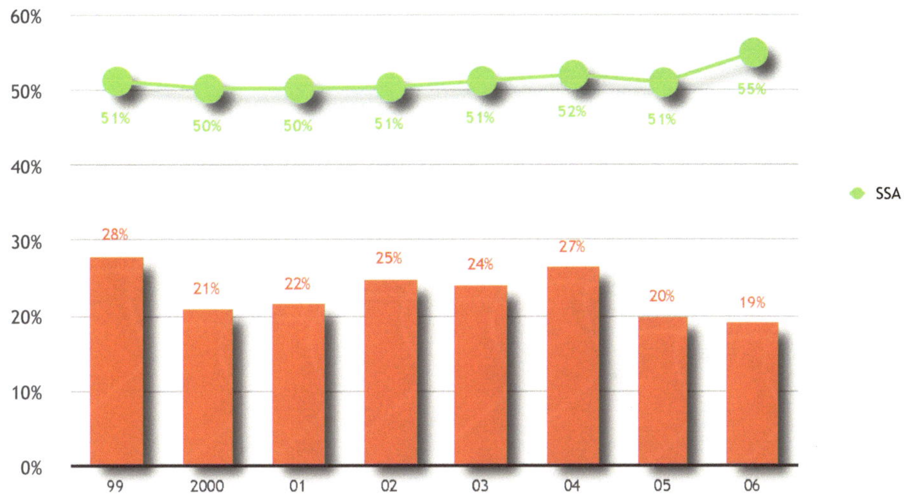


A graphic depiction of the distance between services size on the continent and services size in Nigeria. As much as 36% in 2006.

Nigeria's services sector is small indeed. It was only larger than Liberia's in West Africa, and was bottom also among the oil economies. It shrunk in 03/06 from its level in 99/02.

# 4.13 Productivity in Services as $PPP per Person

**unlock the value within**

Primary Data: World Bank, IMF

|  | 99-02 | 03-06 |
|---|---|---|
| Self-comparison to Preceding Period |  | ▲ |
| Performance in b-Saharan Africa | ▼ | ▼ |
| Performance in West Africa | ▼ | ▼ |
|  | Cape Verde | Cape Verde |
|  | Côte d'Ivoire | Senegal |
|  | Senegal | Côte d'Ivoire |
|  | Mauritania | Mauritania |
|  | Benin | Benin |
|  | Gambia, The | Gambia, The |
|  | Guinea | Guinea |
|  | Ghana | Ghana |
|  | Burkina Faso | Burkina Faso |
|  | Togo | **Nigeria** |
|  | **Nigeria** | Mali |
|  | Mali | Niger |
|  | Niger | Togo |
|  | Guinea-Bissau | Sierra Leone |
|  | Sierra Leone | Guinea-Bissau |
|  | Liberia | Liberia |
| Performance among Oil-Exporters | ▼ | ▼ |
|  | Gabon | Gabon |
|  | Côte d'Ivoire | Congo, Rep. |
|  | Congo, Rep. | Cameroon |
|  | Cameroon | Angola |
|  | Angola | Côte d'Ivoire |
|  | Sudan | Sudan |
|  | Chad | Chad |
|  | **Nigeria** | **Nigeria** |
|  | Equatorial Guinea | Equatorial Guinea |

As with services % GDP, so with services as output per person. 03/06 worse than 99/02; Nigeria worse than Africa; Nigeria worse than West Africa; Nigeria bottom of oil group.

| | |
|---|---|
| ▲ | improved *or* better than average |
| ▼ | worsened *or* worse than average |
| ◁▷ | no change *or* average |

## 4. Economic Productivity

4.37

Productivity in Services per Person of Population in West Africa during 2003/06 ($PPP)

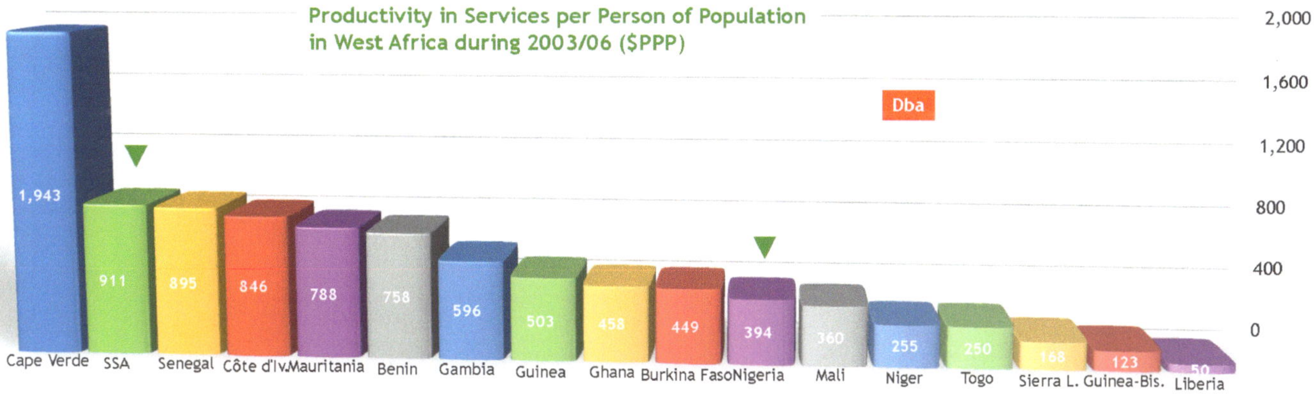


4.38

Productivity in Services per Person of Population in Nigeria and Sub-Saharan Africa from 1999 to 2006 ($PPP)

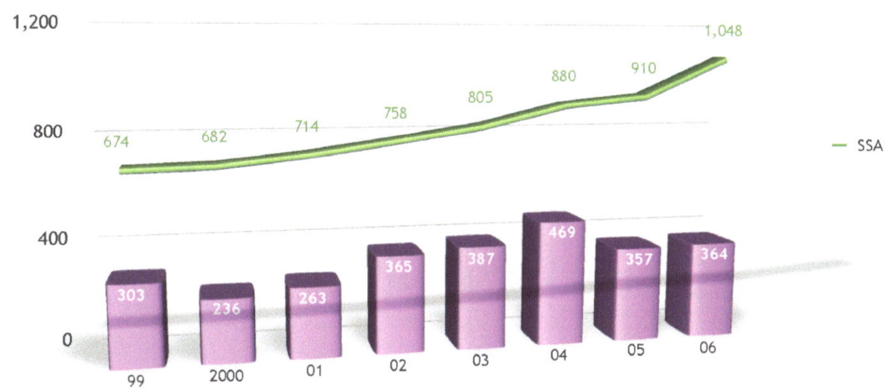


Productivity in Services as $PPP per Person in Sub-Saharan Africa during 2003-06: Rankings

| Rank | Country | Rank | Country | Rank | Country |
|---|---|---|---|---|---|
| 1 | Seychelles | 15 | Benin | 29 | Equatorial Guinea |
| 2 | Mauritius | 16 | Gambia, The | 30 | Mali |
| 3 | Botswana | 17 | Zambia | 31 | Mozambique |
| 4 | South Africa | 18 | Madagascar | 32 | Malawi |
| 5 | Gabon | 19 | Guinea | 33 | Rwanda |
| 6 | Namibia | 20 | Lesotho | 34 | Niger |
| 7 | Cape Verde | 21 | Eritrea | 35 | Togo |
| 8 | Swaziland | 22 | Ghana | 36 | Ethiopia |
| 9 | Congo, Rep. | 23 | Burkina Faso | 37 | Central Afr. Rep. |
| 10 | Cameroon | 24 | Chad | 38 | Sierra Leone |
| 11 | Senegal | 25 | Comoros | 39 | Burundi |
| 12 | Angola | 26 | Uganda | 40 | Guinea-Bissau |
| 13 | Côte d' Ivoire | 27 | Nigeria | 41 | Congo, Dem. Rep. |
| 14 | Kenya | 28 | Tanzania | | |
| TOP | | MIDDLE | | BOTTOM | |

Central Africa
East Africa
Southern Africa
West Africa

But, among Africa's oil economies, Gabon, Congo Rep., Cameroon, Angola and Côte d'Ivoire made it into Africa's top third. Everyone, that is, except Nigeria and 2 others.

# 4.14 Growth in Services Productivity

*force majeure*

| | 99-02 | 03-06 |
|---|---|---|
| Self-comparison to Preceding Period | | ▼ |
| Performance in Sub-Saharan Africa | ▲ | ▼ |

| Performance in West Africa | ▲ | ▼ |
|---|---|---|
| | Sierra Leone | Sierra Leone |
| | Cape Verde | Mali |
| | **Nigeria** | Cape Verde |
| | Mauritania | Senegal |
| | Benin | Burkina Faso |
| | Burkina Faso | Benin |
| | Guinea-Bissau | Ghana |
| | Mali | Niger |
| | Ghana | Gambia, The |
| | Senegal | Guinea |
| | Guinea | Mauritania |
| | Niger | **Nigeria** |
| | Liberia | Côte d'Ivoire |
| | Gambia, The | Guinea-Bissau |
| | Côte d'Ivoire | Liberia |
| | Togo | Togo |

Not encouraging news about the pace of services sector growth. Doesn't look like Nigeria will be catching up in a hurry.

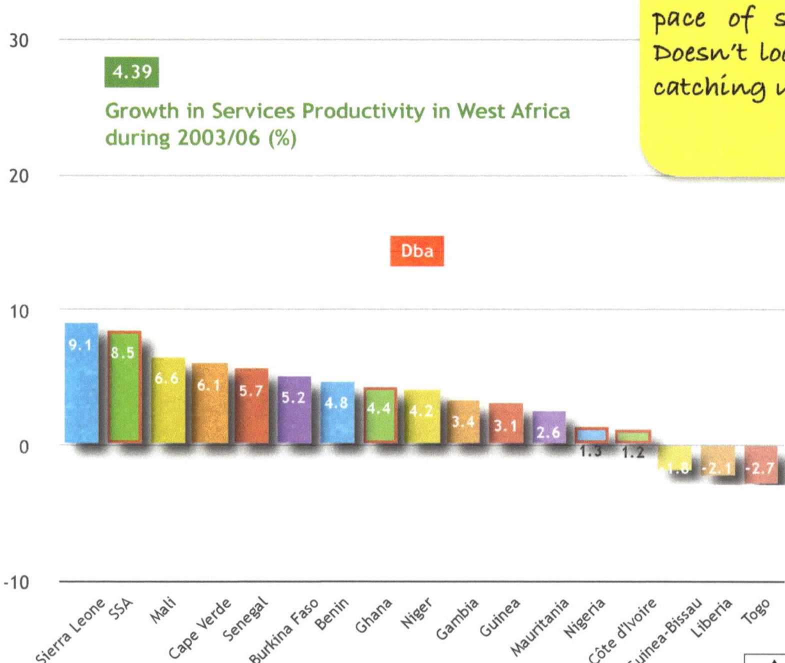


4.39 Growth in Services Productivity in West Africa during 2003/06 (%)

Primary Data: World Bank, IMF

| Performance among Oil-Exporters | ▲ | ▲ |
|---|---|---|
| | Equatorial Guinea | Angola |
| | **Nigeria** | Sudan |
| | Sudan | Cameroon |
| | Chad | **Nigeria** |
| | Cameroon | Côte d'Ivoire |
| | Angola | Congo, Rep. |
| | Côte d'Ivoire | Equatorial Guinea |
| | Congo, Rep. | Gabon |
| | Gabon | Chad |

| | |
|---|---|
| ▲ | improved *or* better than average |
| ▼ | worsened *or* worse than average |
| ◁▷ | no change *or* average |

4.40

**Growth in Services Productivity in Nigeria and Sub-Saharan Africa from 1999 to 2006 (%)**

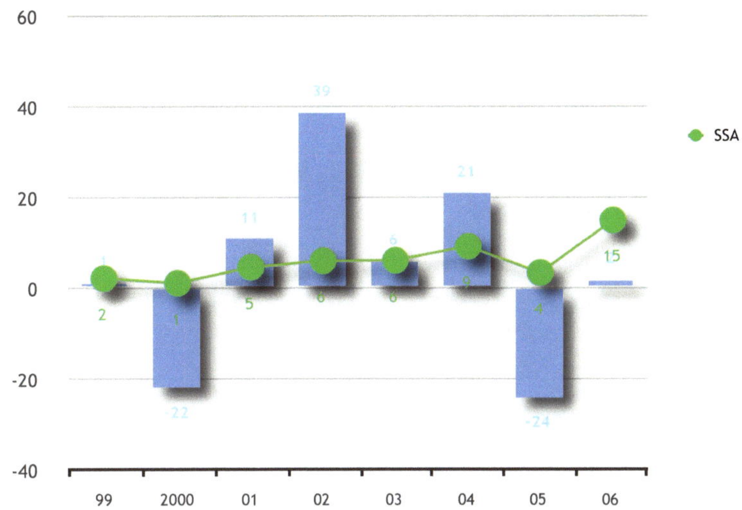


"Shall we grow, or shall we not?," Nigeria's services growth seems to ponder.

Bottom third in Africa.

**Growth in Services Productivity in Sub-Saharan Africa during 2003-06: Rankings**

| Rank | Country | Rank | Country | Rank | Country |
|---|---|---|---|---|---|
| 1 | Madagascar | 15 | Uganda | 29 | Seychelles |
| 2 | Botswana | 16 | Senegal | 30 | Comoros |
| 3 | Sierra Leone | 17 | Mozambique | 31 | Zambia |
| 4 | Angola | 18 | Burundi | 32 | Nigeria |
| 5 | Mauritius | 19 | Congo, Dem. Rep. | 33 | Côte d' Ivoire |
| 6 | South Africa | 20 | Kenya | 34 | Central Afr. Rep. |
| 7 | Ethiopia | 21 | Burkina Faso | 35 | Guinea-Bissau |
| 8 | Namibia | 22 | Benin | 36 | Congo, Rep. |
| 9 | Swaziland | 23 | Ghana | 37 | Equatorial Guinea |
| 10 | Malawi | 24 | Lesotho | 38 | Togo |
| 11 | Rwanda | 25 | Niger | 39 | Eritrea |
| 12 | Mali | 26 | Gambia, The | 40 | Gabon |
| 13 | Cape Verde | 27 | Cameroon | 41 | Chad |
| 14 | Tanzania | 28 | Guinea | | |
| TOP | | MIDDLE | | BOTTOM | |

Central Africa
East Africa
Southern Africa
West Africa

# 4.15 Build-up in Productivity in the 3 Sectors

*they'll need putting together*

Compared to Africa, Nigeria's productivity growth in the 3 sectors has at more than one point outstripped the continent's. But never definitively - except in the industry sector.

full lines: Nigeria
dotted lines: SSA

4.41

Build-up of Agriculture Productivity in Nigeria and Sub-Saharan Africa from 2000 to 2006. 2000=100

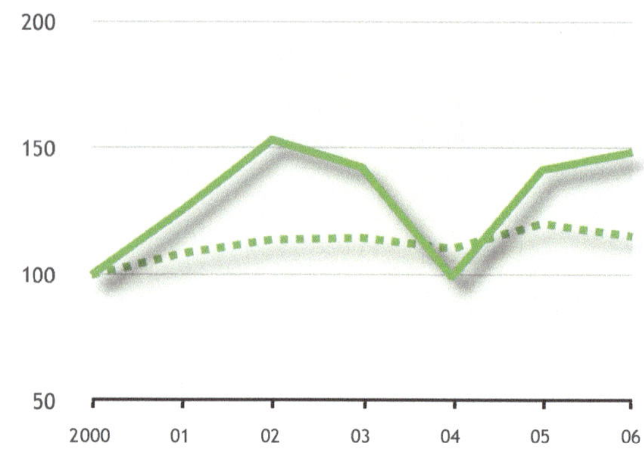


4.42

Build-up of Industry Productivity in Nigeria and Sub-Saharan Africa from 2000 to 2006. 2000=100

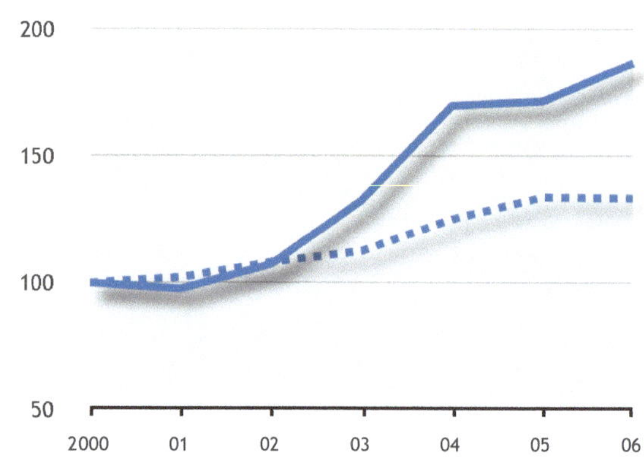


4.43

Build-up of Services Productivity in Nigeria and Sub-Saharan Africa from 2000 to 2006. 2000=100

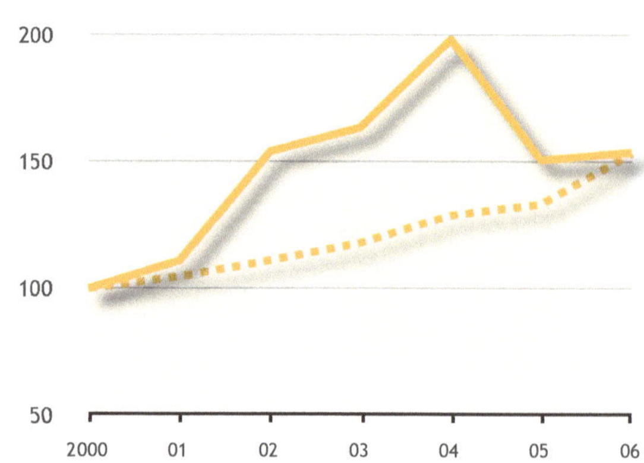


Primary Data: World Bank

4.44

Build-up of Productivity in Agriculture, Industry and Services in Nigeria from 2000 to 2006. 2000=100

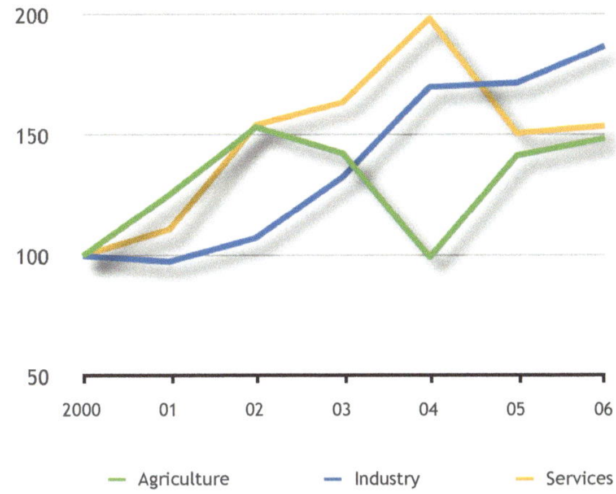


4.45

Build-up of Productivity in Agriculture, Industry and Services in Sub-Saharan Africa from 2000 to 2006. 2000=100

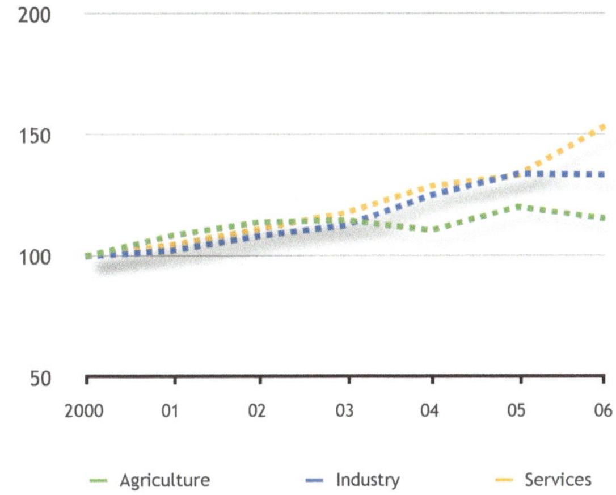


In effect, most of Africa has built up output in the 3 sectors steadily but definitively; climbing throughout, except for a small temporary dip in agriculture during 2004.

Nigeria's progress has been shaky and lacking in confidence. Clearly seen in chart 4.44.

Meantime, the rest of Africa built up productivity with some self-assurance; while Nigeria charted rougher paths. Even though it indeed made effective general upward movement.

On the whole, despite the petrifying hiccups, Nigeria does manage to build in 2006 on levels in 1999. But at no point did it look reassuringly sustainable.

That fast industry growth may not be cause for cheer, because it is down to the easy-money, postpone-the-evil-day, oil industry.

# Leaders & Stragglers

**milk, anyone?**

Nigeria squeezes into the top third. Better than most of the oil states. Albeit without a look of confidence to the job.

## Economic Productivity Rankings: 2003-06

| Rank | Country |
|---|---|
| 1 | Angola |
| 2 | Namibia |
| 3 | Botswana |
| 4 | Mauritius |
| 5 | Cape Verde |
| 6 | Swaziland |
| 7 | Gabon |
| 8 | Seychelles |
| 9 | South Africa |
| 10 | Ghana |
| | Tanzania |
| 11 | Nigeria |
| 12 | Kenya |
| | Equatorial Guinea |

TOP

| Rank | Country |
|---|---|
| 13 | Madagascar |
| 14 | Cameroon |
| 15 | Senegal |
| 16 | Zambia |
| 17 | Benin |
| 18 | Burkina Faso |
| 19 | Côte d' Ivoire |
| 20 | Chad |
| 21 | Congo, Rep. |
| | Gambia, The |
| 22 | Mali |
| 23 | Mozambique |
| 24 | Ethiopia |
| | Rwanda |

MIDDLE

| Rank | Country |
|---|---|
| 25 | Lesotho |
| 26 | Sierra Leone |
| 27 | Togo |
| 28 | Comoros |
| | Malawi |
| 29 | Uganda |
| 30 | Guinea |
| 31 | Eritrea |
| 32 | Congo, Dem. Rep. |
| 33 | Niger |
| 34 | Central Afr. Rep. |
| 35 | Burundi |
| 36 | Guinea-Bissau |

BOTTOM

Central Africa
East Africa
Southern Africa
West Africa

# Wrap-up: Economic Productivity

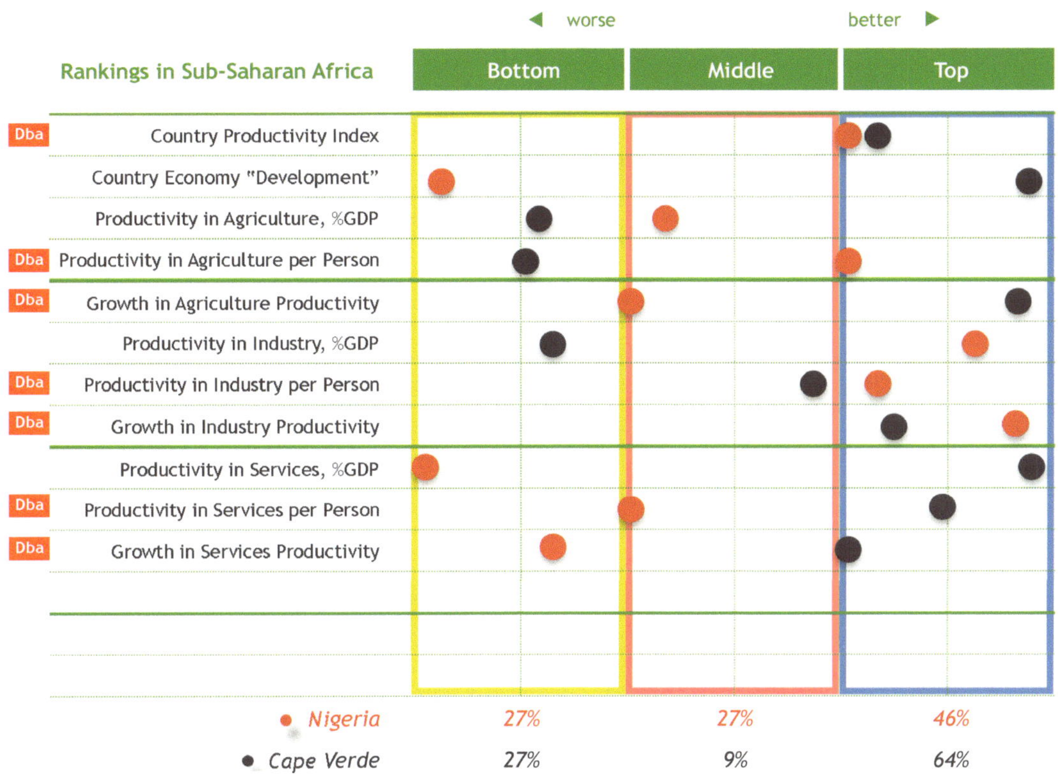


- Cape Verde, no. 1 in West Africa and no. 5 in Africa. Nigeria, no. 3 in West Africa and no. 11 in Africa.
- Nigeria has most of the indicators in the top segment (46%), as does Cape Verde (64%).
- Indeed, Nigeria performs well in the agriculture sector, but it needs to grow that productivity with greater urgency.
- In industry Nigeria is in top shape. However, near 92% of this is made up of oil extraction and exports, while manufacturing constitutes the remaining 8%.
- It is in services that Nigeria plunges. It doesn't manage to leave the bottom section. Cape Verde, by contrast, is in its element there.

# 5. Govt. Earnings & Spending

*cutting the coat, or growing the cloth?*

5.1 Fiscal Deficit & Surplus as % of GDP
5.2 Fiscal Deficit & Surplus as $PPP per Person
5.3 Government Earnings as % of GDP
5.4 Government Earnings per Person
5.5 Government Earnings & Spending as % of GDP
5.6 Government Earnings & Spending per Person
5.7 Growth in Govt. Earnings per Person
5.8 Build-up in Govt. Earnings & Spending
5.9 Current Account Balance as % of GDP
5.10 Debt Service as % of GNI
5.11 Build-up in Debt Service and GNI
Leaders & Stragglers
Wrap-up

The indices in this section involve the principal financial balances of the government. It is an area of macro-economic study that often appears confusing, but its overall intents and significance may be reasonably understood without complication.

## Government Earnings

Governments generally get their income from taxes and duties on goods and services produced within their shores or acquired via importation from the outside. Usually, it may be safely assumed that this is the case, even though there might be instances where a government derives revenue directly from the goods and services it itself produces (e.g. nationalised industries and businesses).

However, the more common trend is for "profit-focused" corporations to be run by the private sector, while the public sector generally renders those services that would otherwise generate profit only at inappropriately great cost to the end users (health, roads, and basic education, for example). Still, these services would not be significant earners of revenue for government, and government earnings would still largely be made up of taxes and duties of diverse sorts.

## Government Spending

Instead, those "unappealing" services borne by the government would often comprise government expenditure. Government spending would then often be services such as health mentioned above, and other infrastructure which only organisations the size and position of governments can provide: education, law & order establishments (security, police, armed forces, etc), and capital projects such as roads, and so on. Rather than a direct revenue-yielding expenditure, these outlays are often indirect incentives that boost aggregate demand (the consumer's purchase of products and services) by providing an enabling environment for the country's economic sectors to churn out products and services that its inhabitants would be financially enabled to purchase. That would usually be because those investments have led to job creation and increase in the inhabitants' purchasing power. And so on, in a production cycle (investment leading to production leading to consumption, and over again, in a continuity).

## Fiscal Deficit/Surplus

Also known as Fiscal Balance and Budget Deficit/Surplus. This is the left-over after government spending is deducted from its earnings, and is an important indicator of government performance.

The deficit or surplus sometimes expresses a government's ability to function on its own resources. Here, the desirable state is a surplus, but a deficit is permissible and, indeed, preferable, if it is due to government investment that will eventually drive domestic consumption (purchase of goods and services) and, consequently, domestic production (provision by industry of those goods and services to meet rising demand).

The size of a surplus or deficit is often expressed as a portion of GDP. We have, in addition, expressed it here as surplus/deficit per inhabitant of population in order to develop a picture of the level of government spending per inhabitant and its potential impact on their quality of life, and so qualify the deficit/surplus more accurately.

## Grants

Here, too, we have chosen the option of including grants - where present - as part of government revenue (they usually come in the shape of non-interest bearing foreign aid), rather than leaving them out. Our reasoning being that, in appraising a government's fiscal performance and discipline, the government should be assessed on the basis of all income at its disposal; and more so when such incomes come at no financial cost. (The volume of these grants is considered in more detail in chapter 8, "Self-Reliance".)

## Which: deficit or surplus?

There isn't an immediate good or bad, desirable or undesirable, interpretation to deficits and surpluses; it all depends on the reasons and purposes behind the shortfall or surplus. Deficits are indeed very good, as explained above, when they indicate a rise in spending by government that spurs on individual and industry spending or investment, because it thereby leads to economic growth. At the same time, though, a deficit might be evocative of financial recklessness.

## Debt Service

The matter of foreign debt is treated more exhaustively in chapter 8, "Self-Reliance". Here, we attempt to express the ability of the economies to sustain their debt levels, with respect to their earning power. Debt levels are usually expressed as percentages of GDP (to assess their size in relation to the overall economy) and as percentages of exports (to assess the ability of the country to offset these foreign debts, since exports are the main source of foreign currency earnings).

We have, instead, chosen to express debt service here as a percentage of GNI (Gross National Income, formerly GNP: Gross National Product), because this would involve both GDP and export earnings, and would also take into account other sources of a country's income besides those two, namely incomes such as remittances and investment earnings from abroad. Our idea being to evaluate the country's debt service levels by comparing it to the economy's total earnings, as it were.

## Current Account Balance

Current Account Balance is surplus or deficit that arises from the external trade transactions involving a country's residents interacting with non-residents. It is the part of "Balance of Payments" record of transactions that does not involve capital projects and investments across borders (e.g. Foreign Direct Investment, addressed in chapter 9). It rather measures the ease or otherwise, with which an economy can generate needed revenue from external trade (imports and exports) in goods and services.

Again, a current account deficit is not necessarily a malaise, but it has to be kept within appropriate limits, if a deficit is inevitable. Oil exporters, for example, will generally have stronger current account balances than their non-oil counterparts. It becomes incumbent on them to use these accumulated savings effectively.

## Build-up of Debt Service and GNI

By tying down both parameters to 100 in a common year (2000 here) and depicting their progress thereafter according to the actual rates of growth recorded during the subsequent years (here, 2001 to 2006), we provide an illustration of the appropriateness or otherwise of the country's pace of debt accumulation, and whether this debt has been transformed into revenue-yielding or value-generating assets and operations. The wider the distance between levels of debt service and levels of GNI build-up, the greater the possibility that debt accumulation has been reckless or ill-advised. At the same time, though, a large gulf might be the result of a deliberate – even if, audacious - move by the country to wipe debt off its books.

**Sources of Primary Data:** AfDB, IMF, World Bank

## Charts

5.1 Fiscal Deficit/Surplus in West Africa (% GDP) during 03/06
5.2 Fiscal Deficit/Surplus in West Africa (% GDP) during 07/08
5.3 Fiscal Deficit/Surplus in Nigeria and Sub-Saharan Africa (% GDP) from 1997 to 2008
5.4 Fiscal Deficit/Surplus per Person in West Africa ($PPP) during 03/06
5.5 Fiscal Deficit/Surplus per Person in West Africa ($PPP) during 07/08
5.6 Fiscal Deficit/Surplus per Person in Nigeria and Sub-Saharan Africa ($PPP) from 1997 to 2008
5.7 Govt. Earnings as % of GDP in West Africa during 2003/06
5.8 Govt. Earnings as % of GDP in Nigeria and Sub-Saharan Africa from 1997 to 2008
5.9 Govt. Earnings per Person ($PPP) in West Africa during 2003/06
5.10 Govt. Earnings per Person ($PPP) in Nigeria and Sub-Saharan Africa from 1997 to 2008
5.11 Govt. Earnings & Spending as % of GDP in West Africa during 2003/06
5.12 Govt. Earnings & Spending per Person ($PPP) in West Africa during 2003/06
5.13 Growth in Govt. Earnings per Person in West Africa during 2003/06
5.14 Build-up in Govt. Earnings & Spending in Nigeria and Sub-Saharan Africa from 2002 to 2008
5.15 Build-up in Govt. Earnings & Spending in Nigeria and Oil Exporters in Sub-Saharan Africa from 2002 to 2008
5.16 Current Account Balance as % of GDP in West Africa during 2003/06
5.17 Current Account Balance as % of GDP in Nigeria and Sub-Saharan Africa from 1999 to 2010
5.18 Debt Service as % of GNI in West Africa during 2003/06
5.19 Debt Service as % of GNI in Nigeria from 1999 to 2006
5.20 Build-up of Debt Service & GNI in Nigeria and Côte d'Ivoire from 2000 to 2006: 2000=100

- **Wrap-up**

# Tables

*1997-2002; 2003-2006; 2007-2008:*
- *self-comparison to preceding period;*
- *performance in S-Saharan Africa;*
- *performance in West Africa;*
- *performance among oil-exporters;*

*for:*

Fiscal Deficit & Surplus as % of GDP

Fiscal Deficit & Surplus per Person ($PPP)

Govt. Earnings as % of GDP

Govt. Earnings per Person ($PPP)

Current Account Balance as % of GDP

*2003-2006; 2007-2008:*
- *self-comparison to preceding period;*
- *performance in S-Saharan Africa;*
- *performance in West Africa;*
- *performance among oil-exporters;*

*for:*

Growth in Govt. Earnings per Person

*1999-2002; 2003-2006:*
- *self-comparison to preceding period;*
- *performance in S-Saharan Africa;*
- *performance in West Africa;*
- *performance among oil-exporters;*

*for:*

Debt Service as % of GNI

- Govt. Earnings as % of GDP in Sub-Saharan Africa during 2003-06: Rankings
- Govt. Earnings per Person ($PPP) in Sub-Saharan Africa during 2003-06: Rankings
- Growth in Govt. Earnings per Person in Sub-Saharan Africa during 2003-06: Rankings
- Gap between GNI and Debt Service Build-up Levels by 2006 in West Africa and among Africa's Oil Exporters: 2000=100
- **Govt. Earnings & Spending Rankings: 2003-06**

# 5.1 Fiscal Deficit & Surplus as % of GDP

***is it good news, or bad?***

| | 97-02 | 03-06 | 07-08 |
|---|---|---|---|
| Self-comparison to Preceding Period | | ▲ | ▼ |
| Performance in Sub-Saharan Africa | ▲ | ▲ | ▲ |
| Performance in West Africa | ▲ | ▲ | ▲ |
| | Benin | Niger | Sierra Leone |
| | Senegal | Mali | **Nigeria** |
| | Côte d'Ivoire | **Nigeria** | Liberia |
| | **Nigeria** | Burkina Faso | Guinea |
| | Togo | Liberia | Côte d'Ivoire |
| | Guinea | Sierra Leone | Gambia, The |
| | Mali | Togo | Benin |
| | Burkina Faso | Benin | Niger |
| | Niger | Côte d'Ivoire | Togo |
| | Gambia, The | Senegal | Cape Verde |
| | Ghana | Ghana | Mali |
| | Sierra Leone | Guinea | Guinea-Bissau |
| | Cape Verde | Cape Verde | Senegal |
| | Guinea-Bissau | Gambia, The | Burkina Faso |
| | Liberia | Guinea-Bissau | Ghana |

Even though Nigeria's balance during 07-08 is a step-down from the preceding years', it still outperformed almost all of West Africa during the 11 years from 1997.

| | 97-02 | 03-06 | 07-08 |
|---|---|---|---|
| Performance among Oil-Exporters | ▼ | ▼ | ▼ |
| | Equatorial Guinea | Equatorial Guinea | Equatorial Guinea |
| | Gabon | Cameroon | Congo, Rep. |
| | Cameroon | Congo, Rep. | Gabon |
| | Côte d'Ivoire | Gabon | Angola |
| | **Nigeria** | **Nigeria** | **Nigeria** |
| | Chad | Angola | Cameroon |
| | Congo, Rep. | Chad | Chad |
| | Angola | Côte d'Ivoire | Côte d'Ivoire |

Something missing, though, when ranked alongside other oil exporters. Nigeria didn't outperform the majority. Rather, it was sat rigidly in the bottom half.

Primary Data: IMF

| | |
|---|---|
| ▲ | "movement towards surplus" OR "above average" |
| ▼ | "movement towards deficit" OR "below average" |
| ◁▷ | no change *or* average |

5.1

Fiscal Deficit/Surplus in West Africa (% GDP) during 03/06

5.2

Fiscal Deficit/Surplus in West Africa (% GDP) during 07/08

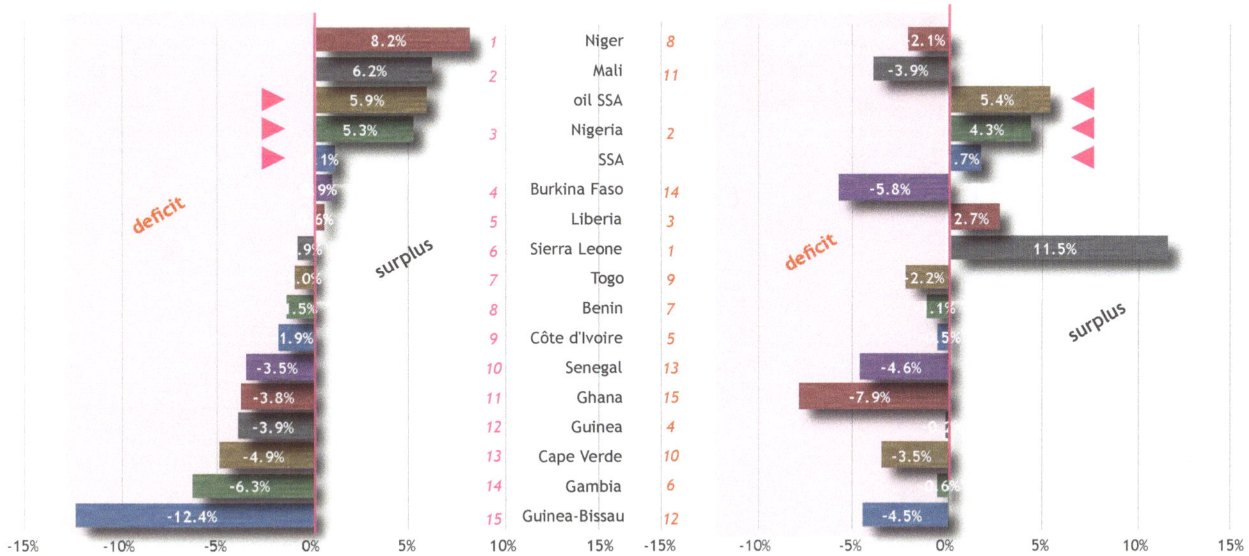


A third of West Africa (5 countries) spent within their means in 03/06. By 07/08, they dropped to 3. Nigeria & Liberia were the only countries running a surplus during both periods.

On the average, across Africa, most govts seemed to exercise fiscal discipline, with surpluses of about 1.1% and 1.7% during 03-06 and 07-08, respectively.

The oil countries, not unexpectedly, ran a high surplus.

5.3

Fiscal Deficit/Surplus in Nigeria and Sub-Saharan Africa (% GDP) from 1997 to 2008

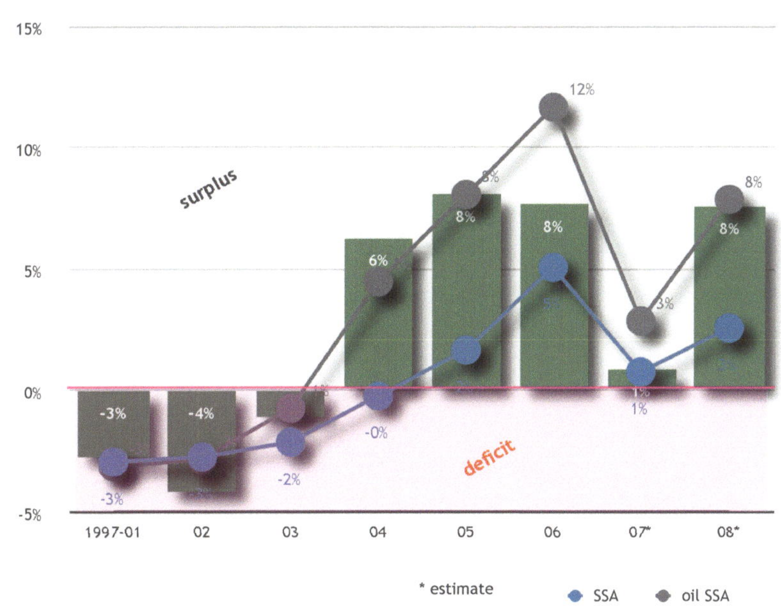


In an interesting group-play, all of Africa seemed to follow an identical trajectory during 1997-2008: deficits in 97-03, surpluses in 04 to 08, but with a big dip in 07.

It is likely this reflects the movement of commodity prices in the international market, particularly in oil and agricultural products.

# 5.2 Fiscal Deficit & Surplus per Person ($PPP)

## it's all he's been left with

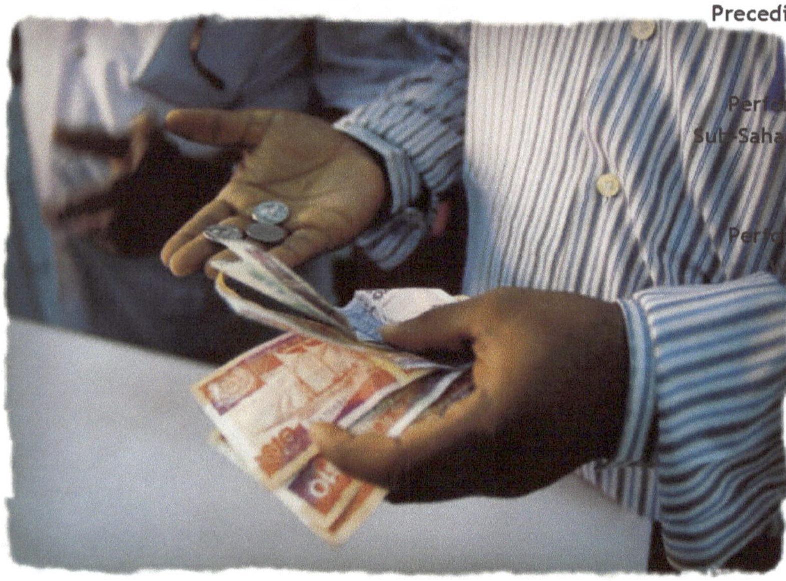

When fiscal balance is expressed as $ per inhabitant, the same picture plays out, as did for balance expressed as % of GDP.

| | 97-02 | 03-06 | 07-08 |
|---|---|---|---|
| Self-comparison to Preceding Period | | ▲ | ▼ |
| Performance in Sub-Saharan Africa | ▲ | ▲ | ▲ |
| Performance in West Africa | ▲ | ▲ | ▲ |
| | Benin | **Nigeria** | **Nigeria** |
| | Senegal | Mali | Sierra Leone |
| | Togo | Niger | Liberia |
| | Niger | Burkina Faso | Guinea |
| | Côte d'Ivoire | Liberia | Côte d'Ivoire |
| | Mali | Sierra Leone | Gambia, The |
| | **Nigeria** | Togo | Niger |
| | Guinea | Benin | Benin |
| | Burkina Faso | Côte d'Ivoire | Togo |
| | Sierra Leone | Guinea | Guinea-Bissau |
| | Gambia, The | Ghana | Mali |
| | Guinea-Bissau | Senegal | Burkina Faso |
| | Ghana | Guinea-Bissau | Senegal |
| | Cape Verde | Gambia, The | Ghana |
| | Liberia | Cape Verde | Cape Verde |

Nigeria better than most of West Africa, but not as good as its fellow oil exporters, and not keeping up in 07-08 with the pre-07 levels.

| | 97-02 | 03-06 | 07-08 |
|---|---|---|---|
| Performance among Oil-Exporters | ▼ | ▼ | ▼ |
| | Equatorial Guinea | Equatorial Guinea | Equatorial Guinea |
| | Gabon | Gabon | Gabon |
| | Cameroon | Congo, Rep. | Congo, Rep. |
| | Côte d'Ivoire | Cameroon | Angola |
| | **Nigeria** | Angola | **Nigeria** |
| | Chad | **Nigeria** | Cameroon |
| | Congo, Rep. | Chad | Chad |
| | Angola | Côte d'Ivoire | Côte d'Ivoire |

Primary Data: IMF

| | |
|---|---|
| ▲ | "movement towards surplus" OR "above average" |
| ▼ | "movement towards deficit" OR "below average" |
| ◁▷ | no change *or* average |

5.4

Fiscal Deficit/Surplus per Person in West Africa ($PPP) during 03/06

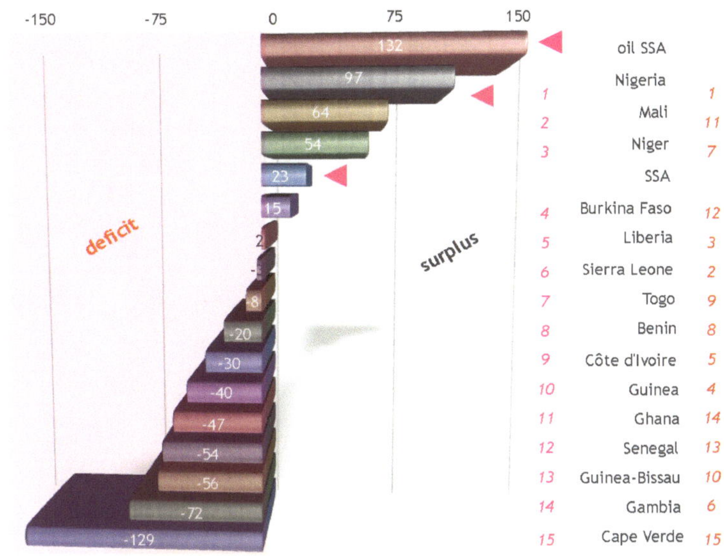


5.5

Fiscal Deficit/Surplus per Person in West Africa ($PPP) during 07/08

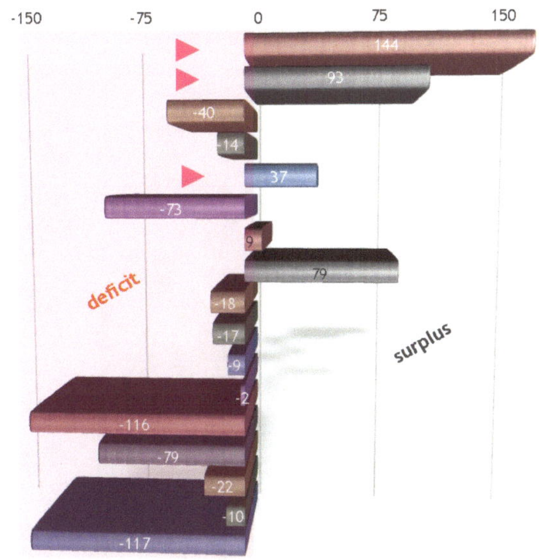


This time, fewer than 5 countries in West Africa spent within their means.

Across Africa, on average, govts ended up with a surplus of $23 and $37 per person in 03-06 and 07-08 respectively.

5.6

Fiscal Deficit/Surplus per Person in Nigeria and Sub-Saharan Africa ($PPP) from 1997 to 2008

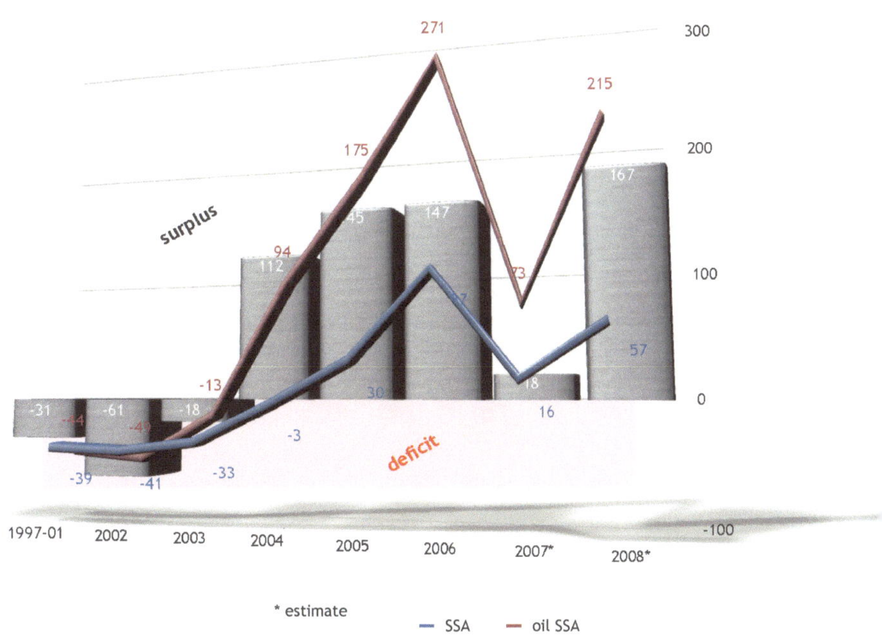


The highest surpluses were registered by the oil economies during both periods.

Again, during the years between 1997 & 2008, Nigeria & most of Africa followed the same trajectory of deficit, surplus, slump but still surplus, then recovery in surplus again.

# 5.3 Govt. Earnings as % of GDP

**there lies your fortune**

| | 97-02 | 03-06 | 07-08 |
|---|---|---|---|
| Self-comparison to Preceding Period | | ▲ | ▼ |
| Performance in Sub-Saharan Africa | ▼ | ▼ | ▼ |
| Performance in West Africa | ▲ | ▲ | ▼ |
| | Cape Verde | Liberia | Liberia |
| | Gambia, The | Gambia, The | Guinea-Bissau |
| | Guinea-Bissau | Cape Verde | Gambia, The |
| | Ghana | Ghana | Cape Verde |
| | **Nigeria** | Guinea-Bissau | Ghana |
| | Senegal | **Nigeria** | Senegal |
| | Côte d'Ivoire | Senegal | Benin |
| | Benin | Mali | Côte d'Ivoire |
| | Sierra Leone | Benin | Mali |
| | Togo | Sierra Leone | Togo |
| | Mali | Togo | **Nigeria** |
| | Burkina Faso | Côte d'Ivoire | Burkina Faso |
| | Guinea | Burkina Faso | Niger |
| | Niger | Niger | Sierra Leone |
| | Liberia | Guinea | Guinea |
| Performance among Oil-Exporters | ▼ | ▼ | ▼ |
| | Angola | Angola | Congo, Rep. |
| | Gabon | Equatorial Guinea | Equatorial Guinea |
| | Congo, Rep. | Congo, Rep. | Angola |
| | Equatorial Guinea | Gabon | Gabon |
| | **Nigeria** | **Nigeria** | Chad |
| | Côte d'Ivoire | Cameroon | Côte d'Ivoire |
| | Cameroon | Côte d'Ivoire | Cameroon |
| | Chad | Chad | **Nigeria** |

Not good news about Nigeria's govt. receipts. If the country kept up surpluses (as the previous sections hold) it must be that it tightened its spending, since it didn't grow revenue.

Indeed, Nigeria's revenue, as a proportion of its economy size, fell to below West Africa and oil exporters levels.

Primary Data: IMF

| | |
|---|---|
| ▲ | increased earnings *or* above average |
| ▼ | decreased earnings *or* below average |
| ◁▷ | no change *or* average |

**5.7**

## Govt. Earnings as % of GDP in West Africa during 2003/06

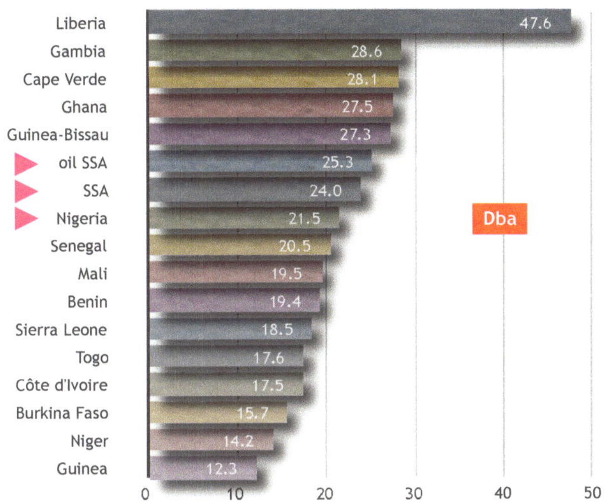


**5.8**

## Govt. Earnings as % of GDP in Nigeria and Sub-Saharan Africa from 1997 to 2008

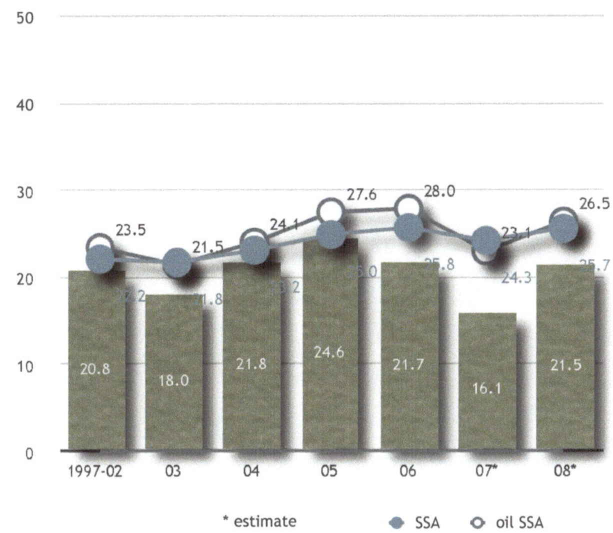


In the end, it sat bang in the middle of Sub-Saharan Africa.

This depleting revenue might have been due to any number of factors, including a possible lax regime of duties and tax collection.

### Govt. Earnings as % of GDP in Sub-Saharan Africa during 2003-06: Rankings

| Rank | Country | Rank | Country | Rank | Country |
|---|---|---|---|---|---|
| 1 | Lesotho | 15 | Guinea-Bissau | 29 | Sierra Leone |
| 2 | Seychelles | 16 | Malawi | 30 | Togo |
| 3 | Botswana | 17 | Rwanda | 31 | Cameroon |
| 4 | Swaziland | 18 | South Africa | 32 | Côte d' Ivoire |
| 5 | Namibia | 19 | Ethiopia | 33 | Congo, Dem. Rep. |
| 6 | Eritrea | 20 | Nigeria | 34 | Comoros |
| 7 | Angola | 21 | Kenya | 35 | Burkina Faso |
| 8 | Burundi | 22 | Uganda | 36 | Chad |
| 9 | Equatorial Guinea | 23 | Senegal | 37 | Tanzania |
| 10 | Congo, Rep. | 24 | Mauritius | 38 | Niger |
| 11 | Gabon | 25 | Mozambique | 39 | Madagascar |
| 12 | Gambia, The | 26 | Mali | 40 | Guinea |
| 13 | Cape Verde | 27 | Benin | 41 | Central Afr. Rep. |
| 14 | Ghana | 28 | Zambia | | |
| TOP | | MIDDLE | | BOTTOM | |

# 5.4 Govt. Earnings per Person ($PPP)

*trickles, or pouring rain?*

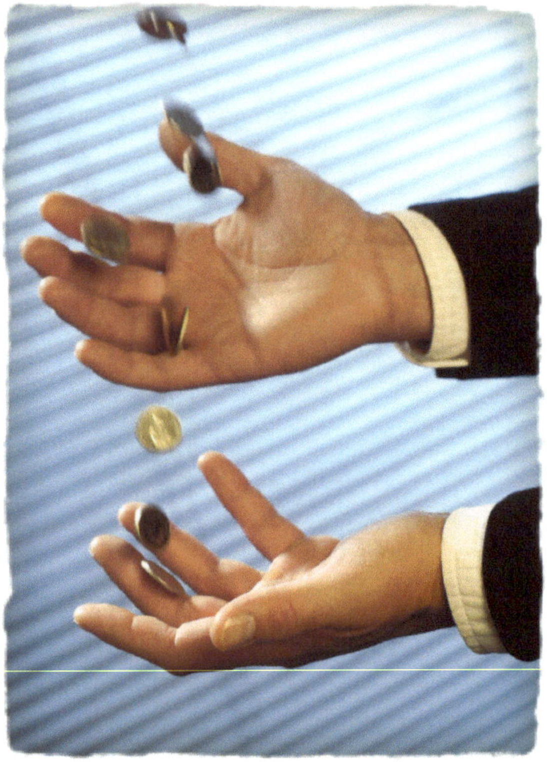

| | 97-02 | 03-06 | 07-08 |
|---|---|---|---|
| Self-comparison to Preceding Period | | ▲ | ▲ |
| Performance in Sub-Saharan Africa | ▼ | ▼ | ▼ |
| Performance in West Africa | ▲ | ▲ | ▲ |

| 97-02 | 03-06 | 07-08 |
|---|---|---|
| Cape Verde | Cape Verde | Cape Verde |
| Côte d'Ivoire | **Nigeria** | Gambia, The |
| Gambia, The | Ghana | **Nigeria** |
| **Nigeria** | Gambia, The | Ghana |
| Senegal | Senegal | Senegal |
| Benin | Côte d'Ivoire | Côte d'Ivoire |
| Ghana | Benin | Benin |
| Burkina Faso | Mali | Burkina Faso |
| Guinea-Bissau | Burkina Faso | Mali |
| Guinea | Liberia | Liberia |
| Mali | Togo | Guinea-Bissau |
| Togo | Guinea | Togo |
| Niger | Guinea-Bissau | Guinea |
| Sierra Leone | Sierra Leone | Niger |
| Liberia | Niger | Sierra Leone |

Same verdict when assessed in money units: decline in Nigeria govt. earnings, although it was one of the better performers in West Africa. It did worse than most of the wider continent.

| | 97-02 | 03-06 | 07-08 |
|---|---|---|---|
| Performance among Oil-Exporters | ▼ | ▼ | ▼ |
| | Gabon | Equatorial Guinea | Equatorial Guinea |
| | Angola | Gabon | Gabon |
| | Equatorial Guinea | Angola | Angola |
| | Congo, Rep. | Congo, Rep. | Congo, Rep. |
| | Côte d'Ivoire | **Nigeria** | Cameroon |
| | Cameroon | Cameroon | **Nigeria** |
| | **Nigeria** | Côte d'Ivoire | Chad |
| | Chad | Chad | Côte d'Ivoire |

Nigeria ended up worse than the oil group, just as it did when earnings was measured in %GDP terms.

Primary Data: IMF

| | |
|---|---|
| ▲ | increased earnings *or* above average |
| ▼ | decreased earnings *or* below average |
| ◁▷ | no change *or* average |

# 5. Govt. Earnings & Spending

5.9

Govt. Earnings per Person ($PPP) in West Africa during 2003/06

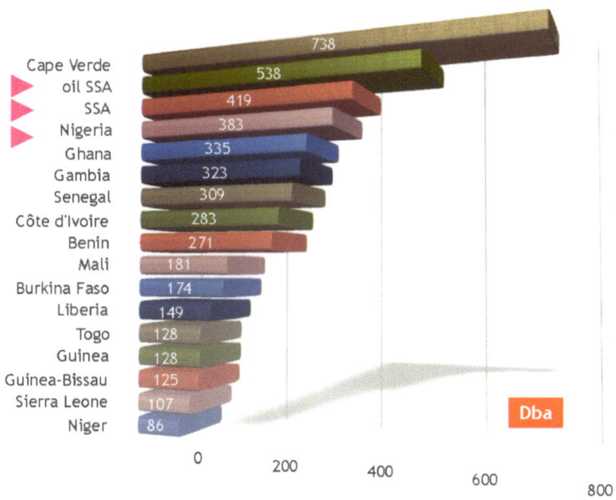


5.10

Govt. Earnings per Person ($PPP) in Nigeria and Sub-Saharan Africa from 1997 to 2008

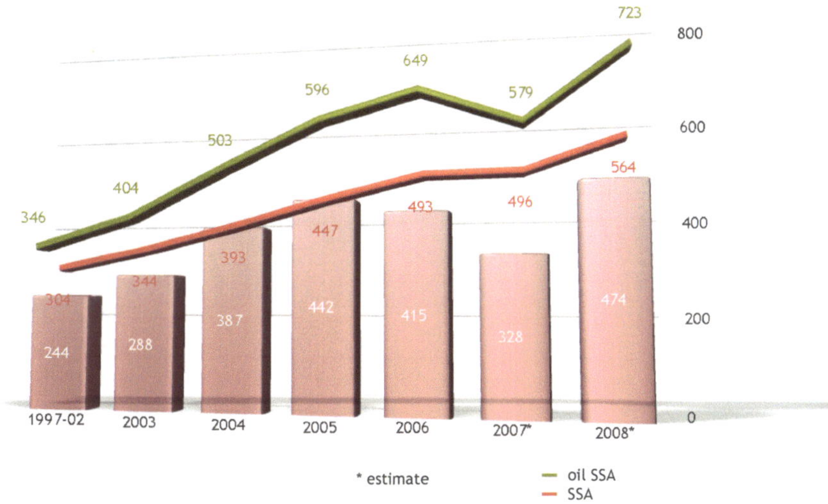


Interesting to see that earnings per person isn't hampered by Nigeria's large population. Indeed, the country ranks higher than when assessed by proportion of GDP.

Yet, it continued below the SSA & oilSSA levels, just as it did on the %GDP scale. Quite likely means that Nigeria isn't pulling its weight: chose to crawl rather than sprint.

A top-third finish for Nigeria within Sub-Saharan Africa, despite its below-average performance on the continent.

Only shows that a few countries on the continent led the pack by such a distance that their combined results put more than half the continent in the shade.

Seychelles: $7,600; Gabon: $4,000; Congo Rep: $1,300; Cape Verde: $740; Nigeria: $380. The first 10 countries pulled near 80% of the continent's total earnings per person.

Govt. Earnings per Person ($PPP) in Sub-Saharan Africa during 2003-06: Rankings

| Rank | Country | Rank | Country | Rank | Country |
|---|---|---|---|---|---|
| 1 | Seychelles | 15 | Ghana | 29 | Uganda |
| 2 | Botswana | 16 | Eritrea | 30 | Tanzania |
| 3 | Equatorial Guinea | 17 | Gambia, The | 31 | Mozambique |
| 4 | Gabon | 18 | Senegal | 32 | Ethiopia |
| 5 | South Africa | 19 | Kenya | 33 | Togo |
| 6 | Mauritius | 20 | Côte d' Ivoire | 34 | Guinea |
| 7 | Swaziland | 21 | Benin | 35 | Burundi |
| 8 | Namibia | 22 | Chad | 36 | Guinea-Bissau |
| 9 | Angola | 23 | Zambia | 37 | Madagascar |
| 10 | Congo, Rep. | 24 | Rwanda | 38 | Sierra Leone |
| 11 | Lesotho | 25 | Mali | 39 | Niger |
| 12 | Cape Verde | 26 | Comoros | 40 | Central Afr. Rep. |
| 13 | Nigeria | 27 | Burkina Faso | 41 | Congo, Dem. Rep. |
| 14 | Cameroon | 28 | Malawi | | |
| | TOP | | MIDDLE | | BOTTOM |

## 5.5 Govt. Earnings & Spending as % of GDP

*wayward cash?*

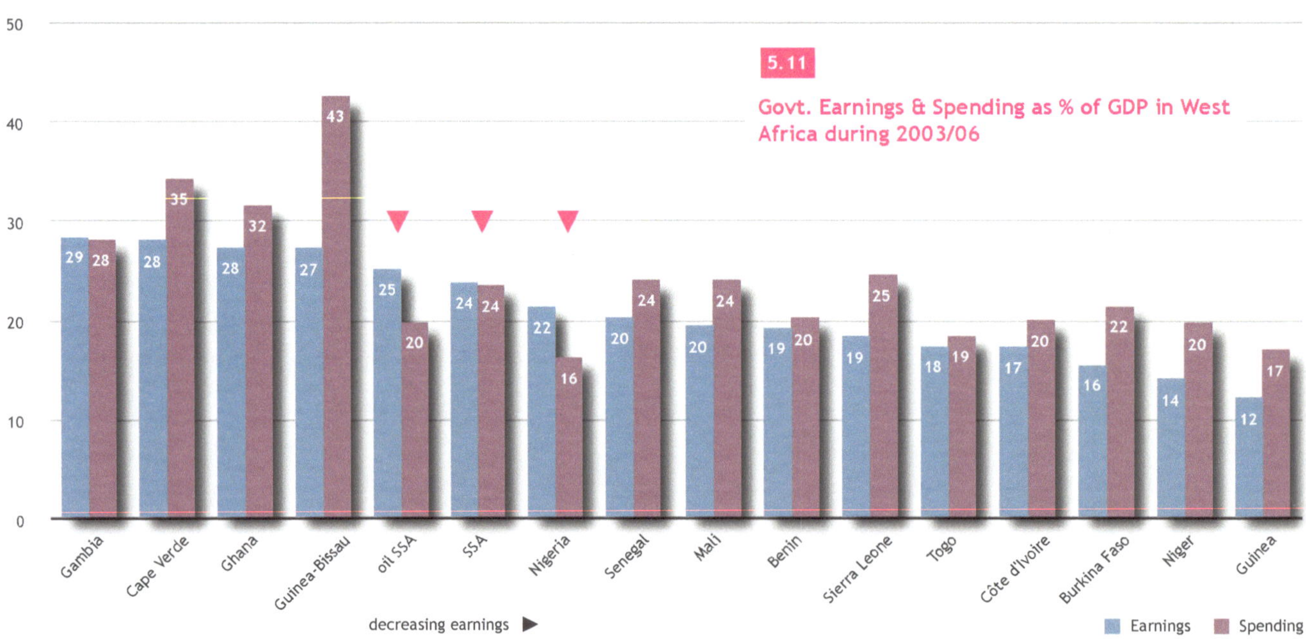


5.11

Govt. Earnings & Spending as % of GDP in West Africa during 2003/06

Primary Data: IMF

Note: figures in this section might differ slightly from those in the preceding ones. Data round-off at source. besides possible inaccuracies, might be to blame. But they do not at all alter the conclusions significantly.

As noted in the intro, not every case of deficit is down to reckless or inopportune spending. But we may still observe the countries where spending overshot earnings.

Only a very few in West Africa ran a surplus. But, while Guinea-Bissau's & Côte d'Ivoire's deficits, for example, did not return economic growth, Cape Verde's did. (See chap. 3)

# 5.6 Govt. Earnings & Spending per Person ($PPP)

**guess which is the heavier**

5.12

Govt. Earnings & Spending per Person ($PPP) in West Africa during 2003/06

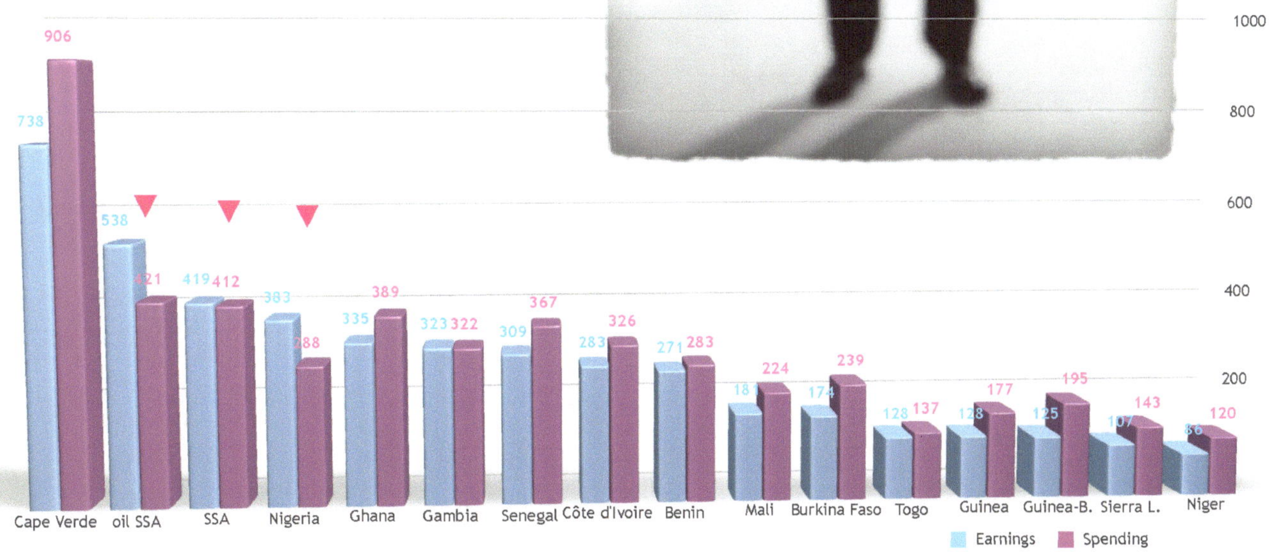


decreasing earnings ▶

Primary Data: IMF

An almost replica picture when earnings & spending are seen as $ per inhabitant. Sierra Leone, Cape Verde & Burkina Faso were the top converters of deficit into economic growth.

# 5.7 Growth in Govt. Earnings per Person

*outgrown the tape measure, hopefully*

| | 03-06 | 07-08 |
|---|---|---|
| Self-comparison to Preceding Period | | ▼ |
| Performance in Sub-Saharan Africa | ▲ | ▲ |
| Performance in West Africa | ▲ | ▲ |
| | Liberia | Guinea-Bissau |
| | Sierra Leone | Gambia, The |
| | Mali | **Nigeria** |
| | **Nigeria** | Ghana |
| | Ghana | Burkina Faso |
| | Niger | Côte d'Ivoire |
| | Cape Verde | Benin |
| | Senegal | Liberia |
| | Benin | Niger |
| | Burkina Faso | Guinea |
| | Gambia, The | Togo |
| | Guinea-Bissau | Senegal |
| | Togo | Cape Verde |
| | Guinea | Mali |
| | Côte d'Ivoire | Sierra Leone |
| Performance among Oil-Exporters | ▼ | ▲ |
| | Equatorial Guinea | **Nigeria** |
| | Chad | Chad |
| | Congo, Rep. | Côte d'Ivoire |
| | Angola | Angola |
| | **Nigeria** | Cameroon |
| | Cameroon | Congo, Rep. |
| | Côte d'Ivoire | Equatorial Guinea |
| | Gabon | Gabon |

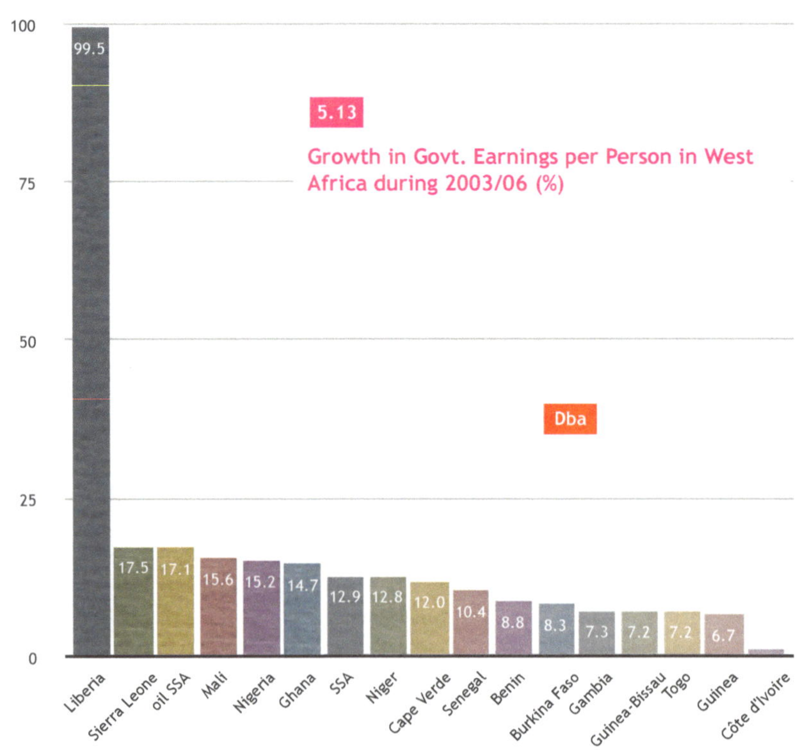


5.13 Growth in Govt. Earnings per Person in West Africa during 2003/06 (%)

Primary Data: IMF

| | |
|---|---|
| ▲ | improved *or* better than average |
| ▼ | worsened *or* worse than average |
| ◁▷ | no change *or* average |

Liberia towers way above everybody else, understandably: reflects the in-pouring of vital economic aid after years of brutal civil war that razed the country to the ground.

Nigeria's growth rate was also in the higher bracket within West Africa, even if it wasn't as determined.

The country ends up in the top-third within the continent, reflecting the relative advantage the Nigeria govt. had with regard to financial resources available and at its disposal.

Growth in Govt. Earnings per Person in Sub-Saharan Africa during 2003-06: Rankings

| Rank | Country | Rank | Country | Rank | Country |
|---|---|---|---|---|---|
| 1 | Equatorial Guinea | 15 | Madagascar | 29 | Benin |
| 2 | Chad | 16 | Ethiopia | 30 | Burkina Faso |
| 3 | Congo, Dem. Rep. | 17 | Malawi | 31 | Seychelles |
| 4 | Mozambique | 18 | Tanzania | 32 | Gambia, The |
| 5 | Congo, Rep. | 19 | Cameroon | 33 | Guinea-Bissau |
| 6 | Swaziland | 20 | Niger | 34 | Togo |
| 7 | Burundi | 21 | Cape Verde | 35 | Kenya |
| 8 | Sierra Leone | 22 | South Africa | 36 | Guinea |
| 9 | Angola | 23 | Rwanda | 37 | Zambia |
| 10 | Botswana | 24 | Namibia | 38 | Comoros |
| 11 | Mali | 25 | Senegal | 39 | Côte d' Ivoire |
| 12 | Nigeria | 26 | Mauritius | 40 | Gabon |
| 13 | Lesotho | 27 | Central Afr. Rep. | 41 | Eritrea |
| 14 | Ghana | 28 | Uganda | | |
| | TOP | | MIDDLE | | BOTTOM |

## 5.8 Build-up in Govt. Earnings & Spending

*did they get their policies confused?*

5.14

Build-up in Govt. Earnings & Spending in Nigeria and Sub-Saharan Africa from 2002 to 2008

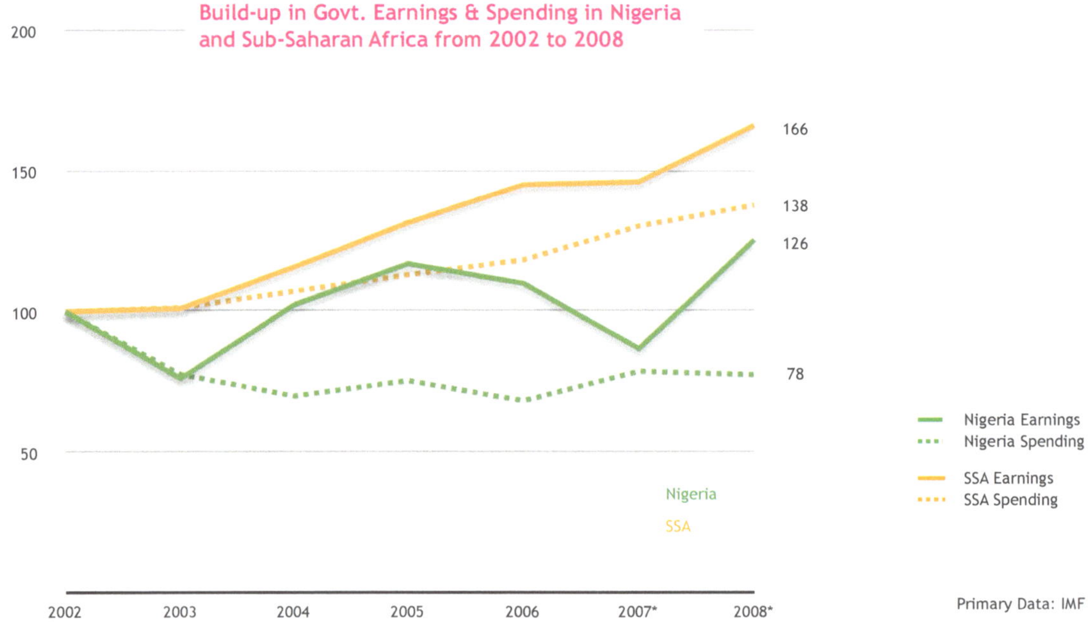


Primary Data: IMF

* estimate

## 5. Govt. Earnings & Spending

Sub-Saharan Africa made a steady climb of its earnings and its spending, almost in tandem, but with a widening surplus, from 2002 to 2008.

Nigeria's progress was an effective climb in earnings build-up, but through some twists and turns. Its spending didn't grow apace, but fell, also thereby widening its surplus.

So, 2 different roads to an end-surplus: Africa steadily spent, while growing earnings at the same time. Nigeria cut spending and grew earnings slower than the continent.

The oil-exporters' travel path is strikingly similar to Nigeria's, with the difference that their cut in spending was temporary, and their growth of earnings more resolute.

5.15

Build-up in Govt. Earnings & Spending in Nigeria and Oil Exporters in Sub-Saharan Africa from 2002 to 2008

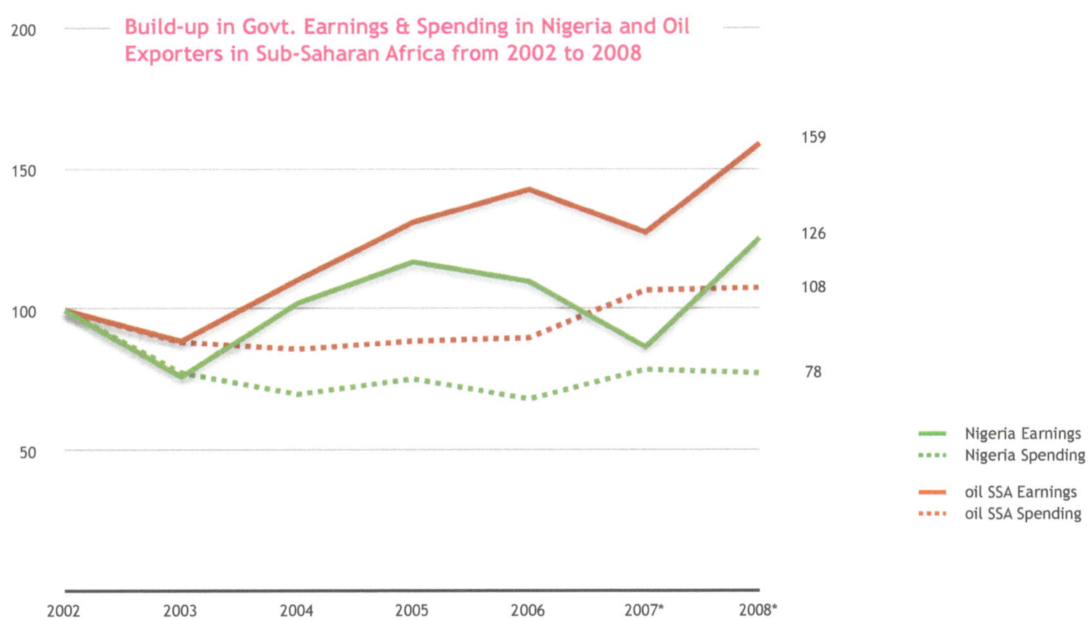


* estimate

# 5.9 Current Account Balance as % of GDP

**that's what the machine said**

Excellent, excellent, & excellent again, for Nigeria. But - to spoil the party - an all too easy performance, built on the straightforward trade in oil export.

Within the oil bloc, Nigeria makes it into the top half, yet you can't help the feeling, deep inside, that it could have done better.

| | 97-02 | 03-06 | 07-08 |
|---|---|---|---|
| Self-comparison to Preceding Period | | ▲ | ▲ |
| Performance in Sub-Saharan Africa | ▲ | ▲ | ▲ |

**Performance in West Africa**

| 97-02 | 03-06 | 07-08 |
|---|---|---|
| ▲ | ▲ | ▲ |
| Côte d'Ivoire | **Nigeria** | **Nigeria** |
| **Nigeria** | Côte d'Ivoire | Guinea-Bissau |
| Gambia, The | Guinea-Bissau | Côte d'Ivoire |
| Guinea | Togo | Sierra Leone |
| Mauritania | Ghana | Benin |
| Senegal | Guinea | Mali |
| Ghana | Sierra Leone | Togo |
| Sierra Leone | Benin | Ghana |
| Niger | Mali | Guinea |
| Togo | Senegal | Senegal |
| Benin | Niger | Burkina Faso |
| Mali | Cape Verde | Gambia, The |
| Liberia | Gambia, The | Mauritania |
| Burkina Faso | Burkina Faso | Niger |
| Cape Verde | Liberia | Cape Verde |
| Guinea-Bissau | Mauritania | Liberia |

**Performance among Oil-Exporters**

| 97-02 | 03-06 | 07-08 |
|---|---|---|
| ▲ | ▲ | ▲ |
| Gabon | Gabon | Gabon |
| Côte d'Ivoire | Angola | Angola |
| **Nigeria** | Congo, Rep. | **Nigeria** |
| Cameroon | **Nigeria** | Congo, Rep. |
| Congo, Rep. | Côte d'Ivoire | Equatorial Guinea |
| Angola | Cameroon | Côte d'Ivoire |
| Sudan | Sudan | Cameroon |
| Equatorial Guinea | Equatorial Guinea | Chad |
| Chad | Chad | Sudan |

Primary Data: IMF

| | |
|---|---|
| ▲ | "movement towards surplus" OR "above average" |
| ▼ | "movement towards deficit" OR "below average" |
| ◁▷ | no change *or* average |

5.16

Current Account Balance as % of GDP in West Africa during 2003/06

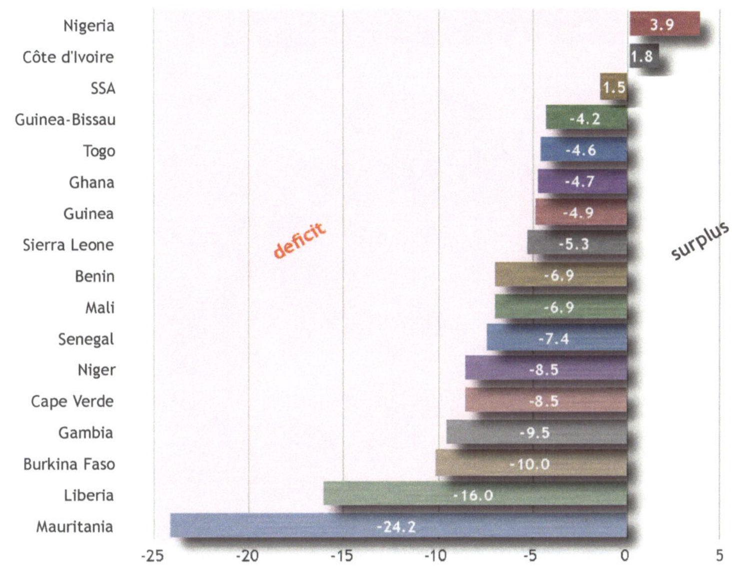


Only the oil producers in West Africa returned a current accounts surplus. The Africa average was a deficit. Oil trade seemed the only fast moving exports item during 03/06.

5.17

Current Account Balance as % of GDP in Nigeria and Sub-Saharan Africa from 1999 to 2010

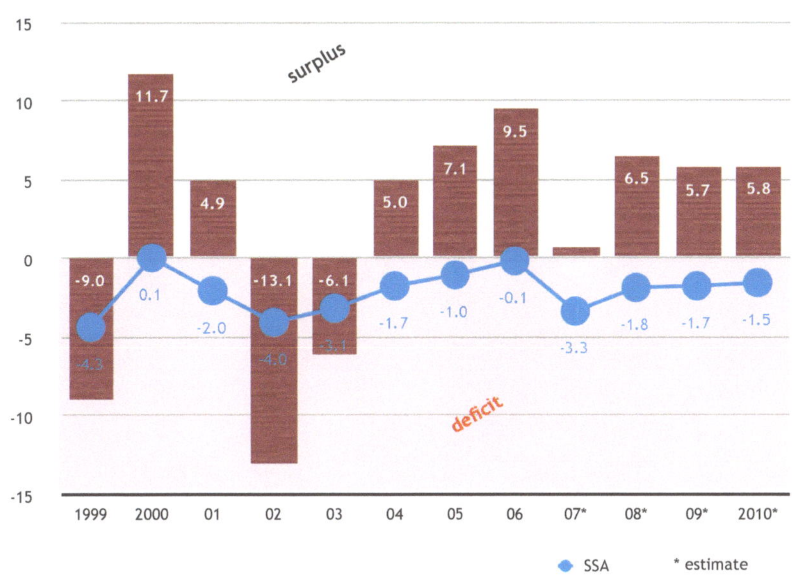


One can almost read the state of oil on the international market, from the current accounts balance of Nigeria: surplus means high price, deficit would imply an oil glut.

# 5.10 Debt Service as % of GNI

## *the debt trap*

| | 99-02 | 03-06 |
|---|---|---|
| Self-comparison to Preceding Period | | ▼ |
| Performance in Sub-Saharan Africa | ▼ | ▼ |
| Performance in West Africa | ▼ | ▼ |
| | Niger | Togo |
| | Togo | Burkina Faso |
| | Burkina Faso | Côte d'Ivoire |
| | Benin | Niger |
| | Sierra Leone | Benin |
| | Mali | Mali |
| | Cape Verde | Sierra Leone |
| | Guinea | Ghana |
| | Ghana | Senegal |
| | Gambia, The | Cape Verde |
| | Senegal | Mauritania |
| | **Nigeria** | Guinea |
| | Mauritania | Gambia, The |
| | Côte d'Ivoire | **Nigeria** |
| | Guinea-Bissau | Guinea-Bissau |

Nigeria went all out on debt repayment during 99-06, esp. during 03-06, when it outpaced all but one country in both West Africa & in the oil bloc, at rate of repayment.

| | 99-02 | 03-06 |
|---|---|---|
| Performance among Oil-Exporters | ▼ | ▼ |
| | Equatorial Guinea | Equatorial Guinea |
| | Sudan | Côte d'Ivoire |
| | Chad | Chad |
| | Congo, Rep. | Sudan |
| | Cameroon | Cameroon |
| | **Nigeria** | Gabon |
| | Côte d'Ivoire | Congo, Rep. |
| | Gabon | **Nigeria** |
| | Angola | Angola |

Primary Data: AfDB, World Bank

| | |
|---|---|
| ▲ | better = low debt service |
| ▼ | worse = high debt service |
| ◁▷ | no change *or* average |

The wisdom behind such high outlays of debt repayment might only be glimpsed 2 or 3 years down the line for Nigeria.

It would have to be seen whether the commitment of such a high portion of GNI to settling otherwise mounting debt would free the economy up so that it flourishes with fresh vigour...

... or whether it would be a belt notch too far and stifle whatever energies might have been remaining for growth.

5.18

Debt Service as % of GNI in West Africa during 2003/06

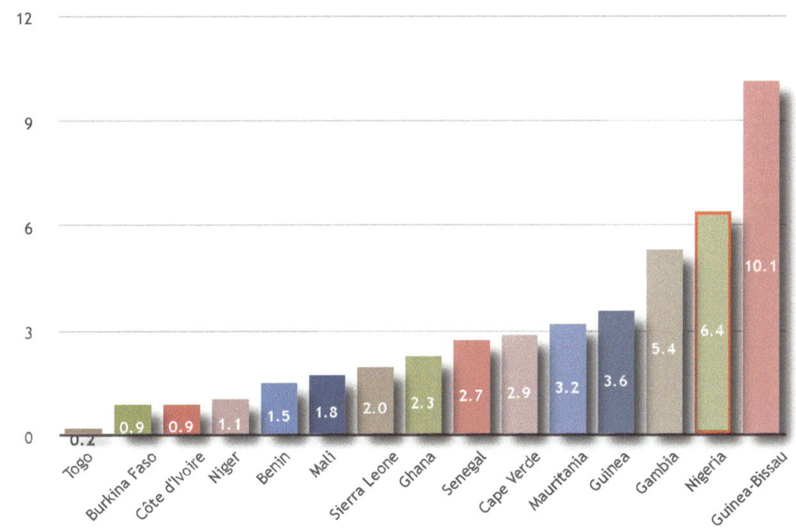


5.19

Debt Service as % of GNI in Nigeria from 1999 to 2006

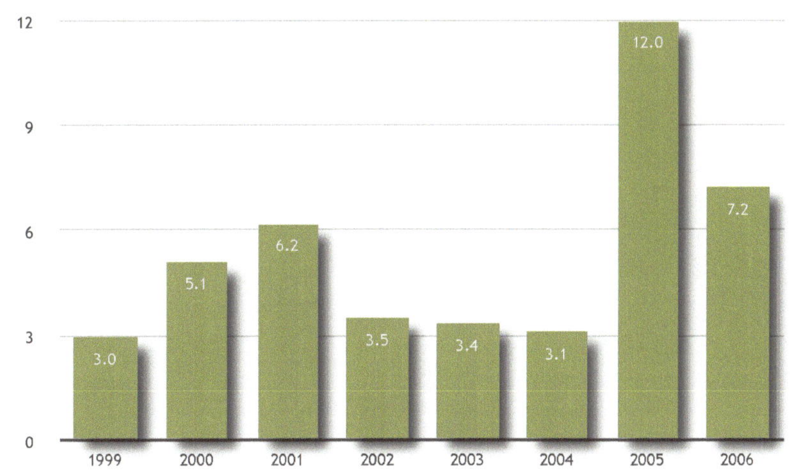

# 5.11 Build-up in Debt Service & GNI

*let's see if they did their maths*

**Gap between *GNI* and *Debt Service* build-up levels by 2006: 2000=100**
**(negative = more debt service than GNI)**

| | West Africa | 2006 |
|---|---|---|
| 1 | Côte d'Ivoire | 146 |
| 2 | Liberia | 126 |
| 3 | Mali | 123 |
| 4 | Ghana | 107 |
| 5 | Togo | 106 |
| 6 | Senegal | 99 |
| 7 | Burkina Faso | 91 |
| 8 | Mauritania | 86 |
| 9 | Sierra Leone | 76 |
| 10 | Benin | 57 |
| 11 | Guinea | 4 |
| 12 | Cape Verde | 4 |
| 13 | Guinea-Bissau | -15 |
| 14 | Gambia | -31 |
| 15 | Niger | -89 |
| 16 | Nigeria | -112 |

| | oil exporters | 2006 |
|---|---|---|
| 7 | Equatorial Guinea | 455 |
| 1 | Angola | 296 |
| 2 | Gabon | 165 |
| 8 | Sudan | 152 |
| 5 | Côte d'Ivoire | 146 |
| 9 | Chad | 113 |
| 3 | Cameroon | 112 |
| 4 | Nigeria | -112 |
| 6 | Congo, Rep.* | -615 |

* 2005

Republic of Congo's approach almost looks an aberration! The widest gap in the oil group, and the 2nd widest on the continent: Seychelles' was 860 percentage points.

Two contrasting approaches, waiting for the jury's verdict in another 4 years or so: Côte d'Ivoire sped up GNI growth faster than it did debt payback; Nigeria took the other road.

5.20

Build-up of Debt Service & GNI in Nigeria and Côte d'Ivoire from 2000 to 2006: 2000=100

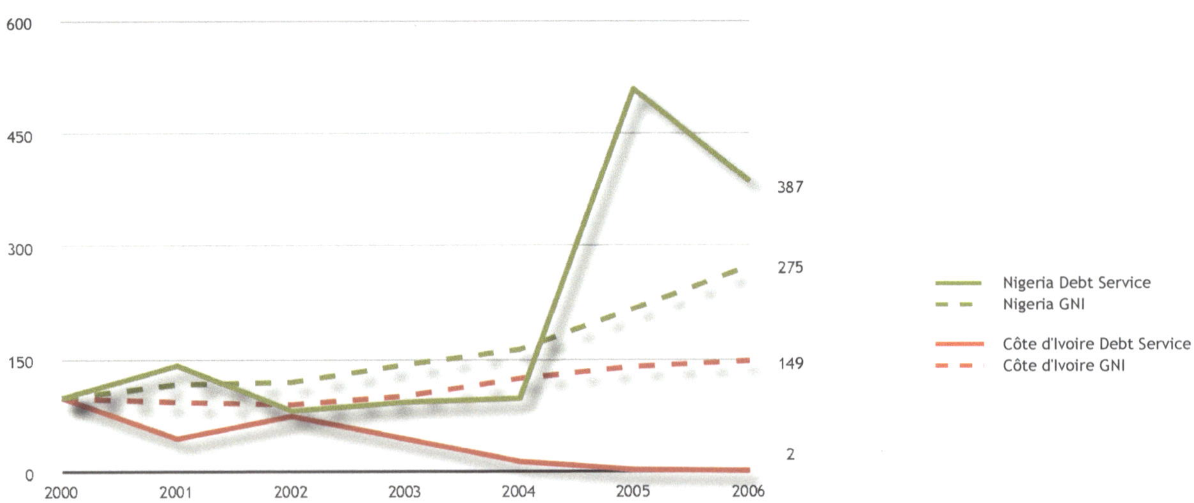


Primary Data: AfDB, World Bank

# Leaders & Stragglers

**were they the right moves?**

In the end, the Nigeria govt. has maintained a level of discipline, compared to the rest of Africa. It tied with South Africa at 8th position. Only Ghana in West Africa did better.

## Govt. Earnings & Spending Rankings: 2003-06

| Rank | Country |
|---|---|
| 1 | Equatorial Guinea |
| 2 | Botswana |
| 3 | Swaziland |
| 4 | Angola |
| | Congo, Rep. |
| | Lesotho |
| 5 | Seychelles |
| 6 | Namibia |
| 7 | Ghana |
| 8 | Nigeria |
| | South Africa |
| 9 | Cape Verde |
| 10 | Burundi |
| 11 | Gabon |

TOP

| Rank | Country |
|---|---|
| 12 | Mauritius |
| 13 | Chad |
| | Mozambique |
| 14 | Gambia, The |
| | Malawi |
| 15 | Mali |
| 16 | Eritrea |
| 17 | Cameroon |
| | Rwanda |
| 18 | Senegal |
| 19 | Ethiopia |
| 20 | Kenya |
| | Sierra Leone |
| 21 | Benin |
| | Congo, Dem. Rep. |

MIDDLE

| Rank | Country |
|---|---|
| 22 | Uganda |
| 23 | Guinea-Bissau |
| 24 | Tanzania |
| 25 | Zambia |
| 26 | Côte d' Ivoire |
| | Madagascar |
| 27 | Burkina Faso |
| 28 | Niger |
| | Togo |
| 29 | Comoros |
| 30 | Central Afr. Rep. |
| 31 | Guinea |

BOTTOM

Central Africa
East Africa
Southern Africa
West Africa

# Wrap-up: Govt. Earnings & Spending

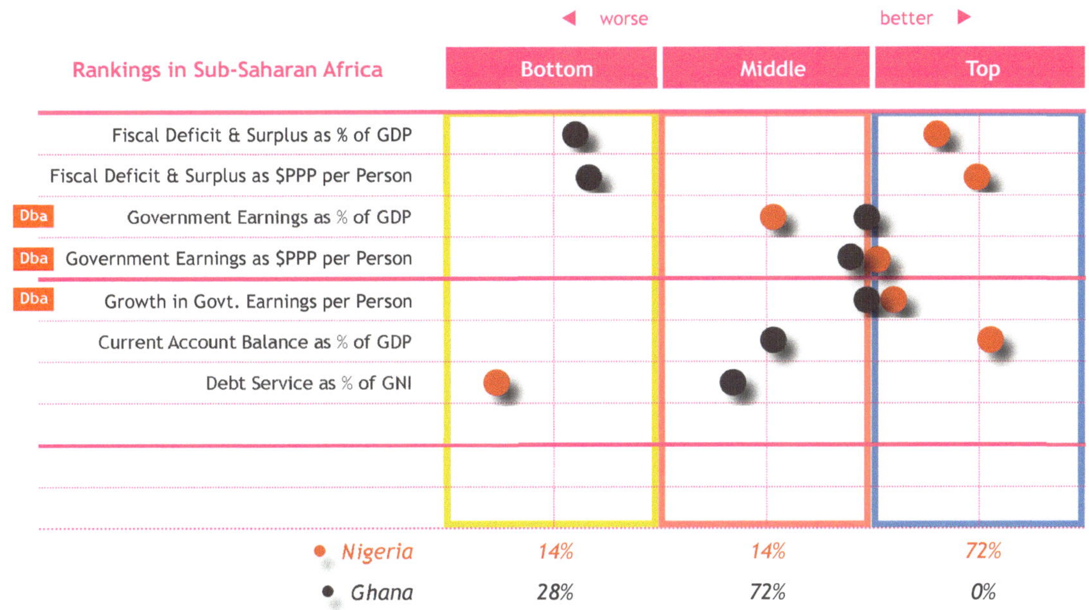


- Ghana just pips Nigeria to the best performer position in West Africa, coming 7th in Africa to Nigeria's 8th position.

- On the face of it, Nigeria does come off looking the prettier of the two countries; top bracket for 72% of the indicators to Ghana's 0%. Even though Ghana has 72% in the middle bracket to Nigeria's 14%, Nigeria still comes away second best.

- The reason for that is this: Nigeria excelled, but not in the right places. The fiscal balances looked good, but they were not the result of a push to grow earnings all round. It did better than Ghana in 2 of those 3 critical indicators, but not by the necessary margin. The gap in size of government earnings considered as %GDP for the 2 countries was too wide, so that it overshadowed the small margins to Nigeria's favour in the other 2 indicators.

# 6. Spending on Health

*so that your staff will be working fit*

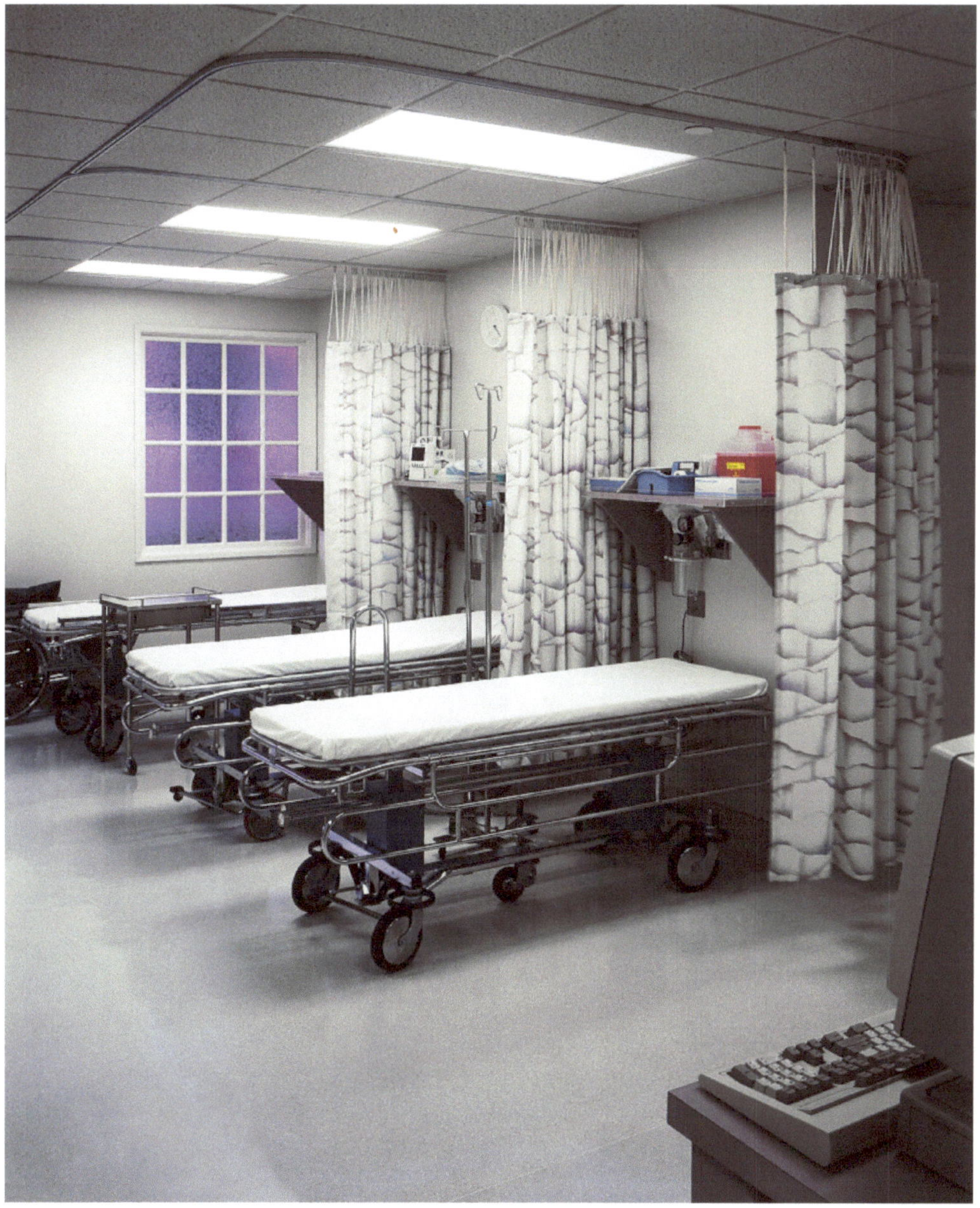


6.1 Total Spending (Govt. & Private) on Health as % GDP

6.2 Total Spending (G & P) on Health per Person

6.3 Build-up of Govt. & Private Spending on Health

6.4 Govt. Spending on Health as % of Total Govt. Spending

6.5 Out-of-Pocket Spending on Health as % of Total Health Spending

6.6 Out-of-Pocket Spending on Health as Part of Total Spending on Health per Person

6.7 Out-of-Pocket as % of Private Spending on Health

6.8 *Out-of-Pocket* & *Other Private* Spending on Health per Person

6.9 *Out-of-Pocket*, *Other Private* and *Govt.* Portions of Total Spending on Health per Person

Leaders & Stragglers

Wrap-up

It is easy to underestimate the impact of the domestic health sector on the economies of Africa. It isn't unlikely that man-hours lost to relatively common and treatable ailments (e.g. malaria) have not been properly quantified, and it isn't uncommon, either, to find that employees effectively are out of work - and so, rendered unproductive to the business and the economy - for considerable periods, compared to other economies, every work-year.

Much of that uncertainty is down to the paucity of accurate information. Health statistics of the working population isn't readily available, and because of the general state of health sectors and their service delivery, workers' efficiency may be hampered not only by direct illness to themselves, but illness to members of their family or household. The end-result is much the same: disruption to work and a dent on their effectiveness and output, which goes on to reflect - inevitably - on the larger economy, once accumulated.

This section attempts to show the quality of health resources available to a population. It compares levels of government and private expenditure on health and thus illustrates the degree of government commitment to the state of health of its residents, and the extent to which the private sector carries (or must carry) the burden of responsibility. It thus provides a snapshot of the challenges and liabilities that the different economies pose to employers and residents.

We have chosen to compare economies here by the expenditure on health undertaken by the two broad groups of providers: government and private sources. The private segment is here split into two major parts: *out-of-pocket* and *other private sector* expenses or outlays. Much of the data headings is self-explanatory, and where brief definitions follow, they are provided by the World Health Organisation (WHO) from where the bulk of the data is sourced.

For the purposes here, a "household" is defined as an individual or a group of persons sharing the same living accommodation, which pool some or all of their income and wealth, and which consume certain types of goods and services collectively (mainly housing and food).

## Total Spending on Health

The sum of government and private expenditure on health.

## Government Spending on Health

The sum of expenditures for health maintenance, restoration or enhancement paid for in cash, or supplied in kind by government entities such as the Ministry of Health, other ministries, parastatals, or social security services.

## Private Spending on Health

The sum of expenditures on health by households; by private entities such as commercial or mutual health insurance and non-profit institutions that serve households; and by resident corporations not controlled by government.

## Out-of-Pocket Spending on Health

Private households' out-of-pocket payment: the expenditure on health by households as direct payments.

## Other Private Spending on Health

The rest of health spending by the private sector after out-of-pocket expenditure. As mentioned above, consists largely of health insurance arrangements and direct expenses by corporations and businesses.

**Sources of Primary Data:** World Bank, WHO

# Charts

6.1 Total Spending (Govt. & Private) on Health as %GDP in West Africa during 2003/06

6.2 Total Spending (Govt. & Private) on Health as %GDP in Nigeria from 2000 to 2006

6.3 Total Spending (Govt. & Private) on Health as %GDP in Sub-Saharan Africa from 2000 to 2006

6.4 Total Spending (Govt. & Private) on Health per Person in West Africa during 2003/06 ($PPP)

6.5 % Breakdown of Total Spending (Govt. & Private) on Health per Person in West Africa during 2003/06 ($PPP)

6.6 Total Spending (Govt. & Private) on Health per Person in Nigeria from 2000 to 2006 ($PPP)

6.7 Total Spending (Govt. & Private) on Health per Person in Mali from 2000 to 2006 ($PPP)

6.8 Build-up of Govt. & Private Spending on Health in Nigeria and Mali from 2000 to 2006: 2000=100

6.9 Govt. Spending on Health as % of Total Govt. Spending in West Africa during 2003/06

6.10 Govt. Spending on Health as % of Total Govt. Spending in Nigeria from 2000 to 2006

6.11 Out-of-Pocket Spending on Health as % of Total Health Spending in West Africa during 2003/06

6.12 Out-of-Pocket Spending on Health as % of Total Health Spending in Nigeria from 2000 to 2006

6.13 Out-of-Pocket Spending on Health as part of Total Health Spending in West Africa during 2003/06

6.14 % Breakdown of Total Health Spending showing Out-of-Pocket Spending on Health in West Africa during 2003/06

6.15 Out-of-Pocket Spending on Health as part of Total Health Spending in Nigeria from 2000 to 2006

6.16 % Breakdown of Total Health Spending showing Out-of-Pocket Spending on Health in Nigeria from 2000 to 2006

6.17 Out-of-Pocket Spending as % of Private Spending on Health in West Africa during 2003/06

6.18 Out-of-Pocket Spending as % of Private Spending on Health in Nigeria from 2000 to 2006

6.19 Out-of-Pocket & other Private Spending on Health per Person in West Africa during 2003/06 ($PPP)

6.20 Out-of-Pocket & other Private Spending on Health per Person in Nigeria from 2000 to 2006 ($PPP)

6.21 Out-of-Pocket & other Private Spending on Health per Person in Mali from 2000 to 2006 ($PPP)

6.22 Breakdown of Total Health Spending into Out-of-Pocket, other Private & Govt. Spending per Person in West Africa during 2003/06 ($PPP)

6.23 % Breakdown of Total Health Spending into Out-of-Pocket, other Private & Govt. Spending per Person in West Africa during 2003/06

6.24 Breakdown of Total Health Spending into Out-of-Pocket, other Private & Govt. Spending per Person in Nigeria from 2000 to 2006 ($PPP)

6.25 Breakdown of Total Health Spending into Out-of-Pocket, other Private & Govt. Spending per Person in Mali from 2000 to 2006 ($PPP)

- **Wrap-up**

# Tables

*2000-2002; 2003-2006:*

- *self-comparison to preceding period;*
- *performance in S-Saharan Africa;*
- *performance in West Africa;*
- *performance among oil-exporters;*

*for:*

Total Spending (Govt. & Private) on Health as % of GDP

Total Spending (Govt. & Private) on Health per Person, $PPP

Govt. Spending on Health as % of Total Govt. Spending

Out-of-Pocket Spending on Health as % of Total Health Spending

Out-of-Pocket as % of Private Spending on Health

- Total Spending on Health as % of GDP during 2003-06: Rankings
- Total Spending on Health per Person ($PPP) during 2003-06: Rankings
- Govt. Spending on Health as % of Total Govt. Spending during 2003-06: Rankings
- Out-of-Pocket Spending on Health as % of Total Health Spending during 2003-06: Rankings
- Out-of-Pocket Spending as % of Private Spending on Health during 2003-06: Rankings
- **Spending on Health Rankings: 2003-06**

# 6.1 Total Spending (Govt. & Private) on Health as % of GDP

## keeping everyone in working order

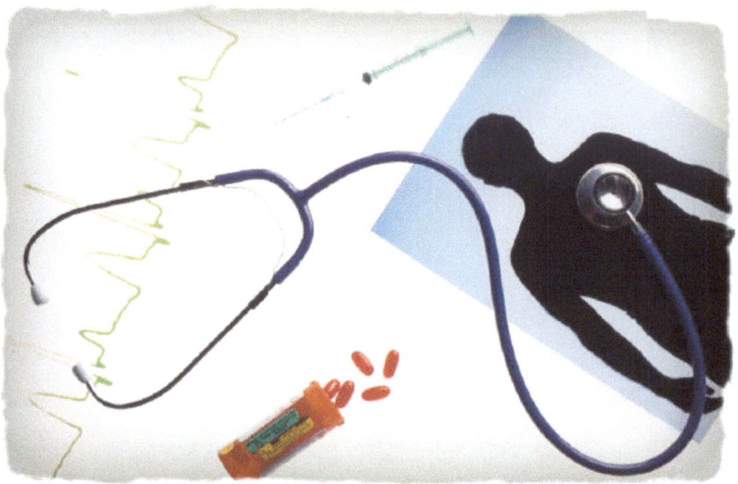

Health spending in Nigeria at all levels and by all quarters is the 3rd worst in West Africa, when compared to the size of the different economies.

Indeed, 03/06 was a big drop in total health spending from the preceding 4 yrs.

| | 00-02 | 03-06 |
|---|---|---|
| Self-comparison to Preceding Period | | ▼ |
| Performance in Sub-Saharan Africa | ▼ | ▼ |
| Performance in West Africa | ▲ | ▼ |

Primary Data: World Bank

| 00-02 | 03-06 |
|---|---|
| Ghana | Burkina Faso |
| Mali | Ghana |
| Guinea-Bissau | Togo |
| Guinea | Guinea-Bissau |
| Gambia, The | Guinea |
| Cape Verde | Mali |
| Burkina Faso | Senegal |
| **Nigeria** | Gambia, The |
| Togo | Cape Verde |
| Benin | Benin |
| Senegal | Sierra Leone |
| Côte d'Ivoire | Niger |
| Sierra Leone | Liberia |
| Niger | **Nigeria** |
| Liberia | Côte d'Ivoire |
| Mauritania | Mauritania |

| Performance among Oil-Exporters | 00-02 | 03-06 |
|---|---|---|
| | ▲ | ▲ |
| | Chad | Chad |
| | Gabon | Gabon |
| | **Nigeria** | Cameroon |
| | Cameroon | **Nigeria** |
| | Côte d'Ivoire | Côte d'Ivoire |
| | Sudan | Sudan |
| | Angola | Congo, Rep. |
| | Equatorial Guinea | Angola |
| | Congo, Rep. | Equatorial Guinea |

6.1

Total Spending (Govt. & Private) on Health as %GDP in West Africa during 2003/06

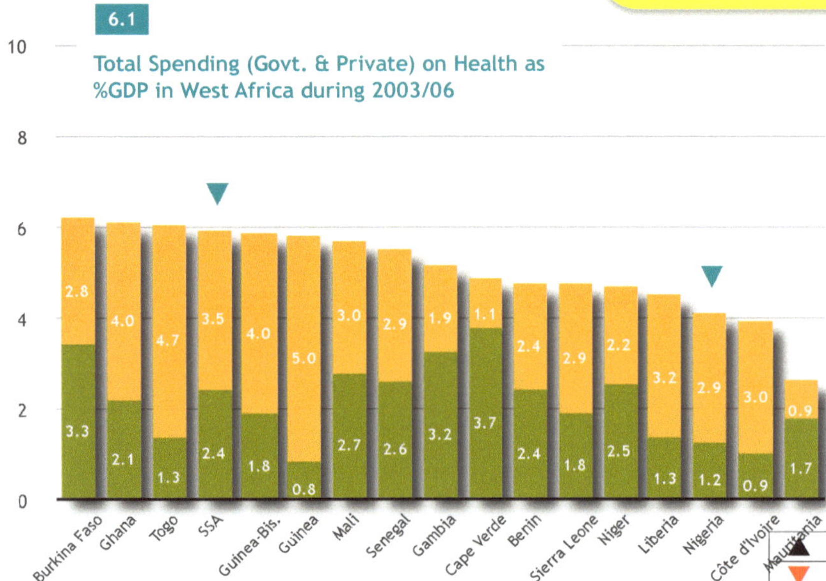


Private
Govt.

Dba

| | |
|---|---|
| ▲ | improved *or* better than average |
| ▼ | worsened *or* worse than average |
| ◁▷ | no change *or* average |

# 6. Spending on Health

**6.2**

**Total Spending (Govt. & Private) on Health as %GDP in Nigeria from 2000 to 2006**

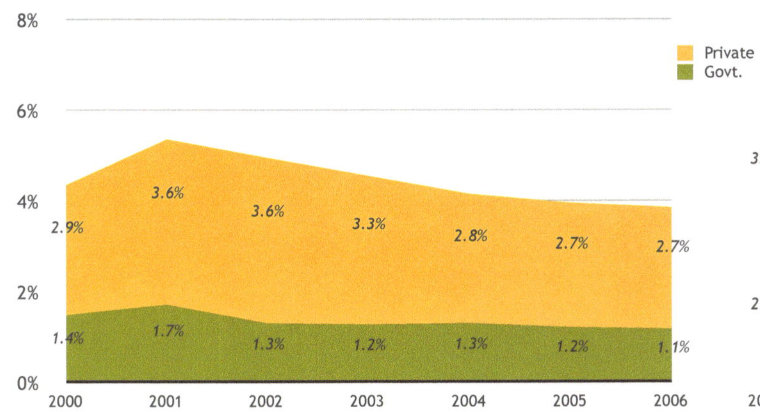


**6.3**

**Total Spending (Govt. & Private) on Health as % GDP in Sub-Saharan Africa from 2000 to 2006**

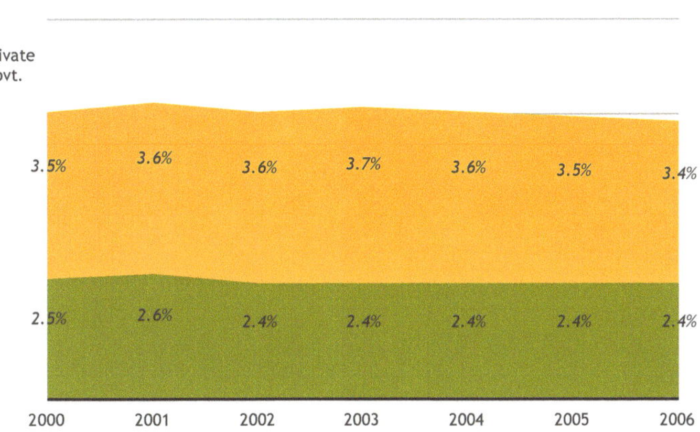


It probably says much for the oil countries that even with that dismal score, Nigeria still makes it into their top half. Too immersed in oil barrels to care?

Total expenditure on health dropped in 2006 from the 2000 level across Africa, but the drop was sharper in Nigeria, where it declined steeply after 2001.

Nigeria fell below 4% of GDP and never went near 6% in 7 yrs. Africa's broke the 6% mark in 2001 and fell just slightly below it in 2006.

Govt. health spending was consistently above 2% in Africa, but consistently less than 2% in Nigeria, dropping to 1% by 2006, compared to Africa's 2.4%.

No surprises, therefore, that Nigeria is in the bottom sector of the Africa table, with health expenditure being worse than every other country, save 7.

**Total Spending on Health as % of GDP during 2003-06: Rankings**

Central Africa
East Africa
Southern Africa
West Africa

| Rank | Country |
|---|---|
| 1 | Malawi |
| 2 | Rwanda |
| 3 | Namibia |
| | South Africa |
| 4 | Botswana |
| 5 | Uganda |
| 6 | Burundi |
| 7 | Zambia |
| 8 | Lesotho |
| 9 | Swaziland |
| 10 | Burkina Faso |
| 11 | Seychelles |
| 12 | Ghana |

TOP

| Rank | Country |
|---|---|
| 13 | Togo |
| 14 | Congo, Dem. Rep. |
| 15 | Guinea-Bissau |
| 16 | Guinea |
| 17 | Mali |
| 18 | Senegal |
| 19 | Tanzania |
| | Chad |
| 20 | Gambia, The |
| 21 | Cape Verde |
| 22 | Benin |
| | Sierra Leone |
| 23 | Niger |
| 24 | Gabon |

MIDDLE

| Rank | Country |
|---|---|
| 25 | Mozambique |
| 26 | Kenya |
| | Cameroon |
| 27 | Ethiopia |
| 28 | Mauritius |
| 29 | Central Afr. Rep. |
| | Nigeria |
| 30 | Côte d' Ivoire |
| 31 | Eritrea |
| 32 | Madagascar |
| 33 | Comoros |
| 34 | Congo, Rep. |
| 35 | Angola |
| 36 | Equatorial Guinea |

BOTTOM

# 6.2 Total Spending (Govt. & Private) on Health per Person, $PPP

## *who's actually coughing up?*

| | 00-02 | 03-06 |
|---|---|---|
| Self-comparison to Preceding Period | | ▼ |
| Performance in Sub-Saharan Africa | ▼ | ▼ |

**6.4**

Total Spending (Govt. & Private) on Health per Person in West Africa during 2003/06 ($PPP)

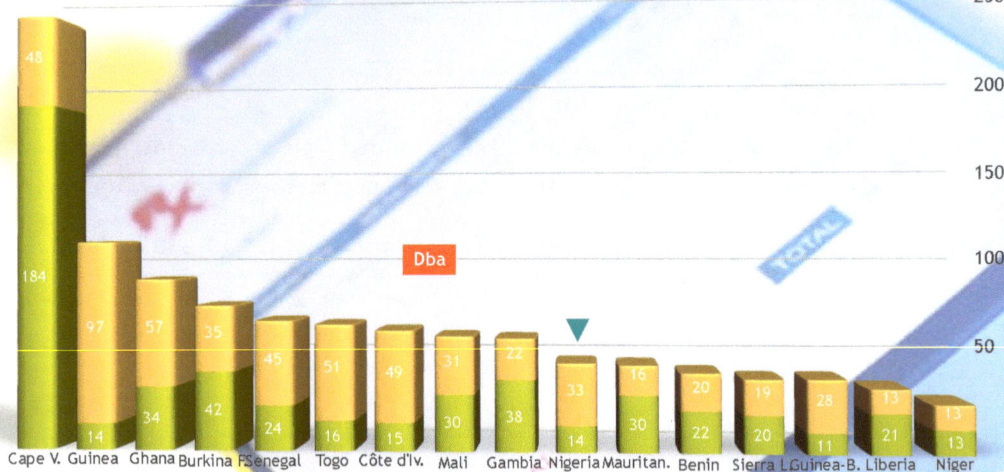


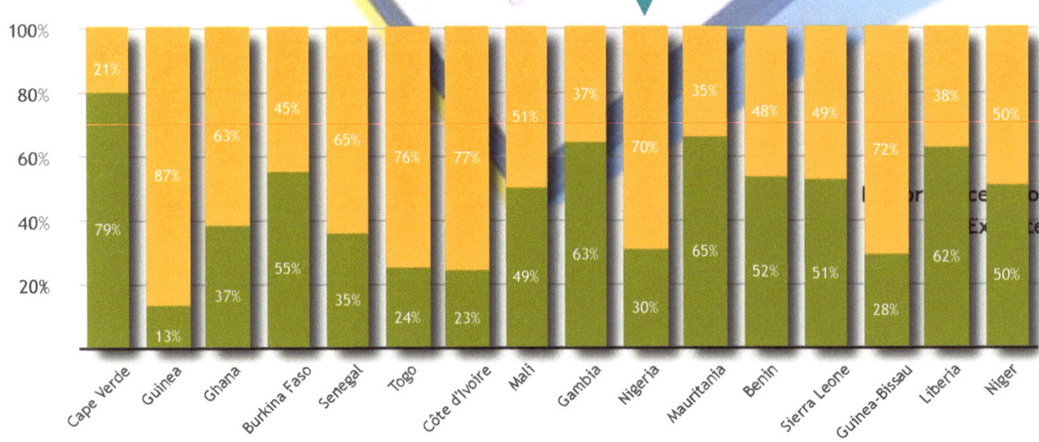


**6.5**

% Breakdown of Total Spending (Govt. & Private) on Health per Person in West Africa during 2003/06 ($PPP)

Private
Govt.

**Performance in West Africa**

| 00-02 | 03-06 |
|---|---|
| ▼ | ▼ |
| Cape Verde | Cape Verde |
| Guinea | Guinea |
| Ghana | Ghana |
| Côte d'Ivoire | Burkina Faso |
| Togo | Senegal |
| Mali | Togo |
| Senegal | Côte d'Ivoire |
| Burkina Faso | Mali |
| Gambia, The | Gambia, The |
| **Nigeria** | **Nigeria** |
| Guinea-Bissau | Mauritania |
| Mauritania | Benin |
| Benin | Sierra Leone |
| Sierra Leone | Guinea-Bissau |
| Liberia | Liberia |
| Niger | Niger |

| 00-02 | 03-06 |
|---|---|
| ◁▷ | ▼ |
| Gabon | Gabon |
| Equatorial Guinea | Equatorial Guinea |
| Côte d'Ivoire | Cameroon |
| Cameroon | Côte d'Ivoire |
| **Nigeria** | Sudan |
| Angola | Angola |
| Sudan | **Nigeria** |
| Chad | Chad |
| Congo, Rep. | Congo, Rep. |

Primary Data: WHO

| | |
|---|---|
| ▲ | improved *or* better than average |
| ▼ | worsened *or* worse than average |
| ◁▷ | no change *or* average |

# 6. Spending on Health

**6.6**

Total Spending (Govt. & Private) on Health per Person in Nigeria from 2000 to 2006 ($PPP)

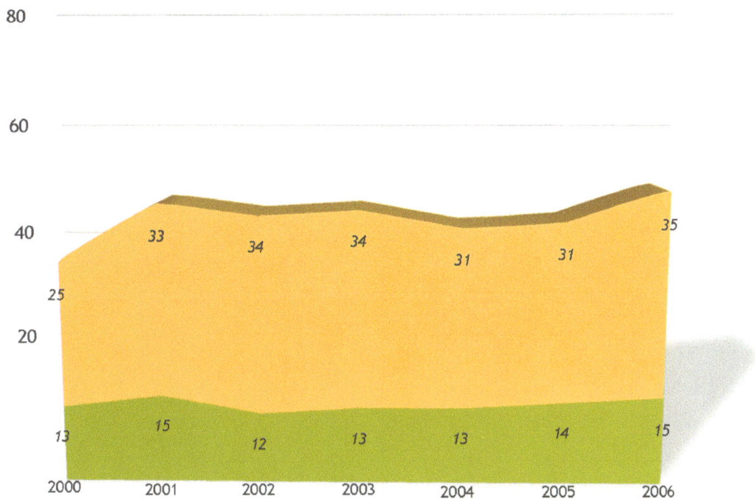


**6.7**

Total Spending (Govt. & Private) on Health per Person in Mali from 2000 to 2006 ($PPP)

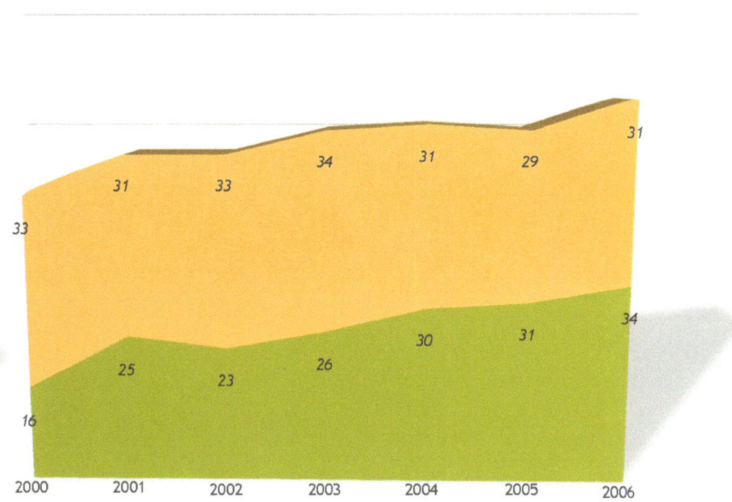


Private
Govt.

Primary Data: WHO

Expressed in real money, Nigeria's total health spending is still worse than average in Africa, West Africa and, this time, in the oil club, too.

And much of that health responsibility is borne by private corporations and households. The govt. contributed just 30%: only better than 4 in West Africa.

This time, the disparity between money spent on health in the country and in the rest of Sub-Saharan Africa is more noticeable.

In Mali for comparison (average in West Africa) govt. spending during 2000-06 grew by 9 times that in Nigeria: $18 per person, against Nigeria's $2.

During the same period, private health spending in Nigeria grew by $10 a head; in Mali it fell instead, by $2. Govt. shouldered more of the burden.

Throughout 2000-2006, in total health expenditure, Mali outspent Nigeria by an average of $13 per person.

## 6. Spending on Health

Total Spending on Health per Person ($PPP) during 2003-06: Rankings

| Rank | Country | Rank | Country | Rank | Country |
|---|---|---|---|---|---|
| 1 | South Africa | 15 | Ghana | 29 | Benin |
| 2 | Seychelles | 16 | Burkina Faso | 30 | Chad |
| 3 | Botswana | 17 | Cameroon | 31 | Sierra Leone |
| 4 | Mauritius | 18 | Senegal | 32 | Guinea-Bissau |
| 5 | Namibia | 19 | Togo | 33 | Tanzania |
| 6 | Swaziland | 20 | Malawi | 34 | Eritrea |
| 7 | Gabon | 21 | Zambia | 35 | Madagascar |
| 8 | Equatorial Guinea | 22 | Côte d' Ivoire | 36 | Comoros |
| 9 | Cape Verde | 23 | Mali | 37 | Congo, Rep. |
| 10 | Rwanda | 24 | Gambia, The | 38 | Niger |
| 11 | Uganda | 25 | Central Afr. Rep. | 39 | Ethiopia |
| 12 | Lesotho | 26 | Angola | 40 | Congo, Dem. Rep. |
| 13 | Guinea | 27 | Mozambique | 41 | Burundi |
| 14 | Kenya | 28 | **Nigeria** | | |
| TOP | | MIDDLE | | BOTTOM | |

Central Africa
East Africa
Southern Africa
West Africa

> And it just about jostles its way into the last position in the middle bracket on the continent. All 5 Southern Africa countries were in the top bracket.

# 6.3 Build-up of Govt. & Private Spending on Health

## *she's keeping a close eye on it*

**6.8**

Build-up of Govt. & Private Spending on Health in Nigeria and Mali from 2000 to 2006: 2000=100

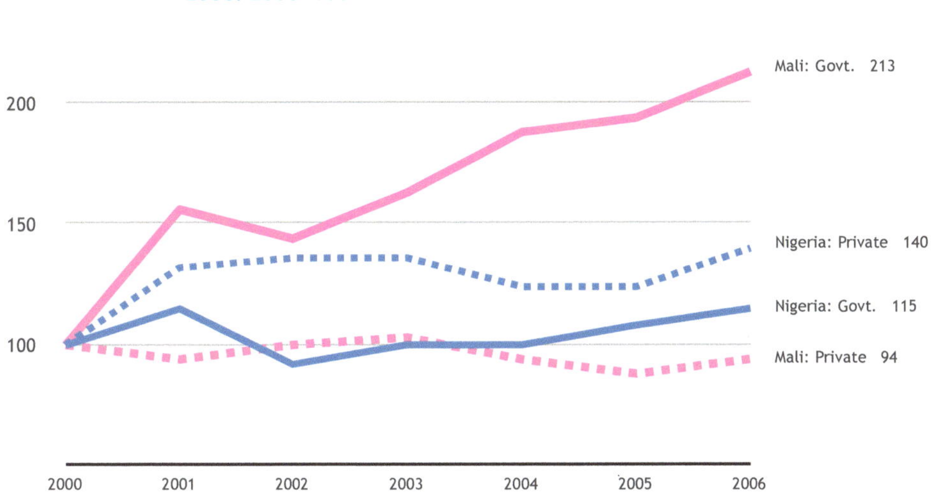


Primary Data: WHO

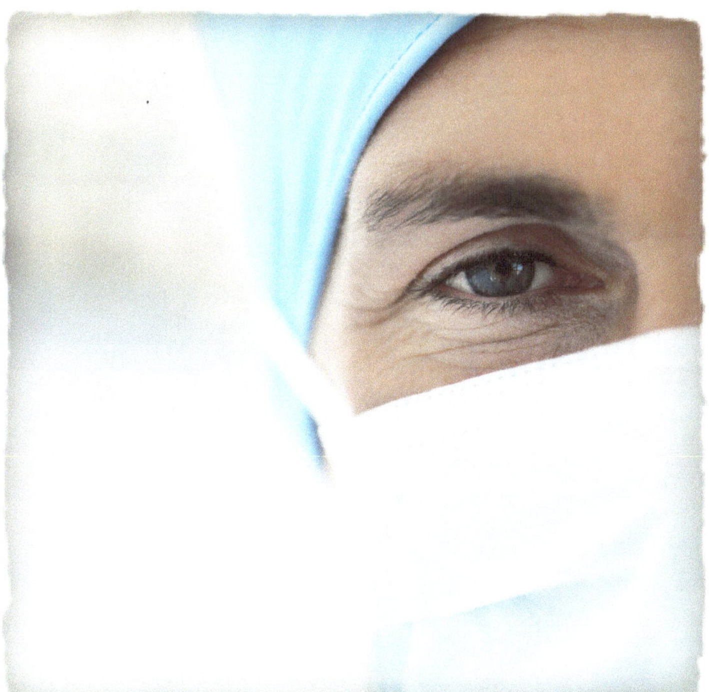

Using Mali again for comparison (average), growth of govt. spending outpaced Nigeria's during 2000-2006, by almost 100 percentage points.

Private sector shell-out in Mali dropped during the same period, by 6 points; in Nigeria it grew by 40 points...

... showing that individuals in Mali saw their health expenses dropping because the govt. shouldered more weight.

It was the opposite in Nigeria: while govt. and private health spending both grew, private spending surpassed the govt.'s by 25 points.

Whereas, Mali's govt. spent 120 percentage points more than the private sector per inhabitant in the 7 yrs from 2000 to 2006.

Their private sector shed weight, instead, during the period (from 100 down to 94 percentage points).

## 6.4 Govt. Spending on Health as % of Total Govt. Spending

*the govt is your friend, sir*

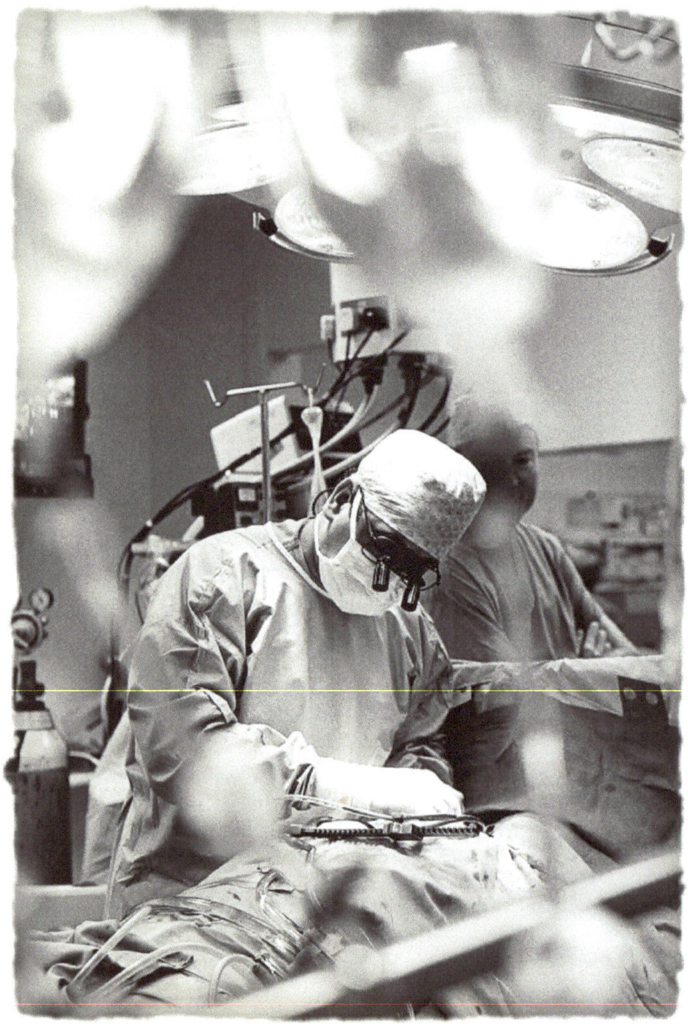

It might have been tempting to put Nigeria's poor per-capita govt. spending on health down to the country's large population.

But not so. Health mattered less and less across 00-06, taking up an increasingly smaller share of the govt. budget.

| | 00-02 | 03-06 |
|---|---|---|
| Self-comparison to Preceding Period | | ▼ |
| Performance in Sub-Saharan Africa | ▼ | ▼ |

| Performance in West Africa | 00-02 | 03-06 |
|---|---|---|
| | ▼ | ▼ |
| | Benin | Liberia |
| | Niger | Burkina Faso |
| | Cape Verde | Benin |
| | Mali | Mali |
| | Ghana | Cape Verde |
| | Burkina Faso | Gambia, The |
| | Senegal | Niger |
| | Gambia, The | Sierra Leone |
| | Liberia | Senegal |
| | Sierra Leone | Ghana |
| | Togo | Togo |
| | Mauritania | Guinea |
| | Côte d'Ivoire | Mauritania |
| | Guinea | Côte d'Ivoire |
| | Guinea-Bissau | Guinea-Bissau |
| | **Nigeria** | **Nigeria** |

| Performance among Oil-Exporters | 00-02 | 03-06 |
|---|---|---|
| | ▼ | ▼ |
| | Gabon | Gabon |
| | Chad | Cameroon |
| | Equatorial Guinea | Chad |
| | Cameroon | Equatorial Guinea |
| | Sudan | Sudan |
| | Côte d'Ivoire | Angola |
| | Congo, Rep. | Côte d'Ivoire |
| | **Nigeria** | Congo, Rep. |
| | Angola | **Nigeria** |

Primary Data: WHO

| | |
|---|---|
| ▲ | improved *or* better than average |
| ▼ | worsened *or* worse than average |
| ◁▷ | no change *or* average |

## 6. Spending on Health

6.9

Govt. Spending on Health as % of Total Govt. Spending in West Africa during 2003/06

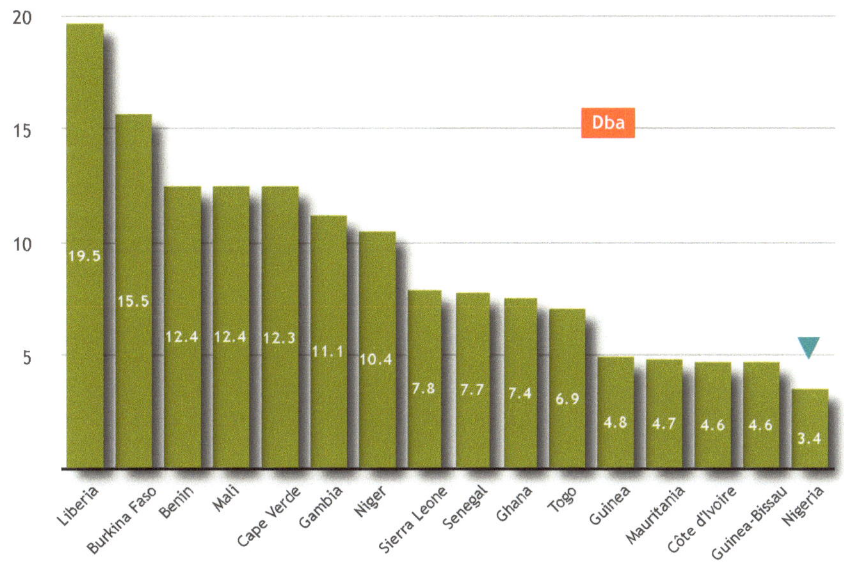


As a % of total govt. expenditure during the period, health wasn't on Nigeria's list of priorities.

It dedicated fewer resources to the health sector than all the other countries of West Africa and the countries of the oil group.

6.10

Govt. Spending on Health as % of Total Govt. Spending in Nigeria from 2000 to 2006

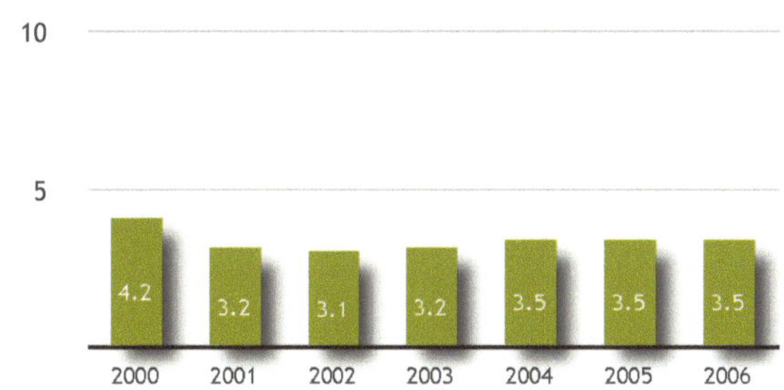


The charts at right are to the same scale. Other West African govts. had health sectors pulling larger chunks of spending; they towered over Nigeria's.

Again, rock-bottom on the continent, inevitably.

Govt. Spending on Health as % of Total Govt. Spending during 2003-06: Rankings

| Rank | Country | Rank | Country | Rank | Country |
|---|---|---|---|---|---|
| 1 | Rwanda | 14 | Central Afr. Rep. | 27 | Senegal |
| 2 | Malawi | 15 | Gambia, The | 28 | Equatorial Guinea |
| 3 | Botswana | 16 | Niger | 29 | Ghana |
| 4 | Burkina Faso | 17 | Ethiopia | 30 | Congo, Dem. Rep. |
| 5 | Gabon | 18 | Cameroon | 31 | Togo |
| 6 | Benin | 19 | Uganda | 32 | Kenya |
| 7 | Mali | 20 | Seychelles | 33 | Guinea |
| 8 | Cape Verde | 21 | Chad | 34 | Angola |
| 9 | Namibia | | South Africa | 35 | Côte d' Ivoire |
| 10 | Tanzania | 22 | Madagascar | | Guinea-Bissau |
| 11 | Mozambique | 23 | Mauritius | 36 | Eritrea |
| 12 | Zambia | 24 | Comoros | 37 | Congo, Rep. |
| 13 | Swaziland | 25 | Lesotho | 38 | **Nigeria** |
| | | 26 | Sierra Leone | 39 | Burundi |
| | TOP | | MIDDLE | | BOTTOM |

Central Africa
East Africa
Southern Africa
West Africa

Primary Data: WHO

# 6.5 Out-of-Pocket Spending on Health as % of Total Health Spending

*he's had to cough up*

An increasingly familiar play-out: Nigeria outdone in health.

Nigerians shouldered the task of their health requirements themselves: they had to spend their own money directly, from their own disposable income.

The situation worsened across the 2000-2006 yrs.

| | 00-02 | 03-06 |
|---|---|---|
| Self-comparison to Preceding Period | | ▼ |
| Performance in Sub-Saharan Africa | ▼ | ▼ |
| Performance in West Africa | ▼ | ▼ |

| 00-02 | 03-06 |
|---|---|
| Cape Verde | Cape Verde |
| Mauritania | Gambia, The |
| Niger | Mauritania |
| Gambia, The | Liberia |
| Guinea-Bissau | Niger |
| Ghana | Burkina Faso |
| Benin | Guinea-Bissau |
| Sierra Leone | Benin |
| Burkina Faso | Sierra Leone |
| Senegal | Ghana |
| Liberia | Mali |
| Mali | Senegal |
| **Nigeria** | **Nigeria** |
| Togo | Togo |
| Côte d'Ivoire | Côte d'Ivoire |
| Guinea | Guinea |

| | 00-02 | 03-06 |
|---|---|---|
| Performance among Oil-Exporters | ▼ | ▼ |

| 00-02 | 03-06 |
|---|---|
| Gabon | Angola |
| Equatorial Guinea | Equatorial Guinea |
| Angola | Gabon |
| Congo, Rep. | Congo, Rep. |
| Chad | Chad |
| **Nigeria** | Sudan |
| Côte d'Ivoire | **Nigeria** |
| Cameroon | Côte d'Ivoire |
| Sudan | Cameroon |

Primary Data: WHO

| | |
|---|---|
| ▲ | improved *or* smaller than average |
| ▼ | worsened *or* higher than average |
| ◁▷ | no change *or* average |

# 6. Spending on Health

6.11

Out-of-Pocket Spending on Health as % of Total Health Spending in West Africa during 2003/06

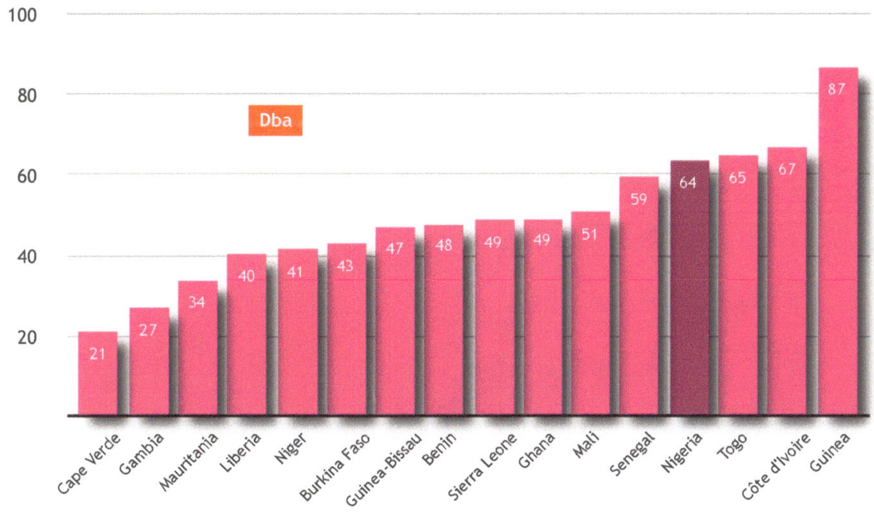


Indeed, the position is staggering: more than 60% of all health spending in Nigeria is funded by the people directly, from their income or savings.

6.12

Out-of-Pocket Spending on Health as % of Total Health Spending in Nigeria from 2000 to 2006

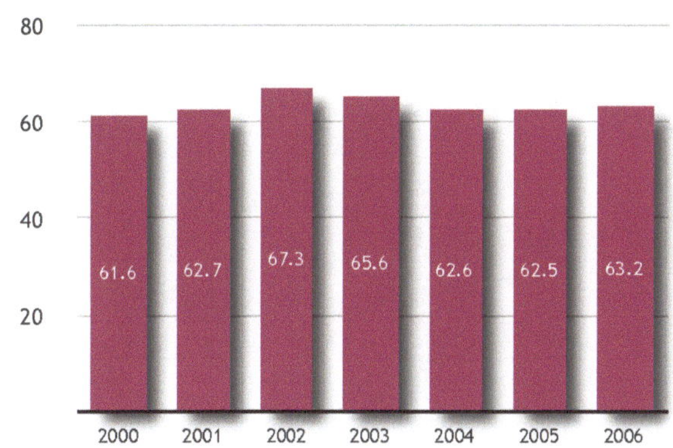


Govt. clinics and medicines account for less than 40% of the citizens' requirements.

Out-of-Pocket Spending on Health as % of Total Health Spending during 2003-06: Rankings

| Rank | Country | Rank | Country | Rank | Country |
|---|---|---|---|---|---|
| 1 | Namibia | 15 | Lesotho | 29 | Ghana |
| 2 | Botswana | 16 | Zambia | 30 | Mali |
| 3 | Malawi | 17 | Ethiopia | 31 | Congo, Rep. |
| 4 | South Africa | 18 | Uganda | 32 | Chad |
| 5 | Mozambique | 19 | Mauritius | 33 | Senegal |
| 6 | Swaziland | 20 | Tanzania | 34 | Central Afr. Rep. |
| 7 | Seychelles | 21 | Niger | 35 | Nigeria |
| 8 | Angola | 22 | Burkina Faso | 36 | Togo |
| 9 | Equatorial Guinea | 23 | Kenya | 37 | Côte d' Ivoire |
| 10 | Rwanda | 24 | Eritrea | 38 | Congo, Dem. Rep. |
| 11 | Madagascar | 25 | Comoros | 39 | Cameroon |
| 12 | Cape Verde | 26 | Guinea-Bissau | 40 | Burundi |
| 13 | Gambia, The | 27 | Benin | 41 | Guinea |
| 14 | Gabon | 28 | Sierra Leone | | |
| LOWEST % | | MIDDLE | | LARGEST % | |

Central Africa
East Africa
Southern Africa
West Africa

Primary Data: WHO

## 6.6 Out-of-Pocket Spending on Health as Part of Total Spending on Health per Person, $PPP

*nice colours, yes?*

The monies spent on health by individuals & households tally with the percentages illustrated in the previous section.

The focus in this section are the disparities in money volumes.

Even though Cape Verde has its people spending a lot more than other residents in all but 1 West African country, its total expenditure on health more than makes up for that extra weight.

At $30 per capita, Nigerians spent just about the West Africa average of personal money on their health. But that wasn't a desirable position, small though the amount was:

reason being that personal money represented the largest source for their health expenses. As seen in the preceding sections, their overall health spending was the worst on show.

# 6. Spending on Health

6.13

Out-of-Pocket Spending on Health as part of Total Health Spending in West Africa during 2003/06 ($PPP)

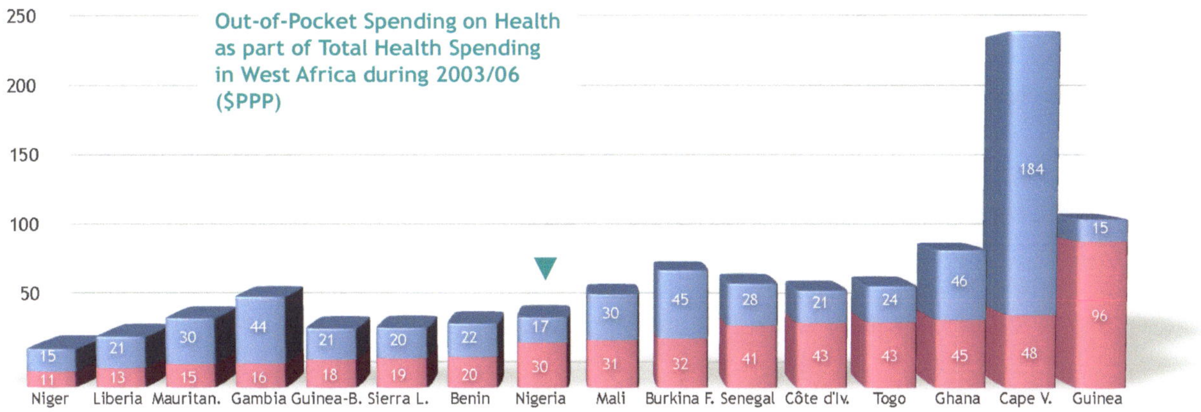


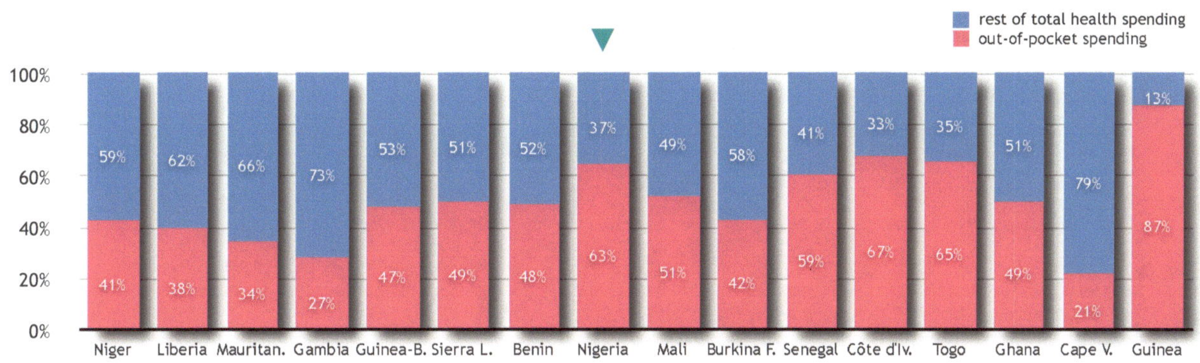


6.14

% Breakdown of Total Health Spending showing Out-of-Pocket Spending on Health in West Africa during 2003/06

Primary Data: WHO

6.15

Out-of-Pocket Spending on Health as part of Total Health Spending in Nigeria from 2000 to 2006 ($PPP)

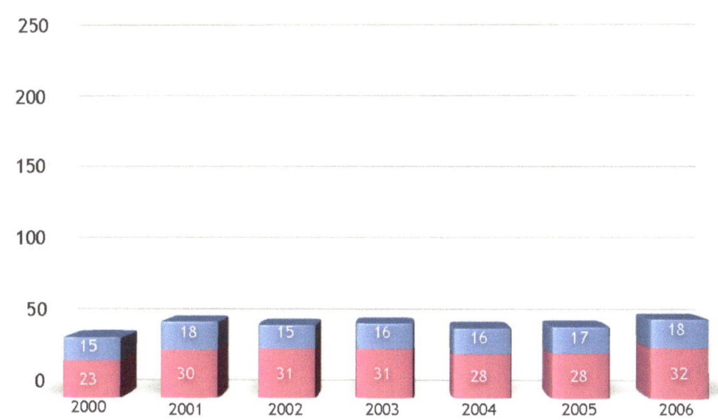


8.16

% Breakdown of Total Health Spending showing Out-of-Pocket Spending on Health in Nigeria from 2000 to 2006

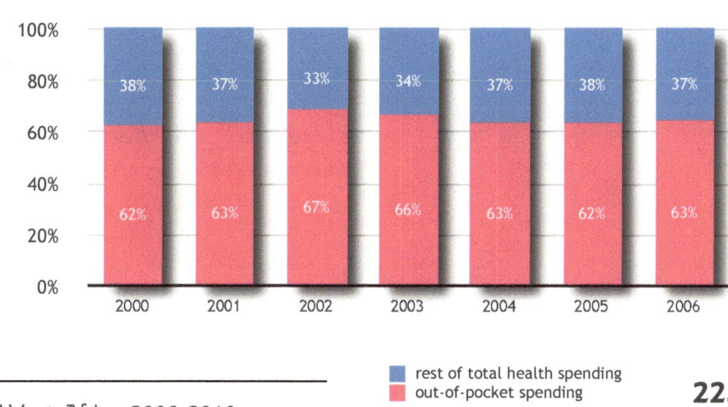

# 6.7 Out-of-Pocket as % of Private Spending on Health

*do you love your insurance company?*

Leaving total spending and looking at just private spending, personal expenditure on health made up a large part of Nigeria's private health spending.

Nigeria was bested by most of Africa, even though it came up average in West Africa.

Among the oil exporters the general situation is a dismal one, because in spite of Nigeria's poor showing, it still came up better than average there.

| | 00-02 | 03-06 |
|---|---|---|
| Self-comparison to Preceding Period | | ◁▷ |
| Performance in Sub-Saharan Africa | ▼ | ▼ |

**Performance in West Africa**

| 00-02 | 03-06 |
|---|---|
| ▲ | ▲ |
| Guinea-Bissau | Guinea-Bissau |
| Ghana | Gambia, The |
| Gambia, The | Ghana |
| Niger | Togo |
| Togo | Niger |
| Côte d'Ivoire | Côte d'Ivoire |
| Senegal | Senegal |
| **Nigeria** | **Nigeria** |
| Burkina Faso | Burkina Faso |
| Liberia | Liberia |
| Guinea | Mali |
| Mali | Guinea |
| Cape Verde | Cape Verde |
| Benin | Benin |
| Mauritania | Mauritania |
| Sierra Leone | Sierra Leone |

**Performance among Oil-Exporters**

| 00-02 | 03-06 |
|---|---|
| ▲ | ▲ |
| Equatorial Guinea | Equatorial Guinea |
| Côte d'Ivoire | Côte d'Ivoire |
| **Nigeria** | **Nigeria** |
| Cameroon | Cameroon |
| Chad | Chad |
| Sudan | Sudan |
| Angola | Angola |
| Congo, Rep. | Congo, Rep. |
| Gabon | Gabon |

Primary Data: WHO

| | |
|---|---|
| ▲ | improved *or* smaller than average |
| ▼ | worsened *or* higher than average |
| ◁▷ | no change *or* average |

**6.17**

Out-of-Pocket Spending as % of Private Spending on Health in West Africa during 2003/06

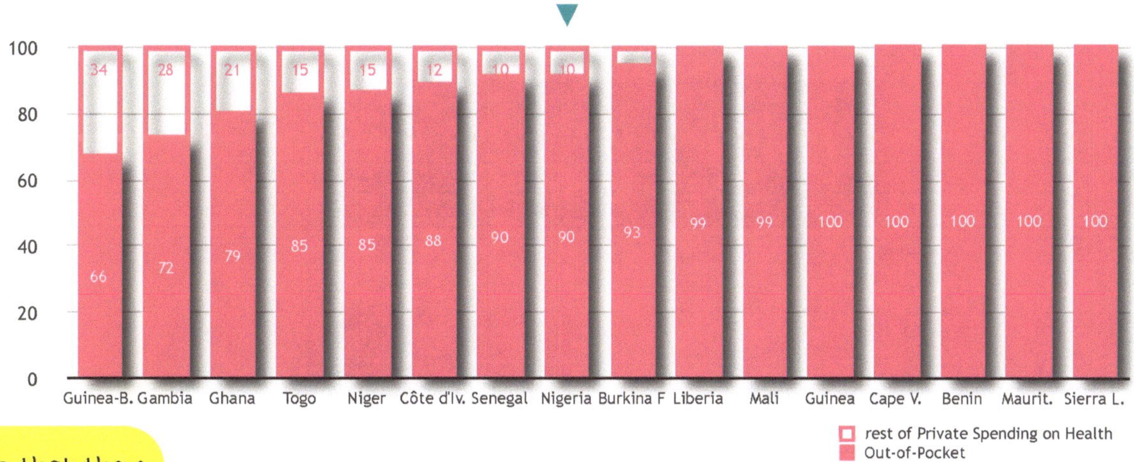


The other inference is that there is no health insurance arrangement through most of West Africa, & certainly through most of the oil exporters:

individuals are forced to pay for health directly, off their pockets, literally.

**6.18**

Out-of-Pocket Spending as % of Private Spending on Health in Nigeria from 2000 to 2006

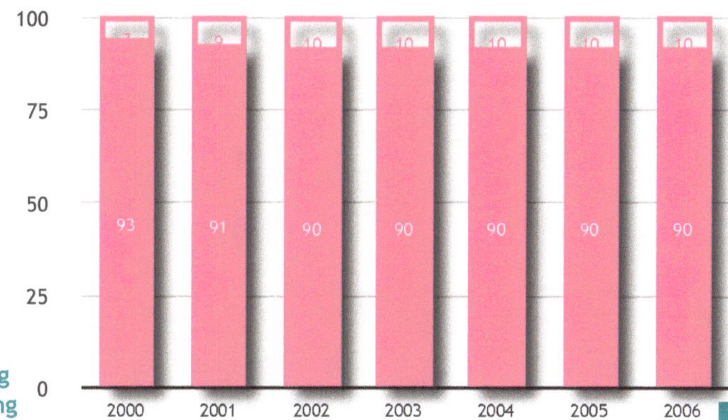


In West Africa, near half the countries have no support scheme for private spending: individuals carry the entire cost of private spending: 100%.

In Nigeria, 10% of private sector spending is provided by insurance schemes or corporate spending. That figure changed little across 2000-2006.

As is seen at right, a large proportion of African countries haven't effective private sector health arrangement schemes.

Out-of-Pocket Spending as % of Private Spending on Health during 2003-06: Rankings

| Rank | Country | Rank | Country | Rank | Country |
|---|---|---|---|---|---|
| 1 | Namibia | 13 | Lesotho | 25 | Senegal |
| 2 | South Africa | 14 | Gambia, The | 26 | **Nigeria** |
| 3 | Botswana | 15 | Zambia | 27 | Burkina Faso |
| 4 | Malawi | 16 | Equatorial Guinea | 28 | Cameroon |
| 5 | Mozambique | 17 | Ghana | 29 | Central Afr. Rep. |
| 6 | Swaziland | 18 | Kenya | 30 | Chad |
| 7 | Rwanda | 19 | Mauritius | 31 | Mali |
| 8 | Uganda | 20 | Ethiopia | 32 | Guinea |
| 9 | Madagascar | 21 | Tanzania | 33 | Cape Verde |
| 10 | Seychelles | 22 | Togo | 34 | Benin |
| 11 | Eritrea | 23 | Niger | 35 | Angola |
| 12 | Guinea-Bissau | 24 | Côte d' Ivoire | | Burundi |
| | | | | | Comoros |
| | | | | | Congo, Dem. Rep. |
| | | | | | Congo, Rep. |
| | | | | | Gabon |
| | | | | | Sierra Leone |
| LOWEST % | | MIDDLE | | LARGEST % | |

Central Africa
East Africa
Southern Africa
West Africa

Primary Data: WHO

## 6.8 *Out-of-Pocket* & *Other Private* Spending on Health per Person

*I paid for the ones on the top shelf*

Much the same observations as in the preceding section. But here, the quantities of money spent can be appreciated better.

# 6. Spending on Health

6.19

Out-of-Pocket & other Private Spending on Health per Person in West Africa during 2003/06, $PPP

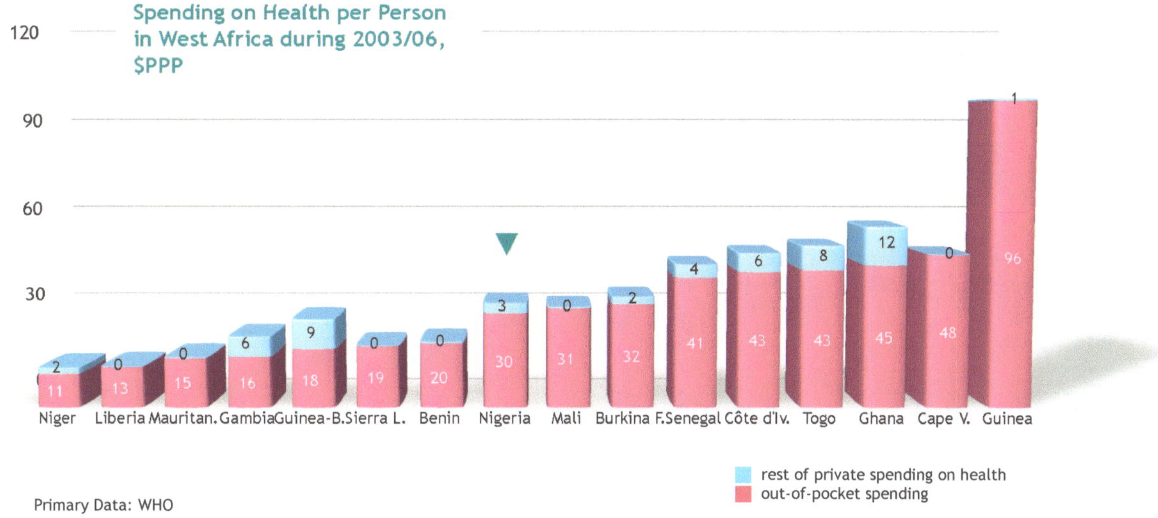


Primary Data: WHO

6.20

Out-of-Pocket & other Private Spending on Health per Person in Nigeria from 2000 to 2006, $PPP

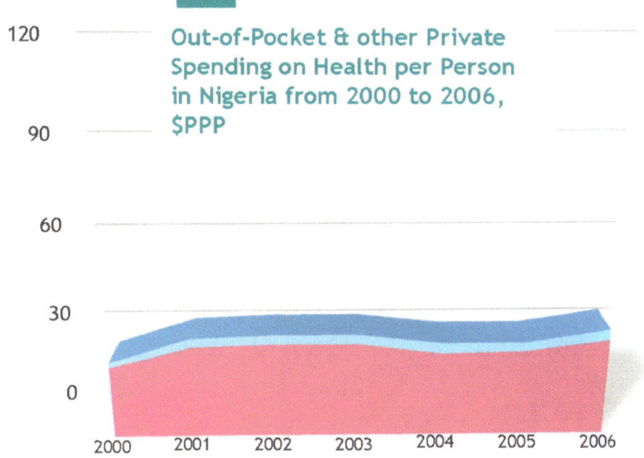


6.21

Out-of-Pocket & other Private Spending on Health per Person in Mali from 2000 to 2006, $PPP

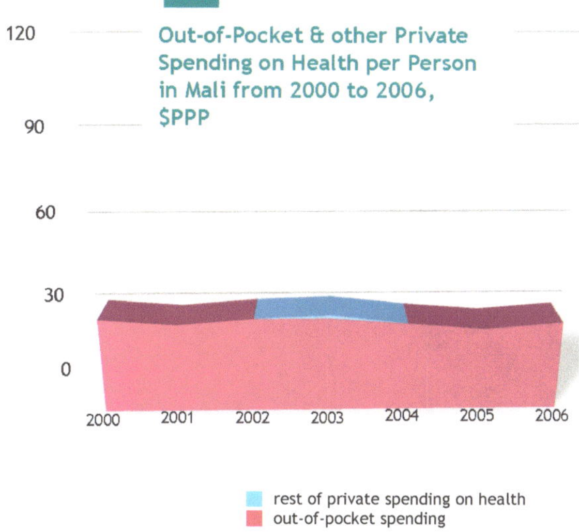


In most of West Africa, "other private sources" account for less than $5 of private spending on health.

The highest was $12 in Ghana, which nonetheless also had one of the highest out-of-pocket levels: $45.

## 6.9 *Out-of-Pocket*, *Other Private* and *Govt.* Portions of Total Spending on Health per Person

*is there a problem here?*

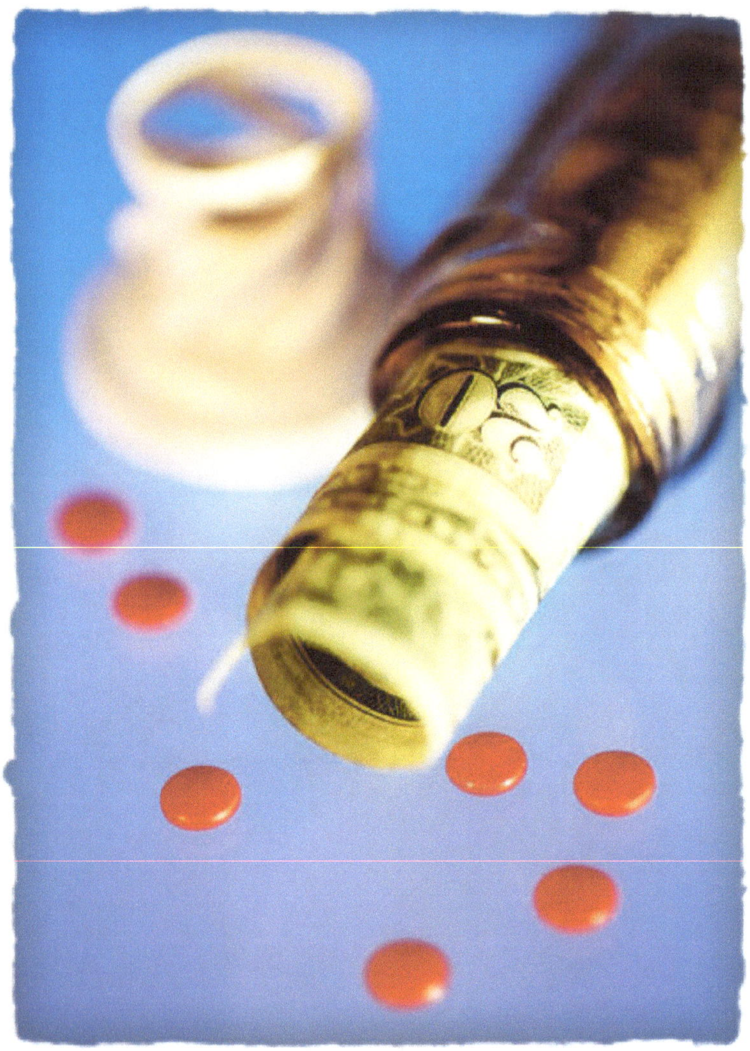

Ghana also had the 3rd highest total spending on health per capita, more of it coming from the private sector ($57) than the govt. ($34).

Guineans spend the most from private coffers ($97; 90%). They have the 2nd largest total spending on health ($111 per pers), after Cape Verde ($232).

In several countries, "other private" spending is near non-existent, their citizens having to shell out from their own pockets, for all non-govt. health expenses.

Nowhere did "other private" spending outweigh out-of-pocket.

Between 2000 & 2006, there was hardly any development in the health insurance sector in Nigeria; instead, out-of-pocket spending grew.

Nigeria govt. spending between 2000 & 2006: no movement. No change in govt. spending in 7 yrs.

Whatever was spent by the govt. in 2000 was just about maintained stagnant throughout the deteriorating sector, 7 yrs. on.

# 6. Spending on Health

6.22

Breakdown of Total Health Spending into Out-of-Pocket, other Private & Govt. Spending per Person in West Africa during 2003/06, $PPP

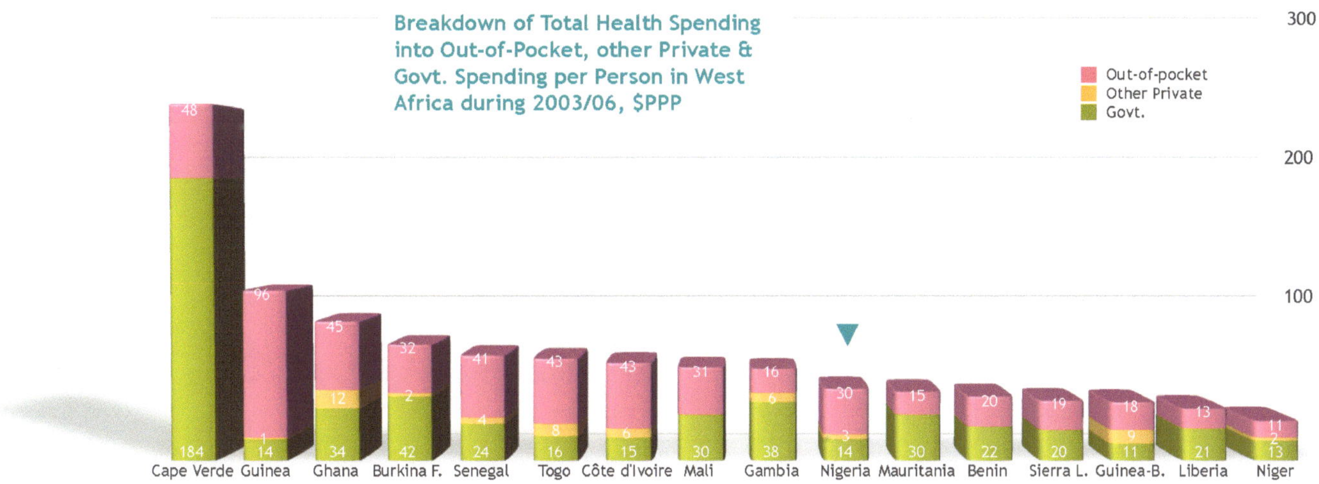


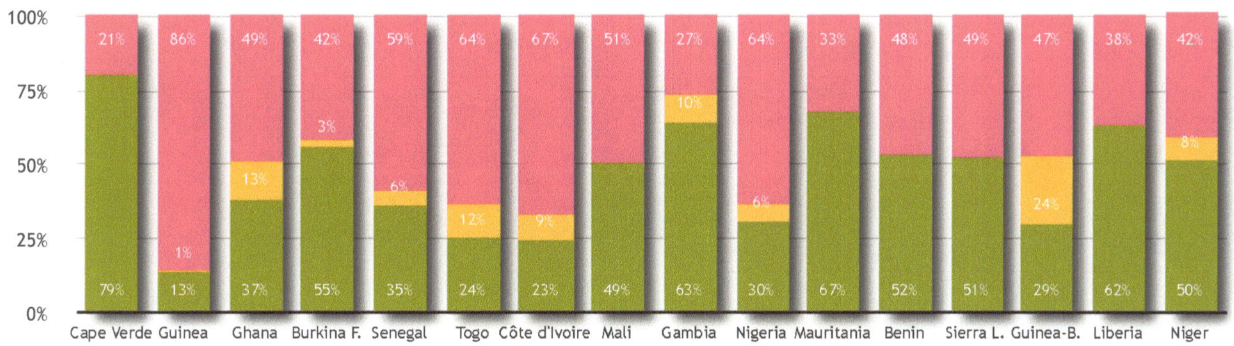


6.23

% Breakdown of Total Health Spending into Out-of-Pocket, other Private & Govt. Spending per Person in West Africa during 2003/06

The most desirable West African country for health purposes is Cape Verde, by several miles.

Primary Data: WHO

Out-of-pocket
Other Private
Govt.

6.24

Breakdown of Total Health Spending into Out-of-Pocket, other Private & Govt. Spending per Person in Nigeria from 2000 to 2006, $PPP

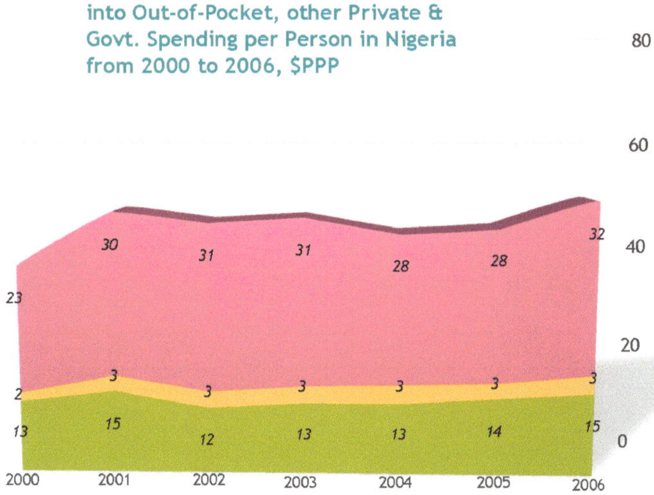


6.25

Breakdown of Total Health Spending into Out-of-Pocket, other Private & Govt. Spending per Person in Mali from 2000 to 2006, $PPP

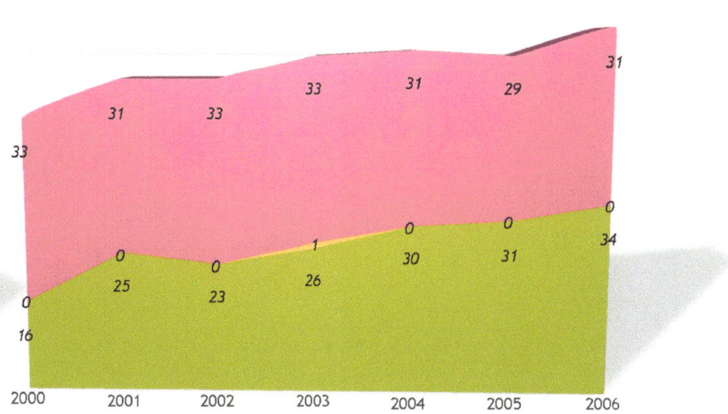

# Leaders & Stragglers

**is yours in working condition?**

In Africa, the most desirable country for health is Botswana, then Namibia and Malawi. Nigeria is 4th from bottom.

## Spending on Health Rankings: 2003-06

| Rank | Country | Rank | Country | Rank | Country |
|---|---|---|---|---|---|
| 1 | Botswana | 15 | Gabon | 29 | Cameroon |
| 2 | Namibia | 16 | Mauritius | 30 | Central Afr. Rep. |
| 3 | Malawi | 17 | Equatorial Guinea | 31 | Chad |
| 4 | Rwanda | 18 | Ghana | 32 | Eritrea |
| 5 | South Africa | 19 | Tanzania | 33 | Guinea |
| 6 | Swaziland | 20 | Mali | 34 | Angola |
| 7 | Seychelles | 21 | Madagascar | 35 | Sierra Leone |
| 8 | Uganda | 22 | Kenya | 36 | Côte d' Ivoire |
| 9 | Zambia | 23 | Guinea-Bissau | 37 | Comoros |
| 10 | Lesotho | 24 | Benin | 38 | **Nigeria** |
| 11 | Mozambique | 25 | Ethiopia | 39 | Congo, Dem. Rep. |
| 12 | Burkina Faso | 26 | Togo | 40 | Burundi |
| 13 | Gambia, The | 27 | Niger | 41 | Congo, Rep. |
| 14 | Cape Verde | 28 | Senegal | | |
| TOP | | MIDDLE | | BOTTOM | |

Central Africa
East Africa
Southern Africa
West Africa

# Wrap-up: Spending on Health

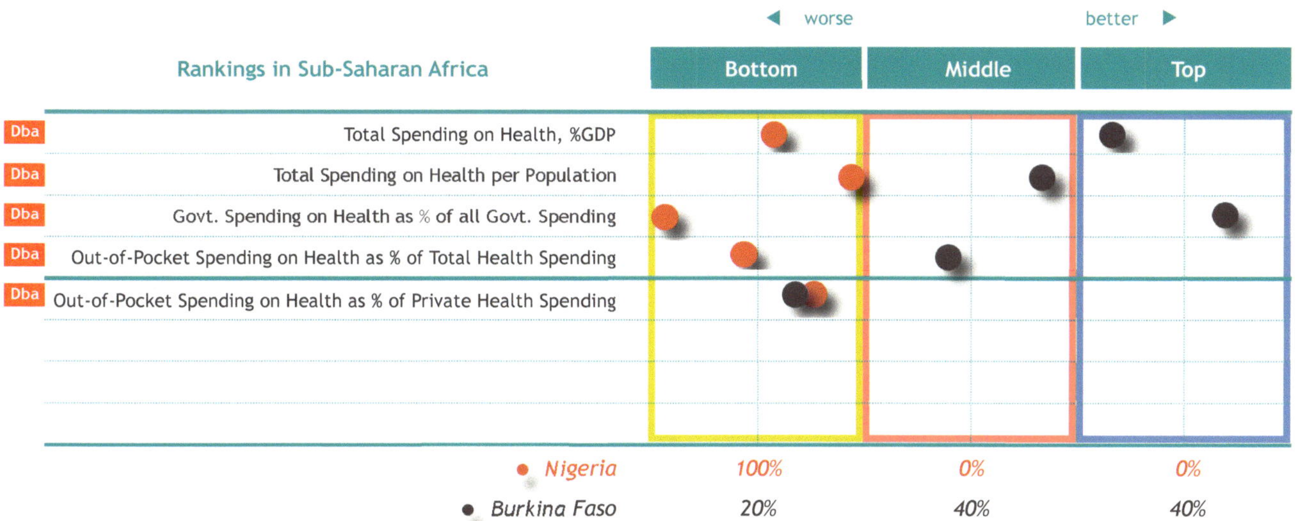


- Burkina Faso, best performer in West Africa, no. 12 in Africa. Nigeria was bottom in West Africa and no. 38 in Africa.
- The reason stands out in stark reality from the boxes: by all 5 measures, Nigeria fails in quality of health services. It spends less than Burkina Faso (and likely, the rest of West Africa) every time.
- Its citizens pay for too much of the services from their own pocket; the government spends too little of its GDP on health while the other expenses it spends on - whatever they are - seem to be of more urgency and take priority over healthcare.
- Whereas Burkina Faso spends bravely out of its public coffers.

# 7. Purchasing Power

**depth of pocket**


7.1 Government Consumption as % of GDP

7.2. Household Consumption as % of GDP

7.3 Government Consumption per Person

7.4 Household Consumption per Person

7.5 Consumption from 1999 to 2007

7.6 Growth in Government Consumption

7.7 Growth in Household Consumption

7.8 Build-up of Govt. & Household Consumption

Leaders & Stragglers

Wrap-up

The purchasing power of a people is usually expressed by the term, "consumption". There are two parts to it: **government** (or public) consumption and **household** (or private) consumption. It is money spent on mainly recurrent expenditure, as distinct from, for example, capital expenditure like projects and investments.

## Government Consumption

The level of government spending tends to reflect the role of the State in an economy. Generally, in mature economies, government consumption hovers between 10% and 20% of GDP. (Although in strongly welfarist societies, e.g. Scandinavia, it tends to be higher.) High expenditure levels are not automatically a positive sign: they could just as easily be beneficial to economic growth as they could be effectively wastes of funds.

## Household Consumption

Usually considerably higher than government consumption, tending towards around 60% of GDP in more developed economies. It reflects the purchasing power and disposable income of the population. Household consumption plays an important role in economic development: it is the main factor that drives production which in turn spurs on investment that again drives production and consumption, in a continuous cycle.

## Consumption per Person

And so, Household Consumption per Person in a virile economy would increase from year to year, or at least would not drop sharply. High private consumption levels usually indicate healthy economies. (In this section, we have again used per population ratios for expression. We believe this is crucial for an accurate assessment of consumption and purchasing power.)

Note: Government/Household Consumption should be distinguished from Government/Private Investments. They both make up spending, but consumption refers to non-capital expenditure, while investments mean capital or infrastructure spending. Dealt with in chapter 9.

**Sources of Primary Data:** IMF, World Bank

# Charts

7.1 Govt. & Household Consumption as % of GDP in West Africa during 2003/06

7.2 Govt. & Household Consumption per Person ($PPP) in West Africa during 2003/06

7.3 Govt. & Household Consumption in Nigeria as % of GDP from 1999-2007

7.4 Govt. & Household Consumption in Sub-Saharan Africa as % of GDP from 1999-2007

7.5 Govt. & Household Consumption per Person in Nigeria ($PPP) from 1999-2007

7.6 Govt. & Household Consumption per Person in Sub-Saharan Africa ($PPP) from 1999-2007

7.7 Growth of Govt. & Household Consumption per Person in West Africa during 2003/06

7.8 Build-up of Govt. & Household Consumption per Person in Nigeria and Sub-Saharan Africa from 2000-07: 2000=100

- **Wrap-up**

# Tables

*1999-2002; 2003-2006:*

- *self-comparison to preceding period;*
- *performance in S-Saharan Africa;*
- *performance in West Africa;*
- *performance among oil-exporters;*

*for:*

Government Consumption as % of GDP

Household Consumption as % of GDP

Government Consumption per Person ($PPP)

Household Consumption per Person ($PPP)

Growth in Government Consumption per Person

Growth in Household Consumption per Person

- Household Consumption per Person in Sub-Saharan Africa during 2003-06: Rankings
- Household Consumption as % of GDP in Sub-Saharan Africa during 2003-06: Rankings
- Growth of Household Consumption per Person in Sub-Saharan Africa during 2003-06: Rankings
- **Purchasing Power Rankings: 2003-06**

# 7.1 Government Consumption as % of GDP

**was it all just a party?**

| | 99-02 | 03-06 |
|---|---|---|
| Self-comparison to Preceding Period | | ◁▷ |
| Performance in Sub-Saharan Africa | ▲ | ▲ |
| Performance in West Africa | ▲ | ▲ |
| | Nigeria | Nigeria |
| | Cape Verde | Mauritania |
| | Mauritania | Ghana |
| | Sierra Leone | Guinea-Bissau |
| | Gambia, The | Benin |
| | Senegal | Senegal |
| | Niger | Cape Verde |
| | Burkina Faso | Sierra Leone |
| | Guinea-Bissau | Burkina Faso |
| | Benin | Niger |
| | Mali | Gambia, The |
| | Ghana | Togo |
| | Togo | Mali |
| | Côte d'Ivoire | Côte d'Ivoire |
| | Guinea | Guinea |
| Performance among Oil-Exporters | ▲ | ▲ |
| | Angola | Angola |
| | Nigeria | Nigeria |
| | Congo, Rep. | Congo, Rep. |
| | Gabon | Sudan |
| | Cameroon | Cameroon |
| | Sudan | Côte d'Ivoire |
| | Chad | Gabon |
| | Côte d'Ivoire | Chad |

Primary Data: World Bank, IMF

7.1 Govt. & Household Consumption as % of GDP in West Africa during 2003/06

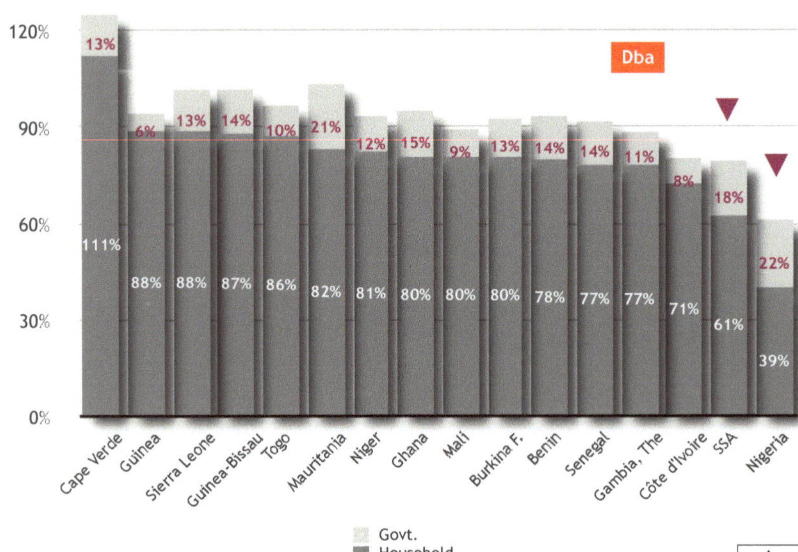


| | |
|---|---|
| ▲ | improved *or* better than average |
| ▼ | worsened *or* worse than average |
| ◁▷ | no change *or* average |

# 7.2 Household Consumption as % of GDP

## *money to burn*

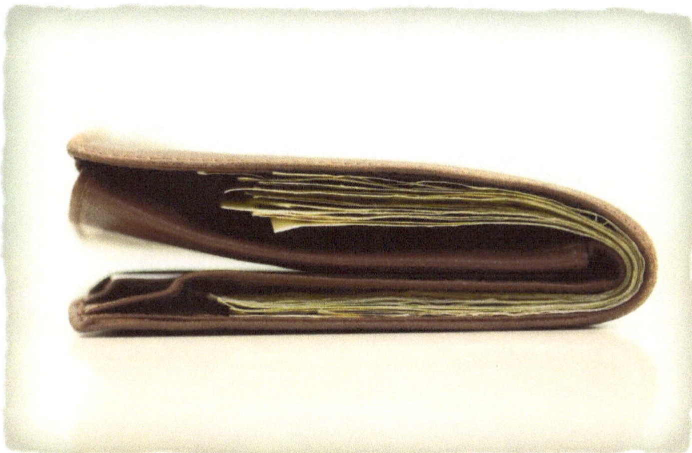

| | 99-02 | 03-06 |
|---|---|---|
| Self-comparison to Preceding Period | | ▼ |
| Performance in Sub-Saharan Africa | ▼ | ▼ |
| Performance in West Africa | ▼ | ▼ |
| | Cape Verde | Cape Verde |
| | Guinea-Bissau | Guinea |
| | Sierra Leone | Sierra Leone |
| | Togo | Guinea-Bissau |
| | Ghana | Togo |
| | Benin | Mauritania |
| | Niger | Niger |
| | Mauritania | Ghana |
| | Burkina Faso | Mali |
| | Guinea | Burkina Faso |
| | Mali | Benin |
| | Senegal | Senegal |
| | Gambia, The | Gambia, The |
| | Côte d'Ivoire | Côte d'Ivoire |
| | **Nigeria** | **Nigeria** |

| | 99-02 | 03-06 |
|---|---|---|
| Performance among Oil-Exporters | ▼ | ▼ |
| | Chad | Sudan |
| | Sudan | Cameroon |
| | Côte d'Ivoire | Côte d'Ivoire |
| | Cameroon | Gabon |
| | Gabon | Chad |
| | **Nigeria** | Angola |
| | Congo, Rep. | **Nigeria** |
| | Angola | Congo, Rep. |

Primary Data: World Bank

A clear depiction of where purchasing power lies. Nigeria is tops in West Africa for govt. consumption, but bottom in household consumption.

A similar situation within the oil group.

Between 1999 and 2006, household consumption dips for Nigeria, while government consumption stays about equal to its preceding high levels.

These suggest Nigerians do not spend as much as their West Africa and oil counterparts in private, household, expenditure.

Reason might be that they are more frugal, but it's more likely that they have a smaller disposable income and are, on the whole, poorer than other Africans.

| | |
|---|---|
| ▲ | improved *or* better than average |
| ▼ | worsened *or* worse than average |
| ◁▷ | no change *or* average |

# 7.3 Government Consumption per Person ($PPP)

***nice... but only if it nourishes***

| | 99-02 | 03-06 |
|---|---|---|
| Self-comparison to Preceding Period | | ▲ |
| Performance in Sub-Saharan Africa | ▲ | ▲ |
| Performance in West Africa | ▲ | ▲ |
| | Cape Verde | **Nigeria** |
| | **Nigeria** | Mauritania |
| | Mauritania | Cape Verde |
| | Senegal | Senegal |
| | Benin | Benin |
| | Gambia, The | Ghana |
| | Côte d'Ivoire | Burkina Faso |
| | Burkina Faso | Côte d'Ivoire |
| | Ghana | Gambia, The |
| | Mali | Mali |
| | Niger | Sierra Leone |
| | Togo | Togo |
| | Guinea-Bissau | Niger |
| | Guinea | Guinea-Bissau |
| | Sierra Leone | Guinea |
| Performance among Oil-Exporters | ▲ | ▲ |
| | Gabon | Angola |
| | Angola | Gabon |
| | Congo, Rep. | Congo, Rep. |
| | **Nigeria** | **Nigeria** |
| | Cameroon | Sudan |
| | Côte d'Ivoire | Cameroon |
| | Sudan | Côte d'Ivoire |
| | Chad | Chad |

Primary Data: World Bank, IMF

7.2

Govt. & Household Consumption per Person ($PPP) in West Africa during 2003/06

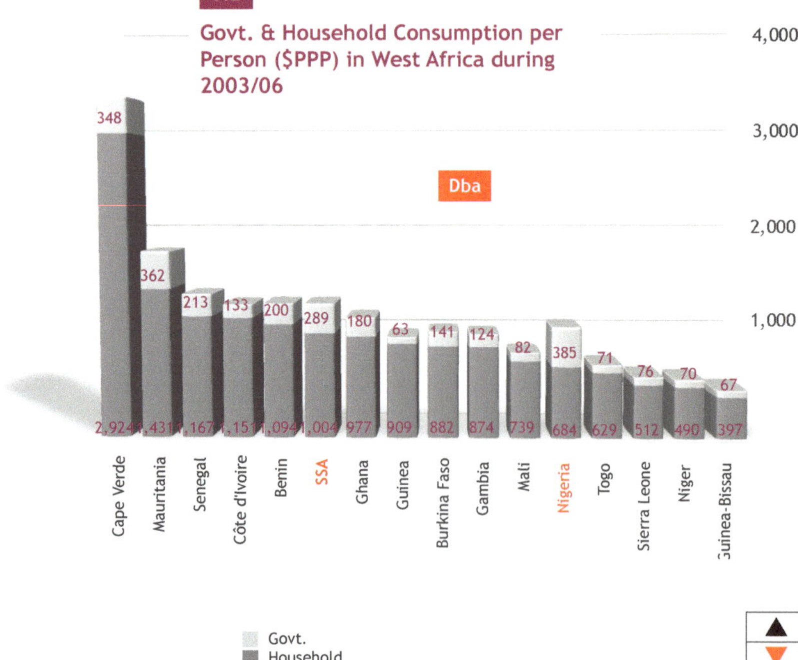


| | |
|---|---|
| ▲ | improved *or* better than average |
| ▼ | worsened *or* worse than average |
| ◁▷ | no change *or* average |

# 7.4 Household Consumption per Person ($PPP)

*because they can afford it*

In money terms per capita, the numbers tell a similar story: rich and spending govt., but a non-spending population, individually effectively poorer than other Africans.

| | 99-02 | 03-06 |
|---|---|---|
| Self-comparison to Preceding Period | | ▲ |
| Performance in Sub-Saharan Africa | ▼ | ▼ |
| Performance in West Africa | ▼ | ▼ |

| 99-02 | 03-06 |
|---|---|
| Cape Verde | Cape Verde |
| Mauritania | Mauritania |
| Côte d'Ivoire | Senegal |
| Benin | Côte d'Ivoire |
| Senegal | Benin |
| Ghana | Ghana |
| Guinea | Guinea |
| Burkina Faso | Burkina Faso |
| Gambia, The | Gambia, The |
| **Nigeria** | Mali |
| Togo | **Nigeria** |
| Mali | Togo |
| Guinea-Bissau | Sierra Leone |
| Niger | Niger |
| Sierra Leone | Guinea-Bissau |

Primary Data: World Bank

| Performance among Oil-Exporters | ▼ | ▼ |
|---|---|---|
| | Gabon | Gabon |
| | Cameroon | Angola |
| | Côte d'Ivoire | Cameroon |
| | Sudan | Sudan |
| | Congo, Rep. | Congo, Rep. |
| | Chad | Côte d'Ivoire |
| | Angola | Chad |
| | **Nigeria** | **Nigeria** |

| | |
|---|---|
| ▲ | improved *or* better than average |
| ▼ | worsened *or* worse than average |
| ◁▷ | no change *or* average |

# 7.5 Consumption from 1999 to 2007

7.3

Govt. & Household Consumption in Nigeria as % of GDP from 1999-2007

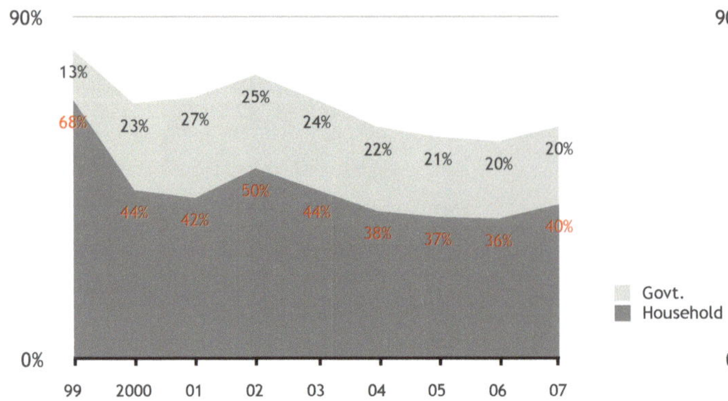


7.4

Govt. & Household Consumption in Sub-Saharan Africa as % of GDP from 1999-2007

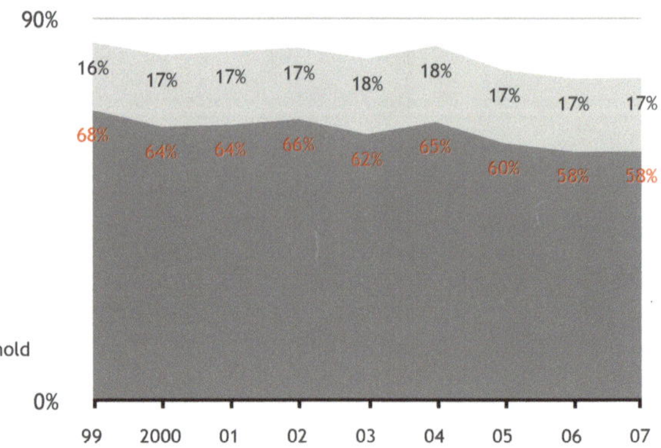


Total consumption, as a % of total economic output, fell across Africa (9%), but it fell deeper in Nigeria (21%).

The levels of personal consumption were every time higher in the rest of Africa (68% ending up as 58%) than Nigeria (68% ending up as 40%).

In money terms, consumption rose in Africa, suggesting a population growing in wealth. Nigeria's residents were poorer (smaller disposable income).

Consumption in GDP terms fell, & in money terms rose, suggesting that the economies can sustain higher spending levels, spurring growth; but only if managed more efficiently.

7.5

Govt. & Household Consumption per Person in Nigeria ($PPP) from 1999-2007

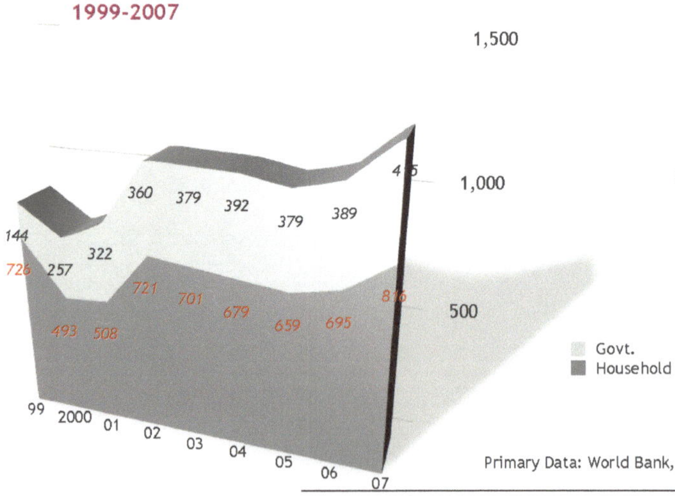


7.6

Govt. & Household Consumption per Person in Sub-Saharan Africa ($PPP) from 1999-2007

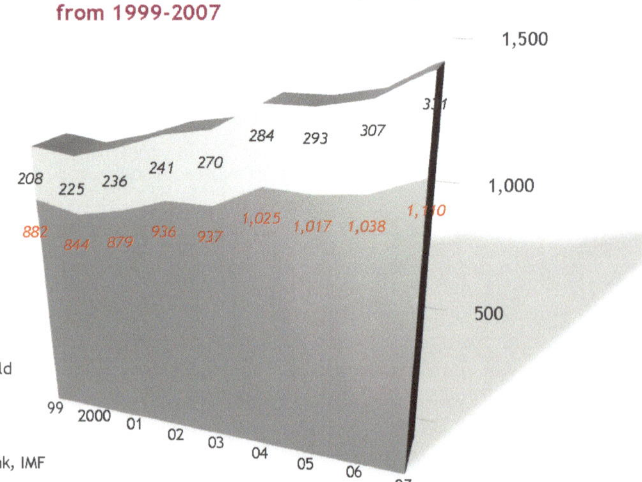


Primary Data: World Bank, IMF

## 7. Purchasing Power

### Household Consumption per Person in Sub-Saharan Africa during 2003-06: Rankings

| Rank | Country | Rank | Country | Rank | Country |
|---|---|---|---|---|---|
| 1 | Seychelles | 15 | Kenya | 29 | Eritrea |
| 2 | Gabon | 16 | Equatorial Guinea | 30 | Uganda |
| 3 | Mauritius | 17 | Lesotho | 31 | Rwanda |
| 4 | South Africa | 18 | Ghana | 32 | Togo |
| 5 | Botswana | 19 | Comoros | 33 | Malawi |
| 6 | Cape Verde | 20 | Chad | 34 | Central Afr. Rep. |
| 7 | Swaziland | 21 | Guinea | 35 | Sierra Leone |
| 8 | Namibia | 22 | Burkina Faso | 36 | Ethiopia |
| 9 | Angola | 23 | Gambia, The | 37 | Mozambique |
| 10 | Cameroon | 24 | Tanzania | 38 | Niger |
| 11 | Senegal | 25 | Madagascar | 39 | Guinea-Bissau |
| 12 | Congo, Rep. | 26 | Mali | 40 | Burundi |
| 13 | Côte d' Ivoire | 27 | Zambia | 41 | Congo, Dem. Rep. |
| 14 | Benin | 28 | Nigeria | | |
| | TOP | | MIDDLE | | BOTTOM |

Not surprising, then, that Nigeria is at best just about average in individual's purchasing power.

This is often camouflaged by the capacity of its huge market to absorb products and services thrown at it.

It should be remembered that its people may be poorer on the whole than other Africans, but even though the percentage of its relatively wealthy is small...

... because of its overall population, that small percentage is still larger in absolute size (no. of persons) than many countries' entire populations.

### Household Consumption as % of GDP in Sub-Saharan Africa during 2003-06: Rankings

| Rank | Country | Rank | Country | Rank | Country |
|---|---|---|---|---|---|
| 1 | Cape Verde | 15 | Niger | 28 | Swaziland |
| 2 | Malawi | 16 | Ghana | 29 | Mauritius |
| 3 | Central Afr. Rep. | 17 | Mali | 30 | Zambia |
| 4 | Lesotho | 18 | Burkina Faso | 31 | South Africa |
| 5 | Congo, Dem. Rep. | 19 | Benin | 32 | Gabon |
| 6 | Guinea | 20 | Senegal | 33 | Chad |
| 7 | Comoros | 21 | Gambia, The | 34 | Seychelles |
| | Sierra Leone | 22 | Uganda | 35 | Namibia |
| 8 | Guinea-Bissau | 23 | Tanzania | 36 | Angola |
| 9 | Togo | 24 | Kenya | 37 | Nigeria |
| 10 | Rwanda | 25 | Mozambique | 38 | Congo, Rep. |
| 11 | Madagascar | 26 | Cameroon | 39 | Botswana |
| 12 | Ethiopia | 27 | Côte d' Ivoire | 40 | Equatorial Guinea |
| 13 | Burundi | | | | |
| 14 | Eritrea | | | | |
| | TOP | | MIDDLE | | BOTTOM |

Primary Data: World Bank, IMF

Central Africa
East Africa
Southern Africa
West Africa

# 7.6 Growth in Government Consumption per Person

**there's more where that came from**

| | 99-02 | 03-06 |
|---|---|---|
| Self-comparison to Preceding Period | | ▼ |
| Performance in Sub-Saharan Africa | ▲ | ▼ |
| Performance in West Africa | ▲ | ▼ |

| ▲ | ▼ |
|---|---|
| **Nigeria** | Guinea-Bissau |
| Sierra Leone | Ghana |
| Guinea | Mali |
| Benin | Mauritania |
| Mauritania | Benin |
| Guinea-Bissau | Cape Verde |
| Senegal | Senegal |
| Cape Verde | Togo |
| Burkina Faso | Burkina Faso |
| Côte d'Ivoire | Niger |
| Gambia, The | Côte d'Ivoire |
| Ghana | Sierra Leone |
| Niger | **Nigeria** |
| Mali | Gambia, The |
| Togo | Guinea |

The Nigerian govt. seems to have begun to cut down its expenses drastically during 2003-06, compared to 1999-02 levels.

Performance among Oil-Exporters

| ▲ | ▼ |
|---|---|
| **Nigeria** | Sudan |
| Angola | Gabon |
| Sudan | Cameroon |
| Chad | Chad |
| Cameroon | Côte d'Ivoire |
| Côte d'Ivoire | **Nigeria** |
| Congo, Rep. | Congo, Rep. |
| Gabon | Angola |

7.7

Growth of Govt. & Household Consumption per Person in West Africa during 2003/06

Primary Data: World Bank, IMF

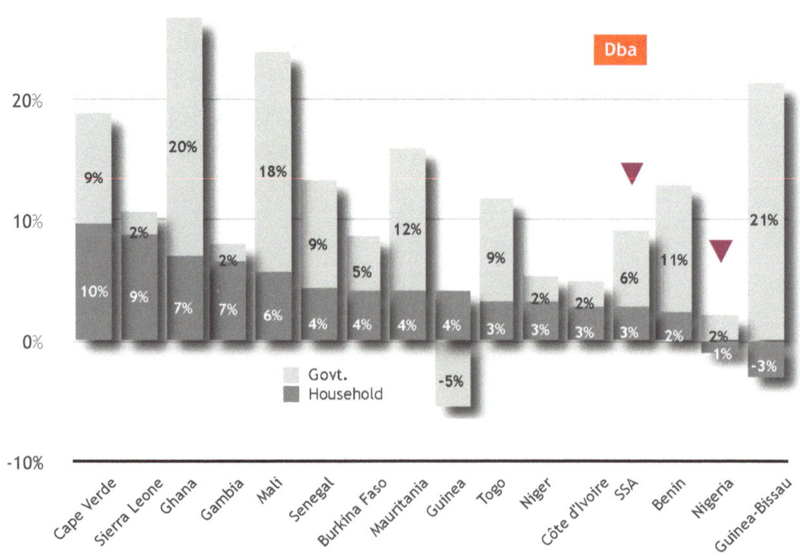


| | |
|---|---|
| ▲ | improved *or* better than average |
| ▼ | worsened *or* worse than average |
| ◁▷ | no change *or* average |

# 7.7 Growth in Household Consumption per Person

**i'd like this... and that... and that...**

But individuals' consumption was not growing, either (or, at best, was growing at a falling rate, and relatively much slower than elsewhere).

Not a good sign. Because it again highlights a progressively weaker private purchasing power.

Without consumption, industry won't grow, putting pressure on GDP, and ultimately shrinking the economy.

| | 99-02 | 03-06 |
|---|---|---|
| Self-comparison to Preceding Period | | ▼ |
| Performance in Sub-Saharan Africa | ▲ | ▼ |
| Performance in West Africa | ▼ | ▼ |

| 99-02 | 03-06 |
|---|---|
| Sierra Leone | Cape Verde |
| Cape Verde | Sierra Leone |
| Burkina Faso | Ghana |
| Mali | Gambia, The |
| Mauritania | Mali |
| Guinea | Senegal |
| Senegal | Burkina Faso |
| Ghana | Mauritania |
| Benin | Guinea |
| Gambia, The | Togo |
| **Nigeria** | Niger |
| Niger | Côte d'Ivoire |
| Togo | Benin |
| Guinea-Bissau | **Nigeria** |
| Côte d'Ivoire | Guinea-Bissau |

Primary Data: World Bank, IMF

| | 99-02 | 03-06 |
|---|---|---|
| Performance among Oil-Exporters | ▼ | ▼ |

| 99-02 | 03-06 |
|---|---|
| Angola | Gabon |
| Gabon | Angola |
| Chad | Congo, Rep. |
| Cameroon | Sudan |
| Sudan | Côte d'Ivoire |
| **Nigeria** | Cameroon |
| Côte d'Ivoire | **Nigeria** |
| Congo, Rep. | Chad |

| | |
|---|---|
| ▲ | improved *or* better than average |
| ▼ | worsened *or* worse than average |
| ◁▷ | no change *or* average |

# 7.8 Build-up of Consumption from 1999 to 2007

Looks like there was a rally to an increased purchasing power in Nigeria between 2000 & 2007, if all the countries are put to the same start level in 2000.

Suggests that pre-2000 levels were so low that even later growth rates could not bring it to par in West Africa, as borne out by the preceding sections above.

**7.8**

**Build-up of Govt. & Household Consumption per Person in Nigeria and Sub-Saharan Africa from 2000-07: 2000=100**

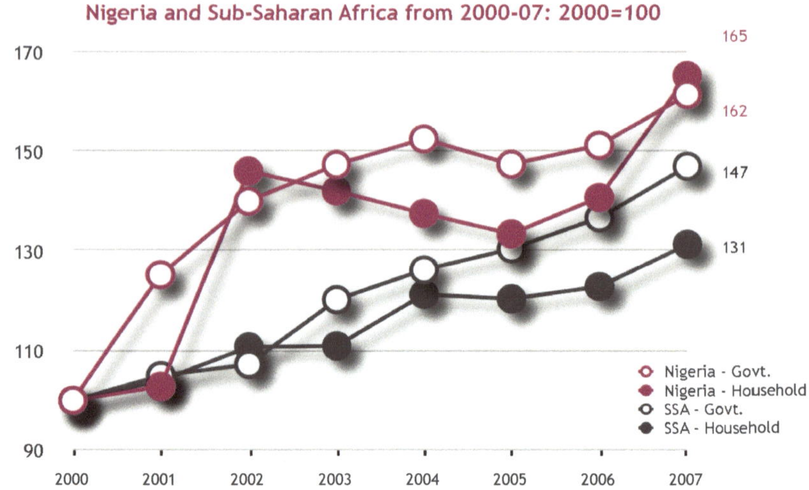


Primary Data: World Bank, IMF

Central Africa
East Africa
Southern Africa
West Africa

Poor growth in household consumption between 2003-06, again as illustrated by the build-up chart above.

**Growth of Household Consumption per Person in Sub-Saharan Africa during 2003-06: Rankings**

| Rank | Country | Rank | Country | Rank | Country |
|---|---|---|---|---|---|
| 1 | Gabon | 15 | Angola | 29 | Niger |
| 2 | Ethiopia | 16 | Congo, Rep. | 30 | Namibia |
| 3 | Madagascar | 17 | Mali | 31 | Côte d' Ivoire |
| 4 | Botswana | 18 | Comoros | 32 | Cameroon |
| 5 | Cape Verde | 19 | Congo, Dem. Rep. | 33 | Benin |
| 6 | Mauritius | 20 | Swaziland | 34 | Zambia |
| 7 | Sierra Leone | 21 | Rwanda | 35 | Burundi |
| 8 | Central Afr. Rep. | 22 | Senegal | 36 | Lesotho |
| 9 | South Africa | 23 | Burkina Faso | 37 | Nigeria |
| 10 | Kenya | 24 | Mozambique | 38 | Chad |
| 11 | Ghana | 25 | Guinea | 39 | Guinea-Bissau |
| 12 | Gambia, The | 26 | Uganda | 40 | Eritrea |
| 13 | Malawi | 27 | Togo | 41 | Equatorial Guinea |
| 14 | Tanzania | 28 | Seychelles | | |
| TOP | | MIDDLE | | BOTTOM | |

# Leaders & Stragglers

**around the world in 80 days**

Bleak verdict, indeed.

Bringing to question issues like:

• an impoverishing larger segment of population; or

• wealth being restricted to a small minority, so that their large consumption notwithstanding, data still reports poor overall purchasing power; or

... a mixture of both.

## Purchasing Power Rankings: 2003-06

| Rank | Country | Rank | Country | Rank | Country |
|---|---|---|---|---|---|
| 1 | Cape Verde | 15 | Senegal | 29 | Cameroon |
| 2 | Gabon | 16 | Swaziland | 30 | Côte d' Ivoire |
| 3 | Mauritius | 17 | Gambia, The | 31 | Namibia |
| 4 | Madagascar | 18 | Lesotho | 32 | Uganda |
| 5 | Comoros | 19 | Mali | 33 | Niger |
| 6 | South Africa | 20 | Angola | 34 | Eritrea |
| 7 | Central Afr. Rep. | 21 | Tanzania | 35 | Guinea-Bissau |
| 8 | Ghana | 22 | Rwanda | 36 | Mozambique |
| 9 | Malawi | 23 | Burkina Faso | 37 | Burundi |
| 10 | Botswana | 24 | Seychelles | 38 | Zambia |
| 11 | Sierra Leone | 25 | Congo, Dem. Rep. | 39 | Chad |
| 12 | Kenya | 26 | Benin | 40 | Equatorial Guinea |
| 13 | Ethiopia | 27 | Congo, Rep. | 41 | Nigeria |
| 14 | Guinea | 28 | Togo | | |
| | TOP | | MIDDLE | | BOTTOM |

Primary Data: World Bank, IMF

Central Africa
East Africa
Southern Africa
West Africa

# Wrap-up: Purchasing Power

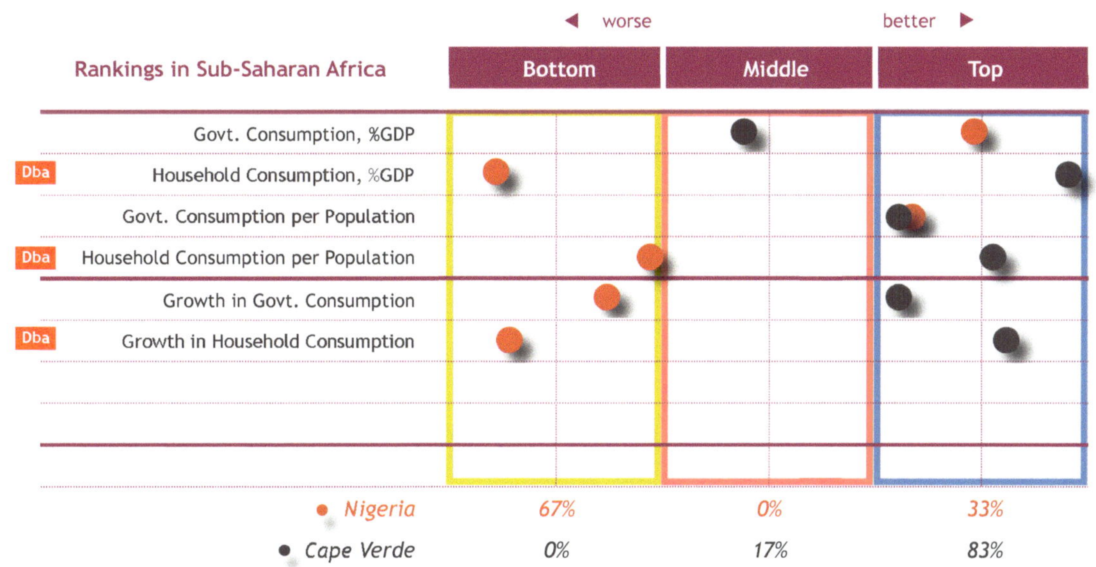


- The people of Cape Verde have the deepest pockets in West Africa and Africa, too. Nigeria is bottom of West Africa and Africa, too.

- Government consumption in Nigeria is healthy enough, the problem is private disposable income. The Nigeria government was cutting back its spending, though, growing it at a falling pace. The contrast couldn't be starker between Nigeria government spending and the purchasing power of the country's people.

- It might be proposed that this is because of its large population, but that won't entirely explain the dismal showing. Government consumption per person of population is very robust, despite that large population.

- Instead, it is more likely that there is a quickly growing gulf between sections of the population, between the rich and the poor, the ranks of the rich narrowing, while that at the other end is increasingly bloated.

# 8. Self-Reliance

*doing it themselves*

8.1 Exports & Imports of Goods & Services

8.2 Growth in Goods Exports and Imports

8.3 Growth in Services Exports and Imports

8.4 Imports Dependence in Merchandise

8.5 Imports Dependence in Services

8.6 Composition of Goods Exports and Imports

8.7 Foreign Reserves (months of imports)

8.8 Foreign Debt (as % of GDP)

8.9 Foreign Debt (as $PPP per Person)

8.10 Service of Foreign Debt (as % of exports)

8.11 Growth of Income & Growth of Debt

8.12 Aid Dependency (as % of GDP)

8.13 Aid Dependency (as $PPP per Person)

Leaders & Stragglers

Wrap-up

Strictly speaking, no economy can be self-reliant. But the more developed the economy, the less reliant it is on external providers for products or services it can efficiently render by itself. Every economy is said to have an areas of "competitive advantage": sectors in which it is well positioned (by natural endowments, for example, or specific skills, etc) to compete favourably with other countries. It would not make sense, for example, for Nigeria to depend on others for crude oil, or the United States to outsource its banking needs to foreign operators.

So, different sectors can be evaluated to see if the economy is operating as efficiently as should be possible in the circumstances. By expressing these indicators in per capita terms, a more accurate picture of self-reliance or the extent of dependence is achieved.

### Imports dependence

The extent on which an economy depends on others to supply goods and services. Usually taken to be an unhealthy situation, unless inescapable. Holland, for example, cannot be expected to grow its own bananas, but would be inefficient if it relied overwhelmingly on others for its dairy needs.

**Net exports:** desirable status; means the country exports more than it imports; results in a positive trade balance.

**Net imports:** the country imports more than it exports; results in a negative trade balance.

By self-sufficient, we mean that the country exports more than it imports, not that it produces all the quantity of the particular products that its consumption level requires.

### Composition of Goods Exports

Three broad sectors: agriculture, fuels & mining, and manufactures. Agriculture and fuels/mining are regarded as "primary" sectors because their products require relatively little further innovation before sale. Manufactures, on the other hand, require innovation and significant further added input or processing; and so, further alteration/transformation. Sturdier and more developed economies are supposed to rely more on the sectors that demand innovation and actual discernible value-added. These economies are generally less susceptible to the vagaries of international commodity prices, which tend to be more fickle since these commodities literally are sold as-is, without the distinguishing qualities of end-processing or transformation that would provide comparatively more attractive value-added qualities.

### Foreign Reserves

Countries usually hold money in foreign reserves, which can be deployed in a number of ways, for a variety of objectives. While huge foreign reserves is the better position, the continuous growing of reserves without appropriate deployment might augur negatively for the country. The volume of reserves is often measured by the number of months of imports it can finance at prevailing import levels. This helps put the amount of reserves in more accurate contexts, since imports would have to be paid for in foreign currency.

### Foreign Debt

Again, strictly speaking, it would be unusual to come across a country (or government) that is without debt. Domestic debt is common and in order, because it is a convenient way for governments to source funds without "capital flight", that is, without having repayment funds leaving the country to creditors abroad. Domestic debt, besides incentives of specifically micro-economic sorts, ensures that the money circulates and stays within the country, stimulating economic development, rather than leaving the country's shores and stimulating economic growth in foreign lands.

However, only rarely do countries manage to source all funds internally. The danger, though, is to have foreign debt grow to unmanageable proportions that would compromise the country's ability to drive internal growth, because it would effectively become committed to an albatross of external debt repayment burdens. Countries in that position jeopardise domestic needs because a disproportionately large chunk of their earnings goes towards servicing foreign debt commitments. This is often a big danger with developing economies.

### Growth of Income & Debt

Income here refers to GNI: Gross National Income, an estimation of the earnings of all of a country's residents and non-residents, i.e. it includes remittances from abroad. Comparing its growth with the growth of debt provides a rough assessment of the country's book balance and sustainability.

### Aid Dependency

Foreign aid is not necessarily restricted to poor countries, although they - understandably - form the bulk of beneficiaries of aid. Usually, countries are either net donors or net recipients. While it would be unexpected for the United States, Switzerland or other west European countries to be beneficiaries of any sort of aid, it is accepted that Hungary, Jordan, Israel and Poland, for example, would be listed as aid recipients of one economic sort or another, despite being rich or developed economies. However, the danger here applies more accurately to the poorer countries of the developing world and the countries of the "transition" economies (mostly the former Soviet Republics and south-east Asia). Excessive dependency on aid is taken to be a sign of a weak economic base and rings alarm bells of fragility.

### Aid Dependency and Country Development

There has been a lot of discussion lately about the appropriateness or otherwise of aid as a channel for the stimulation of social and economic development. Much has been said about the merits and otherwise of a continued pumping of aid into developing country economies. An attempt is made in the earlier part of this book (Part I) to view the question from an empirical perspective, by comparing the pace of economic and social development of African countries, with the amount of aid they received, across 8 to 12 years.

**Sources of Primary Data:** AfDB, IMF, World Bank, WTO

# Charts


8.1 Total Exports and Imports per Person of Population in West Africa during 2003/06. ($US)

8.2 % Breakdown of Exports and Imports into Goods & Services in West Africa during 2003/06

8.3 Total Exports and Imports as % of GDP in West Africa during 2003/06

8.4 Total Exports and Imports per Person of Population in Nigeria from 1999-2006 ($US)

8.5 Total Exports and Imports per Person of Population in Sub-Saharan Africa from 1999-2006 ($US)

8.6 Total Exports and Imports per Person of Population among the Oil Exporters from 1999-2006 ($US)

8.7 Total Exports and Imports as % of GDP in Nigeria from 1999-2006

8.8 Total Exports and Imports as % of GDP in Sub-Saharan Africa from 1999-2006

8.9 Total Exports and Imports as % of GDP among the Oil Exporters from 1999-2006

8.10 Growth on Previous Yr. of Goods Exports and Imports per Person in West Africa during 2003/06

8.11 Build-up of Goods Exports and Imports per Person in Nigeria and Sub-Saharan Africa from 2000-07: 2000=100

8.12 Build-up of Goods Exports and Imports per Person in Nigeria and Oil-Exporting Countries from 2000-07: 2000=100

8.13 Growth on Previous Yr. of Services Exports and Imports per Person in West Africa during 2003/06

8.14 Build-up of Services Exports and Imports per Person in Nigeria and Sub-Saharan Africa from 2000-06: 2000=100

8.15 Build-up of Services Exports and Imports per Person in Nigeria and Oil-Exporting Countries from 2000-06: 2000=100

8.16 Net Goods Exports per Person in West Africa during 2003/06

8.17 Net Goods Exports per Person in Nigeria and Sub-Saharan Africa from 1999-2007

8.18 Net Services Exports per Person in West Africa during 2003/06

8.19 Net Services Exports per Person in Nigeria and Sub-Saharan Africa from 1999-2007

8.20 Composition of Goods Exports and Imports in West Africa during 2003/06

8.21 Composition of Goods Exports and Imports in Nigeria from 1999-2005

8.22 Composition of Services Exports and Imports in West Africa during 2003/06

8.23 Composition of Services Exports and Imports in Nigeria from 1999-2005

8.24 Foreign Reserves (as months of imports) in West Africa during 2003-06

8.25 Foreign Reserves (as months of imports) in Nigeria and Sub-Saharan Africa from 1997 - 2008

8.26 Foreign Debt as % of GDP in West Africa during 2003-06

8.27 Foreign Debt as % of GDP in Nigeria and Sub-Saharan Africa from 1997/01-2008

8.28 Foreign Debt per Person of Population in West Africa during 2003/06 ($PPP)

8.29 Foreign Debt per Person of Population in Nigeria and Sub-Saharan Africa from 1997-2008 ($PPP)

8.30 Service of Foreign Debt as % of Exports in West Africa during 2003/06

8.31 Service of Foreign Debt as % of Exports in Nigeria from 1999-2007

8.32 Growth Rates of Debt and Income in West Africa during 2003/06 (%)

8.33 Net Growth Rate of Debt and Income in West Africa during 2003/06 (%)

8.34 Build-up of Debt and Income in Nigeria and Sub-Saharan Africa from 2000-2006: 2000=100

8.35 Foreign Aid as % of GDP in West Africa during 2003/06

8.36 Foreign Aid as % of GDP in Nigeria and Sub-Saharan Africa from 1999-2007

8.37 Foreign Aid as $PPP per Person in West Africa during 2003/06

8.38 Foreign Aid in Nigeria and Sub-Saharan Africa during 2003/06 as $PPP per Person

- **Wrap-up**

# Tables

*2000-2002; 2003-2006:*
- *self-comparison to preceding period;*
- *performance in S-Saharan Africa;*
- *performance in West Africa;*
- *performance among oil-exporters;*

*for:*

Growth in Total Goods Exports per Population

Growth in Services Exports per Population

---------------------------

*1999-2002; 2003-2006:*
- *self-comparison to preceding period;*
- *performance in S-Saharan Africa;*
- *performance in West Africa;*
- *performance among oil-exporters;*

*for:*

Growth in Total Goods Exports per Population

Imports Dependence in Merchandise

Imports Dependence in Services

Service of Foreign Debt (as % of exports)

---------------------------

*1997-2002; 2003-2006; 2007-2008:*
- *self-comparison to preceding period;*
- *performance in S-Saharan Africa;*
- *performance in West Africa;*
- *performance among oil-exporters;*

*for:*

Foreign Reserves (months of imports)

Foreign Debt (as % of GDP)

Foreign Debt (as $PPP per person)

Aid Dependency (as % of GDP)

Aid Dependency (as $PPP per person)

---------------------------

- Total Exports and Imports per Person of Population in West Africa during 2003/06 ($US)
- Merchandise Imports Dependence per Person in Sub-Saharan Africa during 2003-06: Rankings
- Services Imports Dependence per Person in Sub-Saharan Africa during 2003-06: Rankings
- Foreign Reserves (as months of imports) in Sub-Saharan Africa during 2003-06: Rankings
- Foreign Debt as % of GDP in Sub-Saharan Africa during 2003-06: Rankings
- Foreign Debt per Person of Population in Sub-Saharan Africa during 2003-06: Rankings
- Service of Foreign Debt as % of Exports in Sub-Saharan Africa during 2003-06: Rankings
- Foreign Aid as % of GDP in Sub-Saharan Africa during 2003-06: Rankings
- Foreign Aid in Sub-Saharan Africa as $PPP per Person during 2003-06: Rankings
- Household Consumption as % of GDP in Sub-Saharan Africa during 2003-06: Rankings
- **Self-Reliance Rankings: 2003-06**

# 8.1 Exports & Imports of Goods & Services

## outgoings & incomings

| | EXPORTS per PERSON: $US | | | IMPORTS per PERSON: $US | | |
|---|---|---|---|---|---|---|
| | Goods | Services | Total Exports | Goods | Services | Total Imports |
| Cape Verde | 33 | 513 | 546 | 877 | 406 | 1,283 |
| Côte d'Ivoire | 389 | 35 | 424 | 243 | 103 | 346 |
| oil SSA | 380 | 29 | 408 | 166 | 88 | 254 |
| Nigeria | 305 | 33 | 338 | 120 | 48 | 169 |
| SSA | 236 | 41 | 276 | 209 | 66 | 275 |
| | | | | | | |
| Mauritania | 217 | 22 | 239 | 365 | 105 | 469 |
| Senegal | 127 | 51 | 178 | 255 | 61 | 315 |
| Ghana | 126 | 41 | 167 | 218 | 47 | 265 |
| Togo | 100 | 21 | 121 | 169 | 41 | 210 |
| Mali | 99 | 18 | 117 | 133 | 48 | 181 |
| | | | | | | |
| Guinea | 90 | 4 | 94 | 89 | 22 | 111 |
| Benin | 68 | 23 | 91 | 109 | 32 | 141 |
| Gambia | 6 | 52 | 57 | 138 | 34 | 172 |
| Guinea-Bissau | 47 | 4 | 51 | 56 | 28 | 84 |
| Burkina Faso | 34 | 10 | 43 | 92 | 24 | 116 |
| | | | | | | |
| Niger | 34 | 6 | 40 | 60 | 19 | 79 |
| Sierra Leone | 28 | 11 | 39 | 60 | 15 | 76 |

Primary Data: WTO, World Bank

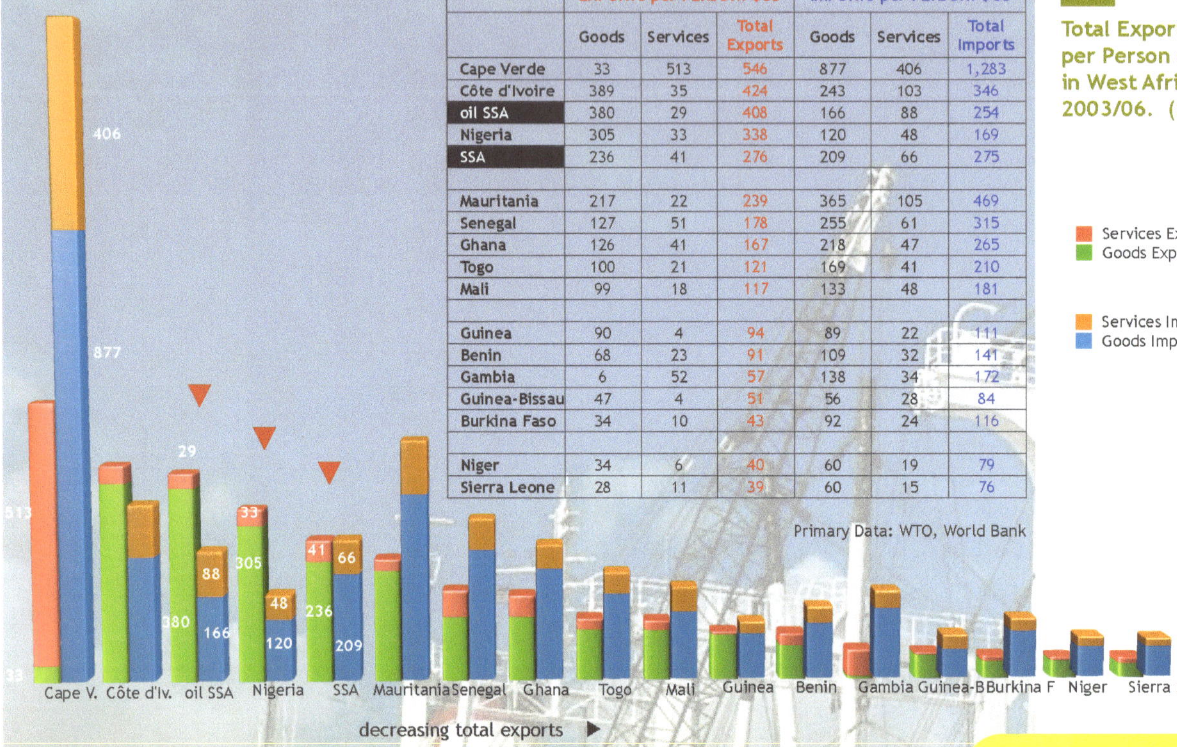


**8.1**

**Total Exports and Imports per Person of Population in West Africa during 2003/06. ($US)**

Services Exports
Goods Exports

Services Imports
Goods Imports

*Nigeria has the 3rd highest volume of total exports per person in West Africa.*

*Most of the exports are merchandise (goods; 90%) and much of that merchandise is crude oil. Only a small % comes from the services sector (10%).*

*The same is true of Africa's oil bloc, 93% goods and 7% services. For the rest of Africa, the ratios were 85% and 15%.*

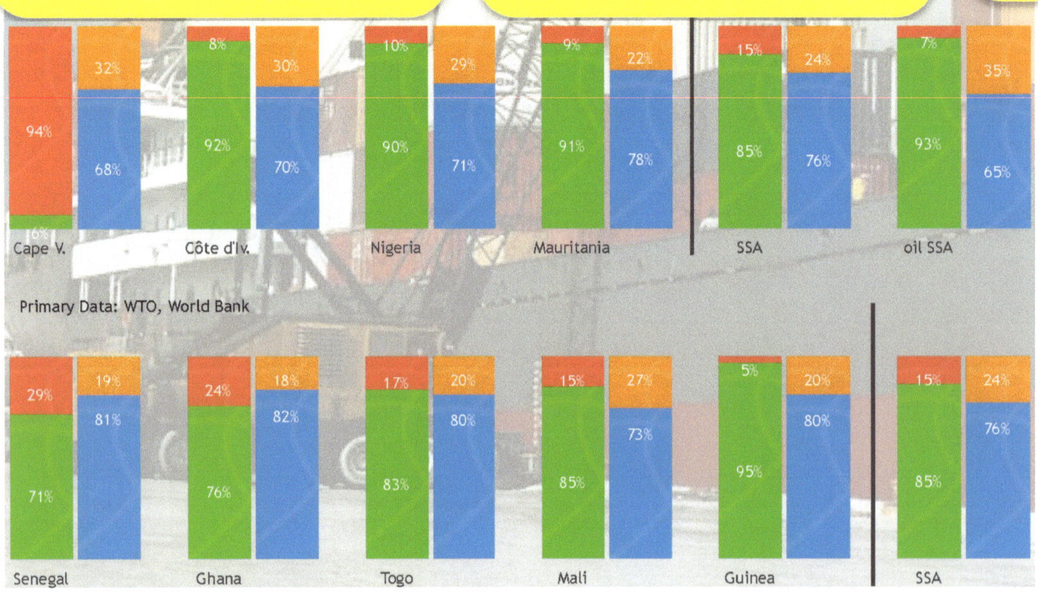


**8.2**

**% Breakdown of Exports and Imports into Goods & Services in West Africa during 2003/06**

Services Exports
Goods Exports

Services Imports
Goods Imports

**8.3**

**Total Exports and Imports as % of GDP in West Africa during 2003/06.**

If taken as a proportion of the country overall economy size, rather than $ per person, Nigeria has the highest volume of exports.

Cape Verde & Gambia are the only countries in West Africa that earn more exports revenue from services and not goods.

And Nigeria is 1 of only 2 countries in West Africa that export more than they import, as a proportion of economy.

The other country, unsurprisingly, is the only other oil country in the group: Côte d'Ivoire.

**8.2**

**% Breakdown of Exports and Imports into Goods & Services in West Africa during 2003/06**

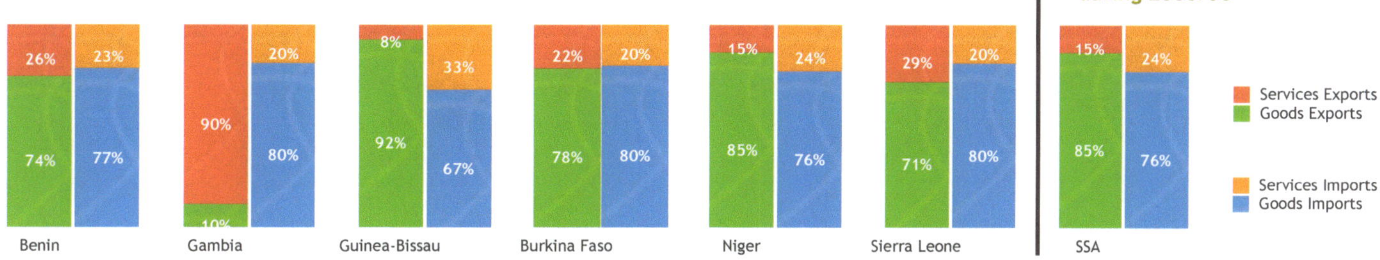

## 8. Self-Reliance

Exports per person in Nigeria has increased at a faster pace than in the rest of Africa. Again, largely oil exports.

8.4

Total Exports and Imports per Person of Population in Nigeria from 1999-2006 ($US)

Nigeria also put increasing distance between exports and imports; good news for its trade balance; better than the Africa average.

8.5

Total Exports and Imports per Person of Population in Sub-Saharan Africa from 1999-2006 ($US)

8.6

Total Exports and Imports per Person of Population among the Oil Exporters from 1999-2006 ($US)

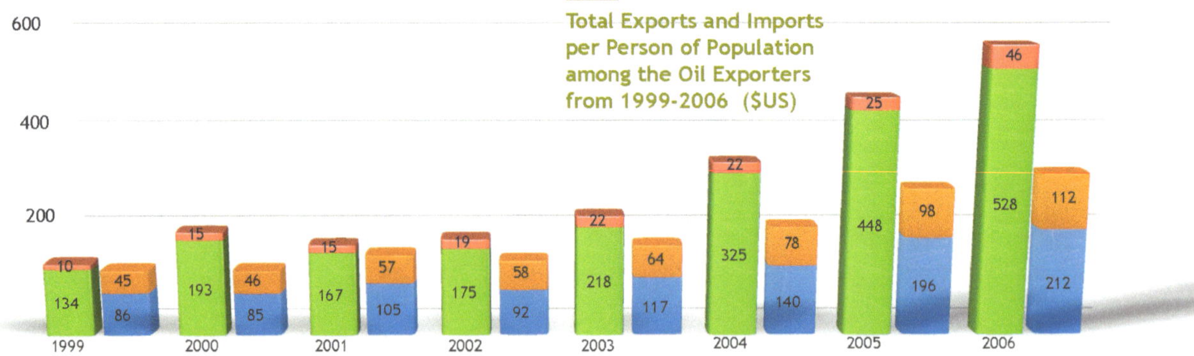


Primary Data: WTO, World Bank

But the other oil economies in Sub-Saharan Africa had their exports growing higher and more rapidly than Nigeria's.

However, their imports have been less curtailed than Nigeria's, growing larger and quicker, too.

## 8. Self-Reliance

With respect to the overall size of the economy, exports have risen in Nigeria but not as rapidly as they did in per person terms.

**8.7**

Total Exports and Imports as % of GDP in Nigeria from 1999-2006

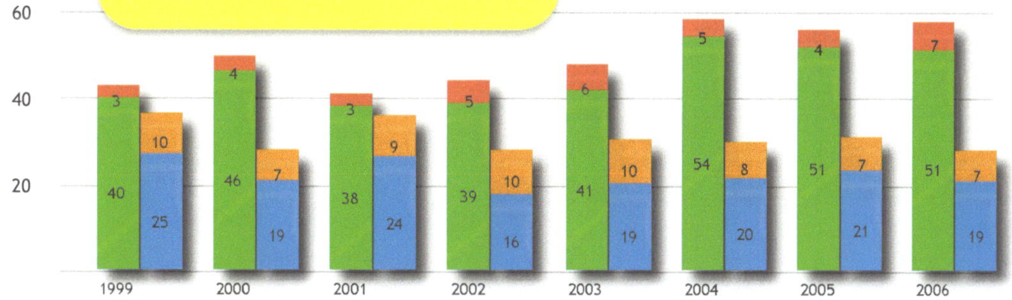


Which suggests that while exports have risen, the rest of the economy has risen as well, but at a slower rate, and so to a smaller extent.

**8.8**

Total Exports and Imports as % of GDP in Sub-Saharan Africa from 1999-2006

Services Exports
Goods Exports

Services Imports
Goods Imports

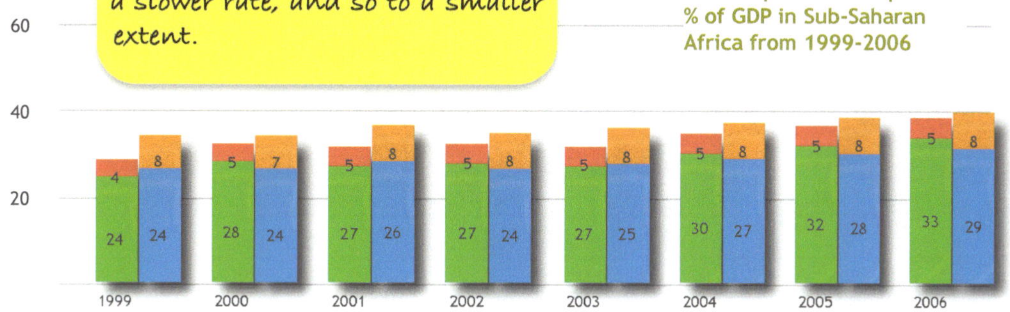


**8.9**

Total Exports and Imports as % of GDP among the Oil Exporters from 1999-2006

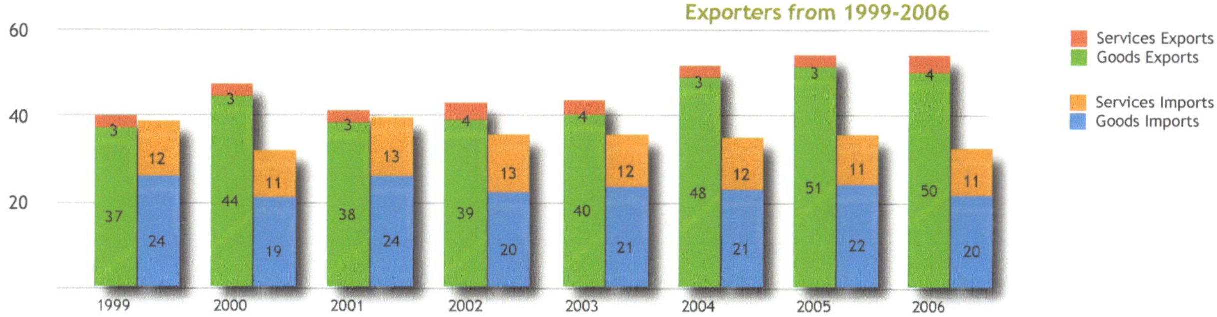


Primary Data: WTO, World Bank

Imports fell in Nigeria, and by more than it did in the other oil economies. While the rest of Africa increased imports levels.

Services Exports
Goods Exports

Services Imports
Goods Imports

## 8.2 Growth in Goods Exports and Imports

**are they leaving faster than they're coming?**

In West Africa, only Mauritania and Sierra Leone grew exports faster than Nigeria during 2003/06.

Among oil exporters, Nigeria stepped up one place, growing exports quicker than 5 of the 9 oil producers.

| Growth in Total Goods Exports per Population | 00-02 | 03-06 |
|---|---|---|
| Self-comparison to Preceding Period | | ▲ |
| Performance in Sub-Saharan Africa | ▲ | ▲ |
| Performance in West Africa | ▲ | ▲ |
| | Sierra Leone | Mauritania |
| | Mali | Sierra Leone |
| | **Nigeria** | **Nigeria** |
| | Côte d'Ivoire | Burkina Faso |
| | Guinea | Ghana |
| | Gambia, The | Cape Verde |
| | Togo | Niger |
| | Ghana | Mali |
| | Guinea-Bissau | Côte d'Ivoire |
| | Benin | Guinea |
| | Senegal | Togo |
| | Burkina Faso | Senegal |
| | Cape Verde | Guinea-Bissau |
| | Niger | Benin |
| | Mauritania | Gambia, The |
| | Liberia | Liberia |
| Performance among Oil-Exporters | ◁▷ | ▲ |
| | Sudan | Chad |
| | Equatorial Guinea | Equatorial Guinea |
| | Angola | Angola |
| | Congo, Rep. | **Nigeria** |
| | **Nigeria** | Sudan |
| | Côte d'Ivoire | Congo, Rep. |
| | Cameroon | Gabon |
| | Gabon | Cameroon |
| | Chad | Côte d'Ivoire |

Primary Data: WTO, World Bank

| | |
|---|---|
| ▲ | improved *or* better than average |
| ▼ | worsened *or* worse than average |
| ◁▷ | no change *or* average |

# 8. Self-Reliance

8.10

Growth on Previous Yr. of Goods Exports and Imports per Person in West Africa during 2003/06

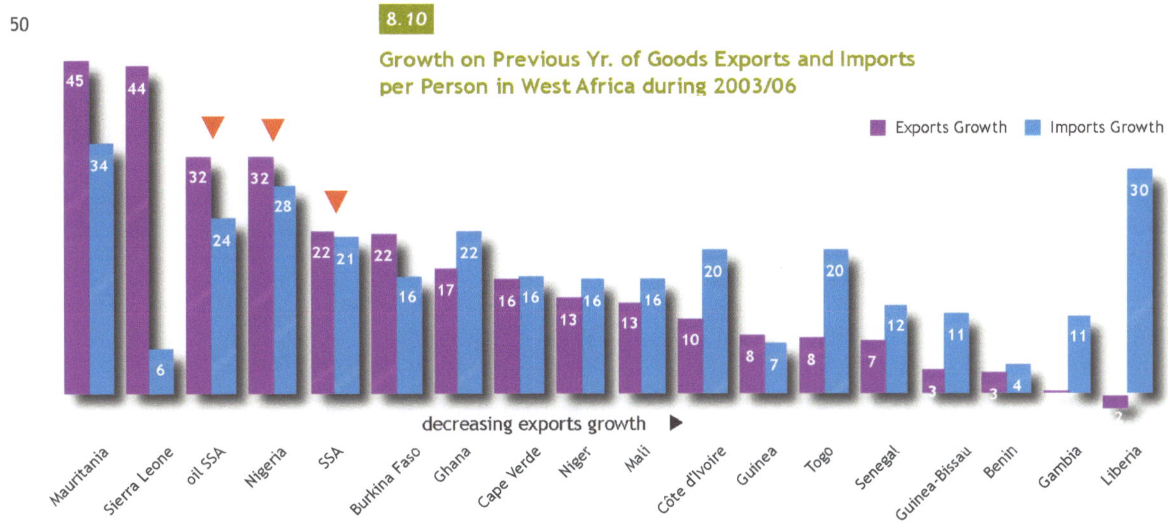


Primary Data: WTO, World Bank

Concretely, focusing on just the period between 2000 and 2007, Nigeria grew exports earnings by a larger volume than the Africa average.

8.11

Build-up of Goods Exports and Imports per Person in Nigeria and Sub-Saharan Africa from 2000-07: 2000=100

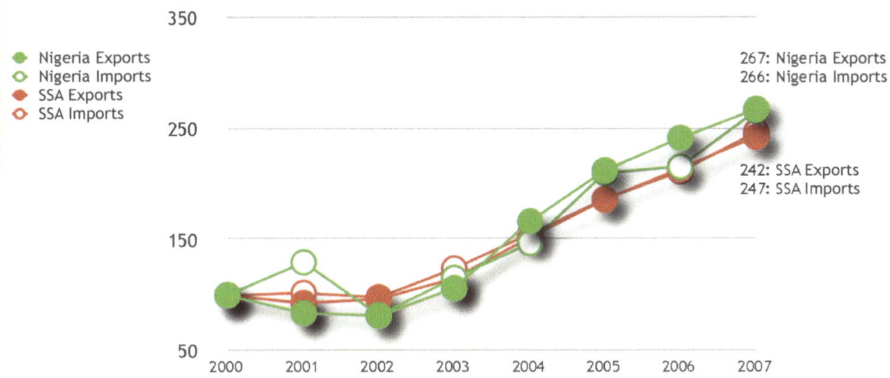


But it didn't do as well as the other oil economies, even though it kept its imports volume growth under tighter check than they did.

8.12

Build-up of Goods Exports and Imports per Person in Nigeria and Oil-Exporting Countries from 2000-07: 2000=100

## 8.3 Growth in Services Exports and Imports

*are they leaving faster than they're coming?*

| Growth in Services Exports per Population | 00-02 | 03-06 |
|---|---|---|
| Self-comparison to Preceding Period | | ▼ |
| Performance in Sub-Saharan Africa | ▲ | ▲ |
| Performance in West Africa | ▲ | ▲ |
| | **Nigeria** | Burkina Faso |
| | Sierra Leone | **Nigeria** |
| | Guinea | Togo |
| | Guinea-Bissau | Cape Verde |
| | Mauritania | Ghana |
| | Mali | Guinea-Bissau |
| | Niger | Mauritania |
| | Cape Verde | Niger |
| | Togo | Benin |
| | Burkina Faso | Senegal |
| | Ghana | Gambia, The |
| | Senegal | Sierra Leone |
| | Côte d'Ivoire | Côte d'Ivoire |
| | Benin | Mali |
| | Gambia, The | Guinea |

Primary Data: WTO, World Bank

Nigeria didn't grow services exports as ruggedly. The pace slowed in 03/06. Though that only cost it a drop of 1 place in West Africa, compared to 00/02.

| Performance among Oil-Exporters | ▲ | ▲ |
|---|---|---|
| | Sudan | Angola |
| | **Nigeria** | Sudan |
| | Cameroon | Equatorial Guinea |
| | Equatorial Guinea | **Nigeria** |
| | Angola | Gabon |
| | Chad | Chad |
| | Congo, Rep. | Congo, Rep. |
| | Côte d'Ivoire | Côte d'Ivoire |
| | Gabon | Cameroon |

It's drop among the oil exporters, however, was worse; the group seem to have grown their non-oil exports earnings by faster margins.

| | |
|---|---|
| ▲ | improved *or* better than average |
| ▼ | worsened *or* worse than average |
| ◁▷ | no change *or* average |

# 8. Self-Reliance

8.13

Growth on Previous Yr. of Services Exports and Imports per Person in West Africa during 2003/06 (%)

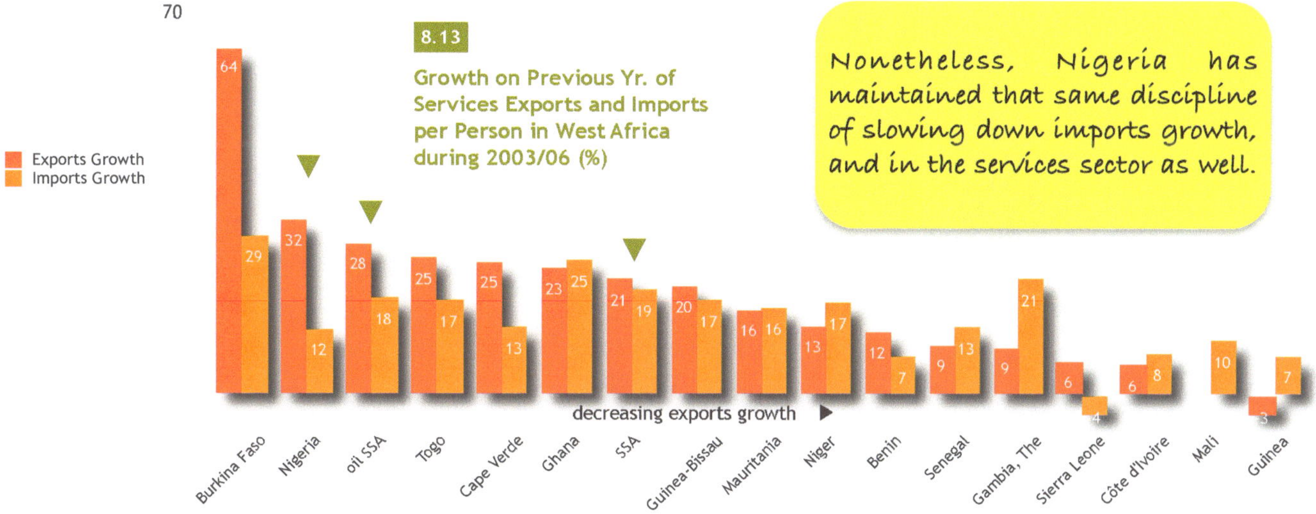


Nonetheless, Nigeria has maintained that same discipline of slowing down imports growth, and in the services sector as well.

Primary Data: WTO, World Bank

8.14

Build-up of Services Exports and Imports per Person in Nigeria and Sub-Saharan Africa from 2000-06: 2000=100

If focus is restricted to 2000-2006, Nigeria's growth of services exports might have been slow on the average, but it did spike in 2006.

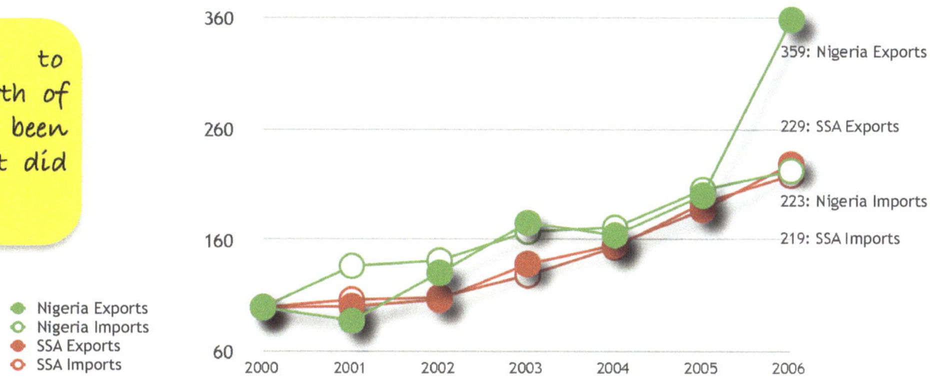


8.15

Build-up of Services Exports and Imports per Person in Nigeria and Oil-Exporting Countries from 2000-06: 2000=100

As it spiked in the other oil economies, too, indicating, quite likely, a spur common across the group between 2005 and 2006.

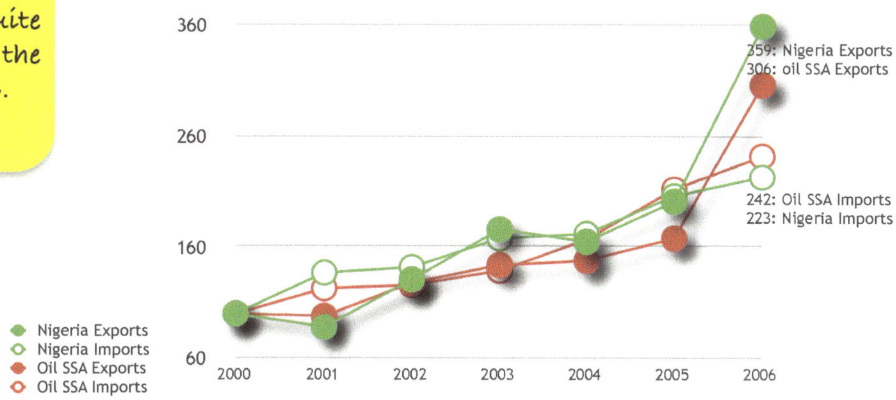

# 8.4 Imports Dependence in Merchandise

## *unable to do without*

Primary Data: WTO, World Bank

| | 99-02 | 03-06 |
|---|---|---|
| Self-comparison to Preceding Period | | ▲ |
| Performance in Sub-Saharan Africa | ▲ | ▲ |
| Performance in West Africa | ▲ | ▲ |
| | Côte d'Ivoire | **Nigeria** |
| | **Nigeria** | Côte d'Ivoire |
| | Guinea | Guinea |
| | Guinea-Bissau | Guinea-Bissau |
| | Niger | Niger |
| | Mali | Sierra Leone |
| | Mauritania | Mali |
| | Sierra Leone | Benin |
| | Togo | Liberia |
| | Burkina Faso | Burkina Faso |
| | Benin | Togo |
| | Liberia | Ghana |
| | Senegal | Senegal |
| | Ghana | Gambia, The |
| | Gambia, The | Mauritania |
| | Cape Verde | Cape Verde |
| Performance among Oil-Exporters | ▼ | ◁▷ |
| | Equatorial Guinea | Equatorial Guinea |
| | Gabon | Gabon |
| | Congo, Rep. | Congo, Rep. |
| | Angola | Angola |
| | Côte d'Ivoire | **Nigeria** |
| | **Nigeria** | Côte d'Ivoire |
| | Cameroon | Chad |
| | Sudan | Cameroon |
| | Chad | Sudan |

Nigeria was the best performer in West Africa in external trade of goods, selling more than it bought.

Among Africa's oil economies, it was out-done. But it saw a modest improvement, nonetheless, of 1 place up, to average position.

| | |
|---|---|
| ▲ | better = less imports dependent |
| ▼ | worse = more imports dependent |
| ◁▷ | no change *or* average |

## 8. Self-Reliance

Only 3 countries in West Africa were "self-sufficient" in external trade during 2003/06: Nigeria, Côte d'Ivoire and Guinea.

8.16

### Net Goods Exports per Person in West Africa during 2003/06

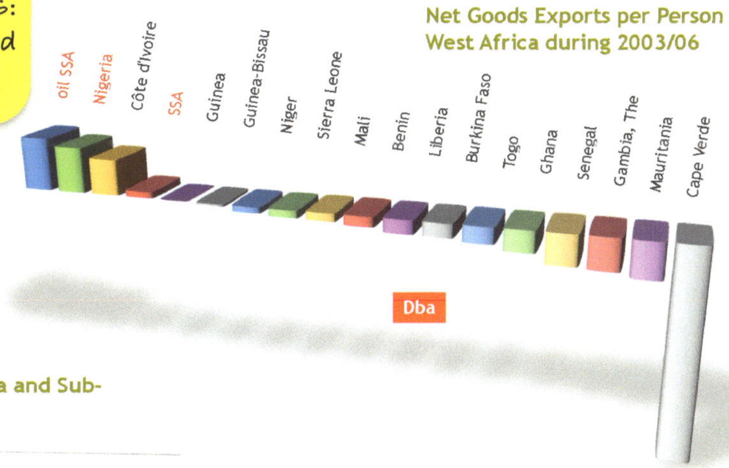


| | $US |
|---|---|
| **oil SSA** | **214** |
| Nigeria | 185 |
| Côte d'Ivoire | 146 |
| **SSA** | **27** |
| Guinea | 1 |
| Guinea-Bissau | -9 |
| Niger | -26 |
| Sierra Leone | -32 |
| Mali | -34 |
| Benin | -41 |
| Liberia | -58 |
| Burkina Faso | -58 |
| Togo | -69 |
| Ghana | -91 |
| Senegal | -128 |
| Gambia, The | -132 |
| Mauritania | -148 |
| Cape Verde | -844 |

Primary Data: WTO, World Bank

8.17

### Net Goods Exports per Person in Nigeria and Sub-Saharan Africa from 1999-2007

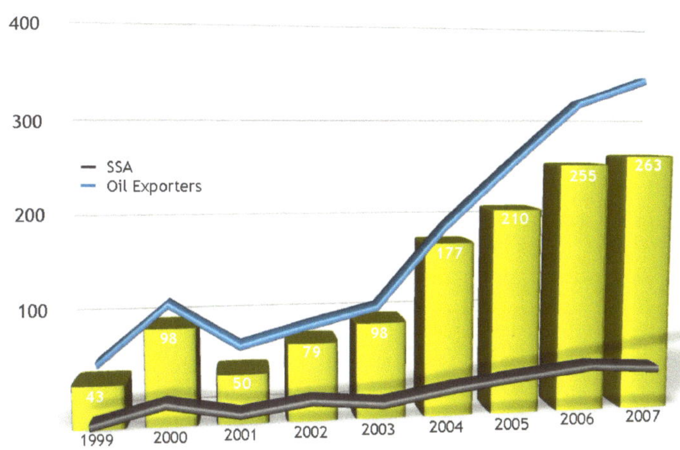


Indeed, Nigeria was more self-sufficient than most of the continent, save the other oil exporters.

### Merchandise Imports Dependence per Person in Sub-Saharan Africa during 2003-06: Rankings

| Rank | Country | Rank | Country | Rank | Country |
|---|---|---|---|---|---|
| 1 | Equatorial Guinea | 15 | Niger | 29 | Togo |
| 2 | Gabon | 16 | Burundi | 30 | Kenya |
| 3 | Congo, Rep. | 17 | Rwanda | 31 | Ghana |
| 4 | Angola | 18 | Zambia | 32 | Eritrea |
| 5 | Botswana | 19 | Mozambique | 33 | Comoros |
| 6 | **Nigeria** | 20 | Sierra Leone | 34 | Senegal |
| 7 | Côte d' Ivoire | 21 | Mali | 35 | Gambia, The |
| 8 | Chad | 22 | Ethiopia | 36 | South Africa |
| 9 | Cameroon | 23 | Madagascar | 37 | Namibia |
| 10 | Guinea | 24 | Malawi | 38 | Lesotho |
| 11 | Congo, Dem. Rep. | 25 | Uganda | 39 | Mauritius |
| 12 | Central Afr. Rep. | 26 | Tanzania | 40 | Cape Verde |
| 13 | Guinea-Bissau | 27 | Benin | 41 | Seychelles |
| 14 | Swaziland | 28 | Burkina Faso | | |
| | Least | | MIDDLE | | Most |

It was the 6th best out of 41 countries. Note that 8 of the top 10 are oil exporters.

Central Africa
East Africa
Southern Africa
West Africa

# 8.5 Imports Dependence in Services

## *mind over matter*

Self-sufficiency in services trade was an improvement for Nigeria in 2003/06 over 1999/02.

That brought Nigeria from a below-average in Africa during 1999/02 to an above-average showing in 2003/06. But most of West Africa did better.

Yet, Nigeria was best among the oil economies, emphasising how neglected the non-oil sectors of these countries are. At least in foreign trade is concerned.

| | 99-02 | 03-06 |
|---|---|---|
| Self-comparison to Preceding Period | | ▲ |
| Performance in Sub-Saharan Africa | ▼ | ▲ |
| Performance in West Africa | ▼ | ▼ |
| | Gambia, The | Cape Verde |
| | Cape Verde | Gambia, The |
| | Ghana | Sierra Leone |
| | Senegal | Ghana |
| | Benin | Benin |
| | Niger | Senegal |
| | Burkina Faso | Niger |
| | Sierra Leone | Burkina Faso |
| | Togo | **Nigeria** |
| | Guinea-Bissau | Liberia |
| | **Nigeria** | Guinea |
| | Guinea | Togo |
| | Mali | Guinea-Bissau |
| | Côte d'Ivoire | Mali |
| | Mauritania | Côte d'Ivoire |
| | Liberia | Mauritania |
| Performance among Oil-Exporters | ▲ | ▲ |
| | Sudan | **Nigeria** |
| | **Nigeria** | Cameroon |
| | Cameroon | Sudan |
| | Chad | Côte d'Ivoire |
| | Côte d'Ivoire | Chad |
| | Angola | Angola |
| | Congo, Rep. | Congo, Rep. |
| | Gabon | Gabon |
| | Equatorial Guinea | Equatorial Guinea |

Primary Data: WTO, World Bank

| | |
|---|---|
| ▲ | better = less imports dependent |
| ▼ | worse = more imports dependent |
| ◁▷ | no change *or* average |

# 8. Self-Reliance

8.18

**Net Services Exports per Person in West Africa during 2003/06**

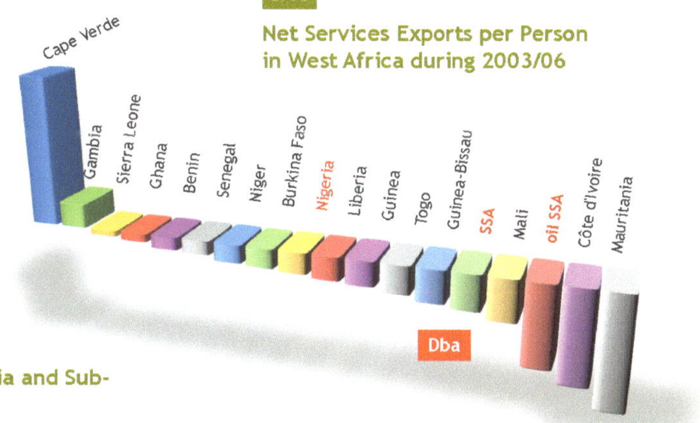


| | $US |
|---|---|
| Cape Verde | 107 |
| Gambia, The | 17 |
| Sierra Leone | -4 |
| Ghana | -6 |
| Benin | -9 |
| Senegal | -10 |
| Niger | -13 |
| Burkina Faso | -14 |
| Nigeria | -15 |
| Liberia | -17 |
| Guinea | -18 |
| Togo | -20 |
| Guinea-Bissau | -24 |
| SSA | -26 |
| Mali | -30 |
| oil SSA | -59 |
| Côte d'Ivoire | -68 |
| Mauritania | -82 |

Primary Data: WTO, World Bank

8.19

**Net Services Exports per Person in Nigeria and Sub-Saharan Africa from 1999-2007**

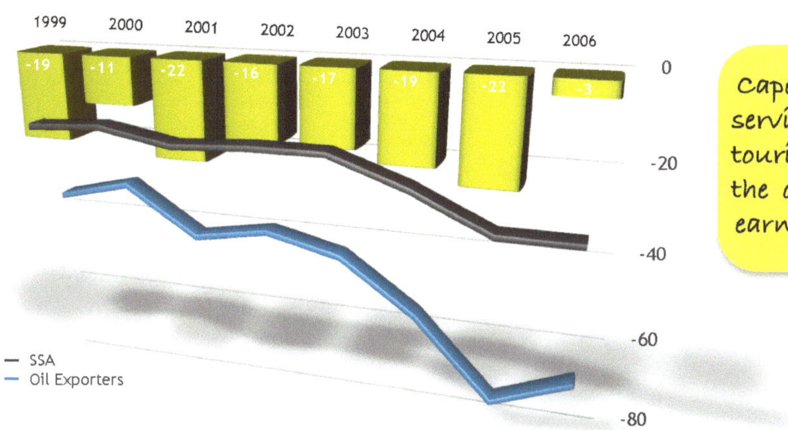


Cape Verde's the top earner in services by a distance; through tourism mainly. Further down, the oil economies are the bottom earners, also by a distance.

Nigeria's trade deficit in services ended up lower in '06 than in '99, after shaky travel in-between. But better - again - than Africa and the oil group.

**Services Imports Dependence per Person in Sub-Saharan Africa during 2003-06: Rankings**

| Rank | Country | Rank | Country | Rank | Country |
|---|---|---|---|---|---|
| 1 | Seychelles | 15 | Uganda | 29 | Zambia |
| 2 | Mauritius | 16 | Burundi | 30 | Central Afr. Rep. |
| 3 | Cape Verde | 17 | Malawi | 31 | Guinea-Bissau |
| 4 | Namibia | 18 | Rwanda | 32 | Mali |
| 5 | Gambia, The | 19 | Botswana | 33 | Cameroon |
| 6 | Kenya | 20 | Niger | 34 | Côte d' Ivoire |
| 7 | Tanzania | 21 | Burkina Faso | 35 | Swaziland |
| 8 | Ethiopia | 22 | Comoros | 36 | Chad |
| 9 | Sierra Leone | 23 | Mozambique | 37 | Angola |
| 10 | Congo, Dem. Rep. | 24 | Lesotho | 38 | Congo, Rep. |
| 11 | Madagascar | 25 | Nigeria | 39 | Gabon |
| 12 | Ghana | 26 | Guinea | 40 | Equatorial Guinea |
| 13 | Benin | 27 | South Africa | N/A | Eritrea |
| 14 | Senegal | 28 | Togo | | |
| | Least | | MIDDLE | | Most |

Central Africa
East Africa
Southern Africa
West Africa

# 8.6 Composition of Goods Exports and Imports

**this is how these break down**

Not much surprise about Nigeria's goods exports composition: 97% oil-related exports.

The surprises, perhaps, are Togo, Senegal, Cape Verde and Gambia, who have a good chunk of export earnings coming from the manufacturing sector.

It may not be unexpected that Nigeria's exports are skewed towards fuels & mining, but it is worrying that its agric. sector is dwarfed by agric. imports.

Besides Cape Verde (which has poor natural resources), Nigeria seems to be the only country that isn't self-sufficient in agriculture.

8.20

Composition of Goods Exports and Imports in West Africa during 2003/06

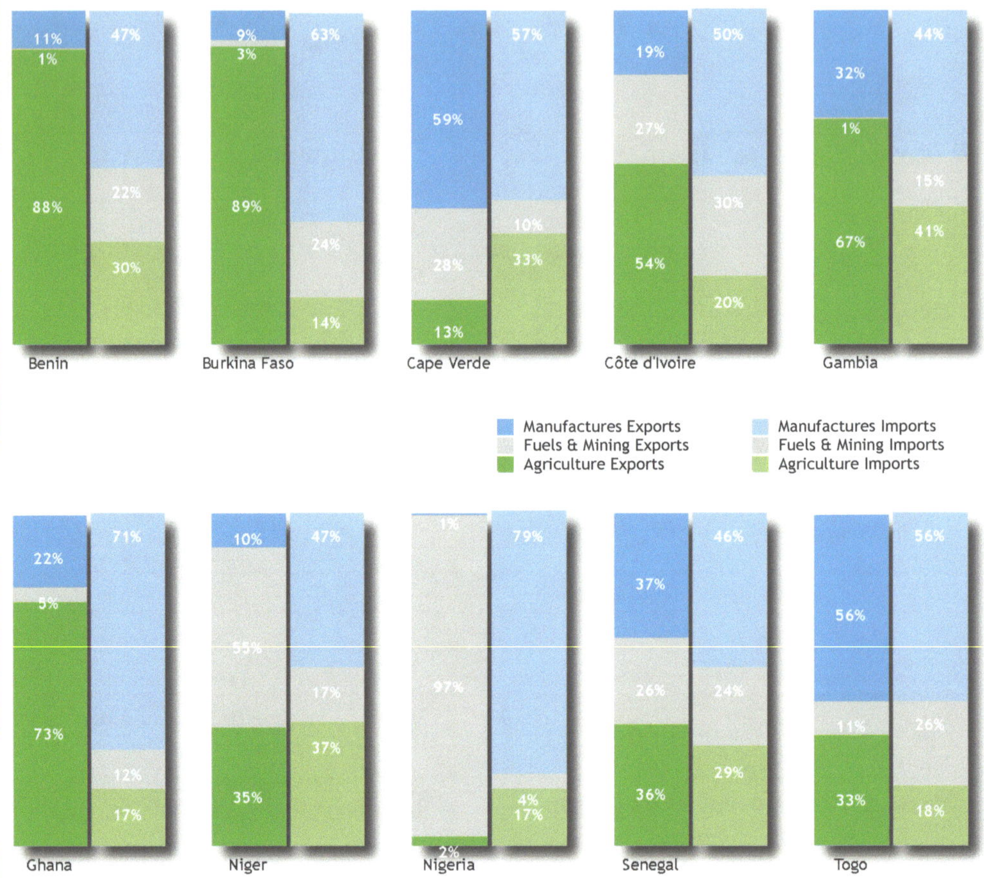


8.21

Primary Data: WTO

Composition of Goods Exports and Imports in Nigeria from 1999-2005

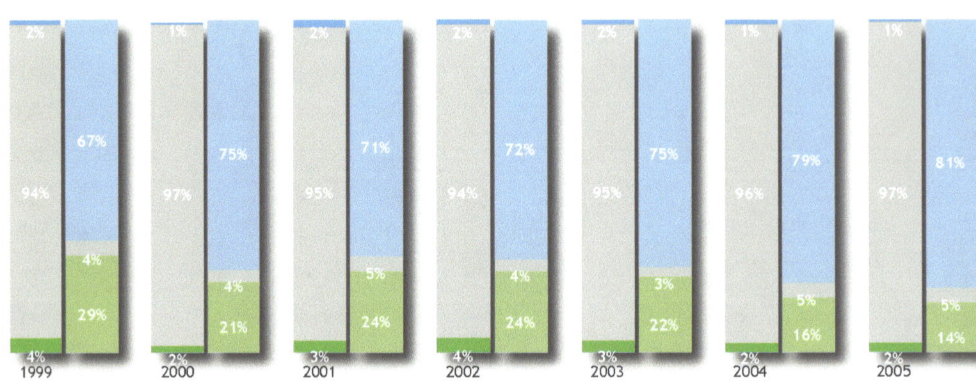

**while these ones break down like so**

8.22

## Composition of Services Exports and Imports in West Africa during 2003/06

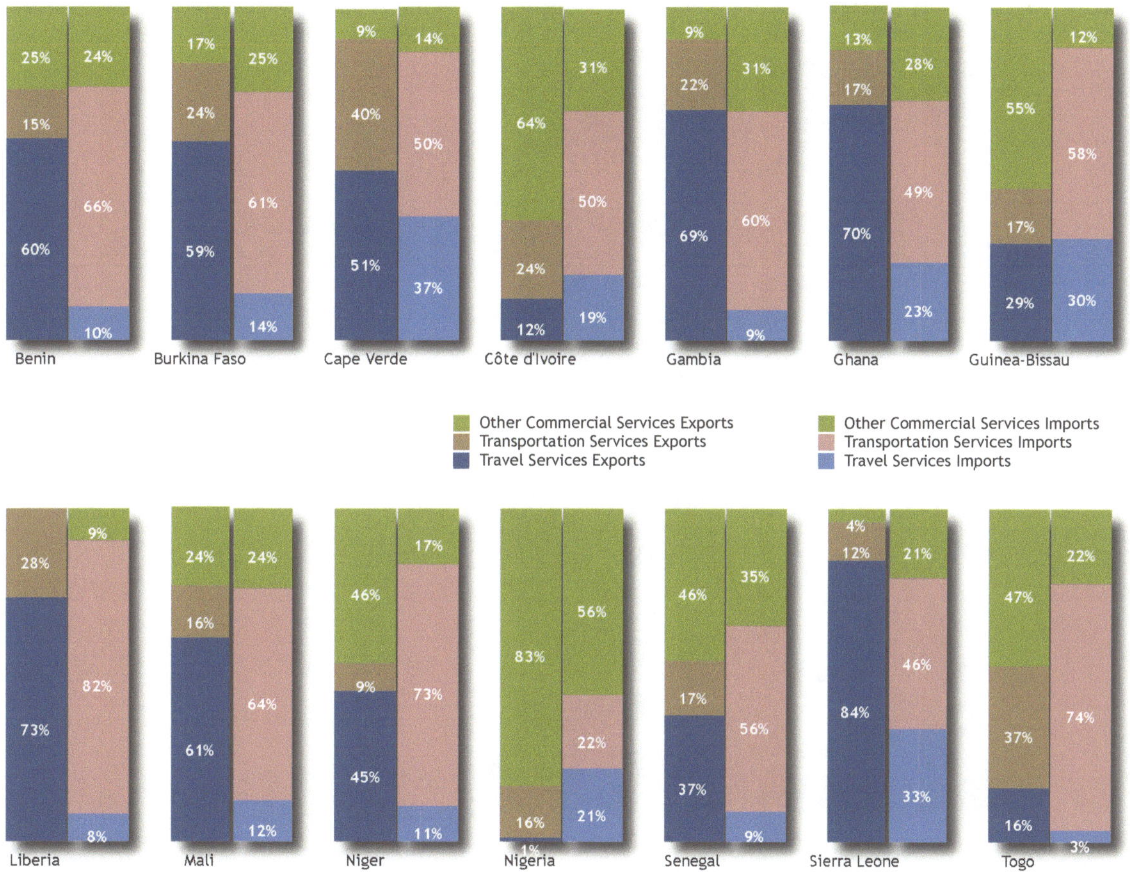


Primary Data: WTO

8.23

## Composition of Services Exports and Imports in Nigeria from 1999-2005

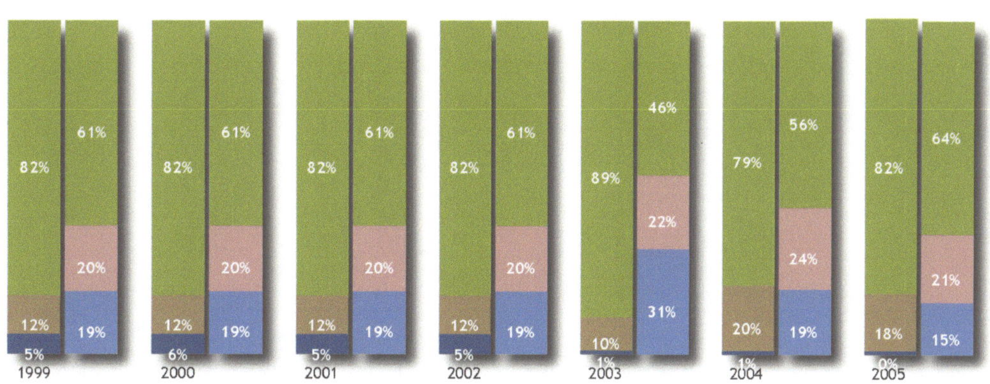

# 8.7 Foreign Reserves (months of imports)

**we've got it stashed away**

| | 97-02 | 03-06 | 07-08 |
|---|---|---|---|
| Self-comparison to Preceding Period | | ▲ | ▲ |
| Performance in Sub-Saharan Africa | ▲ | ▲ | ▲ |

**Performance in West Africa**

| 97-02 | 03-06 | 07-08 |
|---|---|---|
| ▲ | ▲ | ▲ |
| Benin | Benin | **Nigeria** |
| Guinea-Bissau | **Nigeria** | Benin |
| **Nigeria** | Mali | Guinea-Bissau |
| Gambia, The | Burkina Faso | Burkina Faso |
| Burkina Faso | Guinea-Bissau | Mali |
| Mali | Senegal | Sierra Leone |
| Côte d'Ivoire | Gambia, The | Niger |
| Senegal | Sierra Leone | Gambia, The |
| Sierra Leone | Niger | Cape Verde |
| Guinea | Ghana | Senegal |
| Togo | Côte d'Ivoire | Togo |
| Niger | Togo | Côte d'Ivoire |
| Ghana | Cape Verde | Ghana |
| Cape Verde | Guinea | Guinea |
| Liberia | Liberia | Liberia |

Primary Data: IMF

Ever-growing foreign reserves in Nigeria. Thanks to oil. And to some financial discipline, too: other oil exporters didn't do as well.

**Performance among Oil-Exporters**

| 97-02 | 03-06 | 07-08 |
|---|---|---|
| ▲ | ▲ | ▲ |
| **Nigeria** | **Nigeria** | **Nigeria** |
| Côte d'Ivoire | Equatorial Guinea | Equatorial Guinea |
| Chad | Côte d'Ivoire | Angola |
| Angola | Cameroon | Cameroon |
| Cameroon | Gabon | Congo, Rep. |
| Congo, Rep. | Angola | Gabon |
| Gabon | Congo, Rep. | Chad |
| Equatorial Guinea | Chad | Côte d'Ivoire |

| | |
|---|---|
| ▲ | improved *or* better than average |
| ▼ | worsened *or* worse than average |
| ◁▷ | no change *or* average |

# 8. Self-Reliance

After 2003, Nigeria seems to have taken off, swelling its foreign reserves holdings.

8.24

**Foreign Reserves (as months of imports) in West Africa during 2003-06**

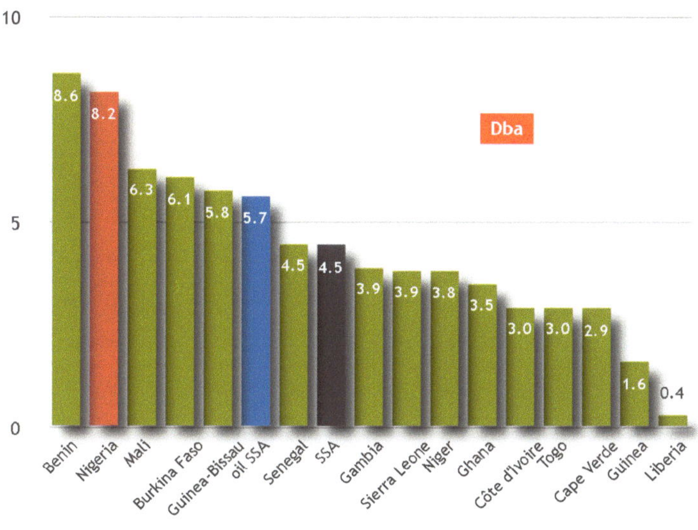


8.25

**Foreign Reserves (as months of imports) in Nigeria and Sub-Saharan Africa from 1997 - 2008**

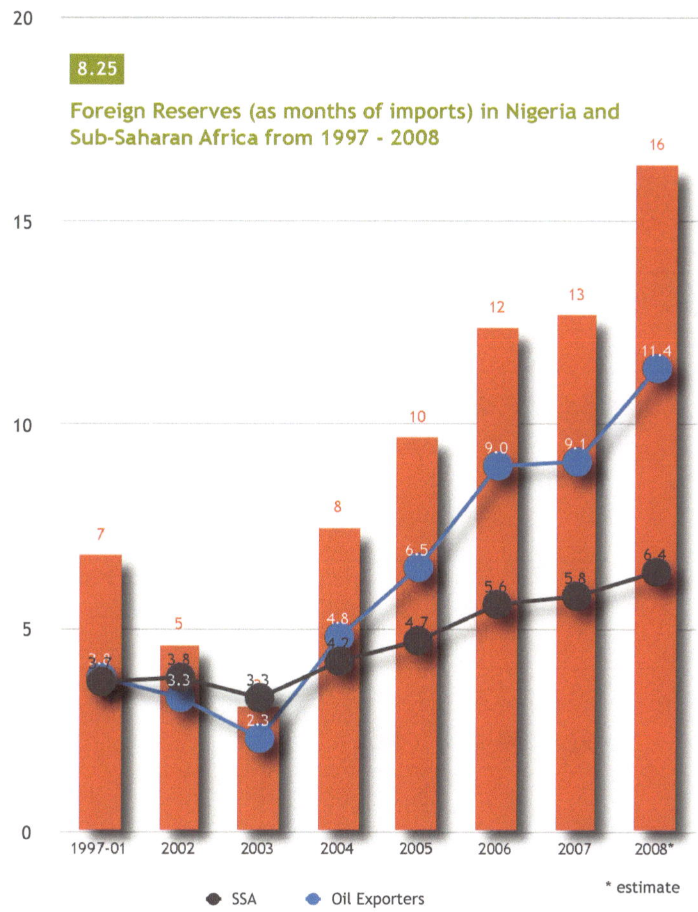


* estimate

Primary Data: IMF

It had the 4th best reserves holdings in Africa during 2003-2006.

**Foreign Reserves (as months of imports) in Sub-Saharan Africa during 2003-06: Rankings**

| Rank | Country | Rank | Country | Rank | Country |
|---|---|---|---|---|---|
| 1 | Botswana | 14 | Lesotho | 27 | Gabon |
| 2 | Comoros | 15 | Mozambique | | South Africa |
| 3 | Benin | 16 | Senegal | 28 | Angola |
| 4 | **Nigeria** | 17 | Burundi | 29 | Zambia |
| 5 | Tanzania | 18 | Gambia, The | 30 | Congo, Rep. |
| 6 | Uganda | 19 | Ethiopia | 31 | Swaziland |
| 7 | Rwanda | 20 | Sierra Leone | 32 | Namibia |
| 8 | Central Afr. Rep. | 21 | Niger | 33 | Guinea |
| 9 | Mali | 22 | Kenya | 34 | Malawi |
| 10 | Burkina Faso | 23 | Ghana | 35 | Chad |
| 11 | Guinea-Bissau | 24 | Côte d' Ivoire | 36 | Seychelles |
| 12 | Equatorial Guinea | | Togo | 37 | Congo, Dem. Rep. |
| 13 | Mauritius | 25 | Cameroon | 38 | Eritrea |
| | | 26 | Cape Verde | | |
| | | | Madagascar | | |
| | TOP | | MIDDLE | | BOTTOM |

Central Africa
East Africa
Southern Africa
West Africa

# 8.8 Foreign Debt (as % of GDP)

## *bills, bills, bills*

| | 97-02 | 03-06 | 07-08 |
|---|---|---|---|
| Self-comparison to Preceding Period | | ▲ | ▲ |
| Performance in Sub-Saharan Africa | ▼ | ▲ | ▲ |
| Performance in West Africa | ▲ | ▲ | ▲ |
| | Cape Verde | **Nigeria** | **Nigeria** |
| | Burkina Faso | Benin | Sierra Leone |
| | **Nigeria** | Burkina Faso | Benin |
| | Senegal | Senegal | Niger |
| | Benin | Niger | Senegal |
| | Côte d'Ivoire | Cape Verde | Burkina Faso |
| | Niger | Mali | Ghana |
| | Togo | Côte d'Ivoire | Mali |
| | Guinea | Ghana | Cape Verde |
| | Mali | Togo | Côte d'Ivoire |
| | Ghana | Guinea | Guinea |
| | Gambia, The | Sierra Leone | Gambia, The |
| | Sierra Leone | Gambia, The | Togo |
| | Guinea-Bissau | Guinea-Bissau | Guinea-Bissau |
| | Liberia | Liberia | Liberia |
| Performance among Oil-Exporters | ▲ | ▲ | ▲ |
| | Equatorial Guinea | Equatorial Guinea | Equatorial Guinea |
| | Cameroon | **Nigeria** | **Nigeria** |
| | Chad | Angola | Cameroon |
| | **Nigeria** | Cameroon | Angola |
| | Angola | Chad | Gabon |
| | Gabon | Gabon | Chad |
| | Côte d'Ivoire | Côte d'Ivoire | Côte d'Ivoire |
| | Congo, Rep. | Congo, Rep. | Congo, Rep. |

Another impressive showing by Nigeria: small foreign debt compared to the continent, and to the other oil producers, also. Only Equatorial Guinea did better.

Nigeria is the least geared in West Africa: relatively little constraints of a debt burden.

Primary Data: IMF

| | |
|---|---|
| ▲ | better = less debt |
| ▼ | worse = more debt |
| ◁▷ | no change *or* average |

# 8. Self-Reliance

8.26

Foreign Debt as % of GDP in West Africa during 2003-06

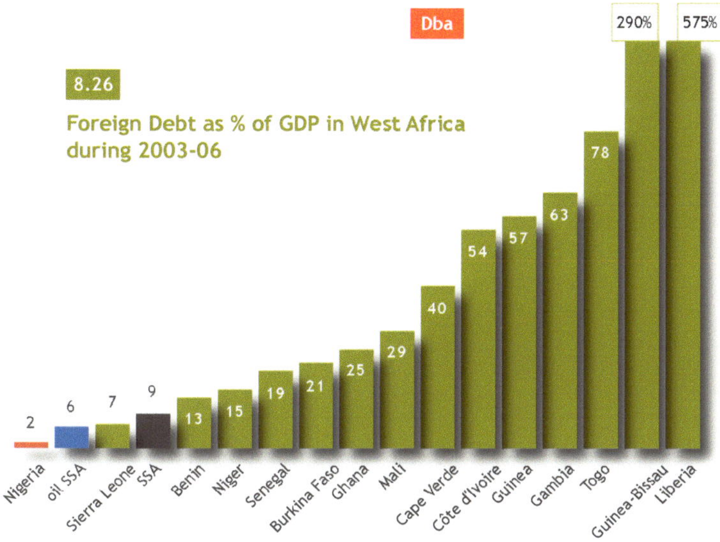


8.27

Foreign Debt as % of GDP in Nigeria and Sub-Saharan Africa from 1997/01-2008

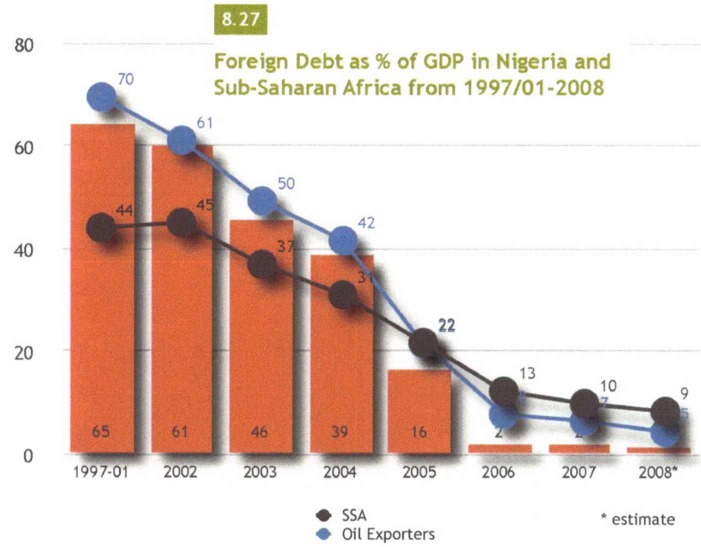


Primary Data: IMF

Spectacular collapsing of its debt since 2001. But the trend was continent-wide: other nations were crashing their debt portfolios, too.

Foreign Debt as % of GDP in Sub-Saharan Africa during 2003-06: Rankings

As a proportion of overall economy size, Nigeria had the 7th smallest debt portfolio in Africa.

| Rank | Country | Rank | Country | Rank | Country |
|---|---|---|---|---|---|
| 1 | South Africa | 15 | Senegal | 29 | Eritrea |
| 2 | Botswana | 16 | Gabon | 30 | Comoros |
| 3 | Namibia | 17 | Tanzania | 31 | Zambia |
| 4 | Equatorial Guinea | 18 | Lesotho | 32 | Central Afr. Rep. |
| 5 | Mauritius | 19 | Niger | 33 | Togo |
| 6 | Swaziland | 20 | Cape Verde | 34 | Guinea |
| 7 | **Nigeria** | 21 | Mozambique | 35 | Malawi |
| 8 | Kenya | 22 | Mali | 36 | Sierra Leone |
| 9 | Angola | 23 | Uganda | 37 | Congo, Rep. |
| 10 | Cameroon | 24 | Ethiopia | 38 | Congo, Dem. Rep. |
| 11 | Benin | 25 | Rwanda | 39 | Gambia, The |
| 12 | Burkina Faso | 26 | Côte d' Ivoire | 40 | Burundi |
| 13 | Chad | 27 | Madagascar | 41 | Guinea-Bissau |
| 14 | Seychelles | 28 | Ghana | | |
| | Least | | MIDDLE | | Most |

Central Africa
East Africa
Southern Africa
West Africa

# 8.9 Foreign Debt (as $PPP per person)

**beware**

| | 97-02 | 03-06 | 07-08 |
|---|---|---|---|
| Self-comparison to Preceding Period | | ▲ | ▲ |
| Performance in Sub-Saharan Africa | ▼ | ▼ | ▲ |
| Performance in West Africa | ▲ | ▲ | ▲ |

| 97-02 | 03-06 | 07-08 |
|---|---|---|
| Benin | Benin | **Nigeria** |
| Guinea-Bissau | **Nigeria** | Benin |
| **Nigeria** | Mali | Guinea-Bissau |
| Gambia, The | Burkina Faso | Burkina Faso |
| Burkina Faso | Guinea-Bissau | Mali |
| Mali | Senegal | Sierra Leone |
| Côte d'Ivoire | Gambia, The | Niger |
| Senegal | Sierra Leone | Gambia, The |
| Sierra Leone | Niger | Cape Verde |
| Guinea | Ghana | Senegal |
| Togo | Côte d'Ivoire | Togo |
| Niger | Togo | Côte d'Ivoire |
| Ghana | Cape Verde | Ghana |
| Cape Verde | Guinea | Guinea |
| Liberia | Liberia | Liberia |

Primary Data: IMF

Expressed as debt per person of population, Nigeria was behind the continent average in 03/06, but it did well in West Africa and within the oil league.

| Performance among Oil-Exporters | 97-02 | 03-06 | 07-08 |
|---|---|---|---|
| | ▲ | ▲ | ▲ |
| | Chad | **Nigeria** | **Nigeria** |
| | **Nigeria** | Chad | Cameroon |
| | Cameroon | Equatorial Guinea | Equatorial Guinea |
| | Côte d'Ivoire | Cameroon | Angola |
| | Angola | Côte d'Ivoire | Chad |
| | Equatorial Guinea | Angola | Côte d'Ivoire |
| | Congo, Rep. | Congo, Rep. | Congo, Rep. |
| | Gabon | Gabon | Gabon |

| | |
|---|---|
| ▲ | better = less debt |
| ▼ | worse = more debt |
| ◁▷ | no change *or* average |

8.28

**Foreign Debt per Person of Population in West Africa during 2003/06 ($PPP)**

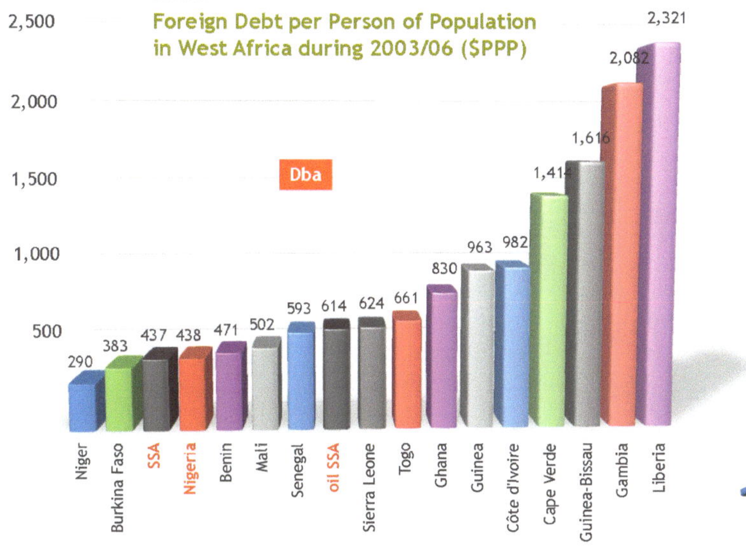


The collapsing debt burden would better the rest of the continent by a distance, after 2005.

8.29

**Foreign Debt per Person of Population in Nigeria and Sub-Saharan Africa from 1997-2008 ($PPP)**

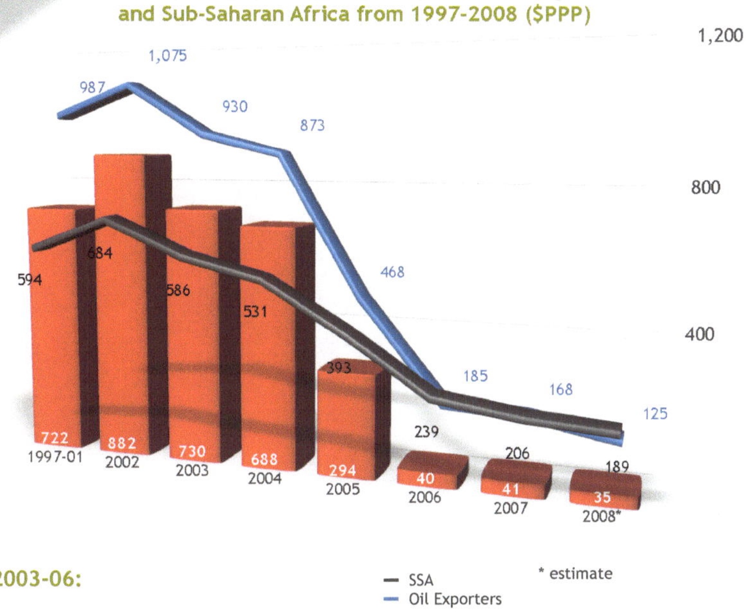


By either measure, % GDP or $ per person, Nigeria's debt baggage was among the 10 smallest in Africa.

**Foreign Debt per Person of Population in Sub-Saharan Africa during 2003-06: Rankings**

| Rank | Country | Rank | Country | Rank | Country |
|---|---|---|---|---|---|
| 1 | South Africa | 15 | Chad | 29 | Ghana |
| 2 | Namibia | 16 | Lesotho | 30 | Comoros |
| 3 | Niger | 17 | Central Afr. Rep. | 31 | Zambia |
| 4 | Ethiopia | 18 | Equatorial Guinea | 32 | Guinea |
| 5 | Mozambique | 19 | Eritrea | 33 | Côte d' Ivoire |
| 6 | Congo, Dem. Rep. | 20 | Madagascar | 34 | Angola |
| 7 | Kenya | 21 | Botswana | 35 | Mauritius |
| 8 | Burkina Faso | 22 | Senegal | 36 | Cape Verde |
| 9 | Rwanda | 23 | Malawi | 37 | Guinea-Bissau |
| 10 | Nigeria | 24 | Cameroon | 38 | Gambia, The |
| 11 | Tanzania | 25 | Swaziland | 39 | Congo, Rep. |
| 12 | Benin | 26 | Sierra Leone | 40 | Gabon |
| 13 | Uganda | 27 | Burundi | 41 | Seychelles |
| 14 | Mali | 28 | Togo | | |
| | Least | | MIDDLE | | Most |

Primary Data: IMF

Central Africa
East Africa
Southern Africa
West Africa

# 8.10 Service of Foreign Debt (as % of exports)

## paying up

Perhaps as a result of the drive to collapse debt burdens, Nigeria's debt repayments have been significantly high, in the years leading to 2006.

But it still does comparatively better than much of the continent, including the oil group.

| | 99-02 | 03-06 |
|---|---|---|
| Self-comparison to Preceding Period | | ▲ |
| Performance in Sub-Saharan Africa | ▲ | ▲ |
| Performance in West Africa | ▲ | ▲ |

| 99-02 | 03-06 |
|---|---|
| Togo | Togo |
| **Nigeria** | Mali |
| Mali | Benin |
| Mauritania | Ghana |
| Niger | Sierra Leone |
| Benin | **Nigeria** |
| Senegal | Burkina Faso |
| Burkina Faso | Guinea-Bissau |
| Guinea | Niger |
| Cape Verde | Guinea |
| Ghana | Côte d'Ivoire |
| Côte d'Ivoire | Senegal |
| Guinea-Bissau | Cape Verde |
| Gambia, The | Mauritania |
| Sierra Leone | Gambia, The |

Primary Data: AfDB

| Performance among Oil-Exporters | 99-02 | 03-06 |
|---|---|---|
| | ▲ | ▲ |
| | Equatorial Guinea | Equatorial Guinea |
| | Sudan | Chad |
| | Congo, Rep. | Sudan |
| | **Nigeria** | **Nigeria** |
| | Cameroon | Congo, Rep. |
| | Gabon | Côte d'Ivoire |
| | Côte d'Ivoire | Cameroon |
| | Chad | Angola |
| | Angola | Gabon |

| | |
|---|---|
| ▲ | better = smaller debt service |
| ▼ | worse = larger debt service |
| ◁▷ | no change *or* average |

8.30

Service of Foreign Debt as % of Exports in West Africa during 2003/06

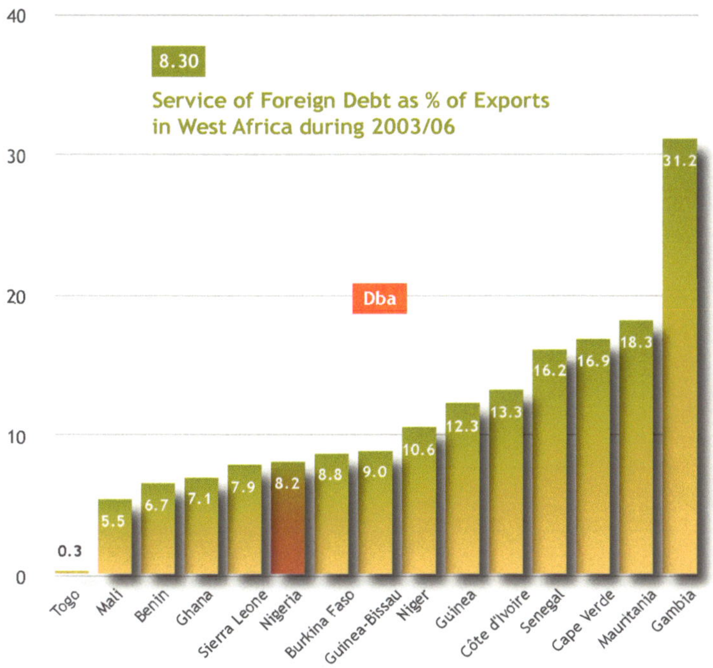


8.31

Service of Foreign Debt as % of Exports in Nigeria from 1999-2007

A massive outlay in 2005 to push a further climb-down in debt burden.

As a whole, during 2003-2006, Nigeria's debt repayment was easier to shoulder than most other countries'. upper-third performance.

Service of Foreign Debt as % of Exports in Sub-Saharan Africa during 2003-06: Rankings

| Rank | Country | Rank | Country | Rank | Country |
|---|---|---|---|---|---|
| 1 | Togo | 15 | Burkina Faso | 29 | Angola |
| 2 | Equatorial Guinea | 16 | Tanzania | 30 | Malawi |
| 3 | Namibia | 17 | Kenya | 31 | Senegal |
| 4 | Central Afr. Rep. | 18 | Guinea-Bissau | 32 | Cape Verde |
| 5 | Chad | 19 | Congo, Rep. | 33 | Rwanda |
| 6 | Mali | 20 | South Africa | 34 | Uganda |
| 7 | Benin | 21 | Zambia | 35 | Gabon |
| 8 | Ghana | 22 | Niger | 36 | Mozambique |
| 9 | Mauritius | 23 | Ethiopia | 37 | Gambia, The |
| 10 | Comoros | 24 | Seychelles | 38 | Madagascar |
| 11 | Sierra Leone | 25 | Guinea | 39 | Eritrea |
| 12 | Nigeria | 26 | Côte d' Ivoire | 40 | Burundi |
| 13 | Lesotho | 27 | Cameroon | N/A | Swaziland |
| 14 | Congo, Dem. Rep. | 28 | Botswana | | |
| | Least | | MIDDLE | | Most |

Primary Data: AfDB

Central Africa
East Africa
Southern Africa
West Africa

# 8.11 Growth of Income & Growth of Debt

**er... are we doing ok?**

8.34

**Build-up of Debt and Income in Nigeria and Sub-Saharan Africa from 2000-2006: 2000=100**

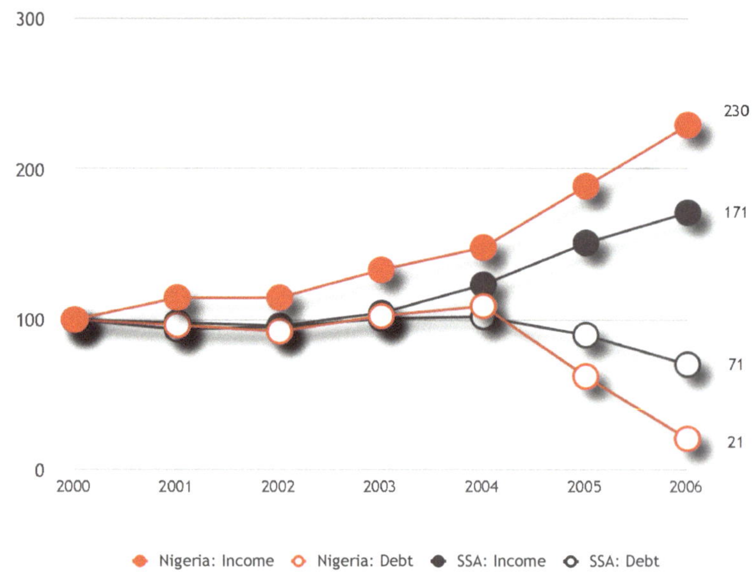


Something about 2005; when there seems to have been a concerted and continent-wide drive to lower debt profiles.

Excellent work by Nigeria, putting a gaping distance between its increasing earnings and falling debt.

**8.32**

**Growth Rates of Debt and Income in West Africa during 2003/06 (%)**

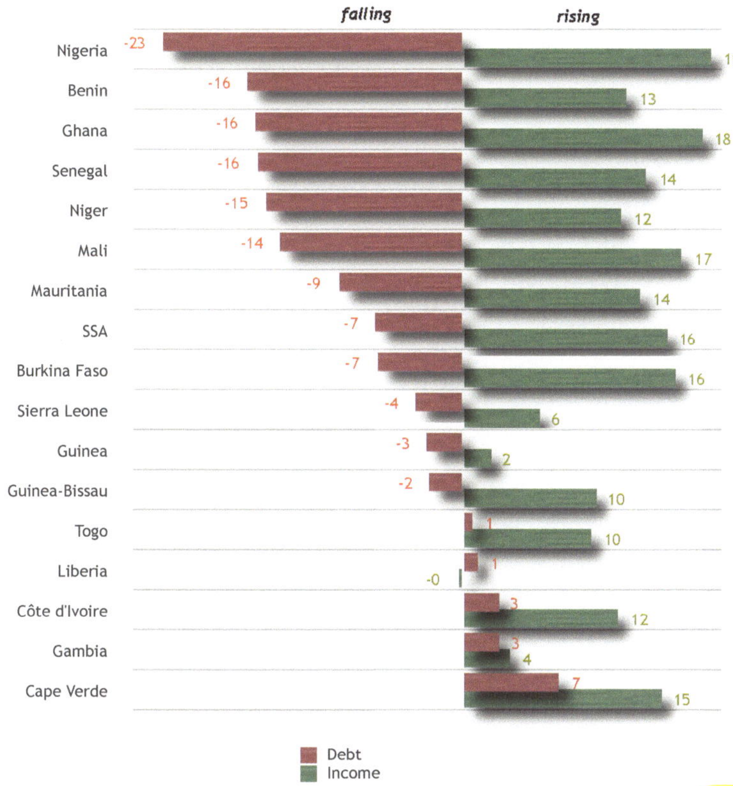


Primary Data: World Bank

**8.33**

**Net Growth Rate of Debt and Income in West Africa during 2003/06 (%)**

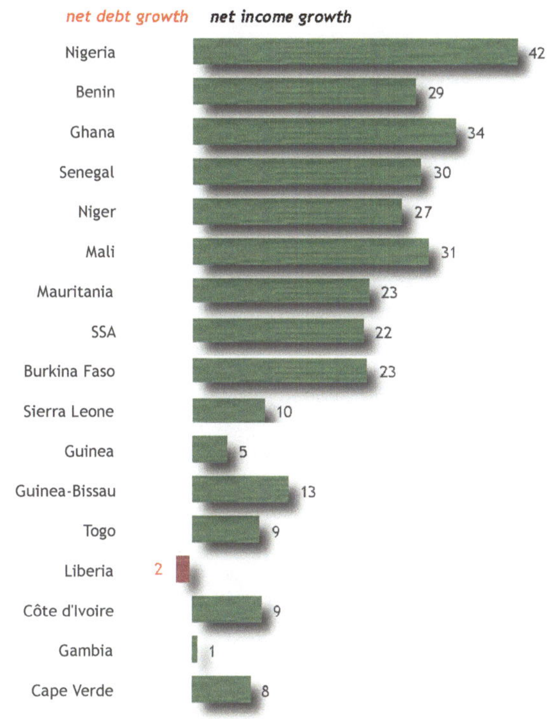


Nigeria out-did everyone else in West Africa. Fastest rate of debt climb-down and fastest rate of income build-up.

Ghana came in 2nd and Mali, 3rd.

Liberia was worst, understandably: it was picking itself up from zero after years of war. It needed both grants and loans to rebuild from scratch.

# 8.12 Aid Dependency (as % of GDP)

## counting on Santa

| | 97-02 | 03-06 | 07-08 |
|---|---|---|---|
| Self-comparison to Preceding Period | | ◁▷ | ◁▷ |
| Performance in Sub-Saharan Africa | ▲ | ▲ | ▲ |
| Performance in West Africa | ▲ | ▲ | ▲ |

| 97-02 | 03-06 | 07-08 |
|---|---|---|
| **Nigeria** | **Nigeria** | **Nigeria** |
| Côte d'Ivoire | Côte d'Ivoire | Guinea |
| Guinea | Guinea | Côte d'Ivoire |
| Mali | Togo | Mali |
| Senegal | Senegal | Senegal |
| Togo | Mali | Togo |
| Benin | Benin | Ghana |
| Niger | Niger | Niger |
| Burkina Faso | Burkina Faso | Benin |
| Ghana | Ghana | Sierra Leone |
| Cape Verde | Cape Verde | Burkina Faso |
| Sierra Leone | Sierra Leone | Cape Verde |
| Gambia, The | Gambia, The | Gambia, The |
| Guinea-Bissau | Guinea-Bissau | Guinea-Bissau |
| Liberia | Liberia | Liberia |

Primary Data: IMF

It could be argued, of course, that Nigeria has no business with foreign aid because of its economic size and potential. It lives up to those expectations.

Performance among Oil-Exporters

| 97-02 | 03-06 | 07-08 |
|---|---|---|
| ▲ | ▲ | ▲ |
| **Nigeria** | Gabon | Gabon |
| Congo, Rep. | **Nigeria** | **Nigeria** |
| Gabon | Côte d'Ivoire | Côte d'Ivoire |
| Cameroon | Angola | Angola |
| Côte d'Ivoire | Equatorial Guinea | Equatorial Guinea |
| Angola | Congo, Rep. | Congo, Rep. |
| Equatorial Guinea | Cameroon | Cameroon |
| Chad | Chad | Chad |

It was bettered within the oil bloc by Gabon.

| | |
|---|---|
| ▲ | better = less dependence |
| ▼ | worse = more dependence |
| ◁▷ | no change *or* average |

8.35

Foreign Aid as % of GDP in West Africa during 2003/06

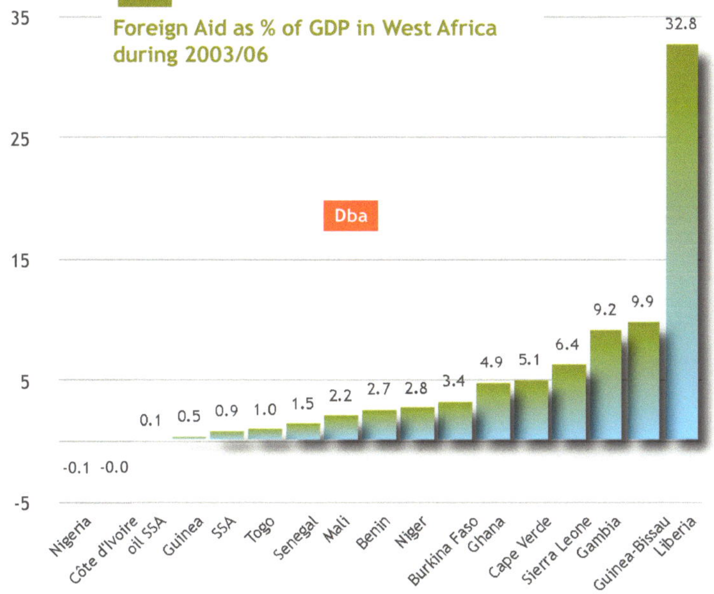


Liberia's position here is understandable. Nigeria and Côte d'Ivoire look to have been net donors, not recipients.

8.36

Foreign Aid as % of GDP in Nigeria and Sub-Saharan Africa from 1999-2007

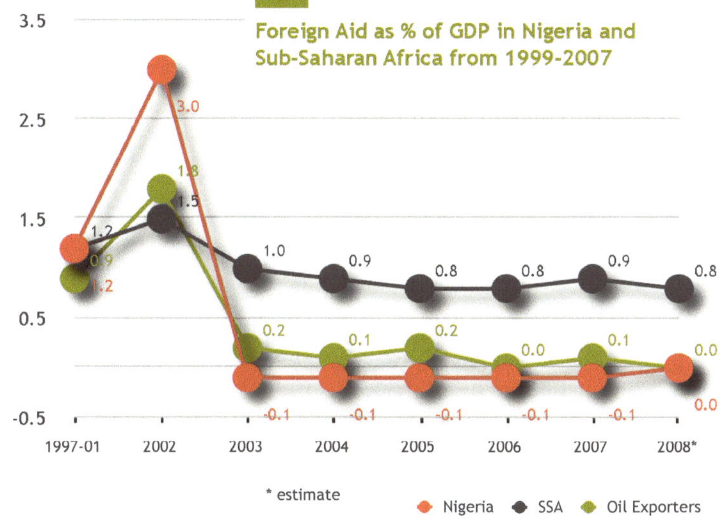


Foreign aid tightened up for the oil economies in 2003. For the rest of Africa, too, but not as sharply.

Foreign Aid as % of GDP in Sub-Saharan Africa during 2003-06: Rankings

| Rank | Country | Rank | Country | Rank | Country |
|---|---|---|---|---|---|
| 1 | South Africa | 15 | Senegal | 29 | Ethiopia |
| 2 | Gabon | 16 | Mali | 30 | Sierra Leone |
| 3 | Nigeria | 17 | Madagascar | 31 | Congo, Dem. Rep. |
| 4 | Côte d' Ivoire | 18 | Seychelles | 32 | Uganda |
| 5 | Angola | 19 | Benin | 33 | Malawi |
| 6 | Kenya | 20 | Niger | 34 | Gambia, The |
| 7 | Mauritius | 21 | Burkina Faso | 35 | Guinea-Bissau |
| 8 | Equatorial Guinea | 22 | Central Afr. Rep. | 36 | Swaziland |
| 9 | Congo, Rep. | 23 | Tanzania | 37 | Namibia |
| 10 | Guinea | 24 | Chad | 38 | Rwanda |
| 11 | Cameroon | 25 | Ghana | 39 | Eritrea |
| 12 | Togo | 26 | Cape Verde | 40 | Burundi |
| 13 | Comoros | 27 | Mozambique | 41 | Lesotho |
| 14 | Zambia | 28 | Botswana | | |
| Least | | MIDDLE | | Most | |

6 of the 10 least aid recipients were oil exporters. Of these 10, South Africa, Gabon and Nigeria were net donors.

Primary Data: IMF

Central Africa
East Africa
Southern Africa
West Africa

# 8.13 Aid Dependency (as $PPP per person)

**beggar thy neighbour**

| | 97-02 | 03-06 | 07-08 |
|---|---|---|---|
| Self-comparison to Preceding Period | | ▲ | ▼ |
| Performance in Sub-Saharan Africa | ▲ | ▲ | ▲ |
| Performance in West Africa | ▲ | ▲ | ▲ |
| | **Nigeria** | **Nigeria** | **Nigeria** |
| | Côte d'Ivoire | Côte d'Ivoire | Guinea |
| | Guinea | Guinea | Mali |
| | Mali | Togo | Togo |
| | Niger | Niger | Niger |
| | Togo | Mali | Senegal |
| | Senegal | Senegal | Sierra Leone |
| | Sierra Leone | Burkina Faso | Côte d'Ivoire |
| | Burkina Faso | Sierra Leone | Ghana |
| | Benin | Benin | Benin |
| | Ghana | Guinea-Bissau | Burkina Faso |
| | Guinea-Bissau | Ghana | Guinea-Bissau |
| | Gambia, The | Gambia, The | Liberia |
| | Cape Verde | Liberia | Gambia, The |
| | Liberia | Cape Verde | Cape Verde |

Primary Data: IMF

| | 97-02 | 03-06 | 07-08 |
|---|---|---|---|
| Performance among Oil-Exporters | ▲ | ▲ | ▲ |
| | **Nigeria** | Gabon | Angola |
| | Cameroon | **Nigeria** | **Nigeria** |
| | Congo, Rep. | Côte d'Ivoire | Equatorial Guinea |
| | Côte d'Ivoire | Angola | Gabon |
| | Gabon | Cameroon | Congo, Rep. |
| | Angola | Congo, Rep. | Cameroon |
| | Chad | Equatorial Guinea | Côte d'Ivoire |
| | Equatorial Guinea | Chad | Chad |

In $ per person, Nigeria was a net donor, not recipient, during 2003-2006. By 2007-2008, it is still a net donor, but by a smaller margin.

| | |
|---|---|
| ▲ | better = less dependence |
| ▼ | worse = more dependence |
| ◁▷ | no change *or* average |

## 8. Self-Reliance

8.37

Foreign Aid as $PPP per Person in West Africa during 2003/06

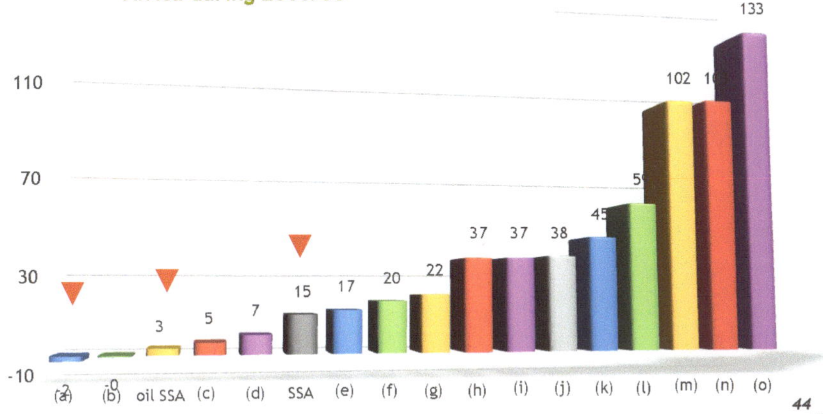


| | | |
|---|---|---|
| (a) | Nigeria | -2 |
| (b) | Côte d'Ivoire | -0 |
| | oil SSA | 3 |
| (c) | Guinea | 5 |
| (d) | Togo | 7 |
| | SSA | 15 |
| (e) | Niger | 17 |
| (f) | Mali | 20 |
| (g) | Senegal | 22 |
| (e) | Burkina Faso | 37 |
| (f) | Sierra Leone | 37 |
| (g) | Benin | 38 |
| (e) | Guinea-Bissau | 45 |
| (f) | Ghana | 59 |
| (g) | Gambia | 102 |
| (e) | Liberia | 103 |
| (f) | Cape Verde | 133 |

8.38

Foreign Aid in Nigeria and Sub-Saharan Africa during 2003/06 as $PPP per Person

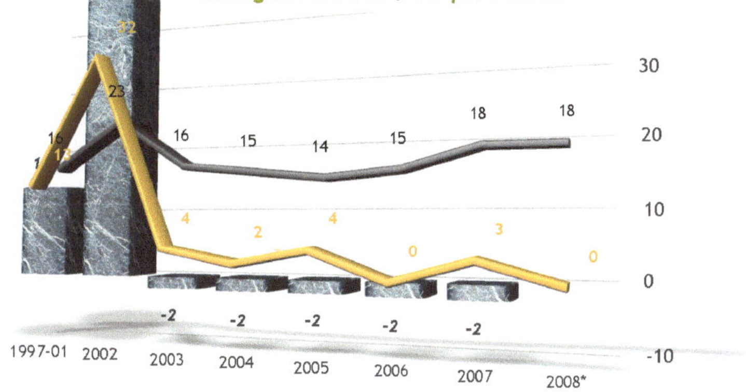


* estimate — Oil Exporters — SSA

Besides Nigeria, the other net donors during 03/06 in Africa were South Africa and Gabon.

Foreign Aid in Sub-Saharan Africa as $PPP per Person during 2003-06: Rankings

| Rank | Country | Rank | Country | Rank | Country |
|---|---|---|---|---|---|
| 1 | South Africa | 15 | Madagascar | 29 | Malawi |
| 2 | Gabon | 16 | Mali | 30 | Ghana |
| 3 | Nigeria | 17 | Senegal | 31 | Burundi |
| 4 | Côte d' Ivoire | 18 | Central Afr. Rep. | 32 | Uganda |
| 5 | Kenya | 19 | Mauritius | 33 | Rwanda |
| 6 | Angola | 20 | Tanzania | 34 | Gambia, The |
| 7 | Guinea | 21 | Burkina Faso | 35 | Eritrea |
| 8 | Togo | 22 | Sierra Leone | 36 | Cape Verde |
| 9 | Cameroon | 23 | Ethiopia | 37 | Lesotho |
| 10 | Congo, Rep. | 24 | Benin | 38 | Seychelles |
| 11 | Comoros | 25 | Equatorial Guinea | 39 | Swaziland |
| 12 | Zambia | 26 | Mozambique | 40 | Namibia |
| 13 | Niger | 27 | Guinea-Bissau | 41 | Botswana |
| 14 | Congo, Dem. Rep. | 28 | Chad | | |
| | Least | | MIDDLE | | Most |

By 07/08 there were a different 3: South Africa and Nigeria again, but Angola rather than Gabon.

Central Africa
East Africa
Southern Africa
West Africa

Primary Data: IMF

# Leaders & Stragglers

**we'll be needing some more, please**

Nigeria turned out to be the most self-reliant in Africa during 2003-2006, beating South Africa - the only larger economy - who came in 4th.

## Self-Reliance Rankings: 2003-06

| Rank | Country | Rank | Country | Rank | Country |
|---|---|---|---|---|---|
| 1 | Nigeria | 15 | Ethiopia | 29 | Rwanda |
| 2 | Kenya | 16 | Angola | 30 | Ghana |
| 3 | Equatorial Guinea | 17 | Côte d' Ivoire | 31 | Congo, Rep. |
| 4 | South Africa | 18 | Namibia | 32 | Zambia |
| 5 | Benin | 19 | Congo, Dem. Rep. | 33 | Lesotho |
| 6 | Tanzania | 20 | Gabon | 34 | Guinea-Bissau |
| 7 | Mauritius | 21 | Togo | 35 | Seychelles |
| 8 | Niger | 22 | Senegal | 36 | Cape Verde |
| 9 | Mali | 23 | Chad | 37 | Malawi |
| 10 | Burkina Faso | 24 | Mozambique | 38 | Burundi |
| 11 | Central Afr. Rep. | 25 | Sierra Leone | 39 | Swaziland |
| 12 | Botswana | 26 | Madagascar | 40 | Gambia, The |
| 13 | Cameroon | 27 | Guinea | 41 | Eritrea |
| 14 | Comoros | 28 | Uganda | | |
| TOP | | MIDDLE | | BOTTOM | |

Central Africa
East Africa
Southern Africa
West Africa

# Wrap-up: Self-Reliance

- This time, Nigeria tops West Africa and the entire Sub-Saharan Africa. The next best West Africa result is from Benin Republic, in 5th place on the continental table.
- It isn't difficult to see why Nigeria stands out: near 70% of all the indicator outcomes are in the top segment; only one of them turns up in the bottom segment of performance. Benin has three there.
- All Nigeria's "critical" indicators are top-bracket finishers, except one. The country relies comparatively little on foreign aid, and is not burdened by debt overhang. Its external trade is robust, even though much of it is due to oil.
- A lot still must be done to improve external trade and exports in the services sector.
- There is a precarious balance though, in the desire for imports. Nigeria manages to stay within reasonable range in its import levels per population, but it is growing those levels dangerously fast. That is the one area where it sank into the bottom segment of performance.

# 9. Investor Confidence

*coming over to stay*


9.1 FDI as % of GDP

9.2 FDI per Person

9.3 Growth in FDI per Person

9.4 FDI as % of Total Capital Investment

9.5 Total Capital Investment as % of GDP

9.6 Total Capital Investment per Person

9.7 Growth in Total Capital Investment per Person

9.8 Private Component of TCI as % of GDP

9.9 Private Component of TCI as Investment per Person

9.10 Growth of Private (& Public) Component of TCI

9.11 Domestic Credit to the Private Sector as % of GDP

9.12 Domestic Credit to the Private Sector in $PPP

9.13 Growth in Domestic Credit to the Private Sector

Leaders & Stragglers

Wrap-up

**Investment** is crucial to any economy. Economies, literally, thrive on the volume of investments they attract. Countries fall over themselves to create environments that would pull investment in to various sectors. Investors will only sink funds where they expect to derive reasonable benefits and rewards. Governments would have to maintain a sane balance to make sure that consumer rights, for example, are well protected, otherwise business will, left to itself, be exploitative. Volume of investment is a strong sign of an economy's strength and viability.

## Foreign Direct Investment (FDI)

The volume of foreign commitment to business enterprises in a host economy. It must be distinguished from acquisition of shares on a stock exchange which generally is taken not to be a firm investment commitment but could easily become "hot money": money withdrawn at the least notice and moved elsewhere. FDI generally involves the acquisition of "immovable assets" (e.g. factories, machinery) and the exercise of some managerial control. An increase in FDI would imply investor confidence in a host country's economic and social climate. By expressing FDI in terms of percentage of GDP, or per person of population, a more accurate picture of economic activity can be obtained. Otherwise the volume of FDI by itself, without reference to country size, could not be a meaningful evaluation.

The FDI figures shown are *net* flows. That is, the net of investment coming into the economy and the ones leaving it. That is why some figures are negative, indicating that there was a net exodus of foreign investment: more FDI leaving than entering, during the period.

## Total Capital investment (TCI)

Refers to the aggregate total of Capital Investment in an economy (again, as distinct from stocks and shares), and so, comprises FDI and more. It is also known as Gross Fixed Capital Formation (GFCF). It may be split into various components to measure and evaluate its make-up.

It would, for example, be a further sign of confidence in the economy if the level of **Private** input into TCI is high or growing. The **Public** (government) component of TCI would not, for simply that fact, necessarily point to a robust economy, since the government's imperatives do not have to be confident expectations of a justifying return on investment.

FDI is part of the private component of this Total Capital Investment. The rest of this private component would be of "domestic origins", i.e. investors from the private sector, domiciled within that economy. In other words,

TCI = Private Investment + Public Investment

Private Investment = FDI + "Domestic Investment"

## Domestic Credit to the Private Sector

This is another indicator of the level of business confidence in an economy; this time from the perspective of commercial institutions in the financial sector. The thinking being that these institutions would tend to lend money to business enterprises when they (the institutions) perceive the economic and business climate to be promising or vibrant.

**Sources of Primary Data:** AfDB, IMF, UNCTAD, World Bank

# Charts

9.1 FDI as % of GDP in West Africa during 2003-06
9.2 FDI as % of GDP in Nigeria and Sub-Saharan Africa from 1999 to 2007
9.3 Share of West Africa and Nigeria in Total FDI of Sub-Saharan Africa (%): 1999 - 2007
9.4 FDI as US$ per Person in West Africa during 2003-06
9.5 FDI as US$ per Person in Nigeria and Sub-Saharan Africa from 1999 to 2007
9.6 Annual Growth in FDI per Person in West Africa during 2003-06 (%)
9.7 Annual Growth in FDI per Person in Nigeria and Sub-Saharan Africa from 2000-2007 (%)
9.8 Build-up of FDI per Person in Nigeria and Sub-Saharan Africa from 2000-2007: 2000=100
9.9 FDI as % of Total Capital Investment in West Africa during 2003-06
9.10 FDI as % of Total Capital Investment in Nigeria and Sub-Saharan Africa from 1999-2006
9.11 Total Capital Investment as % of GDP in West Africa during 2003-06
9.12 Total Capital Investment as % of GDP in Nigeria and Sub-Saharan Africa from 1999-2006
9.13 Total Capital Investment per Person (US$) in West Africa during 2003-06
9.14 Total Capital Investment per Person ($US) in Nigeria and Sub-Saharan Africa from 1999-2006
9.15 Growth in Total Capital Investment per Person (%) in West Africa during 2003-06
9.16 Growth in Total Capital Investment per Person in Nigeria and Sub-Saharan Africa during 2003-06
9.17 Build-up of Total Capital Investment per Person in Nigeria and Sub-Saharan Africa: 2000=100
9.18 Private and Public Components of Total Capital Investment as % GDP in West Africa during 2003-06
9.19 Private and Public Components of Total Capital Investment as % GDP in Nigeria: from 2000-07
9.20 Private and Public Components of Total Capital Investment per Person ($PPP) in West Africa during 2003-06
9.21 Private and Public Components of Total Capital Investment per Person in Nigeria ($PPP): from 2000-07
9.22 Growth of Private and Public Components of Total Capital Investment in West Africa during 2003-06 (%)
9.23 Growth of Private and Public Components of Total Capital Investment in Nigeria (%): from 2000-07
9.24 Build-up of Private and Public Components of Total Capital Investment in Nigeria 2000-07: 2000=100
9.25 Domestic Credit to the Private Sector as % of GDP in West Africa during 2003-06
9.26 Domestic Credit to the Private Sector as % of GDP in Nigeria and Sub-Saharan Africa from 1999-2006
9.27 Domestic Credit to the Private Sector in West Africa ($PPP millions) during 2003-06
9.28 Domestic Credit to the Private Sector in Nigeria in $PPP (millions): from 1999-2006
9.29 Growth in Domestic Credit to the Private Sector during 2003-06 (%)
9.30 Growth in Domestic Credit to the Private Sector in Nigeria and Sub-Saharan Africa from 1999-2006
9.31 Build-up of Domestic Credit to the Private Sector in Nigeria and Sub-Saharan Africa from 2000-06: 2000=100

- **Wrap-up**

# Tables

*1999-2002; 2003-2006:*

- *self-comparison to preceding period;*
- *performance in S-Saharan Africa;*
- *performance in West Africa;*
- *performance among oil-exporters;*

*for:*

FDI as % of GDP

FDI per Person

Growth in FDI per Person

FDI as % of Total Capital Investment

Total Capital Investment as % of GDP

Total Capital Investment per Person

Growth in TCI per Person

Private Component of TCI as % of GDP

Private Component of TCI as Investment per Person

Growth of Private Component of TCI

Domestic Credit to the Private Sector as % of GDP

Domestic Credit to the Private Sector in $PPP

Growth in Domestic Credit to the Private Sector

- FDI as % of GDP in Sub-Saharan Africa during 2003-06: Rankings
- FDI as US$ per Person in Sub-Saharan Africa during 2003-06: Rankings
- Annual Growth in FDI per Person in Sub-Saharan Africa during 2003-06: Rankings
- FDI as % of Total Capital Investment in Sub-Saharan Africa during 2003-06: Rankings
- Total Capital Investment as % of GDP in Sub-Saharan Africa during 2003-06: Rankings
- Total Capital Investment per Person in Sub-Saharan Africa during 2003-06: Rankings
- Growth in Total Capital Investment per Person in Sub-Saharan Africa during 2003-06: Rankings
- Private Component of Total Capital Investment as % of GDP in Sub-Saharan Africa during 2003-06: Rankings
- Private Component of TCI as Investment per Person ($PPP) in Sub-Saharan Africa during 2003-06: Rankings
- Growth of Private Component of Total Capital Investment per Person in Sub-Saharan Africa during 2003-06: Rankings
- Domestic Credit to the Private Sector as % of GDP in Sub-Saharan Africa during 2003-06: Rankings
- Domestic Credit to the Private Sector as $PPP in Sub-Saharan Africa during 2003-06: Rankings
- Growth in Domestic Credit to the Private Sector in Sub-Saharan Africa during 2003-06: Rankings
- **Investor Confidence Rankings: 2003-06**

# 9.1 FDI as % of GDP

*shall we, shall we not?*

| | 99-02 | 03-06 |
|---|---|---|
| Self-comparison to Preceding Period | | ▲ |
| Performance in Sub-Saharan Africa | ▼ | ▲ |
| Performance in West Africa | ▲ | ▲ |
| | Liberia | Mauritania |
| | Gambia, The | Gambia, The |
| | Cape Verde | Cape Verde |
| | Mauritania | **Nigeria** |
| | Mali | Sierra Leone |
| | Togo | Guinea |
| | **Nigeria** | Togo |
| | Côte d'Ivoire | Guinea-Bissau |
| | Ghana | Mali |
| | Senegal | Ghana |
| | Benin | Côte d'Ivoire |
| | Sierra Leone | Benin |
| | Guinea | Senegal |
| | Guinea-Bissau | Niger |
| | Burkina Faso | Burkina Faso |
| | Niger | Liberia |
| Performance among Oil-Exporters | ▼ | ▼ |
| | Equatorial Guinea | Equatorial Guinea |
| | Angola | Chad |
| | Chad | Sudan |
| | Congo, Rep. | Angola |
| | Sudan | Congo, Rep. |
| | **Nigeria** | **Nigeria** |
| | Côte d'Ivoire | Gabon |
| | Cameroon | Cameroon |
| | Gabon | Côte d'Ivoire |

Primary Data: UNCTAD

Nigeria improved on its 99-02 performance, during 03-06. It also did better than the Africa average; whereas it had done worse in 99-02.

Nevertheless, it didn't match up to fellow exporters of crude oil, suggesting that there is still a lot of latent capacity for FDI in the economy.

| | |
|---|---|
| ▲ | improved *or* better than average |
| ▼ | worsened *or* worse than average |
| ◁▷ | no change *or* average |

# 9. Investor Confidence

9.1

FDI as % of GDP in West Africa during 2003-06

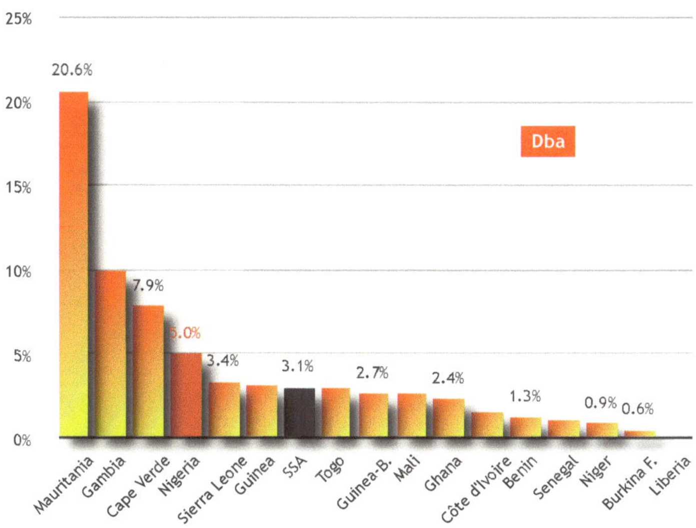


9.2

FDI as % of GDP in Nigeria and Sub-Saharan Africa from 1999 to 2007

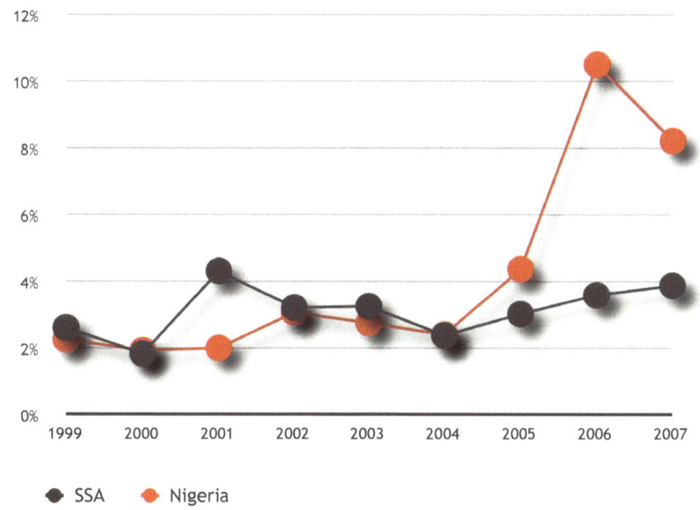


After 2004, FDI moved rapidly to fill that latent capacity. It dipped slightly in 2007, though.

Primary Data: UNCTAD

Central Africa
East Africa
Southern Africa
West Africa

FDI as % of GDP in Sub-Saharan Africa during 2003-06: Rankings

| Rank | Country | Rank | Country | Rank | Country |
|---|---|---|---|---|---|
| 1 | Equatorial Guinea | 15 | Mozambique | 29 | Central Afr. Rep. |
| 2 | Chad | 16 | Tanzania | 30 | Senegal |
| 3 | Seychelles | 17 | Sierra Leone | 31 | Niger |
| 4 | Gambia, The | 18 | Guinea | 32 | Mauritius |
| 5 | Cape Verde | 19 | Malawi | 33 | South Africa |
| 6 | Angola | 20 | Togo | 34 | Burkina Faso |
| 7 | Congo, Rep. | 21 | Madagascar | 35 | Rwanda |
| 8 | Zambia | 22 | Guinea-Bissau | 36 | Eritrea |
| 9 | Nigeria | 23 | Mali | 37 | Kenya |
| 10 | Botswana | 24 | Gabon | 38 | Comoros |
| 11 | Namibia | 25 | Ghana | 39 | Congo, Dem. Rep. |
| 12 | Lesotho | 26 | Cameroon | 40 | Burundi |
| 13 | Ethiopia | 27 | Côte d' Ivoire | 41 | Swaziland |
| 14 | Uganda | 28 | Benin | | |
| TOP | | MIDDLE | | BOTTOM | |

Top-10 performance in Africa; the pack being led by oil exporters. Understandably; as they command foreign investment more easily than the other countries.

# 9.2 FDI per Person

**worth the trouble going all the way?**

| | 99-02 | 03-06 |
|---|---|---|
| Self-comparison to Preceding Period | | ▲ |
| Performance in Sub-Saharan Africa | ▼ | ▲ |
| Performance in West Africa | ▲ | ▲ |
| | Cape Verde | Cape Verde |
| | Gambia, The | Mauritania |
| | Liberia | **Nigeria** |
| | Mauritania | Gambia, The |
| | Côte d'Ivoire | Côte d'Ivoire |
| | **Nigeria** | Mali |
| | Mali | Ghana |
| | Togo | Guinea |
| | Senegal | Togo |
| | Ghana | Sierra Leone |
| | Benin | Senegal |
| | Sierra Leone | Benin |
| | Guinea | Guinea-Bissau |
| | Burkina Faso | Niger |
| | Guinea-Bissau | Burkina Faso |
| | Niger | Liberia |
| Performance among Oil-Exporters | ▼ | ▼ |
| | Equatorial Guinea | Equatorial Guinea |
| | Angola | Gabon |
| | Congo, Rep. | Congo, Rep. |
| | Chad | Chad |
| | Côte d'Ivoire | Angola |
| | Sudan | Sudan |
| | Cameroon | **Nigeria** |
| | **Nigeria** | Cameroon |
| | Gabon | Côte d'Ivoire |

Primary Data: UNCTAD

*Nigeria has commanded an increasing share of Africa's FDI, but still lies bottom of the oil exporters' league. Untapped investment potential.*

**9.3**

**Share of West Africa and Nigeria in Total FDI of Sub-Saharan Africa (%): 1999 - 2007**

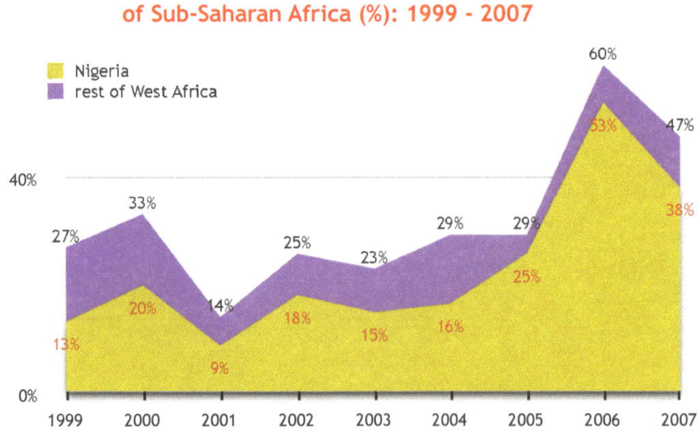


| | |
|---|---|
| ▲ | improved *or* better than average |
| ▼ | worsened *or* worse than average |
| ◁▷ | no change *or* average |

# 9. Investor Confidence

9.4

FDI as US$ per Person in West Africa during 2003-06

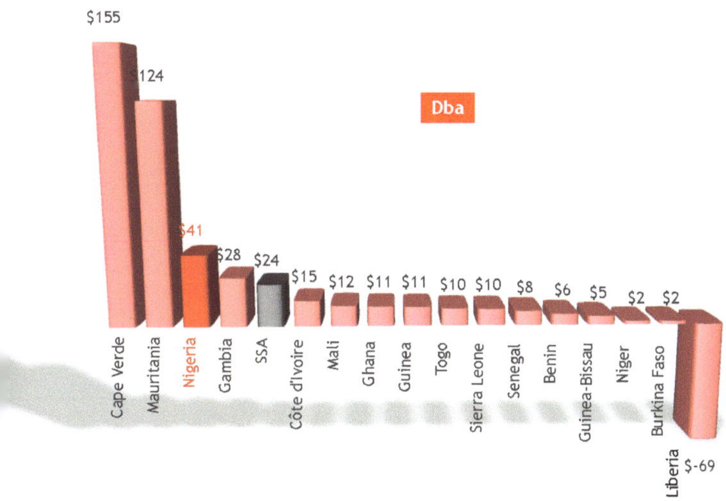


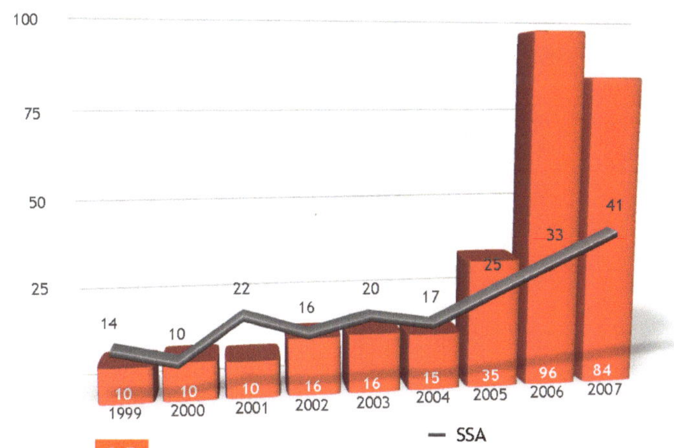


9.5

FDI as US$ per Person in Nigeria and Sub-Saharan Africa from 1999 to 2007

After 2004, Nigeria surpassed the Africa average for FDI per population. A dip in level in 2007, however.

Primary Data: UNCTAD

Central Africa
East Africa
Southern Africa
West Africa

FDI as US$ per Person in Sub-Saharan Africa during 2003-06: Rankings

| Rank | Country | Rank | Country | Rank | Country |
|---|---|---|---|---|---|
| 1 | Equatorial Guinea | 15 | Gambia, The | 29 | Ethiopia |
| 2 | Seychelles | 16 | Cameroon | 30 | Guinea-Bissau |
| 3 | Botswana | 17 | Côte d' Ivoire | 31 | Malawi |
| 4 | Cape Verde | 18 | Mali | 32 | Central Afr. Rep. |
| 5 | Gabon | 19 | Ghana | 33 | Niger |
| 6 | Namibia | 20 | Tanzania | 34 | Burkina Faso |
| 7 | Congo, Rep. | 21 | Uganda | 35 | Kenya |
| 8 | Chad | 22 | Guinea | 36 | Rwanda |
| 9 | Angola | 23 | Mozambique | 37 | Eritrea |
| 10 | Mauritius | 24 | Togo | 38 | Comoros |
| 11 | Nigeria | 25 | Sierra Leone | 39 | Burundi |
| 12 | South Africa | 26 | Senegal | 40 | Congo, Dem. Rep. |
| 13 | Zambia | 27 | Madagascar | 41 | Swaziland |
| 14 | Lesotho | 28 | Benin | | |
| TOP | | MIDDLE | | BOTTOM | |

But it is beaten out of a Top-10 showing in Africa. Smaller countries like Namibia and Chad attracted more foreign money per population.

# 9.3 Growth in FDI per Person

**who had the widest doors?**

| | 99-02 | 03-06 |
|---|---|---|
| Self-comparison to Preceding Period | | ▲ |
| Performance in Sub-Saharan Africa | ▼ | ▲ |

**Performance in West Africa**

| ▼ | ▲ |
|---|---|
| Sierra Leone | Liberia |
| Mauritania | Sierra Leone |
| Mali | Niger |
| Guinea | Guinea-Bissau |
| Cape Verde | Ghana |
| Guinea-Bissau | Senegal |
| Burkina Faso | Mauritania |
| Senegal | **Nigeria** |
| Niger | Benin |
| Togo | Gambia, The |
| Gambia, The | Guinea |
| **Nigeria** | Burkina Faso |
| Benin | Cape Verde |
| Côte d'Ivoire | Togo |
| Ghana | Côte d'Ivoire |
| Liberia | Mali |

9.6

Annual Growth in FDI per Person in West Africa during 2003-06 (%)

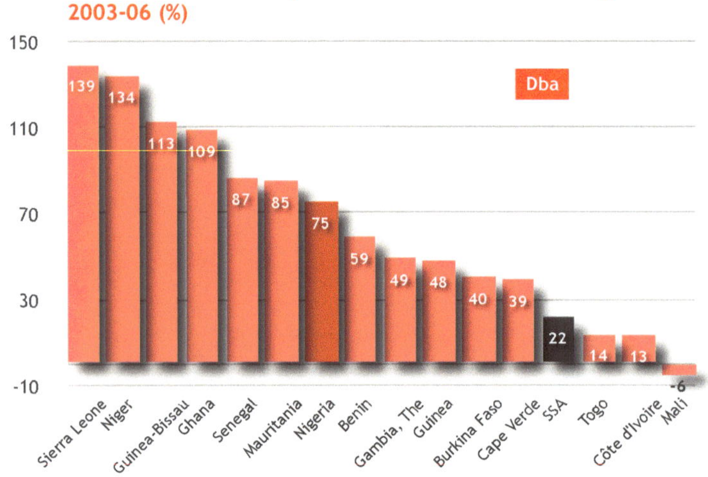


Primary Data: UNCTAD

**Performance among Oil-Exporters**

| ▼ | ▲ |
|---|---|
| Cameroon | Congo, Rep. |
| Congo, Rep. | Gabon |
| Chad | Equatorial Guinea |
| Equatorial Guinea | **Nigeria** |
| Angola | Sudan |
| Sudan | Côte d'Ivoire |
| **Nigeria** | Chad |
| Côte d'Ivoire | Angola |
| Gabon | Cameroon |

*A good showing by West Africa in general, where investment per person grew by more than the Africa average.*

| | |
|---|---|
| ▲ | improved *or* better than average |
| ▼ | worsened *or* worse than average |
| ◁▷ | no change *or* average |

9.7

Annual Growth in FDI per Person in Nigeria and Sub-Saharan Africa from 2000-2007 (%)

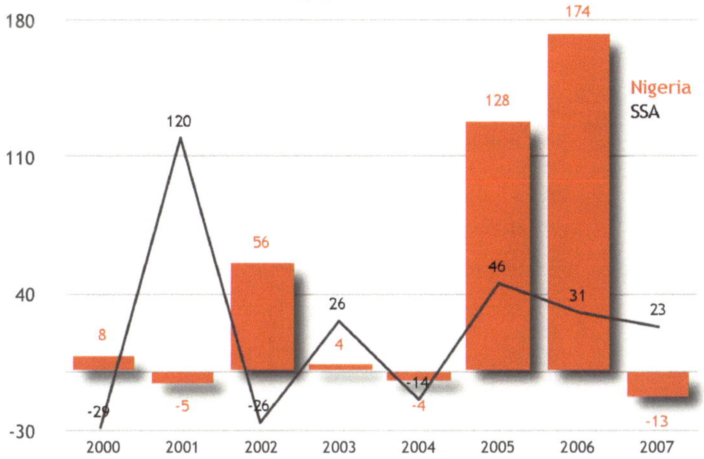


9.8

Build-up of FDI per Person in Nigeria and Sub-Saharan Africa from 2000-2007: 2000=100

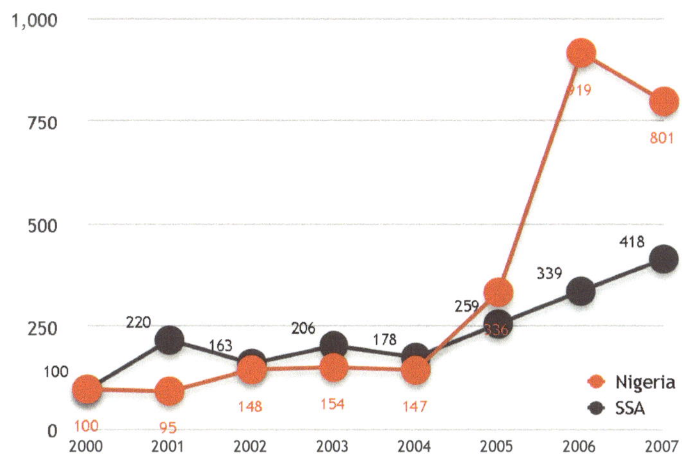


Primary Data: UNCTAD

Nigeria generally grew its FDI during 03-06, better than it did during the previous 4 yrs.

Nigeria's FDI per Population grew by 8 times from 2000 through 2007. The rest of Africa grew by 4 times.

Annual Growth in FDI per Person in Sub-Saharan Africa during 2003-06: Rankings

| Rank | Country | Rank | Country | Rank | Country |
|---|---|---|---|---|---|
| 1 | Congo, Rep. | 15 | Benin | 29 | Togo |
| 2 | Gabon | 16 | Central Afr. Rep. | 30 | Côte d' Ivoire |
| 3 | South Africa | 17 | Kenya | 31 | Swaziland |
| 4 | Sierra Leone | 18 | Gambia, The | 32 | Comoros |
| 5 | Niger | 19 | Guinea | 33 | Tanzania |
| 6 | Guinea-Bissau | 20 | Seychelles | 34 | Botswana |
| 7 | Ghana | 21 | Burkina Faso | 35 | Burundi |
| 8 | Mauritius | 22 | Cape Verde | 36 | Mali |
| 9 | Rwanda | 23 | Lesotho | 37 | Chad |
| 10 | Senegal | 24 | Ethiopia | 38 | Angola |
| 11 | Equatorial Guinea | 25 | Namibia | 39 | Mozambique |
| 12 | Nigeria | 26 | Zambia | 40 | Cameroon |
| 13 | Malawi | 27 | Uganda | 41 | Congo, Dem. Rep. |
| 14 | Madagascar | 28 | Eritrea | | |
| | TOP | | MIDDLE | | BOTTOM |

However, it was behind more than 10 other countries, who did better.

Central Africa
East Africa
Southern Africa
West Africa

# 9.4 FDI as % of Total Capital Investment

**pleased to work with you**

| | 99-02 | 03-06 |
|---|---|---|
| Self-comparison to Preceding Period | | ▼ |
| Performance in Sub-Saharan Africa | ▲ | ▲ |

**Performance in West Africa**

| 99-02 | 03-06 |
|---|---|
| ▲ | ▲ |
| Liberia | Sierra Leone |
| Sierra Leone | Mauritania |
| Gambia, The | **Nigeria** |
| **Nigeria** | Gambia, The |
| Togo | Cape Verde |
| Mauritania | Guinea |
| Cape Verde | Guinea-Bissau |
| Côte d'Ivoire | Côte d'Ivoire |
| Mali | Mali |
| Ghana | Togo |
| Benin | Ghana |
| Senegal | Benin |
| Guinea | Niger |
| Guinea-Bissau | Senegal |
| Niger | Burkina Faso |
| Burkina Faso | Liberia |

Primary Data: UNCTAD

**Performance among Oil-Exporters**

| 99-02 | 03-06 |
|---|---|
| ▲ | ▲ |
| Angola | Equatorial Guinea |
| Chad | Angola |
| Equatorial Guinea | Chad |
| **Nigeria** | **Nigeria** |
| Congo, Rep. | Sudan |
| Sudan | Congo, Rep. |
| Côte d'Ivoire | Côte d'Ivoire |
| Cameroon | Cameroon |
| Gabon | Gabon |

| | |
|---|---|
| ▲ | improved *or* better than average |
| ▼ | worsened *or* worse than average |
| ◁▷ | no change *or* average |

9.9

FDI as % of Total Capital Investment in West Africa during 2003-06

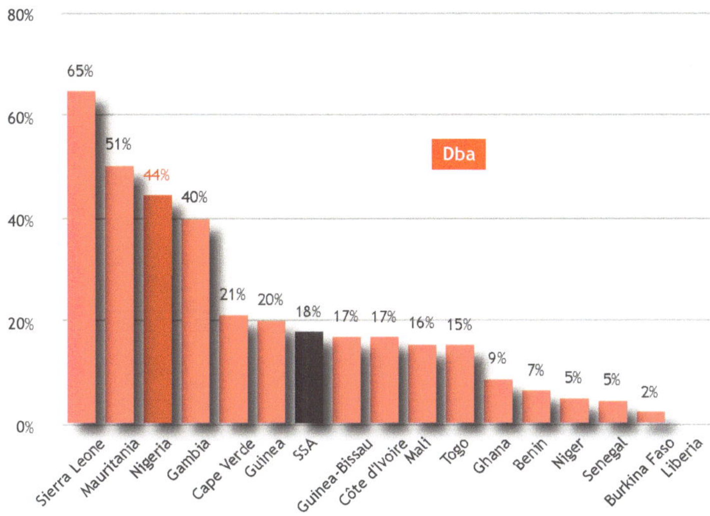


9.10

FDI as % of Total Capital Investment in Nigeria and Sub-Saharan Africa from 1999-2006

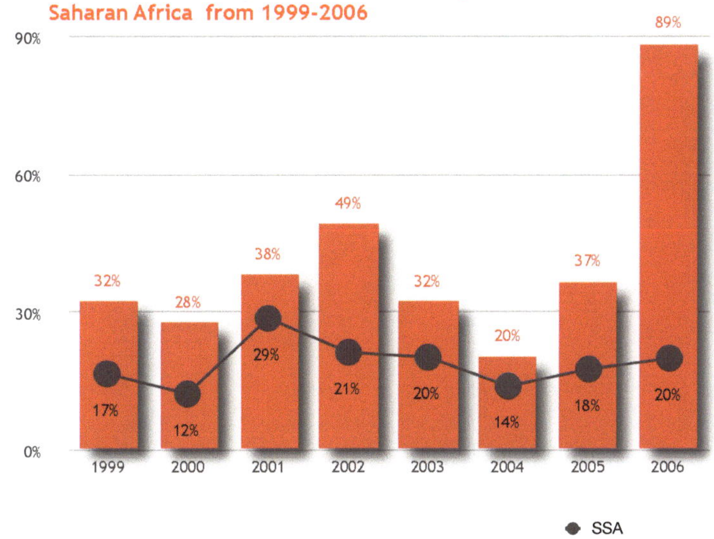


The FDI contribution to overall investment in Nigeria grew - even though in fits and starts - from 1999 through 2006.

FDI as % of Total Capital Investment in Sub-Saharan Africa during 2003-06: Rankings

| Rank | Country | Rank | Country | Rank | Country |
|---|---|---|---|---|---|
| 1 | Seychelles | 15 | Botswana | 29 | Benin |
| 2 | Equatorial Guinea | 16 | Namibia | 30 | Niger |
| 3 | Sierra Leone | 17 | Guinea-Bissau | 31 | South Africa |
| 4 | Angola | 18 | Côte d' Ivoire | 32 | Senegal |
| 5 | Chad | 19 | Tanzania | 33 | Mauritius |
| 6 | Nigeria | 20 | Uganda | 34 | Rwanda |
| 7 | Gambia, The | 21 | Mozambique | 35 | Burkina Faso |
| 8 | Malawi | 22 | Mali | 36 | Comoros |
| 9 | Zambia | 23 | Togo | 37 | Eritrea |
| 10 | Congo, Rep. | 24 | Madagascar | 38 | Congo, Dem. Rep. |
| 11 | Central Afr. Rep. | 25 | Lesotho | 39 | Kenya |
| 12 | Ethiopia | 26 | Cameroon | 40 | Burundi |
| 13 | Cape Verde | 27 | Gabon | 41 | Swaziland |
| 14 | Guinea | 28 | Ghana | | |
| TOP | | MIDDLE | | BOTTOM | |

Nigeria did better than average in Africa, in terms of FDI contribution to overall investment. Top-10.

Primary Data: UNCTAD

Central Africa
East Africa
Southern Africa
West Africa

# 9.5 Total Capital Investment as % of GDP

do the numbers bear that out?

| | 99-02 | 03-06 |
|---|---|---|
| Self-comparison to Preceding Period | | ▲ |
| Performance in Sub-Saharan Africa | ▼ | ▼ |

Primary Data: UNCTAD

| Performance in West Africa | 99-02 | 03-06 |
|---|---|---|
| | ▼ | ▼ |
| | Cape Verde | Mauritania |
| | Burkina Faso | Cape Verde |
| | Senegal | Ghana |
| | Ghana | Gambia, The |
| | Mauritania | Senegal |
| | Gambia, The | Burkina Faso |
| | Guinea | Benin |
| | Mali | Togo |
| | Benin | Mali |
| | Togo | Niger |
| | Guinea-Bissau | Guinea-Bissau |
| | Niger | Guinea |
| | Côte d'Ivoire | Liberia |
| | **Nigeria** | **Nigeria** |
| | Liberia | Côte d'Ivoire |
| | Sierra Leone | Sierra Leone |

| Performance among Oil-Exporters | 99-02 | 03-06 |
|---|---|---|
| | ▼ | ▼ |
| | Equatorial Guinea | Equatorial Guinea |
| | Chad | Chad |
| | Gabon | Congo, Rep. |
| | Congo, Rep. | Gabon |
| | Sudan | Sudan |
| | Cameroon | Cameroon |
| | Angola | **Nigeria** |
| | Côte d'Ivoire | Angola |
| | **Nigeria** | Côte d'Ivoire |

*03/06 was an improvement over the previous 4 yrs. But it still didn't bring Nigeria up to "standard". Worse performance than in most of the continent.*

| | |
|---|---|
| ▲ | improved *or* better than average |
| ▼ | worsened *or* worse than average |
| ◁▷ | no change *or* average |

# 9. Investor Confidence

9.11

**Total Capital Investment as % of GDP in West Africa during 2003-06**

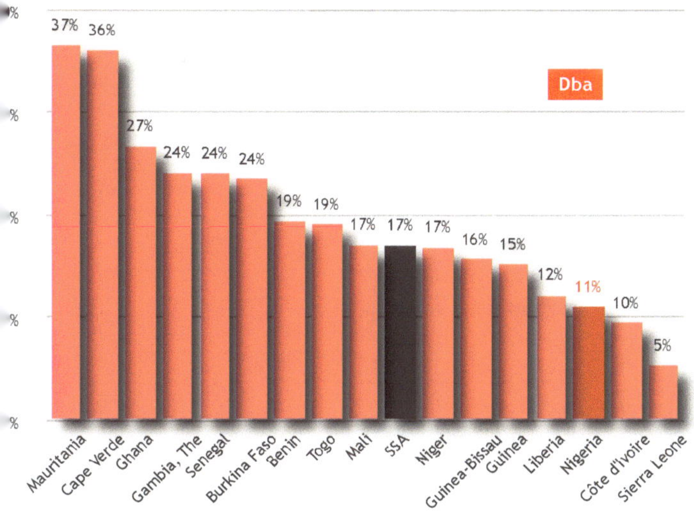


9.12

**Total Capital Investment as % of GDP in Nigeria and Sub-Saharan Africa from 1999-2006**

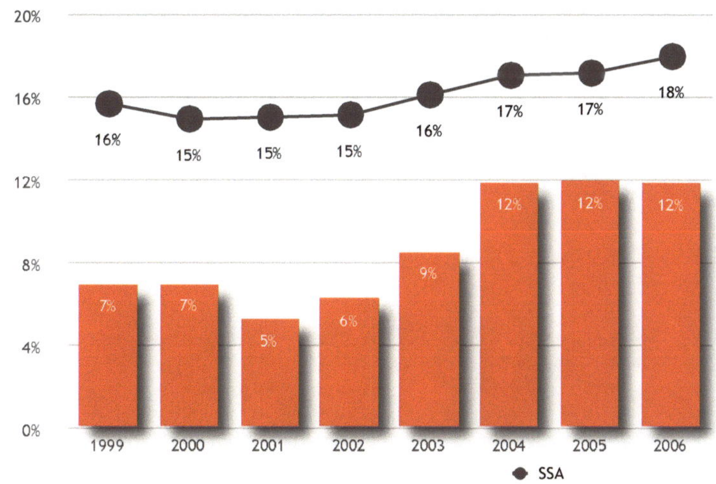


Huge chasm between Africa and Nigeria levels, but closing up towards 2006. Perhaps an indicator again that there's considerable unharnessed potential.

**Total Capital Investment as % of GDP in Sub-Saharan Africa during 2003-06: Rankings**

| Rank | Country | Rank | Country | Rank | Country |
|---|---|---|---|---|---|
| 1 | Equatorial Guinea | 15 | Mauritius | 29 | Niger |
| 2 | Lesotho | 16 | Mozambique | 30 | South Africa |
| 3 | Cape Verde | 17 | Eritrea | 31 | Guinea-Bissau |
| 4 | Chad | 18 | Madagascar | 32 | Congo, Dem. Rep. |
| 5 | Ghana | 19 | Tanzania | 33 | Burundi |
| 6 | Namibia | 20 | Ethiopia | 34 | Guinea |
| 7 | Congo, Rep. | 21 | Rwanda | 35 | Nigeria |
| 8 | Zambia | 22 | Seychelles | 36 | Angola |
| 9 | Botswana | 23 | Benin | 37 | Comoros |
| 10 | Gambia, The | 24 | Cameroon | 38 | Côte d' Ivoire |
| 11 | Senegal | 25 | Togo | 39 | Malawi |
| 12 | Burkina Faso | 26 | Swaziland | 40 | Central Afr. Rep. |
| 13 | Gabon | 27 | Mali | 41 | Sierra Leone |
| 14 | Uganda | 28 | Kenya | | |
| TOP | | MIDDLE | | BOTTOM | |

Primary Data: UNCTAD

Central Africa
East Africa
Southern Africa
West Africa

# 9.6 Total Capital Investment per Person

*home, sweet home?*

Primary Data: UNCTAD

| | 99-02 | 03-06 |
|---|---|---|
| Self-comparison to Preceding Period | | ▲ |
| Performance in Sub-Saharan Africa | ▼ | ▼ |

**Performance in West Africa**

| 99-02 ▼ | 03-06 ▲ |
|---|---|
| Cape Verde | Cape Verde |
| Senegal | Mauritania |
| Mauritania | Senegal |
| Côte d'Ivoire | Ghana |
| Guinea | Benin |
| Ghana | Burkina Faso |
| Benin | Côte d'Ivoire |
| Gambia, The | **Nigeria** |
| Burkina Faso | Mali |
| Mali | Gambia, The |
| Togo | Togo |
| **Nigeria** | Guinea |
| Guinea-Bissau | Niger |
| Niger | Guinea-Bissau |
| Liberia | Liberia |
| Sierra Leone | Sierra Leone |

Also when investment is measured in per capita terms, 03/06 was an improvement over 99/02. Despite that, Nigeria is at rock bottom among oil exporters.

**Performance among Oil-Exporters**

| 99-02 ▼ | 03-06 ▼ |
|---|---|
| Equatorial Guinea | Equatorial Guinea |
| Gabon | Gabon |
| Congo, Rep. | Congo, Rep. |
| Cameroon | Angola |
| Angola | Cameroon |
| Côte d'Ivoire | Sudan |
| Sudan | Chad |
| Chad | Côte d'Ivoire |
| **Nigeria** | **Nigeria** |

| | |
|---|---|
| ▲ | improved *or* better than average |
| ▼ | worsened *or* worse than average |
| ◁▷ | no change *or* average |

# 9. Investor Confidence

9.13

Total Capital Investment per Person (US$) in West Africa during 2003-06

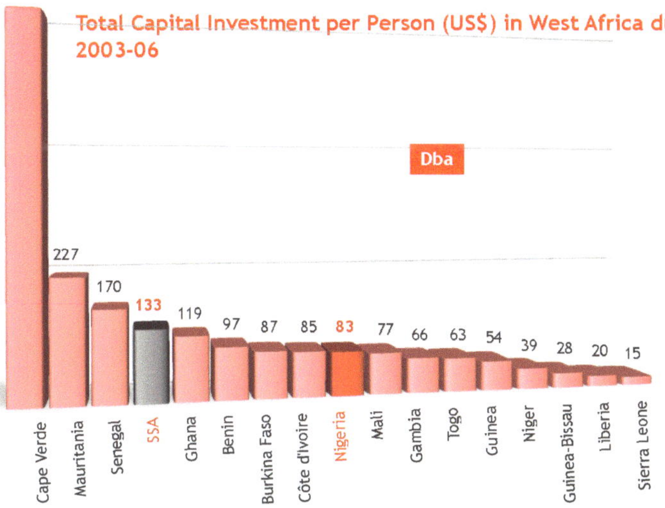


Looks like the Nigeria market can still absorb a lot more capital investment. It falls behind the continent average by a considerable gap.

9.14

Total Capital Investment per Person ($US) in Nigeria and Sub-Saharan Africa from 1999-2006

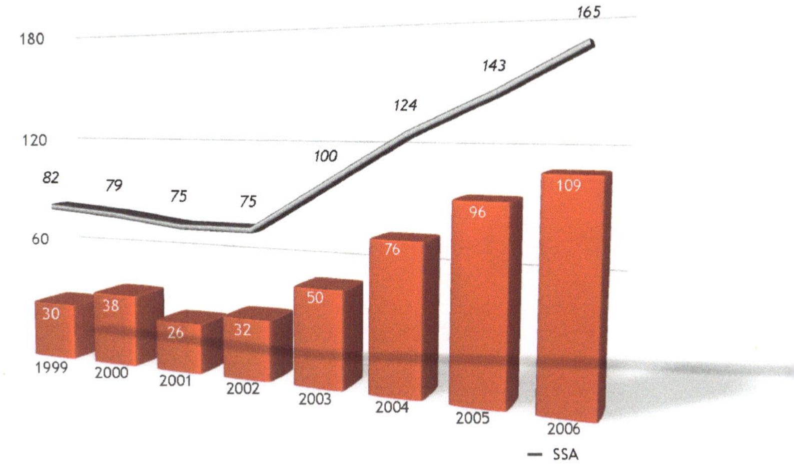


Total Capital Investment per Person in Sub-Saharan Africa during 2003-06: Rankings

| Rank | Country | Rank | Country | Rank | Country |
|---|---|---|---|---|---|
| 1 | Equatorial Guinea | 15 | Zambia | 29 | Madagascar |
| 2 | Seychelles | 16 | Chad | 30 | Guinea |
| 3 | Gabon | 17 | Ghana | 31 | Comoros |
| 4 | Botswana | 18 | Benin | 32 | Eritrea |
| 5 | Mauritius | 19 | Kenya | 33 | Rwanda |
| 6 | South Africa | 20 | Burkina Faso | 34 | Niger |
| 7 | Namibia | 21 | Côte d' Ivoire | 35 | Guinea-Bissau |
| 8 | Cape Verde | 22 | Nigeria | 36 | Ethiopia |
| 9 | Swaziland | 23 | Mali | 37 | Congo, Dem. Rep. |
| 10 | Congo, Rep. | 24 | Uganda | 38 | Central Afr. Rep. |
| 11 | Lesotho | 25 | Mozambique | 39 | Burundi |
| 12 | Angola | 26 | Tanzania | 40 | Sierra Leone |
| 13 | Cameroon | 27 | Gambia, The | 41 | Malawi |
| 14 | Senegal | 28 | Togo | | |
| TOP | | MIDDLE | | BOTTOM | |

Primary Data: UNCTAD

Central Africa
East Africa
Southern Africa
West Africa

# 9.7 Growth in Total Capital Investment per Person

*it's quite safe, actually*

| | 99-02 | 03-06 |
|---|---|---|
| Self-comparison to Preceding Period | | ▲ |
| Performance in Sub-Saharan Africa | ▲ | ▲ |
| Performance in West Africa | ▲ | ▲ |
| | Sierra Leone | **Nigeria** |
| | Guinea-Bissau | Mauritania |
| | Cape Verde | Liberia |
| | **Nigeria** | Ghana |
| | Benin | Niger |
| | Mali | Cape Verde |
| | Mauritania | Burkina Faso |
| | Guinea | Senegal |
| | Niger | Mali |
| | Senegal | Benin |
| | Burkina Faso | Gambia, The |
| | Togo | Togo |
| | Gambia, The | Côte d'Ivoire |
| | Ghana | Guinea |
| | Côte d'Ivoire | Guinea-Bissau |
| | Liberia | Sierra Leone |

Primary Data: UNCTAD

| | 99-02 | 03-06 |
|---|---|---|
| Performance among Oil-Exporters | ◁▷ | ▲ |
| | Chad | Equatorial Guinea |
| | Equatorial Guinea | Angola |
| | Sudan | **Nigeria** |
| | Cameroon | Sudan |
| | **Nigeria** | Congo, Rep. |
| | Gabon | Cameroon |
| | Congo, Rep. | Côte d'Ivoire |
| | Angola | Gabon |
| | Côte d'Ivoire | Chad |

9.15

Growth in Total Capital Investment per Person (%) in West Africa during 2003-06

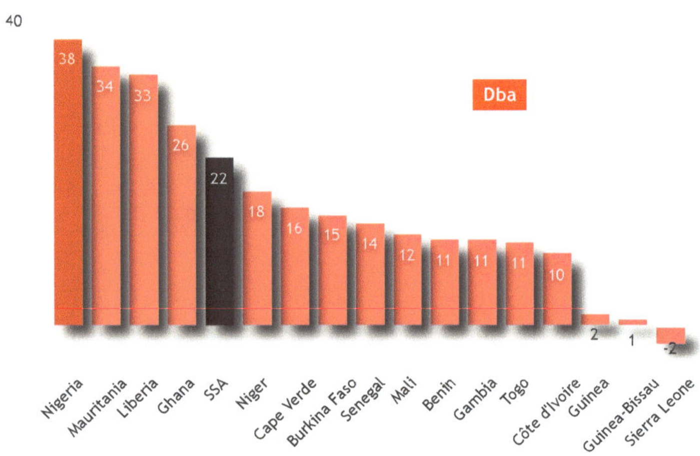


Signs of strong growth for Nigeria. Looks like it's trying to fill in the huge capacity vacuum.

| | |
|---|---|
| ▲ | improved *or* better than average |
| ▼ | worsened *or* worse than average |
| ◁▷ | no change *or* average |

# 9. Investor Confidence

Africa has been getting a growing swathe of investment from about 2001.

**9.16**

**Growth in Total Capital Investment per Person in Nigeria and Sub-Saharan Africa during 2003-06**

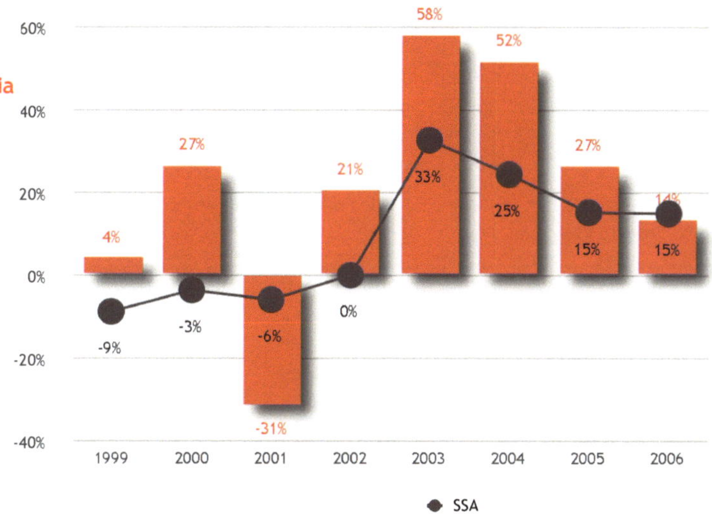


Nigeria's volume of capital investment per population almost tripled between 2000 and 2006, where Africa's doubled.

**9.17**

**Build-up of Total Capital Investment per Person in Nigeria and Sub-Saharan Africa: 2000=100**

Both growth rates - Nigeria & Africa - were slowing significantly from 2003 levels, though.

**Growth in Total Capital Investment per Person in Sub-Saharan Africa during 2003-06: Rankings**

| Rank | Country |
|---|---|
| 1 | Equatorial Guinea |
| 2 | Angola |
| 3 | Seychelles |
| 4 | Nigeria |
| 5 | Burundi |
| 6 | Zambia |
| 7 | Congo, Dem. Rep. |
| 8 | Namibia |
| 9 | Congo, Rep. |
| 10 | South Africa |
| 11 | Ghana |
| 12 | Swaziland |
| 13 | Lesotho |
| 14 | Niger |

TOP

| Rank | Country |
|---|---|
| 15 | Botswana |
| 16 | Mozambique |
| 17 | Uganda |
| 18 | Madagascar |
| 19 | Cape Verde |
| 20 | Kenya |
| 21 | Burkina Faso |
| 22 | Cameroon |
| 23 | Senegal |
| 24 | Comoros |
| 25 | Mali |
| 26 | Benin |
| 27 | Gambia, The |
| 28 | Togo |

MIDDLE

| Rank | Country |
|---|---|
| 29 | Rwanda |
| 30 | Mauritius |
| 31 | Côte d' Ivoire |
| 32 | Ethiopia |
| 33 | Tanzania |
| 34 | Gabon |
| 35 | Chad |
| 36 | Eritrea |
| 37 | Guinea |
| 38 | Guinea-Bissau |
| 39 | Central Afr. Rep. |
| 40 | Sierra Leone |
| 41 | Malawi |

BOTTOM

But Nigeria's was the 4th fastest growing capital investment portfolio in Africa.

Primary Data: UNCTAD

Central Africa
East Africa
Southern Africa
West Africa

# 9.8 Private Component of TCI as % of GDP

*this one's private...*

| | 99-02 | 03-06 |
|---|---|---|
| Self-comparison to Preceding Period | | ▼ |
| Performance in Sub-Saharan Africa | ▲ | ▼ |
| Performance in West Africa | ▲ | ▼ |
| | Cape Verde | Cape Verde |
| | Ghana | Senegal |
| | Senegal | Ghana |
| | **Nigeria** | Burkina Faso |
| | Gambia, The | Gambia, The |
| | Mali | Mali |
| | Togo | Benin |
| | Burkina Faso | Niger |
| | Guinea | **Nigeria** |
| | Benin | Togo |
| | Côte d'Ivoire | Sierra Leone |
| | Niger | Guinea |
| | Mauritania | Côte d'Ivoire |
| | Sierra Leone | Mauritania |
| | Guinea-Bissau | Guinea-Bissau |
| Performance among Oil-Exporters | ▼ | ▼ |
| | Equatorial Guinea | Equatorial Guinea |
| | Chad | Chad |
| | Gabon | Gabon |
| | Cameroon | Sudan |
| | Sudan | Congo, Rep. |
| | Congo, Rep. | Cameroon |
| | **Nigeria** | **Nigeria** |
| | Angola | Côte d'Ivoire |
| | Côte d'Ivoire | Angola |

Primary Data: AfDB

Most of Nigeria's capital investment seems to have come from the public sector (govt.), as overall TCI was growing, even though private investment fell.

Indeed, overwhelmingly so, when placed alongside other countries' proportions. Including the oil exporters'.

| | |
|---|---|
| ▲ | improved *or* better than average |
| ▼ | worsened *or* worse than average |
| ◁▷ | no change *or* average |

## 9. Investor Confidence

9.18

Private and Public Components of Total Capital Investment as % GDP in West Africa during 2003-06

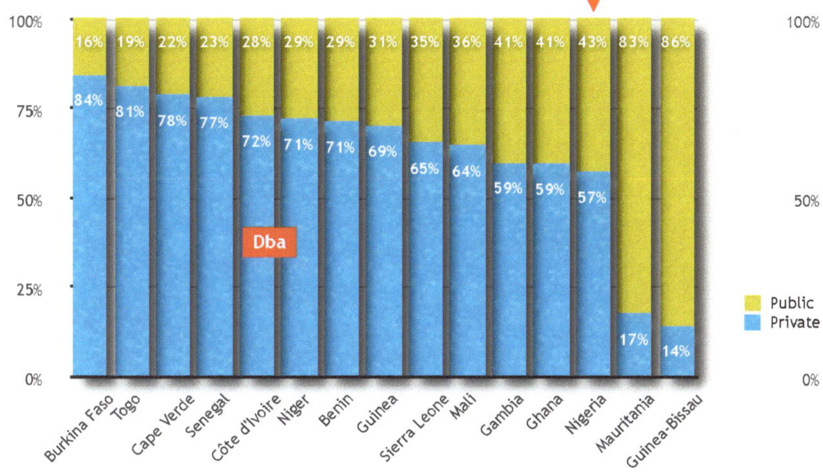


9.19

Private and Public Components of Total Capital Investment as % GDP in Nigeria: from 2000-07

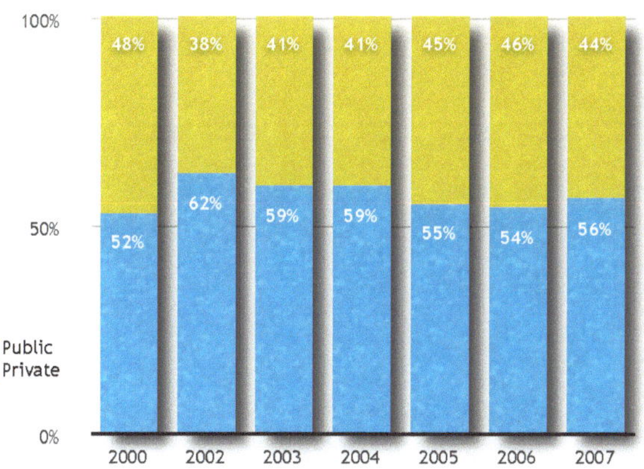


Primary Data: AfDB

The level of private sector involvement in Nigeria's capital investment generally revolved around the 50% mark, smaller than most of West Africa's.

### ... and that one over there's public

Private Component of Total Capital Investment as % of GDP in Sub-Saharan Africa during 2003-06: Rankings

| Rank | Country | Rank | Country | Rank | Country |
|---|---|---|---|---|---|
| 1 | Equatorial Guinea | 15 | South Africa | 29 | Swaziland |
| 2 | Cape Verde | 16 | Cameroon | 30 | Congo, Dem. Rep. |
| 3 | Botswana | 17 | Mauritius | 31 | Togo |
| 4 | Chad | 18 | Burkina Faso | 32 | Sierra Leone |
| 5 | Lesotho | 19 | Gambia, The | 33 | Ethiopia |
| 6 | Namibia | 20 | Mozambique | 34 | Guinea |
| 7 | Malawi | 21 | Mali | 35 | Côte d' Ivoire |
| 8 | Gabon | 22 | Benin | 36 | Comoros |
| 9 | Senegal | 23 | Niger | 37 | Central Afr. Rep. |
| 10 | Uganda | 24 | Tanzania | 38 | Eritrea |
| 11 | Seychelles | 25 | Kenya | 39 | Burundi |
| 12 | Congo, Rep. | 26 | Nigeria | 40 | Angola |
| 13 | Zambia | 27 | Rwanda | 41 | Guinea-Bissau |
| 14 | Ghana | 28 | Madagascar | | |
| TOP | | MIDDLE | | BOTTOM | |

Also smaller than most of SSA. But difficult to say whether this reflects the level of private sector confidence.

Central Africa
East Africa
Southern Africa
West Africa

## 9.9 Private Component of TCI as Investment per Person

**that's me; in the corner**

In per-person measures of private sector participation, however, Nigeria looked good within West Africa.

But that wasn't enough to earn it satisfaction among the oil economies. They did considerably better, both sides of 2003.

| | 99-02 | 03-06 |
|---|---|---|
| Self-comparison to Preceding Period | | ▲ |
| Performance in Sub-Saharan Africa | ▲ | ▲ |
| Performance in West Africa | ▲ | ▲ |

| 99-02 | 03-06 |
|---|---|
| Cape Verde | Cape Verde |
| Senegal | Senegal |
| **Nigeria** | **Nigeria** |
| Ghana | Ghana |
| Benin | Benin |
| Gambia, The | Gambia, The |
| Côte d'Ivoire | Burkina Faso |
| Guinea | Mali |
| Burkina Faso | Côte d'Ivoire |
| Mali | Mauritania |
| Togo | Guinea |
| Mauritania | Niger |
| Niger | Togo |
| Sierra Leone | Sierra Leone |
| Guinea-Bissau | Guinea-Bissau |

Primary Data: AfDB, IMF

| | 99-02 | 03-06 |
|---|---|---|
| Performance among Oil-Exporters | ▼ | ▼ |

| 99-02 | 03-06 |
|---|---|
| Gabon | Equatorial Guinea |
| Equatorial Guinea | Gabon |
| Congo, Rep. | Congo, Rep. |
| Chad | Chad |
| Cameroon | Sudan |
| Sudan | Cameroon |
| Angola | **Nigeria** |
| **Nigeria** | Angola |
| Côte d'Ivoire | Côte d'Ivoire |

| | |
|---|---|
| ▲ | improved *or* better than average |
| ▼ | worsened *or* worse than average |
| ◁▷ | no change *or* average |

# 9. Investor Confidence

9.20

Private and Public Components of Total Capital Investment per Person ($PPP) in West Africa during 2003-06

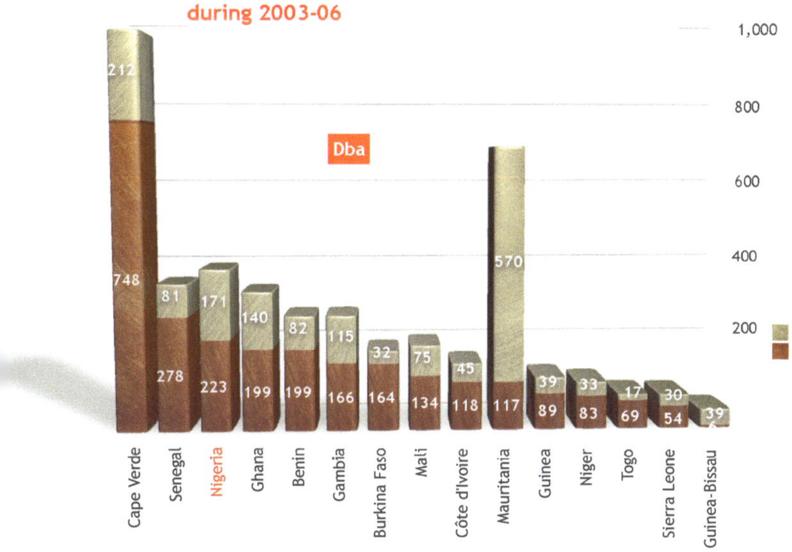


9.21

Private and Public Components of Total Capital Investment per Person in Nigeria ($PPP): from 2000-07

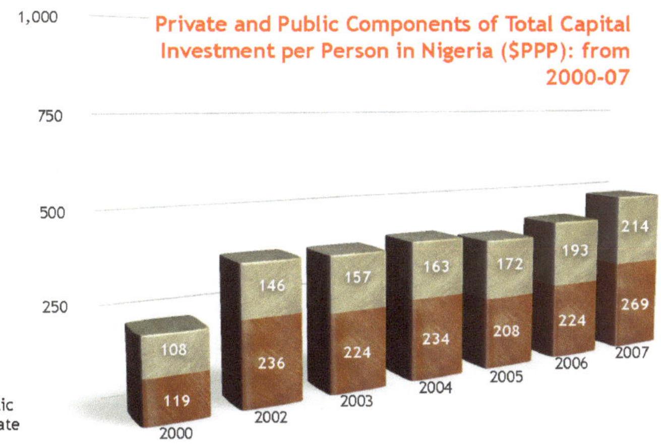


Primary Data: AfDB, IMF

Nigeria doubled the amount of capital invested per person, in both public and private-owned ventures, between 2000 & 2007.

Private Component of TCI as Investment per Person ($PPP) in Sub-Saharan Africa during 2003-06: Rankings

| Rank | Country | Rank | Country | Rank | Country |
|---|---|---|---|---|---|
| 1 | Botswana | 15 | Nigeria | 29 | Mozambique |
| 2 | Equatorial Guinea | 16 | Ghana | 30 | Rwanda |
| 3 | Gabon | 17 | Benin | 31 | Guinea |
| 4 | Seychelles | 18 | Kenya | 32 | Niger |
| 5 | Mauritius | 19 | Zambia | 33 | Togo |
| 6 | South Africa | 20 | Gambia, The | 34 | Sierra Leone |
| 7 | Namibia | 21 | Burkina Faso | 35 | Ethiopia |
| 8 | Cape Verde | 22 | Uganda | 36 | Comoros |
| 9 | Congo, Rep. | 23 | Tanzania | 37 | Eritrea |
| 10 | Swaziland | 24 | Mali | 38 | Central Afr. Rep. |
| 11 | Chad | 25 | Angola | 39 | Congo, Dem. Rep. |
| 12 | Cameroon | 26 | Malawi | 40 | Burundi |
| 13 | Senegal | 27 | Côte d' Ivoire | 41 | Guinea-Bissau |
| 14 | Lesotho | 28 | Madagascar | | |
| | TOP | | MIDDLE | | BOTTOM |

But private sector participation looked healthier in several other countries. Nigeria made the middle category on the continent.

Primary Data: AfDB, IMF

Central Africa
East Africa
Southern Africa
West Africa

# 9.10 Growth of Private (& Public) Component of TCI

**he can't wait**

| | 99-02 | 03-06 |
|---|---|---|
| Self-comparison to Preceding Period | | ▼ |
| Performance in Sub-Saharan Africa | ▲ | ▼ |

Performance in West Africa

| ▲ | ▼ |
|---|---|
| Sierra Leone | Guinea-Bissau |
| **Nigeria** | Niger |
| Togo | Sierra Leone |
| Mauritania | Senegal |
| Cape Verde | Burkina Faso |
| Niger | Benin |
| Gambia, The | Ghana |
| Ghana | Mali |
| Mali | Cape Verde |
| Benin | Mauritania |
| Côte d'Ivoire | Gambia, The |
| Burkina Faso | Guinea |
| Senegal | Côte d'Ivoire |
| Guinea | **Nigeria** |
| Guinea-Bissau | Togo |

Primary Data: AfDB, IMF

*Sharp deterioration in growth of private sector investment during 03/06, compared to the rest of West Africa. And to fellow oil exporters, too.*

**9.22**

**Growth of Private and Public Components of Total Capital Investment in West Africa during 2003-06 (%)**

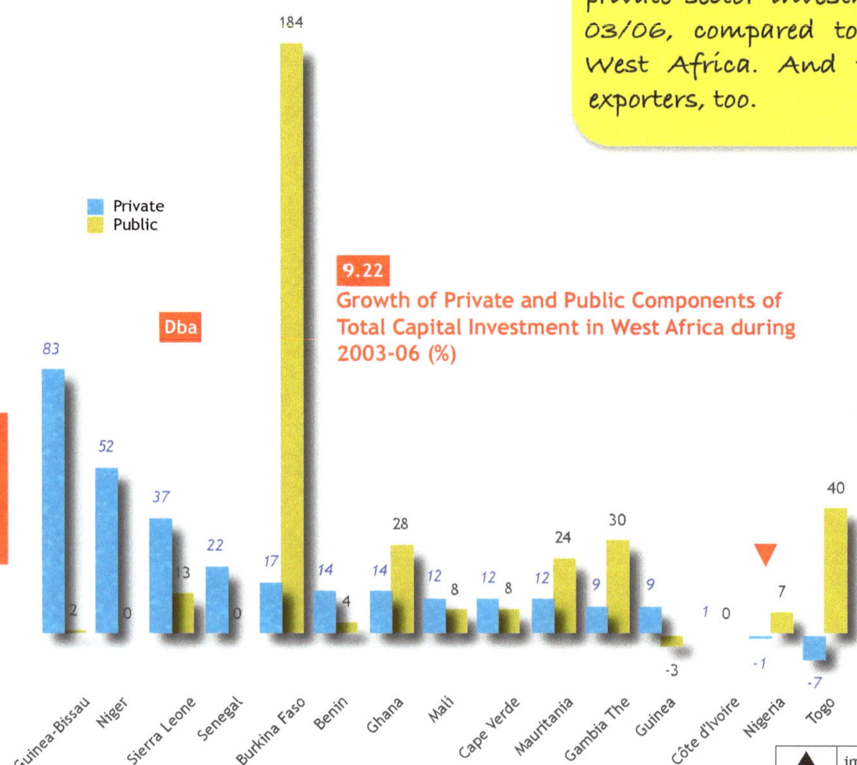


Performance among Oil-Exporters

| ▲ | ▼ |
|---|---|
| Chad | Equatorial Guinea |
| **Nigeria** | Sudan |
| Cameroon | Congo, Rep. |
| Sudan | Côte d'Ivoire |
| Gabon | Cameroon |
| Congo, Rep. | Gabon |
| Côte d'Ivoire | **Nigeria** |
| Equatorial Guinea | Angola |
| Angola | Chad |

| | |
|---|---|
| ▲ | improved *or* better than average |
| ▼ | worsened *or* worse than average |
| ◁▷ | no change *or* average |

# 9. Investor Confidence

**9.23**

**Growth of Private and Public Components of Total Capital Investment in Nigeria (%): from 2000-07**

After sharp growth in 2000/02, subsequent yrs have struggled to even achieve a fifth of that pace in private investment growth. Similar story for public inv., too.

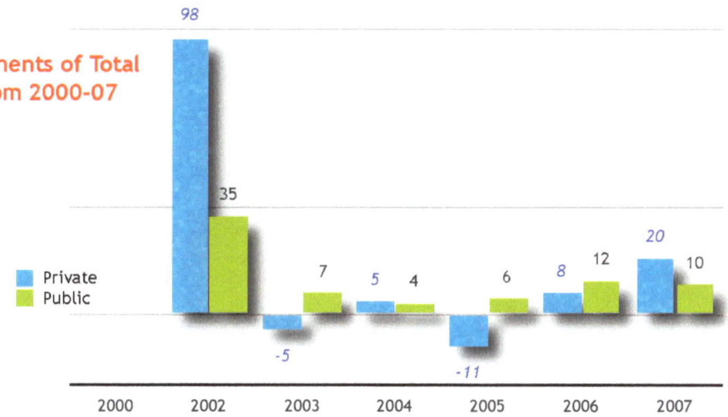


**9.24**

**Build-up of Private and Public Components of Total Capital Investment in Nigeria 2000-07: 2000=100**

The huge leap in 2002 masks the very poor showing during 2003-2007. Bottom position in the continent rankings.

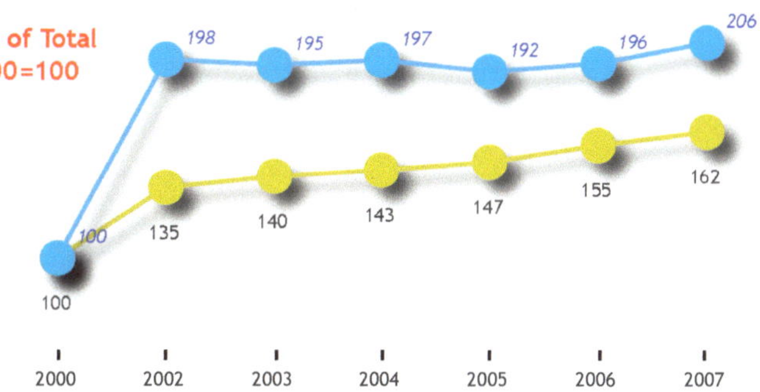


**Growth of Private Component of Total Capital Investment per Person in Sub-Saharan Africa during 2003-06: Rankings**

| Rank | Country | Rank | Country | Rank | Country |
|---|---|---|---|---|---|
| 1 | Malawi | 15 | Benin | 29 | Congo, Rep. |
| 2 | Guinea-Bissau | 16 | Ghana | 30 | Comoros |
| 3 | Niger | 17 | Tanzania | 31 | Côte d' Ivoire |
| 4 | Burundi | 18 | Congo, Dem. Rep. | 32 | Cameroon |
| 5 | Sierra Leone | 19 | Mali | 33 | Botswana |
| 6 | Seychelles | 20 | Uganda | 34 | Gabon |
| 7 | Kenya | 21 | Cape Verde | 35 | Nigeria |
| 8 | Equatorial Guinea | 22 | Central Afr. Rep. | 36 | Swaziland |
| 9 | Zambia | 23 | Gambia, The | 37 | Togo |
| 10 | Madagascar | 24 | Guinea | 38 | Lesotho |
| 11 | Senegal | 25 | Mauritius | 39 | Angola |
| 12 | Namibia | 26 | Rwanda | 40 | Chad |
| 13 | Burkina Faso | 27 | Mozambique | 41 | Eritrea |
| 14 | South Africa | 28 | Ethiopia | | |
| TOP | | MIDDLE | | BOTTOM | |

Primary Data: AfDB, IMF

Central Africa
East Africa
Southern Africa
West Africa

# 9.11 Domestic Credit to the Private Sector as % of GDP

*opening up the bank vaults*

| | 99-02 | 03-06 |
|---|---|---|
| Self-comparison to Preceding Period | | ▼ |
| Performance in Sub-Saharan Africa | ▼ | ▼ |

Performance in West Africa

| 99-02 | 03-06 |
|---|---|
| ▲ | ▲ |
| Cape Verde | Cape Verde |
| Mauritania | Mauritania |
| Senegal | Senegal |
| Mali | Mali |
| Côte d'Ivoire | Togo |
| **Nigeria** | Burkina Faso |
| Togo | Benin |
| Gambia, The | **Nigeria** |
| Burkina Faso | Ghana |
| Ghana | Gambia, The |
| Benin | Côte d'Ivoire |
| Guinea-Bissau | Niger |
| Niger | Liberia |
| Guinea | Sierra Leone |
| Liberia | Guinea |
| Sierra Leone | Guinea-Bissau |

Primary Data: WB, IMF

Level of credit from Nigeria's domestic financial institutions dropped to average within West Africa in 03/06.

Performance among Oil-Exporters

| 99-02 | 03-06 |
|---|---|
| ▲ | ▲ |
| Côte d'Ivoire | **Nigeria** |
| **Nigeria** | Côte d'Ivoire |
| Gabon | Cameroon |
| Cameroon | Gabon |
| Congo, Rep. | Sudan |
| Chad | Angola |
| Equatorial Guinea | Equatorial Guinea |
| Angola | Chad |
| Sudan | Congo, Rep. |

That average performance nonetheless was sufficient to put Nigeria on top of the other oil economies. Dismal performance by the group.

| | |
|---|---|
| ▲ | improved *or* better than average |
| ▼ | worsened *or* worse than average |
| ◁▷ | no change *or* average |

# 9. Investor Confidence

9.25
Domestic Credit to the Private Sector as % of GDP in West Africa during 2003-06

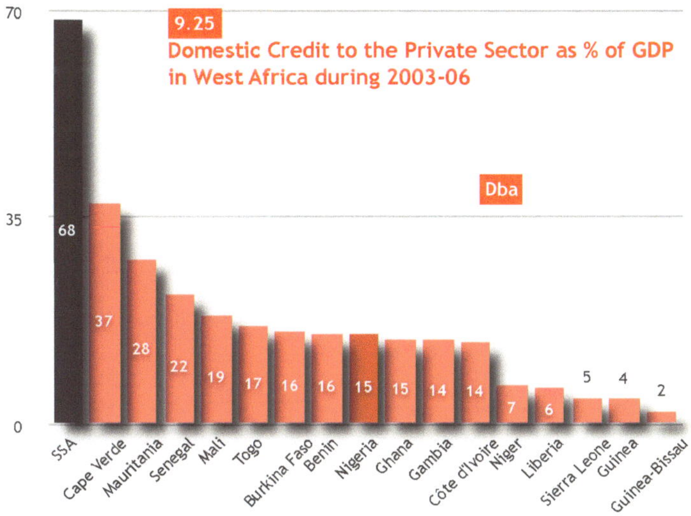


Huge gulf between the continent's and Nigeria's levels of private-sector investment participation.

9.26
Domestic Credit to the Private Sector as % of GDP in Nigeria and Sub-Saharan Africa from 1999-2006

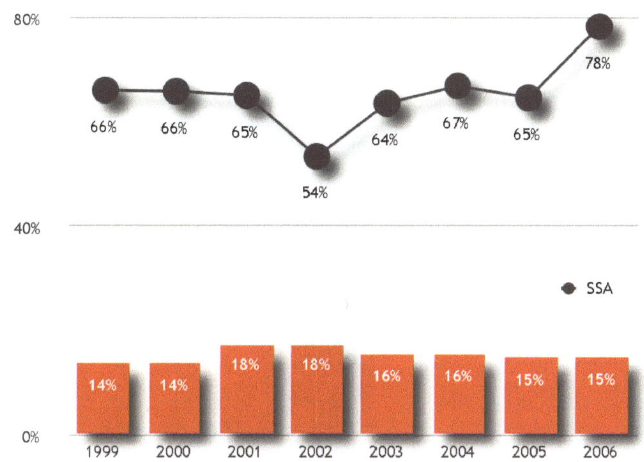


It should be observed, though, that South Africa was responsible for the continent's high % average. Indeed, all the other 46 countries fell below that (weighted ) average.

Domestic Credit to the Private Sector as % of GDP in Sub-Saharan Africa during 2003-06: Rankings

| Rank | Country | Rank | Country | Rank | Country |
|---|---|---|---|---|---|
| 1 | South Africa | 15 | Burkina Faso | 29 | Lesotho |
| 2 | Mauritius | 16 | Benin | 30 | Mozambique |
| 3 | Namibia | 17 | Nigeria | 31 | Uganda |
| 4 | Cape Verde | 18 | Ghana | 32 | Niger |
| 5 | Seychelles | 19 | Gambia, The | 33 | Central Afr. Rep. |
| 6 | Eritrea | 20 | Côte d' Ivoire | 34 | Angola |
| 7 | Ethiopia | 21 | Rwanda | 35 | Sierra Leone |
| 8 | Kenya | 22 | Tanzania | 36 | Guinea |
| 9 | Burundi | 23 | Madagascar | 37 | Equatorial Guinea |
| 10 | Senegal | 24 | Cameroon | 38 | Chad |
| 11 | Swaziland | 25 | Gabon | 39 | Congo, Rep. |
| 12 | Botswana | 26 | Malawi | 40 | Guinea-Bissau |
| 13 | Mali | 27 | Comoros | 41 | Congo, Dem. Rep. |
| 14 | Togo | 28 | Zambia | | |
| TOP | | MIDDLE | | BOTTOM | |

Primary Data: WB, IMF

Central Africa
East Africa
Southern Africa
West Africa

# 9.12 Domestic Credit to the Private Sector in $PPP

**perilous trips to the bank**

| | 99-02 | 03-06 |
|---|---|---|
| Self-comparison to Preceding Period | | ▲ |
| Performance in Sub-Saharan Africa | ▲ | ▲ |
| Performance in West Africa | ▲ | ▲ |

| 99-02 | 03-06 |
|---|---|
| Nigeria | Nigeria |
| Côte d'Ivoire | Côte d'Ivoire |
| Senegal | Senegal |
| Ghana | Ghana |
| Mali | Burkina Faso |
| Burkina Faso | Mali |
| Mauritania | Benin |
| Benin | Mauritania |
| Togo | Togo |
| Guinea | Niger |
| Cape Verde | Cape Verde |
| Niger | Guinea |
| Gambia, The | Gambia, The |
| Sierra Leone | Sierra Leone |
| Liberia | Liberia |
| Guinea-Bissau | Guinea-Bissau |

Primary Data: WB, IMF

Nigeria's excellent performance here isn't surprising, since this measures the volume of investment in itself, and not as a proportion of output or population.

| Performance among Oil-Exporters | 99-02 | 03-06 |
|---|---|---|
| | ▲ | ▲ |
| | Nigeria | Nigeria |
| | Côte d'Ivoire | Côte d'Ivoire |
| | Cameroon | Sudan |
| | Gabon | Angola |
| | Sudan | Cameroon |
| | Angola | Gabon |
| | Congo, Rep. | Equatorial Guinea |
| | Chad | Chad |
| | Equatorial Guinea | Congo, Rep. |

It simply reflects the overall size of the economy.

| | |
|---|---|
| ▲ | improved *or* better than average |
| ▼ | worsened *or* worse than average |
| ◁▷ | no change *or* average |

## 9. Investor Confidence

9.27

Domestic Credit to the Private Sector in West Africa ($PPP millions) during 2003-06

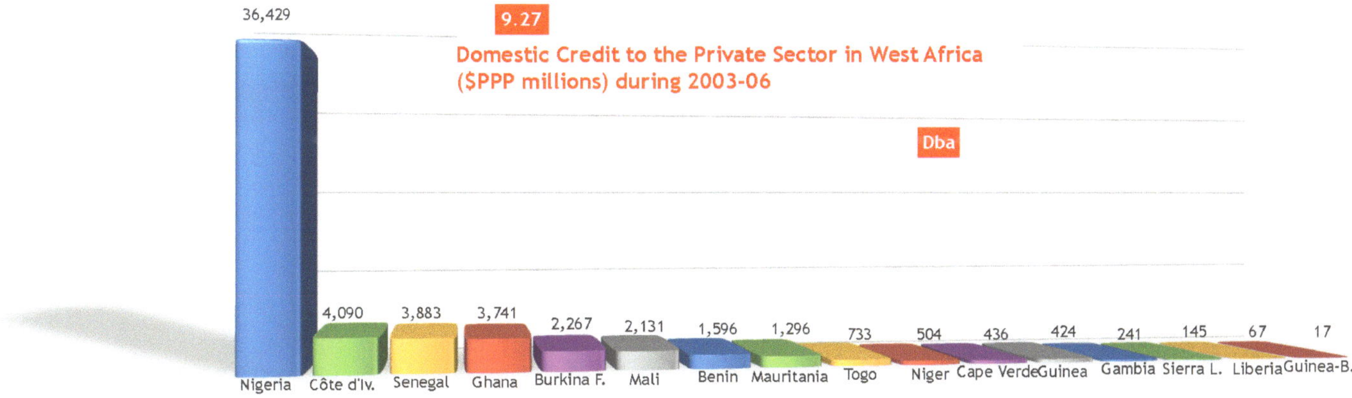


Primary Data: WB, IMF

The vol. of credit facilities has been increasing in Nigeria since 1999.

9.28

Domestic Credit to the Private Sector in Nigeria in $PPP (millions): from 1999-2006

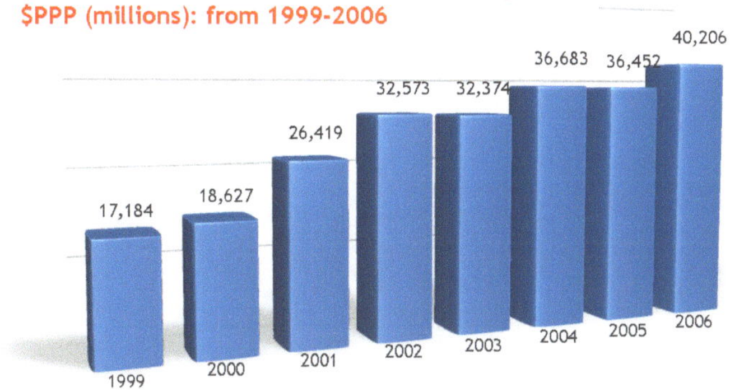


Central Africa
East Africa
Southern Africa
West Africa

Domestic Credit to the Private Sector as $PPP in Sub-Saharan Africa during 2003-06: Rankings

| Rank | Country | Rank | Country | Rank | Country |
|---|---|---|---|---|---|
| 1 | South Africa | 15 | Mali | 29 | Equatorial Guinea |
| 2 | Nigeria | 16 | Uganda | 30 | Cape Verde |
| 3 | Kenya | 17 | Gabon | 31 | Chad |
| 4 | Ethiopia | 18 | Benin | 32 | Guinea |
| 5 | Mauritius | 19 | Madagascar | 33 | Seychelles |
| 6 | Namibia | 20 | Eritrea | 34 | Congo, Rep. |
| 7 | Côte d' Ivoire | 21 | Mozambique | 35 | Congo, Dem. Rep. |
| 8 | Botswana | 22 | Zambia | 36 | Gambia, The |
| 9 | Senegal | 23 | Swaziland | 37 | Lesotho |
| 10 | Tanzania | 24 | Rwanda | 38 | Central Afr. Rep. |
| 11 | Ghana | 25 | Malawi | 39 | Sierra Leone |
| 12 | Angola | 26 | Togo | 40 | Comoros |
| 13 | Cameroon | 27 | Burundi | 41 | Guinea-Bissau |
| 14 | Burkina Faso | 28 | Niger | | |
| TOP | | MIDDLE | | BOTTOM | |

The figures for 03/06
South Africa: $PPP 567bn
Nigeria: $PPP 36bn
Kenya: $PPP 12bn
Ethiopia: $PPP 11bn

Quite a distance between 1st and 2nd positions in vol. of investment. Volume thereafter gradually tapers from Ethiopia's 11 billion until Guinea-Bissau's 0.02 billion.

# 9.13 Growth in Domestic Credit to the Private Sector

## *dashing to the bank manager*

Primary Data: WB, IMF

| | 99-02 | 03-06 |
|---|---|---|
| Self-comparison to Preceding Period | | ▼ |
| Performance in Sub-Saharan Africa | ▲ | ▼ |
| Performance in West Africa | ▲ | ▼ |
| | **Nigeria** | Liberia |
| | Sierra Leone | Guinea-Bissau |
| | Benin | Niger |
| | Gambia, The | Ghana |
| | Mauritania | Sierra Leone |
| | Ghana | Benin |
| | Cape Verde | Togo |
| | Senegal | Burkina Faso |
| | Burkina Faso | Guinea |
| | Niger | Cape Verde |
| | Mali | Senegal |
| | Guinea | Gambia, The |
| | Guinea-Bissau | Mali |
| | Côte d'Ivoire | **Nigeria** |
| | Togo | Mauritania |
| | Liberia | Côte d'Ivoire |
| Performance among Oil-Exporters | ▲ | ▲ |
| | Sudan | Equatorial Guinea |
| | **Nigeria** | Angola |
| | Angola | **Nigeria** |
| | Equatorial Guinea | Chad |
| | Chad | Sudan |
| | Cameroon | Congo, Rep. |
| | Gabon | Cameroon |
| | Côte d'Ivoire | Côte d'Ivoire |
| | Congo, Rep. | Gabon |

*Nigeria drops sharply on credit growth levels during 03/06 from 99/02. Eventual growth level worse than both the West Africa & continent average.*

*Surprisingly, that performance was still good enough to rank it high among the oil exporters. Their collective performance was poor, indeed.*

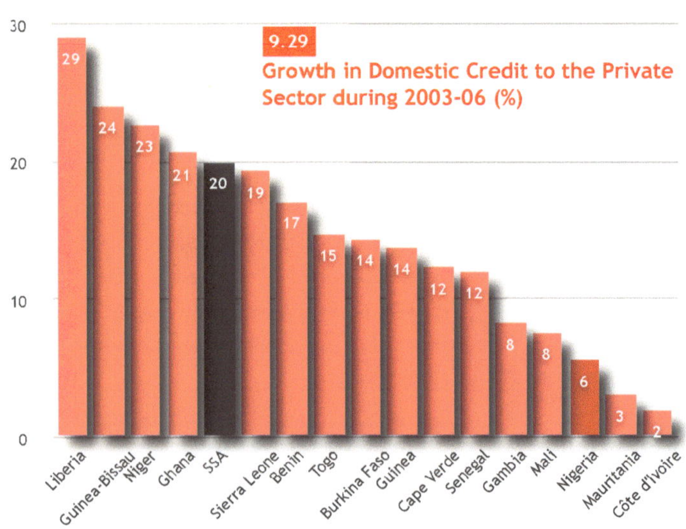


9.29 Growth in Domestic Credit to the Private Sector during 2003-06 (%)

| | |
|---|---|
| ▲ | improved *or* better than average |
| ▼ | worsened *or* worse than average |
| ◁▷ | no change *or* average |

## 9. Investor Confidence

9.30

**Growth in Domestic Credit to the Private Sector in Nigeria and Sub-Saharan Africa from 1999-2006**

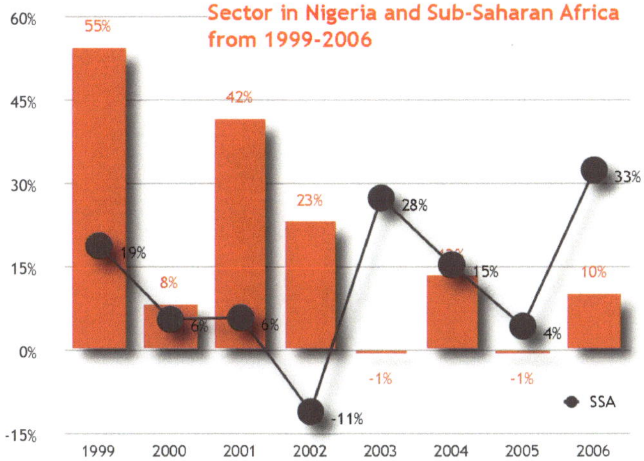


9.31

**Build-up of Domestic Credit to the Private Sector in Nigeria and Sub-Saharan Africa from 2000-06: 2000=100**

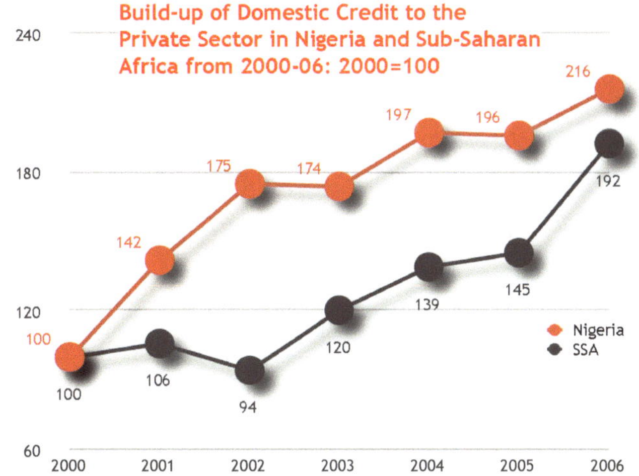


Nonetheless, Nigeria's domestic credit progress since 2000 is encouraging, outstripping the continent average.

**Growth in Domestic Credit to the Private Sector in Sub-Saharan Africa during 2003-06: Rankings**

| Rank | Country | Rank | Country | Rank | Country |
|---|---|---|---|---|---|
| 1 | Mozambique | 15 | Rwanda | 29 | Gambia, The |
| 2 | Congo, Dem. Rep. | 16 | Namibia | 30 | Central Afr. Rep. |
| 3 | Equatorial Guinea | 17 | Togo | 31 | Mali |
| 4 | Malawi | 18 | Burkina Faso | 32 | Comoros |
| 5 | Angola | 19 | Mauritius | 33 | Nigeria |
| 6 | Tanzania | 20 | Ethiopia | 34 | Chad |
| 7 | Seychelles | 21 | Guinea | 35 | Lesotho |
| 8 | Guinea-Bissau | 22 | Uganda | 36 | Congo, Rep. |
| 9 | Niger | 23 | South Africa | 37 | Cameroon |
| 10 | Zambia | 24 | Kenya | 38 | Côte d' Ivoire |
| 11 | Swaziland | 25 | Cape Verde | 39 | Burundi |
| 12 | Ghana | 26 | Senegal | 40 | Eritrea |
| 13 | Sierra Leone | 27 | Madagascar | 41 | Gabon |
| 14 | Benin | 28 | Botswana | | |
| TOP | | MIDDLE | | BOTTOM | |

However, many other countries came off better, even if only by small margins.

Primary Data: WB, IMF

Central Africa
East Africa
Southern Africa
West Africa

# Leaders & Stragglers

wait!
we can
explain!!

## Investor Confidence Rankings: 2003-06

| Rank | Country |
|---|---|
| 1 | Equatorial Guinea |
| 2 | Namibia |
| 3 | Cape Verde |
| 4 | Seychelles |
| 5 | South Africa |
| 6 | Zambia |
| 7 | Botswana |
| 8 | Mauritius |
| 9 | Ghana |
| 10 | Congo, Rep. |
| | Gabon |
| 11 | Gambia, The |
| 12 | Mali |
| | Senegal |

TOP

| Rank | Country |
|---|---|
| 13 | Angola |
| | Lesotho |
| 14 | Chad |
| 15 | Mozambique |
| 16 | Benin |
| | Tanzania |
| 17 | Ethiopia |
| | **Nigeria** |
| 18 | Burundi |
| 19 | Burkina Faso |
| 20 | Kenya |
| 21 | Uganda |
| 22 | Madagascar |
| 23 | Sierra Leone |
| 24 | Malawi |

MIDDLE

| Rank | Country |
|---|---|
| 25 | Guinea-Bissau |
| | Swaziland |
| 26 | Cameroon |
| 27 | Niger |
| 28 | Togo |
| 29 | Côte d' Ivoire |
| 30 | Guinea |
| 31 | Rwanda |
| 32 | Eritrea |
| 33 | Congo, Dem. Rep. |
| 34 | Central Afr. Rep. |
| 35 | Comoros |

BOTTOM

Central Africa
East Africa
Southern Africa
West Africa

*Ranked a joint 17th out of 35 positions (among 41 countries, though); investor confidence wasn't looking that hot in Nigeria.*

# Wrap-up: Investor Confidence

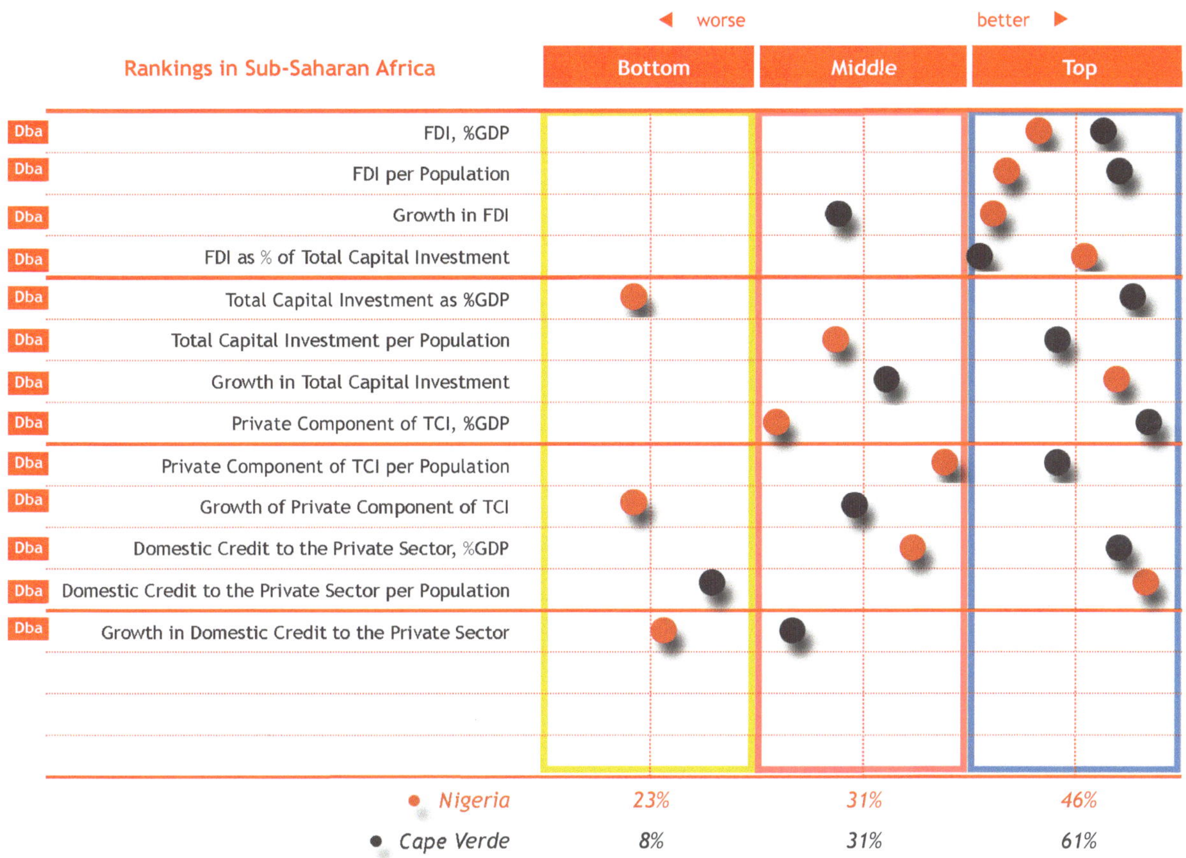


- Within West Africa, investors showed the most confidence in Cape Verde. The country was 3rd most favoured on the continent. Nigeria was 7th out of the 14 countries of West Africa, and joint 17th on the continent.

- All the indicators here are critical. Cape Verde scored more top-bracket points than Nigeria (61% of the indicators, compared to Nigeria's 46%) and less bottom-bracket outcomes (8% against 23%).

- Within its own performance, Nigeria scored highest in the foreign investment areas; all the different FDI indicators ended up in the top-third. But when total investment is considered, the performance drops to average or middle-brackets.

- And so, it appears that the private (domestic) investment portion of Nigeria investment is not a robust performance and has the effect of dragging the overall (total) investment performance down.

- This may suggest that foreigners appear to have more confidence in the Nigerian economy than Nigerians themselves. FDI was more robust than private domestic investment. FDI was also growing considerably faster.

- A consolation, though, might be that it was easier to corner loans from Nigerian financial institutions than in many countries of Africa.

# 10. Regulatory Environment

*do you sense bureaucracy?*


10.1 Ease of Starting a Business: Rank

10.2 Ease of Dealing with Construction Permits: Rank

10.3 Ease of Employing Workers: Rank

10.4 Ease of Registering Property: Rank

10.5 Ease of Getting Credit: Rank

10.6 Extent of Investor Protection: Rank

10.7 Ease of Paying Taxes: Rank

10.8 Ease of External Trade: Rank

10.9 Ease of Enforcing Contracts: Rank

10.10 Ease of Closing a Business: Rank

10.11 Ease of Doing Business: Rank

Leaders & Stragglers

Wrap-up

# Prelims

This chapter attempts to quantify the ease or difficulty entailed in various critical business proedures for entrants into the particular country's economic structure. It involves data collated by the World Bank and the International Finance Corporation (IFC).

The different indicators are appropriately named and their meaning can be followed without difficulty. In this chapter, they comprise ten divisions, which are each broken into segments as shown below.

In the chapter sections which follow, the countries are ranked according to their relative performance. The World Bank/IFC explain that the data refer to the period between April 2007 and June 2008.

### Ease of starting a business

Based on four segments:

- procedures - completed when the final document is submitted
- time - preregistration, registration and postregistration
- cost - as % of income per capita
- paid-in minimum capital - funds deposited in a bank or with a notary before registration

### Ease of dealing with construction permits

Based on three segments:

- procedures - completed when final document is received (construction permits, inspections and utility connections included)
- time - number of days to build a warehouse in a main city
- cost - as % of income per capita

### Ease of employing workers

Four segments:

- ease of hiring - fixed-term contracts, minimum wage regulations
- flexibility of hours - nonstandard work schedules, paid vacation days
- Ease of firing - mandatory legal requirements for dismissals for economic reasons
- firing cost - as weeks of salary; includes notice period and severance payments

### Ease of registering property

Three segments:

- procedures - steps for encumbrance checking, deed and title transfer until property can be sold again or used as collateral
- time - days to transfer property between two companies in main city
- cost - as % of property value

### Ease of getting credit

Two segments:

- strength-of-legal rights index - regulations on non-possessory security interests in movable property
- depth-of-credit information index - scope, quality and accessibility of credit information through public and private credit registeries

### Extent of investor protection

Three segments:

- extent-of-disclosure index - requirements on approval and disclosure of related-party transactions

- extent-of-director liability index - liability of CEO and board of directors in related-party transactions
- ease-of-shareholders suits index - type of evidence that can be collected before and during the trial

### Ease of paying taxes

Three segments:

- payments - number of tax payments per year
- time - number of hours per year to prepare, file returns and pay taxes
- total tax rate - firm tax liability as % of profits before all taxes borne

### Ease of external trade

Three segments:

- documents to export and import - all documents required by customs and other agencies
- time to export and import - document preparation, customs clearance and technical control, ports and terminal handling, inland transport and handling

### Ease of enforcing contracts

Three segments:

- procedures - steps to file claim, obtain and enforce judgment
- time - days to resolve commercial sale dispute before courts
- cost - lawyer, court and enforcement costs as % of claim value

### Ease of closing a business

One segment only:

- recovery rate (cents on the $US) - function of time, cost and other factors such as lending rate and the likelihood of the company continuing to operate

### Ease of doing business

the eventual score and rank of the country across these indicators

**Sources of Primary Data:** AfDB, IMF, UNCTAD, World Bank

# Charts


10.1 Ease of Starting a Business in West Africa: no. of days. 2009
10.2 Ease of Starting a Business in WA: no. of procedures. 2009

10.3 Ease of Dealing with Construction Permits in WA: no. of days. 2009
10.4 Ease of Dealing with Construction Permits in WA: no. of procedures. 2009

10.5 Ease of Employing Workers in WA: ease of hiring. 2009
10.6 Ease of Employing Workers in WA: flexibility of hours. 2009
10.7 Ease of Employing Workers in WA: ease of firing. 2009
10.8 Ease of Employing Workers in WA: cost of firing (no. of weeks' wages). 2009

10.9 Ease of Registering Property in WA: no. of procedures. 2009
10.10 Ease of Registering Property in WA: no. of days. 2009
10.11 Ease of Registering Property in WA: cost (% of property value). 2009

10.12 Extent of Investor Protection in WA: disclosure index. 2009
10.13 Extent of Investor Protection in WA: director liability index. 2009
10.14 Extent of Investor Protection in WA: shareholder suits index. 2009

10.15 Ease of Paying Taxes in WA: no. of payments. 2009
10.16 Ease of Paying Taxes in WA: time required (hours). 2009
10.17 Ease of Paying Taxes in WA: tax on profit (%). 2009
10.18 Ease of Paying Taxes in WA: labour tax & contributions (%). 2009
10.19 Ease of Paying Taxes in WA: other taxes. 2009
10.20 Ease of Paying Taxes in WA: total tax rate (%). 2009

10.21 Ease of External Trade in WA: cost to export 1 container (US$). 2009
10.22 Ease of External Trade in WA: cost to import 1 container (US$). 2009
10.23 Ease of External Trade in WA: no. of documents needed to export. 2009
10.24 Ease of External Trade in WA: no. of documents needed to import. 2009
10.25 Ease of External Trade in WA: time for export (days). 2009
10.26 Ease of External Trade in WA: time for import (days). 2009

10.27 Ease of Enforcing Contracts in WA: no. of procedures. 2009
10.28 Ease of Enforcing Contracts in WA: time in days. 2009
10.29 Ease of Enforcing Contracts in WA: cost (as % of debt in dispute). 2009

10.30 Ease of Closing a Business in WA: recovery rate (cents on the dollar). 2009

- **Wrap-up**

# Tables

*2008; 2009:*
- *self-comparison to preceding period;*
- *performance in S-Saharan Africa;*
- *performance in West Africa;*
- *performance among oil-exporters;*

*for:*

Ease of Starting a Business

Ease of Dealing with Construction Permits

Ease of Employing Workers

Ease of Registering Property

Ease of Getting Credit

Extent of Investor Protection

Ease of Paying Taxes

Ease of External Trade

Ease of Enforcing Contracts

Ease of Closing a Business

- **Regulatory Environment Rankings: 2009**

# 10. Regulatory Environment

# 10.1 Ease of Starting a Business: Rank

| 2008 | 2009 | |
|---|---|---|
| | ▼ | Self-comparison to Preceding Period |
| ▲ | ▲ | Performance in Sub-Saharan Africa |

**Performance in West Africa**

| 2008 ▲ | 2009 ▲ |
|---|---|
| **Nigeria** | Sierra Leone |
| Sierra Leone | Liberia |
| Gambia, The | **Nigeria** |
| Burkina Faso | Senegal |
| Benin | Gambia, The |
| Ghana | Burkina Faso |
| Liberia | Ghana |
| Mali | Mauritania |
| Niger | Benin |
| Côte d'Ivoire | Niger |
| Cape Verde | Mali |
| Senegal | Cape Verde |
| Mauritania | Côte d'Ivoire |
| Guinea | Guinea |
| Togo | Togo |
| Guinea-Bissau | Guinea-Bissau |

**Performance among Oil-Exporters**

| 2008 ▲ | 2009 ▲ |
|---|---|
| **Nigeria** | **Nigeria** |
| Sudan | Sudan |
| Gabon | Gabon |
| Congo, Rep. | Angola |
| Côte d'Ivoire | Congo, Rep. |
| Cameroon | Côte d'Ivoire |
| Equatorial Guinea | Cameroon |
| Angola | Equatorial Guinea |
| Chad | Chad |

| | |
|---|---|
| ▲ | improved *or* better than average |
| ▼ | worsened *or* worse than average |
| ◁▷ | no change *or* average |

*Nigeria dropped from the easiest place to start a business in West Africa in 2008, to 3rd easiest in 2009, behind Sierra Leone and Liberia.*

3 Sierra Leone

9 Liberia

10 Nigeria

| | | | |
|---|---|---|---|
| 11 | Senegal | | |
| 22 | Gambia | 35 | Mali |
| 16 | Burkina Faso | 36 | Cape Verde |
| 22 | Ghana | 38 | Côte d'Ivoire |
| 24 | Mauritania | 42 | Guinea |
| 27 | Benin | 44 | Togo |
| 33 | Niger | 46 | Guinea-Bissau |

2009 rankings of 47 Sub-Saharan Africa Countries

Source: World Bank, IFC

*Those 2 countries perhaps displayed greater urgency in attracting business to their shores after difficult and protracted war years.*

***it's a breeze...***

Overall *Ease of Starting a Business*:
2009 rankings of 47 Sub-Saharan Africa Countries. Source: World Bank, IFC

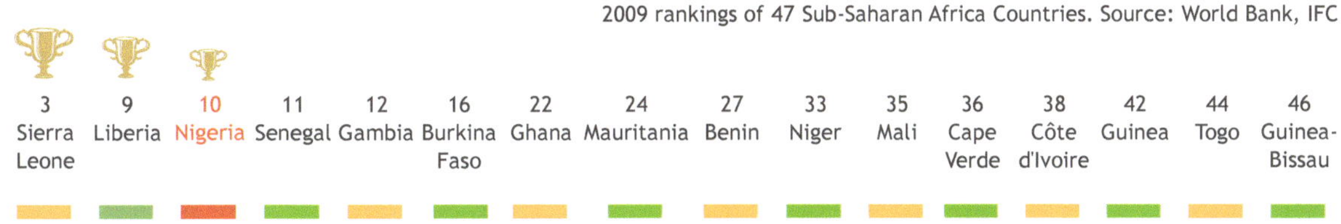


8 days is the duration for completing formalities to set up shop, and 31 is the number of procedures involved, in Nigeria.

**10.1**

**Ease of Starting a Business: no. of days. 2009**

***... right?***

Fewer days in Senegal (4), Burkina Faso (5) and Benin (7). But Nigeria had fewer procedures than many in West Africa.

Source: World Bank, IFC

**10.2**

**Ease of Starting a Business: no. of procedures 2009**

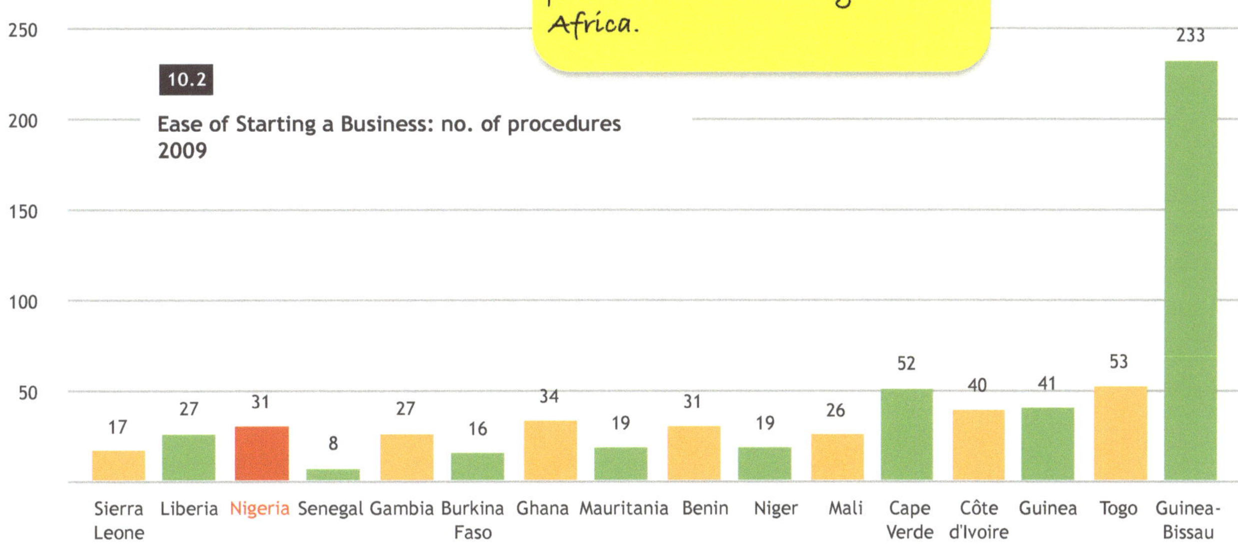

# 10.2 Ease of Dealing with Construction Permits: Rank

| 2008 | 2009 | |
|---|---|---|
| | ▲ | Self-comparison to Preceding Period |
| ▼ | ▼ | Performance in Sub-Saharan Africa |
| ▼ | ▼ | Performance in West Africa |
| Senegal | Gambia, The | |
| Gambia, The | Cape Verde | |
| Cape Verde | Burkina Faso | |
| Mali | Mali | |
| Guinea-Bissau | Guinea-Bissau | |
| Benin | Senegal | |
| Ghana | Benin | |
| Mauritania | Ghana | |
| Togo | Mauritania | |
| Sierra Leone | Togo | |
| Niger | **Nigeria** | |
| Côte d'Ivoire | Niger | |
| Guinea | Côte d'Ivoire | |
| **Nigeria** | Guinea | |
| Burkina Faso | Sierra Leone | |
| Liberia | Liberia | |

| 2008 | 2009 | |
|---|---|---|
| ▼ | ▼ | Performance among Oil-Exporters |
| Gabon | Gabon | |
| Congo, Rep. | Congo, Rep. | |
| Chad | Chad | |
| Equatorial Guinea | Equatorial Guinea | |
| Sudan | Angola | |
| Angola | Sudan | |
| Cameroon | **Nigeria** | |
| Côte d'Ivoire | Cameroon | |
| **Nigeria** | Côte d'Ivoire | |

| | |
|---|---|
| ▲ | improved *or* better than average |
| ▼ | worsened *or* worse than average |
| ◁▷ | no change *or* average |

nice word, that

Improvement in Nigeria from 2008 to 2009. But still below par in the continent and in West Africa, as well. Below par within the oil club also.

2009 rankings of 47 Sub-Saharan Africa Countries

Source: World Bank, IFC

12 Gambia

13 Cape Verde

19 Burkina Faso

19 Mali

| | | | |
|---|---|---|---|
| 20 | Guinea-Bissau | 33 | Nigeria |
| 22 | Senegal | 37 | Niger |
| 25 | Benin | 38 | Côte d'Ivoire |
| 29 | Ghana | 39 | Guinea |
| 29 | Mauritania | 40 | Sierra Leone |
| 30 | Togo | 44 | Liberia |

Overall *Ease of Dealing with Construction Permits*:
2009 rankings of 47 Sub-Saharan Africa Countries. Source: World Bank, IFC

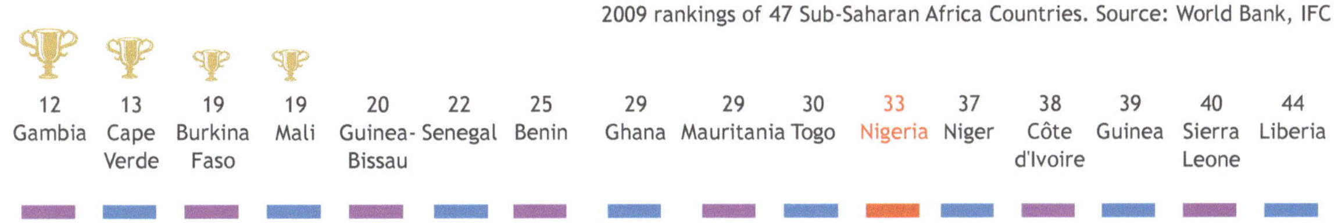


10.3

**Ease of Dealing with Construction Permits: no. of days. 2009**

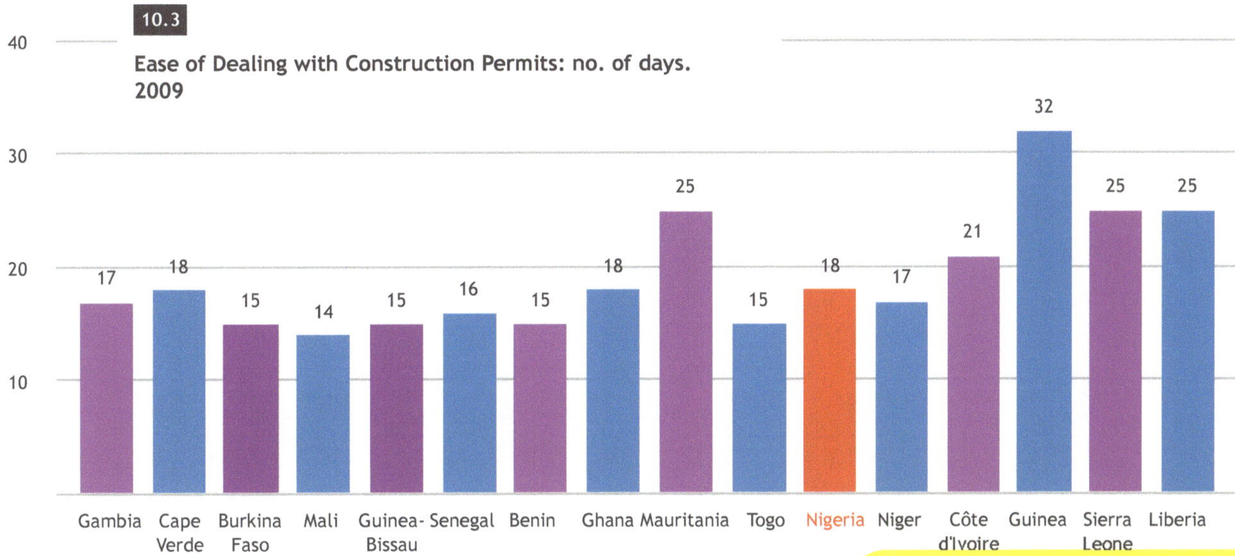


The reason for that is clearly seen here. Too many days of paperwork and too many procedures in Nigeria.

10.4

**Ease of Dealing with Construction Permits: no. of procedures. 2009**

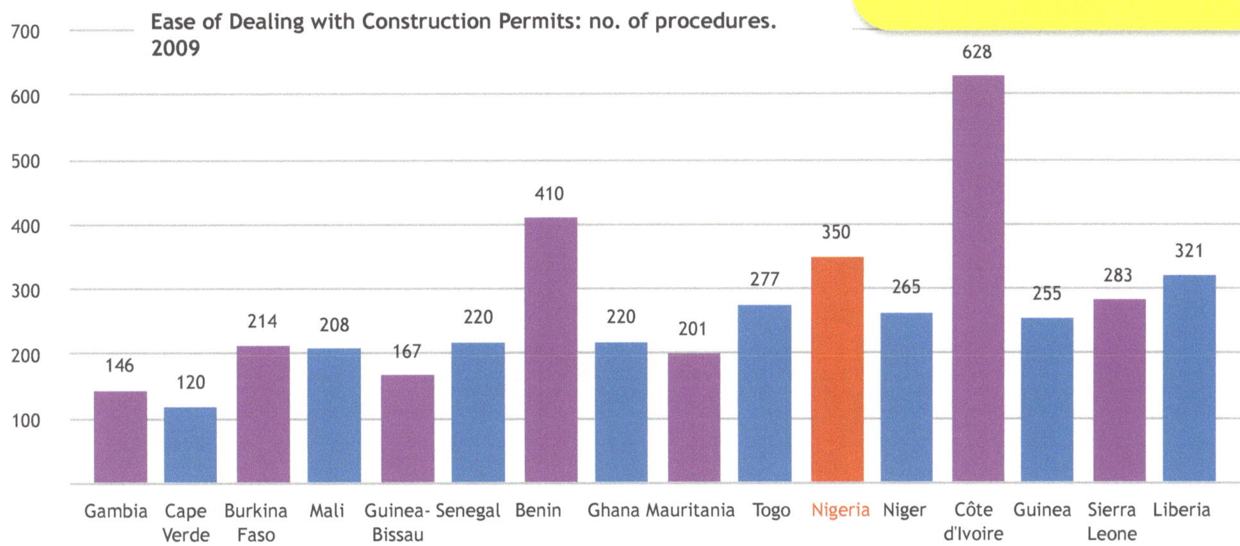

# 10.3 Ease of Employing Workers: Rank

| 2008 | 2009 | |
|---|---|---|
| | ▲ | Self-comparison to Preceding Period |
| ▲ | ▲ | Performance in Sub-Saharan Africa |

**Performance in West Africa**

| 2008 | 2009 |
|---|---|
| ▲ | ▲ |
| Gambia, The | **Nigeria** |
| **Nigeria** | Gambia, The |
| Mali | Burkina Faso |
| Guinea | Mali |
| Liberia | Liberia |
| Côte d'Ivoire | Côte d'Ivoire |
| Benin | Guinea |
| Mauritania | Benin |
| Ghana | Mauritania |
| Cape Verde | Ghana |
| Togo | Togo |
| Burkina Faso | Senegal |
| Senegal | Niger |
| Niger | Cape Verde |
| Sierra Leone | Sierra Leone |
| Guinea-Bissau | Guinea-Bissau |

**Performance among Oil-Exporters**

| 2008 | 2009 |
|---|---|
| ▲ | ▲ |
| **Nigeria** | **Nigeria** |
| Côte d'Ivoire | Côte d'Ivoire |
| Cameroon | Cameroon |
| Chad | Chad |
| Sudan | Sudan |
| Gabon | Gabon |
| Congo, Rep. | Congo, Rep. |
| Angola | Angola |
| Equatorial Guinea | Equatorial Guinea |

| | |
|---|---|
| ▲ | improved *or* better than average |
| ▼ | worsened *or* worse than average |
| ◁▷ | no change *or* average |

## *rules of engagement*

*Engaging staff in West Africa is easiest in Nigeria, the 2nd easiest on the continent.*

2 Nigeria

5 Gambia

6 Burkina Faso

| | |
|---|---|
| 14 | Mali |
| 18 | Liberia |
| 19 | Côte d'Ivoire |
| 20 | Guinea |
| 21 | Benin |
| 23 | Mauritania |
| 31 | Ghana |
| 35 | Togo |
| 38 | Senegal |
| 39 | Niger |
| 40 | Cape Verde |
| 42 | Sierra Leone |
| 45 | Guinea-Bissau |

2009 rankings of 47 Sub-Saharan Africa Countries

Source: World Bank, IFC

Overall *Ease of Employing Workers*:
2009 rankings of 47 Sub-Saharan Africa Countries. Source: World Bank, IFC

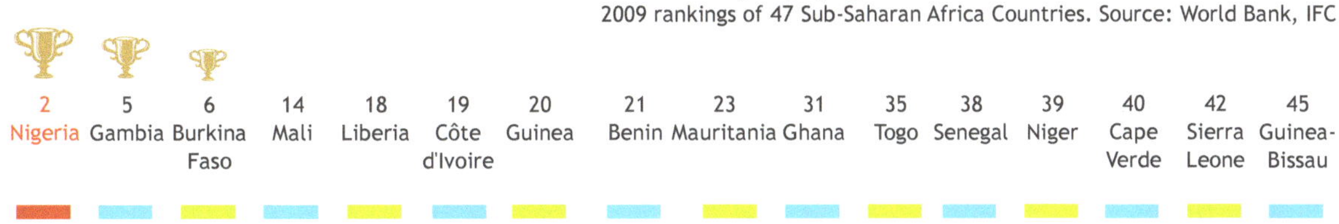


10.5

Ease of Employing Workers: ease of hiring 2009

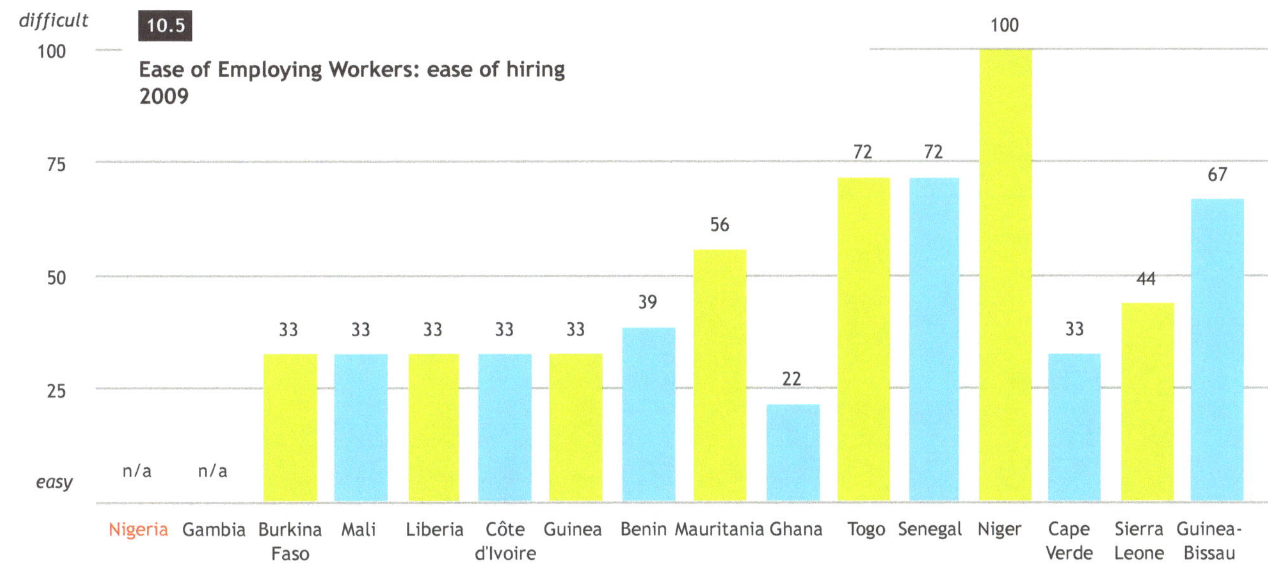


No data for Nigeria here. But Niger is the most difficult country in which to hire people and Burkina Faso & Liberia have the most flexible working hours.

10.6

Ease of Employing Workers: flexibility of hours 2009

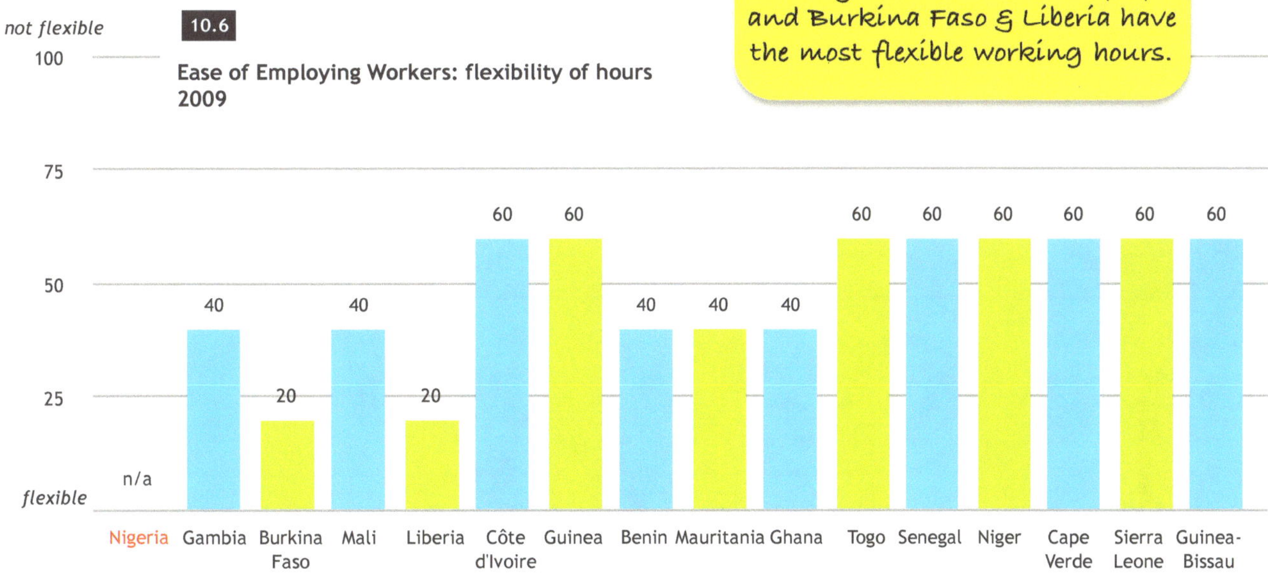

Overall *Ease of Employing Workers*:
2009 rankings of 47 Sub-Saharan Africa Countries. Source: World Bank, IFC

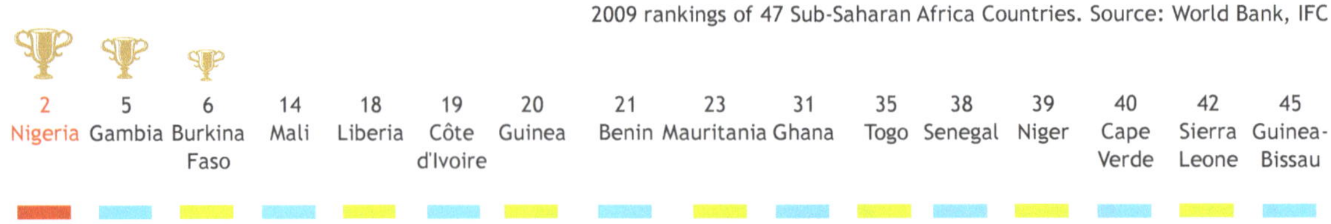


**10.7**

**Ease of Employing Workers: ease of firing 2009**

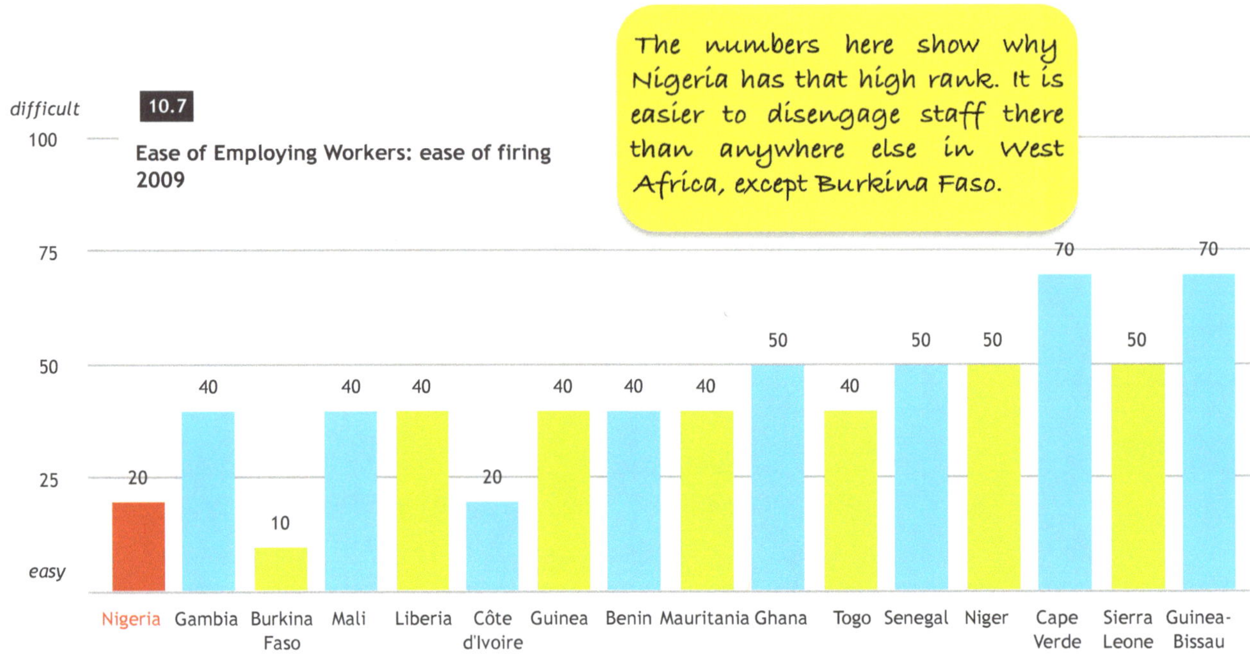


**10.8**

**Ease of Employing Workers: cost of firing (no. of weeks' wages) 2009**

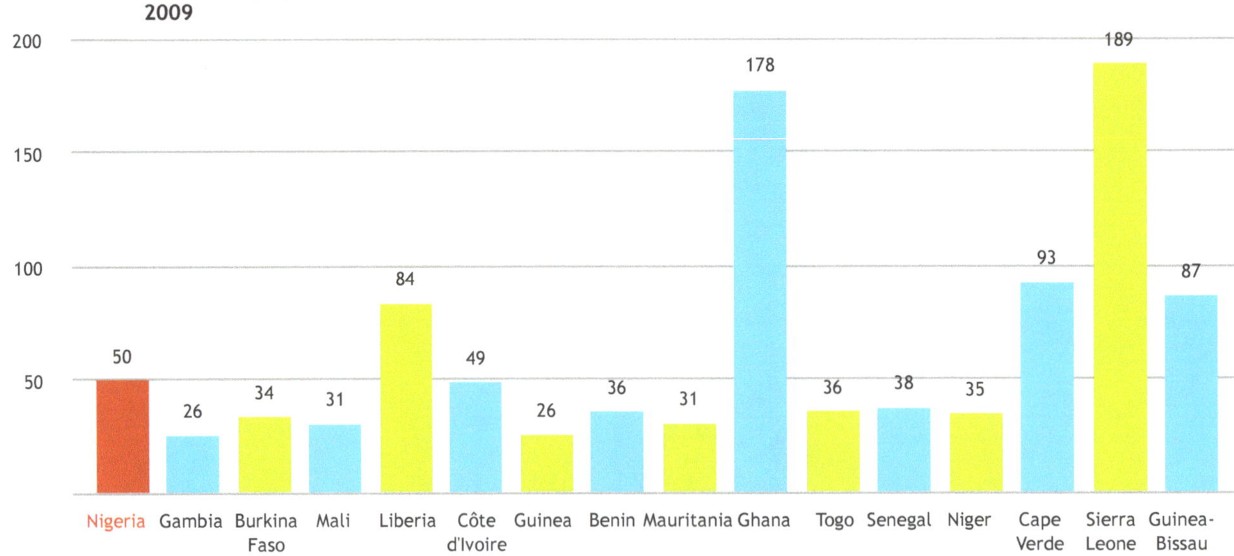

# 10.4 Ease of Registering Property: Rank

**maybe there's a good reason**

| 2008 | 2009 |
|---|---|
| | ◁▷ |

Self-comparison to Preceding Period

| 2008 | 2009 |
|---|---|
| ▼ | ▼ |

Performance in Sub-Saharan Africa

| 2008 | 2009 |
|---|---|
| ▼ | ▼ |
| Ghana | Ghana |
| Mauritania | Mauritania |
| Niger | Niger |
| Mali | Mali |
| Benin | Gambia, The |
| Cape Verde | Benin |
| Gambia, The | Cape Verde |
| Togo | Côte d'Ivoire |
| Guinea | Burkina Faso |
| Côte d'Ivoire | Togo |
| Senegal | Guinea |
| Guinea-Bissau | Senegal |
| Liberia | Sierra Leone |
| Burkina Faso | Guinea-Bissau |
| Sierra Leone | Liberia |
| Nigeria | Nigeria |

Performance in West Africa

| 2008 | 2009 |
|---|---|
| ▼ | ▼ |
| Sudan | Sudan |
| Equatorial Guinea | Equatorial Guinea |
| Chad | Chad |
| Cameroon | Cameroon |
| Gabon | Côte d'Ivoire |
| Côte d'Ivoire | Gabon |
| Angola | Congo, Rep. |
| Congo, Rep. | Angola |
| Nigeria | Nigeria |

Performance among Oil-Exporters

A hassle to register property in Nigeria. Easier everywhere else in Sub-Saharan Africa.

2 Ghana

6 Mauritania

8 Niger

| | | | |
|---|---|---|---|
| 13 | Mali | 36 | Guinea |
| 15 | Gambia | 38 | Senegal |
| 16 | Benin | 39 | Sierra Leone |
| 17 | Cape Verde | 42 | Guinea-Bissau |
| 26 | Côte d'Ivoire | 44 | Liberia |
| 29 | Burkina Faso | 46 | Nigeria |
| 35 | Togo | | |

2009 rankings of 47 Sub-Saharan Africa Countries

Source: World Bank, IFC

| | |
|---|---|
| ▲ | improved *or* better than average |
| ▼ | worsened *or* worse than average |
| ◁▷ | no change *or* average |

Overall *Ease of Registering Property*:
2009 rankings of 47 Sub-Saharan Africa Countries. Source: World Bank, IFC

| 2 | 6 | 8 | 13 | 15 | 16 | 17 | 26 | 29 | 35 | 36 | 38 | 39 | 42 | 44 | 46 |
|---|---|---|---|---|---|---|---|---|---|---|---|---|---|---|---|
| Ghana | Mauritania | Niger | Mali | Gambia | Benin | Cape Verde | Côte d'Ivoire | Burkina Faso | Togo | Guinea | Senegal | Sierra Leone | Guinea-Bissau | Liberia | Nigeria |

**10.9**

**Ease of Registering Property: no. of procedures 2009**

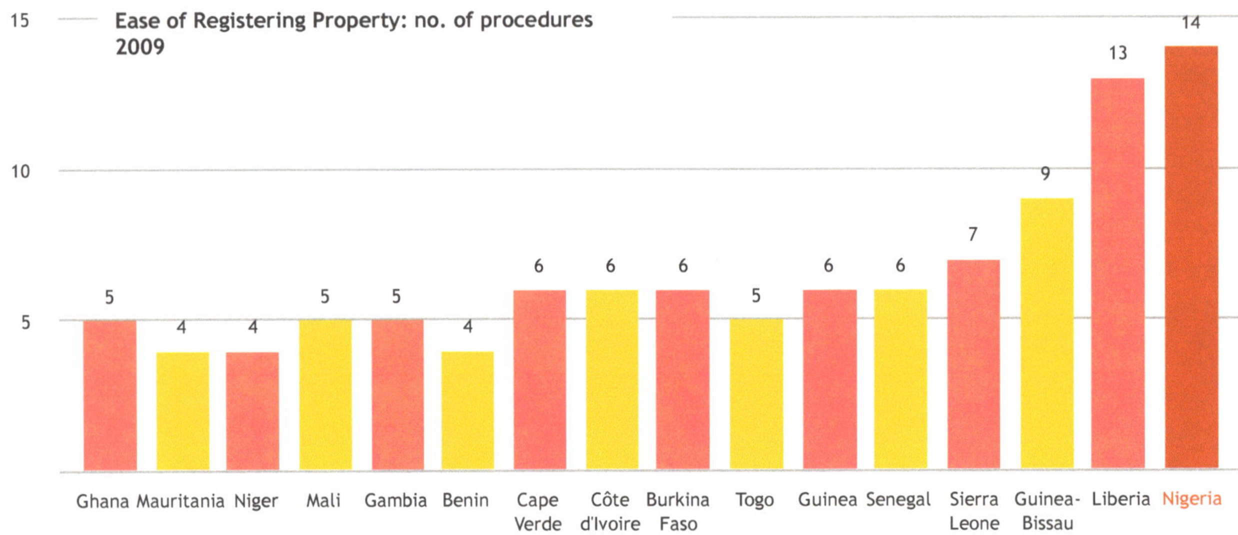


**10.10**

**Ease of Registering Property: no. of days 2009**

There are more procedures in Nigeria than anywhere else, although these take up less time than they do in several other countries.

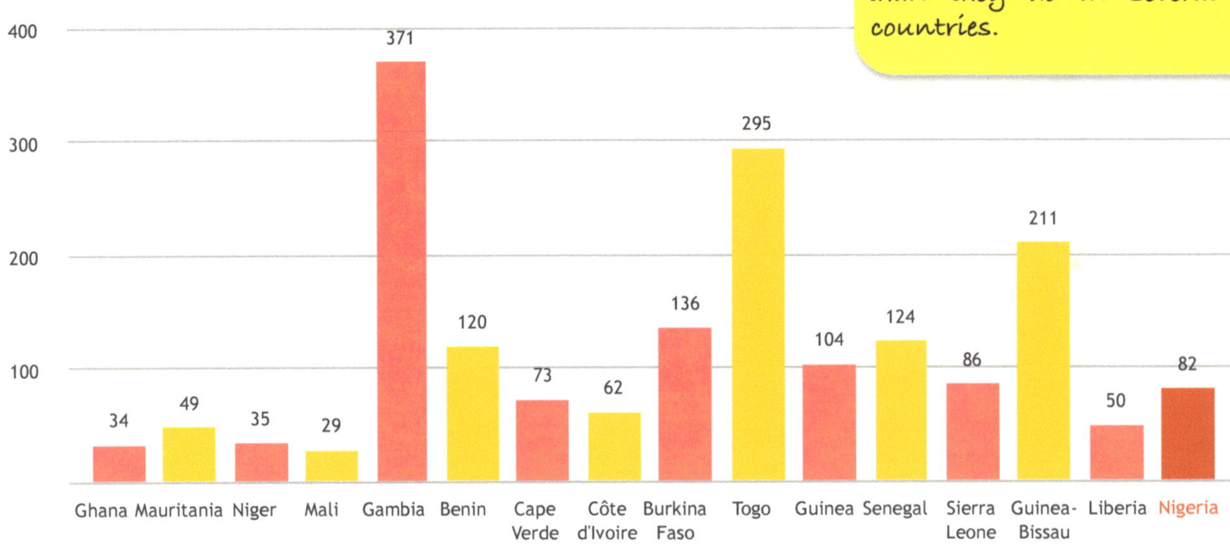

Overall *Ease of Registering Property*:
2009 rankings of 47 Sub-Saharan Africa Countries. Source: World Bank, IFC

| 2 | 6 | 8 | 13 | 15 | 16 | 17 | 26 | 29 | 35 | 36 | 38 | 39 | 42 | 44 | 46 |
|---|---|---|---|---|---|---|---|---|---|---|---|---|---|---|---|
| Ghana | Mauritania | Niger | Mali | Gambia | Benin | Cape Verde | Côte d'Ivoire | Burkina Faso | Togo | Guinea | Senegal | Sierra Leone | Guinea-Bissau | Liberia | Nigeria |

10.11

**Ease of Registering Property: cost (% of property value)**
**2009**

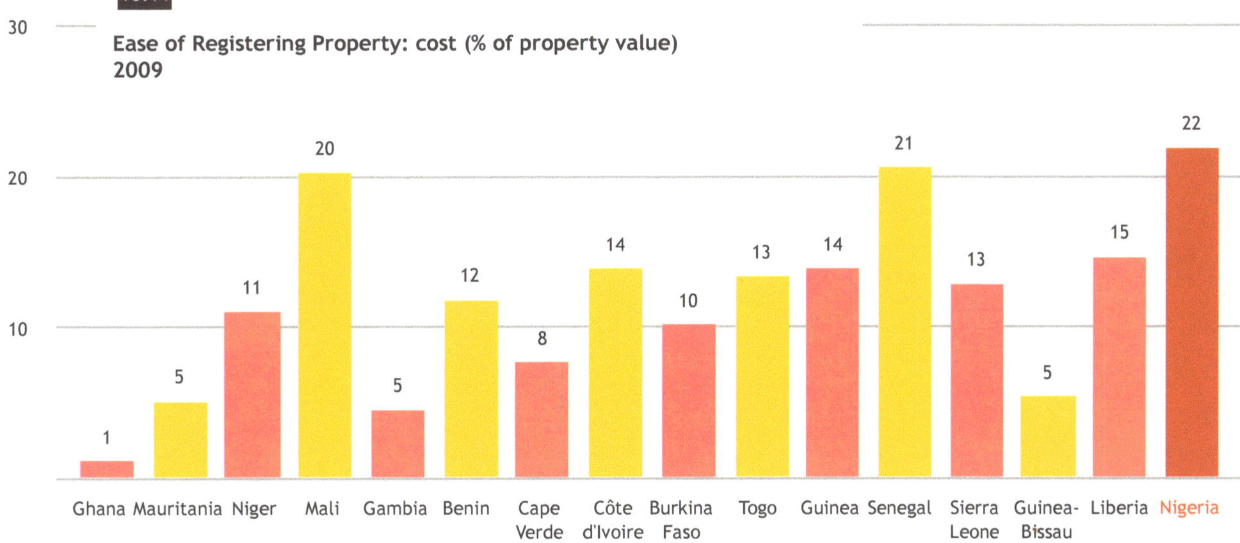


Costs involved in registration are the highest in West Africa and 3rd highest on the continent, after Zimbabwe (25%) and Chad (23%).

# 10.5 Ease of Getting Credit: Rank

| 2008 | 2009 |
|---|---|
| | ▼ |

Self-comparison to Preceding Period

| 2008 | 2009 |
|---|---|
| ▲ | ▲ |

Performance in Sub-Saharan Africa

| 2008 | 2009 |
|---|---|
| ▲ | ▲ |
| Cape Verde | **Nigeria** |
| **Nigeria** | Ghana |
| Ghana | Cape Verde |
| Benin | Gambia, The |
| Burkina Faso | Liberia |
| Mauritania | Benin |
| Sierra Leone | Burkina Faso |
| Gambia, The | Côte d'Ivoire |
| Liberia | Guinea-Bissau |
| Côte d'Ivoire | Mali |
| Guinea-Bissau | Mauritania |
| Mali | Niger |
| Niger | Senegal |
| Senegal | Sierra Leone |
| Togo | Togo |
| Guinea | Guinea |

Performance in West Africa

| 2008 | 2009 |
|---|---|
| ▲ | ▲ |
| Angola | Angola |
| **Nigeria** | **Nigeria** |
| Cameroon | Cameroon |
| Congo, Rep. | Congo, Rep. |
| Gabon | Equatorial Guinea |
| Chad | Gabon |
| Côte d'Ivoire | Sudan |
| Equatorial Guinea | Chad |
| Sudan | Côte d'Ivoire |

Performance among Oil-Exporters

| | |
|---|---|
| ▲ | improved *or* better than average |
| ▼ | worsened *or* worse than average |
| ◁▷ | no change *or* average |

***they'll be wanting your shoe size next***

*Banks and other financial institutions are more welcoming of your business in Nigeria: the best in West Africa; 6th best on the continent.*

**6 Nigeria**

**7 Ghana**

**8 Cape Verde**

9 Gambia
9 Liberia
10 Benin
10 Burkina Faso
10 Côte d'Ivoire
10 Guinea-Bissau
10 Mali
10 Mauritania
10 Niger
10 Senegal
10 Sierra Leone
10 Togo
11 Guinea

2009 rankings of 47 Sub-Saharan Africa Countries

Source: World Bank, IFC

# 10.6 Extent of Investor Protection: Rank

*he's on your side.*
*or isn't he?*

| | 2008 | 2009 |
|---|---|---|
| Self-comparison to Preceding Period | | ◁▷ |
| Performance in Sub-Saharan Africa | ▲ | ▲ |
| Performance in West Africa | ▲ | ▲ |
| | Ghana | Ghana |
| | **Nigeria** | **Nigeria** |
| | Sierra Leone | Sierra Leone |
| | Cape Verde | Cape Verde |
| | Guinea-Bissau | Guinea-Bissau |
| | Burkina Faso | Burkina Faso |
| | Liberia | Liberia |
| | Togo | Mauritania |
| | Mauritania | Togo |
| | Benin | Benin |
| | Côte d'Ivoire | Côte d'Ivoire |
| | Mali | Mali |
| | Niger | Niger |
| | Senegal | Senegal |
| | Gambia, The | Gambia, The |
| | Guinea | Guinea |
| Performance among Oil-Exporters | ▲ | ▲ |
| | Angola | Angola |
| | **Nigeria** | **Nigeria** |
| | Cameroon | Cameroon |
| | Chad | Chad |
| | Equatorial Guinea | Equatorial Guinea |
| | Sudan | Congo, Rep. |
| | Congo, Rep. | Côte d'Ivoire |
| | Côte d'Ivoire | Gabon |
| | Gabon | Sudan |

Its arbitration institutions are 2nd best in West Africa (after Ghana) and 2nd best among the oil exporters, too. They were 4th best in Sub-Saharan Africa.

3 Ghana

**4 Nigeria**
4 Sierra Leone

9 Cape Verde
9 Guinea-Bissau

10 Burkina Faso
10 Liberia
10 Mauritania
10 Togo

11 Benin
11 Côte d'Ivoire
11 Mali
11 Niger

12 Senegal
13 Gambia
13 Guinea

2009 rankings of 47 Sub-Saharan Africa Countries

Source: World Bank, IFC

| | |
|---|---|
| ▲ | improved *or* better than average |
| ▼ | worsened *or* worse than average |
| ◁▷ | no change *or* average |

Overall *Extent of Investor Protection*:
2009 rankings of 47 Sub-Saharan Africa Countries. Source: World Bank, IFC

Shareholders and the public have good access to company information in Nigeria, even though this is true for most of West Africa.

**10.12**

**Extent of Investor Protection: disclosure index 2009**

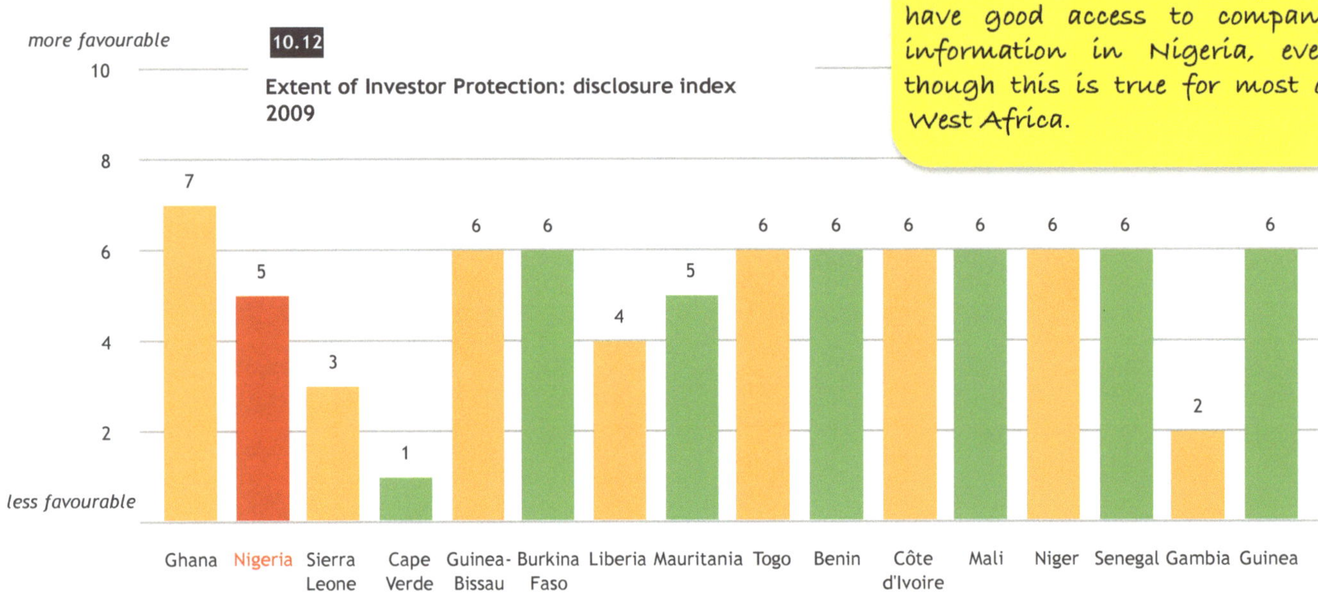


Shareholders may also hold company directors accountable relatively easily. Again, this is true - and is even surpassed - in much of west Africa.

**10.13**

**Extent of Investor Protection: director liability index 2009**

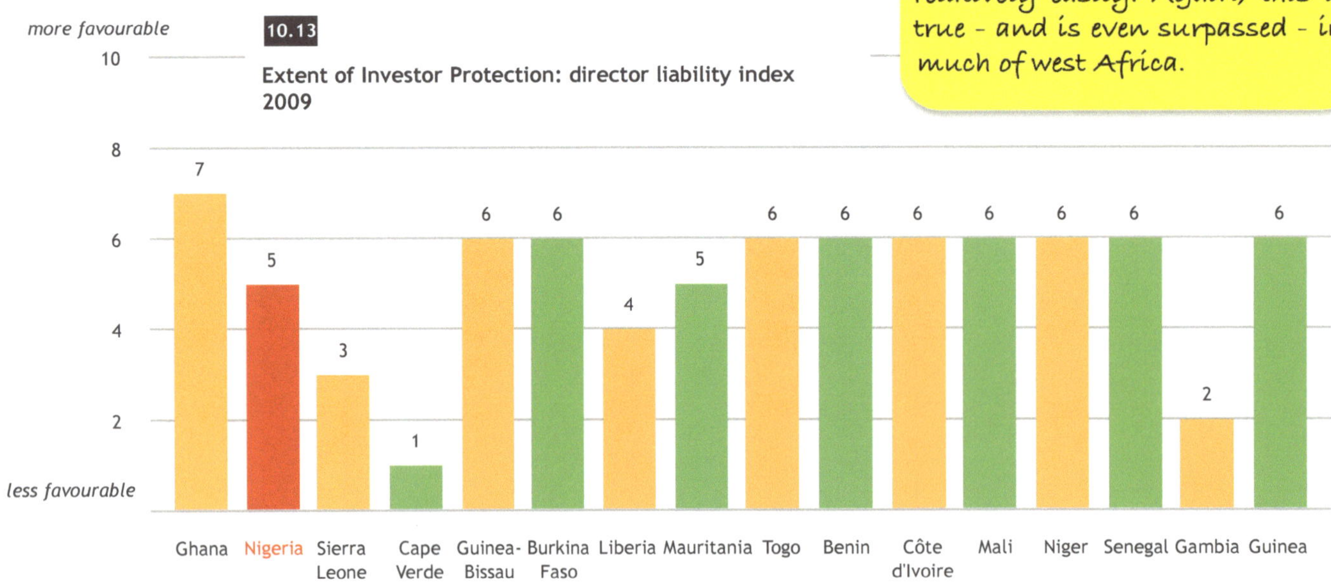

Overall *Extent of Investor Protection*:
2009 rankings of 47 Sub-Saharan Africa Countries. Source: World Bank, IFC

| Ghana | Nigeria | Sierra Leone | Cape Verde | Guinea-Bissau | Burkina Faso | Liberia | Mauritania | Togo | Benin | Côte d'Ivoire | Mali | Niger | Senegal | Gambia | Guinea |
|---|---|---|---|---|---|---|---|---|---|---|---|---|---|---|---|
| 3 | 4 | 4 | 9 | 9 | 10 | 10 | 10 | 10 | 11 | 11 | 11 | 11 | 12 | 13 | 13 |

10.14

**Extent of Investor Protection: shareholder suits index 2009**

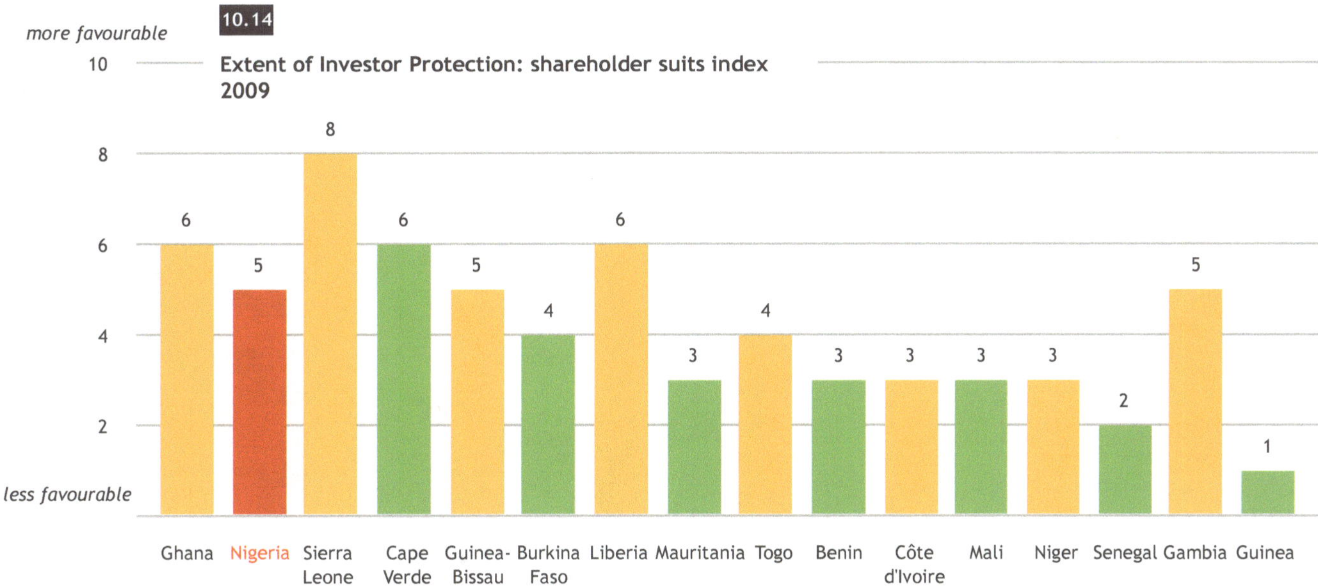


Should the parties opt for court resolution of disputes, evidence is gathered more easily in Nigeria than it is in 9 West African countries.

More easily than obtains in 16 countries of Sub-Saharan Africa.

# 10.7 Ease of Paying Taxes: Rank

*two quick steps and it's done*

| 2008 | 2009 | |
|---|---|---|
| | ▼ | Self-comparison to Preceding Period |
| ▲ | ▼ | Performance in Sub-Saharan Africa |

| ▲ | ▲ | Performance in West Africa |
|---|---|---|
| Ghana | Liberia | |
| **Nigeria** | Ghana | |
| Guinea-Bissau | Cape Verde | |
| Niger | Guinea-Bissau | |
| Cape Verde | Niger | |
| Liberia | **Nigeria** | |
| Burkina Faso | Burkina Faso | |
| Togo | Togo | |
| Côte d'Ivoire | Côte d'Ivoire | |
| Sierra Leone | Mali | |
| Mali | Sierra Leone | |
| Benin | Benin | |
| Guinea | Guinea | |
| Senegal | Senegal | |
| Mauritania | Mauritania | |
| Gambia, The | Gambia, The | |

It is more difficult to comply with tax regulations in Nigeria than most places in Sub-Saharan Africa.

But still easier than is the case in most of the oil exporters.

| ▲ | ▲ | Performance among Oil-Exporters |
|---|---|---|
| Sudan | Sudan | |
| Gabon | Gabon | |
| **Nigeria** | **Nigeria** | |
| Angola | Angola | |
| Chad | Chad | |
| Equatorial Guinea | Côte d'Ivoire | |
| Côte d'Ivoire | Equatorial Guinea | |
| Cameroon | Cameroon | |
| Congo, Rep. | Congo, Rep. | |

| | |
|---|---|
| ▲ | improved *or* better than average |
| ▼ | worsened *or* worse than average |
| ◁▷ | no change *or* average |

12 Liberia

14 Ghana

24 Cape Verde

| | |
|---|---|
| 25 | Guinea-Bissau |
| 26 | Niger |
| 26 | Nigeria |
| 28 | Burkina Faso |
| 29 | Togo |
| 30 | Côte d'Ivoire |
| 33 | Mali |
| 36 | Sierra Leone |
| 38 | Benin |
| 39 | Guinea |
| 40 | Senegal |
| 42 | Mauritania |
| 43 | Gambia |

2009 rankings of 47 Sub-Saharan Africa Countries

Source: World Bank, IFC

Overall *Ease of Paying Taxes*:
2009 rankings of 47 Sub-Saharan Africa Countries. Source: World Bank, IFC

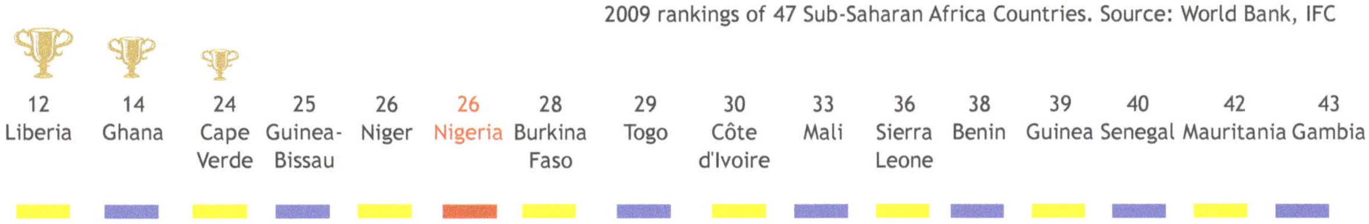


10.15

**Ease of Paying Taxes: no. of payments 2009**

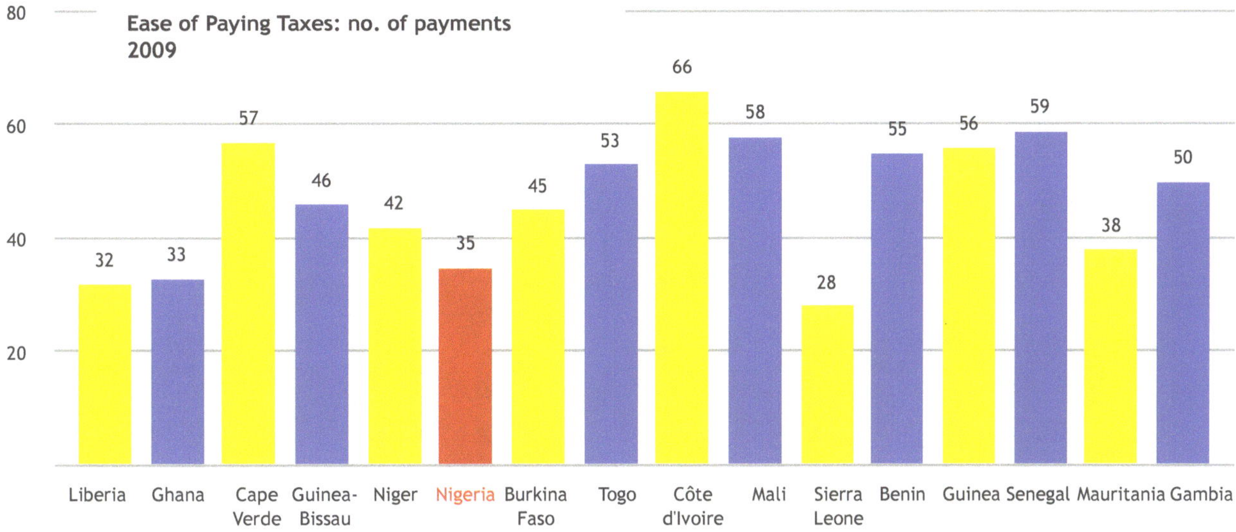


10.16

**Ease of Paying Taxes: time required (hours) 2009**

A major reason for that unflattering ranking would be the no. of hours that the tax procedures involve.

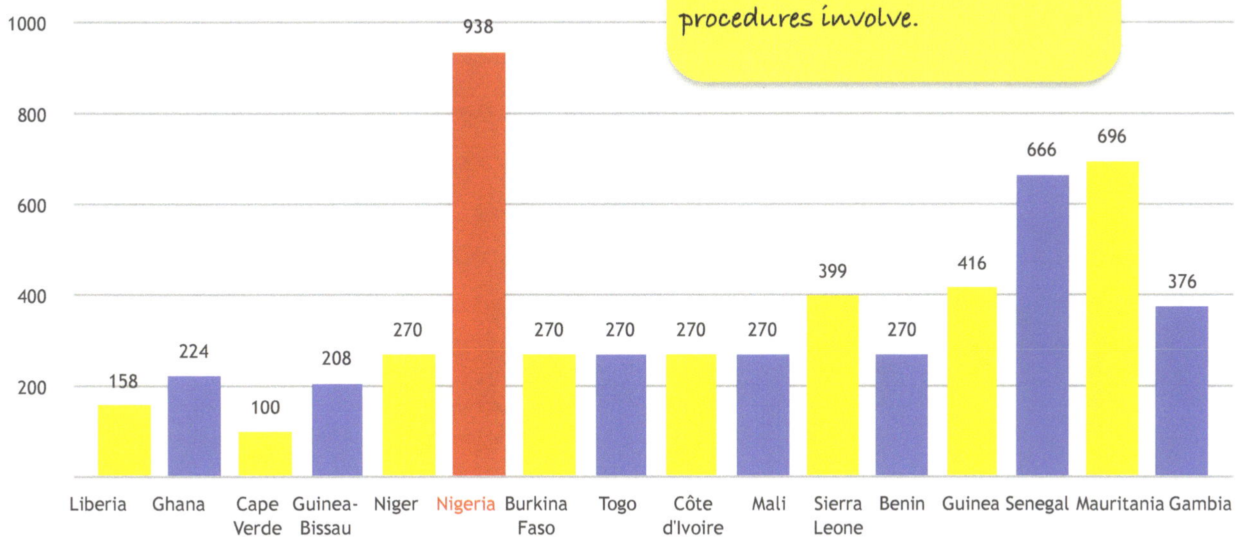

Overall *Ease of Paying Taxes*:
2009 rankings of 47 Sub-Saharan Africa Countries. Source: World Bank, IFC

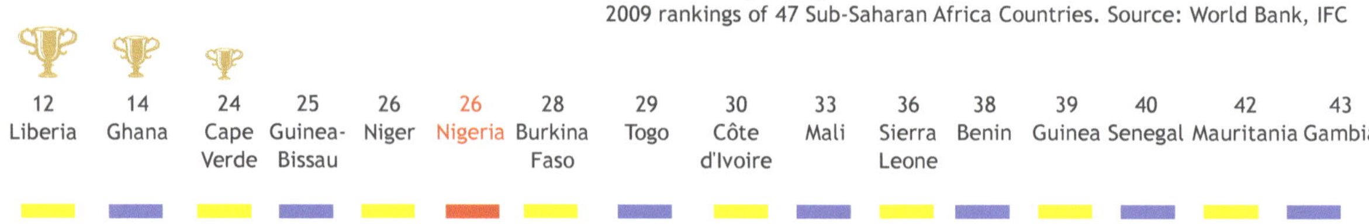


10.17

**Ease of Paying Taxes: tax on profit (%)**
**2009**

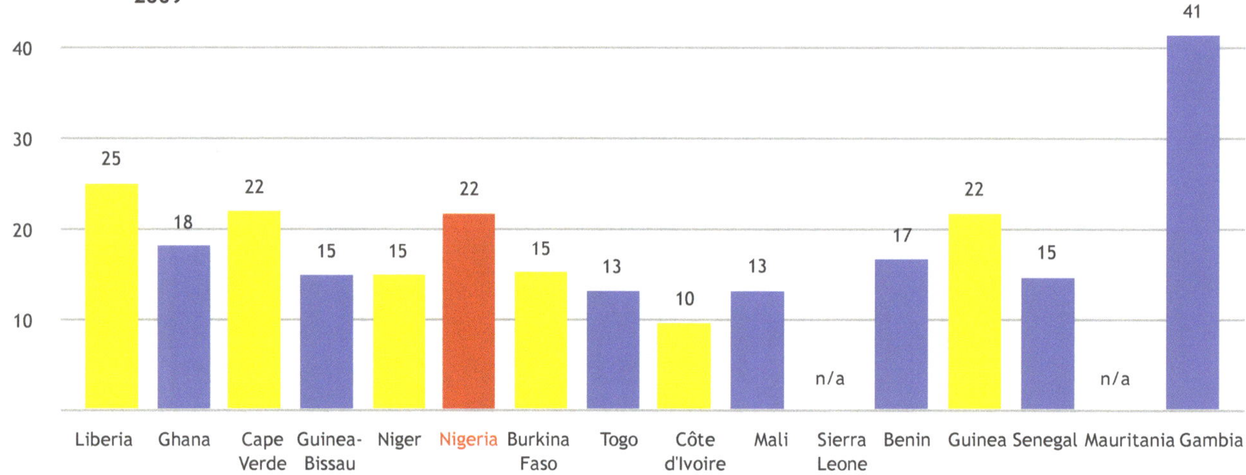


The various applicable tax rates, taken as a whole, compare more or less favourably with the rest of West Africa.

10.18

**Ease of Paying Taxes: labour tax & contributions (%)**
**2009**

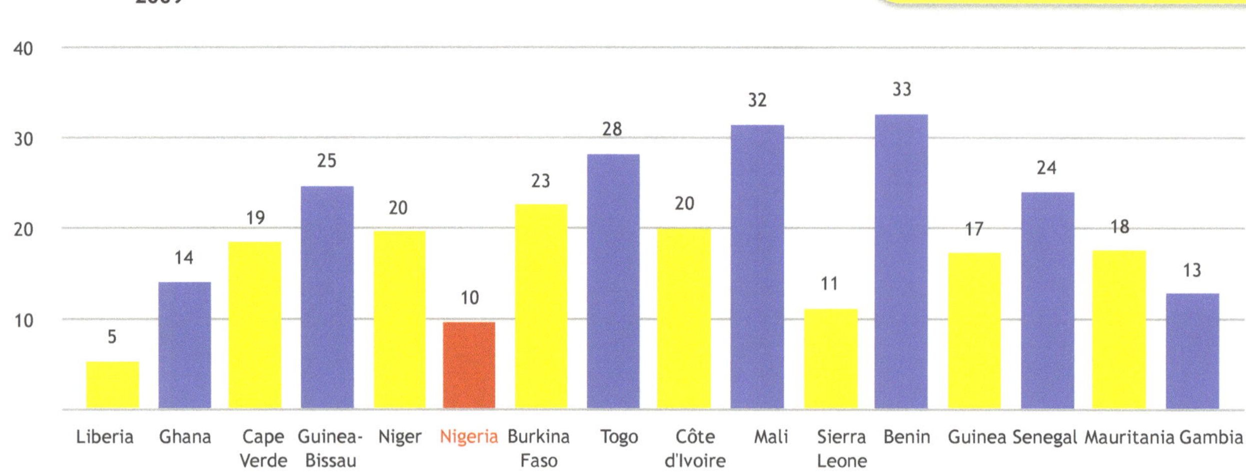

Overall *Ease of Paying Taxes*:
2009 rankings of 47 Sub-Saharan Africa Countries. Source: World Bank, IFC

|  |  |
|---|---|
| 12 | Liberia |
| 14 | Ghana |
| 24 | Cape Verde |
| 25 | Guinea-Bissau |
| 26 | Niger |
| 26 | Nigeria |
| 28 | Burkina Faso |
| 29 | Togo |
| 30 | Côte d'Ivoire |
| 33 | Mali |
| 36 | Sierra Leone |
| 38 | Benin |
| 39 | Guinea |
| 40 | Senegal |
| 42 | Mauritania |
| 43 | Gambia |

10.19

**Ease of Paying Taxes: other taxes 2009**

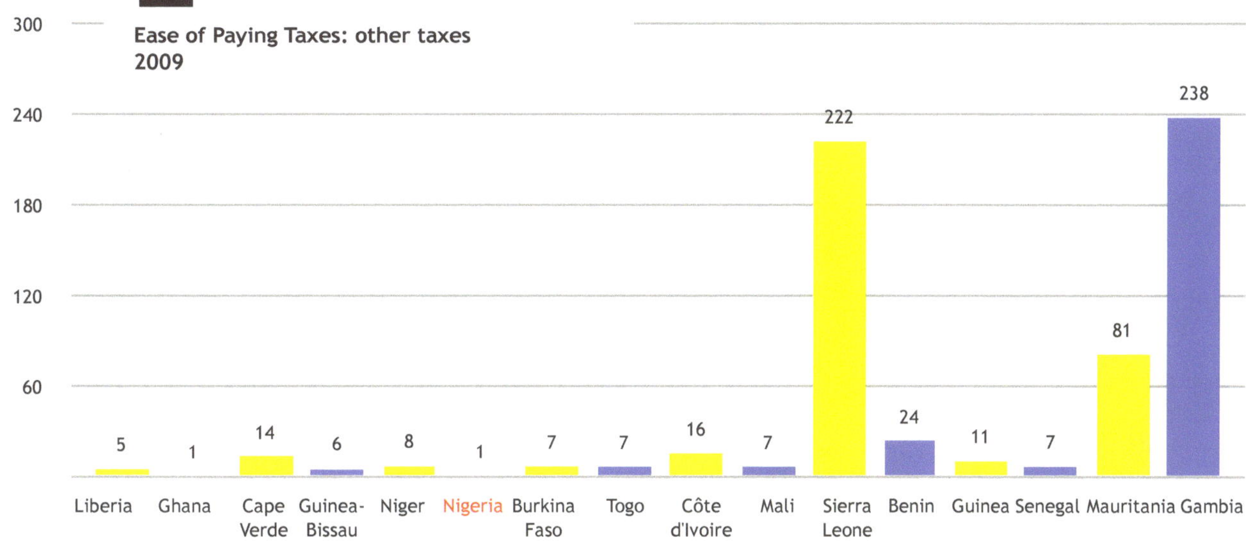


10.20

**Ease of Paying Taxes: total tax rate (%) 2009**

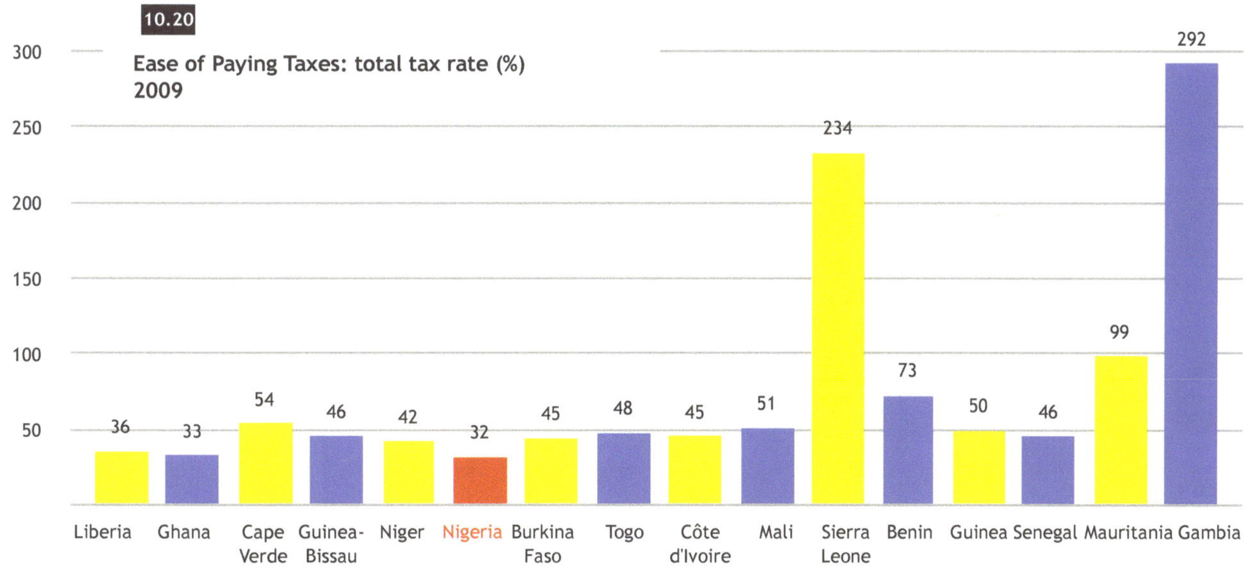

# 10.8 Ease of External Trade: Rank

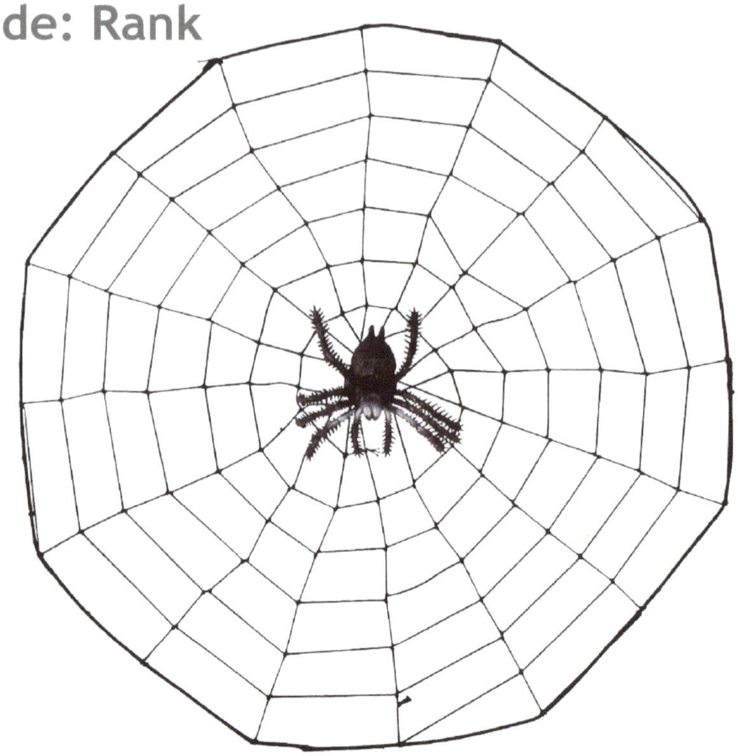

## it's actually simpler elsewhere

| 2008 | 2009 | |
|---|---|---|
| | ◁▷ | Self-comparison to Preceding Period |
| ▲ | ▲ | Performance in Sub-Saharan Africa |

**Performance in West Africa**

| 2008 ▼ | 2009 ▼ |
|---|---|
| Cape Verde | Cape Verde |
| Ghana | Senegal |
| Gambia, The | Gambia, The |
| Togo | Ghana |
| Liberia | Togo |
| Guinea | Guinea |
| Guinea-Bissau | Guinea-Bissau |
| Benin | Liberia |
| Sierra Leone | Benin |
| Senegal | Sierra Leone |
| **Nigeria** | **Nigeria** |
| Côte d'Ivoire | Côte d'Ivoire |
| Mauritania | Mauritania |
| Mali | Mali |
| Niger | Niger |
| Burkina Faso | Burkina Faso |

**Performance among Oil-Exporters**

| 2008 ▲ | 2009 ◁▷ |
|---|---|
| Gabon | Gabon |
| Cameroon | Equatorial Guinea |
| Equatorial Guinea | Cameroon |
| **Nigeria** | Sudan |
| Sudan | **Nigeria** |
| Côte d'Ivoire | Côte d'Ivoire |
| Chad | Chad |
| Angola | Angola |
| Congo, Rep. | Congo, Rep. |

*23rd out of 47 gives Nigeria a shaky pass-mark in Africa, but not in West Africa & the oil bloc, where it is outflanked in the ease of exporting and importing.*

*Cape Verde, Senegal and Gambia are among the top 5 in Africa for ease of external trade. Ghana and Togo are in the top 10.*

| | |
|---|---|
| ▲ | improved *or* better than average |
| ▼ | worsened *or* worse than average |
| ◁▷ | no change *or* average |

3 Cape Verde

4 Senegal

5 Gambia

| | |
|---|---|
| 6 | Ghana |
| 7 | Togo |
| 12 | Guinea |
| 13 | Guinea-Bissau |
| 14 | Liberia |
| 16 | Benin |
| 17 | Sierra Leone |
| 23 | Nigeria |
| 32 | Côte d'Ivoire |
| 33 | Mauritania |
| 38 | Mali |
| 41 | Niger |
| 44 | Burkina Faso |

2009 rankings of 47 Sub-Saharan Africa Countries

Source: World Bank, IFC

Overall *Ease of External Trade*:
2009 rankings of 47 Sub-Saharan Africa Countries. Source: World Bank, IFC

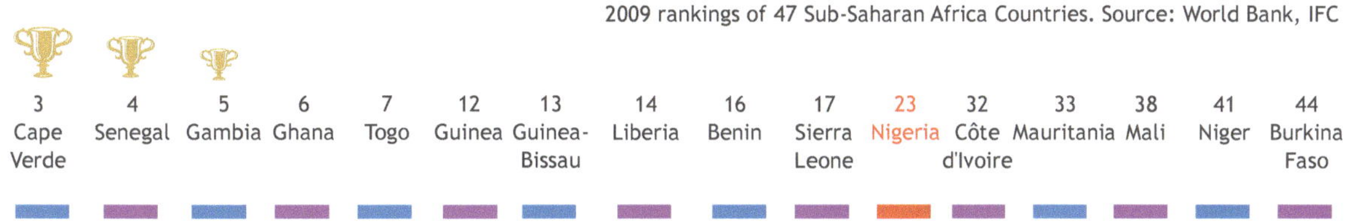


10.21

Ease of External Trade: cost to export 1 container (US$) 2009

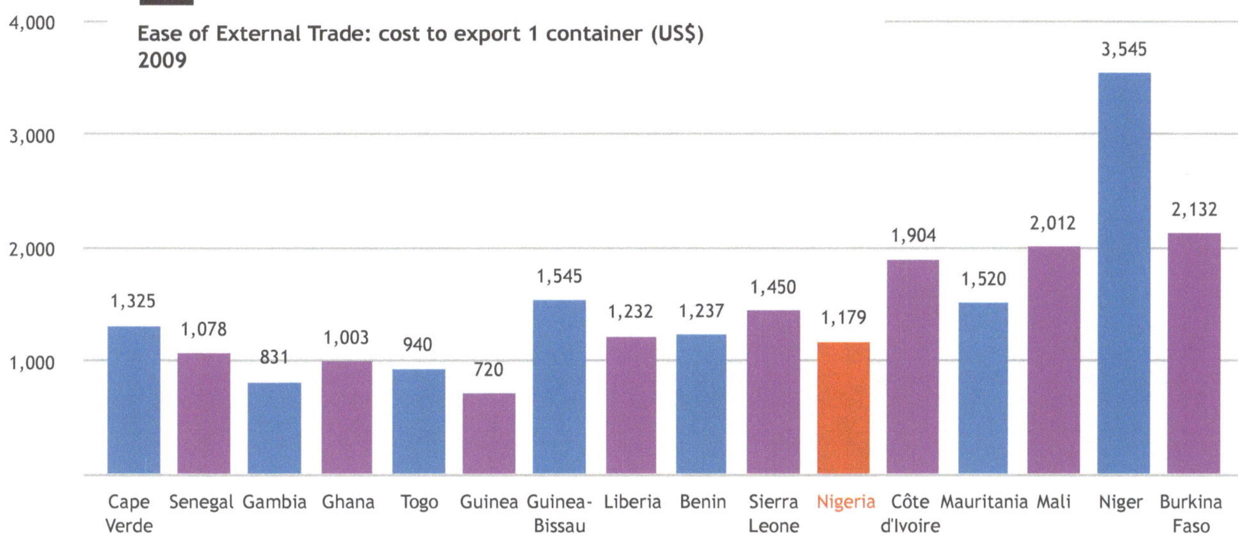


10.22

Ease of External Trade: cost to import 1 container (US$) 2009

Handling charges for exports and imports are in the mid-range when compared to other West Africa.

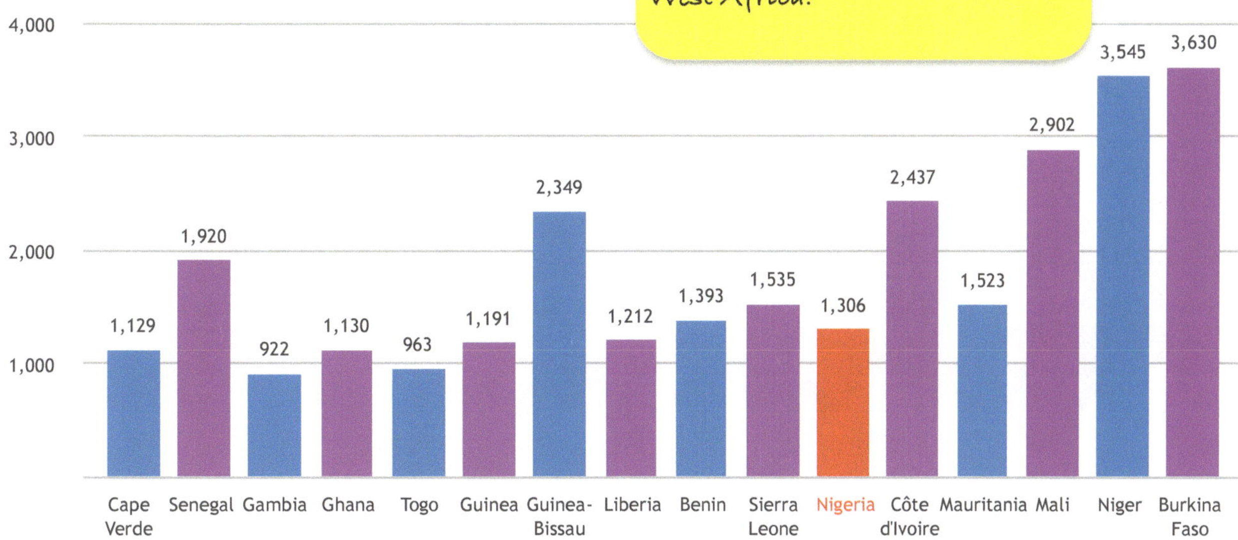

Overall *Ease of External Trade*:
2009 rankings of 47 Sub-Saharan Africa Countries. Source: World Bank, IFC

| 3 | 4 | 5 | 6 | 7 | 12 | 13 | 14 | 16 | 17 | 23 | 32 | 33 | 38 | 41 | 44 |
|---|---|---|---|---|---|---|---|---|---|---|---|---|---|---|---|
| Cape Verde | Senegal | Gambia | Ghana | Togo | Guinea | Guinea-Bissau | Liberia | Benin | Sierra Leone | Nigeria | Côte d'Ivoire | Mauritania | Mali | Niger | Burkina Faso |

10.23

**Ease of External Trade: no. of documents needed to export 2009**

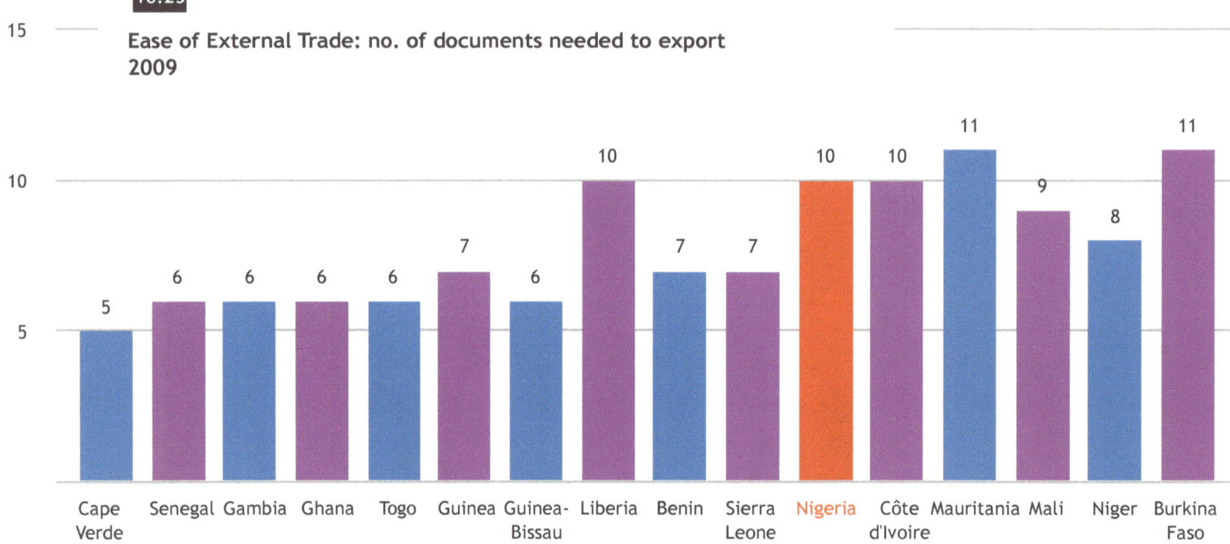


But paperwork is tedious.

10.24

**Ease of External Trade: no. of documents needed to import 2009**

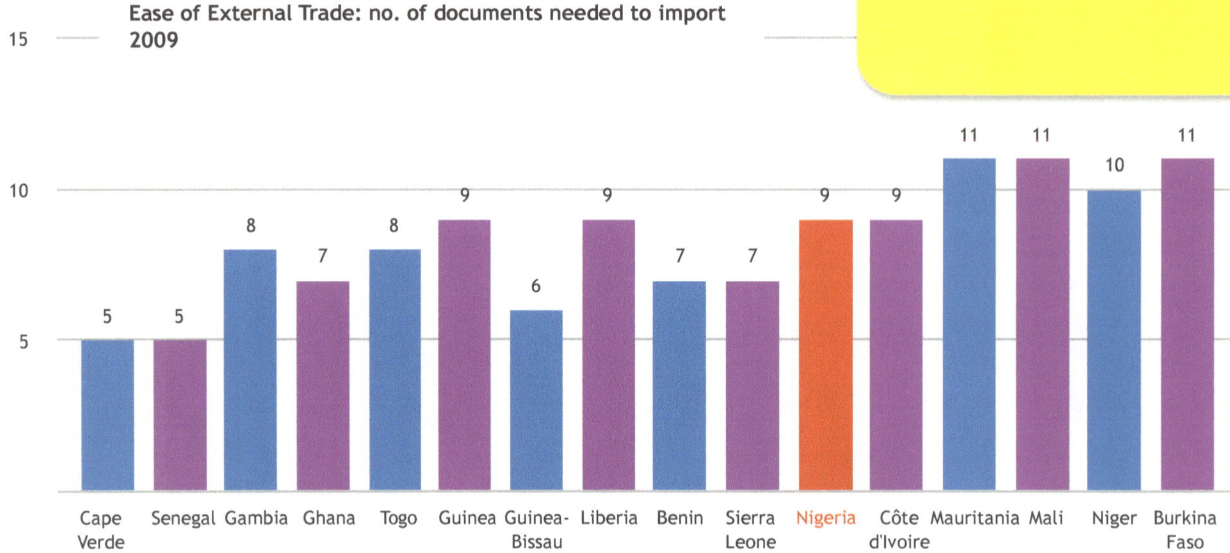

Overall *Ease of External Trade*:
2009 rankings of 47 Sub-Saharan Africa Countries. Source: World Bank, IFC

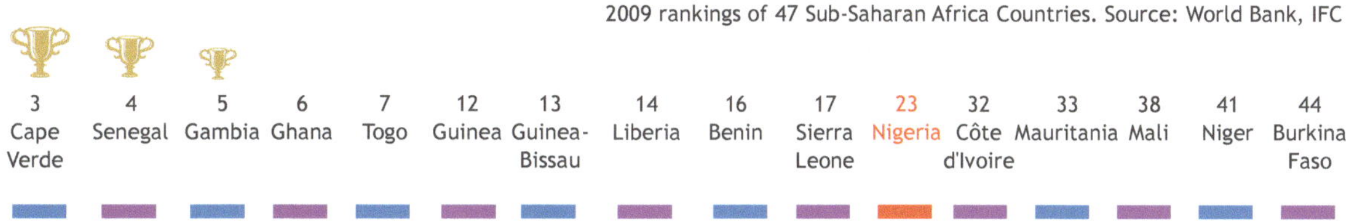


**10.25**

**Ease of External Trade: time for export (days) 2009**

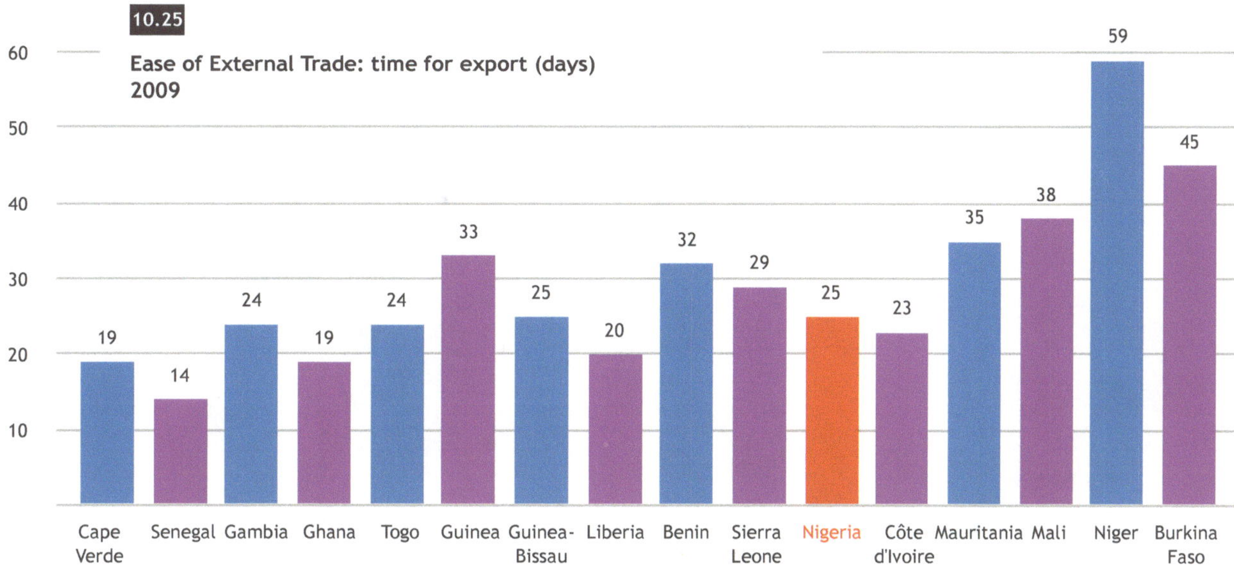


In the end, through-put time is on the high side for both exports and imports processes.

**10.26**

**Ease of External Trade: time for import (days) 2009**

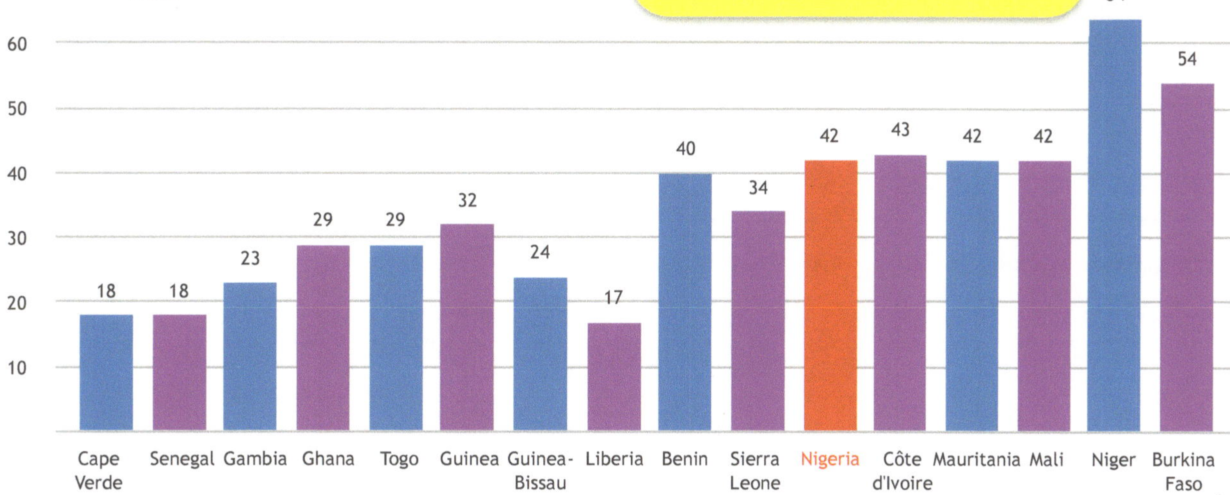

# 10.9 Ease of Enforcing Contracts: Rank

| 2008 | 2009 | |
|---|---|---|
| | ◁▷ | Self-comparison to Preceding Period |
| ▲ | ▲ | Performance in Sub-Saharan Africa |
| ▲ | ▲ | Performance in West Africa |
| Ghana | Cape Verde | |
| Cape Verde | Ghana | |
| Gambia, The | Gambia, The | |
| Mauritania | Mauritania | |
| **Nigeria** | **Nigeria** | |
| Burkina Faso | Burkina Faso | |
| Côte d'Ivoire | Côte d'Ivoire | |
| Guinea | Guinea | |
| Niger | Niger | |
| Guinea-Bissau | Guinea-Bissau | |
| Sierra Leone | Sierra Leone | |
| Senegal | Senegal | |
| Togo | Togo | |
| Mali | Mali | |
| Liberia | Liberia | |
| Benin | Benin | |

| 2008 | 2009 | |
|---|---|---|
| ▲ | ▲ | Performance among Oil-Exporters |
| Equatorial Guinea | Equatorial Guinea | |
| **Nigeria** | **Nigeria** | |
| Côte d'Ivoire | Côte d'Ivoire | |
| Sudan | Sudan | |
| Gabon | Gabon | |
| Congo, Rep. | Congo, Rep. | |
| Chad | Chad | |
| Cameroon | Cameroon | |
| Angola | Angola | |

she's on top of it

Business disputes usually reach suitable resolution in Nigeria. Cape Verde, Ghana & Gambia are again top finishers in West Africa, and in all Africa, too.

2009 rankings of 47 Sub-Saharan Africa Countries

Source: World Bank, IFC

3 Cape Verde

5 Ghana

8 Gambia

| | | | |
|---|---|---|---|
| 14 | Mauritania | 28 | Sierra Leone |
| 16 | Nigeria | 30 | Senegal |
| 20 | Burkina Faso | 33 | Togo |
| 22 | Côte d'Ivoire | 36 | Mali |
| 24 | Guinea | 38 | Liberia |
| 25 | Niger | 45 | Benin |
| 27 | Guinea-Bissau | | |

| | |
|---|---|
| ▲ | improved *or* better than average |
| ▼ | worsened *or* worse than average |
| ◁▷ | no change *or* average |

Overall *Ease of Enforcing Contracts*:
2009 rankings of 47 Sub-Saharan Africa Countries. Source: World Bank, IFC

|  |  |
|---|---|
| 3 | Cape Verde |
| 5 | Ghana |
| 8 | Gambia |
| 14 | Mauritania |
| 16 | Nigeria |
| 20 | Burkina Faso |
| 22 | Côte d'Ivoire |
| 24 | Guinea |
| 25 | Niger |
| 27 | Guinea-Bissau |
| 28 | Sierra Leone |
| 30 | Senegal |
| 33 | Togo |
| 36 | Mali |
| 38 | Liberia |
| 45 | Benin |

10.27

**Ease of Enforcing Contracts: no. of procedures 2009**

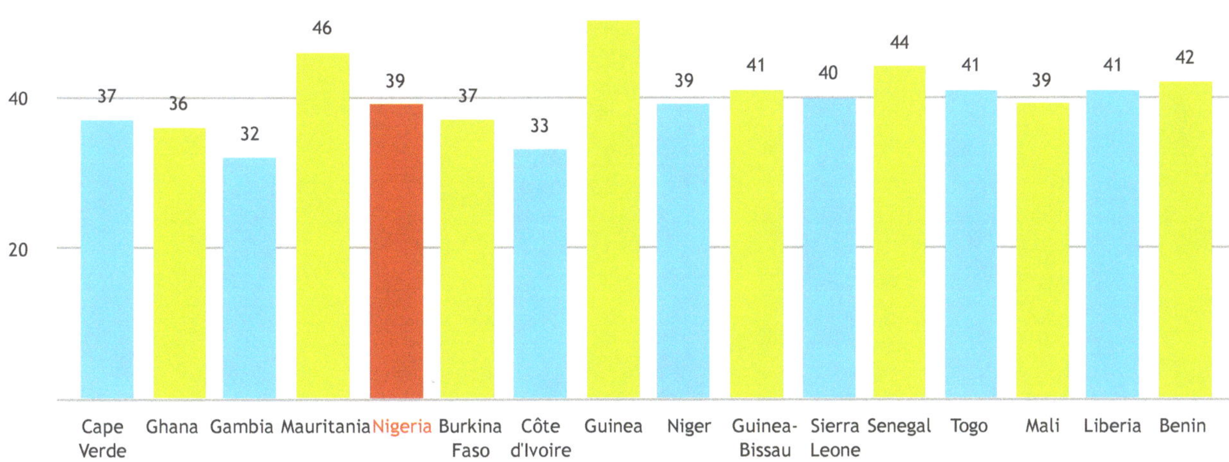


There's little separating West Africa's countries in no. of procedures involved. But in Nigeria it takes many days less than in a lot of West Africa.

10.28

**Ease of Enforcing Contracts: time in days 2009**

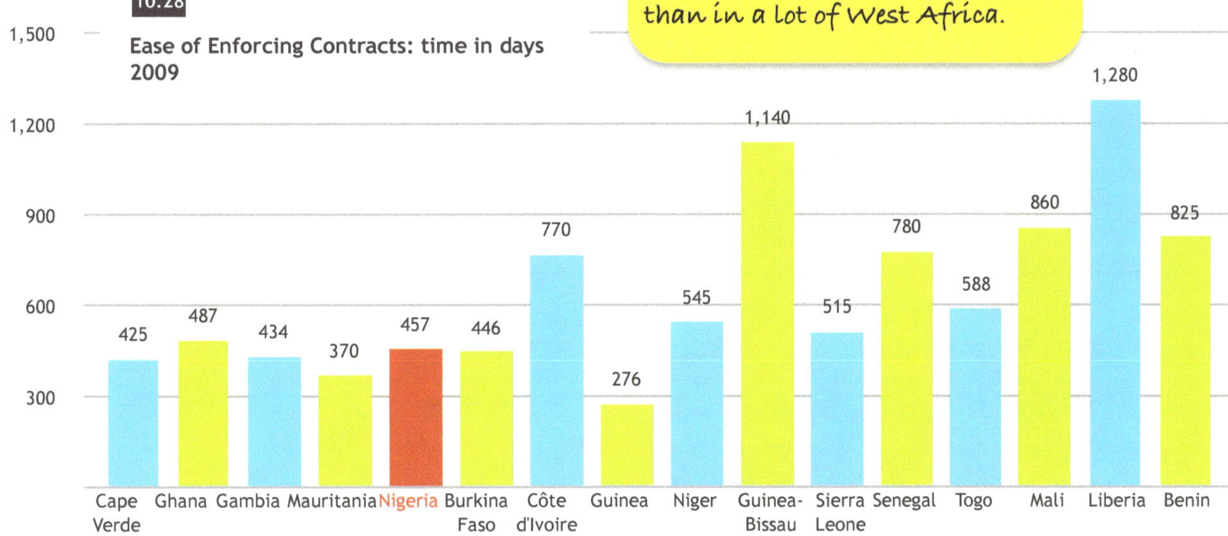

Overall *Ease of Enforcing Contracts*:
2009 rankings of 47 Sub-Saharan Africa Countries. Source: World Bank, IFC

| 3 | 5 | 8 | 14 | 16 | 20 | 22 | 24 | 25 | 27 | 28 | 30 | 33 | 36 | 38 | 45 |
|---|---|---|---|---|---|---|---|---|---|---|---|---|---|---|---|
| Cape Verde | Ghana | Gambia | Mauritania | Nigeria | Burkina Faso | Côte d'Ivoire | Guinea | Niger | Guinea-Bissau | Sierra Leone | Senegal | Togo | Mali | Liberia | Benin |

**10.29**

**Ease of Enforcing Contracts: cost (as % of debt in dispute) 2009**

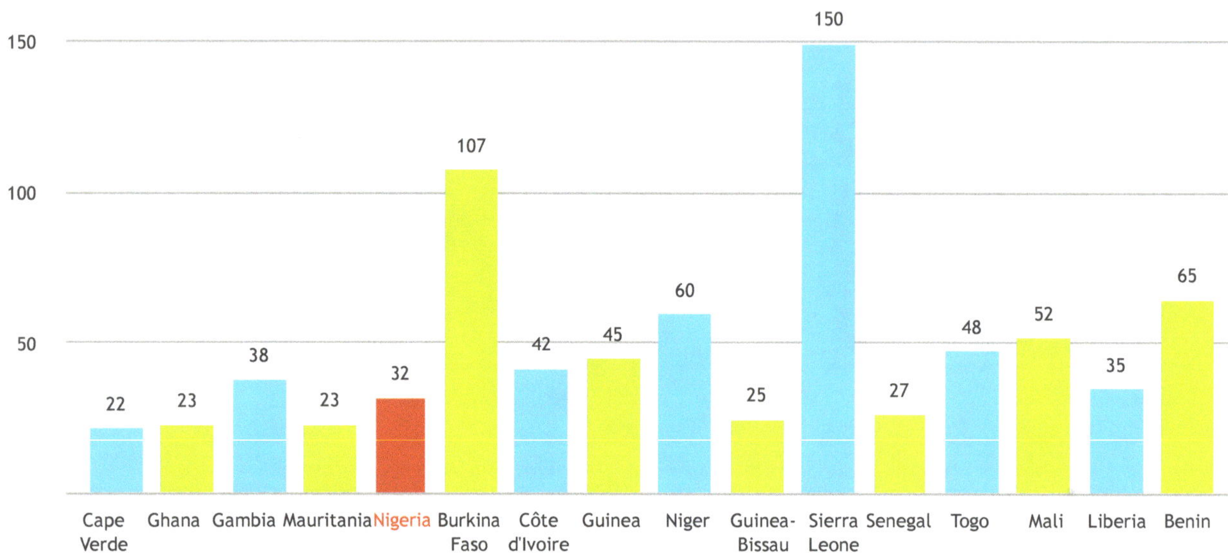


It also costs less than the West Africa average, in Niegria, to bring the dispute to a resolution.

# 10.10 Ease of Closing a Business: Rank

| 2008 | 2009 | |
|---|---|---|
| | ◁▷ | Self-comparison to Preceding Period |
| ▲ | ▲ | Performance in Sub-Saharan Africa |
| ▲ | ▲ | Performance in West Africa |
| Côte d'Ivoire | Côte d'Ivoire | |
| Senegal | Senegal | |
| **Nigeria** | **Nigeria** | |
| Togo | Togo | |
| Burkina Faso | Ghana | |
| Ghana | Guinea | |
| Benin | Burkina Faso | |
| Mali | Mali | |
| Guinea | Gambia, The | |
| Gambia, The | Benin | |
| Niger | Niger | |
| Sierra Leone | Sierra Leone | |
| Mauritania | Liberia | |
| Liberia | Mauritania | |
| Cape Verde | Cape Verde | |
| Guinea-Bissau | Guinea-Bissau | |

good-bye.
it was a pleasure.
honest.

To "up and go" is relatively easy in Nigeria, giving a picture somewhat of "hard to get in but easy to pull out". Tricky to say which one investors would prefer.

| 2008 | 2009 | |
|---|---|---|
| ▲ | ▲ | Performance among Oil-Exporters |
| Côte d'Ivoire | Côte d'Ivoire | |
| **Nigeria** | **Nigeria** | |
| Cameroon | Cameroon | |
| Congo, Rep. | Congo, Rep. | |
| Gabon | Gabon | |
| Angola | Angola | |
| Chad | Chad | |
| Equatorial Guinea | Equatorial Guinea | |
| Sudan | Sudan | |

| | |
|---|---|
| ▲ | improved *or* better than average |
| ▼ | worsened *or* worse than average |
| ◁▷ | no change *or* average |

2009 rankings of 47 Sub-Saharan Africa Countries

Source: World Bank, IFC

5 Côte d'Ivoire

11 Senegal

13 Nigeria

| Rank | Country | Rank | Country |
|---|---|---|---|
| 14 | Togo | 28 | Niger |
| 16 | Ghana | 30 | Sierra Leone |
| 17 | Guinea | 31 | Liberia |
| 18 | Burkina Faso | 32 | Mauritania |
| 20 | Mali | 35 | Cape Verde |
| 22 | Gambia | 35 | Guinea-Bissau |
| 23 | Benin | | |

Overall *Ease of Closing a Business*:
2009 rankings of 47 Sub-Saharan Africa Countries. Source: World Bank, IFC

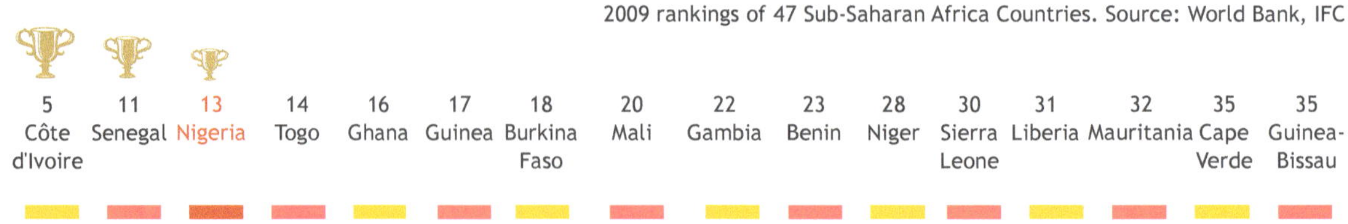


As though to press that point, you stand to recover more of your investment and costs in Nigeria than elsewhere, should you wish to pack and leave.

**10.30**

**Ease of Closing a Business: recovery rate (cents on the dollar) 2009**

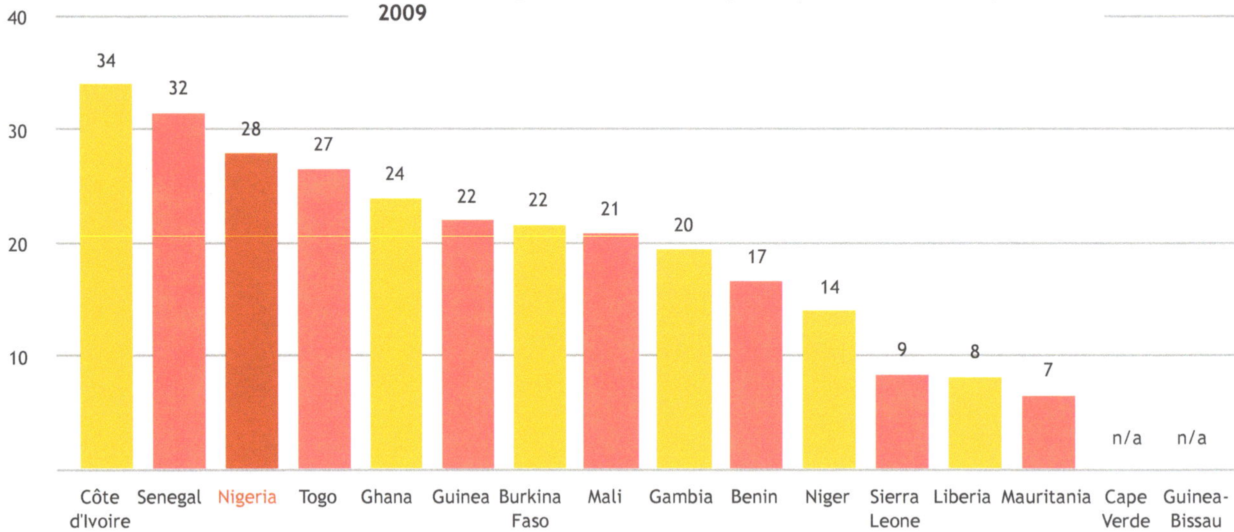

# 10.11 Ease of Doing Business: Rank

*are you in for long nights?*

Nigeria ends up in the upper-third of Sub-Saharan Afr. countries when ranked by the ease of business operations. Only bettered in West Afr. by Ghana.

| | 2008 | 2009 |
|---|---|---|
| Self-comparison to Preceding Period | | ▼ |
| Performance in Sub-Saharan Africa | ▲ | ▲ |
| Performance in West Africa | ▲ | ▲ |
| | Ghana | Ghana |
| | **Nigeria** | **Nigeria** |
| | Gambia, The | Gambia, The |
| | Cape Verde | Cape Verde |
| | Benin | Burkina Faso |
| | Côte d'Ivoire | Senegal |
| | Togo | Sierra Leone |
| | Mauritania | Liberia |
| | Mali | Mauritania |
| | Sierra Leone | Côte d'Ivoire |
| | Burkina Faso | Togo |
| | Senegal | Mali |
| | Guinea | Benin |
| | Niger | Guinea |
| | Liberia | Niger |
| | Guinea-Bissau | Guinea-Bissau |
| Performance among Oil-Exporters | ▲ | ▲ |
| | **Nigeria** | **Nigeria** |
| | Sudan | Sudan |
| | Gabon | Gabon |
| | Cameroon | Côte d'Ivoire |
| | Côte d'Ivoire | Cameroon |
| | Equatorial Guinea | Equatorial Guinea |
| | Angola | Angola |
| | Chad | Chad |
| | Congo, Rep. | Congo, Rep. |

2009 rankings of 47 Sub-Saharan Africa Countries

Source: World Bank, IFC

|  |  |
|---|---|
| 6 | Ghana |
| 12 | Nigeria |
| 15 | Gambia |
| 19 | Cape Verde |
| 22 | Burkina Faso |
| 23 | Senegal |
| 27 | Sierra Leone |
| 28 | Liberia |
| 30 | Mauritania |
| 31 | Côte d'Ivoire |
| 32 | Togo |
| 34 | Mali |
| 37 | Benin |
| 38 | Guinea |
| 39 | Niger |
| 45 | Guinea-Bissau |

| | |
|---|---|
| ▲ | improved *or* better than average |
| ▼ | worsened *or* worse than average |
| ◁▷ | no change *or* average |

# Leaders & Stragglers

*they've cut out the red tape*

## Regulatory Environment Rankings: 2009

| Rank | Country | Rank | Country | Rank | Country |
|---|---|---|---|---|---|
| 1 | Mauritius | 15 | Gambia, The | 29 | Mali |
| 2 | South Africa | 16 | Malawi | 30 | Equatorial Guinea |
| 3 | Botswana | 17 | Rwanda | 31 | Angola |
| 4 | Namibia | 18 | Mozambique | 32 | Benin |
| 5 | Kenya | 19 | Cape Verde | 33 | Guinea |
| 6 | Ghana | 20 | Madagascar | 34 | Niger |
| 7 | Zambia | 21 | Burkina Faso | 35 | Eritrea |
| 8 | Seychelles | 22 | Senegal | 36 | Chad |
| 9 | Swaziland | 23 | Gabon | 37 | Burundi |
| 10 | Uganda | 24 | Comoros | 38 | Congo, Rep. |
| 11 | Ethiopia | 25 | Sierra Leone | 39 | Guinea-Bissau |
| 12 | **Nigeria** | 26 | Côte d' Ivoire | 40 | Central Afr. Rep. |
| 13 | Lesotho | 27 | Togo | 41 | Congo, Dem. Rep. |
| 14 | Tanzania | 28 | Cameroon | | |
| | More Favourable | | MIDDLE | | Less Favourable |

Central Africa
East Africa
Southern Africa
West Africa

Of the top 10 in Sub-Saharan Africa, 5 are East African (including no. 1), 4 Southern African, and 1 West African: Ghana.

# Wrap-up: Regulatory Environment

- Mauritius, then Ghana, and then Nigeria, was the order of the top 3 finishers in West Africa. Mauritius was also the least constrained economy in Africa in which to do business. Ghana was 6th and Nigeria 12th. All 3 countries were the only West Africans in the top-brackets.
- Mauritius' performance was outstanding: 82% of the indicators ended up top-bracket. Nigeria had its majority in the mid-brackets (45%), but next highest was its top-bracket finishers (37%).
- Nigeria was excellent in the ease of starting a business, ease of employing workers, and in the legal and regulatory protection given to investors. But it was very poor at enabling registration of property. And it fared only marginally better in the construction department.
- Otherwise, on the whole, Nigeria was an enabling environment for business, compared to the rest of Sub-Saharan Africa: top-bracket finisher.

# 11. Business Friendliness

here's to us

11.1 Index of Economic Freedoms: Rank

11.2 Personal Income Tax Rate: 2008

11.3 Corporate Tax Rate: 2008

11.4 Voice and Accountability: Rank

11.5 Political Stability: Rank

11.6 Government Effectiveness: Rank

11.7 Regulatory Quality: Rank

11.8 Rule of Law: Rank

11.9 Control of Corruption: Rank

Leaders & Stragglers

Wrap-up

# Prelims

This chapter attempts to encapsulate in figures the extent to which an economy has proven to be welcoming and stimulating for the conduct of business and investment. It relies on data gathered and presented by two groups: *The Heritage Foundation* in conjunction with the *Wall Street Journal* (through their Index of Economic Freedoms); and the *World Bank* (through its Worldwide Governance Indicators).

## Index of Economic Freedom

The Heritage Foundation and The Wall Street Journal have been producing their Index of Economic Freedoms for fourteen years. The methodology and scope have been adjusted and improved through this period. As they explain, the "2008 Index of Economic Freedom covers 162 countries across 10 specific factors of economic freedom (...) the higher the score on a factor, the lower the level of government interference in the economy (...) Taken together, they offer an empirical depiction of a country's degree of economic freedom (...) the key to creating an environment that allows a virtuous cycle of entrepreneurship, innovation, and sustained economic growth and development to flourish. Economies with higher levels of economic freedom enjoy higher living standards."

The 10 Factors of Economic Freedom as presented by them are:

- Business Freedom
- Trade Freedom
- Fiscal Freedom
- Government Size
- Monetary Freedom
- Investment Freedom
- Financial Freedom
- Property Rights
- Freedom from Corruption
- Labour Freedom

## Tax Rates

The top tax rate on individual income, and the top tax rate on corporate income.

## Quality of Governance

The World Bank, with the International Bank for Reconstruction and Development (IBRD), has been collating data about Governance practice throughout the world for a little over ten years now. They divide this set of indices into six areas:

## Voice and Accountability

"The extent to which a country's citizens are able to participate in selecting their government, as well as freedom of expression, freedom of association, and a free media."

## Political Stability and Absence of Violence

"Perceptions of the likelihood that the government will be destabilised or overthrown by unconstitutional or violent means, including domestic violence and terrorism."

## Government Effectiveness

"The quality of public services, the quality of the civil service and the degree of its independence from political pressures, the quality of policy formulation and implementation, and the credibility of the government's commitment to such policies."

## Regulatory Quality

"The ability of the government to formulate and implement sound policies and regulations that permit and promote private sector development."

## Rule of Law

"The extent to which agents have confidence in and abide by the rules of society, and in particular the quality of contract enforcement, the police, and the courts, as well as the likelihood of crime and violence."

## Control of Corruption

"The extent to which public power is exercised for private gain, including both petty and grand forms of corruption, as well as capture of the state by the elite and private interests."

In this chapter we have charted the progress, along the years, of the country in focus across the ranks in Sub-Saharan Africa, dividing the 48 countries into three bands of achievement: the top rank (top third: 1-16), middle rank (middle third: 17-32), and bottom rank (bottom third: 33-48).

(The quotations cited above - enclosed within marks - are as they are given by the agencies mentioned, in the following publications: *2008 Index of Economic Freedom* and *A Decade of Measuring the Quality of Governance*. None of the data in this chapter goes towards evaluating our Dba Index of Country Performance.)

**Sources of Primary Data:** The Heritage Foundation, The Wall Street Journal, the World Bank, IBRD.

# Charts

11.1 Index of Economic Freedom: Nigeria's Ranking in Sub-Saharan Africa from 1999-2008

11.2 Voice and Accountability: Nigeria's Ranking in SSA from 1998-2006

11.3 Political Stability: Nigeria's Ranking in SSA from 1998-2006

11.4 Government Effectiveness: Nigeria's Ranking in SSA from 1998-2006

11.5 Regulatory Quality: Nigeria's Ranking in SSA from 1998-2006

11.6 Rule of Law: Nigeria's Ranking in SSA from 1998-2006

11.7 Control of Corruption: Nigeria's Ranking in SSA from 1998-2006

- **Wrap-up**

# Tables

*2001-2004; 2005-2008:*
- *self-comparison to preceding period;*
- *performance in S-Saharan Africa;*
- *performance in West Africa;*
- *performance among oil-exporters;*

*for:*

Index of Economic Freedoms: Rank

---------------------------

*1998-2002; 2003-2006:*
- *self-comparison to preceding period;*
- *performance in S-Saharan Africa;*
- *performance in West Africa;*
- *performance among oil-exporters;*

*for:*

Voice and Accountability: Rank

Political Stability: Rank

Government Effectiveness: Rank

Regulatory Quality: Rank

Rule of Law: Rank

Control of Corruption: Rank

---------------------------

*2001-2004; 2005-2008:*
- *rank out of 40 African countries over the 2 periods;*

*for:*

Index of Economic Freedoms

---------------------------

*2003-2006; 1998-2002:*
- *rank out of 48 African countries over the 2 periods;*

*for:*

Voice and Accountability: Rank

Political Stability: Rank

Government Effectiveness: Rank

Regulatory Quality: Rank

Rule of Law: Rank

Control of Corruption: Rank

---------------------------

- Personal Income Tax Rate: 2008
- Corporate Tax Rate: 2008

- **Business Friendliness Rankings: 2003-2008**

# 11.1 Index of Economic Freedoms: Rank

| 01-04 | 05-08 | |
|---|---|---|
| | ▲ | Self-comparison to Preceding Period |
| ▼ | ▼ | Performance in Sub-Saharan Africa |
| ▼ | ▼ | Performance in West Africa |
| Mali | Cape Verde | |
| Senegal | Senegal | |
| Burkina Faso | Gambia, The | |
| Ghana | Ghana | |
| Cape Verde | Côte d'Ivoire | |
| Mauritania | Burkina Faso | |
| Côte d'Ivoire | Mauritania | |
| Benin | Mali | |
| Gambia, The | Guinea | |
| Guinea | Benin | |
| Niger | **Nigeria** | |
| **Nigeria** | Niger | |
| Togo | Togo | |
| Guinea-Bissau | Sierra Leone | |
| Sierra Leone | Guinea-Bissau | |

| 01-04 | 05-08 | |
|---|---|---|
| ▲ | ▲ | Performance among Oil-Exporters |
| Gabon | Côte d'Ivoire | |
| Côte d'Ivoire | Gabon | |
| Cameroon | Cameroon | |
| **Nigeria** | **Nigeria** | |
| Equatorial Guinea | Equatorial Guinea | |
| Chad | Chad | |
| Congo, Rep. | Angola | |
| Angola | Congo, Rep. | |

*they won't shackle you*

Not a good verdict. Nigeria improved during 2005-08, over the preceding 4 yrs; but it wasn't enough to match the rest of West Africa, nor the rest of Africa.

That it stayed above water among the oil economies is a sign of their poor rating on the conduciveness of their business and investment culture.

| | |
|---|---|
| ▲ | improved *or* better than average |
| ▼ | worsened *or* worse than average |
| ◁▷ | no change *or* average |

2008 rankings of 40 Sub-Saharan Africa Countries
Source: Heritage Foundation, Wall Street Journal

## *and they won't shackle it, either*

11.1

Index of Economic Freedom: Nigeria's Ranking in SSA 1999-2008

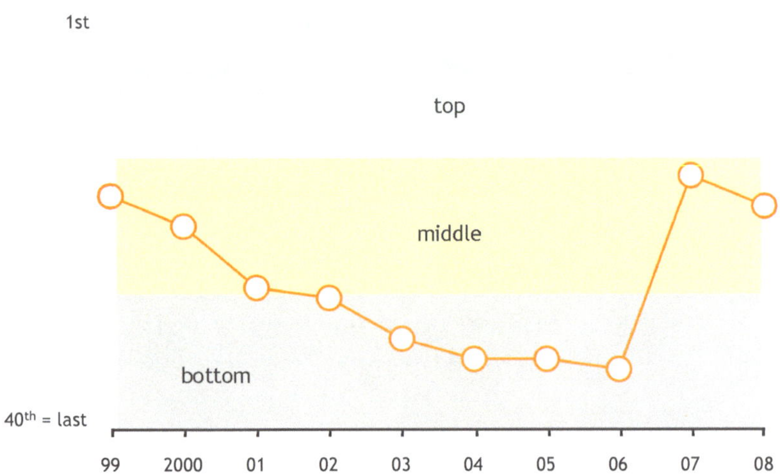


2008 rankings of 40 Sub-Saharan Africa Countries
Source: Heritage Foundation, Wall Street Journal

During 2002-2006 Nigeria fell deeper into the bottom tier in Africa. 2007 saw a leap into a high in the mid-tier. By 2008 it was dropping again.

*now, that's worth celebrating*

## Index of Economic Freedom: Rankings

| Change | Rank | 2005-08 | 2001-04 |
|---|---|---|---|
| | 1 | Botswana | Botswana |
| | 2 | Mauritius | Mauritius |
| ▲ | 3 | Uganda | Namibia |
| | 4 | South Africa | South Africa |
| ▲ | 5 | Madagascar | Uganda |
| ▼ | 6 | Namibia | Swaziland |
| ▼ | 7 | Swaziland | Mali |
| ▲ | 8 | Kenya | Senegal |
| ▲ | 9 | Cape Verde | Burkina Faso |
| ▼ | 10 | Senegal | Mozambique |
| ▲ | 11 | Gambia, The | Kenya |
| | 12 | Tanzania | Tanzania |
| ▲ | 13 | Ghana | Madagascar |
| ▲ | 14 | Zambia | Ghana |
| ▲ | 15 | Côte d' Ivoire | Zambia |
| ▼ | 16 | Burkina Faso | Gabon |
| ▲ | 17 | Mauritania | Cape Verde |
| ▼ | 18 | Mali | Central Afr. Rep. |
| ▼ | 19 | Mozambique | Djibouti |
| ▲ | 20 | Malawi | Mauritania |
| ▲ | 21 | Guinea | Côte d' Ivoire |
| ▼ | 22 | Gabon | Benin |
| ▲ | 23 | Cameroon | Gambia, The |
| ▼ | 24 | Benin | Guinea |
| ▼ | 25 | Djibouti | Malawi |
| ▲ | 26 | **Nigeria** | Cameroon |
| ▲ | 27 | Lesotho | Niger |
| ▲ | 28 | Equatorial Guinea | Ethiopia |
| ▼ | 29 | Central Afr. Rep. | **Nigeria** |
| ▼ | 30 | Ethiopia | Lesotho |
| ▲ | 31 | Rwanda | Equatorial Guinea |
| ▼ | 32 | Niger | Chad |
| ▼ | 33 | Chad | Rwanda |
| | 34 | Togo | Togo |
| ▲ | 35 | Sierra Leone | Congo, Rep. |
| ▲ | 36 | Burundi | Guinea-Bissau |
| ▼ | 37 | Guinea-Bissau | Sierra Leone |
| ▲ | 38 | Angola | Zimbabwe |
| ▼ | 39 | Congo, Rep. | Angola |
| ▼ | 40 | Zimbabwe | Burundi |

| | |
|---|---|
| ▲ | moved up from 2001/04 |
| ▼ | moved down from 2001/04 |
| blank | no change from 2001/04 |

Central Africa
East Africa
Southern Africa
West Africa

2008 rankings of 40 Sub-Saharan Africa Countries
Source: Heritage Foundation, Wall Street Journal

Economic Freedom: 2005-08 was an improvement over 2001-04. Three places up. But still firmly rooted in Africa's bottom half.

## 11.2 Personal Income Tax Rate: 2008

*it's going to cost her*

Tax on personal earnings is higher in most of Sub-Saharan Africa, than it is in Nigeria. At about 25%, Nigeria's is less than half of the highest (Chad: 65%).

It is near twice that of the lowest (Angola, Mauritius: 15%). The least in West Africa is Guinea-Bissau (20%), and the highest, Côte d' Ivoire (60%).

| Rank | Country | % |
|---|---|---|
| 1 | Angola | 15 |
| 1 | Mauritius | 15 |
| 2 | Guinea-Bissau | 20 |
| 3 | Botswana | 25 |
| 3 | Ghana | 25 |
| 3 | Nigeria | 25 |
| 4 | Burkina Faso | 30 |
| 4 | Djibouti | 30 |
| 4 | Kenya | 30 |
| 4 | Madagascar | 30 |
| 4 | Sierra Leone | 30 |
| 4 | Tanzania | 30 |
| 4 | Uganda | 30 |
| 5 | Mozambique | 32 |
| 6 | Swaziland | 33 |
| 7 | Burundi | 35 |
| 7 | Cameroon | 35 |
| 7 | Equatorial Guinea | 35 |
| 7 | Ethiopia | 35 |
| 7 | Gambia, The | 35 |
| 7 | Lesotho | 35 |
| 7 | Namibia | 35 |
| 7 | Rwanda | 35 |
| 7 | Zambia | 35 |
| 8 | Benin | 40 |
| 8 | Guinea | 40 |
| 8 | Malawi | 40 |
| 8 | Mali | 40 |
| 8 | Mauritania | 40 |
| 8 | South Africa | 40 |
| 9 | Cape Verde | 45 |
| 9 | Niger | 45 |
| 10 | Zimbabwe | 47.5 |
| 11 | Central Afr. Rep. | 50 |
| 11 | Congo, Rep. | 50 |
| 11 | Gabon | 50 |
| 11 | Senegal | 50 |
| 12 | Togo | 55 |
| 13 | Côte d' Ivoire | 60 |
| 14 | Chad | 65 |

Source: Heritage Foundation

# 11.3 Corporate Tax Rate: 2008

*and it will cost you, too*

Corporate tax is a closer call, with smaller differences. Nigeria at 30% is in the mid-range.

The lowest - again - is Mauritius (15%), and the highest - again - is Chad (40%).

| Rank | Country | % |
|---|---|---|
| 1 | Mauritius | 15 |
| 2 | Botswana | 25 |
| 2 | Djibouti | 25 |
| 2 | Ghana | 25 |
| 2 | Guinea-Bissau | 25 |
| 2 | Lesotho | 25 |
| 2 | Mauritania | 25 |
| 2 | Senegal | 25 |
| 3 | South Africa | 29 |
| 4 | Cape Verde | 30 |
| 4 | Central Afr. Rep. | 30 |
| 4 | Ethiopia | 30 |
| 4 | Kenya | 30 |
| 4 | Madagascar | 30 |
| 4 | Malawi | 30 |
| 4 | Nigeria | 30 |
| 4 | Rwanda | 30 |
| 4 | Sierra Leone | 30 |
| 4 | Swaziland | 30 |
| 4 | Tanzania | 30 |
| 4 | Uganda | 30 |
| 4 | Zimbabwe | 30 |
| 5 | Mozambique | 32 |
| 6 | Angola | 35 |
| 6 | Burkina Faso | 35 |
| 6 | Burundi | 35 |
| 6 | Côte d' Ivoire | 35 |
| 6 | Equatorial Guinea | 35 |
| 6 | Gabon | 35 |
| 6 | Gambia, The | 35 |
| 6 | Guinea | 35 |
| 6 | Mali | 35 |
| 6 | Namibia | 35 |
| 6 | Niger | 35 |
| 6 | Zambia | 35 |
| 7 | Togo | 37 |
| 8 | Benin | 38 |
| 8 | Congo, Rep. | 38 |
| 9 | Cameroon | 38.5 |
| 10 | Chad | 40 |

Source: Heritage Foundation

# 11.4 Voice and Accountability: Rank

*tough getting yourself heard?*

A poor Nigeria showing.
This indicator measures the influence the country's people have on their govt.

The oil bloc does poorly. Even Nigeria survives in the group, whereas it falls short within the rest of Africa. Perhaps oil and open govt. don't mix.

| | 1998-02 | 2003-06 |
|---|---|---|
| Self-comparison to Preceding Period | | ▲ |
| Performance in Sub-Saharan Africa | ▼ | ▼ |
| Performance in West Africa | ▼ | ▼ |
| | Cape Verde | Cape Verde |
| | Benin | Mali |
| | Mali | Ghana |
| | Senegal | Benin |
| | Ghana | Senegal |
| | Burkina Faso | Niger |
| | Mauritania | Burkina Faso |
| | Niger | Sierra Leone |
| | Gambia, The | Gambia, The |
| | **Nigeria** | Guinea-Bissau |
| | Guinea-Bissau | **Nigeria** |
| | Côte d'Ivoire | Mauritania |
| | Guinea | Liberia |
| | Togo | Guinea |
| | Sierra Leone | Togo |
| | Liberia | Côte d'Ivoire |
| Performance among Oil-Exporters | ▲ | ▲ |
| | Gabon | Gabon |
| | Chad | **Nigeria** |
| | **Nigeria** | Congo, Rep. |
| | Cameroon | Cameroon |
| | Côte d'Ivoire | Angola |
| | Angola | Chad |
| | Congo, Rep. | Côte d'Ivoire |
| | Equatorial Guinea | Equatorial Guinea |
| | Sudan | Sudan |

| | |
|---|---|
| ▲ | improved *or* better than average |
| ▼ | worsened *or* worse than average |
| ◁▷ | no change *or* average |

# 11. Business Friendliness

Rankings of 48 Sub-Saharan Africa Countries
Source: IBRD, World Bank

Central Africa
East Africa
Southern Africa
North Africa
West Africa

| | |
|---|---|
| ▲ | moved up from 98/02 |
| ▼ | moved down from 98/02 |
| blank | no change from 98/02 |

| | Rank | 2003-06 | 1998-2002 |
|---|---|---|---|
| | 1 | Mauritius | Mauritius |
| | 2 | Botswana | Botswana |
| ▲ | 3 | South Africa | Cape Verde |
| ▼ | 4 | Cape Verde | South Africa |
| | 5 | Namibia | Namibia |
| ▼ | 6 | Mali | Sao Tome & Princ. |
| ▼ | 7 | Ghana | Benin |
| ▼ | 8 | Sao Tome & Princ. | Mali |
| | 9 | Seychelles | Seychelles |
| ▼ | 10 | Benin | Madagascar |
| | 11 | Senegal | Senegal |
| ▲ | 12 | Lesotho | Ghana |
| ▼ | 13 | Madagascar | Mozambique |
| ▼ | 14 | Mozambique | Malawi |
| ▲ | 15 | Kenya | Gabon |
| ▲ | 16 | Niger | Tanzania |
| ▲ | 17 | Zambia | Burkina Faso |
| ▲ | 18 | Comoros | Lesotho |
| ▼ | 19 | Tanzania | Zambia |
| ▼ | 20 | Burkina Faso | Comoros |
| ▼ | 21 | Malawi | Mauritania |
| ▲ | 22 | Sierra Leone | Central Afr. Rep. |
| ▲ | 23 | Gambia, The | Niger |
| ▲ | 24 | Guinea-Bissau | Kenya |
| ▲ | 25 | Uganda | Gambia, The |
| ▼ | 26 | Gabon | Djibouti |
| ▲ | 27 | **Nigeria** | Chad |
| ▼ | 28 | Djibouti | **Nigeria** |
| ▼ | 29 | Mauritania | Uganda |
| ▲ | 30 | Congo, Rep. | Ethiopia |
| ▲ | 31 | Cameroon | Guinea-Bissau |
| ▲ | 32 | Burundi | Cameroon |
| ▼ | 33 | Ethiopia | Côte d' Ivoire |
| ▲ | 34 | Liberia | Zimbabwe |
| ▲ | 35 | Angola | Guinea |
| ▼ | 36 | Guinea | Togo |
| ▼ | 37 | Chad | Sierra Leone |
| ▲ | 38 | Rwanda | Swaziland |
| ▼ | 39 | Central Afr. Rep. | Angola |
| ▼ | 40 | Swaziland | Liberia |
| ▼ | 41 | Togo | Congo, Rep. |
| ▼ | 42 | Côte d' Ivoire | Eritrea |
| ▼ | 43 | Zimbabwe | Rwanda |
| ▲ | 44 | Equatorial Guinea | Burundi |
| ▲ | 45 | Sudan | Equatorial Guinea |
| ▲ | 46 | Congo, Dem. Rep. | Sudan |
| | 47 | Somalia | Somalia |
| ▼ | 48 | Eritrea | Congo, Dem. Rep. |

11.2

Voice and Accountability: Nigeria's Ranking in SSA. 1998-2006

Nigeria stayed average on the continent; worse than many, but better than a number. Moved up one notch from 1998-2002 levels.

# 11.5 Political Stability: Rank

*are you feeling the love?*

Touchy topic in Nigeria: there are as many opinions as there are thinkers. Applying empirical methods as here, a poor outing again is the picture.

This time, Nigeria performs poorly within the oil club, too.

| | 1998-02 | 2003-06 |
|---|---|---|
| Self-comparison to Preceding Period | | ▼ |
| Performance in Sub-Saharan Africa | ▼ | ▼ |

| Performance in West Africa | 1998-02 ▼ | 2003-06 ▼ |
|---|---|---|
| | Cape Verde | Cape Verde |
| | Benin | Gambia, The |
| | Gambia, The | Benin |
| | Mali | Ghana |
| | Mauritania | Mali |
| | Ghana | Burkina Faso |
| | Burkina Faso | Senegal |
| | Togo | Mauritania |
| | Niger | Niger |
| | Senegal | Guinea-Bissau |
| | Côte d'Ivoire | Sierra Leone |
| | Guinea | Togo |
| | Guinea-Bissau | Guinea |
| | **Nigeria** | Liberia |
| | Sierra Leone | **Nigeria** |
| | Liberia | Côte d'Ivoire |

| Performance among Oil-Exporters | 1998-02 ▼ | 2003-06 ▼ |
|---|---|---|
| | Gabon | Gabon |
| | Equatorial Guinea | Equatorial Guinea |
| | Cameroon | Cameroon |
| | Côte d'Ivoire | Angola |
| | Congo, Rep. | Congo, Rep. |
| | **Nigeria** | Chad |
| | Chad | **Nigeria** |
| | Angola | Côte d'Ivoire |
| | Sudan | Sudan |

| | |
|---|---|
| ▲ | improved *or* better than average |
| ▼ | worsened *or* worse than average |
| ◁▷ | no change *or* average |

# 11. Business Friendliness

Rankings of 48 Sub-Saharan Africa Countries
Source: IBRD, World Bank

- Central Africa
- East Africa
- Southern Africa
- North Africa
- West Africa

| | |
|---|---|
| ▲ | moved up from 98/02 |
| ▼ | moved down from 98/02 |
| blank | no change from 98/02 |

| | Rank | 2003-06 | 1998-2002 |
|---|---|---|---|
| ▲ | 1 | Botswana | Mauritius |
| ▼ | 2 | Mauritius | Seychelles |
| ▼ | 3 | Seychelles | Cape Verde |
| ▼ | 4 | Cape Verde | Botswana |
| ▲ | 5 | Namibia | Sao Tome & Princ. |
| ▼ | 6 | Sao Tome & Princ. | Benin |
| | 7 | Gambia, The | Gambia, The |
| ▲ | 8 | Lesotho | Mali |
| ▼ | 9 | Benin | Mauritania |
| ▲ | 10 | Ghana | Mozambique |
| ▼ | 11 | Mozambique | Comoros |
| | 12 | Gabon | Gabon |
| ▼ | 13 | Mali | Namibia |
| | 14 | Madagascar | Madagascar |
| ▲ | 15 | Zambia | Swaziland |
| ▼ | 16 | Swaziland | Lesotho |
| ▲ | 17 | Malawi | Ghana |
| | 18 | Burkina Faso | Burkina Faso |
| ▲ | 19 | South Africa | Equatorial Guinea |
| ▼ | 20 | Comoros | Tanzania |
| ▼ | 21 | Equatorial Guinea | Togo |
| ▲ | 22 | Senegal | Zambia |
| ▼ | 23 | Mauritania | Niger |
| ▼ | 24 | Tanzania | Malawi |
| ▼ | 25 | Niger | South Africa |
| | 26 | Cameroon | Cameroon |
| | 27 | Djibouti | Djibouti |
| ▲ | 28 | Guinea-Bissau | Senegal |
| ▲ | 29 | Sierra Leone | Côte d' Ivoire |
| ▼ | 30 | Togo | Ethiopia |
| ▲ | 31 | Eritrea | Kenya |
| ▲ | 32 | Rwanda | Guinea |
| ▲ | 33 | Angola | Guinea-Bissau |
| ▼ | 34 | Guinea | Eritrea |
| | 35 | Congo, Rep. | Congo, Rep. |
| ▼ | 36 | Kenya | **Nigeria** |
| ▲ | 37 | Central Afr. Rep. | Zimbabwe |
| | 38 | Chad | Chad |
| ▲ | 39 | Uganda | Central Afr. Rep. |
| ▼ | 40 | Ethiopia | Uganda |
| ▼ | 41 | Zimbabwe | Sierra Leone |
| ▲ | 42 | Liberia | Rwanda |
| ▲ | 43 | Burundi | Angola |
| ▼ | 44 | **Nigeria** | Liberia |
| ▼ | 45 | Côte d' Ivoire | Sudan |
| ▼ | 46 | Sudan | Burundi |
| ▲ | 47 | Congo, Dem. Rep. | Somalia |
| ▼ | 48 | Somalia | Congo, Dem. Rep. |

11.3

Political Stability: Nigeria's Ranking in SSA. 1998-2006

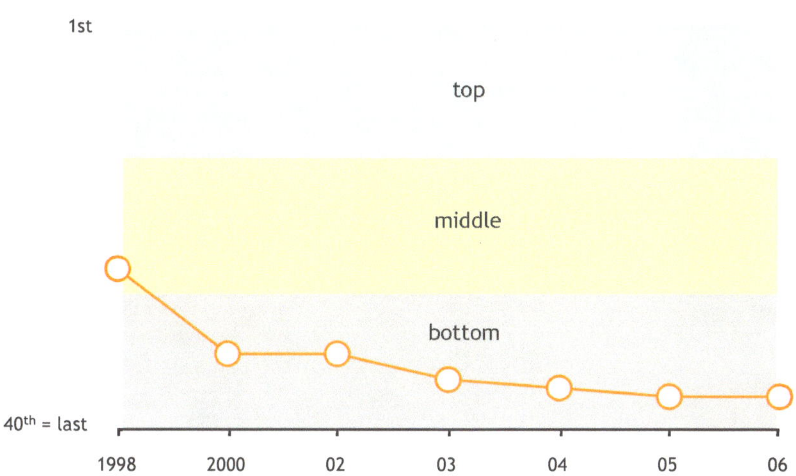


The trend isn't a pretty picture, either: gradual descent in rank, and entrenched in the bottom tier.

# 11.6 Government Effectiveness: Rank

**the waiting game**

Quality of governance in Nigeria improved across 1999-2006. Alas, not substantially enough to better other African countries.

But the oil economies did worse.

| | 1998-02 | 2003-06 |
|---|---|---|
| Self-comparison to Preceding Period | | ▲ |
| Performance in Sub-Saharan Africa | ▼ | ▼ |
| Performance in West Africa | ▼ | ▼ |
| | Cape Verde | Cape Verde |
| | Senegal | Senegal |
| | Ghana | Ghana |
| | Mauritania | Mauritania |
| | Benin | Mali |
| | Gambia, The | Benin |
| | Burkina Faso | Gambia, The |
| | Mali | Burkina Faso |
| | Côte d'Ivoire | Niger |
| | Guinea | **Nigeria** |
| | **Nigeria** | Guinea |
| | Togo | Sierra Leone |
| | Niger | Côte d'Ivoire |
| | Guinea-Bissau | Guinea-Bissau |
| | Sierra Leone | Liberia |
| | Liberia | Togo |
| Performance among Oil-Exporters | ◁▷ | ▲ |
| | Gabon | Gabon |
| | Chad | Cameroon |
| | Côte d'Ivoire | **Nigeria** |
| | Cameroon | Angola |
| | **Nigeria** | Chad |
| | Sudan | Sudan |
| | Angola | Congo, Rep. |
| | Equatorial Guinea | Côte d'Ivoire |
| | Congo, Rep. | Equatorial Guinea |

| | |
|---|---|
| ▲ | improved *or* better than average |
| ▼ | worsened *or* worse than average |
| ◁▷ | no change *or* average |

# 11. Business Friendliness

Rankings of 48 Sub-Saharan Africa Countries
Source: IBRD, World Bank

Central Africa
East Africa
Southern Africa
North Africa
West Africa

| | |
|---|---|
| ▲ | moved up from 98/02 |
| ▼ | moved down from 98/02 |
| blank | no change from 98/02 |

| | Rank | 2003-06 | 1998-2002 |
|---|---|---|---|
| ▲ | 1 | Botswana | South Africa |
| ▼ | 2 | South Africa | Botswana |
| | 3 | Mauritius | Mauritius |
| | 4 | Namibia | Namibia |
| ▲ | 5 | Cape Verde | Seychelles |
| ▼ | 6 | Seychelles | Cape Verde |
| | 7 | Senegal | Senegal |
| | 8 | Ghana | Ghana |
| ▲ | 9 | Madagascar | Mauritania |
| | 10 | Lesotho | Lesotho |
| ▼ | 11 | Mauritania | Mozambique |
| ▲ | 12 | Mali | Benin |
| ▼ | 13 | Mozambique | Gabon |
| ▲ | 14 | Tanzania | Malawi |
| ▼ | 15 | Benin | Tanzania |
| ▲ | 16 | Uganda | Madagascar |
| ▲ | 17 | Gambia, The | Uganda |
| ▼ | 18 | Gabon | Gambia, The |
| ▲ | 19 | Burkina Faso | Sao Tome & Princ. |
| ▲ | 20 | Kenya | Swaziland |
| ▲ | 21 | Ethiopia | Burkina Faso |
| ▼ | 22 | Sao Tome & Princ. | Chad |
| ▲ | 23 | Rwanda | Kenya |
| ▲ | 24 | Djibouti | Mali |
| ▼ | 25 | Malawi | Côte d' Ivoire |
| ▲ | 26 | Niger | Cameroon |
| ▼ | 27 | Swaziland | Zambia |
| ▼ | 28 | Cameroon | Zimbabwe |
| ▼ | 29 | Zambia | Eritrea |
| ▲ | 30 | Nigeria | Djibouti |
| ▼ | 31 | Eritrea | Ethiopia |
| ▲ | 32 | Angola | Guinea |
| ▼ | 33 | Chad | Rwanda |
| ▼ | 34 | Guinea | Nigeria |
| ▲ | 35 | Sudan | Togo |
| ▲ | 36 | Sierra Leone | Niger |
| ▲ | 37 | Congo, Rep. | Sudan |
| ▲ | 38 | Burundi | Guinea-Bissau |
| ▼ | 39 | Côte d' Ivoire | Angola |
| ▲ | 40 | Equatorial Guinea | Comoros |
| ▼ | 41 | Guinea-Bissau | Equatorial Guinea |
| ▼ | 42 | Zimbabwe | Congo, Rep. |
| ▲ | 43 | Liberia | Burundi |
| ▼ | 44 | Togo | Sierra Leone |
| | 45 | Central Afr. Rep. | Central Afr. Rep. |
| ▲ | 46 | Congo, Dem. Rep. | Liberia |
| ▼ | 47 | Comoros | Congo, Dem. Rep. |
| | 48 | Somalia | Somalia |

11.4

Government Effectiveness: Nigeria's Ranking in SSA. 1998-2006

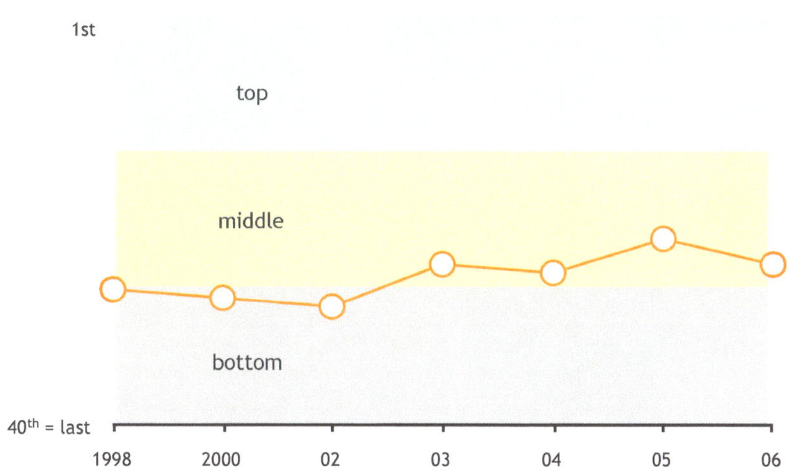


A hesitant climb in 2003 out of the bottom tier and into the average group. But not a confident resurgence; still teetered near the borderline.

# 11.7 Regulatory Quality: Rank

**there's a watching umpire**

Still no respite for Nigeria.

Poor regulation of private (and also, public) sector business practice.

Yet again, the oil economies do badly in Africa.

| | 1998-02 | 2003-06 |
|---|---|---|
| Self-comparison to Preceding Period | | ▼ |
| Performance in Sub-Saharan Africa | ▼ | ▼ |
| Performance in West Africa | ▼ | ▼ |
| | Burkina Faso | Mauritania |
| | Cape Verde | Cape Verde |
| | Benin | Ghana |
| | Senegal | Senegal |
| | Ghana | Burkina Faso |
| | Mali | Gambia, The |
| | Gambia, The | Benin |
| | Côte d'Ivoire | Mali |
| | Mauritania | Niger |
| | Guinea | Togo |
| | Niger | Côte d'Ivoire |
| | Togo | Guinea |
| | **Nigeria** | **Nigeria** |
| | Guinea-Bissau | Guinea-Bissau |
| | Sierra Leone | Sierra Leone |
| | Liberia | Liberia |
| Performance among Oil-Exporters | ◁▷ | ◁▷ |
| | Gabon | Gabon |
| | Côte d'Ivoire | Cameroon |
| | Cameroon | Côte d'Ivoire |
| | Chad | Chad |
| | **Nigeria** | **Nigeria** |
| | Congo, Rep. | Congo, Rep. |
| | Sudan | Sudan |
| | Equatorial Guinea | Angola |
| | Angola | Equatorial Guinea |

| | |
|---|---|
| ▲ | improved *or* better than average |
| ▼ | worsened *or* worse than average |
| ◁▷ | no change *or* average |

# 11. Business Friendliness

Rankings of 48 Sub-Saharan Africa Countries
Source: IBRD, World Bank

- Central Africa
- East Africa
- Southern Africa
- North Africa
- West Africa

| | |
|---|---|
| ▲ | moved up from 98/02 |
| ▼ | moved down from 98/02 |
| blank | no change from 98/02 |

| | Rank | 2003-06 | 1998-2002 |
|---|---|---|---|
| | 1 | Botswana | Botswana |
| ▲ | 2 | South Africa | Mauritius |
| ▼ | 3 | Mauritius | Namibia |
| ▼ | 4 | Namibia | South Africa |
| | 5 | Uganda | Uganda |
| ▲ | 6 | Mauritania | Gabon |
| ▲ | 7 | Kenya | Burkina Faso |
| | 8 | Cape Verde | Cape Verde |
| ▲ | 9 | Ghana | Benin |
| | 10 | Senegal | Senegal |
| ▲ | 11 | Madagascar | Ghana |
| ▼ | 12 | Burkina Faso | Mali |
| ▼ | 13 | Gabon | Zambia |
| ▲ | 14 | Tanzania | Mozambique |
| | 15 | Gambia, The | Gambia, The |
| ▼ | 16 | Benin | Côte d' Ivoire |
| ▼ | 17 | Mali | Malawi |
| ▼ | 18 | Mozambique | Mauritania |
| ▼ | 19 | Malawi | Kenya |
| ▲ | 20 | Niger | Swaziland |
| | 21 | Lesotho | Lesotho |
| ▲ | 22 | Seychelles | Tanzania |
| ▼ | 23 | Swaziland | Madagascar |
| ▼ | 24 | Zambia | Guinea |
| ▲ | 25 | Rwanda | Cameroon |
| ▼ | 26 | Cameroon | Niger |
| ▲ | 27 | Sao Tome & Princ. | Togo |
| ▲ | 28 | Djibouti | Seychelles |
| ▼ | 29 | Togo | Sao Tome & Princ. |
| ▼ | 30 | Côte d' Ivoire | Eritrea |
| ▲ | 31 | Ethiopia | Djibouti |
| ▼ | 32 | Guinea | Chad |
| ▼ | 33 | Chad | **Nigeria** |
| ▼ | 34 | **Nigeria** | Rwanda |
| ▲ | 35 | Guinea-Bissau | Central Afr. Rep. |
| ▲ | 36 | Congo, Rep. | Ethiopia |
| ▲ | 37 | Sierra Leone | Comoros |
| ▲ | 38 | Sudan | Guinea-Bissau |
| ▲ | 39 | Burundi | Congo, Rep. |
| ▲ | 40 | Angola | Zimbabwe |
| ▼ | 41 | Central Afr. Rep. | Sudan |
| ▲ | 42 | Equatorial Guinea | Burundi |
| ▼ | 43 | Comoros | Sierra Leone |
| ▼ | 44 | Eritrea | Equatorial Guinea |
| ▲ | 45 | Congo, Dem. Rep. | Angola |
| | 46 | Liberia | Liberia |
| ▼ | 47 | Zimbabwe | Congo, Dem. Rep. |
| | 48 | Somalia | Somalia |

11.5

Regulatory Quality: Nigeria's Ranking in SSA. 1998-2006

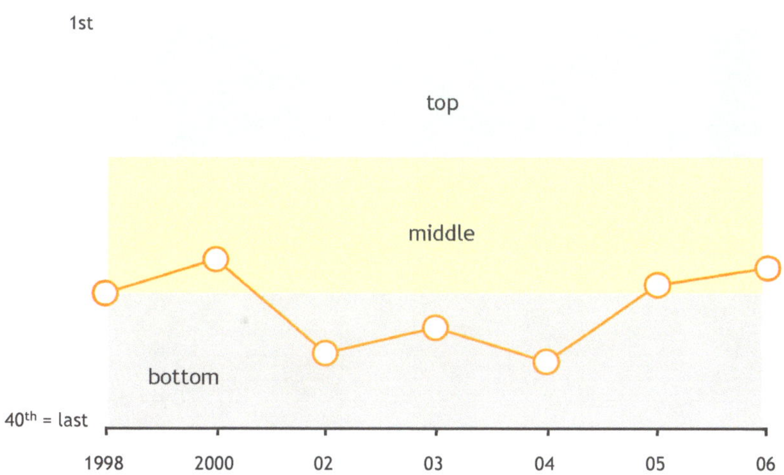


Things began to look up in Nigeria during 2005. But unclear how strong a break-out from the bottom that movement connoted.

# 11.8 Rule of Law: Rank

***hopefully, more than a mantra***

Rule of Law performance: not good news for Nigeria.
Better picture almost everywhere else in West Africa, and among the oil economies as well.

| | 1998-02 | 2003-06 |
|---|---|---|
| Self-comparison to Preceding Period | | ▼ |
| Performance in Sub-Saharan Africa | ▼ | ▼ |

| Performance in West Africa | 1998-02 | 2003-06 |
|---|---|---|
| | ▼ | ▼ |
| | Cape Verde | Cape Verde |
| | Senegal | Mali |
| | Gambia, The | Gambia, The |
| | Ghana | Ghana |
| | Benin | Senegal |
| | Mauritania | Mauritania |
| | Mali | Burkina Faso |
| | Burkina Faso | Benin |
| | Togo | Niger |
| | Niger | Togo |
| | Côte d'Ivoire | Sierra Leone |
| | Guinea | Guinea-Bissau |
| | **Nigeria** | Guinea |
| | Sierra Leone | **Nigeria** |
| | Guinea-Bissau | Liberia |
| | Liberia | Côte d'Ivoire |

| Performance among Oil-Exporters | 1998-02 | 2003-06 |
|---|---|---|
| | ▼ | ▼ |
| | Gabon | Gabon |
| | Chad | Cameroon |
| | Côte d'Ivoire | Chad |
| | Cameroon | Equatorial Guinea |
| | Equatorial Guinea | Congo, Rep. |
| | **Nigeria** | Angola |
| | Congo, Rep. | **Nigeria** |
| | Sudan | Sudan |
| | Angola | Côte d'Ivoire |

| | |
|---|---|
| ▲ | improved *or* better than average |
| ▼ | worsened *or* worse than average |
| ◁▷ | no change *or* average |

Rankings of 48 Sub-Saharan Africa Countries
Source: IBRD, World Bank

- Central Africa
- East Africa
- Southern Africa
- North Africa
- West Africa

| | |
|---|---|
| ▲ | moved up from 98/02 |
| ▼ | moved down from 98/02 |
| blank | no change from 98/02 |

| | Rank | 2003-06 | 1998-2002 |
|---|---|---|---|
| | 1 | Mauritius | Mauritius |
| ▲ | 2 | Botswana | Cape Verde |
| ▼ | 3 | Cape Verde | Seychelles |
| ▼ | 4 | Seychelles | Botswana |
| ▲ | 5 | South Africa | Namibia |
| ▼ | 6 | Namibia | South Africa |
| | 7 | Lesotho | Lesotho |
| ▲ | 8 | Mali | Senegal |
| | 9 | Gambia, The | Gambia, The |
| ▲ | 10 | Madagascar | Ghana |
| ▼ | 11 | Ghana | Benin |
| ▼ | 12 | Senegal | Gabon |
| ▲ | 13 | Malawi | Sao Tome & Princ. |
| ▲ | 14 | Tanzania | Eritrea |
| | 15 | Mauritania | Mauritania |
| ▼ | 16 | Sao Tome & Princ. | Madagascar |
| ▲ | 17 | Burkina Faso | Mali |
| ▼ | 18 | Gabon | Tanzania |
| ▼ | 19 | Benin | Malawi |
| | 20 | Zambia | Zambia |
| ▼ | 21 | Eritrea | Swaziland |
| ▲ | 22 | Uganda | Burkina Faso |
| ▲ | 23 | Mozambique | Togo |
| ▲ | 24 | Ethiopia | Uganda |
| ▲ | 25 | Rwanda | Mozambique |
| | 26 | Djibouti | Djibouti |
| ▼ | 27 | Swaziland | Ethiopia |
| | 28 | Niger | Niger |
| ▲ | 29 | Comoros | Chad |
| | 30 | Kenya | Kenya |
| ▼ | 31 | Togo | Zimbabwe |
| ▲ | 32 | Cameroon | Côte d' Ivoire |
| ▲ | 33 | Sierra Leone | Cameroon |
| ▲ | 34 | Burundi | Guinea |
| ▲ | 35 | Guinea-Bissau | Comoros |
| ▼ | 36 | Chad | Rwanda |
| | 37 | Equatorial Guinea | Equatorial Guinea |
| ▼ | 38 | Guinea | **Nigeria** |
| ▲ | 39 | Congo, Rep. | Sierra Leone |
| ▲ | 40 | Angola | Central Afr. Rep. |
| ▼ | 41 | **Nigeria** | Congo, Rep. |
| ▲ | 42 | Liberia | Guinea-Bissau |
| ▲ | 43 | Sudan | Burundi |
| ▼ | 44 | Côte d' Ivoire | Sudan |
| ▼ | 45 | Central Afr. Rep. | Angola |
| ▼ | 46 | Zimbabwe | Liberia |
| | 47 | Congo, Dem. Rep. | Congo, Dem. Rep. |
| | 48 | Somalia | Somalia |

11.6

Rule of Law: Nigeria's Ranking in SSA. 1998-2006

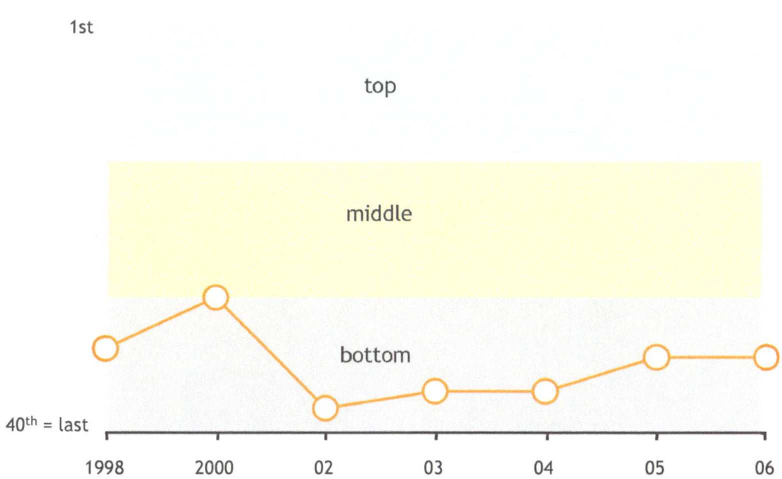


Brief climb-out attempt in 2000. Then a fall, back onto the bottom tier. During 03/06, only Liberia and Côte d' Ivoire did worse in West Africa.

# 11.9 Control of Corruption: Rank

## *disappearing act*

*Another tetchy topic, and another poor Nigeria showing. There was a cleaner climate everywhere else in West Africa.*

| | 1998-02 | 2003-06 |
|---|---|---|
| Self-comparison to Preceding Period | | ▼ |
| Performance in Sub-Saharan Africa | ▼ | ▼ |
| Performance in West Africa | ▼ | ▼ |
| | Cape Verde | Cape Verde |
| | Burkina Faso | Burkina Faso |
| | Mauritania | Mauritania |
| | Senegal | Ghana |
| | Ghana | Senegal |
| | Gambia, The | Mali |
| | Mali | Gambia, The |
| | Côte d'Ivoire | Benin |
| | Togo | Togo |
| | Benin | Guinea |
| | Guinea | Niger |
| | Sierra Leone | Sierra Leone |
| | Guinea-Bissau | Guinea-Bissau |
| | Niger | Liberia |
| | **Nigeria** | Côte d'Ivoire |
| | Liberia | **Nigeria** |
| Performance among Oil-Exporters | ▼ | ▼ |
| | Côte d'Ivoire | Gabon |
| | Gabon | Cameroon |
| | Chad | Congo, Rep. |
| | Sudan | Côte d'Ivoire |
| | Congo, Rep. | Angola |
| | Cameroon | Chad |
| | **Nigeria** | Sudan |
| | Angola | **Nigeria** |
| | Equatorial Guinea | Equatorial Guinea |

| | |
|---|---|
| ▲ | improved *or* better than average |
| ▼ | worsened *or* worse than average |
| ◁▷ | no change *or* average |

Rankings of 48 Sub-Saharan Africa Countries
Source: IBRD, World Bank

Central Africa
East Africa
Southern Africa
North Africa
West Africa

| | |
|---|---|
| ▲ | moved up from 98/02 |
| ▼ | moved down from 98/02 |
| blank | no change from 98/02 |

| | Rank | 2003-06 | 1998-2002 |
|---|---|---|---|
| | 1 | Botswana | Botswana |
| ▲ | 2 | South Africa | Eritrea |
| ▲ | 3 | Cape Verde | South Africa |
| | 4 | Mauritius | Mauritius |
| | 5 | Seychelles | Seychelles |
| | 6 | Namibia | Namibia |
| ▲ | 7 | Madagascar | Cape Verde |
| | 8 | Burkina Faso | Burkina Faso |
| ▲ | 9 | Lesotho | Mauritania |
| ▼ | 10 | Eritrea | Swaziland |
| ▼ | 11 | Mauritania | Lesotho |
| ▲ | 12 | Ghana | Madagascar |
| | 13 | Senegal | Senegal |
| ▲ | 14 | Mali | Sao Tome & Princ. |
| ▲ | 15 | Rwanda | Ghana |
| ▼ | 16 | Swaziland | Gambia, The |
| ▼ | 17 | Gambia, The | Ethiopia |
| ▲ | 18 | Mozambique | Mali |
| ▼ | 19 | Ethiopia | Côte d' Ivoire |
| ▲ | 20 | Gabon | Malawi |
| ▼ | 21 | Sao Tome & Princ. | Gabon |
| ▲ | 22 | Tanzania | Togo |
| ▲ | 23 | Djibouti | Benin |
| ▼ | 24 | Benin | Mozambique |
| ▲ | 25 | Uganda | Rwanda |
| ▼ | 26 | Malawi | Guinea |
| ▲ | 27 | Comoros | Djibouti |
| ▼ | 28 | Togo | Chad |
| ▲ | 29 | Zambia | Sierra Leone |
| ▼ | 30 | Guinea | Zimbabwe |
| ▲ | 31 | Kenya | Zambia |
| ▲ | 32 | Cameroon | Guinea-Bissau |
| ▲ | 33 | Niger | Uganda |
| ▲ | 34 | Burundi | Sudan |
| ▲ | 35 | Congo, Rep. | Comoros |
| ▼ | 36 | Sierra Leone | Niger |
| ▼ | 37 | Guinea-Bissau | Tanzania |
| ▲ | 38 | Liberia | Kenya |
| ▼ | 39 | Côte d' Ivoire | Congo, Rep. |
| ▲ | 40 | Angola | Burundi |
| ▲ | 41 | Central Afr. Rep. | Cameroon |
| ▼ | 42 | Chad | Central Afr. Rep. |
| ▼ | 43 | Sudan | **Nigeria** |
| ▼ | 44 | Zimbabwe | Angola |
| ▼ | 45 | **Nigeria** | Somalia |
| | 46 | Congo, Dem. Rep. | Congo, Dem. Rep. |
| ▲ | 47 | Equatorial Guinea | Liberia |
| ▼ | 48 | Somalia | Equatorial Guinea |

11.7

Control of Corruption: Nigeria's Ranking in SSA. 1998-2006

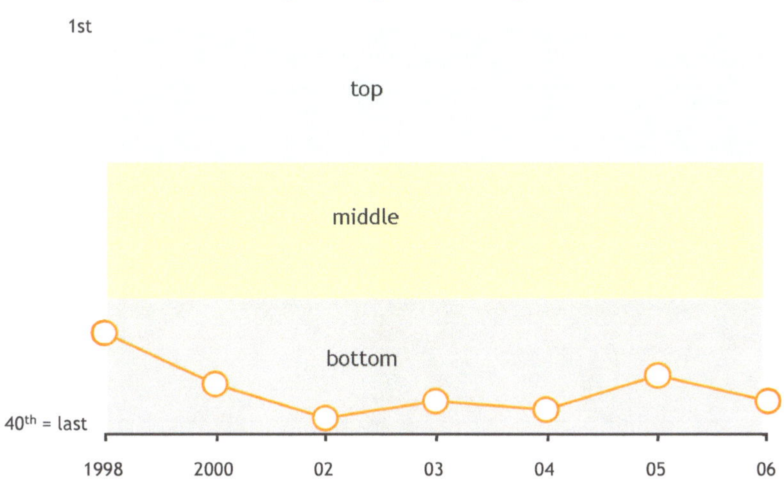


Stranded at the bottom.

## Leaders & Stragglers

**Never mind the red, it's mostly green**

### Business Friendliness Rankings: 2003-08

| Rank | Country |
|---|---|
| 1 | Mauritius |
| 2 | Botswana |
| 3 | South Africa |
| 4 | Cape Verde |
| 5 | Namibia |
| 6 | Ghana |
| 7 | Madagascar |
| 8 | Senegal |
| 9 | Lesotho |
| 10 | Mali |
| 11 | Tanzania |
| 12 | Burkina Faso |
| 13 | Mozambique |

TOP

| Rank | Country |
|---|---|
| 14 | Gambia, The |
| 15 | Uganda |
| 16 | Kenya |
| 17 | Benin |
| 18 | Malawi |
| 19 | Swaziland |
| 20 | Zambia |
| 21 | Gabon |
| 22 | Rwanda |
| 23 | Niger |
| 24 | Ethiopia |
| 25 | Guinea-Bissau |

MIDDLE

| Rank | Country |
|---|---|
| 26 | Cameroon |
| 27 | Sierra Leone |
| 28 | **Nigeria** |
| 29 | Guinea |
| 30 | Angola |
| 31 | Togo |
| 32 | Equatorial Guinea |
| 33 | Burundi |
| 34 | Côte d' Ivoire |
| 35 | Congo, Rep. |
| 36 | Central Afr. Rep. |
| 37 | Chad |
| n/a | Comoros |
| n/a | Congo, Dem. Rep. |
| n/a | Eritrea |
| n/a | Seychelles |

BOTTOM

Central Africa
East Africa
Southern Africa
West Africa

Many parameters here have already been represented in previous sections, so this end-table outcome doesn't go towards the final definitive rankings.

But it is still worth noting that Nigeria is 4th from bottom in West Africa & needs to make its business environment more endearing to stakeholders.

Cape Verde, Ghana, Senegal & Mali are the most business friendly environments in West Africa and count among the top 10 in Sub-Saharan Africa.

# Wrap-up: Business Friendliness

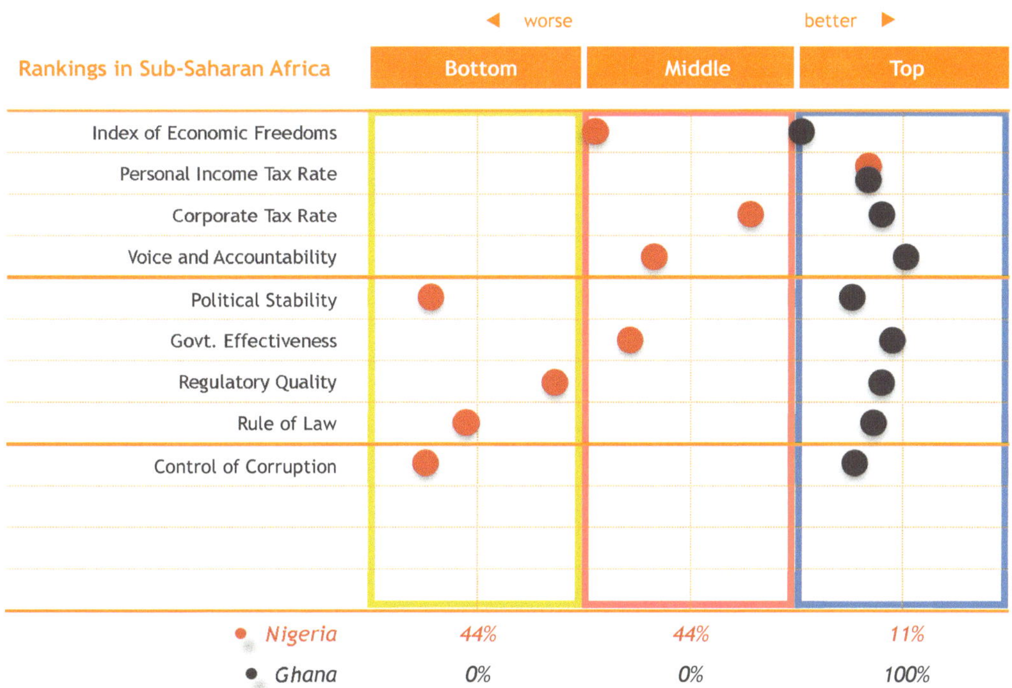


- Comparing Nigeria with Ghana this time, the reason for the gulf in friendliness ranking is easy to see. Ghana scores top-bracket performance in every area. Nigeria ends up mainly in the middle and bottom-brackets.

- Nigeria does best in level of personal income tax, followed by level of company taxes. But it is dragged down by very poor scores for political environment, rule of law and control of corruption,

- Ghana outdoes Nigeria in every measure and does best in voice & accountability. Then government effectiveness and company tax rates.

# 12. The Final Ratings

*and the winners are...*

## The Dba Ranking and Dba Rating

This final chapter brings all the preceding analyses to a culmination. It assesses 41 Sub-Saharan Africa economies (out of 48) across 56 critical socio-economic indicators among the 200 employed for this DBWA 2009-2010 compilation - the so-called Dba [dee-bee-aay] indicators. The outcome is the 2009-2010 Dba Rankings and Ratings.

All 48 Sub-Saharan Africa economies are involved in this study, but 7 of the economies were missing data among the critical 56 indicators. They are Djibouti, Liberia, Mauritania, São Tomé & Príncipe, Somalia, Sudan and Zimbabwe. And so, they are not included in the ensuing Dba ranking and ratings.

(Note, though, that appendix B, which follows this chapter is exhaustive and carries individual tables for near all indicators employed in this study, including the 56 critical indices, showing how all the countries with that specific data available, stack up. Hence, wherever their data is at hand, the 7 countries absent from the final rankings, are also shown there, in the position they occupy according to their performance, although without final assigned ratings.)

## Methodology

The procedure for this final rankings is straightforward: each of the book's main chapters ends with a final table-ranking of performance across the critical indicators in that chapter. The aggregate scores across these critical indicators, through all the main chapters, are evaluated, and rankings derived from the countries' relative performance positions. These are the *Dba Rankings*.

*Dba Ratings* range from one star to five stars, out of five. The country aggregate scores go from 0 for worst performance, to 10 for best performance. That range is divided into 5 equal sections, that is: 0 to 1.99, 2 to 3.99, 4 to 5.99, 6 to 7.99 and 8 to 10. These divisions carry the ratings of 1, 2, 3, 4 and 5 stars, respectively; all out of the maximum 5. A 5-star rating would mean "excellent", down to a 1-star rating meaning "worst".

## Assessments, not Final Say

Please note that the Dba rankings and ratings are purely assessments according to a specific body of indicators and specific methods of evaluation; and they have been well described in the main chapters of this volume and in its appendix A. They are not hard-and-fast allocations, and do not attempt to recommend a particular country for specific business purposes.

Nonetheless, they are intended as a guide, while decisions or steps taken are the responsibility of the business owners themselves. The *Dba Rankings* and *Ratings*, however, do have the immense advantage of being entirely transparent, so that where the user is familiar with aspects of a specific economy, they may feel comfortable to make allowances for that country's good or poor performance in a particular area, and effectively attach a weight to an indicator different from the equal weighting assigned across them in the Dba evaluation. The user may thereby make appropriate allowances for countries' performances in coming to a business decision, should they so wish.

# Tables

Dba Ranking by Rank

Dba Ranking by Rating

Dba Ranking by Country

Dba Ranking by Sub-Region

# 12.1 Dba Ranking by Rank

| Rank | Country | Rating |
|---|---|---|
| 1 | Botswana | ★★★★☆ |
| 2 | South Africa | ★★★★☆ |
| 3 | Namibia | ★★★★☆ |
| 4 | Mauritius | ★★★★☆ |
| 5 | Cape Verde | ★★★★☆ |
| 6 | Equatorial Guinea | ★★★★☆ |
| 7 | Seychelles | ★★★★☆ |
| 8 | Ghana | ★★★☆☆ |
| 9 | Gabon | ★★★☆☆ |
| 10 | Nigeria | ★★★☆☆ |
| 11 | Senegal | ★★★☆☆ |
| 12 | Kenya | ★★★☆☆ |
| 13 | Tanzania | ★★★☆☆ |
| 14 | Angola | ★★★☆☆ |

TOP

Central Africa
East Africa
Southern Africa
West Africa

| Rank | Country | Rating |
|---|---|---|
| 15 | Swaziland | ★★★☆☆ |
| 16 | Lesotho | ★★★☆☆ |
| 17 | Uganda | ★★★☆☆ |
| 18 | Zambia | ★★★☆☆ |
| 19 | Gambia, The | ★★★☆☆ |
| 20 | Benin | ★★★☆☆ |
| 21 | Burkina Faso | ★★★☆☆ |
| 22 | Cameroon | ★★★☆☆ |
| 23 | Madagascar | ★★★☆☆ |
| 24 | Congo, Rep. | ★★★☆☆ |
| 25 | Ethiopia | ★★★☆☆ |
| 26 | Mali | ★★★☆☆ |
| 27 | Mozambique | ★★★☆☆ |
| 28 | Malawi | ★★★☆☆ |

MIDDLE

| Rank | Country | Rating |
|---|---|---|
| 29 | Chad | ★★★☆☆ |
| 30 | Rwanda | ★★★☆☆ |
| 31 | Togo | ★★★☆☆ |
| 32 | Côte d' Ivoire | ★★★☆☆ |
| 33 | Niger | ★★☆☆☆ |
| 34 | Sierra Leone | ★★☆☆☆ |
| 35 | Comoros | ★★☆☆☆ |
| 36 | Guinea | ★★☆☆☆ |
| 37 | Congo, Dem. Rep. | ★★☆☆☆ |
| 38 | Central Afr. Rep. | ★★☆☆☆ |
| 39 | Guinea-Bissau | ★★☆☆☆ |
| 40 | Eritrea | ★★☆☆☆ |
| 41 | Burundi | ★★☆☆☆ |

BOTTOM

There are no 5-star finishers. But neither are there any 1-stars. Instead, the 41 countries breakdown like this: 7 4-stars, 25 3-stars & 9 2-stars.

Central Africa & East Africa have 2 countries each in the top-10. The bottom-10 has 2 Central Africans, 3 East Africans, & 5 West Africans.

Nigeria is in 10th place, & is the 3rd highest ranked West African country after Cape Verde & Ghana.

The top-10 involve countries from all 4 sub-regions, with the smallest, Southern Africa, and one of the largest, West Africa, leading with 3 countries each.

Africa's best 3 performers are Botswana, South Africa & Namibia, all Southern Africans. They are followed by Mauritius, Cape Verde, & Equatorial Guinea.

The 3 Southerners make up the top-3 places.

# 12.2 Dba Ranking by Rating

Central Africa
East Africa
Southern Africa
West Africa

| Rank | Country | Score | Rating |
|---|---|---|---|
| 1 | Botswana | 6.985 | ★★★★☆ |
| 2 | South Africa | 6.941 | ★★★★☆ |
| 3 | Namibia | 6.779 | ★★★★☆ |
| 4 | Mauritius | 6.535 | ★★★★☆ |
| 5 | Cape Verde | 6.299 | ★★★★☆ |
| 6 | Equatorial Guinea | 6.275 | ★★★★☆ |
| 7 | Seychelles | 6.207 | ★★★★☆ |

7 countries: 17%

| Rank | Country | Score | Rating |
|---|---|---|---|
| 8 | Ghana | 5.738 | ★★★☆☆ |
| 9 | Gabon | 5.696 | ★★★☆☆ |
| 10 | **Nigeria** | 5.548 | ★★★☆☆ |
| 11 | Senegal | 5.504 | ★★★☆☆ |
| 12 | Kenya | 5.461 | ★★★☆☆ |
| 13 | Tanzania | 5.37 | ★★★☆☆ |
| 14 | Angola | 5.283 | ★★★☆☆ |
| 15 | Swaziland | 5.096 | ★★★☆☆ |
| 16 | Lesotho | 5.025 | ★★★☆☆ |
| 17 | Uganda | 4.998 | ★★★☆☆ |
| 18 | Zambia | 4.985 | ★★★☆☆ |
| 19 | Gambia, The | 4.919 | ★★★☆☆ |
| 20 | Benin | 4.91 | ★★★☆☆ |
| 21 | Burkina Faso | 4.902 | ★★★☆☆ |
| 22 | Cameroon | 4.901 | ★★★☆☆ |
| 23 | Madagascar | 4.809 | ★★★☆☆ |
| 24 | Congo, Rep. | 4.759 | ★★★☆☆ |
| 25 | Ethiopia | 4.721 | ★★★☆☆ |
| 26 | Mali | 4.715 | ★★★☆☆ |
| 27 | Mozambique | 4.685 | ★★★☆☆ |
| 28 | Malawi | 4.528 | ★★★☆☆ |
| 29 | Chad | 4.452 | ★★★☆☆ |
| 30 | Rwanda | 4.402 | ★★★☆☆ |
| 31 | Togo | 4.235 | ★★★☆☆ |
| 32 | Côte d' Ivoire | 4.146 | ★★★☆☆ |

25 countries: 61%

| Rank | Country | Score | Rating |
|---|---|---|---|
| 33 | Niger | 3.738 | ★★☆☆☆ |
| 34 | Sierra Leone | 3.701 | ★★☆☆☆ |
| 35 | Comoros | 3.689 | ★★☆☆☆ |
| 36 | Guinea | 3.335 | ★★☆☆☆ |
| 37 | Congo, Dem. Rep. | 3.161 | ★★☆☆☆ |
| 38 | Central Afr. Rep. | 2.951 | ★★☆☆☆ |
| 39 | Guinea-Bissau | 2.935 | ★★☆☆☆ |
| 40 | Eritrea | 2.866 | ★★☆☆☆ |
| 41 | Burundi | 2.638 | ★★☆☆☆ |

9 countries: 22%

East and West Africa have the same number of countries among the 41: 14 each. And they break down across the 3 rating categories differently:

| | 4-stars | 3-stars | 2-stars |
|---|---|---|---|
| East | 14% | 64% | 22% |
| West | 7% | 64% | 29% |

A large majority of the 41 countries fall into the 3-star rating category (61%), followed by the 2-star (22%), then the 4-star superior finishers (17%).

# 12.3 Dba Ranking by Country

| Rank | Country | Rating |
|---|---|---|
| 14 | Angola | ★★★☆☆ |
| 20 | Benin | ★★★☆☆ |
| 1 | Botswana | ★★★★☆ |
| 21 | Burkina Faso | ★★★☆☆ |
| 41 | Burundi | ★★☆☆☆ |
| 22 | Cameroon | ★★★☆☆ |
| 5 | Cape Verde | ★★★★☆ |
| 38 | Central Afr. Rep. | ★★☆☆☆ |
| 29 | Chad | ★★★☆☆ |
| 35 | Comoros | ★★☆☆☆ |
| 37 | Congo, Dem. Rep. | ★★☆☆☆ |
| 24 | Congo, Rep. | ★★★☆☆ |
| 32 | Côte d' Ivoire | ★★★☆☆ |
| 6 | Equatorial Guinea | ★★★★☆ |
| 40 | Eritrea | ★★☆☆☆ |
| 25 | Ethiopia | ★★★☆☆ |
| 9 | Gabon | ★★★☆☆ |
| 19 | Gambia, The | ★★★☆☆ |
| 8 | Ghana | ★★★☆☆ |
| 36 | Guinea | ★★☆☆☆ |
| 39 | Guinea-Bissau | ★★☆☆☆ |

| Rank | Country | Rating |
|---|---|---|
| 12 | Kenya | ★★★☆☆ |
| 16 | Lesotho | ★★★☆☆ |
| 23 | Madagascar | ★★★☆☆ |
| 28 | Malawi | ★★★☆☆ |
| 26 | Mali | ★★★☆☆ |
| 4 | Mauritius | ★★★★☆ |
| 27 | Mozambique | ★★★☆☆ |
| 3 | Namibia | ★★★★☆ |
| 33 | Niger | ★★☆☆☆ |
| 10 | **Nigeria** | ★★★☆☆ |
| 30 | Rwanda | ★★★☆☆ |
| 11 | Senegal | ★★★☆☆ |
| 7 | Seychelles | ★★★★☆ |
| 34 | Sierra Leone | ★★☆☆☆ |
| 2 | South Africa | ★★★★☆ |
| 15 | Swaziland | ★★★☆☆ |
| 13 | Tanzania | ★★★☆☆ |
| 31 | Togo | ★★★☆☆ |
| 17 | Uganda | ★★★☆☆ |
| 18 | Zambia | ★★★☆☆ |

Central Africa
East Africa
Southern Africa
West Africa

*nice country, that*

# 12.4 Dba Ranking by Sub-Region

| Rank | Country | Rating |
|---|---|---|
| 6 | Equatorial Guinea | ★★★★☆ |
| 9 | Gabon | ★★★☆☆ |
| 14 | Angola | ★★★☆☆ |
| 22 | Cameroon | ★★★☆☆ |
| 24 | Congo, Rep. | ★★★☆☆ |
| 29 | Chad | ★★★☆☆ |
| 37 | Congo, Dem. Rep. | ★★☆☆☆ |
| 38 | Central Afr. Rep. | ★★☆☆☆ |

CENTRAL AFRICA

| Rank | Country | Rating |
|---|---|---|
| 5 | Cape Verde | ★★★★☆ |
| 8 | Ghana | ★★★☆☆ |
| 10 | Nigeria | ★★★☆☆ |
| 11 | Senegal | ★★★☆☆ |
| 19 | Gambia, The | ★★★☆☆ |
| 20 | Benin | ★★★☆☆ |
| 21 | Burkina Faso | ★★★☆☆ |
| 26 | Mali | ★★★☆☆ |
| 31 | Togo | ★★★☆☆ |
| 32 | Côte d' Ivoire | ★★★☆☆ |
| 33 | Niger | ★★☆☆☆ |
| 34 | Sierra Leone | ★★☆☆☆ |
| 36 | Guinea | ★★☆☆☆ |
| 39 | Guinea-Bissau | ★★☆☆☆ |

WEST AFRICA

| Rank | Country | Rating |
|---|---|---|
| 4 | Mauritius | ★★★★☆ |
| 7 | Seychelles | ★★★★☆ |
| 12 | Kenya | ★★★☆☆ |
| 13 | Tanzania | ★★★☆☆ |
| 17 | Uganda | ★★★☆☆ |
| 18 | Zambia | ★★★☆☆ |
| 23 | Madagascar | ★★★☆☆ |
| 25 | Ethiopia | ★★★☆☆ |
| 27 | Mozambique | ★★★☆☆ |
| 28 | Malawi | ★★★☆☆ |
| 30 | Rwanda | ★★★☆☆ |
| 35 | Comoros | ★★☆☆☆ |
| 40 | Eritrea | ★★☆☆☆ |
| 41 | Burundi | ★★☆☆☆ |

EAST AFRICA

| Rank | Country | Rating |
|---|---|---|
| 1 | Botswana | ★★★★☆ |
| 2 | South Africa | ★★★★☆ |
| 3 | Namibia | ★★★★☆ |
| 15 | Swaziland | ★★★☆☆ |
| 16 | Lesotho | ★★★☆☆ |

SOUTHERN AFRICA

The top 6 economies in Central Africa - out of 8 - are oil exporters.

Not so in West Africa, where there are 2 oil exporters - Nigeria & Côte d'Ivoire - and they end up far apart. Quite likely a result of the civil war in Côte d'Ivoire.

All the sub-regions, save Southern Africa, have their countries spanning across three tiers of performance: 4-star, 3-star and 2-star.

Only Southern Africa has a majority of its countries chalking up a 4-star rating. It is the smallest sub-region, though.

| | 4-stars | 3-stars | 2-stars |
|---|---|---|---|
| Central | 12% | 63% | 25% |
| East | 14% | 64% | 22% |
| Southern | 60% | 40% | 0% |
| West | 7% | 64% | 29% |

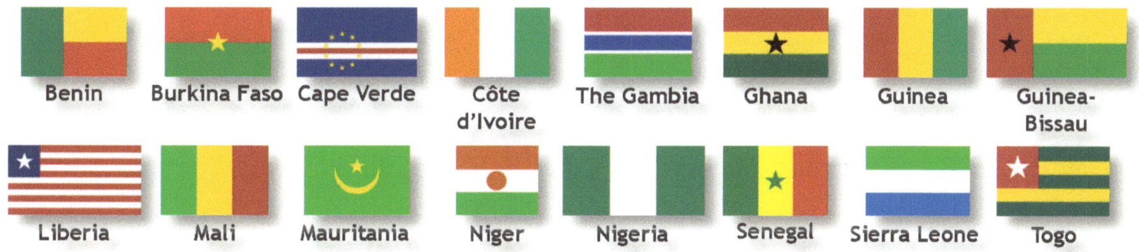

# Part III:

# Appendices

# A. Dba Index & Rankings & Ratings

# A1 Dba

***The Dba [dee-be-ay] Index*** is an assessment of the economic and business environment prevailing in the countries that make up Sub-Saharan Africa. The letters stand for **D**oing **b**usiness in **a**frica and it is the first assessment and innovation of the sort.

The index ranges from zero to 10, representing worst and best, and it expresses the countries' performance across an array of relevant parameters, evaluated over the latest continuous four years with definitive data, within the preceding 6 years in the build-up to the index's reference year. In other words, Dba 2009-2010 considers country performance across 2003 to 2009, using any continuous four years during the period with confirmed and not provisional data. This is done with a view to presenting accurate scenarios and persisting trends that are of importance to investors, businesses, governments and other myriad purposes for which a clear and concise picture of the region's economic and social situation is crucial.

## 56 "Critical" Indicators

A total of 56 "critical" macro and socio-economic indices are employed, selected from the 200 involved in the in-depth compilation of country analyses in the book, *Doing Business in West Africa 2009-2010*. All of them are taken from the latest data held by various leading multilateral agencies like the World Bank and the World Health Organisation, that is available at the time of evaluation. The sources of these indicators are always identified.

In almost every case, these indices are analysed and adapted to enable a comparative evaluation of each country in the context of the sub-continent. So, for example, rather than use just size of GDP outright for cross-country comparisons, GDP per person of population is applied, instead. That is a more accurate measure of country output; what is being assessed there is the efficiency with which the country deploys its resources and factors of production in producing the volume of GDP. Otherwise, countries like Nigeria and South Africa would stand out for the sheer volume of their GDP, whereas, when that performance is rated across their populations, South Africa ranks considerably higher than Nigeria, in terms of GDP per person of population. That ranking shows that economic productivity in South Africa is more efficient and robust.

The same applies to Foreign Direct Investment (FDI), Manufacturing Output, etc. They are all better evaluated as a proportion of either the overall size of the economy (percentage of GDP) or its population (per person). Both evaluations are applied throughout our *Doing Business in Africa* series. In effect, ratios are the important parameters for comparison.

## 11 Specific Areas

These 56 indicators come from the same 11 areas of assessment into which we have split the countries' broad spectrum of economic and national life, as would interest the business practitioner or other user of the book and index:

- General Size
- Quality of life
- Economic strength
- Economic productivity
- Government earning and spending
- Spending on health
- Purchasing power
- Self-reliance
- Investor confidence
- Regulatory environment
- Business friendliness

## Methodology

(This is protected by relevant patent, copyright and trademark laws.)

All the countries are ranked for each of the 56 indices, based on their performance in the specific area during four years leading to the Dba publication year. So, for instance, 'Dba 2009-2010' involves the countries' performance with respect to each index, across the latest 4 contiguous years of definitive data between 2003 and 2009. The same four years are applied for the same indicator across all the countries, so that every country's performance is evaluated for the same base years.

The highest ranking would imply the best performing, and the lowest the worst performing, of the 48 countries that make up Sub-Saharan Africa. In the end, each country's aggregate ranking across the entire spectrum of 56 indices would be its Dba index for that reference year.

It is clear, therefore, that Dba is not an absolute scoring of country performance, but is instead an assessment of the country's performance relative to others in the Sub-Saharan Africa region. In other words, while a country may perform well or poorly in a given sector, its overall relative score would help express its performance in a total context, which - in the end - is usually what matters for investors and businesses.

## 41 of the Continent's 48 Countries

However, not every country had sufficient data available for a Dba evaluation. Our criterion was that missing data must not constitute more than 5% of the total applied; in this case, 3 out of 56. Domestic data from the individual countries (usually their Office of Statistics and Central Banks) was deliberately avoided, as this was not likely to provide a satisfactory common and objective basis for cross-country comparison and assessment. It was important to use external and "detached" assessors, which the multilaterals like the IMF, World Bank, UNICEF and so on, suitably represent.

7 of the 48 countries ended up outside the scope of Dba 2009-2010, for insufficient data. They are: Djibouti, Liberia, Mauritania, Sao Tome & Principe, Somalia, Sudan and Zimbabwe. However, these seven countries are assessed in every indicator for which they had data, and their performance can be gleaned from the respective indicator ranking tables supplied in the body of the book and in appendix B.

## Unequivocal, yet Flexible

It should be borne in mind, though, that while the Dba Index is a wide-spanning comparative assessment of country performance, other factors about a particular country that ranks poorly (whether out of the 41 included or the 7 omitted) might still recommend them for whatever purpose the investor or user is concerned with. Their specific performance in a particular area can be seen in the rest of the book and might very well be a deciding factor.

One advantage of our Dba Index is that its procedure is transparent, and its user may choose to adapt it further to their needs by assigning a weight or level of importance to particular areas different from that which the index itself assumed. (So far, the 56 indices carry equal weighting; this will be adjusted as appropriate over subsequent Dba editions.)

To the best of our knowledge, there isn't yet anywhere else, as comprehensive and rigourous a ranking as the Dba Index, None provides a level comparable to its in-depth macro and socio-economy wide comparative evaluations of country performance in Sub-Saharan Africa.

# B. performance tables

| | Surface Area | | Population (IMF estimates) 2009 | | Population Density (UNPD estimates) 2005-2010 |
|---|---|---|---|---|---|
| | *largest* | | *largest* | | *most dense* |
| 1 | Sudan | 1 | Nigeria | 1 | Mauritius |
| 2 | Congo, Dem. Rep. | 2 | Ethiopia | 2 | Comoros |
| 3 | Chad | 3 | Congo, Dem. Rep. | 3 | Rwanda |
| 4 | Niger | 4 | South Africa | 4 | Burundi |
| 5 | Angola | 5 | Tanzania | 5 | Sao Tome & Principe |
| 6 | Mali | 6 | Sudan | 6 | Nigeria |
| 7 | South Africa | 7 | Kenya | 7 | Gambia, The |
| 8 | Ethiopia | 8 | Uganda | 8 | Cape Verde |
| 9 | Mauritania | 9 | Ghana | 9 | Uganda |
| 10 | Tanzania | 10 | Mozambique | 10 | Malawi |
| 11 | Nigeria | 11 | Cameroon | 11 | Togo |
| 12 | Namibia | 12 | Cote d'Ivoire | 12 | Ghana |
| 13 | Mozambique | 13 | Madagascar | 13 | Sierra Leone |
| 14 | Zambia | 14 | Angola | 14 | Benin |
| 15 | Somalia | 15 | Burkina Faso | 15 | Ethiopia |
| 16 | Central African Rep. | 16 | Niger | 16 | Lesotho |
| 17 | Madagascar | 17 | Malawi | 16 | Swaziland |
| 18 | Botswana | 18 | Mali | 17 | Kenya |
| 19 | Kenya | 19 | Senegal | 18 | Senegal |
| 20 | Cameroon | 20 | Zambia | 19 | Cote d'Ivoire |
| 21 | Zimbabwe | 21 | Guinea | 20 | Burkina Faso |
| 22 | Congo, Rep. | 22 | Chad | 21 | Guinea-Bissau |
| 23 | Cote d'Ivoire | 23 | Rwanda | 22 | Tanzania |
| 24 | Burkina Faso | 24 | Benin | 23 | Eritrea |
| 25 | Gabon | 25 | Burundi | 24 | South Africa |
| 26 | Guinea | 26 | Togo | 25 | Cameroon |
| 27 | Uganda | 27 | Sierra Leone | 25 | Guinea |
| 28 | Ghana | 28 | Eritrea | 26 | Djibouti |
| 29 | Senegal | 29 | Central African Rep. | 27 | Liberia |
| 30 | Malawi | 30 | Liberia | 28 | Zimbabwe |
| 31 | Eritrea | 31 | Congo, Rep. | 29 | Madagascar |
| 32 | Benin | 32 | Mauritania | 30 | Congo, Dem. Rep. |
| 33 | Liberia | 33 | Lesotho | 30 | Mozambique |
| 34 | Sierra Leone | 34 | Namibia | 31 | Equatorial Guinea |
| 35 | Togo | 35 | Guinea-Bissau | 32 | Zambia |
| 36 | Guinea-Bissau | 36 | Gambia, The | 33 | Sudan |
| 37 | Lesotho | 37 | Botswana | 34 | Angola |
| 38 | Equatorial Guinea | 38 | Gabon | 34 | Somalia |
| 39 | Burundi | 39 | Mauritius | 35 | Congo, Rep. |
| 40 | Rwanda | 40 | Equatorial Guinea | 36 | Niger |
| 41 | Djibouti | 41 | Swaziland | 37 | Mali |
| 42 | Swaziland | 42 | Djibouti | 38 | Chad |
| 43 | Gambia, The | 43 | Comoros | 39 | Central African Rep. |
| 44 | Cape Verde | 44 | Cape Verde | 40 | Gabon |
| 45 | Comoros | 45 | Sao Tome & Principe | 41 | Botswana |
| 46 | Mauritius | 46 | Seychelles | 41 | Mauritania |
| 47 | Sao Tome & Principe | n/a | Somalia | 42 | Namibia |
| 48 | Seychelles | n/a | Zimbabwe | n/a | Seychelles |
| | *smallest* | | *smallest* | | *least dense* |

# appendix B1: performance tables - region overview

### Urban Population

UNPD estimates

| | 2005-2010 | |
|---|---|---|
| largest | 1 | Nigeria |
| | 2 | South Africa |
| | 3 | Congo, Dem. Rep. |
| | 4 | Sudan |
| | 5 | Ethiopia |
| | 6 | Ghana |
| | 7 | Cameroon |
| | 8 | Tanzania |
| | 9 | Angola |
| | 10 | Cote d'Ivoire |
| | 11 | Kenya |
| | 12 | Mozambique |
| | 13 | Madagascar |
| | 14 | Senegal |
| | 15 | Zimbabwe |
| | 16 | Zambia |
| | 17 | Uganda |
| | 18 | Mali |
| | 19 | Benin |
| | 20 | Guinea |
| | 21 | Somalia |
| | 22 | Burkina Faso |
| | 23 | Chad |
| | 24 | Togo |
| | 25 | Malawi |
| | 26 | Niger |
| | 27 | Congo, Rep. |
| | 28 | Liberia |
| | 29 | Sierra Leone |
| | 30 | Rwanda |
| | 31 | Central African Rep. |
| | 32 | Mauritania |
| | 33 | Gabon |
| | 34 | Botswana |
| | 35 | Eritrea |
| | 36 | Gambia, The |
| | 37 | Burundi |
| | 38 | Namibia |
| | 39 | Djibouti |
| | 40 | Mauritius |
| | 41 | Guinea-Bissau |
| | 42 | Lesotho |
| | 43 | Cape Verde |
| | 44 | Swaziland |
| | 45 | Comoros |
| | 46 | Equatorial Guinea |
| | 47 | Sao Tome & Principe |
| | 48 | Seychelles |
| smallest | | |

### Urban % of Total Population

UNPD estimates

| | 2005-2010 | |
|---|---|---|
| highest | 1 | Djibouti |
| | 2 | Gabon |
| | 3 | Congo, Rep. |
| | 4 | South Africa |
| | 5 | Sao Tome & Principe |
| | 6 | Liberia |
| | 7 | Cape Verde |
| | 8 | Botswana |
| | 9 | Cameroon |
| | 10 | Angola |
| | 11 | Gambia, The |
| | 12 | Seychelles |
| | 13 | Ghana |
| | 14 | Cote d'Ivoire |
| | 15 | Nigeria |
| | 16 | Sudan |
| | 17 | Mauritius |
| | 18 | Senegal |
| | 19 | Togo |
| | 20 | Benin |
| | 21 | Mauritania |
| | 22 | Equatorial Guinea |
| | 23 | Central African Rep. |
| | 24 | Sierra Leone |
| | 25 | Zimbabwe |
| | 26 | Namibia |
| | 27 | Mozambique |
| | 28 | Somalia |
| | 29 | Zambia |
| | | SSA average |
| | 30 | Guinea |
| | 31 | Congo, Dem. Rep. |
| | 32 | Mali |
| | 33 | Guinea-Bissau |
| | 34 | Madagascar |
| | 35 | Comoros |
| | 36 | Chad |
| | 37 | Tanzania |
| | 38 | Lesotho |
| | 39 | Swaziland |
| | 40 | Kenya |
| | 41 | Eritrea |
| | 42 | Burkina Faso |
| | 43 | Malawi |
| | 44 | Rwanda |
| | 45 | Ethiopia |
| | 46 | Niger |
| | 47 | Uganda |
| lowest | 48 | Burundi |

### Growth Rate of Urban Population

UNPD estimates

| | 2005-2010 | |
|---|---|---|
| highest | 1 | Burundi |
| | 2 | Liberia |
| | 3 | Eritrea |
| | 4 | Malawi |
| | 5 | Congo, Dem. Rep. |
| | 6 | Burkina Faso |
| | 7 | Mali |
| | 8 | Chad |
| | 9 | Angola |
| | 9 | Uganda |
| | 10 | Togo |
| | 11 | Sudan |
| | 11 | Ethiopia |
| | 12 | Rwanda |
| | 13 | Tanzania |
| | 14 | Somalia |
| | 15 | Gambia, The |
| | 16 | Mozambique |
| | 17 | Benin |
| | 18 | Kenya |
| | 19 | Niger |
| | 20 | Madagascar |
| | 21 | Nigeria |
| | | SSA average |
| | 22 | Guinea |
| | 23 | Lesotho |
| | 24 | Ghana |
| | 24 | Cape Verde |
| | 25 | Cameroon |
| | 26 | Guinea-Bissau |
| | 27 | Cote d'Ivoire |
| | 28 | Senegal |
| | 29 | Mauritania |
| | 30 | Sao Tome & Principe |
| | 31 | Namibia |
| | 32 | Sierra Leone |
| | 33 | Equatorial Guinea |
| | 34 | Congo, Rep. |
| | 35 | Comoros |
| | 36 | Botswana |
| | 37 | Zambia |
| | 38 | Central African Rep. |
| | 39 | Zimbabwe |
| | 40 | Djibouti |
| | 41 | Gabon |
| | 42 | Swaziland |
| | 43 | Seychelles |
| | 44 | South Africa |
| lowest | 45 | Mauritius |

### Rural Population

UNPD estimates

| | 2005-2010 | |
|---|---|---|
| largest | 1 | Nigeria |
| | 2 | Ethiopia |
| | 3 | Congo, Dem. Rep. |
| | 4 | Tanzania |
| | 5 | Kenya |
| | 6 | Uganda |
| | 7 | Sudan |
| | 8 | South Africa |
| | 9 | Madagascar |
| | 10 | Mozambique |
| | 11 | Niger |
| | 12 | Burkina Faso |
| | 13 | Ghana |
| | 14 | Malawi |
| | 15 | Cote d'Ivoire |
| | 16 | Mali |
| | 17 | Zimbabwe |
| | 18 | Cameroon |
| | 19 | Rwanda |
| | 20 | Chad |
| | 21 | Burundi |
| | 22 | Zambia |
| | 23 | Angola |
| | 24 | Senegal |
| | 25 | Guinea |
| | 26 | Somalia |
| | 27 | Benin |
| | 28 | Eritrea |
| | 29 | Togo |
| | 30 | Sierra Leone |
| | 31 | Central African Rep. |
| | 32 | Mauritania |
| | 33 | Liberia |
| | 34 | Lesotho |
| | 35 | Congo, Rep. |
| | 36 | Namibia |
| | 37 | Guinea-Bissau |
| | 38 | Swaziland |
| | 39 | Botswana |
| | 40 | Gambia, The |
| | 41 | Mauritius |
| | 42 | Comoros |
| | 43 | Equatorial Guinea |
| | 44 | Cape Verde |
| | 45 | Gabon |
| | 46 | Djibouti |
| | 47 | Sao Tome & Principe |
| | 48 | Seychelles |
| smallest | | |

### Rural % of Total Population

UNPD estimates

| | 2005-2010 | |
|---|---|---|
| highest | 1 | Burundi |
| | 2 | Uganda |
| | 3 | Niger |
| | 4 | Ethiopia |
| | 5 | Rwanda |
| | 6 | Malawi |
| | 7 | Burkina Faso |
| | 8 | Eritrea |
| | 9 | Kenya |
| | 10 | Swaziland |
| | 11 | Lesotho |
| | 12 | Tanzania |
| | 13 | Chad |
| | 14 | Comoros |
| | 15 | Madagascar |
| | 16 | Guinea-Bissau |
| | 17 | Mali |
| | 18 | Congo, Dem. Rep. |
| | 19 | Guinea |
| | 20 | Zambia |
| | | SSA average |
| | 21 | Somalia |
| | 22 | Mozambique |
| | 23 | Namibia |
| | 24 | Zimbabwe |
| | 25 | Sierra Leone |
| | 26 | Central African Rep. |
| | 27 | Equatorial Guinea |
| | 28 | Mauritania |
| | 29 | Benin |
| | 30 | Togo |
| | 31 | Senegal |
| | 32 | Mauritius |
| | 33 | Sudan |
| | 34 | Nigeria |
| | 35 | Cote d'Ivoire |
| | 36 | Ghana |
| | 37 | Seychelles |
| | 38 | Gambia, The |
| | 39 | Angola |
| | 40 | Cameroon |
| | 41 | Botswana |
| | 42 | Cape Verde |
| | 43 | Liberia |
| | 44 | Sao Tome & Principe |
| | 45 | South Africa |
| | 46 | Congo, Rep. |
| | 47 | Gabon |
| lowest | 48 | Djibouti |

## Growth Rate of Rural Population

UNPD estimates

| | | 2005-2010 |
|---|---|---|
| highest | 1 | Burundi |
| | 2 | Niger |
| | 3 | Uganda |
| | 4 | Guinea-Bissau |
| | 5 | Liberia |
| | 6 | Eritrea |
| | 7 | Rwanda |
| | 8 | Burkina Faso |
| | 8 | Comoros |
| | 9 | Benin |
| | 10 | Kenya |
| | 11 | Congo, Dem. Rep. |
| | 12 | Chad |
| | 13 | Somalia |
| | 14 | Madagascar |
| | 15 | Mali |
| | 15 | Mauritania |
| | 16 | Ethiopia |
| | 17 | Equatorial Guinea |
| | 18 | Senegal |
| | 19 | Malawi |
| | 20 | Tanzania |
| | 21 | Zambia |
| | | SSA average |
| | 22 | Central African Rep. |
| | 23 | Sierra Leone |
| | 24 | Togo |
| | 25 | Guinea |
| | 26 | Congo, Rep. |
| | 27 | Nigeria |
| | 28 | Mozambique |
| | 29 | Angola |
| | 29 | Gambia, The |
| | 30 | Mauritius |
| | 31 | Sudan |
| | 32 | Cote d'Ivoire |
| | 33 | Ghana |
| | 34 | Cape Verde |
| | 35 | Namibia |
| | 36 | Swaziland |
| | 37 | Zimbabwe |
| | 38 | Cameroon |
| | 39 | Lesotho |
| | 40 | Sao Tome & Principe |
| | 41 | Seychelles |
| | 42 | Botswana |
| | 43 | South Africa |
| | 44 | Djibouti |
| lowest | 45 | Gabon |

## GDP $PPP

IMF estimates

| | | 2009 |
|---|---|---|
| largest | 1 | South Africa |
| | 2 | Nigeria |
| | 3 | Angola |
| | 4 | Sudan |
| | 5 | Ethiopia |
| | 6 | Kenya |
| | 7 | Tanzania |
| | 8 | Cameroon |
| | 9 | Ghana |
| | 10 | Cote d'Ivoire |
| | 11 | Uganda |
| | 12 | Botswana |
| | 13 | Senegal |
| | 14 | Congo, Dem. Rep. |
| | 15 | Gabon |
| | 16 | Madagascar |
| | 17 | Mozambique |
| | 18 | Burkina Faso |
| | 19 | Zambia |
| | 20 | Equatorial Guinea |
| | 21 | Chad |
| | 22 | Congo, Rep. |
| | 23 | Mauritius |
| | 24 | Mali |
| | 25 | Benin |
| | 26 | Malawi |
| | 27 | Guinea |
| | 28 | Namibia |
| | 29 | Niger |
| | 30 | Rwanda |
| | 31 | Mauritania |
| | 32 | Swaziland |
| | 33 | Togo |
| | 34 | Sierra Leone |
| | 35 | Eritrea |
| | 36 | Lesotho |
| | 37 | Central African Rep. |
| | 38 | Burundi |
| | 39 | Gambia, The |
| | 40 | Djibouti |
| | 41 | Cape Verde |
| | 42 | Liberia |
| | 43 | Seychelles |
| | 44 | Guinea-Bissau |
| | 45 | Comoros |
| | 46 | Sao Tome & Principe |
| | n/a | Somalia |
| | n/a | Zimbabwe |
| smallest | | |

## Economic Productivity

Primary data: IMF

| | | 2009 |
|---|---|---|
| highest | 1 | Botswana |
| | 2 | Seychelles |
| | 3 | Gabon |
| | 4 | Equatorial Guinea |
| | 5 | Mauritius |
| | 6 | South Africa |
| | 7 | Angola |
| | 8 | Namibia |
| | 9 | Swaziland |
| | 10 | Congo, Rep. |
| | 11 | Cape Verde |
| | 12 | Sudan |
| | 13 | Djibouti |
| | 14 | Nigeria |
| | 15 | Mauritania |
| | 16 | Cameroon |
| | 17 | Cote d'Ivoire |
| | 18 | Senegal |
| | 19 | Kenya |
| | 20 | Sao Tome & Principe |
| | 21 | Chad |
| | 22 | Benin |
| | 23 | Ghana |
| | 24 | Gambia, The |
| | 25 | Zambia |
| | 26 | Tanzania |
| | 27 | Lesotho |
| | 28 | Burkina Faso |
| | 29 | Madagascar |
| | 30 | Comoros |
| | 31 | Guinea |
| | 32 | Mali |
| | 33 | Uganda |
| | 34 | Rwanda |
| | 35 | Mozambique |
| | 36 | Ethiopia |
| | 37 | Malawi |
| | 38 | Togo |
| | 39 | Central African Rep. |
| | 40 | Eritrea |
| | 41 | Sierra Leone |
| | 42 | Niger |
| | 43 | Guinea-Bissau |
| | 44 | Burundi |
| | 45 | Liberia |
| | 46 | Congo, Dem. Rep. |
| | n/a | Somalia |
| | n/a | Zimbabwe |
| lowest | | |

## Female % of the Labour Force

World Bank

| | | 2006 |
|---|---|---|
| highest | 1 | Mozambique |
| | 2 | Burundi |
| | 3 | Rwanda |
| | 4 | Malawi |
| | 5 | Tanzania |
| | 6 | Mali |
| | 7 | Uganda |
| | 8 | Madagascar |
| | 9 | Ghana |
| | 10 | Guinea |
| | 11 | Burkina Faso |
| | 12 | Chad |
| | 13 | Central African Rep. |
| | 14 | Angola |
| | 15 | Ethiopia |
| | 16 | Kenya |
| | 17 | Namibia |
| | 18 | Zimbabwe |
| | 19 | Lesotho |
| | 20 | Gabon |
| | 21 | Zambia |
| | 22 | Niger |
| | | SSA average |
| | 23 | Congo, Dem. Rep. |
| | 24 | Senegal |
| | 25 | Eritrea |
| | 26 | Gambia, The |
| | 27 | Guinea-Bissau |
| | 28 | Botswana |
| | 29 | Congo, Rep. |
| | 30 | Comoros |
| | 31 | Liberia |
| | 32 | Cameroon |
| | 33 | Djibouti |
| | 34 | Somalia |
| | 35 | Mauritania |
| | 36 | Sierra Leone |
| | 37 | Benin |
| | 38 | South Africa |
| | 39 | Equatorial Guinea |
| | 40 | Togo |
| | 41 | Mauritius |
| | 42 | Nigeria |
| | 43 | Cape Verde |
| | 44 | Swaziland |
| | 45 | Cote d'Ivoire |
| | 46 | Sao Tome & Principe |
| | 47 | Sudan |
| lowest | n/a | Seychelles |

# B2 performance tables - quality of life

## Human Development Index

UNDP

*high development index*

| | 2003-2005 |
|---|---|
| 1 | Seychelles |
| 2 | Mauritius |
| 3 | Cape Verde |
| 4 | South Africa |
| 5 | Gabon |
| 6 | Equatorial Guinea |
| 7 | Namibia |
| 7 | São Tomé & Príncipe |
| 8 | Botswana |
| 9 | Comoros |
| 10 | Ghana |
| 11 | Congo, Rep. |
| 12 | Sudan |
| 13 | Madagascar |
| 14 | Swaziland |
| 15 | Cameroon |
| 16 | Lesotho |
| 17 | Togo |
| 17 | Uganda |
| 18 | Mauritania |
| 19 | Zimbabwe |
| 20 | Djibouti |
| | SSA average |
| 21 | Kenya |
| 22 | Gambia, The |
| 23 | Senegal |
| 24 | Eritrea |
| 24 | Nigeria |
| 25 | Guinea |
| 26 | Rwanda |
| 27 | Angola |
| 28 | Tanzania |
| 29 | Benin |
| 30 | Côte d'Ivoire |
| 31 | Malawi |
| 32 | Zambia |
| 33 | Congo, Dem. Rep. |
| 34 | Burundi |
| 35 | Mozambique |
| 36 | Ethiopia |
| 37 | Central African Rep. |
| 37 | Chad |
| 38 | Guinea-Bissau |
| 39 | Mali |
| 40 | Burkina Faso |
| 41 | Niger |
| 42 | Sierra Leone |
| n/a | Liberia |
| n/a | Somalia |

*low development index*

## Life Expectancy

Primary data: UNICEF

*high life expectancy*

| | 2003-2006 |
|---|---|
| 1 | Mauritius |
| 2 | Cape Verde |
| 3 | Sao Tome & Principe |
| 4 | Comoros |
| 5 | Ghana |
| 6 | Senegal |
| 6 | Sudan |
| 7 | Gambia, The |
| 8 | Madagascar |
| 9 | Mauritania |
| 10 | Gabon |
| 11 | Eritrea |
| 12 | Togo |
| 13 | Benin |
| 14 | Guinea |
| 15 | Congo, Rep. |
| 16 | Djibouti |
| 17 | Mali |
| 18 | Burkina Faso |
| 18 | Ethiopia |
| 18 | Uganda |
| 19 | Kenya |
| 20 | Niger |
| 21 | South Africa |
| 22 | Namibia |
| 22 | Somalia |
| 23 | Cameroon |
| | SSA average |
| 24 | Tanzania |
| 25 | Equatorial Guinea |
| 25 | Nigeria |
| 26 | Chad |
| 27 | Côte d'Ivoire |
| 27 | Guinea-Bissau |
| 28 | Burundi |
| 29 | Congo, Dem. Rep. |
| 30 | Rwanda |
| 31 | Liberia |
| 32 | Malawi |
| 33 | Angola |
| 33 | Mozambique |
| 34 | Central African Rep. |
| 35 | Sierra Leone |
| 36 | Botswana |
| 37 | Zambia |
| 38 | Zimbabwe |
| 39 | Lesotho |
| 40 | Swaziland |
| n/a | Seychelles |

*low life expectancy*

## Under-5 Child Mortality

Primary data: UNICEF

*least deaths*

| | 2003-2006 |
|---|---|
| 1 | Seychelles |
| 2 | Mauritius |
| 3 | Cape Verde |
| 4 | Namibia |
| 5 | South Africa |
| 6 | Comoros |
| 7 | Eritrea |
| 8 | Sudan |
| 9 | Gabon |
| 10 | Lesotho |
| 11 | Ghana |
| 12 | Congo, Rep. |
| 12 | Sao Tome & Principe |
| 13 | Botswana |
| 14 | Madagascar |
| 14 | Kenya |
| 15 | Zimbabwe |
| 16 | Gambia, The |
| 17 | Senegal |
| 17 | Djibouti |
| 17 | Togo |
| 18 | Tanzania |
| 19 | Uganda |
| 20 | Mauritania |
| 21 | Mozambique |
| 22 | Malawi |
| 23 | Benin |
| 24 | Cameroon |
| 25 | Ethiopia |
| 26 | Guinea |
| 27 | Swaziland |
| | SSA average |
| 28 | Côte d'Ivoire |
| 29 | Zambia |
| 30 | Central African Rep. |
| 31 | Burundi |
| 32 | Equatorial Guinea |
| 33 | Rwanda |
| 34 | Nigeria |
| 35 | Burkina Faso |
| 36 | Guinea-Bissau |
| 37 | Chad |
| 38 | Congo, Dem. Rep. |
| 38 | Somalia |
| 39 | Mali |
| 40 | Liberia |
| 41 | Niger |
| 42 | Angola |
| 43 | Sierra Leone |

*most deaths*

### % of 1-yr olds Immunised against Measles

Primary data: UNICEF

| | Rank | 2003-2006 |
|---|---|---|
| highest | 1 | Seychelles |
| | 2 | Mauritius |
| | 3 | Tanzania |
| | 4 | Botswana |
| | 5 | Gambia, The |
| | 6 | Rwanda |
| | 7 | Sao Tome & Principe |
| | 8 | Uganda |
| | 9 | Eritrea |
| | 10 | Benin |
| | 11 | Zambia |
| | 12 | Zimbabwe |
| | 13 | Ghana |
| | 13 | South Africa |
| | 14 | Burkina Faso |
| | 15 | Malawi |
| | 16 | Mali |
| | 17 | Lesotho |
| | 18 | Mozambique |
| | 19 | Burundi |
| | 20 | Kenya |
| | 21 | Liberia |
| | 22 | Comoros |
| | 23 | Guinea-Bissau |
| | 23 | Swaziland |
| | 23 | Togo |
| | 24 | Namibia |
| | 25 | Senegal |
| | 25 | Sierra Leone |
| | 26 | Niger |
| | 27 | Cape Verde |
| | 28 | Cameroon |
| | | SSA average |
| | 29 | Congo, Dem. Rep. |
| | 30 | Djibouti |
| | 30 | Mauritania |
| | 31 | Guinea |
| | 32 | Sudan |
| | 33 | Ethiopia |
| | 34 | Congo, Rep. |
| | 35 | Madagascar |
| | 36 | Côte d'Ivoire |
| | 37 | Gabon |
| | 38 | Angola |
| | 39 | Equatorial Guinea |
| | 40 | Nigeria |
| | 41 | Chad |
| | 42 | Somalia |
| lowest | 43 | Central African Rep. |

### % of 1-yr olds Immunised against Tuberculosis

Primary data: UNICEF

| | Rank | 2003-2006 |
|---|---|---|
| highest | 1 | Benin |
| | 1 | Botswana |
| | 1 | Seychelles |
| | 2 | Sao Tome & Principe |
| | 3 | South Africa |
| | 4 | Mauritius |
| | 5 | Zimbabwe |
| | 6 | Malawi |
| | 7 | Gambia, The |
| | 7 | Ghana |
| | 8 | Burkina Faso |
| | 9 | Zambia |
| | 10 | Eritrea |
| | 10 | Tanzania |
| | 10 | Uganda |
| | 11 | Togo |
| | 12 | Rwanda |
| | 12 | Senegal |
| | 13 | Lesotho |
| | 14 | Gabon |
| | 15 | Kenya |
| | 16 | Mozambique |
| | 17 | Namibia |
| | 18 | Mauritania |
| | 18 | Swaziland |
| | 19 | Burundi |
| | 19 | Sierra Leone |
| | 20 | Guinea-Bissau |
| | 21 | Guinea |
| | 22 | Comoros |
| | 23 | Cameroon |
| | 24 | Congo, Dem. Rep. |
| | | SSA average |
| | 25 | Congo, Rep. |
| | 26 | Cape Verde |
| | 26 | Mali |
| | 27 | Ethiopia |
| | 28 | Niger |
| | 29 | Equatorial Guinea |
| | 30 | Madagascar |
| | 31 | Djibouti |
| | 32 | Central African Rep. |
| | 33 | Liberia |
| | 34 | Angola |
| | 35 | Côte d'Ivoire |
| | 36 | Sudan |
| | 37 | Somalia |
| | 38 | Nigeria |
| lowest | 39 | Chad |

### % of Population with Access to Safe Water

Primary data: UNICEF

| | Rank | 2004-2006 |
|---|---|---|
| highest | 1 | Mauritius |
| | 2 | Botswana |
| | 3 | Gabon |
| | 3 | Seychelles |
| | 4 | Namibia |
| | 5 | Comoros |
| | 6 | South Africa |
| | 7 | Côte d'Ivoire |
| | 8 | Gambia, The |
| | 9 | Zimbabwe |
| | 10 | Cape Verde |
| | 11 | Burundi |
| | 11 | Lesotho |
| | 11 | Sao Tome & Principe |
| | 12 | Senegal |
| | 13 | Ghana |
| | 14 | Malawi |
| | 14 | Rwanda |
| | 15 | Djibouti |
| | 16 | Sudan |
| | 17 | Benin |
| | 17 | Uganda |
| | 18 | Cameroon |
| | 19 | Central African Rep. |
| | 20 | Liberia |
| | 20 | Swaziland |
| | 20 | Tanzania |
| | 21 | Burkina Faso |
| | 21 | Kenya |
| | 22 | Eritrea |
| | 23 | Guinea-Bissau |
| | 24 | Congo, Rep. |
| | 24 | Zambia |
| | 25 | Sierra Leone |
| | 26 | Angola |
| | 26 | Mauritania |
| | 27 | Togo |
| | 28 | Nigeria |
| | 29 | Guinea |
| | 29 | Madagascar |
| | 29 | Mali |
| | 30 | Congo, Dem. Rep. |
| | 30 | Niger |
| | 31 | Equatorial Guinea |
| | 31 | Mozambique |
| | 32 | Chad |
| | 33 | Somalia |
| | 34 | Ethiopia |
| lowest | | |

### % of Population with Access to Sanitation

Primary data: UNICEF

| | Rank | 2004-2006 |
|---|---|---|
| highest | 1 | Mauritius |
| | 2 | Djibouti |
| | 3 | South Africa |
| | 4 | Malawi |
| | 5 | Senegal |
| | 6 | Zambia |
| | 7 | Equatorial Guinea |
| | 7 | Gambia, The |
| | 7 | Zimbabwe |
| | 8 | Cameroon |
| | 9 | Swaziland |
| | 10 | Tanzania |
| | 11 | Mali |
| | 12 | Nigeria |
| | 13 | Cape Verde |
| | 13 | Kenya |
| | 13 | Uganda |
| | 14 | Botswana |
| | 14 | Rwanda |
| | 15 | Sierra Leone |
| | 16 | Côte d'Ivoire |
| | 16 | Lesotho |
| | 17 | Burundi |
| | 17 | Gabon |
| | 18 | Guinea-Bissau |
| | 18 | Togo |
| | 19 | Madagascar |
| | 19 | Mauritania |
| | 19 | Sudan |
| | 20 | Benin |
| | 20 | Comoros |
| | 21 | Mozambique |
| | 22 | Angola |
| | 23 | Congo, Dem. Rep. |
| | 24 | Central African Rep. |
| | 24 | Congo, Rep. |
| | 24 | Liberia |
| | 25 | Somalia |
| | 26 | Namibia |
| | 26 | Sao Tome & Principe |
| | 27 | Ghana |
| | 27 | Guinea |
| | 28 | Burkina Faso |
| | 28 | Ethiopia |
| | 28 | Niger |
| | 29 | Chad |
| | 29 | Eritrea |
| | n/a | Seychelles |
| lowest | | |

### Total Number of Phone Subscribers (fixed & mobile) per 100 persons of Population

ITU

| | Rank | 2007 |
|---|---|---|
| highest | 1 | Mauritius |
| | 2 | Seychelles |
| | 3 | Cape Verde |
| | 4 | South Africa |
| | 5 | Botswana |
| | 6 | Namibia |
| | 7 | Sao Tome & Principe |
| | 8 | Gambia, The |
| | 9 | Nigeria |
| | 10 | Swaziland |
| | 11 | Lesotho |
| | 12 | Gabon |
| | 13 | Zimbabwe |
| | 14 | Comoros |
| | 15 | Senegal |
| | 16 | Equatorial Guinea |
| | | SSA average |
| | 17 | Ghana |
| | 18 | Djibouti |
| | 19 | Côte d'Ivoire |
| | 20 | Togo |
| | 21 | Malawi |
| | 22 | Benin |
| | 23 | Somalia |
| | 24 | Mauritania |
| | 25 | Ethiopia |
| | 26 | Sudan |
| | 27 | Eritrea |
| | 28 | Cameroon |
| | 29 | Zambia |
| | 30 | Kenya |
| | 31 | Burkina Faso |
| | 32 | Mali |
| | 33 | Madagascar |
| | 34 | Angola |
| | 35 | Tanzania |
| | 36 | Uganda |
| | 37 | Burundi |
| | 38 | Congo, Rep. |
| | 39 | Guinea |
| | 39 | Mozambique |
| | 40 | Central African Rep. |
| | 41 | Guinea-Bissau |
| | 42 | Rwanda |
| | 43 | Niger |
| | 44 | Chad |
| | 45 | Congo, Dem. Rep. |
| | n/a | Liberia |
| lowest | n/a | Sierra Leone |

# appendix B2: performance tables - quality of life

## Number of Mobile Phone Subscribers per 100 persons of Population

ITU

highest

| Rank | 2007 |
|---|---|
| 1 | Seychelles |
| 2 | Gabon |
| 3 | South Africa |
| 4 | Botswana |
| 5 | Mauritius |
| 6 | Gambia, The |
| 7 | Equatorial Guinea |
| 8 | Mauritania |
| 9 | Namibia |
| 10 | Côte d'Ivoire |
| 11 | Congo, Rep. |
| 12 | Senegal |
| 13 | Swaziland |
| 14 | Ghana |
| 15 | Kenya |
| 16 | Cape Verde |
| 17 | Nigeria |
| 18 | Cameroon |
| 19 | Lesotho |
| 20 | Zambia |
| 21 | Benin |
| 22 | Tanzania |
| 23 | Mali |
| 24 | Angola |
| 25 | Sudan |
| 26 | Sao Tome & Principe |
| | SSA average |
| 27 | Togo |
| 28 | Guinea-Bissau |
| 29 | Mozambique |
| 30 | Liberia |
| 31 | Uganda |
| 32 | Sierra Leone |
| 33 | Madagascar |
| 34 | Burkina Faso |
| 35 | Congo, Dem. Rep. |
| 36 | Zimbabwe |
| 37 | Chad |
| 38 | Malawi |
| 39 | Rwanda |
| 40 | Somalia |
| 41 | Niger |
| 42 | Djibouti |
| 43 | Comoros |
| 44 | Central African Rep. |
| 45 | Burundi |
| 46 | Guinea |
| 47 | Ethiopia |
| 48 | Eritrea |

lowest

## Total Adult Literacy Rate

AfDB

highest

| Rank | 2007 |
|---|---|
| 1 | Zimbabwe |
| 2 | Equatorial Guinea |
| 3 | Kenya |
| 4 | South Africa |
| 5 | Congo, Rep. |
| 6 | Mauritius |
| 7 | Namibia |
| 8 | Lesotho |
| 9 | Swaziland |
| 10 | Zambia |
| 11 | Botswana |
| 12 | Tanzania |
| 13 | Cape Verde |
| 14 | Ghana |
| 15 | Cameroon |
| 16 | Rwanda |
| 17 | Uganda |
| 18 | Nigeria |
| 19 | Djibouti |
| 19 | Madagascar |
| 20 | Congo, Dem. Rep. |
| 21 | Malawi |
| 22 | Togo |
| 23 | Sudan |
| 24 | Eritrea |
| 25 | Liberia |
| 26 | Comoros |
| 27 | Central African Rep. |
| 28 | Burundi |
| 29 | Côte d'Ivoire |
| 30 | Chad |
| 31 | Mozambique |
| 32 | Ethiopia |
| 32 | Guinea-Bissau |
| 33 | Benin |
| 34 | Gambia, The |
| 35 | Senegal |
| 36 | Mauritania |
| 37 | Mali |
| 38 | Burkina Faso |
| 39 | Niger |
| n/a | Gabon |
| n/a | Angola |
| n/a | Guinea |
| n/a | Sao Tome & Principe |
| n/a | Seychelles |
| n/a | Sierra Leone |
| n/a | Somalia |

lowest

## Number of Internet Users per 100 persons of Population

ITU

highest

| Rank | 2007 |
|---|---|
| 1 | Seychelles |
| 2 | Mauritius |
| 3 | Sao Tome & Principe |
| 4 | South Africa |
| 5 | Zimbabwe |
| 6 | Kenya |
| 7 | Nigeria |
| 8 | Senegal |
| 9 | Uganda |
| 10 | Cape Verde |
| 11 | Gambia, The |
| 12 | Gabon |
| 13 | Togo |
| 14 | Namibia |
| 15 | Botswana |
| 16 | Zambia |
| 17 | Swaziland |
| 18 | Sudan |
| | SSA average |
| 19 | Lesotho |
| 20 | Ghana |
| 21 | Comoros |
| 22 | Guinea-Bissau |
| 23 | Cameroon |
| 24 | Eritrea |
| 25 | Congo, Rep. |
| 26 | Benin |
| 27 | Côte d'Ivoire |
| 28 | Equatorial Guinea |
| 29 | Djibouti |
| 30 | Somalia |
| 31 | Rwanda |
| 32 | Malawi |
| 32 | Tanzania |
| 33 | Mauritania |
| 34 | Mozambique |
| 35 | Mali |
| 36 | Burundi |
| 37 | Angola |
| 37 | Chad |
| 38 | Burkina Faso |
| 39 | Madagascar |
| 40 | Guinea |
| 41 | Congo, Dem. Rep. |
| 42 | Ethiopia |
| 43 | Central African Rep. |
| 44 | Niger |
| 45 | Sierra Leone |
| n/a | Liberia |

lowest

## Number of Personal Computers per 100 persons of Population

AfDB

highest

| Rank | 2006 |
|---|---|
| 1 | Seychelles |
| 2 | Mauritius |
| 3 | Namibia |
| 4 | Sudan |
| 5 | Cape Verde |
| 6 | South Africa |
| 7 | Zimbabwe |
| 8 | Botswana |
| 9 | Sao Tome & Principe |
| 10 | Swaziland |
| 11 | Gabon |
| 12 | Togo |
| 13 | Mauritania |
| 14 | Djibouti |
| | Africa average |
| 15 | Senegal |
| 16 | Gambia, The |
| 17 | Equatorial Guinea |
| 18 | Côte d'Ivoire |
| 19 | Uganda |
| 20 | Kenya |
| 20 | Mozambique |
| 21 | Zambia |
| 22 | Cameroon |
| 23 | Tanzania |
| 24 | Somalia |
| 25 | Nigeria |
| 26 | Angola |
| 26 | Burundi |
| 27 | Comoros |
| 28 | Eritrea |
| 29 | Benin |
| 30 | Ghana |
| 31 | Madagascar |
| 32 | Congo, Rep. |
| 33 | Guinea |
| 34 | Mali |
| 35 | Ethiopia |
| 36 | Central African Rep. |
| 37 | Burkina Faso |
| 38 | Rwanda |
| 39 | Guinea-Bissau |
| 39 | Malawi |
| 40 | Chad |
| 41 | Lesotho |
| 41 | Niger |
| 42 | Congo, Dem. Rep. |
| n/a | Liberia |
| n/a | Sierra Leone |

lowest

## Net Migration per Population

UNPD

people mostly coming into the country

| Rank | 2000-2005 |
|---|---|
| 1 | Sierra Leone |
| 2 | Eritrea |
| 3 | Burundi |
| 4 | Chad |
| 5 | Gambia, The |
| 6 | Somalia |
| 7 | Benin |
| 8 | Angola |
| 9 | Botswana |
| 10 | Mauritania |
| 11 | Burkina Faso |
| 12 | Gabon |
| 13 | Rwanda |
| 14 | South Africa |
| 15 | Guinea-Bissau |
| 16 | Kenya |
| 17 | Cameroon |
| 18 | Ghana |
| 18 | Djibouti |
| 19 | Equatorial Guinea |
| 20 | Mauritius |
| 21 | Uganda |
| 22 | Madagascar |
| 22 | Namibia |
| 22 | Togo |
| 23 | Mozambique |
| 23 | Nigeria |
| | SSA average |
| 23 | Ethiopia |
| 23 | Malawi |
| 24 | Niger |
| 25 | Congo, Rep. |
| 26 | Congo, Dem. Rep. |
| 27 | Swaziland |
| 28 | Zimbabwe |
| 29 | Zambia |
| 30 | Senegal |
| 30 | Tanzania |
| 31 | Cape Verde |
| 31 | Central African Rep. |
| 32 | Mali |
| 33 | Comoros |
| 34 | Sudan |
| 35 | Lesotho |
| 36 | Côte d'Ivoire |
| 37 | Liberia |
| 38 | Sao Tome & Principe |
| 39 | Guinea |
| n/a | Seychelles |

people mostly leaving the country

# B3 performance tables - economic strength

GDP $PPP (IMF)

| Rank | 1999-2002 | 2003-2006 | 2007-2010 |
|---|---|---|---|
| largest | | | |
| 1 | South Africa | South Africa | South Africa |
| 2 | Nigeria | Nigeria | Nigeria |
| 3 | Sudan | Sudan | Angola |
| 4 | Kenya | Angola | Sudan |
| 5 | Angola | Kenya | Ethiopia |
| 6 | Ethiopia | Ethiopia | Kenya |
| 7 | Tanzania | Tanzania | Tanzania |
| 8 | Cameroon | Cameroon | Cameroon |
| 9 | Côte d'Ivoire | Côte d'Ivoire | Ghana |
| 10 | Ghana | Ghana | Côte d'Ivoire |
| 11 | Uganda | Uganda | Uganda |
| 12 | Botswana | Botswana | Botswana |
| 13 | Gabon | Senegal | Senegal |
| 14 | Senegal | Gabon | Congo, Dem. Rep. |
| 15 | Madagascar | Congo, Dem. Rep. | Gabon |
| 16 | Congo, Dem. Rep. | Madagascar | Madagascar |
| 17 | Burkina Faso | Burkina Faso | Mozambique |
| 18 | Zambia | Mozambique | Burkina Faso |
| 19 | Mauritius | Chad | Zambia |
| 20 | Mozambique | Zambia | Equatorial Guinea |
| 21 | Congo, Rep. | Equatorial Guinea | Chad |
| 22 | Mali | Mauritius | Mauritius |
| 23 | Guinea | Congo, Rep. | Congo, Rep. |
| 24 | Benin | Mali | Mali |
| 25 | Chad | Benin | Benin |
| 26 | Namibia | Guinea | Malawi |
| 27 | Malawi | Namibia | Guinea |
| 28 | Niger | Malawi | Namibia |
| 29 | Equatorial Guinea | Niger | Niger |
| 30 | Rwanda | Rwanda | Rwanda |
| 31 | Swaziland | Mauritania | Mauritania |
| 32 | Mauritania | Swaziland | Swaziland |
| 33 | Togo | Togo | Togo |
| 34 | Eritrea | Eritrea | Sierra Leone |
| 35 | Zimbabwe | Sierra Leone | Eritrea |
| 36 | Central African Rep. | Central African Rep. | Lesotho |
| 37 | Lesotho | Lesotho | Central African Rep. |
| 38 | Burundi | Burundi | Burundi |
| 39 | Sierra Leone | Zimbabwe | Gambia, The |
| 40 | Gambia, The | Gambia, The | Zimbabwe |
| 41 | Liberia | Djibouti | Djibouti |
| 42 | Djibouti | Cape Verde | Cape Verde |
| 43 | Seychelles | Seychelles | Liberia |
| 44 | Cape Verde | Liberia | Seychelles |
| 45 | Guinea-Bissau | Guinea-Bissau | Guinea-Bissau |
| 46 | Comoros | Comoros | Comoros |
| 47 | São Tomé & Príncipe | São Tomé & Príncipe | São Tomé & Príncipe |
| n/a | Somalia | Somalia | Somalia |
| smallest | | | |

# appendix B3: performance tables - economic strength

## GDP per Person $PPP

Primary data: IMF

| | | 1999-2002 |
|---|---|---|
| largest | 1 | Seychelles |
| | 2 | Gabon |
| | 3 | Botswana |
| | 4 | Mauritius |
| | 5 | South Africa |
| | 6 | Equatorial Guinea |
| | 7 | Swaziland |
| | 8 | Namibia |
| | 9 | Congo, Rep. |
| | 10 | Angola |
| | 11 | Cape Verde |
| | 12 | Djibouti |
| | 13 | Cameroon |
| | 14 | Côte d'Ivoire |
| | 15 | Mauritania |
| | | SSA average |
| | 16 | Sudan |
| | 17 | Senegal |
| | 18 | Kenya |
| | 19 | Nigeria |
| | 20 | Benin |
| | 21 | São Tomé & Príncipe |
| | 22 | Ghana |
| | 23 | Lesotho |
| | 24 | Comoros |
| | 25 | Gambia, The |
| | 26 | Guinea |
| | 27 | Chad |
| | 28 | Zambia |
| | 29 | Burkina Faso |
| | 30 | Eritrea |
| | 31 | Tanzania |
| | 32 | Mali |
| | 33 | Madagascar |
| | 34 | Uganda |
| | 35 | Togo |
| | 36 | Central African Rep. |
| | 37 | Rwanda |
| | 38 | Malawi |
| | 39 | Mozambique |
| | 40 | Niger |
| | 41 | Guinea-Bissau |
| | 42 | Ethiopia |
| | 43 | Liberia |
| | 44 | Sierra Leone |
| | 45 | Burundi |
| | 46 | Zimbabwe |
| | 47 | Congo, Dem. Rep. |
| smallest | n/a | Somalia |

## GDP per Person $PPP

Primary data: IMF

| | | 2003-2006 |
|---|---|---|
| largest | 1 | Seychelles |
| | 2 | Botswana |
| | 3 | Gabon |
| | 4 | Equatorial Guinea |
| | 5 | Mauritius |
| | 6 | South Africa |
| | 7 | Namibia |
| | 8 | Swaziland |
| | 9 | Angola |
| | 10 | Congo, Rep. |
| | 11 | Cape Verde |
| | 12 | Djibouti |
| | 13 | Cameroon |
| | 14 | Nigeria |
| | 15 | Mauritania |
| | | SSA average |
| | 16 | Sudan |
| | 17 | Côte d'Ivoire |
| | 18 | Senegal |
| | 19 | Chad |
| | 20 | Kenya |
| | 21 | Benin |
| | 22 | São Tomé & Príncipe |
| | 23 | Ghana |
| | 24 | Zambia |
| | 25 | Gambia, The |
| | 26 | Lesotho |
| | 27 | Burkina Faso |
| | 28 | Comoros |
| | 29 | Tanzania |
| | 30 | Guinea |
| | 31 | Mali |
| | 32 | Madagascar |
| | 33 | Uganda |
| | 34 | Eritrea |
| | 35 | Rwanda |
| | 36 | Togo |
| | 37 | Mozambique |
| | 38 | Malawi |
| | 39 | Central African Rep. |
| | 40 | Ethiopia |
| | 41 | Niger |
| | 42 | Sierra Leone |
| | 43 | Guinea-Bissau |
| | 44 | Burundi |
| | 45 | Liberia |
| | 46 | Congo, Dem. Rep. |
| | 47 | Zimbabwe |
| smallest | n/a | Somalia |

## GDP per Person $PPP

Primary data: IMF

| | | 2007-2010 |
|---|---|---|
| largest | 1 | Botswana |
| | 2 | Seychelles |
| | 3 | Gabon |
| | 4 | Equatorial Guinea |
| | 5 | Mauritius |
| | 6 | South Africa |
| | 7 | Angola |
| | 8 | Namibia |
| | 9 | Swaziland |
| | 10 | Congo, Rep. |
| | 11 | Cape Verde |
| | 12 | Djibouti |
| | 13 | Sudan |
| | 14 | Nigeria |
| | | SSA average |
| | 15 | Cameroon |
| | 16 | Mauritania |
| | 17 | Côte d'Ivoire |
| | 18 | Senegal |
| | 19 | Kenya |
| | 20 | Chad |
| | 21 | São Tomé & Príncipe |
| | 22 | Benin |
| | 23 | Ghana |
| | 24 | Gambia, The |
| | 25 | Zambia |
| | 26 | Tanzania |
| | 27 | Lesotho |
| | 28 | Burkina Faso |
| | 29 | Madagascar |
| | 30 | Comoros |
| | 31 | Guinea |
| | 32 | Mali |
| | 33 | Uganda |
| | 34 | Rwanda |
| | 35 | Mozambique |
| | 36 | Ethiopia |
| | 37 | Malawi |
| | 38 | Togo |
| | 39 | Eritrea |
| | 40 | Central African Rep. |
| | 41 | Sierra Leone |
| | 42 | Niger |
| | 43 | Guinea-Bissau |
| | 44 | Burundi |
| | 45 | Liberia |
| | 46 | Congo, Dem. Rep. |
| | 47 | Zimbabwe |
| smallest | n/a | Somalia |

## Growth in GDP per Person

Primary data: IMF

| | | 2000-2002 |
|---|---|---|
| largest | 1 | Equatorial Guinea |
| | 2 | Sierra Leone |
| | 3 | Nigeria |
| | 4 | Botswana |
| | 5 | Mozambique |
| | 6 | Sudan |
| | 7 | Cape Verde |
| | 8 | Angola |
| | 9 | Chad |
| | 10 | Mauritius |
| | 11 | Tanzania |
| | 12 | São Tomé & Príncipe |
| | | SSA average |
| | 13 | Congo, Rep. |
| | 14 | South Africa |
| | 15 | Namibia |
| | 16 | Uganda |
| | 17 | Mali |
| | 18 | Ethiopia |
| | 19 | Zambia |
| | 20 | Ghana |
| | 21 | Benin |
| | 22 | Burkina Faso |
| | 23 | Cameroon |
| | 24 | Guinea |
| | 25 | Liberia |
| | 26 | Senegal |
| | 27 | Rwanda |
| | 28 | Niger |
| | 29 | Lesotho |
| | 30 | Comoros |
| | 31 | Gambia, The |
| | 32 | Djibouti |
| | 33 | Kenya |
| | 34 | Mauritania |
| | 35 | Seychelles |
| | 36 | Swaziland |
| | 37 | Central African Rep. |
| | 38 | Burundi |
| | 39 | Gabon |
| | 40 | Malawi |
| | 41 | Madagascar |
| | 42 | Côte d'Ivoire |
| | 43 | Togo |
| | 44 | Eritrea |
| | 45 | Congo, Dem. Rep. |
| | 46 | Zimbabwe |
| | 47 | Guinea-Bissau |
| smallest | n/a | Somalia |

## Growth in GDP per Person

Primary data: IMF

| | | 2003-2006 |
|---|---|---|
| largest | 1 | Chad |
| | 2 | Equatorial Guinea |
| | 3 | Angola |
| | 4 | Madagascar |
| | 5 | Ethiopia |
| | 6 | Botswana |
| | 7 | Sierra Leone |
| | 8 | Sudan |
| | 9 | Mozambique |
| | 10 | Mauritania |
| | 11 | Tanzania |
| | 12 | Nigeria |
| | 13 | Cape Verde |
| | 14 | South Africa |
| | 15 | Namibia |
| | 16 | Rwanda |
| | 17 | Malawi |
| | | SSA average |
| | 18 | Congo, Dem. Rep. |
| | 19 | Gambia, The |
| | 20 | São Tomé & Príncipe |
| | 21 | Ghana |
| | 22 | Zambia |
| | 23 | Mauritius |
| | 24 | Mali |
| | 25 | Congo, Rep. |
| | 26 | Burkina Faso |
| | 27 | Kenya |
| | 28 | Togo |
| | 29 | Senegal |
| | 30 | Uganda |
| | 31 | Niger |
| | 32 | Swaziland |
| | 33 | Lesotho |
| | 34 | Djibouti |
| | 35 | Benin |
| | 36 | Burundi |
| | 37 | Cameroon |
| | 38 | Comoros |
| | 39 | Gabon |
| | 40 | Central African Rep. |
| | 41 | Guinea-Bissau |
| | 42 | Côte d'Ivoire |
| | 43 | Guinea |
| | 44 | Seychelles |
| | 45 | Eritrea |
| | 46 | Liberia |
| | 47 | Zimbabwe |
| smallest | n/a | Somalia |

# appendix B3: performance tables - economic strength

## Growth in GDP per Person

Primary data: IMF

| | | 2007-2010 |
|---|---|---|
| largest | 1 | Angola |
| | 2 | Sudan |
| | 3 | Congo, Dem. Rep. |
| | 4 | Botswana |
| | 5 | Ethiopia |
| | 6 | Tanzania |
| | 7 | Liberia |
| | 8 | Cape Verde |
| | 9 | Malawi |
| | 10 | Mauritius |
| | 11 | Equatorial Guinea |
| | 12 | Nigeria |
| | 13 | Madagascar |
| | 14 | Mozambique |
| | | SSA average |
| | 15 | Ghana |
| | 16 | Congo, Rep. |
| | 17 | Djibouti |
| | 18 | Seychelles |
| | 19 | São Tomé & Príncipe |
| | 20 | Sierra Leone |
| | 21 | Gambia, The |
| | 22 | Namibia |
| | 23 | Rwanda |
| | 24 | Zambia |
| | 25 | Lesotho |
| | 26 | South Africa |
| | 27 | Burundi |
| | 28 | Uganda |
| | 29 | Senegal |
| | 30 | Burkina Faso |
| | 31 | Central African Rep. |
| | 32 | Kenya |
| | 33 | Gabon |
| | 34 | Mauritania |
| | 35 | Côte d'Ivoire |
| | 36 | Benin |
| | 37 | Mali |
| | 38 | Cameroon |
| | 39 | Guinea |
| | 40 | Niger |
| | 41 | Togo |
| | 42 | Swaziland |
| | 43 | Guinea-Bissau |
| | 44 | Comoros |
| | 45 | Eritrea |
| | 46 | Chad |
| | n/a | Zimbabwe |
| smallest | n/a | Somalia |

## GNI per Person

World Bank

| | | 1992-2002 |
|---|---|---|
| largest | 1 | Seychelles |
| | 2 | Gabon |
| | 3 | Botswana |
| | 4 | Mauritius |
| | 5 | Equatorial Guinea |
| | 6 | South Africa |
| | 7 | Swaziland |
| | 8 | Namibia |
| | 9 | Angola |
| | 10 | Cape Verde |
| | 11 | Congo, Rep. |
| | 12 | Djibouti |
| | 13 | Cameroon |
| | 14 | Côte d'Ivoire |
| | 15 | Mauritania |
| | 16 | Lesotho |
| | | SSA average |
| | 17 | Senegal |
| | 18 | Kenya |
| | 19 | Sudan |
| | 20 | Nigeria |
| | 21 | Benin |
| | 22 | Comoros |
| | 23 | Guinea |
| | 24 | Ghana |
| | 25 | Zambia |
| | 26 | Gambia, The |
| | 27 | Burkina Faso |
| | 28 | Chad |
| | 29 | Mali |
| | 30 | Madagascar |
| | 31 | Tanzania |
| | 32 | Eritrea |
| | 32 | Togo |
| | 32 | Uganda |
| | 33 | Central African Rep. |
| | 34 | Malawi |
| | 35 | Rwanda |
| | 36 | Niger |
| | 37 | Ethiopia |
| | 38 | Mozambique |
| | 39 | Guinea-Bissau |
| | 40 | Sierra Leone |
| | 41 | Burundi |
| | 42 | Liberia |
| | 43 | Congo, Dem. Rep. |
| | n/a | São Tomé & Príncipe |
| | n/a | Somalia |
| smallest | n/a | Zimbabwe |

## GNI per Person

World Bank

| | | 2003-2006 |
|---|---|---|
| largest | 1 | Seychelles |
| | 2 | Equatorial Guinea |
| | 3 | Gabon |
| | 4 | Botswana |
| | 5 | Mauritius |
| | 6 | South Africa |
| | 7 | Namibia |
| | 8 | Swaziland |
| | 9 | Angola |
| | 10 | Cape Verde |
| | 11 | Congo, Rep. |
| | 12 | Djibouti |
| | 13 | Cameroon |
| | 14 | Mauritania |
| | 15 | Lesotho |
| | 16 | Sudan |
| | | SSA average |
| | 17 | Côte d'Ivoire |
| | 18 | Senegal |
| | 19 | Kenya |
| | 20 | Nigeria |
| | 21 | Benin |
| | 22 | Ghana |
| | 23 | Chad |
| | 23 | Comoros |
| | 24 | Guinea |
| | 25 | Zambia |
| | 26 | Burkina Faso |
| | 27 | Gambia, The |
| | 28 | Mali |
| | 29 | Tanzania |
| | 30 | Uganda |
| | 31 | Madagascar |
| | 32 | Togo |
| | 33 | Eritrea |
| | 34 | Rwanda |
| | 35 | Central African Rep. |
| | 36 | Malawi |
| | 37 | Mozambique |
| | 38 | Niger |
| | 39 | Sierra Leone |
| | 40 | Ethiopia |
| | 41 | Guinea-Bissau |
| | 42 | Burundi |
| | 43 | Congo, Dem. Rep. |
| | 43 | Liberia |
| | n/a | São Tomé & Príncipe |
| | n/a | Somalia |
| smallest | n/a | Zimbabwe |

## Growth in GNI per Person

Primary data: World Bank

| | | 2000-2002 |
|---|---|---|
| largest | 1 | Equatorial Guinea |
| | 2 | Sierra Leone |
| | 3 | Liberia |
| | 4 | Angola |
| | 5 | Sudan |
| | 6 | Mozambique |
| | 7 | Congo, Rep. |
| | 8 | Mauritius |
| | 9 | Tanzania |
| | 10 | Namibia |
| | 11 | Ethiopia |
| | 12 | Cape Verde |
| | 13 | Botswana |
| | 14 | Rwanda |
| | 15 | Mauritania |
| | 16 | Zambia |
| | 17 | Uganda |
| | 18 | Guinea |
| | 19 | Benin |
| | 20 | South Africa |
| | 21 | Ghana |
| | 22 | Chad |
| | 23 | Mali |
| | 24 | Cameroon |
| | 25 | Burkina Faso |
| | | SSA average |
| | 26 | Comoros |
| | 27 | Senegal |
| | 28 | Lesotho |
| | 29 | Djibouti |
| | 30 | Niger |
| | 31 | Gambia, The |
| | 32 | Gabon |
| | 33 | Kenya |
| | 34 | Burundi |
| | 35 | Central African Rep. |
| | 36 | Togo |
| | 37 | Swaziland |
| | 38 | Guinea-Bissau |
| | 39 | Seychelles |
| | 40 | Nigeria |
| | 41 | Congo, Dem. Rep. |
| | 42 | Madagascar |
| | 43 | Côte d'Ivoire |
| | 44 | Malawi |
| | 45 | Eritrea |
| | n/a | São Tomé & Príncipe |
| | n/a | Somalia |
| smallest | n/a | Zimbabwe |

## Growth in GNI per Person

Primary data: World Bank

| | | 2003-2006 |
|---|---|---|
| largest | 1 | Equatorial Guinea |
| | 2 | Angola |
| | 3 | Sudan |
| | 4 | Chad |
| | 5 | Botswana |
| | 6 | Nigeria |
| | 7 | Ethiopia |
| | 8 | Djibouti |
| | 9 | Lesotho |
| | 10 | Ghana |
| | 11 | Sierra Leone |
| | 12 | Tanzania |
| | 13 | Congo, Dem. Rep. |
| | 14 | Madagascar |
| | 15 | South Africa |
| | 16 | Gambia, The |
| | 17 | Mauritius |
| | 18 | Burkina Faso |
| | 19 | Mozambique |
| | | SSA average |
| | 20 | Malawi |
| | 21 | Cape Verde |
| | 22 | Mali |
| | 23 | Kenya |
| | 24 | Namibia |
| | 25 | Congo, Rep. |
| | 26 | Mauritania |
| | 27 | Senegal |
| | 28 | Cameroon |
| | 29 | Uganda |
| | 30 | Rwanda |
| | 31 | Zambia |
| | 32 | Swaziland |
| | 33 | Niger |
| | 34 | Guinea |
| | 35 | Seychelles |
| | 36 | Benin |
| | 37 | Togo |
| | 38 | Comoros |
| | 39 | Guinea-Bissau |
| | 40 | Côte d'Ivoire |
| | 41 | Central African Rep. |
| | 42 | Burundi |
| | 43 | Eritrea |
| | 44 | Gabon |
| | 45 | Liberia |
| | n/a | São Tomé & Príncipe |
| | n/a | Somalia |
| smallest | n/a | Zimbabwe |

# appendix B3: performance tables - economic strength

### Real GDP Growth

IMF

| | | 1999-2002 |
|---|---|---|
| highest | 1 | Equatorial Guinea |
| | 2 | Liberia |
| | 3 | Sierra Leone |
| | 4 | Nigeria |
| | 5 | Mozambique |
| | 6 | Cape Verde |
| | 7 | Rwanda |
| | 8 | Botswana |
| | 9 | Uganda |
| | 10 | Angola |
| | 11 | Sudan |
| | 12 | Tanzania |
| | 13 | Ethiopia |
| | 14 | Benin |
| | 15 | Burkina Faso |
| | 16 | Chad |
| | | SSA average |
| | 17 | São Tomé & Príncipe |
| | 18 | Mauritius |
| | 19 | Cameroon |
| | 20 | Ghana |
| | 21 | Mali |
| | 22 | Namibia |
| | 23 | Guinea |
| | 24 | Senegal |
| | 25 | Gambia, The |
| | 26 | Zambia |
| | 27 | Congo, Rep. |
| | 28 | South Africa |
| | 29 | Mauritania |
| | 30 | Niger |
| | 31 | Comoros |
| | 32 | Guinea-Bissau |
| | 33 | Djibouti |
| | 34 | Kenya |
| | 35 | Swaziland |
| | 36 | Lesotho |
| | 37 | Seychelles |
| | 38 | Central African Rep. |
| | 39 | Burundi |
| | 40 | Madagascar |
| | 41 | Malawi |
| | 42 | Eritrea |
| | 43 | Togo |
| | 44 | Côte d'Ivoire |
| | 45 | Gabon |
| | 46 | Congo, Dem. Rep. |
| | 47 | Zimbabwe |
| lowest | n/a | Somalia |

### Real GDP Growth

IMF

| | | 2003-2006 |
|---|---|---|
| highest | 1 | Chad |
| | 2 | Angola |
| | 3 | Equatorial Guinea |
| | 4 | Nigeria |
| | 5 | Sierra Leone |
| | 6 | Mozambique |
| | 7 | Ethiopia |
| | 8 | Sudan |
| | 9 | Tanzania |
| | 10 | Mauritania |
| | 11 | Congo, Dem. Rep. |
| | 12 | Madagascar |
| | 13 | Gambia, The |
| | 14 | Cape Verde |
| | 15 | Burkina Faso |
| | | SSA average |
| | 16 | São Tomé & Príncipe |
| | 17 | Ghana |
| | 18 | Zambia |
| | 19 | Uganda |
| | 20 | Mali |
| | 21 | Botswana |
| | 22 | Senegal |
| | 23 | Niger |
| | 24 | Malawi |
| | 25 | Kenya |
| | 26 | Namibia |
| | 27 | South Africa |
| | 28 | Congo, Rep. |
| | 29 | Rwanda |
| | 30 | Lesotho |
| | 31 | Mauritius |
| | 32 | Djibouti |
| | 33 | Benin |
| | 34 | Cameroon |
| | 35 | Togo |
| | 36 | Swaziland |
| | 37 | Burundi |
| | 38 | Guinea |
| | 39 | Gabon |
| | 40 | Comoros |
| | 41 | Guinea-Bissau |
| | 42 | Côte d'Ivoire |
| | 43 | Eritrea |
| | 44 | Central African Rep. |
| | 45 | Seychelles |
| | 46 | Liberia |
| | 47 | Zimbabwe |
| lowest | n/a | Somalia |

### Real GDP Growth

IMF

| | | 2007-2010 |
|---|---|---|
| highest | 1 | Angola |
| | 2 | Liberia |
| | 3 | Sudan |
| | 4 | Congo, Dem. Rep. |
| | 5 | Ethiopia |
| | 6 | Equatorial Guinea |
| | 7 | Tanzania |
| | 8 | Nigeria |
| | 9 | Madagascar |
| | 10 | Cape Verde |
| | 11 | Congo, Rep. |
| | 12 | Ghana |
| | 13 | Mozambique |
| | 14 | Malawi |
| | 15 | Uganda |
| | 16 | Djibouti |
| | | SSA average |
| | 17 | Sierra Leone |
| | 18 | Gambia, The |
| | 19 | São Tomé & Príncipe |
| | 20 | Zambia |
| | 21 | Rwanda |
| | 22 | Mauritius |
| | 23 | Senegal |
| | 24 | Lesotho |
| | 25 | Burundi |
| | 26 | Benin |
| | 27 | Burkina Faso |
| | 28 | Botswana |
| | 29 | Central African Rep. |
| | 30 | Mauritania |
| | 31 | Namibia |
| | 32 | Seychelles |
| | 33 | South Africa |
| | 34 | Mali |
| | 35 | Kenya |
| | 36 | Cameroon |
| | 37 | Niger |
| | 38 | Guinea |
| | 39 | Gabon |
| | 40 | Côte d'Ivoire |
| | 41 | Togo |
| | 42 | Guinea-Bissau |
| | 43 | Eritrea |
| | 44 | Swaziland |
| | 45 | Comoros |
| | 46 | Chad |
| | 47 | Zimbabwe |
| lowest | n/a | Somalia |

### Inflation

IMF

| | | 1999-2002 |
|---|---|---|
| lowest rate | 1 | Ethiopia |
| | 2 | Gabon |
| | 3 | Djibouti |
| | 4 | Burkina Faso |
| | 5 | Rwanda |
| | 6 | Senegal |
| | 7 | Niger |
| | 8 | Congo, Rep. |
| | 9 | Cape Verde |
| | 10 | Central African Rep. |
| | 11 | Mali |
| | 12 | Uganda |
| | 13 | Togo |
| | 14 | Côte d'Ivoire |
| | 15 | Benin |
| | 16 | Cameroon |
| | 17 | Chad |
| | 18 | Guinea-Bissau |
| | 19 | Comoros |
| | 20 | Gambia, The |
| | 21 | Seychelles |
| | 22 | Guinea |
| | 23 | Equatorial Guinea |
| | 24 | Mauritius |
| | 25 | Mauritania |
| | 26 | Kenya |
| | 27 | Tanzania |
| | 28 | South Africa |
| | 29 | Botswana |
| | 30 | Sierra Leone |
| | 31 | Swaziland |
| | 32 | Lesotho |
| | 33 | Burundi |
| | 34 | Sudan |
| | 35 | Namibia |
| | 36 | São Tomé & Príncipe |
| | 37 | Mozambique |
| | 38 | Madagascar |
| | 39 | Liberia |
| | 40 | Nigeria |
| | | SSA average |
| | 41 | Eritrea |
| | 42 | Ghana |
| | 43 | Zambia |
| | 44 | Malawi |
| | 45 | Zimbabwe |
| | 46 | Angola |
| highest rate | 47 | Congo, Dem. Rep. |
| | n/a | Somalia |

### Inflation

IMF

| | | 2003-2006 |
|---|---|---|
| lowest rate | 1 | Gabon |
| | 2 | Guinea-Bissau |
| | 3 | Mali |
| | 4 | Senegal |
| | 5 | Cape Verde |
| | 6 | Niger |
| | 7 | Seychelles |
| | 8 | Cameroon |
| | 9 | Togo |
| | 10 | Chad |
| | 11 | Burkina Faso |
| | 12 | Côte d'Ivoire |
| | 13 | Benin |
| | 14 | Djibouti |
| | 15 | Central African Rep. |
| | 16 | Congo, Rep. |
| | 17 | Comoros |
| | 18 | South Africa |
| | 19 | Namibia |
| | 20 | Mauritius |
| | 21 | Tanzania |
| | 22 | Swaziland |
| | 23 | Equatorial Guinea |
| | 24 | Lesotho |
| | 25 | Uganda |
| | 26 | Liberia |
| | 27 | Sudan |
| | 28 | Mauritania |
| | | SSA average |
| | 29 | Burundi |
| | 30 | Botswana |
| | 31 | Rwanda |
| | 32 | Gambia, The |
| | 33 | Madagascar |
| | 34 | Ethiopia |
| | 35 | Sierra Leone |
| | 36 | Mozambique |
| | 37 | Kenya |
| | 38 | Malawi |
| | 39 | Congo, Dem. Rep. |
| | 40 | Nigeria |
| | 41 | São Tomé & Príncipe |
| | 42 | Ghana |
| | 43 | Zambia |
| | 44 | Eritrea |
| | 45 | Guinea |
| | 46 | Angola |
| highest rate | 47 | Zimbabwe |
| | n/a | Somalia |

| Inflation (IMF) | | Exchange Rate Stability (Primary data: IMF) | | Exchange Rate Stability (Primary data: IMF) | |
|---|---|---|---|---|---|
| 2007-2010 | | 1999-2006 | | 2003-2010 | |
| *lowest rate* | | *most stable* | | *most stable* | |
| 1 | Chad | 1 | Liberia | 1 | Liberia |
| 2 | Cameroon | 2 | Seychelles | 2 | Sudan |
| 3 | Niger | 3 | Sudan | 3 | Lesotho |
| 4 | Benin | 4 | Ethiopia | 4 | Swaziland |
| 5 | Mali | 5 | Botswana | 5 | Botswana |
| 6 | Central African Rep. | 6 | Lesotho | 6 | South Africa |
| 7 | Burkina Faso | 7 | Swaziland | 7 | Gambia, The |
| 8 | Côte d'Ivoire | 8 | South Africa | 8 | Namibia |
| 9 | Comoros | 9 | Namibia | 9 | Seychelles |
| 10 | Guinea-Bissau | 10 | Djibouti | 10 | Ethiopia |
| 11 | Congo, Rep. | 11 | Mauritius | 11 | Eritrea |
| 12 | Cape Verde | 12 | Eritrea | 12 | Mauritius |
| 13 | Togo | 13 | Gambia, The | 13 | Cape Verde |
| 14 | Senegal | 14 | Kenya | 14 | Cameroon |
| 15 | Gabon | 15 | Cape Verde | 15 | Comoros |
| 16 | Djibouti | 16 | Senegal | 16 | Benin |
| 17 | Equatorial Guinea | 17 | Cameroon | 17 | Guinea-Bissau |
| 18 | Gambia, The | 18 | Benin | 18 | Mali |
| 19 | Uganda | 19 | Niger | 19 | Djibouti |
| 20 | Mozambique | 20 | Côte d'Ivoire | 20 | Central African Rep. |
| 21 | Tanzania | 21 | Burkina Faso | 21 | Kenya |
| 22 | Mauritania | 22 | Mali | 22 | Burkina Faso |
| 23 | Sudan | 23 | Guinea-Bissau | 23 | Senegal |
| 24 | Rwanda | 24 | Central African Rep. | 24 | Niger |
| 25 | South Africa | 25 | Comoros | 25 | Côte d'Ivoire |
| 26 | Namibia | 26 | Malawi | 26 | Togo |
| 27 | Malawi | 27 | Togo | 27 | Malawi |
| 28 | Botswana | 28 | Nigeria | 28 | Angola |
| | SSA average | 29 | Mauritania | 29 | Nigeria |
| 29 | Zambia | 30 | Angola | 30 | Mauritania |
| 30 | Lesotho | 31 | Gabon | 31 | Chad |
| 31 | Madagascar | 32 | Rwanda | 32 | Rwanda |
| 32 | Swaziland | 33 | Chad | 33 | Gabon |
| 33 | Nigeria | 34 | Tanzania | 34 | Tanzania |
| 34 | Burundi | 35 | Congo, Rep. | 35 | Congo, Rep. |
| 35 | Ghana | 36 | Burundi | 36 | Burundi |
| 36 | Kenya | 37 | Uganda | 37 | Congo, Dem. Rep. |
| 37 | Mauritius | 38 | Equatorial Guinea | 38 | Equatorial Guinea |
| 38 | Liberia | 39 | Congo, Dem. Rep. | 39 | Uganda |
| 39 | Angola | 40 | Madagascar | 40 | Madagascar |
| 40 | Eritrea | 41 | Zimbabwe | 41 | Sierra Leone |
| 41 | Sierra Leone | 42 | Sierra Leone | 42 | Zambia |
| 42 | Seychelles | 43 | Guinea | 43 | Guinea |
| 43 | São Tomé & Príncipe | 44 | Zambia | 44 | Ghana |
| 44 | Guinea | 45 | São Tomé & Príncipe | 45 | Mozambique |
| 45 | Congo, Dem. Rep. | 46 | Ghana | 46 | São Tomé & Príncipe |
| 46 | Ethiopia | 47 | Mozambique | 47 | Zimbabwe |
| 47 | Zimbabwe | n/a | Somalia | n/a | Somalia |
| *highest rate* | | *least stable* | | *least stable* | |

# B4 performance tables - economic productivity

**Productivity Index**

Primary data: IMF

| | | 1999-2002 |
|---|---|---|
| highest | 1 | Seychelles |
| | 2 | Gabon |
| | 3 | Botswana |
| | 4 | Mauritius |
| | 5 | South Africa |
| | 6 | Equatorial Guinea |
| | 7 | Swaziland |
| | 8 | Namibia |
| | 9 | Congo, Rep. |
| | 10 | Angola |
| | 11 | Cape Verde |
| | 12 | Djibouti |
| | 13 | Cameroon |
| | 14 | Côte d'Ivoire |
| | 15 | Mauritania |
| | | SSA=1.00 |
| | 16 | Sudan |
| | 17 | Senegal |
| | 18 | Kenya |
| | 19 | Nigeria |
| | 20 | Benin |
| | 21 | São Tomé & Príncipe |
| | 22 | Ghana |
| | 23 | Lesotho |
| | 24 | Comoros |
| | 25 | Gambia, The |
| | 26 | Guinea |
| | 27 | Chad |
| | 28 | Zambia |
| | 29 | Burkina Faso |
| | 30 | Eritrea |
| | 31 | Tanzania |
| | 32 | Mali |
| | 33 | Madagascar |
| | 34 | Uganda |
| | 35 | Togo |
| | 36 | Central African Rep. |
| | 37 | Rwanda |
| | 38 | Malawi |
| | 39 | Niger |
| | 40 | Mozambique |
| | 41 | Guinea-Bissau |
| | 42 | Ethiopia |
| | 43 | Liberia |
| | 44 | Sierra Leone |
| | 45 | Burundi |
| | 46 | Zimbabwe |
| | 47 | Congo, Dem. Rep. |
| lowest | n/a | Somalia |

**Productivity Index**

Primary data: IMF

| | | 2003-2006 |
|---|---|---|
| highest | 1 | Seychelles |
| | 2 | Botswana |
| | 3 | Gabon |
| | 4 | Equatorial Guinea |
| | 5 | Mauritius |
| | 6 | South Africa |
| | 7 | Namibia |
| | 8 | Swaziland |
| | 9 | Angola |
| | 10 | Congo, Rep. |
| | 11 | Cape Verde |
| | 12 | Djibouti |
| | 13 | Cameroon |
| | 14 | Nigeria |
| | 15 | Mauritania |
| | | SSA=1.00 |
| | 16 | Sudan |
| | 17 | Côte d'Ivoire |
| | 18 | Senegal |
| | 19 | Chad |
| | 20 | Kenya |
| | 21 | Benin |
| | 22 | São Tomé & Príncipe |
| | 23 | Ghana |
| | 24 | Zambia |
| | 25 | Gambia, The |
| | 26 | Lesotho |
| | 27 | Burkina Faso |
| | 28 | Comoros |
| | 29 | Tanzania |
| | 30 | Guinea |
| | 31 | Mali |
| | 32 | Madagascar |
| | 33 | Uganda |
| | 34 | Eritrea |
| | 35 | Rwanda |
| | 36 | Togo |
| | 37 | Mozambique |
| | 38 | Malawi |
| | 39 | Central African Rep. |
| | 40 | Niger |
| | 41 | Ethiopia |
| | 42 | Sierra Leone |
| | 43 | Guinea-Bissau |
| | 44 | Burundi |
| | 45 | Liberia |
| | 46 | Congo, Dem. Rep. |
| | 47 | Zimbabwe |
| lowest | n/a | Somalia |

**Productivity Index**

Primary data: IMF

| | | 2007-2010 |
|---|---|---|
| highest | 1 | Botswana |
| | 2 | Seychelles |
| | 3 | Gabon |
| | 4 | Equatorial Guinea |
| | 5 | Mauritius |
| | 6 | South Africa |
| | 7 | Angola |
| | 8 | Namibia |
| | 9 | Swaziland |
| | 10 | Congo, Rep. |
| | 11 | Cape Verde |
| | 12 | Djibouti |
| | 13 | Sudan |
| | 14 | Nigeria |
| | | SSA=1.00 |
| | 15 | Cameroon |
| | 16 | Mauritania |
| | 17 | Côte d'Ivoire |
| | 18 | Senegal |
| | 19 | Kenya |
| | 20 | Chad |
| | 21 | São Tomé & Príncipe |
| | 22 | Benin |
| | 23 | Ghana |
| | 24 | Gambia, The |
| | 25 | Zambia |
| | 26 | Tanzania |
| | 27 | Lesotho |
| | 28 | Burkina Faso |
| | 29 | Madagascar |
| | 30 | Comoros |
| | 31 | Guinea |
| | 32 | Mali |
| | 33 | Uganda |
| | 34 | Rwanda |
| | 35 | Mozambique |
| | 36 | Ethiopia |
| | 37 | Malawi |
| | 38 | Togo |
| | 39 | Eritrea |
| | 40 | Central African Rep. |
| | 41 | Sierra Leone |
| | 42 | Niger |
| | 43 | Guinea-Bissau |
| | 44 | Burundi |
| | 45 | Liberia |
| | 46 | Congo, Dem. Rep. |
| | n/a | Somalia |
| lowest | n/a | Zimbabwe |

### Size of Services Sector as % of Total Economy

World Bank

| | | 2003-2006 |
|---|---|---|
| largest | 1 | Djibouti |
| | 2 | Cape Verde |
| | 3 | Seychelles |
| | 4 | South Africa |
| | 5 | Mauritius |
| | 6 | São Tomé & Príncipe |
| | 7 | Zimbabwe |
| | 8 | Namibia |
| | 9 | Senegal |
| | 10 | Eritrea |
| | 11 | Madagascar |
| | 12 | Benin |
| | 13 | Gambia, The |
| | 14 | Kenya |
| | | SSA |
| | 15 | Côte d'Ivoire |
| | 16 | Guinea |
| | 17 | Cameroon |
| | 18 | Zambia |
| | 19 | Uganda |
| | 20 | Mozambique |
| | 21 | Mauritania |
| | 22 | Malawi |
| | 23 | Botswana |
| | 24 | Niger |
| | 25 | Burundi |
| | 26 | Swaziland |
| | 27 | Lesotho |
| | 28 | Burkina Faso |
| | 29 | Ethiopia |
| | 30 | Sudan |
| | 31 | Mali |
| | 32 | Rwanda |
| | 33 | Ghana |
| | 34 | Tanzania |
| | 35 | Comoros |
| | 36 | Gabon |
| | 37 | Togo |
| | 38 | Chad |
| | 39 | Sierra Leone |
| | 40 | Central African Rep. |
| | 41 | Congo, Rep. |
| | 42 | Congo, Dem. Rep. |
| | 43 | Guinea-Bissau |
| | 44 | Nigeria |
| | 45 | Angola |
| | 46 | Liberia |
| | 47 | Equatorial Guinea |
| smallest | n/a | Somalia |

### Productivity in Agriculture as % of GDP

World Bank

| | | 1999-2002 |
|---|---|---|
| highest | 1 | Liberia |
| | 2 | Guinea-Bissau |
| | 3 | Central African Rep. |
| | 4 | Sierra Leone |
| | 5 | Congo, Dem. Rep. |
| | 6 | Comoros |
| | 7 | Ethiopia |
| | 8 | Tanzania |
| | 9 | Sudan |
| | 10 | Rwanda |
| | 11 | Burundi |
| | 12 | Chad |
| | 13 | Mali |
| | 14 | Niger |
| | 15 | Malawi |
| | 16 | Togo |
| | 17 | Benin |
| | 18 | Uganda |
| | 19 | Ghana |
| | 20 | Gambia, The |
| | 21 | Kenya |
| | 22 | Burkina Faso |
| | 23 | Nigeria |
| | 24 | Madagascar |
| | 25 | Mauritania |
| | 26 | Mozambique |
| | 27 | Côte d'Ivoire |
| | 28 | Zambia |
| | 29 | Cameroon |
| | 30 | Guinea |
| | 31 | São Tomé & Príncipe |
| | | SSA average |
| | 32 | Senegal |
| | 33 | Eritrea |
| | 34 | Zimbabwe |
| | 35 | Lesotho |
| | 36 | Swaziland |
| | 37 | Namibia |
| | 38 | Cape Verde |
| | 39 | Equatorial Guinea |
| | 40 | Mauritius |
| | 41 | Angola |
| | 42 | Gabon |
| | 43 | Congo, Rep. |
| | 44 | South Africa |
| | 45 | Djibouti |
| | 46 | Seychelles |
| | 47 | Botswana |
| lowest | n/a | Somalia |

### Productivity in Agriculture as % of GDP

World Bank

| | | 2003-2006 |
|---|---|---|
| highest | 1 | Liberia |
| | 2 | Guinea-Bissau |
| | 3 | Central African Rep. |
| | 4 | Comoros |
| | 5 | Congo, Dem. Rep. |
| | 6 | Sierra Leone |
| | 7 | Ethiopia |
| | 8 | Tanzania |
| | 9 | Togo |
| | 10 | Rwanda |
| | 11 | Niger |
| | 12 | Burundi |
| | 13 | Ghana |
| | 14 | Mali |
| | 15 | Malawi |
| | 16 | Sudan |
| | 17 | Uganda |
| | 18 | Gambia, The |
| | 19 | Benin |
| | 20 | Burkina Faso |
| | 21 | Madagascar |
| | 22 | Kenya |
| | 23 | Mozambique |
| | 24 | Chad |
| | 25 | Côte d'Ivoire |
| | 26 | Zambia |
| | 27 | Mauritania |
| | 28 | Nigeria |
| | 29 | Cameroon |
| | 30 | São Tomé & Príncipe |
| | 31 | Zimbabwe |
| | 32 | Guinea |
| | 33 | Eritrea |
| | 34 | Lesotho |
| | 35 | Senegal |
| | | SSA average |
| | 36 | Swaziland |
| | 37 | Namibia |
| | 38 | Cape Verde |
| | 39 | Angola |
| | 40 | Mauritius |
| | 41 | Gabon |
| | 42 | Congo, Rep. |
| | 43 | Equatorial Guinea |
| | 44 | Djibouti |
| | 45 | South Africa |
| | 46 | Seychelles |
| | 47 | Botswana |
| lowest | n/a | Somalia |

### Productivity in Agriculture as $PPP per Person

IMF, World Bank

| | | 1999-2002 |
|---|---|---|
| highest | 1 | Gabon |
| | 2 | Sudan |
| | 3 | Swaziland |
| | 4 | Mauritius |
| | 5 | Comoros |
| | 6 | Equatorial Guinea |
| | 7 | Seychelles |
| | 8 | Benin |
| | 9 | Mauritania |
| | 10 | Kenya |
| | 11 | Cameroon |
| | 12 | Chad |
| | 13 | Côte d'Ivoire |
| | 14 | Namibia |
| | 15 | Nigeria |
| | 16 | Tanzania |
| | 17 | Ghana |
| | 18 | Central African Rep. |
| | 19 | Gambia, The |
| | 20 | Mali |
| | 21 | Burkina Faso |
| | 22 | Liberia |
| | 23 | Guinea-Bissau |
| | | SSA average |
| | 24 | Rwanda |
| | 25 | Uganda |
| | 26 | Togo |
| | 27 | Botswana |
| | 28 | South Africa |
| | 29 | Senegal |
| | 30 | Malawi |
| | 31 | Madagascar |
| | 32 | São Tomé & Príncipe |
| | 33 | Ethiopia |
| | 34 | Zambia |
| | 35 | Guinea |
| | 36 | Niger |
| | 37 | Cape Verde |
| | 38 | Sierra Leone |
| | 39 | Angola |
| | 40 | Congo, Rep. |
| | 41 | Lesotho |
| | 42 | Eritrea |
| | 43 | Burundi |
| | 44 | Mozambique |
| | 45 | Congo, Dem. Rep. |
| | 46 | Djibouti |
| | 47 | Zimbabwe |
| lowest | n/a | Somalia |

### Productivity in Agriculture as $PPP per Person

IMF, World Bank

| | | 2003-2006 |
|---|---|---|
| highest | 1 | Gabon |
| | 2 | Sudan |
| | 3 | Mauritius |
| | 4 | Comoros |
| | 5 | Swaziland |
| | 6 | Namibia |
| | 7 | Tanzania |
| | 8 | Ghana |
| | 9 | Benin |
| | 10 | Seychelles |
| | 11 | Equatorial Guinea |
| | 12 | Cameroon |
| | 13 | Kenya |
| | 14 | Nigeria |
| | 15 | Mauritania |
| | 16 | Côte d'Ivoire |
| | 17 | Central African Rep. |
| | 18 | Chad |
| | 19 | Gambia, The |
| | 20 | Burkina Faso |
| | 21 | Mali |
| | 22 | Angola |
| | 23 | Rwanda |
| | 24 | Togo |
| | 25 | Botswana |
| | 26 | Ethiopia |
| | 27 | Guinea-Bissau |
| | | SSA average |
| | 28 | Uganda |
| | 29 | Sierra Leone |
| | 30 | São Tomé & Príncipe |
| | 31 | Madagascar |
| | 32 | Zambia |
| | 33 | Senegal |
| | 34 | South Africa |
| | 35 | Niger |
| | 36 | Malawi |
| | 37 | Cape Verde |
| | 38 | Liberia |
| | 39 | Mozambique |
| | 40 | Lesotho |
| | 41 | Guinea |
| | 42 | Congo, Rep. |
| | 43 | Eritrea |
| | 44 | Congo, Dem. Rep. |
| | 45 | Burundi |
| | 46 | Djibouti |
| | 47 | Zimbabwe |
| lowest | n/a | Somalia |

# appendix B4: performance tables - economic productivity

### Growth in Agriculture Productivity

IMF, World Bank

| | | 1999-2002 |
|---|---|---|
| highest | 1 | São Tomé & Príncipe |
| | 2 | Comoros |
| | 3 | Mozambique |
| | 4 | Seychelles |
| | 5 | South Africa |
| | 6 | Zambia |
| | 7 | Tanzania |
| | 8 | Liberia |
| | 9 | Namibia |
| | 10 | Nigeria |
| | 11 | Gambia, The |
| | 12 | Chad |
| | 13 | Ghana |
| | 14 | Sierra Leone |
| | 15 | Sudan |
| | 16 | Burkina Faso |
| | 17 | Djibouti |
| | 18 | Central African Rep. |
| | 19 | Mauritius |
| | | SSA average |
| | 20 | Malawi |
| | 21 | Lesotho |
| | 22 | Togo |
| | 23 | Guinea |
| | 24 | Benin |
| | 25 | Côte d'Ivoire |
| | 26 | Madagascar |
| | 27 | Rwanda |
| | 28 | Niger |
| | 29 | Kenya |
| | 30 | Cameroon |
| | 31 | Congo, Dem. Rep. |
| | 32 | Ethiopia |
| | 33 | Angola |
| | 34 | Botswana |
| | 35 | Senegal |
| | 36 | Mauritania |
| | 37 | Uganda |
| | 38 | Burundi |
| | 39 | Mali |
| | 40 | Cape Verde |
| | 41 | Swaziland |
| | 42 | Guinea-Bissau |
| | 43 | Gabon |
| | 44 | Equatorial Guinea |
| | 45 | Congo, Rep. |
| | 46 | Zimbabwe |
| | 47 | Eritrea |
| lowest | n/a | Somalia |

### Growth in Agriculture Productivity

IMF, World Bank

| | | 2003-2006 |
|---|---|---|
| highest | 1 | Angola |
| | 2 | Cape Verde |
| | 3 | Ethiopia |
| | 4 | Gambia, The |
| | 5 | Eritrea |
| | 6 | Togo |
| | 7 | Mozambique |
| | 8 | Tanzania |
| | 9 | Ghana |
| | 10 | Mali |
| | 11 | Sierra Leone |
| | 12 | Namibia |
| | 13 | Madagascar |
| | 14 | Zimbabwe |
| | 15 | Rwanda |
| | 16 | Uganda |
| | 17 | Senegal |
| | 18 | Zambia |
| | 19 | Niger |
| | 20 | Guinea-Bissau |
| | 21 | Lesotho |
| | 22 | Burkina Faso |
| | 23 | Djibouti |
| | 24 | Malawi |
| | 25 | Congo, Dem. Rep. |
| | 26 | Botswana |
| | 27 | Kenya |
| | 28 | Benin |
| | 29 | Nigeria |
| | 30 | Central African Rep. |
| | 31 | São Tomé & Príncipe |
| | 32 | Seychelles |
| | 33 | Sudan |
| | | SSA average |
| | 34 | Comoros |
| | 35 | Cameroon |
| | 36 | Mauritius |
| | 37 | Burundi |
| | 38 | Swaziland |
| | 39 | Côte d'Ivoire |
| | 40 | Gabon |
| | 41 | South Africa |
| | 42 | Congo, Rep. |
| | 43 | Chad |
| | 44 | Guinea |
| | 45 | Mauritania |
| | 46 | Liberia |
| | 47 | Equatorial Guinea |
| lowest | n/a | Somalia |

### Productivity in Industry as % of GDP

World Bank

| | | 1999-2002 |
|---|---|---|
| highest | 1 | Equatorial Guinea |
| | 2 | Angola |
| | 3 | Congo, Rep. |
| | 4 | Botswana |
| | 5 | Gabon |
| | 6 | Swaziland |
| | 7 | Nigeria |
| | 8 | Lesotho |
| | 9 | Cameroon |
| | 10 | South Africa |
| | 11 | Guinea |
| | 12 | Mauritius |
| | | SSA average |
| | 13 | Namibia |
| | 14 | Seychelles |
| | 15 | Mauritania |
| | 16 | Sierra Leone |
| | 17 | Zambia |
| | 18 | Ghana |
| | 19 | Senegal |
| | 20 | Côte d'Ivoire |
| | 21 | Eritrea |
| | 22 | Mozambique |
| | 23 | Zimbabwe |
| | 24 | Mali |
| | 25 | Burkina Faso |
| | 26 | Rwanda |
| | 27 | Uganda |
| | 28 | Congo, Dem. Rep. |
| | 29 | Sudan |
| | 30 | Burundi |
| | 31 | Malawi |
| | 32 | Togo |
| | 33 | Niger |
| | 34 | Kenya |
| | 35 | São Tomé & Príncipe |
| | 36 | Cape Verde |
| | 37 | Central African Rep. |
| | 38 | Tanzania |
| | 39 | Djibouti |
| | 40 | Madagascar |
| | 41 | Benin |
| | 42 | Ethiopia |
| | 43 | Gambia, The |
| | 44 | Chad |
| | 45 | Guinea-Bissau |
| | 46 | Comoros |
| | 47 | Liberia |
| lowest | n/a | Somalia |

### Productivity in Industry as % of GDP

World Bank

| | | 2003-2006 |
|---|---|---|
| highest | 1 | Equatorial Guinea |
| | 2 | Angola |
| | 3 | Congo, Rep. |
| | 4 | Gabon |
| | 5 | Nigeria |
| | 6 | Botswana |
| | 7 | Swaziland |
| | 8 | Chad |
| | 9 | Lesotho |
| | 10 | Guinea |
| | 11 | Mauritania |
| | | SSA average |
| | 12 | Cameroon |
| | 13 | South Africa |
| | 14 | Zambia |
| | 15 | Namibia |
| | 16 | Mauritius |
| | 17 | Seychelles |
| | 18 | Mozambique |
| | 19 | Sudan |
| | 20 | Congo, Dem. Rep. |
| | 21 | Ghana |
| | 22 | Sierra Leone |
| | 23 | Eritrea |
| | 24 | Côte d'Ivoire |
| | 25 | Senegal |
| | 26 | Mali |
| | 27 | Zimbabwe |
| | 28 | Togo |
| | 29 | Burkina Faso |
| | 30 | Rwanda |
| | 31 | Uganda |
| | 32 | São Tomé & Príncipe |
| | 33 | Burundi |
| | 34 | Malawi |
| | 35 | Kenya |
| | 36 | Cape Verde |
| | 37 | Niger |
| | 38 | Tanzania |
| | 39 | Djibouti |
| | 40 | Madagascar |
| | 41 | Central African Rep. |
| | 42 | Liberia |
| | 43 | Ethiopia |
| | 44 | Gambia, The |
| | 45 | Benin |
| | 46 | Guinea-Bissau |
| | 47 | Comoros |
| lowest | n/a | Somalia |

### Productivity in Industry as $PPP per Person

IMF, World Bank

| | | 1992-2002 |
|---|---|---|
| highest | 1 | Gabon |
| | 2 | Botswana |
| | 3 | Equatorial Guinea |
| | 4 | Seychelles |
| | 5 | Mauritius |
| | 6 | South Africa |
| | 7 | Congo, Rep. |
| | 8 | Angola |
| | 9 | Swaziland |
| | 10 | Namibia |
| | 11 | Cameroon |
| | 12 | Nigeria |
| | | SSA average |
| | 13 | Mauritania |
| | 14 | Lesotho |
| | 15 | Côte d'Ivoire |
| | 16 | Cape Verde |
| | 17 | Senegal |
| | 18 | Guinea |
| | 19 | Djibouti |
| | 20 | Sudan |
| | 21 | Ghana |
| | 22 | Zambia |
| | 23 | Kenya |
| | 24 | Eritrea |
| | 25 | Burkina Faso |
| | 26 | São Tomé & Príncipe |
| | 27 | Mali |
| | 28 | Benin |
| | 29 | Uganda |
| | 30 | Gambia, The |
| | 31 | Tanzania |
| | 32 | Rwanda |
| | 33 | Chad |
| | 34 | Mozambique |
| | 35 | Togo |
| | 36 | Comoros |
| | 37 | Central African Rep. |
| | 38 | Madagascar |
| | 39 | Malawi |
| | 40 | Sierra Leone |
| | 41 | Niger |
| | 42 | Ethiopia |
| | 43 | Guinea-Bissau |
| | 44 | Burundi |
| | 45 | Zimbabwe |
| | 46 | Congo, Dem. Rep. |
| | 47 | Liberia |
| lowest | n/a | Somalia |

# appendix B4: performance tables - economic productivity

### Productivity in Industry as $PPP per Person

IMF, World Bank

| | | 2003-2006 |
|---|---|---|
| highest | 1 | Equatorial Guinea |
| | 2 | Gabon |
| | 3 | Botswana |
| | 4 | Seychelles |
| | 5 | Mauritius |
| | 6 | Angola |
| | 7 | South Africa |
| | 8 | Congo, Rep. |
| | 9 | Swaziland |
| | 10 | Namibia |
| | 11 | Nigeria |
| | 12 | Chad |
| | 13 | Cameroon |
| | 14 | Mauritania |
| | | SSA average |
| | 15 | Lesotho |
| | 16 | Sudan |
| | 17 | Cape Verde |
| | 18 | Côte d'Ivoire |
| | 19 | Senegal |
| | 20 | Guinea |
| | 21 | Zambia |
| | 22 | Djibouti |
| | 23 | Ghana |
| | 24 | Kenya |
| | 25 | São Tomé & Príncipe |
| | 26 | Burkina Faso |
| | 27 | Mali |
| | 28 | Eritrea |
| | 29 | Benin |
| | 30 | Mozambique |
| | 31 | Tanzania |
| | 32 | Togo |
| | 33 | Uganda |
| | 34 | Rwanda |
| | 35 | Gambia, The |
| | 36 | Sierra Leone |
| | 37 | Madagascar |
| | 38 | Comoros |
| | 39 | Malawi |
| | 40 | Niger |
| | 41 | Central African Rep. |
| | 42 | Ethiopia |
| | 43 | Congo, Dem. Rep. |
| | 44 | Burundi |
| | 45 | Guinea-Bissau |
| | 46 | Zimbabwe |
| | 47 | Liberia |
| lowest | n/a | Somalia |

### Growth in Industry Productivity

IMF, World Bank

| | | 1999-2002 |
|---|---|---|
| highest | 1 | Equatorial Guinea |
| | 2 | Mali |
| | 3 | Nigeria |
| | 4 | Sudan |
| | 5 | Congo, Rep. |
| | 6 | Angola |
| | 7 | São Tomé & Príncipe |
| | 8 | Mozambique |
| | 9 | Uganda |
| | 10 | Sierra Leone |
| | 11 | Burkina Faso |
| | 12 | Ethiopia |
| | 13 | Chad |
| | 14 | Botswana |
| | 15 | Seychelles |
| | 16 | Cape Verde |
| | 17 | Namibia |
| | 18 | Tanzania |
| | | SSA average |
| | 19 | Cameroon |
| | 20 | Rwanda |
| | 21 | Senegal |
| | 22 | Mauritius |
| | 23 | South Africa |
| | 24 | Benin |
| | 25 | Djibouti |
| | 26 | Lesotho |
| | 27 | Gambia, The |
| | 28 | Ghana |
| | 29 | Guinea |
| | 30 | Burundi |
| | 31 | Swaziland |
| | 32 | Eritrea |
| | 33 | Mauritania |
| | 34 | Niger |
| | 35 | Gabon |
| | 36 | Kenya |
| | 37 | Comoros |
| | 38 | Zambia |
| | 39 | Madagascar |
| | 40 | Togo |
| | 41 | Côte d'Ivoire |
| | 42 | Guinea-Bissau |
| | 43 | Congo, Dem. Rep. |
| | 44 | Malawi |
| | 45 | Central African Rep. |
| | 46 | Zimbabwe |
| | 47 | Liberia |
| lowest | n/a | Somalia |

### Growth in Industry Productivity

IMF, World Bank

| | | 2003-2006 |
|---|---|---|
| highest | 1 | Chad |
| | 2 | Mauritania |
| | 3 | Liberia |
| | 4 | Sudan |
| | 5 | Nigeria |
| | 6 | São Tomé & Príncipe |
| | 7 | Congo, Dem. Rep. |
| | 8 | Equatorial Guinea |
| | 9 | Togo |
| | 10 | Zambia |
| | 11 | Angola |
| | 12 | Madagascar |
| | 13 | Mozambique |
| | 14 | Cape Verde |
| | 15 | Malawi |
| | 16 | Congo, Rep. |
| | 17 | Tanzania |
| | 18 | Sierra Leone |
| | 19 | Ethiopia |
| | 20 | Botswana |
| | 21 | Kenya |
| | 22 | Gabon |
| | 23 | Burkina Faso |
| | 24 | Rwanda |
| | 25 | Ghana |
| | 26 | Namibia |
| | | SSA average |
| | 27 | Côte d'Ivoire |
| | 28 | Djibouti |
| | 29 | Guinea |
| | 30 | Lesotho |
| | 31 | Burundi |
| | 32 | South Africa |
| | 33 | Niger |
| | 34 | Swaziland |
| | 35 | Cameroon |
| | 36 | Comoros |
| | 37 | Benin |
| | 38 | Senegal |
| | 39 | Mauritius |
| | 40 | Mali |
| | 41 | Gambia, The |
| | 42 | Central African Rep. |
| | 43 | Zimbabwe |
| | 44 | Uganda |
| | 45 | Guinea-Bissau |
| | 46 | Seychelles |
| | 47 | Eritrea |
| lowest | n/a | Somalia |

### Productivity in Manufacturing as $US per Person

AfDB, World Bank

| | | 1999-2002 |
|---|---|---|
| highest | 1 | Seychelles |
| | 2 | Mauritius |
| | 3 | South Africa |
| | 4 | Swaziland |
| | 5 | Namibia |
| | 6 | Gabon |
| | 7 | Botswana |
| | 8 | Côte d'Ivoire |
| | 9 | Cameroon |
| | 10 | Lesotho |
| | 11 | Zimbabwe |
| | 12 | Cape Verde |
| | 13 | Senegal |
| | 14 | Kenya |
| | 15 | Congo, Rep. |
| | 16 | Mauritania |
| | 17 | Zambia |
| | 18 | Burkina Faso |
| | 19 | Sudan |
| | 20 | Mozambique |
| | 21 | Benin |
| | 22 | Tanzania |
| | 23 | Madagascar |
| | 24 | Ghana |
| | 25 | Uganda |
| | 26 | Central African Rep. |
| | 27 | Togo |
| | 28 | Eritrea |
| | 29 | Angola |
| | 30 | Guinea-Bissau |
| | 31 | Djibouti |
| | 32 | Mali |
| | 33 | Comoros |
| | 34 | Malawi |
| | 35 | Rwanda |
| | 36 | São Tomé & Príncipe |
| | 37 | Gambia, The |
| | 38 | Guinea |
| | 39 | Nigeria |
| | 40 | Burundi |
| | 41 | Niger |
| | 42 | Ethiopia |
| | 43 | Equatorial Guinea |
| | 44 | Sierra Leone |
| | 45 | Congo, Dem. Rep. |
| | 46 | Chad |
| | n/a | Liberia |
| | n/a | Somalia |
| lowest | | |

### Productivity in Manufacturing as $US per Person

AfDB, World Bank

| | | 2003-2006 |
|---|---|---|
| highest | 1 | Seychelles |
| | 2 | Mauritius |
| | 3 | South Africa |
| | 4 | Swaziland |
| | 5 | Namibia |
| | 6 | Gabon |
| | 7 | Botswana |
| | 8 | Cameroon |
| | 9 | Côte d'Ivoire |
| | 10 | Lesotho |
| | 11 | Cape Verde |
| | 12 | Senegal |
| | 13 | Congo, Rep. |
| | 14 | Zimbabwe |
| | 15 | Kenya |
| | 16 | Mozambique |
| | 17 | Zambia |
| | 18 | Burkina Faso |
| | 19 | Tanzania |
| | 20 | Benin |
| | 21 | Angola |
| | 22 | Sudan |
| | 23 | Ghana |
| | 24 | Togo |
| | 25 | Mauritania |
| | 26 | Madagascar |
| | 27 | Uganda |
| | 28 | Eritrea |
| | 29 | Djibouti |
| | 30 | Rwanda |
| | 31 | Mali |
| | 32 | Nigeria |
| | 33 | Comoros |
| | 34 | Central African Rep. |
| | 35 | Malawi |
| | 36 | Guinea-Bissau |
| | 37 | Gambia, The |
| | 38 | Guinea |
| | 39 | São Tomé & Príncipe |
| | 40 | Burundi |
| | 41 | Niger |
| | 42 | Equatorial Guinea |
| | 43 | Ethiopia |
| | 44 | Sierra Leone |
| | 45 | Congo, Dem. Rep. |
| | 46 | Chad |
| | n/a | Liberia |
| | n/a | Somalia |
| lowest | | |

### Productivity in Other Industry as $US per Person

AfDB, World Bank

highest

| | 1999-2002 |
|---|---|
| 1 | Equatorial Guinea |
| 2 | Gabon |
| 3 | Botswana |
| 4 | Seychelles |
| 5 | Congo, Rep. |
| 6 | Angola |
| 7 | South Africa |
| 8 | Namibia |
| 9 | Mauritius |
| 10 | Nigeria |
| 11 | Cape Verde |
| 12 | Guinea |
| 13 | Lesotho |
| 14 | Djibouti |
| 15 | Swaziland |
| 16 | Cameroon |
| 17 | Mauritania |
| 18 | Sudan |
| 19 | São Tomé & Príncipe |
| 20 | Mali |
| 21 | Zambia |
| 22 | Ghana |
| 23 | Senegal |
| 24 | Côte d'Ivoire |
| 25 | Tanzania |
| 26 | Zimbabwe |
| 27 | Comoros |
| 28 | Mozambique |
| 29 | Central African Rep. |
| 30 | Uganda |
| 31 | Togo |
| 32 | Kenya |
| 33 | Gambia, The |
| 34 | Eritrea |
| 35 | Sierra Leone |
| 36 | Burkina Faso |
| 37 | Benin |
| 38 | Rwanda |
| 39 | Congo, Dem. Rep. |
| 40 | Niger |
| 41 | Ethiopia |
| 42 | Malawi |
| 43 | Burundi |
| 44 | Chad |
| 45 | Guinea-Bissau |
| 46 | Madagascar |
| n/a | Liberia |
| n/a | Somalia |

lowest

### Productivity in Other Industry as $US per Person

AfDB, World Bank

highest

| | 2003-2006 |
|---|---|
| 1 | Equatorial Guinea |
| 2 | Gabon |
| 3 | Botswana |
| 4 | Congo, Rep. |
| 5 | Angola |
| 6 | South Africa |
| 7 | Namibia |
| 8 | Mauritius |
| 9 | Nigeria |
| 10 | Cape Verde |
| 11 | Lesotho |
| 12 | Guinea |
| 13 | Djibouti |
| 14 | Mauritania |
| 15 | Swaziland |
| 16 | Sudan |
| 17 | Cameroon |
| 18 | Zambia |
| 19 | São Tomé & Príncipe |
| 20 | Mali |
| 21 | Ghana |
| 22 | Chad |
| 23 | Senegal |
| 24 | Tanzania |
| 25 | Côte d'Ivoire |
| 26 | Mozambique |
| 27 | Sierra Leone |
| 28 | Uganda |
| 29 | Comoros |
| 30 | Togo |
| 31 | Central African Rep. |
| 32 | Kenya |
| 33 | Gambia, The |
| 34 | Burkina Faso |
| 35 | Rwanda |
| 36 | Benin |
| 37 | Zimbabwe |
| 38 | Eritrea |
| 39 | Congo, Dem. Rep. |
| 40 | Ethiopia |
| 41 | Niger |
| 42 | Malawi |
| 43 | Burundi |
| 44 | Guinea-Bissau |
| 45 | Madagascar |
| 45 | Seychelles |
| n/a | Liberia |
| n/a | Somalia |

lowest

### Growth in Manufacturing Productivity

AfDB, World Bank

highest

| | 1999-2002 |
|---|---|
| 1 | Mozambique |
| 2 | Equatorial Guinea |
| 3 | Congo, Rep. |
| 4 | Togo |
| 5 | Angola |
| 6 | Burkina Faso |
| 7 | Uganda |
| 8 | Guinea |
| 9 | Cameroon |
| 10 | Nigeria |
| 11 | Benin |
| 12 | Tanzania |
| 13 | Lesotho |
| 14 | Seychelles |
| 15 | Ethiopia |
| 16 | Zambia |
| 17 | Ghana |
| 18 | Mauritius |
| 19 | Namibia |
| 20 | South Africa |
| 21 | Gabon |
| 22 | Comoros |
| 23 | Sierra Leone |
| 24 | Senegal |
| 25 | Botswana |
| 26 | Burundi |
| 27 | Central African Rep. |
| 28 | Mali |
| 29 | Gambia, The |
| 30 | Swaziland |
| 31 | Cape Verde |
| 32 | Rwanda |
| 33 | São Tomé & Príncipe |
| 34 | Eritrea |
| 35 | Djibouti |
| 36 | Kenya |
| 37 | Madagascar |
| 38 | Congo, Dem. Rep. |
| 39 | Niger |
| 40 | Mauritania |
| 41 | Malawi |
| 42 | Guinea-Bissau |
| 43 | Côte d'Ivoire |
| 44 | Chad |
| 45 | Sudan |
| 46 | Zimbabwe |
| n/a | Liberia |
| n/a | Somalia |

lowest

### Growth in Manufacturing Productivity

AfDB, World Bank

highest

| | 2003-2006 |
|---|---|
| 1 | Equatorial Guinea |
| 2 | Angola |
| 3 | Mozambique |
| 4 | Tanzania |
| 5 | Congo, Rep. |
| 6 | Congo, Dem. Rep. |
| 7 | Nigeria |
| 8 | Cape Verde |
| 9 | Madagascar |
| 10 | Rwanda |
| 11 | Togo |
| 12 | Burkina Faso |
| 13 | Zambia |
| 14 | Malawi |
| 15 | Kenya |
| 16 | Ethiopia |
| 17 | Ghana |
| 18 | South Africa |
| 19 | Djibouti |
| 20 | Uganda |
| 21 | Gabon |
| 22 | Burundi |
| 23 | Botswana |
| 24 | Sudan |
| 25 | Swaziland |
| 26 | Comoros |
| 27 | Mali |
| 28 | Eritrea |
| 29 | Cameroon |
| 30 | Gambia, The |
| 31 | Namibia |
| 32 | Chad |
| 33 | Niger |
| 34 | Central African Rep. |
| 35 | Mauritius |
| 36 | Lesotho |
| 37 | Benin |
| 38 | Guinea |
| 39 | São Tomé & Príncipe |
| 40 | Mauritania |
| 41 | Côte d'Ivoire |
| 42 | Guinea-Bissau |
| 43 | Sierra Leone |
| 44 | Senegal |
| 45 | Seychelles |
| 46 | Zimbabwe |
| n/a | Liberia |
| n/a | Somalia |

lowest

### Growth in Other Industry Productivity

AfDB, World Bank

highest

| | 1999-2002 |
|---|---|
| 1 | Equatorial Guinea |
| 2 | Guinea-Bissau |
| 3 | Sudan |
| 4 | Chad |
| 5 | Mali |
| 6 | Burkina Faso |
| 7 | Mozambique |
| 8 | Mauritius |
| 9 | Botswana |
| 10 | Tanzania |
| 11 | Uganda |
| 12 | Cape Verde |
| 13 | Angola |
| 14 | Gambia, The |
| 15 | Ethiopia |
| 16 | Burundi |
| 17 | Senegal |
| 18 | Rwanda |
| 19 | Central African Rep. |
| 20 | Guinea |
| 21 | Swaziland |
| 22 | São Tomé & Príncipe |
| 23 | Zambia |
| 24 | Lesotho |
| 25 | Seychelles |
| 26 | Ghana |
| 27 | Congo, Dem. Rep. |
| 28 | Djibouti |
| 29 | Namibia |
| 30 | Mauritania |
| 31 | Eritrea |
| 32 | Comoros |
| 33 | Benin |
| 34 | Sierra Leone |
| 35 | South Africa |
| 36 | Malawi |
| 37 | Kenya |
| 38 | Côte d'Ivoire |
| 39 | Congo, Rep. |
| 40 | Niger |
| 41 | Nigeria |
| 42 | Togo |
| 43 | Cameroon |
| 44 | Gabon |
| 45 | Zimbabwe |
| 46 | Madagascar |
| n/a | Liberia |
| n/a | Somalia |

lowest

# appendix B4: performance tables - economic productivity

## Growth in Other Industry Productivity

AfDB, World Bank

*highest*

| | 2003-2006 |
|---|---|
| 1 | Chad |
| 2 | Sudan |
| 3 | Equatorial Guinea |
| 4 | Sierra Leone |
| 5 | Malawi |
| 6 | Mauritania |
| 7 | Zambia |
| 8 | Namibia |
| 9 | Burundi |
| 10 | Mozambique |
| 11 | Angola |
| 12 | Tanzania |
| 13 | Rwanda |
| 14 | Burkina Faso |
| 15 | Lesotho |
| 16 | Uganda |
| 17 | Congo, Dem. Rep. |
| 18 | Côte d'Ivoire |
| 19 | Nigeria |
| 20 | Cape Verde |
| 21 | Ethiopia |
| 22 | Senegal |
| 23 | São Tomé & Príncipe |
| 24 | Botswana |
| 25 | Djibouti |
| 26 | Togo |
| 27 | Ghana |
| 28 | South Africa |
| 29 | Gambia, The |
| 30 | Mauritius |
| 31 | Benin |
| 32 | Kenya |
| 33 | Congo, Rep. |
| 34 | Niger |
| 35 | Guinea |
| 36 | Central African Rep. |
| 37 | Madagascar |
| 38 | Swaziland |
| 39 | Mali |
| 40 | Gabon |
| 41 | Comoros |
| 42 | Eritrea |
| 43 | Cameroon |
| 44 | Guinea-Bissau |
| 45 | Zimbabwe |
| 46 | Seychelles |
| n/a | Liberia |
| n/a | Somalia |
| | |

*lowest*

## Productivity in Services as % of GDP

World Bank

*highest*

| | 1999-2002 |
|---|---|
| 1 | Djibouti |
| 2 | Cape Verde |
| 3 | Seychelles |
| 4 | South Africa |
| 5 | São Tomé & Príncipe |
| 6 | Mauritius |
| 7 | Zimbabwe |
| 8 | Namibia |
| 9 | Eritrea |
| 10 | Senegal |
| 11 | Madagascar |
| 12 | Gambia, The |
| 13 | Côte d'Ivoire |
| 14 | Zambia |
| 15 | Mozambique |
| 16 | Kenya |
| | SSA average |
| 17 | Benin |
| 18 | Guinea |
| 19 | Chad |
| 20 | Togo |
| 21 | Cameroon |
| 22 | Mauritania |
| 23 | Malawi |
| 24 | Uganda |
| 25 | Niger |
| 26 | Burkina Faso |
| 27 | Gabon |
| 28 | Lesotho |
| 29 | Comoros |
| 30 | Ethiopia |
| 31 | Botswana |
| 32 | Burundi |
| 33 | Swaziland |
| 34 | Ghana |
| 35 | Tanzania |
| 36 | Rwanda |
| 37 | Sudan |
| 38 | Mali |
| 39 | Guinea-Bissau |
| 40 | Central African Rep. |
| 41 | Congo, Rep. |
| 42 | Congo, Dem. Rep. |
| 43 | Nigeria |
| 44 | Angola |
| 45 | Sierra Leone |
| 46 | Liberia |
| 47 | Equatorial Guinea |
| n/a | Somalia |

*lowest*

## Productivity in Services as % of GDP

World Bank

*highest*

| | 2003-2006 |
|---|---|
| 1 | Djibouti |
| 2 | Cape Verde |
| 3 | Seychelles |
| 4 | South Africa |
| 5 | Mauritius |
| 6 | São Tomé & Príncipe |
| 7 | Namibia |
| 8 | Senegal |
| 9 | Eritrea |
| 10 | Zimbabwe |
| 11 | Madagascar |
| 12 | Benin |
| 13 | Gambia, The |
| 14 | Kenya |
| | SSA average |
| 15 | Côte d'Ivoire |
| 16 | Guinea |
| 17 | Cameroon |
| 18 | Zambia |
| 19 | Uganda |
| 20 | Mozambique |
| 21 | Mauritania |
| 22 | Malawi |
| 23 | Botswana |
| 24 | Niger |
| 25 | Burundi |
| 26 | Swaziland |
| 27 | Lesotho |
| 28 | Burkina Faso |
| 29 | Ethiopia |
| 30 | Sudan |
| 31 | Mali |
| 32 | Rwanda |
| 33 | Ghana |
| 34 | Tanzania |
| 35 | Comoros |
| 36 | Gabon |
| 37 | Togo |
| 38 | Chad |
| 39 | Sierra Leone |
| 40 | Central African Rep. |
| 41 | Congo, Rep. |
| 42 | Congo, Dem. Rep. |
| 43 | Guinea-Bissau |
| 44 | Angola |
| 45 | Nigeria |
| 46 | Liberia |
| 47 | Equatorial Guinea |
| n/a | Somalia |

*lowest*

## Productivity in Services as $PPP per Person

IMF, World Bank

*highest*

| | 1999-2002 |
|---|---|
| 1 | Seychelles |
| 2 | Gabon |
| 3 | Mauritius |
| 4 | South Africa |
| 5 | Botswana |
| 6 | Namibia |
| 7 | Cape Verde |
| 8 | Swaziland |
| 9 | Djibouti |
| 10 | Côte d'Ivoire |
| 11 | Congo, Rep. |
| 12 | Cameroon |
| 13 | Senegal |
| | SSA average |
| 14 | São Tomé & Príncipe |
| 15 | Kenya |
| 16 | Mauritania |
| 17 | Angola |
| 18 | Benin |
| 19 | Gambia, The |
| 20 | Sudan |
| 21 | Eritrea |
| 22 | Zambia |
| 23 | Guinea |
| 24 | Chad |
| 25 | Madagascar |
| 26 | Lesotho |
| 27 | Comoros |
| 28 | Ghana |
| 29 | Burkina Faso |
| 30 | Tanzania |
| 31 | Togo |
| 32 | Uganda |
| 33 | Nigeria |
| 34 | Mali |
| 35 | Equatorial Guinea |
| 36 | Mozambique |
| 37 | Malawi |
| 38 | Rwanda |
| 39 | Niger |
| 40 | Ethiopia |
| 41 | Central African Rep. |
| 42 | Guinea-Bissau |
| 43 | Zimbabwe |
| 44 | Burundi |
| 45 | Sierra Leone |
| 46 | Liberia |
| 47 | Congo, Dem. Rep. |
| n/a | Somalia |

*lowest*

## Productivity in Services as $PPP per Person

IMF, World Bank

*highest*

| | 2003-2006 |
|---|---|
| 1 | Seychelles |
| 2 | Mauritius |
| 3 | Botswana |
| 4 | South Africa |
| 5 | Gabon |
| 6 | Namibia |
| 7 | Cape Verde |
| 8 | Swaziland |
| 9 | Djibouti |
| 10 | Congo, Rep. |
| 11 | Cameroon |
| | SSA average |
| 12 | Senegal |
| 13 | Angola |
| 14 | Côte d'Ivoire |
| 15 | Mauritania |
| 16 | São Tomé & Príncipe |
| 17 | Kenya |
| 18 | Benin |
| 19 | Sudan |
| 20 | Gambia, The |
| 21 | Zambia |
| 22 | Madagascar |
| 23 | Guinea |
| 24 | Lesotho |
| 25 | Eritrea |
| 26 | Ghana |
| 27 | Burkina Faso |
| 28 | Chad |
| 29 | Comoros |
| 30 | Uganda |
| 31 | Nigeria |
| 32 | Tanzania |
| 33 | Equatorial Guinea |
| 34 | Mali |
| 35 | Mozambique |
| 36 | Malawi |
| 37 | Rwanda |
| 38 | Niger |
| 39 | Togo |
| 40 | Ethiopia |
| 41 | Central African Rep. |
| 42 | Sierra Leone |
| 43 | Burundi |
| 44 | Guinea-Bissau |
| 45 | Zimbabwe |
| 46 | Congo, Dem. Rep. |
| 47 | Liberia |
| n/a | Somalia |

*lowest*

### Growth in Services Productivity

IMF, World Bank

| | | 1999-2002 |
|---|---|---|
| highest | 1 | Sierra Leone |
| | 2 | São Tomé & Príncipe |
| | 3 | Uganda |
| | 4 | Cape Verde |
| | 5 | Ethiopia |
| | 6 | Equatorial Guinea |
| | 7 | Botswana |
| | 8 | Mozambique |
| | 9 | Nigeria |
| | 10 | Mauritius |
| | 11 | Mauritania |
| | 12 | Benin |
| | 13 | Burkina Faso |
| | 14 | Guinea-Bissau |
| | 15 | Zambia |
| | 16 | Tanzania |
| | 17 | Sudan |
| | 18 | Mali |
| | 19 | Ghana |
| | 20 | Senegal |
| | 21 | Chad |
| | 22 | Central African Rep. |
| | | SSA average |
| | 23 | Guinea |
| | 24 | Rwanda |
| | 25 | Cameroon |
| | 26 | South Africa |
| | 27 | Niger |
| | 28 | Burundi |
| | 29 | Kenya |
| | 30 | Liberia |
| | 31 | Namibia |
| | 32 | Gambia, The |
| | 33 | Zimbabwe |
| | 34 | Swaziland |
| | 35 | Seychelles |
| | 36 | Eritrea |
| | 37 | Djibouti |
| | 38 | Angola |
| | 39 | Lesotho |
| | 40 | Madagascar |
| | 41 | Malawi |
| | 42 | Côte d'Ivoire |
| | 43 | Congo, Dem. Rep. |
| | 44 | Comoros |
| | 45 | Congo, Rep. |
| | 46 | Togo |
| | 47 | Gabon |
| lowest | n/a | Somalia |

### Growth in Services Productivity

IMF, World Bank

| | | 2003-2006 |
|---|---|---|
| highest | 1 | Madagascar |
| | 2 | Botswana |
| | 3 | Sierra Leone |
| | 4 | Angola |
| | 5 | Sudan |
| | | SSA average |
| | 6 | Mauritius |
| | 7 | South Africa |
| | 8 | Ethiopia |
| | 9 | Namibia |
| | 10 | Swaziland |
| | 11 | Malawi |
| | 12 | Rwanda |
| | 13 | Mali |
| | 14 | Cape Verde |
| | 15 | Tanzania |
| | 16 | Uganda |
| | 17 | Senegal |
| | 18 | Mozambique |
| | 19 | Burundi |
| | 20 | Congo, Dem. Rep. |
| | 21 | Kenya |
| | 22 | Burkina Faso |
| | 23 | São Tomé & Príncipe |
| | 24 | Benin |
| | 25 | Ghana |
| | 26 | Djibouti |
| | 27 | Lesotho |
| | 28 | Niger |
| | 29 | Gambia, The |
| | 30 | Cameroon |
| | 31 | Guinea |
| | 32 | Seychelles |
| | 33 | Mauritania |
| | 34 | Comoros |
| | 35 | Zambia |
| | 36 | Nigeria |
| | 37 | Côte d'Ivoire |
| | 38 | Central African Rep. |
| | 39 | Guinea-Bissau |
| | 40 | Congo, Rep. |
| | 41 | Liberia |
| | 42 | Equatorial Guinea |
| | 43 | Togo |
| | 44 | Eritrea |
| | 45 | Gabon |
| | 46 | Chad |
| | 47 | Zimbabwe |
| lowest | n/a | Somalia |

### Fiscal Balance as % of GDP

IMF

greatest balance

| Rank | 1997-2002 |
|---|---|
| 1 | Equatorial Guinea |
| 2 | Botswana |
| 3 | Gabon |
| 4 | Benin |
| 5 | Senegal |
| 6 | Cameroon |
| 7 | Tanzania |
| 8 | Central African Rep. |
| 9 | Kenya |
| 9 | Swaziland |
| 10 | Côte d'Ivoire |
| 11 | Rwanda |
| 12 | South Africa |
| 13 | Nigeria |
| 14 | Togo |
| | SSA average |
| 15 | Comoros |
| 15 | Guinea |
| 16 | Namibia |
| 17 | Mali |
| 17 | Uganda |
| 18 | Burkina Faso |
| 18 | Lesotho |
| 19 | Niger |
| 20 | Mozambique |
| 21 | Madagascar |
| 22 | Burundi |
| 23 | Zambia |
| 24 | Congo, Dem. Rep. |
| 25 | Chad |
| 25 | Mauritius |
| 26 | Gambia, The |
| 27 | Ethiopia |
| 28 | Malawi |
| 29 | Congo, Rep. |
| 30 | Ghana |
| 31 | Zimbabwe |
| 32 | Sierra Leone |
| 33 | Cape Verde |
| 34 | Guinea-Bissau |
| 35 | Seychelles |
| 36 | Angola |
| 37 | São Tomé & Príncipe |
| 38 | Eritrea |
| n/a | Djibouti |
| n/a | Liberia |
| n/a | Mauritania |
| n/a | Somalia |
| n/a | Sudan |

least balance

### Fiscal Balance as % of GDP

IMF

greatest balance

| Rank | 2003-2006 |
|---|---|
| 1 | Equatorial Guinea |
| 2 | Cameroon |
| 3 | Congo, Rep. |
| 4 | Gabon |
| 5 | Niger |
| 6 | Mali |
| 7 | Madagascar |
| 8 | Lesotho |
| 9 | Nigeria |
| 10 | Botswana |
| 11 | Angola |
| 12 | Zambia |
| | SSA average |
| 13 | Burkina Faso |
| 14 | Liberia |
| 15 | Swaziland |
| 16 | Central African Rep. |
| 17 | Rwanda |
| 18 | São Tomé & Príncipe |
| 19 | Sierra Leone |
| 20 | South Africa |
| 21 | Togo |
| 22 | Seychelles |
| 23 | Benin |
| 24 | Kenya |
| 25 | Chad |
| 26 | Côte d'Ivoire |
| 26 | Uganda |
| 27 | Comoros |
| 28 | Namibia |
| 29 | Tanzania |
| 30 | Malawi |
| 31 | Mozambique |
| 32 | Senegal |
| 33 | Congo, Dem. Rep. |
| 34 | Ghana |
| 35 | Guinea |
| 36 | Burundi |
| 37 | Ethiopia |
| 38 | Cape Verde |
| 39 | Mauritius |
| 40 | Zimbabwe |
| 41 | Gambia, The |
| 42 | Guinea-Bissau |
| 43 | Eritrea |
| n/a | Djibouti |
| n/a | Mauritania |
| n/a | Somalia |
| n/a | Sudan |

least balance

### Fiscal Balance as % of GDP

IMF

greatest balance

| Rank | 2007-2008 |
|---|---|
| 1 | São Tomé & Príncipe |
| 2 | Equatorial Guinea |
| 3 | Congo, Rep. |
| 4 | Lesotho |
| 5 | Sierra Leone |
| 6 | Gabon |
| 7 | Botswana |
| 8 | Angola |
| 9 | Nigeria |
| 10 | Cameroon |
| 11 | Chad |
| 12 | Liberia |
| 13 | Namibia |
| | SSA average |
| 14 | South Africa |
| 15 | Burundi |
| 16 | Central African Rep. |
| 17 | Congo, Dem. Rep. |
| 18 | Guinea |
| 19 | Côte d'Ivoire |
| 20 | Gambia, The |
| 21 | Swaziland |
| 22 | Rwanda |
| 23 | Benin |
| 24 | Malawi |
| 25 | Zambia |
| 26 | Niger |
| 27 | Comoros |
| 27 | Togo |
| 28 | Uganda |
| 29 | Mauritius |
| 30 | Ethiopia |
| 31 | Cape Verde |
| 32 | Kenya |
| 33 | Tanzania |
| 34 | Mali |
| 35 | Madagascar |
| 36 | Guinea-Bissau |
| 37 | Senegal |
| 38 | Burkina Faso |
| 39 | Mozambique |
| 40 | Ghana |
| 41 | Seychelles |
| 42 | Eritrea |
| 43 | Zimbabwe |
| n/a | Djibouti |
| n/a | Mauritania |
| n/a | Somalia |
| n/a | Sudan |

least balance

# appendix B5: performance tables - govt. earnings & spending

## Fiscal Balance as $PPP per Person

Primary data: IMF

| | | 1997-2002 |
|---|---|---|
| largest | 1 | Equatorial Guinea |
| | 2 | Gabon |
| | 3 | Botswana |
| | 4 | Benin |
| | 5 | Senegal |
| | 6 | Central African Rep. |
| | 7 | Tanzania |
| | 8 | Congo, Dem. Rep. |
| | 9 | Rwanda |
| | 10 | Burundi |
| | 11 | Cameroon |
| | 12 | Kenya |
| | 13 | Togo |
| | 14 | Niger |
| | 15 | Mozambique |
| | 16 | Zimbabwe |
| | 17 | Uganda |
| | 18 | Côte d'Ivoire |
| | 19 | Mali |
| | 20 | Nigeria |
| | 21 | Ethiopia |
| | 22 | Madagascar |
| | 23 | Guinea |
| | 24 | Comoros |
| | 25 | Burkina Faso |
| | 26 | Sierra Leone |
| | 27 | Lesotho |
| | | SSA average |
| | 28 | Malawi |
| | 29 | Zambia |
| | 30 | Chad |
| | 31 | Swaziland |
| | 32 | Gambia, The |
| | 33 | Guinea-Bissau |
| | 34 | Ghana |
| | 35 | Namibia |
| | 36 | South Africa |
| | 37 | São Tomé & Príncipe |
| | 38 | Congo, Rep. |
| | 39 | Cape Verde |
| | 40 | Eritrea |
| | 41 | Angola |
| | 42 | Mauritius |
| | 43 | Seychelles |
| | n/a | Djibouti |
| | n/a | Liberia |
| | n/a | Mauritania |
| | n/a | Somalia |
| smallest | n/a | Sudan |

## Fiscal Balance as $PPP per Person

Primary data: IMF

| | | 2003-2006 |
|---|---|---|
| largest | 1 | Equatorial Guinea |
| | 2 | Gabon |
| | 3 | Botswana |
| | 4 | Congo, Rep. |
| | 5 | Cameroon |
| | 6 | Angola |
| | 7 | Nigeria |
| | 8 | Lesotho |
| | 9 | Madagascar |
| | 10 | Mali |
| | 11 | Niger |
| | 12 | Zambia |
| | 13 | Swaziland |
| | | SSA average |
| | 14 | Burkina Faso |
| | 15 | Liberia |
| | 16 | Central African Rep. |
| | 17 | Sierra Leone |
| | 18 | Rwanda |
| | 19 | São Tomé & Príncipe |
| | 20 | Togo |
| | 21 | Congo, Dem. Rep. |
| | 22 | Zimbabwe |
| | 23 | Burundi |
| | 24 | Uganda |
| | 25 | Malawi |
| | 26 | Benin |
| | 27 | Mozambique |
| | 28 | Comoros |
| | 29 | Chad |
| | 30 | Kenya |
| | 31 | Ethiopia |
| | 32 | Côte d'Ivoire |
| | 33 | Tanzania |
| | 34 | Guinea |
| | 35 | Ghana |
| | 36 | Senegal |
| | 37 | Guinea-Bissau |
| | 38 | Gambia, The |
| | 39 | South Africa |
| | 40 | Namibia |
| | 41 | Eritrea |
| | 42 | Cape Verde |
| | 43 | Seychelles |
| | 44 | Mauritius |
| | n/a | Djibouti |
| | n/a | Mauritania |
| | n/a | Somalia |
| smallest | n/a | Sudan |

## Fiscal Balance as $PPP per Person

Primary data: IMF

| | | 2007-2008 |
|---|---|---|
| largest | 1 | Equatorial Guinea |
| | 2 | Gabon |
| | 3 | São Tomé & Príncipe |
| | 4 | Botswana |
| | 5 | Congo, Rep. |
| | 6 | Angola |
| | 7 | Lesotho |
| | 8 | Nigeria |
| | 9 | Namibia |
| | 10 | South Africa |
| | 11 | Cameroon |
| | 12 | Sierra Leone |
| | 13 | Chad |
| | | SSA average |
| | 14 | Liberia |
| | 15 | Central African Rep. |
| | 16 | Burundi |
| | 17 | Congo, Dem. Rep. |
| | 18 | Guinea |
| | 19 | Rwanda |
| | 20 | Côte d'Ivoire |
| | 21 | Gambia, The |
| | 22 | Malawi |
| | 23 | Niger |
| | 24 | Benin |
| | 25 | Togo |
| | 26 | Zimbabwe |
| | 27 | Guinea-Bissau |
| | 28 | Comoros |
| | 29 | Zambia |
| | 30 | Ethiopia |
| | 31 | Uganda |
| | 32 | Mali |
| | 33 | Swaziland |
| | 34 | Madagascar |
| | 35 | Tanzania |
| | 36 | Mozambique |
| | 37 | Kenya |
| | 38 | Eritrea |
| | 39 | Burkina Faso |
| | 40 | Senegal |
| | 41 | Ghana |
| | 42 | Cape Verde |
| | 43 | Mauritius |
| | 44 | Seychelles |
| | n/a | Djibouti |
| | n/a | Mauritania |
| | n/a | Somalia |
| smallest | n/a | Sudan |

## Govt. Earnings - incl. Grants - as % of GDP

IMF

| | | 1997-2002 |
|---|---|---|
| highest | 1 | Lesotho |
| | 2 | Seychelles |
| | 3 | Angola |
| | 4 | Namibia |
| | 5 | Botswana |
| | 6 | Eritrea |
| | 7 | São Tomé & Príncipe |
| | 8 | Swaziland |
| | 9 | Gabon |
| | 10 | Cape Verde |
| | 11 | Congo, Rep. |
| | 12 | Gambia, The |
| | 13 | Guinea-Bissau |
| | 14 | Zimbabwe |
| | 15 | Burundi |
| | 16 | Equatorial Guinea |
| | 17 | Malawi |
| | 18 | South Africa |
| | | SSA average |
| | 19 | Ghana |
| | 20 | Nigeria |
| | 21 | Zambia |
| | 22 | Kenya |
| | 23 | Rwanda |
| | 24 | Mauritius |
| | 25 | Ethiopia |
| | 26 | Senegal |
| | 27 | Uganda |
| | 28 | Côte d'Ivoire |
| | 29 | Benin |
| | 30 | Sierra Leone |
| | 31 | Mozambique |
| | 32 | Togo |
| | 33 | Mali |
| | 34 | Burkina Faso |
| | 35 | Comoros |
| | 36 | Cameroon |
| | 37 | Tanzania |
| | 38 | Central African Rep. |
| | 39 | Guinea |
| | 40 | Niger |
| | 41 | Madagascar |
| | 42 | Chad |
| | 43 | Congo, Dem. Rep. |
| | n/a | Djibouti |
| | n/a | Liberia |
| | n/a | Mauritania |
| | n/a | Somalia |
| lowest | n/a | Sudan |

## Govt. Earnings - incl. Grants - as % of GDP

IMF

| | | 2003-2006 |
|---|---|---|
| highest | 1 | Lesotho |
| | 2 | São Tomé & Príncipe |
| | 3 | Seychelles |
| | 4 | Liberia |
| | 5 | Botswana |
| | 6 | Swaziland |
| | 7 | Namibia |
| | 8 | Eritrea |
| | 9 | Angola |
| | 10 | Burundi |
| | 11 | Equatorial Guinea |
| | 12 | Congo, Rep. |
| | 13 | Zimbabwe |
| | 14 | Gabon |
| | 15 | Gambia, The |
| | 16 | Cape Verde |
| | 17 | Ghana |
| | 18 | Guinea-Bissau |
| | 19 | Malawi |
| | 20 | Rwanda |
| | | SSA average |
| | 21 | South Africa |
| | 22 | Ethiopia |
| | 23 | Nigeria |
| | 24 | Kenya |
| | 25 | Uganda |
| | 26 | Senegal |
| | 27 | Mauritius |
| | 28 | Mozambique |
| | 29 | Mali |
| | 30 | Benin |
| | 31 | Zambia |
| | 32 | Sierra Leone |
| | 33 | Togo |
| | 34 | Cameroon |
| | 35 | Côte d'Ivoire |
| | 36 | Congo, Dem. Rep. |
| | 37 | Comoros |
| | 38 | Burkina Faso |
| | 39 | Chad |
| | 40 | Tanzania |
| | 41 | Niger |
| | 42 | Madagascar |
| | 43 | Guinea |
| | 44 | Central African Rep. |
| | n/a | Djibouti |
| | n/a | Mauritania |
| | n/a | Somalia |
| lowest | n/a | Sudan |

### Govt. Earnings - incl. Grants - as % of GDP

IMF

| | | 2007-2008 |
|---|---|---|
| highest | 1 | Lesotho |
| | 2 | Swaziland |
| | 3 | São Tomé & Príncipe |
| | 4 | Liberia |
| | 5 | Seychelles |
| | 6 | Namibia |
| | 7 | Botswana |
| | 8 | Congo, Rep. |
| | 9 | Equatorial Guinea |
| | 10 | Burundi |
| | 11 | Angola |
| | 12 | Guinea-Bissau |
| | 13 | Malawi |
| | 14 | Gambia, The |
| | 15 | Gabon |
| | 16 | Zimbabwe |
| | 17 | Cape Verde |
| | 18 | Mozambique |
| | 19 | Ghana |
| | 19 | South Africa |
| | 20 | Eritrea |
| | | SSA average |
| | 21 | Rwanda |
| | 22 | Chad |
| | 23 | Senegal |
| | 24 | Zambia |
| | 25 | Benin |
| | 26 | Côte d'Ivoire |
| | 27 | Kenya |
| | 28 | Congo, Dem. Rep. |
| | 29 | Mauritius |
| | 30 | Ethiopia |
| | 31 | Cameroon |
| | 32 | Mali |
| | 33 | Togo |
| | 33 | Uganda |
| | 34 | Nigeria |
| | 35 | Tanzania |
| | 36 | Burkina Faso |
| | 37 | Niger |
| | 38 | Comoros |
| | 39 | Sierra Leone |
| | 40 | Guinea |
| | 41 | Central African Rep. |
| | 42 | Madagascar |
| | n/a | Djibouti |
| | n/a | Mauritania |
| | n/a | Somalia |
| lowest | n/a | Sudan |

### Govt. Spending as % of GDP

IMF

| | | 1997-2002 |
|---|---|---|
| highest | 1 | Eritrea |
| | 2 | Angola |
| | 3 | Seychelles |
| | 4 | São Tomé & Príncipe |
| | 5 | Lesotho |
| | 6 | Cape Verde |
| | 7 | Botswana |
| | 8 | Guinea-Bissau |
| | 9 | Namibia |
| | 10 | Congo, Rep. |
| | 11 | Zimbabwe |
| | 12 | Gabon |
| | 13 | Zambia |
| | 14 | Malawi |
| | 15 | Swaziland |
| | 16 | Ghana |
| | 17 | South Africa |
| | 18 | Gambia, The |
| | | SSA average |
| | 19 | Burundi |
| | 19 | Mauritius |
| | 20 | Mozambique |
| | 21 | Ethiopia |
| | 22 | Sierra Leone |
| | 23 | Nigeria |
| | 24 | Burkina Faso |
| | 24 | Kenya |
| | 25 | Comoros |
| | 26 | Mali |
| | 27 | Uganda |
| | 28 | Rwanda |
| | 29 | Côte d'Ivoire |
| | 30 | Senegal |
| | 31 | Niger |
| | 32 | Chad |
| | 33 | Benin |
| | 34 | Madagascar |
| | 35 | Equatorial Guinea |
| | 36 | Togo |
| | 37 | Guinea |
| | 38 | Central African Rep. |
| | 39 | Cameroon |
| | 40 | Tanzania |
| | 41 | Congo, Dem. Rep. |
| | n/a | Djibouti |
| | n/a | Liberia |
| | n/a | Mauritania |
| | n/a | Somalia |
| lowest | n/a | Sudan |

### Govt. Spending as % of GDP

IMF

| | | 2003-2006 |
|---|---|---|
| highest | 1 | Eritrea |
| | 2 | Seychelles |
| | 3 | São Tomé & Príncipe |
| | 4 | Lesotho |
| | 5 | Guinea-Bissau |
| | 6 | Zimbabwe |
| | 7 | Burundi |
| | 8 | Angola |
| | 9 | Botswana |
| | 10 | Cape Verde |
| | 11 | Namibia |
| | 12 | Swaziland |
| | 13 | Ghana |
| | 14 | Malawi |
| | 15 | Gambia, The |
| | 16 | Congo, Rep. |
| | 17 | Zambia |
| | 18 | Mozambique |
| | 19 | South Africa |
| | 20 | Mauritius |
| | 21 | Ethiopia |
| | 22 | Sierra Leone |
| | 23 | Senegal |
| | 24 | Mali |
| | 25 | Rwanda |
| | | SSA average |
| | 26 | Kenya |
| | 27 | Gabon |
| | 28 | Madagascar |
| | 28 | Uganda |
| | 29 | Burkina Faso |
| | 30 | Comoros |
| | 31 | Benin |
| | 32 | Côte d'Ivoire |
| | 33 | Niger |
| | 34 | Tanzania |
| | 35 | Equatorial Guinea |
| | 36 | Togo |
| | 37 | Congo, Dem. Rep. |
| | 38 | Guinea |
| | 39 | Chad |
| | 40 | Nigeria |
| | 41 | Cameroon |
| | 42 | Central African Rep. |
| | n/a | Djibouti |
| | n/a | Liberia |
| | n/a | Mauritania |
| | n/a | Somalia |
| lowest | n/a | Sudan |

### Govt. Earnings as $PPP per Person

Primary data: IMF

| | | 1997-2002 |
|---|---|---|
| highest | 1 | Seychelles |
| | 2 | Gabon |
| | 3 | Botswana |
| | 4 | Namibia |
| | 5 | South Africa |
| | 6 | Mauritius |
| | 7 | Swaziland |
| | 8 | Angola |
| | 9 | Equatorial Guinea |
| | 10 | Congo, Rep. |
| | 11 | Lesotho |
| | 12 | Cape Verde |
| | 13 | São Tomé & Príncipe |
| | 14 | Eritrea |
| | | SSA average |
| | 15 | Côte d'Ivoire |
| | 16 | Kenya |
| | 17 | Gambia, The |
| | 18 | Cameroon |
| | 19 | Nigeria |
| | 20 | Senegal |
| | 21 | Benin |
| | 22 | Ghana |
| | 23 | Zambia |
| | 24 | Comoros |
| | 25 | Malawi |
| | 26 | Burkina Faso |
| | 27 | Guinea-Bissau |
| | 28 | Rwanda |
| | 29 | Uganda |
| | 30 | Guinea |
| | 31 | Mali |
| | 32 | Togo |
| | 33 | Tanzania |
| | 34 | Chad |
| | 35 | Ethiopia |
| | 36 | Central African Rep. |
| | 37 | Madagascar |
| | 38 | Mozambique |
| | 39 | Burundi |
| | 40 | Zimbabwe |
| | 41 | Niger |
| | 42 | Sierra Leone |
| | 43 | Congo, Dem. Rep. |
| | n/a | Djibouti |
| | n/a | Liberia |
| | n/a | Mauritania |
| | n/a | Somalia |
| lowest | n/a | Sudan |

### Govt. Earnings as $PPP per Person

Primary data: IMF

| | | 2003-2006 |
|---|---|---|
| highest | 1 | Seychelles |
| | 2 | Botswana |
| | 3 | Equatorial Guinea |
| | 4 | Gabon |
| | 5 | South Africa |
| | 6 | Mauritius |
| | 7 | Swaziland |
| | 8 | Namibia |
| | 9 | Angola |
| | 10 | Congo, Rep. |
| | 11 | Lesotho |
| | 12 | São Tomé & Príncipe |
| | 13 | Cape Verde |
| | | SSA average |
| | 14 | Nigeria |
| | 15 | Cameroon |
| | 16 | Ghana |
| | 17 | Eritrea |
| | 18 | Gambia, The |
| | 19 | Senegal |
| | 20 | Kenya |
| | 21 | Côte d'Ivoire |
| | 22 | Benin |
| | 23 | Chad |
| | 24 | Zambia |
| | 25 | Rwanda |
| | 26 | Mali |
| | 27 | Comoros |
| | 28 | Burkina Faso |
| | 29 | Malawi |
| | 30 | Uganda |
| | 31 | Tanzania |
| | 32 | Liberia |
| | 33 | Mozambique |
| | 34 | Ethiopia |
| | 35 | Togo |
| | 36 | Guinea |
| | 37 | Burundi |
| | 38 | Guinea-Bissau |
| | 39 | Madagascar |
| | 40 | Sierra Leone |
| | 41 | Niger |
| | 42 | Central African Rep. |
| | 43 | Zimbabwe |
| | 44 | Congo, Dem. Rep. |
| | n/a | Djibouti |
| | n/a | Mauritania |
| | n/a | Somalia |
| lowest | n/a | Sudan |

### Govt. Earnings as $PPP per Person

Primary data: IMF

highest

| | 2007-2008 |
|---|---|
| 1 | Seychelles |
| 2 | Botswana |
| 3 | Equatorial Guinea |
| 4 | Gabon |
| 5 | Swaziland |
| 6 | Namibia |
| 7 | South Africa |
| 8 | Mauritius |
| 9 | Angola |
| 10 | Congo, Rep. |
| 11 | Lesotho |
| 12 | São Tomé & Príncipe |
| 13 | Cape Verde |
| | SSA average |
| 14 | Cameroon |
| 15 | Gambia, The |
| 16 | Nigeria |
| 17 | Chad |
| 18 | Ghana |
| 19 | Senegal |
| 20 | Côte d'Ivoire |
| 21 | Kenya |
| 22 | Benin |
| 23 | Zambia |
| 24 | Malawi |
| 25 | Tanzania |
| 26 | Mozambique |
| 27 | Rwanda |
| 28 | Burkina Faso |
| 29 | Mali |
| 30 | Liberia |
| 31 | Eritrea |
| 32 | Uganda |
| 33 | Comoros |
| 34 | Ethiopia |
| 35 | Guinea-Bissau |
| 36 | Togo |
| 37 | Guinea |
| 38 | Burundi |
| 39 | Madagascar |
| 40 | Niger |
| 41 | Sierra Leone |
| 42 | Central African Rep. |
| 43 | Congo, Dem. Rep. |
| 44 | Zimbabwe |
| n/a | Djibouti |
| n/a | Mauritania |
| n/a | Somalia |
| n/a | Sudan |

lowest

### Govt. Spending as $PPP per Person

Primary data: IMF

highest

| | 1997-2002 |
|---|---|
| 1 | Seychelles |
| 2 | Gabon |
| 3 | Botswana |
| 4 | Mauritius |
| 5 | South Africa |
| 6 | Angola |
| 7 | Namibia |
| 8 | Swaziland |
| 9 | Congo, Rep. |
| 10 | Equatorial Guinea |
| 11 | Cape Verde |
| 12 | Eritrea |
| 13 | São Tomé & Príncipe |
| 14 | Lesotho |
| | SSA average |
| 15 | Côte d'Ivoire |
| 16 | Kenya |
| 17 | Zambia |
| 18 | Nigeria |
| 19 | Ghana |
| 20 | Cameroon |
| 21 | Gambia, The |
| 22 | Senegal |
| 23 | Comoros |
| 24 | Benin |
| 25 | Burkina Faso |
| 26 | Guinea-Bissau |
| 27 | Chad |
| 28 | Malawi |
| 29 | Guinea |
| 30 | Mali |
| 31 | Uganda |
| 32 | Madagascar |
| 33 | Rwanda |
| 34 | Togo |
| 35 | Mozambique |
| 36 | Ethiopia |
| 37 | Tanzania |
| 38 | Central African Rep. |
| 39 | Niger |
| 40 | Sierra Leone |
| 41 | Zimbabwe |
| 42 | Burundi |
| 43 | Congo, Dem. Rep. |
| n/a | Djibouti |
| n/a | Liberia |
| n/a | Mauritania |
| n/a | Somalia |
| n/a | Sudan |

lowest

### Govt. Spending as $PPP per Person

Primary data: IMF

highest

| | 2003-2006 |
|---|---|
| 1 | Seychelles |
| 2 | Botswana |
| 3 | Gabon |
| 4 | Mauritius |
| 5 | South Africa |
| 6 | Equatorial Guinea |
| 7 | Namibia |
| 8 | Swaziland |
| 9 | Angola |
| 10 | Congo, Rep. |
| 11 | Cape Verde |
| 12 | São Tomé & Príncipe |
| 13 | Lesotho |
| 14 | Eritrea |
| | SSA average |
| 15 | Ghana |
| 16 | Senegal |
| 17 | Kenya |
| 18 | Côte d'Ivoire |
| 19 | Gambia, The |
| 20 | Zambia |
| 21 | Cameroon |
| 22 | Nigeria |
| 23 | Benin |
| 24 | Burkina Faso |
| 25 | Chad |
| 26 | Mali |
| 27 | Comoros |
| 28 | Malawi |
| 29 | Tanzania |
| 30 | Madagascar |
| 31 | Guinea-Bissau |
| 32 | Rwanda |
| 33 | Uganda |
| 34 | Mozambique |
| 35 | Guinea |
| 36 | Ethiopia |
| 37 | Sierra Leone |
| 38 | Togo |
| 39 | Burundi |
| 40 | Niger |
| 41 | Central African Rep. |
| 42 | Zimbabwe |
| 43 | Congo, Dem. Rep. |
| n/a | Djibouti |
| n/a | Liberia |
| n/a | Mauritania |
| n/a | Somalia |
| n/a | Sudan |

lowest

### Growth in Govt. Earnings per Person

Primary data: IMF

highest

| | 2003-2006 |
|---|---|
| 1 | Liberia |
| 2 | Equatorial Guinea |
| 3 | São Tomé & Príncipe |
| 4 | Chad |
| 5 | Congo, Dem. Rep. |
| 6 | Mozambique |
| 7 | Congo, Rep. |
| 8 | Swaziland |
| 9 | Burundi |
| 10 | Sierra Leone |
| 11 | Angola |
| 12 | Botswana |
| 13 | Mali |
| 14 | Nigeria |
| 15 | Lesotho |
| 16 | Ghana |
| 17 | Madagascar |
| 18 | Ethiopia |
| 19 | Malawi |
| 20 | Tanzania |
| 21 | Cameroon |
| | SSA average |
| 22 | Niger |
| 23 | Cape Verde |
| 24 | South Africa |
| 25 | Rwanda |
| 26 | Namibia |
| 27 | Senegal |
| 28 | Mauritius |
| 29 | Central African Rep. |
| 30 | Uganda |
| 31 | Benin |
| 32 | Burkina Faso |
| 33 | Seychelles |
| 34 | Gambia, The |
| 35 | Guinea-Bissau |
| 36 | Togo |
| 37 | Kenya |
| 38 | Guinea |
| 39 | Zambia |
| 40 | Comoros |
| 41 | Zimbabwe |
| 42 | Côte d'Ivoire |
| 43 | Gabon |
| 44 | Eritrea |
| n/a | Djibouti |
| n/a | Mauritania |
| n/a | Somalia |
| n/a | Sudan |

lowest

### Growth in Govt. Earnings per Person

Primary data: IMF

highest

| | 2007-2008 |
|---|---|
| 1 | Guinea-Bissau |
| 2 | Gambia, The |
| 3 | Tanzania |
| 4 | São Tomé & Príncipe |
| 5 | Mozambique |
| 6 | Lesotho |
| 7 | Rwanda |
| 8 | Ethiopia |
| 9 | Zambia |
| 10 | Nigeria |
| 11 | Mauritius |
| 12 | Ghana |
| 13 | Swaziland |
| 14 | Chad |
| 15 | Burkina Faso |
| 16 | Malawi |
| 17 | Madagascar |
| 18 | Côte d'Ivoire |
| 19 | Benin |
| 20 | Congo, Dem. Rep. |
| 21 | Liberia |
| 22 | South Africa |
| 23 | Niger |
| | SSA average |
| 24 | Namibia |
| 25 | Angola |
| 26 | Guinea |
| 27 | Togo |
| 28 | Botswana |
| 29 | Senegal |
| 30 | Uganda |
| 31 | Cape Verde |
| 32 | Kenya |
| 33 | Cameroon |
| 34 | Mali |
| 35 | Congo, Rep. |
| 36 | Comoros |
| 37 | Equatorial Guinea |
| 38 | Gabon |
| 39 | Sierra Leone |
| 40 | Central African Rep. |
| 41 | Seychelles |
| 42 | Burundi |
| 43 | Eritrea |
| 44 | Zimbabwe |
| n/a | Djibouti |
| n/a | Mauritania |
| n/a | Somalia |
| n/a | Sudan |

lowest

### Current Account Balance as % of GDP

IMF

largest

| | 1999-2002 |
|---|---|
| 1 | Gabon |
| 2 | Botswana |
| 3 | Namibia |
| 4 | Mauritius |
| 5 | Zimbabwe |
| 6 | Côte d'Ivoire |
| 7 | South Africa |
| 8 | Comoros |
| 9 | Kenya |
| 10 | Nigeria |
| 11 | Central African Rep. |
| 12 | Swaziland |
| | SSA average |
| 13 | Gambia, The |
| 14 | Congo, Dem. Rep. |
| 15 | Cameroon |
| 16 | Congo, Rep. |
| 17 | Djibouti |
| 18 | Eritrea |
| 19 | Guinea |
| 20 | Madagascar |
| 21 | Ethiopia |
| 22 | Mauritania |
| 23 | Senegal |
| 24 | Burundi |
| 25 | Tanzania |
| 26 | Ghana |
| 27 | Sierra Leone |
| 28 | Uganda |
| 29 | Niger |
| 30 | Rwanda |
| 31 | Togo |
| 32 | Benin |
| 33 | Mali |
| 34 | Malawi |
| 35 | Angola |
| 36 | Liberia |
| 37 | Sudan |
| 38 | Burkina Faso |
| 39 | Cape Verde |
| 40 | Guinea-Bissau |
| 41 | Mozambique |
| 42 | Seychelles |
| 43 | Zambia |
| 44 | São Tomé & Príncipe |
| 45 | Lesotho |
| 46 | Equatorial Guinea |
| 47 | Chad |
| n/a | Somalia |

smallest

### Current Account Balance as % of GDP

IMF

largest

| | 2003-2006 |
|---|---|
| 1 | Gabon |
| 2 | Botswana |
| 3 | Angola |
| 4 | Namibia |
| 5 | Congo, Rep. |
| 6 | Nigeria |
| 7 | Côte d'Ivoire |
| 8 | Eritrea |
| 9 | Swaziland |
| 10 | Kenya |
| 11 | Mauritius |
| | SSA average |
| 12 | Cameroon |
| 13 | Mozambique |
| 14 | Djibouti |
| 15 | Central African Rep. |
| 16 | Congo, Dem. Rep. |
| 17 | South Africa |
| 18 | Uganda |
| 19 | Guinea-Bissau |
| 20 | Togo |
| 21 | Ghana |
| 22 | Guinea |
| 23 | Rwanda |
| 24 | Tanzania |
| 25 | Comoros |
| 26 | Lesotho |
| 27 | Ethiopia |
| 28 | Sierra Leone |
| 29 | Benin |
| 30 | Mali |
| 31 | Zimbabwe |
| 32 | Senegal |
| 33 | Madagascar |
| 34 | Niger |
| 35 | Cape Verde |
| 36 | Malawi |
| 37 | Zambia |
| 38 | Burundi |
| 39 | Gambia, The |
| 40 | Burkina Faso |
| 41 | Sudan |
| 42 | Seychelles |
| 43 | Equatorial Guinea |
| 44 | Liberia |
| 45 | Chad |
| 46 | São Tomé & Príncipe |
| 47 | Mauritania |
| n/a | Somalia |

smallest

### Current Account Balance as % of GDP

IMF

largest

| | 2007-2010 |
|---|---|
| 1 | Gabon |
| 2 | Namibia |
| 3 | Angola |
| 4 | Botswana |
| 5 | Lesotho |
| 6 | Nigeria |
| 7 | Congo, Rep. |
| 8 | Guinea-Bissau |
| 9 | Equatorial Guinea |
| 10 | Côte d'Ivoire |
| 11 | Cameroon |
| 12 | Zimbabwe |
| 13 | Swaziland |
| | SSA average |
| 14 | Comoros |
| 15 | Malawi |
| 16 | Chad |
| 17 | Kenya |
| 18 | Eritrea |
| 19 | Zambia |
| 20 | Ethiopia |
| 21 | Sierra Leone |
| 22 | Benin |
| 23 | Central African Rep. |
| 24 | Mauritius |
| 25 | Mali |
| 26 | Uganda |
| 27 | Togo |
| 28 | South Africa |
| 29 | Sudan |
| 30 | Ghana |
| 31 | Tanzania |
| 32 | Rwanda |
| 33 | Mozambique |
| 34 | Guinea |
| 35 | Senegal |
| 36 | Burkina Faso |
| 37 | Gambia, The |
| 38 | Mauritania |
| 39 | Niger |
| 40 | Burundi |
| 41 | Cape Verde |
| 42 | Congo, Dem. Rep. |
| 43 | Madagascar |
| 44 | Djibouti |
| 45 | Liberia |
| 46 | São Tomé & Príncipe |
| 47 | Seychelles |
| n/a | Somalia |

smallest

### Debt Service as % of GNI

AfDB, World Bank

highest

| | 1999-2002 |
|---|---|
| 1 | Equatorial Guinea |
| 2 | Eritrea |
| 3 | Uganda |
| 4 | Rwanda |
| 5 | Central African Rep. |
| 6 | Niger |
| 7 | Togo |
| 8 | Sudan |
| 9 | Botswana |
| 10 | Burkina Faso |
| 11 | Mozambique |
| 12 | Comoros |
| 13 | Chad |
| 14 | South Africa |
| 15 | Ethiopia |
| 16 | Tanzania |
| 17 | Djibouti |
| 18 | Congo, Rep. |
| 19 | Swaziland |
| 20 | Benin |
| 21 | Burundi |
| 22 | Madagascar |
| 23 | Malawi |
| 24 | Sierra Leone |
| 25 | Cameroon |
| 26 | Zimbabwe |
| 27 | Mali |
| 28 | Cape Verde |
| 29 | Kenya |
| 30 | Guinea |
| 31 | Ghana |
| 32 | Gambia, The |
| 33 | Senegal |
| 34 | Zambia |
| 35 | Nigeria |
| 36 | Seychelles |
| 37 | Mauritius |
| 38 | Lesotho |
| 39 | Mauritania |
| 40 | Côte d'Ivoire |
| 41 | Guinea-Bissau |
| 42 | Gabon |
| 43 | Angola |
| n/a | Congo, Dem. Rep. |
| n/a | Liberia |
| n/a | Namibia |
| n/a | São Tomé & Príncipe |
| n/a | Somalia |

lowest

### Debt Service as % of GNI

AfDB, World Bank

highest

| | 2003-2006 |
|---|---|
| 1 | Togo |
| 2 | Equatorial Guinea |
| 3 | Zimbabwe |
| 4 | Botswana |
| 5 | Tanzania |
| 6 | Mozambique |
| 7 | Burkina Faso |
| 8 | Côte d'Ivoire |
| 9 | Ethiopia |
| 10 | Comoros |
| 11 | Niger |
| 12 | Rwanda |
| 13 | South Africa |
| 14 | Chad |
| 15 | Uganda |
| 16 | Central African Rep. |
| 17 | Madagascar |
| 18 | Sudan |
| 19 | Benin |
| 20 | Mali |
| 21 | Swaziland |
| 22 | Sierra Leone |
| 23 | Eritrea |
| 24 | Djibouti |
| 25 | Ghana |
| 26 | Kenya |
| 27 | Malawi |
| 28 | Cameroon |
| 29 | Senegal |
| 30 | Cape Verde |
| 31 | Mauritania |
| 32 | Mauritius |
| 33 | Guinea |
| 34 | Gabon |
| 35 | Congo, Rep. |
| 36 | Lesotho |
| 37 | Zambia |
| 38 | Gambia, The |
| 39 | Burundi |
| 40 | Nigeria |
| 41 | Seychelles |
| 42 | Guinea-Bissau |
| 43 | Angola |
| n/a | Congo, Dem. Rep. |
| n/a | Liberia |
| n/a | Namibia |
| n/a | São Tomé & Príncipe |
| n/a | Somalia |

lowest

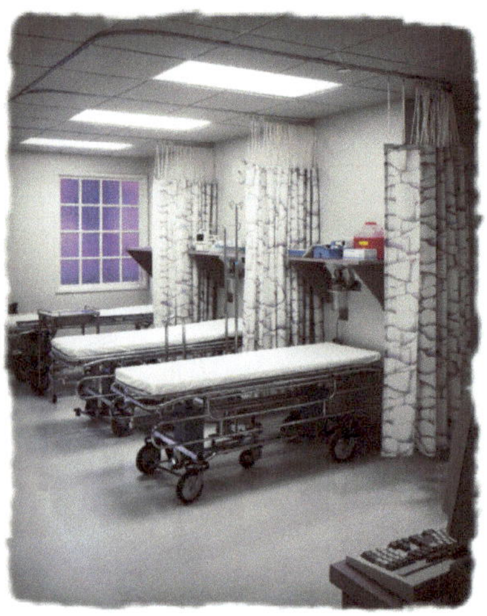

### Total Expenditure on Health as % of GDP

World Bank

| | | 2000-2002 |
|---|---|---|
| *largest* | 1 | South Africa |
| | 2 | São Tomé & Príncipe |
| | 3 | Malawi |
| | 4 | Zimbabwe |
| | 5 | Uganda |
| | 6 | Namibia |
| | 7 | Ghana |
| | 8 | Lesotho |
| | 9 | Djibouti |
| | 9 | Chad |
| | 10 | Mali |
| | 11 | Zambia |
| | | SSA average |
| | 12 | Swaziland |
| | 13 | Guinea-Bissau |
| | 14 | Guinea |
| | 15 | Gambia, The |
| | 16 | Ethiopia |
| | 17 | Gabon |
| | 18 | Seychelles |
| | 19 | Mozambique |
| | 20 | Cape Verde |
| | 20 | Burkina Faso |
| | 21 | Nigeria |
| | 22 | Togo |
| | 23 | Cameroon |
| | 23 | Eritrea |
| | 24 | Benin |
| | 25 | Senegal |
| | 26 | Botswana |
| | 27 | Kenya |
| | 28 | Rwanda |
| | 28 | Côte d'Ivoire |
| | 29 | Sierra Leone |
| | 30 | Tanzania |
| | 30 | Central African Rep. |
| | 31 | Mauritius |
| | 32 | Niger |
| | 33 | Burundi |
| | 34 | Liberia |
| | 35 | Congo, Dem. Rep. |
| | 35 | Sudan |
| | 36 | Madagascar |
| | 37 | Mauritania |
| | 38 | Angola |
| | 39 | Comoros |
| | 40 | Equatorial Guinea |
| | 41 | Congo, Rep. |
| *smallest* | n/a | Somalia |

### Total Expenditure on Health as % of GDP

World Bank

| | | 2003-2006 |
|---|---|---|
| *largest* | 1 | Malawi |
| | 2 | Zimbabwe |
| | 3 | São Tomé & Príncipe |
| | 4 | Rwanda |
| | 5 | Namibia |
| | 5 | South Africa |
| | 6 | Botswana |
| | 7 | Uganda |
| | 8 | Burundi |
| | 9 | Zambia |
| | 10 | Djibouti |
| | 11 | Lesotho |
| | 12 | Swaziland |
| | 13 | Burkina Faso |
| | 14 | Seychelles |
| | 15 | Ghana |
| | 16 | Togo |
| | | SSA average |
| | 17 | Congo, Dem. Rep. |
| | 18 | Guinea-Bissau |
| | 19 | Guinea |
| | 20 | Mali |
| | 21 | Senegal |
| | 22 | Tanzania |
| | 22 | Chad |
| | 23 | Gambia, The |
| | 24 | Cape Verde |
| | 25 | Benin |
| | 25 | Sierra Leone |
| | 26 | Niger |
| | 27 | Gabon |
| | 28 | Mozambique |
| | 29 | Kenya |
| | 29 | Cameroon |
| | 30 | Liberia |
| | 31 | Ethiopia |
| | 32 | Mauritius |
| | 33 | Central African Rep. |
| | 33 | Nigeria |
| | 34 | Côte d'Ivoire |
| | 35 | Sudan |
| | 36 | Eritrea |
| | 37 | Madagascar |
| | 38 | Comoros |
| | 39 | Mauritania |
| | 40 | Congo, Rep. |
| | 41 | Angola |
| | 42 | Equatorial Guinea |
| *smallest* | n/a | Somalia |

### Total Govt. Expenditure on Health as % of GDP

World Bank

| | | 2000-2002 |
|---|---|---|
| *largest* | 1 | São Tomé & Príncipe |
| | 2 | Malawi |
| | 3 | Lesotho |
| | 4 | Namibia |
| | 5 | Djibouti |
| | 6 | Seychelles |
| | 7 | Gabon |
| | 8 | Cape Verde |
| | 9 | Swaziland |
| | 10 | Zambia |
| | 11 | Mozambique |
| | 12 | South Africa |
| | 13 | Zimbabwe |
| | 14 | Ethiopia |
| | 15 | Eritrea |
| | 16 | Botswana |
| | 17 | Chad |
| | 18 | Ghana |
| | | SSA average |
| | 19 | Mali |
| | 20 | Benin |
| | 21 | Angola |
| | 22 | Madagascar |
| | 23 | Mauritius |
| | 24 | Sierra Leone |
| | 25 | Burkina Faso |
| | 26 | Gambia, The |
| | 27 | Kenya |
| | 28 | Uganda |
| | 29 | Niger |
| | 30 | Rwanda |
| | 31 | Mauritania |
| | 32 | Equatorial Guinea |
| | 33 | Senegal |
| | 34 | Tanzania |
| | 35 | Central African Rep. |
| | 36 | Guinea-Bissau |
| | 37 | Nigeria |
| | 38 | Comoros |
| | 39 | Congo, Rep. |
| | 40 | Cameroon |
| | 41 | Liberia |
| | 42 | Togo |
| | 43 | Sudan |
| | 44 | Côte d'Ivoire |
| | 45 | Guinea |
| | 46 | Burundi |
| | 47 | Congo, Dem. Rep. |
| *smallest* | n/a | Somalia |

# appendix B6: performance tables - spending on health

### Total Govt. Expenditure on Health as % of GDP

World Bank

| | 2003-2006 |
|---|---|
| largest 1 | Malawi |
| 2 | Zimbabwe |
| 3 | São Tomé & Príncipe |
| 4 | Rwanda |
| 5 | Namibia |
| 6 | South Africa |
| 7 | Botswana |
| 8 | Uganda |
| 9 | Burundi |
| 10 | Zambia |
| 11 | Djibouti |
| 12 | Lesotho |
| 13 | Swaziland |
| 14 | Burkina Faso |
| 15 | Seychelles |
| 16 | Ghana |
| 17 | Togo |
| | SSA average |
| 18 | Congo, Dem. Rep. |
| 19 | Guinea-Bissau |
| 20 | Guinea |
| 21 | Mali |
| 22 | Senegal |
| 23 | Tanzania |
| 24 | Chad |
| 25 | Gambia, The |
| 26 | Cape Verde |
| 27 | Benin |
| 28 | Sierra Leone |
| 29 | Niger |
| 30 | Gabon |
| 31 | Mozambique |
| 32 | Kenya |
| 33 | Cameroon |
| 34 | Liberia |
| 35 | Ethiopia |
| 36 | Mauritius |
| 37 | Central African Rep. |
| 38 | Nigeria |
| 39 | Côte d'Ivoire |
| 40 | Sudan |
| 41 | Eritrea |
| 42 | Madagascar |
| 43 | Comoros |
| 44 | Mauritania |
| 45 | Congo, Rep. |
| 46 | Angola |
| 47 | Equatorial Guinea |
| smallest n/a | Somalia |

### Total Private Expenditure on Health as % of GDP

World Bank

| | 2000-2002 |
|---|---|
| largest 1 | Uganda |
| 2 | South Africa |
| 3 | Guinea |
| 4 | Zimbabwe |
| 5 | Ghana |
| 6 | Guinea-Bissau |
| 7 | Togo |
| 8 | Mali |
| 9 | Cameroon |
| 10 | Chad |
| | SSA average |
| 11 | Nigeria |
| 12 | Gambia, The |
| 13 | Côte d'Ivoire |
| 14 | Congo, Dem. Rep. |
| 15 | Burundi |
| 16 | Malawi |
| 17 | Senegal |
| 18 | Burkina Faso |
| 19 | Zambia |
| 20 | Kenya |
| 21 | Benin |
| 22 | Liberia |
| 23 | Central African Rep. |
| 24 | Sudan |
| 25 | Swaziland |
| 26 | Namibia |
| 27 | Ethiopia |
| 28 | Tanzania |
| 29 | Rwanda |
| 30 | Sierra Leone |
| 31 | Eritrea |
| 32 | Djibouti |
| 33 | Botswana |
| 34 | Mauritius |
| 35 | Niger |
| 36 | Lesotho |
| 37 | Mozambique |
| 38 | Gabon |
| 39 | São Tomé & Príncipe |
| 40 | Seychelles |
| 41 | Madagascar |
| 42 | Comoros |
| 43 | Cape Verde |
| 44 | Congo, Rep. |
| 45 | Mauritania |
| 46 | Equatorial Guinea |
| 47 | Angola |
| smallest n/a | Somalia |

### Total Private Expenditure on Health as % of GDP

World Bank

| | 2003-2006 |
|---|---|
| largest 1 | Burundi |
| 2 | Uganda |
| 3 | South Africa |
| 4 | Guinea |
| 5 | Zimbabwe |
| 6 | Congo, Dem. Rep. |
| 7 | Togo |
| 8 | Namibia |
| 9 | Guinea-Bissau |
| 10 | Ghana |
| 11 | Rwanda |
| 12 | Cameroon |
| | SSA average |
| 13 | Malawi |
| 14 | Liberia |
| 15 | Mali |
| 16 | Côte d'Ivoire |
| 17 | Senegal |
| 18 | Sierra Leone |
| 19 | Nigeria |
| 20 | Burkina Faso |
| 21 | Lesotho |
| 22 | Zambia |
| 23 | Chad |
| 24 | Central African Rep. |
| 25 | Sudan |
| 26 | Kenya |
| 27 | Benin |
| 28 | Swaziland |
| 29 | Tanzania |
| 30 | Niger |
| 31 | Eritrea |
| 32 | Mauritius |
| 33 | Gambia, The |
| 34 | Djibouti |
| 35 | Ethiopia |
| 36 | Botswana |
| 37 | Mozambique |
| 38 | Seychelles |
| 39 | Gabon |
| 40 | Comoros |
| 41 | Madagascar |
| 42 | São Tomé & Príncipe |
| 43 | Cape Verde |
| 44 | Congo, Rep. |
| 45 | Mauritania |
| 46 | Equatorial Guinea |
| 47 | Angola |
| smallest n/a | Somalia |

### Total Expenditure on Health per Person $PPP

Primary data: WHO

| | 2000-2002 |
|---|---|
| largest 1 | South Africa |
| 2 | Seychelles |
| 3 | Mauritius |
| 4 | Namibia |
| 5 | Botswana |
| 6 | Gabon |
| 7 | Swaziland |
| 8 | Equatorial Guinea |
| 9 | Cape Verde |
| 10 | Zimbabwe |
| 11 | Lesotho |
| 12 | Uganda |
| 13 | Guinea |
| 14 | Ghana |
| 15 | Kenya |
| 16 | São Tomé & Príncipe |
| 17 | Côte d'Ivoire |
| 18 | Djibouti |
| 19 | Cameroon |
| 20 | Rwanda |
| 21 | Togo |
| 22 | Zambia |
| 23 | Mali |
| 24 | Senegal |
| 25 | Burkina Faso |
| 26 | Central African Rep. |
| 27 | Gambia, The |
| 28 | Nigeria |
| 29 | Guinea-Bissau |
| 30 | Mauritania |
| 31 | Angola |
| 32 | Mozambique |
| 33 | Sudan |
| 34 | Chad |
| 35 | Benin |
| 35 | Malawi |
| 36 | Eritrea |
| 37 | Sierra Leone |
| 38 | Madagascar |
| 39 | Congo, Rep. |
| 39 | Liberia |
| 40 | Comoros |
| 41 | Tanzania |
| 42 | Niger |
| 43 | Ethiopia |
| 44 | Burundi |
| 45 | Congo, Dem. Rep. |
| n/a | Somalia |
| smallest | |

### Total Expenditure on Health per Person $PPP

Primary data: WHO

| | 2003-2006 |
|---|---|
| largest 1 | South Africa |
| 2 | Seychelles |
| 3 | Botswana |
| 4 | Mauritius |
| 5 | Namibia |
| 6 | Swaziland |
| 7 | Gabon |
| 8 | Equatorial Guinea |
| 9 | Cape Verde |
| 10 | Zimbabwe |
| 11 | Rwanda |
| 12 | Uganda |
| 13 | São Tomé & Príncipe |
| 14 | Lesotho |
| 15 | Guinea |
| 16 | Kenya |
| 17 | Ghana |
| 18 | Djibouti |
| 19 | Burkina Faso |
| 20 | Cameroon |
| 21 | Senegal |
| 22 | Togo |
| 23 | Malawi |
| 24 | Zambia |
| 25 | Côte d'Ivoire |
| 26 | Mali |
| 27 | Gambia, The |
| 28 | Central African Rep. |
| 28 | Sudan |
| 29 | Angola |
| 30 | Mozambique |
| 31 | Nigeria |
| 32 | Mauritania |
| 33 | Benin |
| 34 | Chad |
| 35 | Sierra Leone |
| 36 | Guinea-Bissau |
| 37 | Tanzania |
| 38 | Eritrea |
| 39 | Liberia |
| 40 | Madagascar |
| 41 | Comoros |
| 42 | Congo, Rep. |
| 43 | Niger |
| 44 | Ethiopia |
| 45 | Congo, Dem. Rep. |
| 46 | Burundi |
| n/a | Somalia |
| smallest | |

# appendix B6: performance tables - spending on health

| | Total Govt. Expenditure on Health per Person $PPP | | Total Govt. Expenditure on Health per Person $PPP | | Total Private Expenditure on Health per Person $PPP | | Total Private Expenditure on Health per Person $PPP | | Govt. Expenditure on Health as % of Total Govt. Expenditure | |
|---|---|---|---|---|---|---|---|---|---|---|
| | Primary data: WHO | | Primary data: WHO | | Primary data: WHO | | Primary data: WHO | | Primary data: WHO | |
| | 1999-2002 | | 2003-2006 | | 2000-2002 | | 2003-2006 | | 1999-2002 | |
| largest / largest / largest / largest / highest | 1 | Seychelles | 1 | Seychelles | 1 | South Africa | 1 | South Africa | 1 | Gabon |
| | 2 | South Africa | 2 | Botswana | 2 | Mauritius | 2 | Mauritius | 2 | Namibia |
| | 3 | Namibia | 3 | South Africa | 3 | Seychelles | 3 | Seychelles | 3 | Benin |
| | 4 | Gabon | 4 | Mauritius | 4 | Swaziland | 4 | Botswana | 4 | Malawi |
| | 5 | Mauritius | 5 | Namibia | 5 | Namibia | 5 | Swaziland | 5 | Chad |
| | 6 | Botswana | 6 | Swaziland | 6 | Botswana | 6 | Namibia | 6 | Tanzania |
| | 7 | Swaziland | 7 | Equatorial Guinea | 7 | Zimbabwe | 7 | Guinea | 7 | Djibouti |
| | 8 | Equatorial Guinea | 8 | Gabon | 8 | Guinea | 8 | Uganda | 8 | Mozambique |
| | 9 | Cape Verde | 9 | Cape Verde | 9 | Uganda | 9 | Zimbabwe | 9 | Equatorial Guinea |
| | 10 | São Tomé & Príncipe | 10 | São Tomé & Príncipe | 10 | Gabon | 10 | Gabon | 10 | Niger |
| | 11 | Lesotho | 11 | Rwanda | 11 | Côte d'Ivoire | 11 | Equatorial Guinea | 11 | Madagascar |
| | 12 | Zimbabwe | 12 | Lesotho | 12 | Ghana | 12 | Rwanda | 12 | Swaziland |
| | 13 | Djibouti | 13 | Djibouti | 13 | Lesotho | 13 | Ghana | 13 | Zambia |
| | 14 | Kenya | 14 | Zimbabwe | 14 | Cameroon | 14 | Cameroon | 14 | Cape Verde |
| | 15 | Angola | 15 | Malawi | 15 | Cape Verde | 15 | Lesotho | 14 | Mali |
| | 16 | Ghana | 16 | Kenya | 16 | Kenya | 16 | Togo | 15 | Ethiopia |
| | 17 | Zambia | 16 | Burkina Faso | 17 | Togo | 17 | Kenya | 16 | Ghana |
| | 18 | Uganda | 17 | Angola | 18 | Equatorial Guinea | 18 | Côte d'Ivoire | 17 | Burkina Faso |
| | 19 | Mauritania | 18 | Uganda | 19 | Guinea-Bissau | 19 | Cape Verde | 18 | Central African Rep. |
| | 20 | Rwanda | 19 | Gambia, The | 20 | Mali | 20 | Senegal | 19 | Uganda |
| | 21 | Mozambique | 20 | Zambia | 20 | Senegal | 21 | Burkina Faso | 20 | Zimbabwe |
| | 22 | Gambia, The | 21 | Ghana | 21 | Rwanda | 22 | Sudan | 21 | Rwanda |
| | 23 | Malawi | 22 | Mozambique | 22 | Nigeria | 23 | Central African Rep. | 22 | South Africa |
| | 24 | Mali | 23 | Mali | 23 | Burkina Faso | 24 | Nigeria | 23 | Botswana |
| | 25 | Burkina Faso | 23 | Mauritania | 24 | Central African Rep. | 25 | Mali | 24 | São Tomé & Príncipe |
| | 25 | Central African Rep. | 24 | Senegal | 25 | Sudan | 26 | Zambia | 25 | Senegal |
| | 26 | Senegal | 25 | Benin | 26 | Gambia, The | 27 | Guinea-Bissau | 26 | Gambia, The |
| | 26 | Madagascar | 26 | Cameroon | 27 | Djibouti | 28 | Chad | 27 | Cameroon |
| | 27 | Côte d'Ivoire | 27 | Liberia | 28 | Zambia | 29 | Eritrea | 28 | Mauritius |
| | 28 | Benin | 28 | Sierra Leone | 29 | Chad | 30 | Djibouti | 29 | Comoros |
| | 29 | Cameroon | 29 | Central African Rep. | 30 | Eritrea | 31 | Gambia, The | 30 | Seychelles |
| | 30 | Guinea | 29 | Madagascar | 31 | Benin | 32 | Benin | 30 | Sudan |
| | 31 | Eritrea | 30 | Tanzania | 32 | Liberia | 33 | Sierra Leone | 31 | Liberia |
| | 31 | Sierra Leone | 31 | Sudan | 33 | Sierra Leone | 34 | São Tomé & Príncipe | 32 | Sierra Leone |
| | 32 | Congo, Rep. | 32 | Comoros | 34 | Tanzania | 35 | Malawi | 33 | Lesotho |
| | 33 | Chad | 33 | Togo | 35 | Malawi | 36 | Tanzania | 34 | Kenya |
| | 34 | Comoros | 34 | Chad | 36 | São Tomé & Príncipe | 37 | Mozambique | 35 | Togo |
| | 35 | Nigeria | 35 | Côte d'Ivoire | 36 | Mozambique | 38 | Congo, Rep. | 36 | Mauritania |
| | 36 | Togo | 36 | Guinea | 37 | Mauritania | 39 | Mauritania | 37 | Côte d'Ivoire |
| | 36 | Niger | 36 | Congo, Rep. | 38 | Congo, Rep. | 40 | Comoros | 38 | Guinea |
| | 37 | Sudan | 37 | Nigeria | 38 | Comoros | 41 | Liberia | 39 | Congo, Rep. |
| | 38 | Liberia | 38 | Niger | 39 | Burundi | 42 | Madagascar | 40 | Guinea-Bissau |
| | 38 | Tanzania | 39 | Guinea-Bissau | 40 | Madagascar | 42 | Niger | 41 | Nigeria |
| | 39 | Ethiopia | 39 | Eritrea | 40 | Niger | 43 | Burundi | 42 | Angola |
| | 40 | Guinea-Bissau | 40 | Ethiopia | 40 | Congo, Dem. Rep. | 44 | Congo, Dem. Rep. | 43 | Eritrea |
| | 41 | Burundi | 41 | Congo, Dem. Rep. | 41 | Ethiopia | 45 | Ethiopia | 44 | Burundi |
| | 42 | Congo, Dem. Rep. | 42 | Burundi | 42 | Angola | 46 | Angola | 45 | Congo, Dem. Rep. |
| smallest / smallest / smallest / smallest / lowest | n/a | Somalia | n/a | Somalia | n/a | Somalia | n/a | Somalia | n/a | Somalia |

# appendix B6: performance tables - spending on health

## Govt. Expenditure on Health as % of Total Govt. Expenditure

Primary data: WHO

highest

| | 2003-2006 |
|---|---|
| 1 | Rwanda |
| 2 | Liberia |
| 3 | Malawi |
| 4 | Botswana |
| 5 | Burkina Faso |
| 6 | Gabon |
| 7 | São Tomé & Príncipe |
| 8 | Djibouti |
| 9 | Benin |
| 10 | Mali |
| 11 | Cape Verde |
| 12 | Namibia |
| 13 | Tanzania |
| 14 | Mozambique |
| 15 | Zambia |
| 16 | Swaziland |
| 17 | Central African Rep. |
| 18 | Gambia, The |
| 19 | Niger |
| 20 | Ethiopia |
| 21 | Cameroon |
| 22 | Uganda |
| 23 | Seychelles |
| 24 | Chad |
| 24 | South Africa |
| 25 | Madagascar |
| 26 | Mauritius |
| 27 | Zimbabwe |
| 28 | Comoros |
| 29 | Lesotho |
| 30 | Sierra Leone |
| 31 | Senegal |
| 32 | Equatorial Guinea |
| 33 | Ghana |
| 34 | Congo, Dem. Rep. |
| 35 | Sudan |
| 36 | Togo |
| 37 | Kenya |
| 38 | Guinea |
| 39 | Angola |
| 40 | Mauritania |
| 41 | Côte d'Ivoire |
| 41 | Guinea-Bissau |
| 42 | Eritrea |
| 43 | Congo, Rep. |
| 44 | Nigeria |
| 45 | Burundi |
| n/a | Somalia |

lowest

## Out-of-Pocket Expenditure as % of Total Health Expenditure

Primary data: WHO

smallest

| | 1999-2002 |
|---|---|
| 1 | Namibia |
| 2 | South Africa |
| 3 | Botswana |
| 4 | Mozambique |
| 5 | Seychelles |
| 6 | Swaziland |
| 7 | São Tomé & Príncipe |
| 8 | Malawi |
| 9 | Madagascar |
| 10 | Rwanda |
| 11 | Cape Verde |
| 12 | Gabon |
| 13 | Equatorial Guinea |
| 14 | Angola |
| 15 | Zimbabwe |
| 16 | Mauritania |
| 17 | Djibouti |
| 18 | Lesotho |
| 19 | Zambia |
| 20 | Mauritius |
| 21 | Eritrea |
| 22 | Ethiopia |
| 23 | Uganda |
| 24 | Niger |
| 25 | Kenya |
| 26 | Congo, Rep. |
| 27 | Gambia, The |
| 28 | Comoros |
| 29 | Tanzania |
| 30 | Guinea-Bissau |
| 31 | Ghana |
| 32 | Benin |
| 33 | Sierra Leone |
| 34 | Burkina Faso |
| 35 | Central African Rep. |
| 36 | Senegal |
| 37 | Liberia |
| 38 | Chad |
| 39 | Mali |
| 40 | Nigeria |
| 41 | Togo |
| 42 | Côte d'Ivoire |
| 43 | Cameroon |
| 44 | Sudan |
| 45 | Burundi |
| 46 | Guinea |
| 47 | Congo, Dem. Rep. |
| n/a | Somalia |

largest

## Out-of-Pocket Expenditure as % of Total Health Expenditure

Primary data: WHO

smallest

| | 2003-2006 |
|---|---|
| 1 | Namibia |
| 2 | Botswana |
| 3 | Malawi |
| 4 | South Africa |
| 5 | São Tomé & Príncipe |
| 6 | Mozambique |
| 7 | Swaziland |
| 8 | Seychelles |
| 9 | Angola |
| 10 | Equatorial Guinea |
| 11 | Rwanda |
| 12 | Madagascar |
| 13 | Cape Verde |
| 14 | Djibouti |
| 15 | Gambia, The |
| 16 | Gabon |
| 17 | Lesotho |
| 18 | Zimbabwe |
| 19 | Zambia |
| 20 | Ethiopia |
| 21 | Mauritania |
| 22 | Uganda |
| 23 | Mauritius |
| 24 | Tanzania |
| 25 | Liberia |
| 26 | Niger |
| 27 | Burkina Faso |
| 28 | Kenya |
| 29 | Eritrea |
| 30 | Comoros |
| 31 | Guinea-Bissau |
| 32 | Benin |
| 33 | Sierra Leone |
| 34 | Ghana |
| 35 | Mali |
| 36 | Congo, Rep. |
| 37 | Chad |
| 38 | Senegal |
| 39 | Central African Rep. |
| 40 | Sudan |
| 41 | Nigeria |
| 42 | Togo |
| 43 | Côte d'Ivoire |
| 44 | Congo, Dem. Rep. |
| 45 | Cameroon |
| 46 | Burundi |
| 47 | Guinea |
| n/a | Somalia |

largest

## Out-of-Pocket Expenditure as % of Private Health Expenditure

Primary data: WHO

smallest

| | 1999-2002 |
|---|---|
| 1 | South Africa |
| 2 | Namibia |
| 3 | Botswana |
| 4 | Mozambique |
| 5 | Swaziland |
| 6 | Malawi |
| 7 | Rwanda |
| 8 | Zimbabwe |
| 9 | Madagascar |
| 10 | Uganda |
| 11 | Guinea-Bissau |
| 12 | Seychelles |
| 13 | Eritrea |
| 14 | Lesotho |
| 15 | Mauritius |
| 16 | Zambia |
| 17 | Ghana |
| 18 | Kenya |
| 19 | Ethiopia |
| 20 | Tanzania |
| 21 | Equatorial Guinea |
| 22 | Gambia, The |
| 23 | Niger |
| 24 | Togo |
| 25 | Côte d'Ivoire |
| 26 | Senegal |
| 27 | Nigeria |
| 28 | Cameroon |
| 29 | Burkina Faso |
| 30 | Central African Rep. |
| 31 | Chad |
| 32 | Sudan |
| 33 | Djibouti |
| 34 | Liberia |
| 35 | Guinea |
| 36 | Mali |
| 37 | Cape Verde |
| 38 | Benin |
| 39 | Angola |
| 39 | Burundi |
| 39 | Comoros |
| 39 | Congo, Dem. Rep. |
| 39 | Congo, Rep. |
| 39 | Gabon |
| 39 | Mauritania |
| 39 | São Tomé & Príncipe |
| 39 | Sierra Leone |
| n/a | Somalia |

largest

## Out-of-Pocket Expenditure as % of Private Health Expenditure

Primary data: WHO

smallest

| | 2003-2006 |
|---|---|
| 1 | Namibia |
| 2 | South Africa |
| 3 | Botswana |
| 4 | Malawi |
| 5 | Mozambique |
| 6 | Swaziland |
| 7 | Rwanda |
| 8 | Uganda |
| 9 | Zimbabwe |
| 10 | Madagascar |
| 11 | Seychelles |
| 12 | Eritrea |
| 13 | Guinea-Bissau |
| 14 | Lesotho |
| 15 | Gambia, The |
| 16 | Zambia |
| 17 | Equatorial Guinea |
| 18 | Ghana |
| 19 | Kenya |
| 20 | Mauritius |
| 21 | Ethiopia |
| 22 | Tanzania |
| 23 | Togo |
| 24 | Niger |
| 25 | Côte d'Ivoire |
| 26 | Senegal |
| 27 | Nigeria |
| 28 | Burkina Faso |
| 29 | Cameroon |
| 30 | Central African Rep. |
| 31 | Chad |
| 32 | Sudan |
| 33 | Djibouti |
| 34 | Liberia |
| 35 | Mali |
| 36 | Guinea |
| 37 | Cape Verde |
| 38 | Benin |
| 39 | Angola |
| 39 | Burundi |
| 39 | Comoros |
| 39 | Congo, Dem. Rep. |
| 39 | Congo, Rep. |
| 39 | Gabon |
| 39 | Mauritania |
| 39 | São Tomé & Príncipe |
| 39 | Sierra Leone |
| n/a | Somalia |

largest

# B7 performance tables - purchasing power

### Govt. Consumption as $PPP per Person

IMF, World Bank

| | | 1999-2002 |
|---|---|---|
| highest | 1 | Seychelles |
| | 2 | Botswana |
| | 3 | Gabon |
| | 4 | South Africa |
| | 5 | Angola |
| | 6 | Mauritius |
| | 7 | Namibia |
| | 8 | Swaziland |
| | 9 | Eritrea |
| | 10 | Congo, Rep. |
| | 11 | Cape Verde |
| | 12 | Nigeria |
| | | SSA average |
| | 13 | Mauritania |
| | 14 | Kenya |
| | 15 | Lesotho |
| | 16 | Senegal |
| | 17 | Cameroon |
| | 18 | Comoros |
| | 19 | Benin |
| | 20 | Gambia, The |
| | 21 | Côte d'Ivoire |
| | 22 | Burkina Faso |
| | 23 | Zambia |
| | 24 | Sudan |
| | 25 | Ghana |
| | 26 | Uganda |
| | 27 | Ethiopia |
| | 28 | Malawi |
| | 29 | Mali |
| | 30 | Central African Rep. |
| | 31 | Chad |
| | 32 | Tanzania |
| | 33 | Rwanda |
| | 34 | Niger |
| | 35 | Togo |
| | 36 | Guinea-Bissau |
| | 37 | Guinea |
| | 38 | Burundi |
| | 39 | Madagascar |
| | 40 | Sierra Leone |
| | 41 | Mozambique |
| | 42 | Zimbabwe |
| | 43 | Congo, Dem. Rep. |
| | 44 | Equatorial Guinea |
| | n/a | Djibouti |
| | n/a | Liberia |
| | n/a | São Tomé & Príncipe |
| lowest | n/a | Somalia |

### Govt. Consumption as $PPP per Person

IMF, World Bank

| | | 2003-2006 |
|---|---|---|
| highest | 1 | Botswana |
| | 2 | Seychelles |
| | 3 | South Africa |
| | 4 | Mauritius |
| | 5 | Namibia |
| | 6 | Angola |
| | 7 | Swaziland |
| | 8 | Gabon |
| | 9 | Congo, Rep. |
| | 10 | Eritrea |
| | 11 | Nigeria |
| | 12 | Mauritania |
| | 13 | Cape Verde |
| | | SSA average |
| | 14 | Sudan |
| | 15 | Equatorial Guinea |
| | 16 | Kenya |
| | 17 | Senegal |
| | 18 | Cameroon |
| | 19 | Benin |
| | 20 | Ghana |
| | 21 | Lesotho |
| | 22 | Burkina Faso |
| | 23 | Tanzania |
| | 24 | Zambia |
| | 25 | Côte d'Ivoire |
| | 26 | Gambia, The |
| | 27 | Uganda |
| | 28 | Comoros |
| | 29 | Malawi |
| | 30 | Rwanda |
| | 31 | Ethiopia |
| | 32 | Chad |
| | 33 | Mali |
| | 34 | Madagascar |
| | 35 | Sierra Leone |
| | 36 | Burundi |
| | 37 | Central African Rep. |
| | 38 | Togo |
| | 39 | Mozambique |
| | 40 | Niger |
| | 41 | Guinea-Bissau |
| | 42 | Guinea |
| | 43 | Zimbabwe |
| | 44 | Congo, Dem. Rep. |
| | n/a | Djibouti |
| | n/a | Liberia |
| | n/a | São Tomé & Príncipe |
| lowest | n/a | Somalia |

### Household Consumption as $PPP per Person

IMF, World Bank

| | | 1999-2002 |
|---|---|---|
| highest | 1 | Seychelles |
| | 2 | Gabon |
| | 3 | Mauritius |
| | 4 | South Africa |
| | 5 | Botswana |
| | 6 | Swaziland |
| | 7 | Cape Verde |
| | 8 | Namibia |
| | 9 | Mauritania |
| | 10 | Cameroon |
| | 11 | Côte d'Ivoire |
| | 12 | Sudan |
| | 13 | Benin |
| | 14 | Congo, Rep. |
| | 15 | Senegal |
| | 16 | Lesotho |
| | 17 | Kenya |
| | | SSA average |
| | 18 | Chad |
| | 19 | Angola |
| | 20 | Ghana |
| | 21 | Comoros |
| | 22 | Guinea |
| | 23 | Burkina Faso |
| | 24 | Gambia, The |
| | 25 | Zambia |
| | 26 | Tanzania |
| | 27 | Eritrea |
| | 28 | São Tomé & Príncipe |
| | 29 | Madagascar |
| | 30 | Nigeria |
| | 31 | Togo |
| | 32 | Mali |
| | 33 | Uganda |
| | 34 | Rwanda |
| | 35 | Central African Rep. |
| | 36 | Malawi |
| | 37 | Guinea-Bissau |
| | 38 | Niger |
| | 39 | Mozambique |
| | 40 | Ethiopia |
| | 41 | Sierra Leone |
| | 42 | Burundi |
| | 43 | Congo, Dem. Rep. |
| | 44 | Zimbabwe |
| | n/a | Djibouti |
| | n/a | Liberia |
| | n/a | São Tomé & Príncipe |
| lowest | n/a | Somalia |

# appendix B7: performance tables - purchasing power

### Household Consumption as $PPP per Person

IMF, World Bank

highest

| | 2003-2006 |
|---|---|
| 1 | Seychelles |
| 2 | Gabon |
| 3 | Mauritius |
| 4 | South Africa |
| 5 | Botswana |
| 6 | Cape Verde |
| 7 | Swaziland |
| 8 | Namibia |
| 9 | Mauritania |
| 10 | Angola |
| 11 | Cameroon |
| 12 | Sudan |
| 13 | Senegal |
| 14 | Congo, Rep. |
| 15 | Côte d'Ivoire |
| 16 | Benin |
| 17 | Kenya |
| 18 | Equatorial Guinea |
| | SSA average |
| 19 | Lesotho |
| 20 | Ghana |
| 21 | Comoros |
| 22 | Chad |
| 23 | Guinea |
| 24 | Burkina Faso |
| 25 | Gambia, The |
| 26 | Tanzania |
| 27 | Madagascar |
| 28 | Mali |
| 29 | Zambia |
| 30 | Nigeria |
| 31 | Eritrea |
| 32 | Uganda |
| 33 | Rwanda |
| 34 | Togo |
| 35 | Malawi |
| 36 | Central African Rep. |
| 37 | Sierra Leone |
| 38 | Ethiopia |
| 39 | Mozambique |
| 40 | Niger |
| 41 | Guinea-Bissau |
| 42 | Burundi |
| 43 | Congo, Dem. Rep. |
| 44 | Zimbabwe |
| n/a | Djibouti |
| n/a | Liberia |
| n/a | São Tomé & Príncipe |
| n/a | Somalia |

lowest

### Govt. Consumption as % of GDP

World Bank

highest

| | 1999-2002 |
|---|---|
| 1 | Eritrea |
| 2 | Angola |
| 3 | Botswana |
| 4 | Namibia |
| 5 | Seychelles |
| 6 | Nigeria |
| 7 | Swaziland |
| 8 | Ethiopia |
| 9 | Burundi |
| 10 | South Africa |
| 11 | Lesotho |
| | SSA average |
| 12 | Cape Verde |
| 13 | Kenya |
| 14 | Comoros |
| 15 | Congo, Rep. |
| 16 | Malawi |
| 17 | Mauritania |
| 18 | Sierra Leone |
| 19 | Uganda |
| 20 | Zimbabwe |
| 21 | Gambia, The |
| 22 | Gabon |
| 23 | Senegal |
| 24 | Niger |
| 25 | Mauritius |
| 26 | Burkina Faso |
| 27 | Guinea-Bissau |
| 28 | Zambia |
| 29 | Central African Rep. |
| 30 | Benin |
| 31 | Rwanda |
| 32 | Mali |
| 33 | Ghana |
| 34 | Mozambique |
| 35 | Cameroon |
| 35 | Togo |
| 36 | Tanzania |
| 37 | Sudan |
| 38 | Madagascar |
| 39 | Chad |
| 40 | Côte d'Ivoire |
| 41 | Congo, Dem. Rep. |
| 42 | Guinea |
| n/a | Equatorial Guinea |
| n/a | Djibouti |
| n/a | Liberia |
| n/a | São Tomé & Príncipe |
| n/a | Somalia |

lowest

### Govt. Consumption as % of GDP

World Bank

highest

| | 2003-2006 |
|---|---|
| 1 | Eritrea |
| 2 | Botswana |
| 3 | Angola |
| 4 | Namibia |
| 5 | Seychelles |
| 6 | Swaziland |
| 7 | Nigeria |
| 8 | Burundi |
| 8 | Zimbabwe |
| 9 | Mauritania |
| 10 | South Africa |
| | SSA average |
| 11 | Kenya |
| 12 | Malawi |
| 13 | Ethiopia |
| 14 | Congo, Rep. |
| 15 | Lesotho |
| 16 | Sudan |
| 17 | Ghana |
| 18 | Uganda |
| 19 | Guinea-Bissau |
| 20 | Mauritius |
| 21 | Benin |
| 22 | Senegal |
| 23 | Rwanda |
| 24 | Cape Verde |
| 25 | Sierra Leone |
| 26 | Tanzania |
| 27 | Burkina Faso |
| 28 | Zambia |
| 29 | Niger |
| 30 | Central African Rep. |
| 31 | Comoros |
| 32 | Gambia, The |
| 33 | Cameroon |
| 34 | Mozambique |
| 35 | Togo |
| 36 | Madagascar |
| 37 | Mali |
| 38 | Côte d'Ivoire |
| 39 | Gabon |
| 40 | Congo, Dem. Rep. |
| 41 | Guinea |
| 42 | Chad |
| 43 | Equatorial Guinea |
| n/a | Djibouti |
| n/a | Liberia |
| n/a | São Tomé & Príncipe |
| n/a | Somalia |

lowest

### Household Consumption as % of GDP

World Bank

highest

| | 1999-2002 |
|---|---|
| 1 | Lesotho |
| 2 | Cape Verde |
| 3 | Guinea-Bissau |
| 4 | Sierra Leone |
| 5 | Chad |
| 6 | Togo |
| 7 | Burundi |
| 8 | Congo, Dem. Rep. |
| 9 | Rwanda |
| 10 | Malawi |
| 11 | Comoros |
| 12 | Ghana |
| 13 | Benin |
| 14 | Tanzania |
| 15 | Madagascar |
| 16 | Niger |
| 17 | Mauritania |
| 18 | Burkina Faso |
| 19 | Sudan |
| 20 | Guinea |
| 21 | Mozambique |
| 22 | Uganda |
| 23 | Central African Rep. |
| 23 | Ethiopia |
| 24 | Mali |
| 25 | Senegal |
| 26 | Zambia |
| 27 | Eritrea |
| 28 | Gambia, The |
| 29 | Zimbabwe |
| 30 | Kenya |
| 31 | Swaziland |
| 32 | Côte d'Ivoire |
| 33 | Cameroon |
| | SSA average |
| 34 | Mauritius |
| 35 | South Africa |
| 36 | Namibia |
| 37 | Gabon |
| 38 | Seychelles |
| 39 | Nigeria |
| 40 | Congo, Rep. |
| 41 | Angola |
| 42 | Botswana |
| n/a | Equatorial Guinea |
| n/a | Djibouti |
| n/a | Liberia |
| n/a | São Tomé & Príncipe |
| n/a | Somalia |

lowest

### Household Consumption as % of GDP

World Bank

highest

| | 2003-2006 |
|---|---|
| 1 | Cape Verde |
| 2 | Malawi |
| 3 | Central African Rep. |
| 4 | Lesotho |
| 5 | Congo, Dem. Rep. |
| 6 | Guinea |
| 7 | Comoros |
| 7 | Sierra Leone |
| 8 | Guinea-Bissau |
| 9 | Togo |
| 10 | Rwanda |
| 11 | Madagascar |
| 12 | Ethiopia |
| 13 | Burundi |
| 14 | Eritrea |
| 15 | Mauritania |
| 16 | Niger |
| 17 | Ghana |
| 18 | Mali |
| 19 | Burkina Faso |
| 20 | Benin |
| 21 | Senegal |
| 22 | Gambia, The |
| 23 | Uganda |
| 24 | Tanzania |
| 25 | Kenya |
| 26 | Sudan |
| 27 | Mozambique |
| 28 | Cameroon |
| 29 | Côte d'Ivoire |
| 30 | Zimbabwe |
| 31 | Swaziland |
| 32 | Mauritius |
| 33 | Zambia |
| 34 | South Africa |
| 35 | Gabon |
| 36 | Chad |
| | SSA average |
| 37 | Seychelles |
| 38 | Namibia |
| 39 | Angola |
| 40 | Nigeria |
| 41 | Congo, Rep. |
| 42 | Botswana |
| 43 | Equatorial Guinea |
| n/a | Djibouti |
| n/a | Liberia |
| n/a | São Tomé & Príncipe |
| n/a | Somalia |

lowest

# appendix B7: performance tables - purchasing power

### Growth in Govt. Consumption

IMF, World Bank

| | | 1999-2002 |
|---|---|---|
| highest | 1 | Nigeria |
| | 2 | Sierra Leone |
| | 3 | Ethiopia |
| | 4 | Angola |
| | 5 | Guinea |
| | 6 | Sudan |
| | 7 | Chad |
| | 8 | Mozambique |
| | 9 | Benin |
| | 10 | Botswana |
| | 11 | Tanzania |
| | 12 | Mauritania |
| | 13 | Uganda |
| | 14 | Guinea-Bissau |
| | 15 | Rwanda |
| | 16 | Senegal |
| | 17 | Cape Verde |
| | 18 | Cameroon |
| | | SSA average |
| | 19 | Mauritius |
| | 20 | Burkina Faso |
| | 21 | Burundi |
| | 22 | Côte d'Ivoire |
| | 23 | South Africa |
| | 24 | Gambia, The |
| | 25 | Comoros |
| | 26 | Ghana |
| | 27 | Kenya |
| | 28 | Central African Rep. |
| | 29 | Madagascar |
| | 30 | Zambia |
| | 31 | Namibia |
| | 32 | Congo, Rep. |
| | 33 | Niger |
| | 34 | Malawi |
| | 35 | Swaziland |
| | 36 | Eritrea |
| | 37 | Seychelles |
| | 38 | Mali |
| | 39 | Lesotho |
| | 40 | Zimbabwe |
| | 41 | Togo |
| | 42 | Congo, Dem. Rep. |
| | 43 | Gabon |
| | n/a | Equatorial Guinea |
| | n/a | Djibouti |
| | n/a | Liberia |
| | n/a | São Tomé & Príncipe |
| lowest | n/a | Somalia |

### Growth in Govt. Consumption

IMF, World Bank

| | | 2003-2006 |
|---|---|---|
| highest | 1 | Burundi |
| | 2 | Sudan |
| | 3 | Congo, Dem. Rep. |
| | 4 | Guinea-Bissau |
| | 5 | Ghana |
| | 6 | Mali |
| | 7 | Tanzania |
| | 8 | Swaziland |
| | 9 | Gabon |
| | 10 | Madagascar |
| | 11 | Mauritania |
| | 12 | Malawi |
| | 13 | Benin |
| | 14 | Cape Verde |
| | 15 | Mauritius |
| | 16 | Senegal |
| | 17 | Rwanda |
| | 18 | Togo |
| | 19 | Eritrea |
| | 20 | South Africa |
| | 21 | Mozambique |
| | 22 | Zimbabwe |
| | | SSA average |
| | 23 | Seychelles |
| | 24 | Botswana |
| | 25 | Burkina Faso |
| | 26 | Uganda |
| | 27 | Kenya |
| | 28 | Cameroon |
| | 29 | Namibia |
| | 30 | Niger |
| | 31 | Chad |
| | 32 | Côte d'Ivoire |
| | 33 | Sierra Leone |
| | 34 | Nigeria |
| | 35 | Lesotho |
| | 36 | Gambia, The |
| | 37 | Central African Rep. |
| | 38 | Ethiopia |
| | 39 | Zambia |
| | 40 | Congo, Rep. |
| | 41 | Angola |
| | 42 | Guinea |
| | 43 | Comoros |
| | 44 | Equatorial Guinea |
| | n/a | Djibouti |
| | n/a | Liberia |
| | n/a | São Tomé & Príncipe |
| lowest | n/a | Somalia |

### Growth in Household Consumption

IMF, World Bank

| | | 1999-2002 |
|---|---|---|
| highest | 1 | Angola |
| | 2 | Gabon |
| | 3 | Sierra Leone |
| | 4 | Cape Verde |
| | 5 | Mozambique |
| | 6 | Burkina Faso |
| | 7 | Chad |
| | 8 | Malawi |
| | 9 | Ethiopia |
| | 10 | Seychelles |
| | 11 | Mauritius |
| | 12 | Mali |
| | 13 | Mauritania |
| | 14 | Guinea |
| | 15 | Botswana |
| | 16 | Senegal |
| | 17 | Ghana |
| | 18 | Uganda |
| | 19 | Benin |
| | 20 | Namibia |
| | 21 | Cameroon |
| | 22 | South Africa |
| | 23 | Zimbabwe |
| | 24 | Sudan |
| | 25 | Gambia, The |
| | 26 | Nigeria |
| | 27 | Burundi |
| | 28 | Eritrea |
| | 29 | Rwanda |
| | 30 | Niger |
| | | SSA average |
| | 31 | Tanzania |
| | 32 | Kenya |
| | 33 | Zambia |
| | 34 | Comoros |
| | 35 | Central African Rep. |
| | 36 | Togo |
| | 37 | Lesotho |
| | 38 | Madagascar |
| | 39 | Guinea-Bissau |
| | 40 | Swaziland |
| | 41 | Congo, Dem. Rep. |
| | 42 | Côte d'Ivoire |
| | 43 | Congo, Rep. |
| | n/a | Equatorial Guinea |
| | n/a | Djibouti |
| | n/a | Liberia |
| | n/a | São Tomé & Príncipe |
| lowest | n/a | Somalia |

### Growth in Household Consumption

IMF, World Bank

| | | 2003-2006 |
|---|---|---|
| highest | 1 | Gabon |
| | 2 | Ethiopia |
| | 3 | Madagascar |
| | 4 | Botswana |
| | 5 | Cape Verde |
| | 6 | Mauritius |
| | 7 | Sierra Leone |
| | 8 | Central African Rep. |
| | 9 | South Africa |
| | 10 | Kenya |
| | 11 | Ghana |
| | 12 | Gambia, The |
| | 13 | Malawi |
| | 14 | Tanzania |
| | 15 | Angola |
| | 16 | Congo, Rep. |
| | 17 | Mali |
| | 18 | Sudan |
| | 19 | Comoros |
| | 20 | Congo, Dem. Rep. |
| | 21 | Swaziland |
| | 22 | Rwanda |
| | 23 | Senegal |
| | 24 | Burkina Faso |
| | 25 | Mozambique |
| | 26 | Mauritania |
| | 27 | Guinea |
| | 28 | Uganda |
| | 29 | Togo |
| | 30 | Seychelles |
| | 31 | Niger |
| | 32 | Namibia |
| | 33 | Côte d'Ivoire |
| | | SSA average |
| | 34 | Cameroon |
| | 35 | Benin |
| | 36 | Zambia |
| | 37 | Burundi |
| | 38 | Lesotho |
| | 39 | Nigeria |
| | 40 | Chad |
| | 41 | Guinea-Bissau |
| | 42 | Eritrea |
| | 43 | Zimbabwe |
| | 44 | Equatorial Guinea |
| | n/a | Djibouti |
| | n/a | Liberia |
| | n/a | São Tomé & Príncipe |
| lowest | n/a | Somalia |

# B8 performance tables - self-reliance

### Total Exports per Person $US

WTO

greatest

| 1999-2002 | |
|---|---|
| 1 | Seychelles |
| 2 | Equatorial Guinea |
| 3 | Mauritius |
| 4 | Gabon |
| 5 | Botswana |
| 6 | Swaziland |
| 7 | Namibia |
| 8 | South Africa |
| 9 | Congo, Rep. |
| 10 | Angola |
| 11 | Côte d'Ivoire |
| 12 | Cape Verde |
| | SSA average |
| 13 | Nigeria |
| 14 | Lesotho |
| 15 | Cameroon |
| 16 | Mauritania |
| 17 | Djibouti |
| 18 | Senegal |
| 19 | Ghana |
| 20 | Zambia |
| 21 | São Tomé & Príncipe |
| 22 | Guinea |
| 23 | Kenya |
| 24 | Comoros |
| 25 | Togo |
| 26 | Mali |
| 27 | Benin |
| 28 | Madagascar |
| 29 | Gambia, The |
| 30 | Sudan |
| 31 | Mozambique |
| 32 | Guinea-Bissau |
| 33 | Tanzania |
| 34 | Central African Rep. |
| 35 | Malawi |
| 36 | Niger |
| 37 | Uganda |
| 38 | Chad |
| 39 | Burkina Faso |
| 40 | Congo, Dem. Rep. |
| 41 | Ethiopia |
| 42 | Rwanda |
| 43 | Sierra Leone |
| 44 | Burundi |
| n/a | Eritrea |
| n/a | Liberia |
| n/a | Somalia |
| n/a | Zimbabwe |

smallest

### Total Exports per Person $US

WTO

greatest

| 2003-2006 | |
|---|---|
| 1 | Equatorial Guinea |
| 2 | Seychelles |
| 3 | Gabon |
| 4 | Mauritius |
| 5 | Botswana |
| 6 | Swaziland |
| 7 | Angola |
| 8 | Congo, Rep. |
| 9 | South Africa |
| 10 | Namibia |
| 11 | Cape Verde |
| 12 | Côte d'Ivoire |
| 13 | Lesotho |
| 14 | Nigeria |
| | SSA average |
| 15 | Mauritania |
| 16 | Chad |
| 17 | Cameroon |
| 18 | Zambia |
| 19 | Senegal |
| 20 | Djibouti |
| 21 | Ghana |
| 22 | São Tomé & Príncipe |
| 23 | Kenya |
| 24 | Togo |
| 25 | Mali |
| 26 | Sudan |
| 27 | Mozambique |
| 28 | Guinea |
| 29 | Benin |
| 30 | Comoros |
| 31 | Madagascar |
| 32 | Tanzania |
| 33 | Gambia, The |
| 34 | Guinea-Bissau |
| 35 | Malawi |
| 36 | Burkina Faso |
| 37 | Uganda |
| 38 | Niger |
| 39 | Sierra Leone |
| 40 | Congo, Dem. Rep. |
| 41 | Central African Rep. |
| 42 | Ethiopia |
| 43 | Rwanda |
| 44 | Burundi |
| n/a | Eritrea |
| n/a | Liberia |
| n/a | Somalia |
| n/a | Zimbabwe |

smallest

### Total Imports per Person $US

WTO

smallest

| 1999-2002 | |
|---|---|
| 1 | Congo, Dem. Rep. |
| 2 | Burundi |
| 3 | Ethiopia |
| 4 | Rwanda |
| 5 | Niger |
| 6 | Sierra Leone |
| 7 | Central African Rep. |
| 8 | Guinea-Bissau |
| 9 | Tanzania |
| 10 | Burkina Faso |
| 11 | Malawi |
| 12 | Sudan |
| 13 | Uganda |
| 14 | Madagascar |
| 15 | Mozambique |
| 16 | Guinea |
| 17 | Nigeria |
| 18 | Kenya |
| 19 | Benin |
| 20 | Mali |
| 21 | Chad |
| 22 | Togo |
| 23 | Comoros |
| 24 | Zambia |
| 25 | Gambia, The |
| 26 | Cameroon |
| | SSA average |
| 27 | Ghana |
| 28 | Senegal |
| 29 | Mauritania |
| 30 | Côte d'Ivoire |
| 31 | São Tomé & Príncipe |
| 32 | Djibouti |
| 33 | Angola |
| 34 | Lesotho |
| 35 | Congo, Rep. |
| 36 | South Africa |
| 37 | Cape Verde |
| 38 | Namibia |
| 39 | Swaziland |
| 40 | Gabon |
| 41 | Botswana |
| 42 | Mauritius |
| 43 | Equatorial Guinea |
| 44 | Seychelles |
| n/a | Eritrea |
| n/a | Liberia |
| n/a | Somalia |
| n/a | Zimbabwe |

greatest

### Total Imports per Person $US

WTO

*smallest*

| 2003-2006 | |
|---|---|
| 1 | Congo, Dem. Rep. |
| 2 | Burundi |
| 3 | Rwanda |
| 4 | Ethiopia |
| 5 | Central African Rep. |
| 6 | Sierra Leone |
| 7 | Niger |
| 8 | Guinea-Bissau |
| 9 | Uganda |
| 10 | Malawi |
| 11 | Tanzania |
| 12 | Guinea |
| 13 | Madagascar |
| 14 | Burkina Faso |
| 15 | Mozambique |
| 16 | Benin |
| 17 | Nigeria |
| 18 | Gambia, The |
| 19 | Kenya |
| 20 | Mali |
| 21 | Sudan |
| 22 | Togo |
| 23 | Cameroon |
| 24 | Chad |
| 25 | Comoros |
| 26 | Zambia |
| 27 | Ghana |
| | SSA average |
| 28 | Senegal |
| 29 | Côte d'Ivoire |
| 30 | Djibouti |
| 31 | São Tomé & Príncipe |
| 32 | Mauritania |
| 33 | Lesotho |
| 34 | Angola |
| 35 | Congo, Rep. |
| 36 | Cape Verde |
| 37 | Namibia |
| 38 | South Africa |
| 39 | Gabon |
| 40 | Botswana |
| 41 | Swaziland |
| 42 | Mauritius |
| 43 | Equatorial Guinea |
| 44 | Seychelles |
| n/a | Eritrea |
| n/a | Liberia |
| n/a | Somalia |
| n/a | Zimbabwe |

*greatest*

### Goods Exports per Person $US

WTO

*greatest*

| 1999-2002 | |
|---|---|
| 1 | Equatorial Guinea |
| 2 | Seychelles |
| 3 | Gabon |
| 4 | Botswana |
| 5 | Mauritius |
| 6 | Swaziland |
| 7 | South Africa |
| 8 | Congo, Rep. |
| 9 | Namibia |
| 10 | Angola |
| 11 | Côte d'Ivoire |
| 12 | Nigeria |
| 13 | Lesotho |
| 14 | Mauritania |
| | SSA average |
| 15 | Cameroon |
| 16 | Senegal |
| 17 | Zambia |
| 18 | Ghana |
| 19 | Guinea |
| 20 | Togo |
| 21 | Mali |
| 22 | Kenya |
| 23 | Benin |
| 24 | Sudan |
| 25 | Madagascar |
| 26 | Djibouti |
| 27 | Guinea-Bissau |
| 28 | Central African Rep. |
| 29 | Malawi |
| 30 | Mozambique |
| 31 | Comoros |
| 32 | Niger |
| 33 | Cape Verde |
| 34 | Chad |
| 35 | Tanzania |
| 36 | São Tomé & Príncipe |
| 37 | Burkina Faso |
| 38 | Uganda |
| 39 | Congo, Dem. Rep. |
| 40 | Gambia, The |
| 41 | Rwanda |
| 42 | Ethiopia |
| 43 | Burundi |
| 44 | Sierra Leone |
| n/a | Eritrea |
| n/a | Liberia |
| n/a | Somalia |
| n/a | Zimbabwe |

*smallest*

### Goods Exports per Person $US

WTO

*greatest*

| 2003-2006 | |
|---|---|
| 1 | Equatorial Guinea |
| 2 | Seychelles |
| 3 | Gabon |
| 4 | Botswana |
| 5 | Swaziland |
| 6 | Mauritius |
| 7 | Angola |
| 8 | Congo, Rep. |
| 9 | South Africa |
| 10 | Namibia |
| 11 | Côte d'Ivoire |
| 12 | Lesotho |
| 13 | Nigeria |
| | SSA average |
| 14 | Chad |
| 15 | Mauritania |
| 16 | Zambia |
| 17 | Cameroon |
| 18 | Senegal |
| 19 | Ghana |
| 20 | Sudan |
| 21 | Togo |
| 22 | Mali |
| 23 | Guinea |
| 24 | Kenya |
| 25 | Mozambique |
| 26 | Benin |
| 27 | Djibouti |
| 28 | Madagascar |
| 29 | Guinea-Bissau |
| 30 | Tanzania |
| 31 | Malawi |
| 32 | Niger |
| 33 | Burkina Faso |
| 34 | Congo, Dem. Rep. |
| 35 | Cape Verde |
| 36 | Central African Rep. |
| 37 | São Tomé & Príncipe |
| 38 | Comoros |
| 39 | Sierra Leone |
| 40 | Uganda |
| 41 | Rwanda |
| 42 | Ethiopia |
| 43 | Burundi |
| 44 | Gambia, The |
| n/a | Eritrea |
| n/a | Liberia |
| n/a | Somalia |
| n/a | Zimbabwe |

*smallest*

### Goods Imports per Person $US

WTO

*smallest*

| 1999-2002 | |
|---|---|
| 1 | Congo, Dem. Rep. |
| 2 | Burundi |
| 3 | Ethiopia |
| 4 | Rwanda |
| 5 | Central African Rep. |
| 6 | Sierra Leone |
| 7 | Niger |
| 8 | Guinea-Bissau |
| 9 | Tanzania |
| 10 | Malawi |
| 11 | Sudan |
| 12 | Madagascar |
| 13 | Uganda |
| 14 | Burkina Faso |
| 15 | Mozambique |
| 16 | Nigeria |
| 17 | Guinea |
| 18 | Chad |
| 19 | Mali |
| 20 | Benin |
| 21 | Comoros |
| 22 | Kenya |
| 23 | Cameroon |
| 24 | Zambia |
| 25 | Togo |
| 26 | Gambia, The |
| | SSA average |
| 27 | Ghana |
| 28 | Mauritania |
| 29 | Côte d'Ivoire |
| 30 | Senegal |
| 31 | Congo, Rep. |
| 32 | São Tomé & Príncipe |
| 33 | Angola |
| 34 | Djibouti |
| 35 | Lesotho |
| 36 | Cape Verde |
| 37 | South Africa |
| 38 | Gabon |
| 39 | Namibia |
| 40 | Swaziland |
| 41 | Botswana |
| 42 | Equatorial Guinea |
| 43 | Mauritius |
| 44 | Seychelles |
| n/a | Eritrea |
| n/a | Liberia |
| n/a | Somalia |
| n/a | Zimbabwe |

*greatest*

### Goods Imports per Person $US

WTO

*smallest*

| 2003-2006 | |
|---|---|
| 1 | Burundi |
| 2 | Congo, Dem. Rep. |
| 3 | Central African Rep. |
| 4 | Rwanda |
| 5 | Ethiopia |
| 6 | Guinea-Bissau |
| 7 | Niger |
| 8 | Sierra Leone |
| 9 | Uganda |
| 10 | Malawi |
| 11 | Tanzania |
| 12 | Madagascar |
| 13 | Guinea |
| 14 | Burkina Faso |
| 15 | Chad |
| 16 | Benin |
| 17 | Mozambique |
| 18 | Nigeria |
| 19 | Mali |
| 20 | Gambia, The |
| 21 | Sudan |
| 22 | Cameroon |
| 23 | Kenya |
| 24 | Comoros |
| 25 | Togo |
| 26 | Zambia |
| | SSA average |
| 27 | Ghana |
| 28 | Côte d'Ivoire |
| 29 | Senegal |
| 30 | São Tomé & Príncipe |
| 31 | Djibouti |
| 32 | Congo, Rep. |
| 33 | Mauritania |
| 34 | Angola |
| 35 | Lesotho |
| 36 | Cape Verde |
| 37 | Gabon |
| 38 | Namibia |
| 39 | South Africa |
| 40 | Botswana |
| 41 | Swaziland |
| 42 | Mauritius |
| 43 | Equatorial Guinea |
| 44 | Seychelles |
| n/a | Eritrea |
| n/a | Liberia |
| n/a | Somalia |
| n/a | Zimbabwe |

*greatest*

# appendix B8: performance tables - self-reliance

## Services Exports per Person $US

WTO

| | | 1999-2002 |
|---|---|---|
| greatest | 1 | Seychelles |
| | 2 | Mauritius |
| | 3 | Cape Verde |
| | 4 | Botswana |
| | 5 | Namibia |
| | 6 | Gabon |
| | 7 | Swaziland |
| | 8 | South Africa |
| | 9 | Djibouti |
| | 10 | São Tomé & Príncipe |
| | 11 | Comoros |
| | 12 | Gambia, The |
| | 13 | Congo, Rep. |
| | 14 | Cameroon |
| | 15 | Senegal |
| | 16 | Equatorial Guinea |
| | 17 | Côte d'Ivoire |
| | 18 | Ghana |
| | 19 | Kenya |
| | | SSA average |
| | 20 | Tanzania |
| | 21 | Benin |
| | 22 | Lesotho |
| | 23 | Madagascar |
| | 24 | Mozambique |
| | 25 | Angola |
| | 26 | Nigeria |
| | 27 | Mauritania |
| | 28 | Mali |
| | 29 | Zambia |
| | 30 | Togo |
| | 31 | Uganda |
| | 32 | Sierra Leone |
| | 33 | Ethiopia |
| | 34 | Guinea |
| | 35 | Rwanda |
| | 36 | Malawi |
| | 37 | Niger |
| | 38 | Chad |
| | 39 | Guinea-Bissau |
| | 40 | Burkina Faso |
| | 41 | Central African Rep. |
| | 42 | Sudan |
| | 43 | Congo, Dem. Rep. |
| | 44 | Burundi |
| | n/a | Eritrea |
| | n/a | Liberia |
| | n/a | Somalia |
| smallest | n/a | Zimbabwe |

## Services Exports per Person $US

WTO

| | | 2003-2006 |
|---|---|---|
| greatest | 1 | Seychelles |
| | 2 | Mauritius |
| | 3 | Cape Verde |
| | 4 | Botswana |
| | 5 | Swaziland |
| | 6 | Namibia |
| | 7 | South Africa |
| | 8 | Djibouti |
| | 9 | Gabon |
| | 10 | São Tomé & Príncipe |
| | 11 | Equatorial Guinea |
| | 12 | Congo, Rep. |
| | 13 | Comoros |
| | 14 | Gambia, The |
| | 15 | Senegal |
| | 16 | Cameroon |
| | 17 | Ghana |
| | | SSA average |
| | 18 | Kenya |
| | 19 | Côte d'Ivoire |
| | 20 | Angola |
| | 21 | Nigeria |
| | 22 | Tanzania |
| | 23 | Lesotho |
| | 24 | Benin |
| | 25 | Mauritania |
| | 26 | Madagascar |
| | 27 | Togo |
| | 28 | Mali |
| | 29 | Zambia |
| | 30 | Mozambique |
| | 31 | Uganda |
| | 32 | Sierra Leone |
| | 33 | Ethiopia |
| | 34 | Burkina Faso |
| | 35 | Rwanda |
| | 36 | Niger |
| | 37 | Chad |
| | 38 | Guinea |
| | 39 | Guinea-Bissau |
| | 40 | Malawi |
| | 41 | Congo, Dem. Rep. |
| | 42 | Central African Rep. |
| | 43 | Sudan |
| | 44 | Burundi |
| | n/a | Eritrea |
| | n/a | Liberia |
| | n/a | Somalia |
| smallest | n/a | Zimbabwe |

## Services Imports per Person $US

WTO

| | | 1999-2002 |
|---|---|---|
| smallest | 1 | Burundi |
| | 2 | Congo, Dem. Rep. |
| | 3 | Ethiopia |
| | 4 | Burkina Faso |
| | 5 | Niger |
| | 6 | Rwanda |
| | 7 | Malawi |
| | 8 | Sudan |
| | 9 | Sierra Leone |
| | 10 | Tanzania |
| | 11 | Uganda |
| | 12 | Guinea-Bissau |
| | 13 | Kenya |
| | 14 | Lesotho |
| | 15 | Togo |
| | 16 | Guinea |
| | 17 | Madagascar |
| | 18 | Central African Rep. |
| | 19 | Ghana |
| | 20 | Benin |
| | 21 | Mozambique |
| | 22 | Nigeria |
| | 23 | Zambia |
| | 24 | Mali |
| | | SSA average |
| | 25 | Senegal |
| | 26 | Comoros |
| | 27 | Chad |
| | 28 | Gambia, The |
| | 29 | Cameroon |
| | 30 | São Tomé & Príncipe |
| | 31 | Mauritania |
| | 32 | Côte d'Ivoire |
| | 33 | Djibouti |
| | 34 | South Africa |
| | 35 | Namibia |
| | 36 | Angola |
| | 37 | Swaziland |
| | 38 | Cape Verde |
| | 39 | Congo, Rep. |
| | 40 | Botswana |
| | 41 | Mauritius |
| | 42 | Gabon |
| | 43 | Equatorial Guinea |
| | 44 | Seychelles |
| | n/a | Eritrea |
| | n/a | Liberia |
| | n/a | Somalia |
| greatest | n/a | Zimbabwe |

## Services Imports per Person $US

WTO

| | | 2003-2006 |
|---|---|---|
| smallest | 1 | Congo, Dem. Rep. |
| | 2 | Burundi |
| | 3 | Ethiopia |
| | 4 | Sierra Leone |
| | 5 | Malawi |
| | 6 | Niger |
| | 7 | Rwanda |
| | 8 | Guinea |
| | 9 | Burkina Faso |
| | 10 | Uganda |
| | 11 | Kenya |
| | 12 | Tanzania |
| | 13 | Central African Rep. |
| | 14 | Madagascar |
| | 15 | Guinea-Bissau |
| | 16 | Mozambique |
| | 17 | Benin |
| | 18 | Gambia, The |
| | 19 | Zambia |
| | 20 | Lesotho |
| | 21 | Togo |
| | 22 | Sudan |
| | 23 | Ghana |
| | 24 | Mali |
| | 25 | Nigeria |
| | 26 | Senegal |
| | | SSA average |
| | 27 | Comoros |
| | 28 | Cameroon |
| | 29 | Djibouti |
| | 30 | Côte d'Ivoire |
| | 31 | Mauritania |
| | 32 | São Tomé & Príncipe |
| | 33 | Chad |
| | 34 | Namibia |
| | 35 | South Africa |
| | 36 | Angola |
| | 37 | Swaziland |
| | 38 | Cape Verde |
| | 39 | Congo, Rep. |
| | 40 | Botswana |
| | 41 | Gabon |
| | 42 | Mauritius |
| | 43 | Equatorial Guinea |
| | 44 | Seychelles |
| | n/a | Eritrea |
| | n/a | Liberia |
| | n/a | Somalia |
| greatest | n/a | Zimbabwe |

## Total Exports as % of GDP

World Bank, WTO

| | | 1999-2002 |
|---|---|---|
| largest | 1 | Equatorial Guinea |
| | 2 | Swaziland |
| | 3 | Angola |
| | 4 | Congo, Rep. |
| | 5 | Seychelles |
| | 6 | Mauritius |
| | 7 | Gabon |
| | 8 | Botswana |
| | 9 | Namibia |
| | 10 | Nigeria |
| | 11 | Côte d'Ivoire |
| | 12 | Ghana |
| | 13 | Lesotho |
| | 14 | Mauritania |
| | | SSA average |
| | 15 | Togo |
| | 16 | Zambia |
| | 17 | Guinea-Bissau |
| | 18 | Mali |
| | 19 | South Africa |
| | 20 | Senegal |
| | 21 | Malawi |
| | 22 | Madagascar |
| | 23 | Cameroon |
| | 24 | Guinea |
| | 25 | Benin |
| | 26 | Cape Verde |
| | 27 | Congo, Dem. Rep. |
| | 28 | Kenya |
| | 29 | Comoros |
| | 30 | Mozambique |
| | 31 | Gambia, The |
| | 32 | Djibouti |
| | 33 | Niger |
| | 34 | Tanzania |
| | 35 | Central African Rep. |
| | 36 | Chad |
| | 37 | São Tomé & Príncipe |
| | 38 | Sudan |
| | 39 | Uganda |
| | 40 | Ethiopia |
| | 41 | Burkina Faso |
| | 42 | Sierra Leone |
| | 43 | Burundi |
| | 44 | Rwanda |
| | n/a | Eritrea |
| | n/a | Liberia |
| | n/a | Somalia |
| smallest | n/a | Zimbabwe |

# appendix B8: performance tables - self-reliance

### Total Exports as % of GDP

World Bank, WTO

| | | 2003-2006 |
|---|---|---|
| largest | 1 | Swaziland |
| | 2 | Equatorial Guinea |
| | 3 | Seychelles |
| | 4 | Congo, Rep. |
| | 5 | Angola |
| | 6 | Mauritius |
| | 7 | Nigeria |
| | 8 | Gabon |
| | 9 | Lesotho |
| | 10 | Côte d'Ivoire |
| | 11 | Botswana |
| | 12 | Chad |
| | 13 | Namibia |
| | 14 | Ghana |
| | 15 | Togo |
| | 16 | Mauritania |
| | | SSA average |
| | 17 | Mozambique |
| | 18 | Zambia |
| | 19 | Congo, Dem. Rep. |
| | 20 | Guinea-Bissau |
| | 21 | Cape Verde |
| | 22 | South Africa |
| | 23 | Madagascar |
| | 24 | Mali |
| | 25 | Senegal |
| | 26 | Guinea |
| | 27 | Kenya |
| | 28 | Tanzania |
| | 29 | Cameroon |
| | 30 | Gambia, The |
| | 31 | Malawi |
| | 32 | Djibouti |
| | 33 | Benin |
| | 34 | Sierra Leone |
| | 35 | São Tomé & Príncipe |
| | 36 | Niger |
| | 37 | Sudan |
| | 38 | Uganda |
| | 39 | Ethiopia |
| | 40 | Comoros |
| | 41 | Burkina Faso |
| | 42 | Central African Rep. |
| | 43 | Rwanda |
| | 44 | Burundi |
| | n/a | Eritrea |
| | n/a | Liberia |
| | n/a | Somalia |
| smallest | n/a | Zimbabwe |

### Total Imports as % of GDP

World Bank, WTO

| | | 1999-2002 |
|---|---|---|
| smallest | 1 | Sudan |
| | 2 | Rwanda |
| | 3 | Central African Rep. |
| | 4 | Congo, Dem. Rep. |
| | 5 | Burundi |
| | 6 | Tanzania |
| | 7 | Cameroon |
| | 8 | Guinea |
| | 9 | Ethiopia |
| | 10 | South Africa |
| | 11 | Burkina Faso |
| | 12 | Niger |
| | 13 | Kenya |
| | 14 | Nigeria |
| | 15 | Uganda |
| | 16 | Madagascar |
| | | SSA average |
| | 17 | Comoros |
| | 18 | Sierra Leone |
| | 19 | Gabon |
| | 20 | Côte d'Ivoire |
| | 21 | Benin |
| | 22 | Guinea-Bissau |
| | 23 | Mozambique |
| | 24 | Malawi |
| | 25 | Zambia |
| | 26 | Senegal |
| | 27 | Botswana |
| | 28 | Djibouti |
| | 29 | Mali |
| | 30 | São Tomé & Príncipe |
| | 31 | Togo |
| | 32 | Mauritania |
| | 33 | Congo, Rep. |
| | 34 | Gambia, The |
| | 35 | Namibia |
| | 36 | Ghana |
| | 37 | Chad |
| | 38 | Cape Verde |
| | 39 | Mauritius |
| | 40 | Angola |
| | 41 | Equatorial Guinea |
| | 42 | Seychelles |
| | 43 | Swaziland |
| | 44 | Lesotho |
| | n/a | Eritrea |
| | n/a | Liberia |
| | n/a | Somalia |
| largest | n/a | Zimbabwe |

### Total Imports as % of GDP

World Bank, WTO

| | | 2003-2006 |
|---|---|---|
| smallest | 1 | Central African Rep. |
| | 2 | Cameroon |
| | 3 | Rwanda |
| | 4 | Sudan |
| | 5 | Nigeria |
| | 6 | Guinea |
| | 7 | Benin |
| | 8 | Burkina Faso |
| | 9 | Gabon |
| | 10 | South Africa |
| | 11 | Niger |
| | 12 | Uganda |
| | 13 | Kenya |
| | 14 | Tanzania |
| | | SSA average |
| | 15 | Sierra Leone |
| | 16 | Comoros |
| | 17 | Congo, Dem. Rep. |
| | 18 | Botswana |
| | 19 | Côte d'Ivoire |
| | 20 | Mali |
| | 21 | Zambia |
| | 22 | Madagascar |
| | 23 | Ethiopia |
| | 24 | Malawi |
| | 25 | Senegal |
| | 26 | Burundi |
| | 27 | Guinea-Bissau |
| | 28 | Angola |
| | 29 | Mozambique |
| | 30 | Chad |
| | 31 | Namibia |
| | 32 | Congo, Rep. |
| | 33 | Djibouti |
| | 34 | Equatorial Guinea |
| | 35 | Ghana |
| | 36 | São Tomé & Príncipe |
| | 37 | Gambia, The |
| | 38 | Togo |
| | 39 | Cape Verde |
| | 40 | Mauritius |
| | 41 | Mauritania |
| | 42 | Swaziland |
| | 43 | Lesotho |
| | 44 | Seychelles |
| | n/a | Eritrea |
| | n/a | Liberia |
| | n/a | Somalia |
| largest | n/a | Zimbabwe |

### Goods Exports as % of GDP

World Bank, WTO

| | | 1999-2002 |
|---|---|---|
| largest | 1 | Equatorial Guinea |
| | 2 | Angola |
| | 3 | Swaziland |
| | 4 | Congo, Rep. |
| | 5 | Gabon |
| | 6 | Botswana |
| | 7 | Nigeria |
| | 8 | Côte d'Ivoire |
| | 9 | Mauritius |
| | 10 | Namibia |
| | 11 | Lesotho |
| | 12 | Mauritania |
| | 13 | Seychelles |
| | 14 | Ghana |
| | 15 | Guinea-Bissau |
| | 16 | Togo |
| | 17 | Zambia |
| | | SSA average |
| | 18 | Mali |
| | 19 | South Africa |
| | 20 | Malawi |
| | 21 | Guinea |
| | 22 | Senegal |
| | 23 | Congo, Dem. Rep. |
| | 24 | Madagascar |
| | 25 | Cameroon |
| | 26 | Benin |
| | 27 | Central African Rep. |
| | 28 | Kenya |
| | 29 | Niger |
| | 30 | Mozambique |
| | 31 | Chad |
| | 32 | Sudan |
| | 33 | Tanzania |
| | 34 | Uganda |
| | 35 | Burkina Faso |
| | 36 | Comoros |
| | 37 | Ethiopia |
| | 38 | Burundi |
| | 39 | Djibouti |
| | 40 | São Tomé & Príncipe |
| | 41 | Rwanda |
| | 42 | Gambia, The |
| | 43 | Sierra Leone |
| | 44 | Cape Verde |
| | n/a | Eritrea |
| | n/a | Liberia |
| | n/a | Somalia |
| smallest | n/a | Zimbabwe |

### Goods Exports as % of GDP

World Bank, WTO

| | | 2003-2006 |
|---|---|---|
| largest | 1 | Equatorial Guinea |
| | 2 | Swaziland |
| | 3 | Congo, Rep. |
| | 4 | Angola |
| | 5 | Gabon |
| | 6 | Nigeria |
| | 7 | Lesotho |
| | 8 | Côte d'Ivoire |
| | 9 | Chad |
| | 10 | Seychelles |
| | 11 | Botswana |
| | 12 | Mauritius |
| | 13 | Namibia |
| | 14 | Mauritania |
| | 15 | Togo |
| | | SSA average |
| | 16 | Ghana |
| | 17 | Zambia |
| | 18 | Mozambique |
| | 19 | Congo, Dem. Rep. |
| | 20 | Guinea-Bissau |
| | 21 | Guinea |
| | 22 | Mali |
| | 23 | South Africa |
| | 24 | Malawi |
| | 25 | Madagascar |
| | 26 | Senegal |
| | 27 | Cameroon |
| | 28 | Kenya |
| | 29 | Sudan |
| | 30 | Niger |
| | 31 | Benin |
| | 32 | Tanzania |
| | 33 | Sierra Leone |
| | 34 | Central African Rep. |
| | 35 | Uganda |
| | 36 | Burkina Faso |
| | 37 | Ethiopia |
| | 38 | Burundi |
| | 39 | Djibouti |
| | 40 | Rwanda |
| | 41 | Comoros |
| | 42 | São Tomé & Príncipe |
| | 43 | Gambia, The |
| | 44 | Cape Verde |
| | n/a | Eritrea |
| | n/a | Liberia |
| | n/a | Somalia |
| smallest | n/a | Zimbabwe |

# appendix B8: performance tables - self-reliance

## Goods Imports as % of GDP

World Bank, WTO

| | | 1999-2002 |
|---|---|---|
| smallest | 1 | Central African Rep. |
| | 2 | Rwanda |
| | 3 | Sudan |
| | 4 | Cameroon |
| | 5 | Congo, Dem. Rep. |
| | 6 | Tanzania |
| | 7 | Gabon |
| | 8 | Guinea |
| | 9 | Burundi |
| | 10 | Ethiopia |
| | 11 | Nigeria |
| | 12 | Niger |
| | 13 | Sierra Leone |
| | 14 | Madagascar |
| | 15 | Comoros |
| | 16 | Burkina Faso |
| | 17 | South Africa |
| | 18 | Uganda |
| | 19 | Kenya |
| | 20 | Congo, Rep. |
| | 21 | Côte d'Ivoire |
| | | SSA average |
| | 22 | Guinea-Bissau |
| | 23 | Benin |
| | 24 | Mozambique |
| | 25 | Zambia |
| | 26 | Malawi |
| | 27 | Mali |
| | 28 | Botswana |
| | 29 | Senegal |
| | 30 | Djibouti |
| | 31 | São Tomé & Príncipe |
| | 32 | Mauritania |
| | 33 | Angola |
| | 34 | Equatorial Guinea |
| | 35 | Togo |
| | 36 | Gambia, The |
| | 37 | Chad |
| | 38 | Cape Verde |
| | 39 | Namibia |
| | 40 | Mauritius |
| | 41 | Ghana |
| | 42 | Seychelles |
| | 43 | Swaziland |
| | 44 | Lesotho |
| | n/a | Eritrea |
| | n/a | Liberia |
| | n/a | Somalia |
| largest | n/a | Zimbabwe |

## Goods Imports as % of GDP

World Bank, WTO

| | | 2003-2006 |
|---|---|---|
| smallest | 1 | Central African Rep. |
| | 2 | Cameroon |
| | 3 | Gabon |
| | 4 | Rwanda |
| | 5 | Nigeria |
| | 6 | Sudan |
| | 7 | Chad |
| | 8 | Benin |
| | 9 | Guinea |
| | 10 | Congo, Rep. |
| | 11 | Burkina Faso |
| | 12 | Niger |
| | 13 | Uganda |
| | 14 | Comoros |
| | 15 | Tanzania |
| | 16 | South Africa |
| | | SSA average |
| | 17 | Sierra Leone |
| | 18 | Côte d'Ivoire |
| | 19 | Angola |
| | 20 | Kenya |
| | 21 | Mali |
| | 22 | Botswana |
| | 23 | Congo, Dem. Rep. |
| | 24 | Guinea-Bissau |
| | 25 | Madagascar |
| | 26 | Ethiopia |
| | 27 | Equatorial Guinea |
| | 28 | Burundi |
| | 29 | Zambia |
| | 30 | Senegal |
| | 31 | Malawi |
| | 32 | Mozambique |
| | 33 | Djibouti |
| | 34 | Namibia |
| | 35 | São Tomé & Príncipe |
| | 36 | Cape Verde |
| | 37 | Ghana |
| | 38 | Mauritius |
| | 39 | Gambia, The |
| | 40 | Togo |
| | 41 | Mauritania |
| | 42 | Seychelles |
| | 43 | Swaziland |
| | 44 | Lesotho |
| | n/a | Eritrea |
| | n/a | Liberia |
| | n/a | Somalia |
| largest | n/a | Zimbabwe |

## Services Exports as % of GDP

World Bank, WTO

| | | 1999-2002 |
|---|---|---|
| largest | 1 | Seychelles |
| | 2 | Mauritius |
| | 3 | Cape Verde |
| | 4 | Gambia, The |
| | 5 | Comoros |
| | 6 | Djibouti |
| | 7 | Swaziland |
| | 8 | São Tomé & Príncipe |
| | 9 | Ghana |
| | 10 | Namibia |
| | 11 | Tanzania |
| | 12 | Mozambique |
| | 13 | Madagascar |
| | 14 | Senegal |
| | 15 | Cameroon |
| | 16 | Kenya |
| | 17 | Botswana |
| | 18 | Benin |
| | 19 | Ethiopia |
| | 20 | Congo, Rep. |
| | 21 | Sierra Leone |
| | | SSA average |
| | 22 | Côte d'Ivoire |
| | 23 | Mali |
| | 24 | Lesotho |
| | 25 | South Africa |
| | 26 | Togo |
| | 27 | Nigeria |
| | 28 | Zambia |
| | 29 | Uganda |
| | 30 | Gabon |
| | 31 | Mauritania |
| | 32 | Rwanda |
| | 33 | Angola |
| | 34 | Malawi |
| | 35 | Guinea-Bissau |
| | 36 | Niger |
| | 37 | Chad |
| | 38 | Congo, Dem. Rep. |
| | 39 | Guinea |
| | 40 | Burkina Faso |
| | 41 | Equatorial Guinea |
| | 42 | Central African Rep. |
| | 43 | Sudan |
| | 44 | Burundi |
| | n/a | Eritrea |
| | n/a | Liberia |
| | n/a | Somalia |
| smallest | n/a | Zimbabwe |

## Services Exports as % of GDP

World Bank, WTO

| | | 2003-2006 |
|---|---|---|
| largest | 1 | Seychelles |
| | 2 | Cape Verde |
| | 3 | Mauritius |
| | 4 | Gambia, The |
| | 5 | Djibouti |
| | 6 | São Tomé & Príncipe |
| | 7 | Swaziland |
| | 8 | Tanzania |
| | 9 | Comoros |
| | 10 | Ghana |
| | 11 | Madagascar |
| | 12 | Namibia |
| | 13 | Botswana |
| | 14 | Kenya |
| | 15 | Ethiopia |
| | 16 | Senegal |
| | 17 | Togo |
| | 18 | Sierra Leone |
| | 19 | Nigeria |
| | 20 | Mozambique |
| | 21 | Cameroon |
| | 22 | Uganda |
| | | SSA average |
| | 23 | Benin |
| | 24 | South Africa |
| | 25 | Congo, Rep. |
| | 26 | Mali |
| | 27 | Côte d'Ivoire |
| | 28 | Lesotho |
| | 29 | Mauritania |
| | 30 | Rwanda |
| | 31 | Zambia |
| | 32 | Congo, Dem. Rep. |
| | 33 | Niger |
| | 34 | Burkina Faso |
| | 35 | Guinea-Bissau |
| | 36 | Gabon |
| | 37 | Malawi |
| | 38 | Angola |
| | 39 | Chad |
| | 40 | Guinea |
| | 41 | Equatorial Guinea |
| | 42 | Central African Rep. |
| | 43 | Burundi |
| | 44 | Sudan |
| | n/a | Eritrea |
| | n/a | Liberia |
| | n/a | Somalia |
| smallest | n/a | Zimbabwe |

## Services Imports as % of GDP

World Bank, WTO

| | | 1999-2002 |
|---|---|---|
| smallest | 1 | Burundi |
| | 2 | South Africa |
| | 3 | Sudan |
| | 4 | Burkina Faso |
| | 5 | Kenya |
| | 6 | Lesotho |
| | 7 | Congo, Dem. Rep. |
| | 8 | Guinea |
| | 9 | Rwanda |
| | 10 | Ethiopia |
| | 11 | Niger |
| | 12 | Tanzania |
| | | SSA average |
| | 13 | Benin |
| | 14 | Uganda |
| | 15 | Senegal |
| | 16 | Botswana |
| | 17 | Nigeria |
| | 18 | Ghana |
| | 19 | Togo |
| | 20 | Namibia |
| | 21 | Cameroon |
| | 22 | Malawi |
| | 23 | Zambia |
| | 24 | Comoros |
| | 25 | Central African Rep. |
| | 26 | Madagascar |
| | 27 | Djibouti |
| | 28 | Sierra Leone |
| | 29 | São Tomé & Príncipe |
| | 30 | Côte d'Ivoire |
| | 31 | Mozambique |
| | 32 | Guinea-Bissau |
| | 33 | Mali |
| | 34 | Gambia, The |
| | 35 | Mauritania |
| | 36 | Gabon |
| | 37 | Swaziland |
| | 38 | Mauritius |
| | 39 | Cape Verde |
| | 40 | Chad |
| | 41 | Seychelles |
| | 42 | Congo, Rep. |
| | 43 | Angola |
| | 44 | Equatorial Guinea |
| | n/a | Eritrea |
| | n/a | Liberia |
| | n/a | Somalia |
| largest | n/a | Zimbabwe |

## Services Imports as % of GDP

World Bank, WTO

smallest

| | 2003-2006 |
|---|---|
| 1 | Kenya |
| 2 | South Africa |
| 3 | Guinea |
| 4 | Sudan |
| 5 | Burkina Faso |
| 6 | Lesotho |
| 7 | Namibia |
| 8 | Benin |
| 9 | Zambia |
| 10 | Sierra Leone |
| 11 | Congo, Dem. Rep. |
| 12 | Malawi |
| 13 | Niger |
| 14 | Botswana |
| | SSA average |
| 15 | Central African Rep. |
| 16 | Nigeria |
| 17 | Tanzania |
| 18 | Cameroon |
| 19 | Rwanda |
| 20 | Senegal |
| 21 | Uganda |
| 22 | Ethiopia |
| 23 | Madagascar |
| 24 | Mozambique |
| 25 | Ghana |
| 26 | Djibouti |
| 27 | Mali |
| 28 | Comoros |
| 29 | Côte d'Ivoire |
| 30 | Gambia, The |
| 31 | Burundi |
| 32 | Togo |
| 33 | Gabon |
| 34 | Swaziland |
| 35 | Guinea-Bissau |
| 36 | Mauritania |
| 37 | São Tomé & Príncipe |
| 38 | Mauritius |
| 39 | Angola |
| 40 | Cape Verde |
| 41 | Equatorial Guinea |
| 42 | Chad |
| 43 | Congo, Rep. |
| 44 | Seychelles |
| n/a | Eritrea |
| n/a | Liberia |
| n/a | Somalia |
| n/a | Zimbabwe |

largest

## Growth in Goods Exports

World Bank, WTO

largest

| | 2000-2002 |
|---|---|
| 1 | Sierra Leone |
| 2 | Eritrea |
| 3 | Mozambique |
| 4 | Sudan |
| 5 | Equatorial Guinea |
| 6 | São Tomé & Príncipe |
| 7 | Comoros |
| 8 | Lesotho |
| 9 | Tanzania |
| 10 | Angola |
| 11 | Seychelles |
| 12 | Congo, Rep. |
| 13 | Mali |
| 14 | Zimbabwe |
| 15 | Nigeria |
| 16 | Congo, Dem. Rep. |
| 17 | Djibouti |
| 18 | Rwanda |
| | SSA average |
| 19 | Côte d'Ivoire |
| 20 | Mauritius |
| 21 | Kenya |
| 22 | South Africa |
| 23 | Guinea |
| 24 | Cameroon |
| 25 | Swaziland |
| 26 | Gambia, The |
| 27 | Togo |
| 28 | Ghana |
| 29 | Guinea-Bissau |
| 30 | Zambia |
| 31 | Benin |
| 32 | Madagascar |
| 33 | Senegal |
| 34 | Central African Rep. |
| 35 | Gabon |
| 36 | Ethiopia |
| 37 | Burkina Faso |
| 38 | Cape Verde |
| 39 | Botswana |
| 40 | Niger |
| 41 | Malawi |
| 42 | Uganda |
| 43 | Namibia |
| 44 | Mauritania |
| 45 | Chad |
| 46 | Burundi |
| 47 | Liberia |
| n/a | Somalia |

smallest

## Growth in Goods Exports

World Bank, WTO

largest

| | 2003-2006 |
|---|---|
| 1 | Chad |
| 2 | Mauritania |
| 3 | Zambia |
| 4 | Sierra Leone |
| 5 | Equatorial Guinea |
| 6 | Angola |
| 7 | Nigeria |
| 8 | Sudan |
| 9 | Mozambique |
| 10 | Congo, Rep. |
| 11 | Namibia |
| 12 | Swaziland |
| | SSA average |
| 13 | Burkina Faso |
| 14 | Rwanda |
| 15 | Gabon |
| 16 | Madagascar |
| 17 | Lesotho |
| 18 | Ethiopia |
| 19 | Ghana |
| 20 | South Africa |
| 21 | Uganda |
| 22 | Congo, Dem. Rep. |
| 23 | Cameroon |
| 24 | Botswana |
| 25 | Cape Verde |
| 26 | Burundi |
| 27 | Seychelles |
| 28 | Niger |
| 29 | Tanzania |
| 30 | Mali |
| 31 | Djibouti |
| 32 | Côte d'Ivoire |
| 33 | Kenya |
| 34 | Guinea |
| 35 | Togo |
| 36 | Senegal |
| 37 | Mauritius |
| 38 | Malawi |
| 39 | Guinea-Bissau |
| 40 | Benin |
| 41 | Central African Rep. |
| 42 | Gambia, The |
| 43 | Zimbabwe |
| 44 | Liberia |
| 45 | São Tomé & Príncipe |
| 46 | Eritrea |
| 47 | Comoros |
| n/a | Somalia |

smallest

## Growth in Goods Imports

World Bank, WTO

smallest

| | 2000-2002 |
|---|---|
| 1 | Liberia |
| 2 | Côte d'Ivoire |
| 3 | Ghana |
| 4 | Uganda |
| 5 | São Tomé & Príncipe |
| 6 | Zimbabwe |
| 7 | Gambia, The |
| 8 | Botswana |
| 9 | Swaziland |
| 10 | Namibia |
| 11 | Central African Rep. |
| 12 | Togo |
| 13 | Benin |
| 14 | Lesotho |
| 15 | Rwanda |
| 16 | Nigeria |
| 17 | Mauritius |
| 18 | Comoros |
| 19 | Congo, Rep. |
| 20 | Djibouti |
| 21 | Madagascar |
| 22 | Eritrea |
| | SSA average |
| 23 | Tanzania |
| 24 | Malawi |
| 25 | Burkina Faso |
| 26 | Seychelles |
| 27 | Niger |
| 28 | South Africa |
| 29 | Burundi |
| 30 | Mali |
| 31 | Cape Verde |
| 32 | Kenya |
| 33 | Ethiopia |
| 34 | Guinea-Bissau |
| 35 | Gabon |
| 36 | Angola |
| 37 | Guinea |
| 38 | Senegal |
| 39 | Mozambique |
| 40 | Cameroon |
| 41 | Mauritania |
| 42 | Equatorial Guinea |
| 43 | Zambia |
| 44 | Sudan |
| 45 | Congo, Dem. Rep. |
| 46 | Sierra Leone |
| 47 | Chad |
| n/a | Somalia |

largest

## Growth in Goods Imports

World Bank, WTO

smallest

| | 2003-2006 |
|---|---|
| 1 | Eritrea |
| 2 | Chad |
| 3 | Benin |
| 4 | Sierra Leone |
| 5 | Zimbabwe |
| 6 | Guinea |
| 7 | Gambia, The |
| 8 | Guinea-Bissau |
| 9 | Cameroon |
| 10 | Malawi |
| 11 | Senegal |
| 12 | Djibouti |
| 13 | Central African Rep. |
| 14 | Mauritius |
| 15 | Botswana |
| 16 | Mozambique |
| 17 | Gabon |
| 18 | Niger |
| 19 | Mali |
| 20 | Lesotho |
| 21 | Cape Verde |
| 22 | Burkina Faso |
| 23 | Seychelles |
| 24 | Rwanda |
| 25 | Namibia |
| 26 | Comoros |
| 27 | Côte d'Ivoire |
| 28 | Kenya |
| 29 | Togo |
| 30 | Uganda |
| | SSA average |
| 31 | Angola |
| 32 | São Tomé & Príncipe |
| 33 | Ghana |
| 34 | Congo, Dem. Rep. |
| 35 | Zambia |
| 36 | Tanzania |
| 37 | South Africa |
| 38 | Swaziland |
| 39 | Congo, Rep. |
| 40 | Ethiopia |
| 41 | Nigeria |
| 42 | Liberia |
| 43 | Burundi |
| 44 | Madagascar |
| 45 | Sudan |
| 46 | Mauritania |
| 47 | Equatorial Guinea |
| n/a | Somalia |

largest

### Growth in Services Exports

World Bank, WTO

| | | 2000-2002 |
|---|---|---|
| largest | 1 | Sudan |
| | 2 | Swaziland |
| | 3 | Nigeria |
| | 4 | Sierra Leone |
| | 5 | Guinea |
| | 6 | Cameroon |
| | 7 | Guinea-Bissau |
| | 8 | Congo, Dem. Rep. |
| | 9 | Burundi |
| | 10 | Mauritania |
| | 11 | Mali |
| | 12 | Equatorial Guinea |
| | 13 | Angola |
| | 14 | Tanzania |
| | 15 | Niger |
| | 16 | Botswana |
| | 17 | Cape Verde |
| | 18 | Chad |
| | 19 | Togo |
| | 20 | Burkina Faso |
| | 21 | Mozambique |
| | 22 | Djibouti |
| | 23 | Ghana |
| | 24 | Seychelles |
| | | SSA average |
| | 25 | Mauritius |
| | 26 | Zambia |
| | 27 | Ethiopia |
| | 28 | Congo, Rep. |
| | 29 | Uganda |
| | 30 | Senegal |
| | 31 | Malawi |
| | 32 | Kenya |
| | 33 | Côte d'Ivoire |
| | 34 | South Africa |
| | 35 | Namibia |
| | 36 | Madagascar |
| | 37 | Benin |
| | 38 | Lesotho |
| | 39 | São Tomé & Príncipe |
| | 40 | Gambia, The |
| | 41 | Central African Rep. |
| | 42 | Comoros |
| | 43 | Gabon |
| | n/a | Eritrea |
| | n/a | Liberia |
| | n/a | Rwanda |
| | n/a | Somalia |
| smallest | n/a | Zimbabwe |

### Growth in Services Exports

World Bank, WTO

| | | 2003-2006 |
|---|---|---|
| largest | 1 | Angola |
| | 2 | Burkina Faso |
| | 3 | Sudan |
| | 4 | Swaziland |
| | 5 | Equatorial Guinea |
| | 6 | Nigeria |
| | 7 | São Tomé & Príncipe |
| | 8 | Congo, Dem. Rep. |
| | 9 | Togo |
| | 10 | South Africa |
| | 11 | Cape Verde |
| | 12 | Kenya |
| | 13 | Gabon |
| | 14 | Ghana |
| | 15 | Central African Rep. |
| | | SSA average |
| | 16 | Chad |
| | 17 | Guinea-Bissau |
| | 18 | Uganda |
| | 19 | Zambia |
| | 20 | Madagascar |
| | 21 | Namibia |
| | 22 | Burundi |
| | 23 | Ethiopia |
| | 24 | Mauritania |
| | 25 | Malawi |
| | 26 | Lesotho |
| | 27 | Botswana |
| | 28 | Comoros |
| | 29 | Niger |
| | 30 | Congo, Rep. |
| | 31 | Benin |
| | 32 | Tanzania |
| | 33 | Senegal |
| | 34 | Gambia, The |
| | 35 | Mauritius |
| | 36 | Seychelles |
| | 37 | Sierra Leone |
| | 38 | Côte d'Ivoire |
| | 39 | Djibouti |
| | 40 | Cameroon |
| | 41 | Mozambique |
| | 42 | Mali |
| | 43 | Guinea |
| | n/a | Eritrea |
| | n/a | Liberia |
| | n/a | Rwanda |
| | n/a | Somalia |
| smallest | n/a | Zimbabwe |

### Growth in Services Imports

World Bank, WTO

| | | 2000-2002 |
|---|---|---|
| smallest | 1 | Namibia |
| | 2 | Guinea |
| | 3 | Tanzania |
| | 4 | Gambia, The |
| | 5 | Central African Rep. |
| | 6 | Gabon |
| | 7 | Djibouti |
| | 8 | Benin |
| | 9 | Sierra Leone |
| | 10 | South Africa |
| | 11 | Ghana |
| | 12 | Burkina Faso |
| | 13 | Lesotho |
| | 14 | Botswana |
| | 15 | Niger |
| | 16 | Comoros |
| | 17 | Senegal |
| | 18 | Congo, Rep. |
| | 19 | Mali |
| | 20 | São Tomé & Príncipe |
| | 21 | Côte d'Ivoire |
| | 22 | Togo |
| | 23 | Mauritius |
| | | SSA average |
| | 24 | Ethiopia |
| | 25 | Kenya |
| | 26 | Zambia |
| | 27 | Malawi |
| | 28 | Guinea-Bissau |
| | 29 | Congo, Dem. Rep. |
| | 30 | Cape Verde |
| | 31 | Uganda |
| | 32 | Angola |
| | 33 | Mauritania |
| | 34 | Seychelles |
| | 35 | Equatorial Guinea |
| | 36 | Nigeria |
| | 37 | Mozambique |
| | 38 | Madagascar |
| | 39 | Swaziland |
| | 40 | Cameroon |
| | 41 | Burundi |
| | 42 | Chad |
| | 43 | Sudan |
| | n/a | Eritrea |
| | n/a | Liberia |
| | n/a | Rwanda |
| | n/a | Somalia |
| largest | n/a | Zimbabwe |

### Growth in Services Imports

World Bank, WTO

| | | 2003-2006 |
|---|---|---|
| smallest | 1 | Sierra Leone |
| | 2 | Malawi |
| | 3 | Madagascar |
| | 4 | Cameroon |
| | 5 | Mozambique |
| | 6 | Central African Rep. |
| | 7 | Benin |
| | 8 | Guinea |
| | 9 | Côte d'Ivoire |
| | 10 | Seychelles |
| | 11 | Djibouti |
| | 12 | Mali |
| | 13 | Zambia |
| | 14 | Gabon |
| | 15 | Nigeria |
| | 16 | Botswana |
| | 17 | Senegal |
| | 18 | Cape Verde |
| | 19 | Uganda |
| | 20 | Mauritius |
| | 21 | Lesotho |
| | 22 | Mauritania |
| | 23 | Congo, Dem. Rep. |
| | 24 | Tanzania |
| | 25 | Niger |
| | 26 | Togo |
| | 27 | Guinea-Bissau |
| | 28 | Swaziland |
| | 29 | Namibia |
| | 30 | Ethiopia |
| | 31 | Kenya |
| | | SSA average |
| | 32 | Chad |
| | 33 | Comoros |
| | 34 | Gambia, The |
| | 35 | Angola |
| | 36 | Ghana |
| | 37 | South Africa |
| | 38 | Equatorial Guinea |
| | 39 | Burkina Faso |
| | 40 | Congo, Rep. |
| | 41 | Sudan |
| | 42 | São Tomé & Príncipe |
| | 43 | Burundi |
| | n/a | Eritrea |
| | n/a | Liberia |
| | n/a | Rwanda |
| | n/a | Somalia |
| largest | n/a | Zimbabwe |

### Imports Dependence in Goods (Net Goods Exports per Person)

World Bank, WTO

| | | 1999-2002 |
|---|---|---|
| least dependent | 1 | Equatorial Guinea |
| | 2 | Gabon |
| | 3 | Congo, Rep. |
| | 4 | Botswana |
| | 5 | Angola |
| | 6 | Côte d'Ivoire |
| | 7 | Nigeria |
| | 8 | South Africa |
| | | SSA average |
| | 9 | Guinea |
| | 10 | Central African Rep. |
| | 11 | Cameroon |
| | 12 | Congo, Dem. Rep. |
| | 13 | Guinea-Bissau |
| | 14 | Zimbabwe |
| | 15 | Sudan |
| | 16 | Madagascar |
| | 17 | Niger |
| | 18 | Burundi |
| | 19 | Ethiopia |
| | 20 | Malawi |
| | 21 | Zambia |
| | 22 | Mali |
| | 23 | Rwanda |
| | 24 | Mauritania |
| | 25 | Tanzania |
| | 26 | Sierra Leone |
| | 27 | Togo |
| | 28 | Uganda |
| | 29 | Burkina Faso |
| | 30 | Benin |
| | 31 | Mozambique |
| | 32 | Kenya |
| | 33 | Liberia |
| | 34 | Chad |
| | 35 | Swaziland |
| | 36 | Senegal |
| | 37 | Comoros |
| | 38 | Ghana |
| | 39 | Gambia, The |
| | 40 | Eritrea |
| | 41 | Namibia |
| | 42 | São Tomé & Príncipe |
| | 43 | Djibouti |
| | 44 | Lesotho |
| | 45 | Mauritius |
| most dependent | 46 | Cape Verde |
| | 47 | Seychelles |
| | n/a | Somalia |

# appendix B8: performance tables - self-reliance

### Imports Dependence in Goods (Net Goods Exports per Person)

World Bank, WTO

*least dependent*

| | 2003-2006 |
|---|---|
| 1 | Equatorial Guinea |
| 2 | Gabon |
| 3 | Congo, Rep. |
| 4 | Angola |
| 5 | Botswana |
| 6 | Nigeria |
| 7 | Côte d'Ivoire |
| 8 | Chad |
| | SSA average |
| 9 | Cameroon |
| 10 | Guinea |
| 11 | Congo, Dem. Rep. |
| 12 | Central African Rep. |
| 13 | Guinea-Bissau |
| 14 | Swaziland |
| 15 | Zimbabwe |
| 16 | Niger |
| 17 | Burundi |
| 18 | Rwanda |
| 19 | Zambia |
| 20 | Mozambique |
| 21 | Sierra Leone |
| 22 | Sudan |
| 23 | Mali |
| 24 | Ethiopia |
| 25 | Madagascar |
| 26 | Malawi |
| 27 | Uganda |
| 28 | Tanzania |
| 29 | Benin |
| 30 | Liberia |
| 31 | Burkina Faso |
| 32 | Togo |
| 33 | Kenya |
| 34 | Ghana |
| 35 | Eritrea |
| 36 | Comoros |
| 37 | Senegal |
| 38 | Gambia, The |
| 39 | Mauritania |
| 40 | South Africa |
| 41 | Namibia |
| 42 | Djibouti |
| 43 | São Tomé & Príncipe |
| 44 | Lesotho |
| 45 | Mauritius |
| 46 | Cape Verde |
| 47 | Seychelles |
| n/a | Somalia |

*most dependent*

### Imports Dependence in Services (Net Services Exports per Person)

World Bank, WTO

*least dependent*

| | 1999-2002 |
|---|---|
| 1 | Seychelles |
| 2 | Mauritius |
| 3 | Djibouti |
| 4 | Comoros |
| 5 | São Tomé & Príncipe |
| 6 | Gambia, The |
| 7 | Kenya |
| 8 | Tanzania |
| 9 | Cape Verde |
| 10 | Ethiopia |
| 11 | Ghana |
| 12 | Burundi |
| 13 | Congo, Dem. Rep. |
| 14 | Lesotho |
| 15 | Senegal |
| 16 | Benin |
| 17 | Niger |
| 18 | Madagascar |
| 19 | Rwanda |
| 20 | Burkina Faso |
| 21 | Sierra Leone |
| 22 | Mozambique |
| 23 | Uganda |
| 24 | Malawi |
| 25 | South Africa |
| 26 | Togo |
| 27 | Sudan |
| 28 | Guinea-Bissau |
| | SSA average |
| 29 | Nigeria |
| 30 | Cameroon |
| 31 | Guinea |
| 32 | Zambia |
| 33 | Namibia |
| 34 | Central African Rep. |
| 35 | Mali |
| 36 | Chad |
| 37 | Côte d'Ivoire |
| 38 | Mauritania |
| 39 | Swaziland |
| 40 | Botswana |
| 41 | Angola |
| 42 | Congo, Rep. |
| 43 | Gabon |
| 44 | Equatorial Guinea |
| n/a | Eritrea |
| n/a | Liberia |
| n/a | Somalia |
| n/a | Zimbabwe |

*most dependent*

### Imports Dependence in Services (Net Services Exports per Person)

World Bank, WTO

*least dependent*

| | 2003-2006 |
|---|---|
| 1 | Seychelles |
| 2 | Mauritius |
| 3 | Cape Verde |
| 4 | Namibia |
| 5 | Djibouti |
| 6 | Gambia, The |
| 7 | Kenya |
| 8 | Tanzania |
| 9 | Ethiopia |
| 10 | Sierra Leone |
| 11 | Congo, Dem. Rep. |
| 12 | Madagascar |
| 13 | Ghana |
| 14 | Benin |
| 15 | Senegal |
| 16 | Uganda |
| 17 | Burundi |
| 18 | Malawi |
| 19 | Rwanda |
| 20 | Botswana |
| 21 | Niger |
| 22 | Burkina Faso |
| 23 | Comoros |
| 24 | Mozambique |
| 25 | Lesotho |
| 26 | Nigeria |
| 27 | Guinea |
| 28 | South Africa |
| 29 | Togo |
| 30 | Zambia |
| 31 | Central African Rep. |
| 32 | Guinea-Bissau |
| 33 | São Tomé & Príncipe |
| | SSA average |
| 34 | Mali |
| 35 | Cameroon |
| 36 | Sudan |
| 37 | Côte d'Ivoire |
| 38 | Mauritania |
| 39 | Swaziland |
| 40 | Chad |
| 41 | Angola |
| 42 | Congo, Rep. |
| 43 | Gabon |
| 44 | Equatorial Guinea |
| n/a | Eritrea |
| n/a | Liberia |
| n/a | Somalia |
| n/a | Zimbabwe |

*most dependent*

### Foreign Reserves (as Months of Imports)

IMF

*most number of months*

| | 1997-2002 |
|---|---|
| 1 | Botswana |
| 2 | Comoros |
| 3 | Benin |
| 4 | Central African Rep. |
| 5 | Uganda |
| 6 | Lesotho |
| 7 | Guinea-Bissau |
| 8 | Nigeria |
| 9 | Gambia, The |
| 10 | Mozambique |
| 11 | Burkina Faso |
| 12 | Rwanda |
| 12 | Tanzania |
| 13 | Mali |
| 14 | Burundi |
| 15 | São Tomé & Príncipe |
| 16 | Mauritius |
| | SSA average |
| 17 | Ethiopia |
| 17 | Malawi |
| 18 | Côte d'Ivoire |
| 18 | Kenya |
| 18 | Senegal |
| 18 | Sierra Leone |
| 18 | Swaziland |
| 19 | Madagascar |
| 20 | Guinea |
| 21 | Togo |
| 22 | Chad |
| 23 | South Africa |
| 24 | Namibia |
| 24 | Niger |
| 25 | Zambia |
| 26 | Ghana |
| 27 | Eritrea |
| 28 | Angola |
| 28 | Cape Verde |
| 28 | Congo, Dem. Rep. |
| 29 | Cameroon |
| 29 | Seychelles |
| 30 | Zimbabwe |
| 31 | Congo, Rep. |
| 31 | Gabon |
| 32 | Equatorial Guinea |
| n/a | Djibouti |
| n/a | Liberia |
| n/a | Mauritania |
| n/a | Somalia |
| n/a | Sudan |

*least number of months*

### Foreign Reserves (as Months of Imports)

IMF

*most number of months*

| | 2003-2006 |
|---|---|
| 1 | Botswana |
| 2 | Comoros |
| 3 | Benin |
| 4 | Nigeria |
| 5 | Tanzania |
| 6 | Uganda |
| 7 | Rwanda |
| 8 | Central African Rep. |
| 9 | Mali |
| 10 | Burkina Faso |
| 11 | Guinea-Bissau |
| 12 | Equatorial Guinea |
| 13 | Mauritius |
| 14 | Lesotho |
| 15 | Mozambique |
| 16 | São Tomé & Príncipe |
| 17 | Senegal |
| | SSA average |
| 18 | Burundi |
| 19 | Gambia, The |
| 20 | Ethiopia |
| 21 | Sierra Leone |
| 22 | Niger |
| 23 | Kenya |
| 24 | Ghana |
| 25 | Côte d'Ivoire |
| 25 | Togo |
| 26 | Cameroon |
| 27 | Cape Verde |
| 27 | Madagascar |
| 28 | Gabon |
| 28 | South Africa |
| 29 | Angola |
| 30 | Zambia |
| 31 | Congo, Rep. |
| 32 | Swaziland |
| 33 | Namibia |
| 34 | Guinea |
| 35 | Malawi |
| 36 | Chad |
| 37 | Seychelles |
| 38 | Congo, Dem. Rep. |
| 39 | Zimbabwe |
| 40 | Liberia |
| 41 | Eritrea |
| n/a | Djibouti |
| n/a | Mauritania |
| n/a | Somalia |
| n/a | Sudan |

*least number of months*

# appendix B8: performance tables - self-reliance

| | Foreign Reserves (as Months of Imports) — IMF — 2007-2008 | | Foreign Debt as % of GDP — IMF — 1997-2002 | | Foreign Debt as % of GDP — IMF — 2003-2006 | | Foreign Debt as % of GDP — IMF — 2007-2008 | | Foreign Debt as $PPP per Person — Primary data: IMF — 1997-2002 | |
|---|---|---|---|---|---|---|---|---|---|---|
| most number of months / smallest | 1 | Botswana | 1 | Namibia | 1 | South Africa | 1 | Equatorial Guinea | 1 | Zimbabwe |
| | 2 | Nigeria | 2 | South Africa | 2 | Botswana | 2 | South Africa | 2 | Namibia |
| | 3 | Benin | 3 | Botswana | 3 | Namibia | 3 | Nigeria | 3 | South Africa |
| | 4 | Comóros | 4 | Swaziland | 4 | Equatorial Guinea | 4 | Botswana | 4 | Ethiopia |
| | 5 | Equatorial Guinea | 5 | Mauritius | 5 | Mauritius | 5 | Cameroon | 5 | Eritrea |
| | 6 | Uganda | 6 | Seychelles | 6 | Swaziland | 6 | Namibia | 6 | Uganda |
| | 7 | Lesotho | 7 | Zimbabwe | 7 | Nigeria | 7 | Angola | 7 | Rwanda |
| | 8 | Guinea-Bissau | 8 | Kenya | | SSA average | 8 | Zambia | 8 | Mozambique |
| | 9 | Angola | 9 | Eritrea | 8 | Kenya | 9 | Sierra Leone | 9 | Burundi |
| | 10 | Rwanda | 10 | Equatorial Guinea | 9 | Angola | 10 | Mauritius | 10 | Niger |
| | | SSA average | | SSA average | 10 | Cameroon | | SSA average | 11 | Kenya |
| | 11 | Burkina Faso | 11 | Cape Verde | 11 | Benin | 11 | Swaziland | 12 | Burkina Faso |
| | 12 | Cameroon | 12 | Burkina Faso | 12 | Burkina Faso | 12 | Ethiopia | 13 | Central African Rep. |
| | 13 | Mali | 13 | Uganda | 13 | Chad | 13 | Benin | 14 | Tanzania |
| | 14 | São Tomé & Príncipe | 14 | Cameroon | 14 | Seychelles | 14 | Uganda | 15 | Chad |
| | 15 | Tanzania | 15 | Chad | 15 | Senegal | 15 | Niger | 16 | Sierra Leone |
| | 16 | Congo, Rep. | 16 | Ethiopia | 16 | Gabon | 16 | Tanzania | 17 | Swaziland |
| | 17 | Sierra Leone | 16 | Nigeria | 17 | Tanzania | 17 | Rwanda | 18 | Congo, Dem. Rep. |
| | 18 | Niger | 17 | Angola | 18 | Lesotho | 18 | Kenya | | SSA average |
| | 19 | Mozambique | 18 | Senegal | 19 | Niger | 19 | Gabon | 19 | Togo |
| | 20 | Gambia, The | 19 | Lesotho | 20 | Zimbabwe | 20 | Senegal | 20 | Lesotho |
| | 21 | Gabon | 20 | Benin | 21 | Cape Verde | 21 | Zimbabwe | 21 | Mali |
| | 22 | Cape Verde | 21 | Gabon | 22 | Mozambique | 22 | Burkina Faso | 22 | Nigeria |
| | 23 | Senegal | 22 | Tanzania | 23 | Mali | 23 | Malawi | 23 | Malawi |
| | 24 | Burundi | 23 | Rwanda | 24 | Uganda | 24 | Ghana | 24 | Benin |
| | 24 | Mauritius | 24 | Côte d'Ivoire | 25 | Ethiopia | 25 | Madagascar | 25 | Botswana |
| | 25 | Kenya | 25 | Central African Rep. | 26 | Rwanda | 26 | Chad | 26 | Madagascar |
| | 26 | Chad | 26 | Mozambique | 27 | Côte d'Ivoire | 27 | Mali | 27 | Senegal |
| | 27 | South Africa | 27 | Niger | 28 | Madagascar | 28 | Mozambique | 28 | Guinea |
| | 27 | Swaziland | 28 | Togo | 29 | Ghana | 29 | Seychelles | 29 | Comoros |
| | 28 | Togo | 29 | Guinea | 30 | Eritrea | 30 | Lesotho | 30 | Cameroon |
| | 29 | Zambia | 30 | Mali | 31 | Comoros | 31 | Cape Verde | 31 | Cape Verde |
| | 30 | Côte d'Ivoire | 31 | Comoros | 32 | Zambia | 32 | Congo, Dem. Rep. | 32 | Ghana |
| | 31 | Namibia | 32 | Madagascar | 33 | Central African Rep. | 33 | Comoros | 33 | Côte d'Ivoire |
| | 32 | Madagascar | 33 | Ghana | 34 | Togo | 34 | Côte d'Ivoire | 34 | Gambia, The |
| | 33 | Ghana | 34 | Gambia, The | 35 | Guinea | 35 | Guinea | 35 | Angola |
| | 34 | Malawi | 35 | Malawi | 36 | Malawi | 36 | Congo, Rep. | 36 | Mauritius |
| | 35 | Central African Rep. | 36 | Burundi | 37 | Sierra Leone | 37 | Eritrea | 37 | Zambia |
| | 36 | Ethiopia | 37 | Sierra Leone | 38 | Congo, Rep. | 38 | Gambia, The | 38 | Equatorial Guinea |
| | 37 | Guinea | 38 | Congo, Rep. | 39 | Congo, Dem. Rep. | 39 | Central African Rep. | 39 | Guinea-Bissau |
| | 38 | Zimbabwe | 39 | Zambia | 40 | Gambia, The | 40 | Togo | 40 | Seychelles |
| | 39 | Seychelles | 40 | Congo, Dem. Rep. | 41 | Burundi | 41 | São Tomé & Príncipe | 41 | São Tomé & Príncipe |
| | 40 | Liberia | 41 | São Tomé & Príncipe | 42 | São Tomé & Príncipe | 42 | Burundi | 42 | Congo, Rep. |
| | 41 | Congo, Dem. Rep. | 42 | Guinea-Bissau | 43 | Guinea-Bissau | 43 | Guinea-Bissau | 43 | Gabon |
| | 42 | Eritrea | 43 | Liberia | 44 | Liberia | 44 | Liberia | n/a | Liberia |
| least number of months / largest | n/a | Djibouti | n/a | Djibouti | n/a | Djibouti | n/a | Djibouti | n/a | Djibouti |
| | n/a | Mauritania | n/a | Mauritania | n/a | Mauritania | n/a | Mauritania | n/a | Mauritania |
| | n/a | Somalia | n/a | Somalia | n/a | Somalia | n/a | Somalia | n/a | Somalia |
| | n/a | Sudan | n/a | Sudan | n/a | Sudan | n/a | Sudan | n/a | Sudan |

## Foreign Debt as $PPP per Person

Primary data: IMF

| | | 2003-2006 |
|---|---|---|
| smallest | 1 | Zimbabwe |
| | 2 | South Africa |
| | 3 | Namibia |
| | 4 | Niger |
| | 5 | Ethiopia |
| | 6 | Mozambique |
| | 7 | Congo, Dem. Rep. |
| | 8 | Kenya |
| | 9 | Burkina Faso |
| | | SSA average |
| | 10 | Rwanda |
| | 11 | Nigeria |
| | 12 | Tanzania |
| | 13 | Benin |
| | 14 | Uganda |
| | 15 | Mali |
| | 16 | Chad |
| | 17 | Lesotho |
| | 18 | Central African Rep. |
| | 19 | Equatorial Guinea |
| | 20 | Eritrea |
| | 21 | Madagascar |
| | 22 | Botswana |
| | 23 | Senegal |
| | 24 | Malawi |
| | 25 | Cameroon |
| | 26 | Swaziland |
| | 27 | Sierra Leone |
| | 28 | Burundi |
| | 29 | Togo |
| | 30 | Ghana |
| | 31 | Comoros |
| | 32 | Zambia |
| | 33 | Guinea |
| | 34 | Côte d'Ivoire |
| | 35 | Angola |
| | 36 | Mauritius |
| | 37 | Cape Verde |
| | 38 | Guinea-Bissau |
| | 39 | Gambia, The |
| | 40 | Liberia |
| | 41 | São Tomé & Príncipe |
| | 42 | Congo, Rep. |
| | 43 | Gabon |
| | 44 | Seychelles |
| | n/a | Djibouti |
| | n/a | Mauritania |
| | n/a | Somalia |
| largest | n/a | Sudan |

## Foreign Debt as $PPP per Person

Primary data: IMF

| | | 2007-2008 |
|---|---|---|
| smallest | 1 | Nigeria |
| | 2 | Sierra Leone |
| | 3 | Zambia |
| | 4 | Ethiopia |
| | 5 | Niger |
| | 6 | Cameroon |
| | 7 | Uganda |
| | 8 | Rwanda |
| | 9 | Equatorial Guinea |
| | 10 | Congo, Dem. Rep. |
| | 11 | South Africa |
| | 12 | Malawi |
| | 13 | Tanzania |
| | | SSA average |
| | 14 | Benin |
| | 15 | Burkina Faso |
| | 16 | Mozambique |
| | 17 | Kenya |
| | 18 | Madagascar |
| | 19 | Namibia |
| | 20 | Mali |
| | 21 | Senegal |
| | 22 | Angola |
| | 23 | Ghana |
| | 24 | Chad |
| | 25 | Eritrea |
| | 26 | Botswana |
| | 27 | Central African Rep. |
| | 28 | Lesotho |
| | 29 | Burundi |
| | 30 | Swaziland |
| | 31 | Comoros |
| | 32 | Guinea |
| | 33 | Togo |
| | 34 | Gambia, The |
| | 35 | Côte d'Ivoire |
| | 36 | Mauritius |
| | 37 | Cape Verde |
| | 38 | Guinea-Bissau |
| | 39 | São Tomé & Príncipe |
| | 40 | Liberia |
| | 41 | Congo, Rep. |
| | 42 | Gabon |
| | 43 | Seychelles |
| | 44 | Zimbabwe |
| | n/a | Djibouti |
| | n/a | Mauritania |
| | n/a | Somalia |
| largest | n/a | Sudan |

## Service of Foreign Debt as % of Exports

AfDB

| | | 1999-2002 |
|---|---|---|
| lowest | 1 | Equatorial Guinea |
| | 2 | Namibia |
| | 3 | Togo |
| | 4 | Central African Rep. |
| | 5 | Comoros |
| | 6 | Djibouti |
| | 7 | Sudan |
| | 8 | Mauritius |
| | 9 | Congo, Rep. |
| | 10 | Nigeria |
| | 11 | Mali |
| | 12 | Mauritania |
| | 13 | Cameroon |
| | 14 | Niger |
| | 15 | Zimbabwe |
| | 16 | Benin |
| | 17 | Seychelles |
| | 18 | Senegal |
| | 19 | Zambia |
| | 20 | South Africa |
| | 21 | Burkina Faso |
| | 22 | Guinea |
| | 23 | Eritrea |
| | 24 | Cape Verde |
| | 25 | Ghana |
| | 26 | Madagascar |
| | 27 | Gabon |
| | 28 | Kenya |
| | 29 | Lesotho |
| | 30 | Côte d'Ivoire |
| | 31 | Chad |
| | 32 | Malawi |
| | 33 | Botswana |
| | 34 | Uganda |
| | 35 | Tanzania |
| | 36 | Guinea-Bissau |
| | 37 | Gambia, The |
| | 38 | Rwanda |
| | 39 | São Tomé & Príncipe |
| | 40 | Angola |
| | 41 | Congo, Dem. Rep. |
| | 42 | Mozambique |
| | 43 | Sierra Leone |
| | 44 | Ethiopia |
| | 45 | Burundi |
| | n/a | Liberia |
| | n/a | Somalia |
| | n/a | Swaziland |
| highest | | |

## Service of Foreign Debt as % of Exports

AfDB

| | | 2003-2006 |
|---|---|---|
| lowest | 1 | Togo |
| | 2 | Equatorial Guinea |
| | 3 | Namibia |
| | 4 | Central African Rep. |
| | 5 | Chad |
| | 6 | Mali |
| | 7 | Benin |
| | 8 | Ghana |
| | 9 | Sudan |
| | 10 | Mauritius |
| | 11 | Comoros |
| | 12 | Sierra Leone |
| | 13 | Nigeria |
| | 14 | Djibouti |
| | 15 | Lesotho |
| | 16 | Congo, Dem. Rep. |
| | 17 | Burkina Faso |
| | 18 | Tanzania |
| | 19 | Kenya |
| | 20 | Guinea-Bissau |
| | 21 | Congo, Rep. |
| | 22 | South Africa |
| | 23 | Zambia |
| | 24 | Niger |
| | 25 | Zimbabwe |
| | 26 | Ethiopia |
| | 27 | Seychelles |
| | 28 | Guinea |
| | 29 | Côte d'Ivoire |
| | 30 | Cameroon |
| | 31 | Botswana |
| | 32 | Angola |
| | 33 | Malawi |
| | 34 | Senegal |
| | 35 | Cape Verde |
| | 36 | Mauritania |
| | 37 | Rwanda |
| | 38 | Uganda |
| | 39 | Gabon |
| | 40 | Mozambique |
| | 41 | Gambia, The |
| | 42 | Madagascar |
| | 43 | Eritrea |
| | 44 | São Tomé & Príncipe |
| | 45 | Burundi |
| | n/a | Liberia |
| | n/a | Somalia |
| | n/a | Swaziland |
| highest | | |

## Growth in Foreign Debt per Person

Primary data: World Bank

| | | 1999-2002 |
|---|---|---|
| slowest | 1 | Mozambique |
| | 2 | Guinea-Bissau |
| | 3 | Ethiopia |
| | 4 | Congo, Dem. Rep. |
| | 5 | Angola |
| | 6 | Côte d'Ivoire |
| | 7 | Gabon |
| | 8 | Equatorial Guinea |
| | 9 | Mali |
| | 10 | Cameroon |
| | 11 | Kenya |
| | 12 | Zimbabwe |
| | | SSA average |
| | 13 | Mauritania |
| | 14 | Tanzania |
| | 15 | Guinea |
| | 16 | Botswana |
| | 17 | Zambia |
| | 18 | Uganda |
| | 19 | Nigeria |
| | 20 | Lesotho |
| | 21 | Senegal |
| | 22 | Congo, Rep. |
| | 23 | Liberia |
| | 24 | Madagascar |
| | 25 | Mauritius |
| | 26 | South Africa |
| | 27 | Niger |
| | 28 | Sudan |
| | 29 | Rwanda |
| | 30 | Togo |
| | 31 | Burkina Faso |
| | 32 | Sierra Leone |
| | 33 | Swaziland |
| | 34 | Benin |
| | 35 | Burundi |
| | 36 | Ghana |
| | 37 | Djibouti |
| | 38 | Chad |
| | 39 | Malawi |
| | 40 | Comoros |
| | 41 | Gambia, The |
| | 42 | Central African Rep. |
| | 43 | Seychelles |
| | 44 | Cape Verde |
| | 45 | Eritrea |
| | n/a | Namibia |
| | n/a | São Tomé & Príncipe |
| fastest | n/a | Somalia |

# appendix B8: performance tables - self-reliance

### Growth in Foreign Debt per Person

Primary data: World Bank

*slowest*

| | 2003-2006 |
|---|---|
| 1 | Nigeria |
| 2 | Madagascar |
| 3 | Cameroon |
| 4 | Zambia |
| 5 | Ethiopia |
| 6 | Rwanda |
| 7 | Malawi |
| 8 | Uganda |
| 9 | Benin |
| 10 | Ghana |
| 11 | Senegal |
| 12 | Niger |
| 13 | Mali |
| 14 | Mozambique |
| 15 | Tanzania |
| 16 | Mauritania |
| | SSA average |
| 17 | Burkina Faso |
| 18 | Botswana |
| 19 | Sierra Leone |
| 20 | Guinea |
| 21 | Central African Rep. |
| 22 | Guinea-Bissau |
| 23 | Comoros |
| 24 | Kenya |
| 25 | Congo, Dem. Rep. |
| 26 | Equatorial Guinea |
| 27 | Lesotho |
| 28 | Burundi |
| 29 | Angola |
| 30 | Sudan |
| 31 | Togo |
| 32 | Liberia |
| 33 | Côte d'Ivoire |
| 34 | Gambia, The |
| 35 | Congo, Rep. |
| 36 | Mauritius |
| 37 | Gabon |
| 38 | Chad |
| 39 | Zimbabwe |
| 40 | Eritrea |
| 41 | Cape Verde |
| 42 | Djibouti |
| 43 | South Africa |
| 44 | Swaziland |
| 45 | Seychelles |
| n/a | Namibia |
| n/a | São Tomé & Príncipe |
| n/a | Somalia |

*fastest*

### Aid Dependency (Foreign Aid as % of GDP)

IMF

*lowest*

| | 1997-2002 |
|---|---|
| 1 | South Africa |
| 2 | Nigeria |
| 3 | Mauritius |
| 4 | Congo, Rep. |
| 5 | Gabon |
| 6 | Cameroon |
| 6 | Kenya |
| 7 | Côte d'Ivoire |
| 8 | Zimbabwe |
| 9 | Madagascar |
| 10 | Angola |
| | SSA average |
| 11 | Guinea |
| 12 | Equatorial Guinea |
| 13 | Mali |
| 13 | Zambia |
| 14 | Senegal |
| 14 | Seychelles |
| 15 | Comoros |
| 16 | Togo |
| 17 | Benin |
| 17 | Niger |
| 18 | Burkina Faso |
| 18 | Chad |
| 19 | Ghana |
| 20 | Botswana |
| 21 | Central African Rep. |
| 22 | Ethiopia |
| 23 | Tanzania |
| 24 | Congo, Dem. Rep. |
| 25 | Mozambique |
| 26 | Uganda |
| 27 | Burundi |
| 28 | Cape Verde |
| 29 | Malawi |
| 30 | Sierra Leone |
| 31 | Swaziland |
| 32 | Gambia, The |
| 33 | Rwanda |
| 34 | Eritrea |
| 35 | Namibia |
| 36 | Guinea-Bissau |
| 37 | Lesotho |
| 38 | São Tomé & Príncipe |
| n/a | Liberia |
| n/a | Djibouti |
| n/a | Mauritania |
| n/a | Somalia |
| n/a | Sudan |

*highest*

### Aid Dependency (Foreign Aid as % of GDP)

IMF

*lowest*

| | 2003-2006 |
|---|---|
| 1 | South Africa |
| 2 | Gabon |
| 3 | Nigeria |
| 4 | Côte d'Ivoire |
| 5 | Angola |
| 6 | Kenya |
| 7 | Mauritius |
| 8 | Equatorial Guinea |
| 9 | Congo, Rep. |
| 10 | Guinea |
| 11 | Cameroon |
| 12 | Zimbabwe |
| | SSA average |
| 13 | Togo |
| 14 | Comoros |
| 15 | Zambia |
| 16 | Senegal |
| 17 | Mali |
| 18 | Madagascar |
| 19 | Seychelles |
| 20 | Benin |
| 21 | Niger |
| 22 | Burkina Faso |
| 23 | Central African Rep. |
| 23 | Tanzania |
| 24 | Chad |
| 25 | Ghana |
| 26 | Cape Verde |
| 27 | Mozambique |
| 28 | Botswana |
| 29 | Ethiopia |
| 30 | Sierra Leone |
| 31 | Congo, Dem. Rep. |
| 32 | Uganda |
| 33 | Malawi |
| 34 | Gambia, The |
| 35 | Guinea-Bissau |
| 36 | Swaziland |
| 37 | Namibia |
| 38 | Rwanda |
| 39 | Eritrea |
| 40 | Burundi |
| 41 | Lesotho |
| 42 | São Tomé & Príncipe |
| 43 | Liberia |
| n/a | Djibouti |
| n/a | Mauritania |
| n/a | Somalia |
| n/a | Sudan |

*highest*

### Aid Dependency (Foreign Aid as % of GDP)

IMF

*lowest*

| | 2007-2008 |
|---|---|
| 1 | South Africa |
| 2 | Angola |
| 3 | Nigeria |
| 4 | Equatorial Guinea |
| 5 | Gabon |
| 6 | Kenya |
| 7 | Congo, Rep. |
| 8 | Guinea |
| 9 | Madagascar |
| 9 | Mauritius |
| 10 | Zimbabwe |
| | SSA average |
| 11 | Cameroon |
| 12 | Côte d'Ivoire |
| 12 | Mali |
| 12 | Senegal |
| 13 | Togo |
| 14 | Eritrea |
| 15 | Chad |
| 15 | Seychelles |
| 16 | Comoros |
| 17 | Zambia |
| 18 | Ghana |
| 18 | Niger |
| 19 | Benin |
| 20 | Central African Rep. |
| 20 | Tanzania |
| 21 | Sierra Leone |
| 22 | Burkina Faso |
| 23 | Congo, Dem. Rep. |
| 24 | Cape Verde |
| 25 | Uganda |
| 26 | Ethiopia |
| 27 | Botswana |
| 28 | Gambia, The |
| 29 | Mozambique |
| 30 | Rwanda |
| 31 | Malawi |
| 32 | Namibia |
| 33 | Guinea-Bissau |
| 34 | Burundi |
| 35 | Swaziland |
| 36 | São Tomé & Príncipe |
| 37 | Liberia |
| 38 | Lesotho |
| n/a | Djibouti |
| n/a | Mauritania |
| n/a | Somalia |
| n/a | Sudan |

*highest*

### Aid Dependency (Foreign Aid as $PPP per Person)

Primary data: IMF

*lowest*

| | 1999-2002 |
|---|---|
| 1 | South Africa |
| 2 | Nigeria |
| 3 | Zimbabwe |
| 4 | Kenya |
| 5 | Cameroon |
| 6 | Congo, Rep. |
| 7 | Côte d'Ivoire |
| 8 | Madagascar |
| 9 | Mauritius |
| 10 | Guinea |
| 11 | Congo, Dem. Rep. |
| 12 | Mali |
| 13 | Niger |
| | SSA average |
| 14 | Togo |
| 15 | Zambia |
| 16 | Ethiopia |
| 17 | Burundi |
| 18 | Comoros |
| 19 | Central African Rep. |
| 20 | Senegal |
| 21 | Gabon |
| 22 | Mozambique |
| 23 | Angola |
| 24 | Sierra Leone |
| 25 | Burkina Faso |
| 26 | Chad |
| 27 | Benin |
| 28 | Tanzania |
| 29 | Ghana |
| 30 | Malawi |
| 31 | Uganda |
| 32 | Rwanda |
| 33 | Guinea-Bissau |
| 34 | Equatorial Guinea |
| 35 | Eritrea |
| 36 | Gambia, The |
| 37 | Cape Verde |
| 38 | Lesotho |
| 39 | São Tomé & Príncipe |
| 40 | Seychelles |
| 41 | Swaziland |
| 42 | Botswana |
| 43 | Namibia |
| n/a | Liberia |
| n/a | Djibouti |
| n/a | Mauritania |
| n/a | Somalia |
| n/a | Sudan |

*highest*

**Aid Dependency (Foreign Aid as $PPP per Person)**

Primary data: IMF

| | | 2003-2006 | | 2007-2008 |
|---|---|---|---|---|
| lowest | 1 | South Africa | 1 | South Africa |
| | 2 | Gabon | 2 | Angola |
| | 3 | Nigeria | 3 | Nigeria |
| | 4 | Côte d'Ivoire | 4 | Zimbabwe |
| | 5 | Zimbabwe | 5 | Kenya |
| | 6 | Kenya | 6 | Guinea |
| | 7 | Angola | 7 | Madagascar |
| | 8 | Guinea | 8 | Equatorial Guinea |
| | 9 | Togo | 9 | Gabon |
| | 10 | Cameroon | 10 | Congo, Rep. |
| | 11 | Congo, Rep. | 11 | Congo, Dem. Rep. |
| | 12 | Comoros | 12 | Mali |
| | | SSA average | 13 | Togo |
| | 13 | Zambia | 14 | Eritrea |
| | 14 | Niger | | SSA average |
| | 15 | Congo, Dem. Rep. | 15 | Niger |
| | 16 | Madagascar | 16 | Cameroon |
| | 17 | Mali | 17 | Central African Rep. |
| | 18 | Senegal | 18 | Senegal |
| | 19 | Central African Rep. | 19 | Sierra Leone |
| | 20 | Mauritius | 20 | Côte d'Ivoire |
| | 21 | Tanzania | 21 | Comoros |
| | 22 | Burkina Faso | 22 | Zambia |
| | 23 | Sierra Leone | 23 | Chad |
| | 24 | Ethiopia | 24 | Ghana |
| | 25 | Benin | 25 | Tanzania |
| | 26 | Equatorial Guinea | 26 | Benin |
| | 27 | Mozambique | 27 | Burkina Faso |
| | 28 | Guinea-Bissau | 28 | Uganda |
| | 29 | Chad | 29 | Mauritius |
| | 30 | Malawi | 30 | Ethiopia |
| | 31 | Ghana | 31 | Guinea-Bissau |
| | 32 | Burundi | 32 | Burundi |
| | 33 | Uganda | 33 | Mozambique |
| | 34 | Rwanda | 34 | Rwanda |
| | 35 | Gambia, The | 35 | Malawi |
| | 36 | Liberia | 36 | Liberia |
| | 37 | Eritrea | 37 | Gambia, The |
| | 38 | Cape Verde | 38 | Cape Verde |
| | 39 | Lesotho | 39 | São Tomé & Príncipe |
| | 40 | São Tomé & Príncipe | 40 | Seychelles |
| | 41 | Seychelles | 41 | Lesotho |
| | 42 | Swaziland | 42 | Namibia |
| | 43 | Namibia | 43 | Swaziland |
| | 44 | Botswana | 44 | Botswana |
| | n/a | Djibouti | n/a | Djibouti |
| | n/a | Mauritania | n/a | Mauritania |
| | n/a | Somalia | n/a | Somalia |
| highest | n/a | Sudan | n/a | Sudan |

# B9 performance tables - investor confidence

### FDI as % of GDP

UNCTAD

| | | 1999-2002 |
|---|---|---|
| largest | 1 | Equatorial Guinea |
| | 2 | Angola |
| | 3 | Chad |
| | 4 | Liberia |
| | 5 | Gambia, The |
| | 6 | Congo, Rep. |
| | 7 | Seychelles |
| | 8 | Mozambique |
| | 9 | São Tomé & Príncipe |
| | 10 | Cape Verde |
| | 11 | Swaziland |
| | 12 | Namibia |
| | 13 | Eritrea |
| | 14 | Mauritania |
| | 15 | Zambia |
| | 16 | Sudan |
| | 17 | Tanzania |
| | 18 | Lesotho |
| | 19 | Mali |
| | 20 | Togo |
| | | SSA average |
| | 21 | Uganda |
| | 22 | Ethiopia |
| | 23 | Botswana |
| | 24 | Nigeria |
| | 25 | Côte d'Ivoire |
| | 26 | Ghana |
| | 27 | South Africa |
| | 28 | Malawi |
| | 29 | Cameroon |
| | 30 | Mauritius |
| | 31 | Madagascar |
| | 32 | Senegal |
| | 33 | Benin |
| | 34 | Sierra Leone |
| | 35 | Congo, Dem. Rep. |
| | 36 | Guinea |
| | 37 | Guinea-Bissau |
| | 38 | Djibouti |
| | 39 | Burkina Faso |
| | 40 | Zimbabwe |
| | 41 | Niger |
| | 42 | Rwanda |
| | 43 | Burundi |
| | 44 | Central African Rep. |
| | 45 | Kenya |
| | 46 | Comoros |
| | 47 | Somalia |
| smallest | 48 | Gabon |

### FDI as % of GDP

UNCTAD

| | | 2003-2006 |
|---|---|---|
| largest | 1 | Equatorial Guinea |
| | 2 | São Tomé & Príncipe |
| | 3 | Mauritania |
| | 4 | Chad |
| | 5 | Seychelles |
| | 6 | Gambia, The |
| | 7 | Djibouti |
| | 8 | Sudan |
| | 9 | Cape Verde |
| | 10 | Angola |
| | 11 | Congo, Rep. |
| | 12 | Zambia |
| | 13 | Nigeria |
| | 14 | Botswana |
| | 15 | Namibia |
| | 16 | Lesotho |
| | 17 | Ethiopia |
| | 18 | Uganda |
| | 19 | Mozambique |
| | 20 | Tanzania |
| | 21 | Sierra Leone |
| | 22 | Guinea |
| | | SSA average |
| | 23 | Malawi |
| | 24 | Togo |
| | 25 | Madagascar |
| | 26 | Guinea-Bissau |
| | 27 | Mali |
| | 28 | Gabon |
| | 29 | Ghana |
| | 30 | Cameroon |
| | 31 | Zimbabwe |
| | 32 | Côte d'Ivoire |
| | 33 | Benin |
| | 34 | Central African Rep. |
| | 35 | Somalia |
| | 36 | Senegal |
| | 37 | Niger |
| | 38 | Mauritius |
| | 39 | South Africa |
| | 40 | Burkina Faso |
| | 41 | Rwanda |
| | 42 | Eritrea |
| | 43 | Kenya |
| | 44 | Comoros |
| | 45 | Congo, Dem. Rep. |
| | 46 | Burundi |
| | 47 | Swaziland |
| smallest | 48 | Liberia |

### FDI as $US per Person

Primary data: UNCTAD

| | | 1999-2002 |
|---|---|---|
| largest | 1 | Equatorial Guinea |
| | 2 | Seychelles |
| | 3 | Angola |
| | 4 | Namibia |
| | 5 | Cape Verde |
| | 6 | Swaziland |
| | 7 | Botswana |
| | 8 | Mauritius |
| | 9 | Congo, Rep. |
| | 10 | South Africa |
| | 11 | Chad |
| | 12 | Gambia, The |
| | 13 | Liberia |
| | 14 | São Tomé & Príncipe |
| | 15 | Mauritania |
| | 16 | Lesotho |
| | | SSA average |
| | 17 | Mozambique |
| | 18 | Côte d'Ivoire |
| | 19 | Sudan |
| | 20 | Zambia |
| | 21 | Cameroon |
| | 22 | Nigeria |
| | 23 | Tanzania |
| | 24 | Mali |
| | 25 | Eritrea |
| | 26 | Togo |
| | 27 | Senegal |
| | 28 | Ghana |
| | 29 | Uganda |
| | 30 | Benin |
| | 31 | Djibouti |
| | 32 | Madagascar |
| | 33 | Malawi |
| | 34 | Sierra Leone |
| | 35 | Guinea |
| | 36 | Ethiopia |
| | 37 | Zimbabwe |
| | 38 | Kenya |
| | 39 | Congo, Dem. Rep. |
| | 40 | Burkina Faso |
| | 41 | Guinea-Bissau |
| | 42 | Central African Rep. |
| | 43 | Rwanda |
| | 44 | Niger |
| | 45 | Comoros |
| | 46 | Burundi |
| | 47 | Somalia |
| smallest | 48 | Gabon |

# appendix B9: performance tables - investor confidence

## FDI as $US per Person

Primary data: UNCTAD

| | | 2003-2006 |
|---|---|---|
| largest | 1 | Equatorial Guinea |
| | 2 | Seychelles |
| | 3 | Botswana |
| | 4 | Cape Verde |
| | 5 | Gabon |
| | 6 | Namibia |
| | 7 | Mauritania |
| | 8 | São Tomé & Príncipe |
| | 9 | Congo, Rep. |
| | 10 | Djibouti |
| | 11 | Chad |
| | 12 | Angola |
| | 13 | Sudan |
| | 14 | Mauritius |
| | 15 | Nigeria |
| | 16 | South Africa |
| | 17 | Zambia |
| | 18 | Lesotho |
| | 19 | Gambia, The |
| | | SSA average |
| | 20 | Cameroon |
| | 21 | Côte d'Ivoire |
| | 22 | Mali |
| | 23 | Ghana |
| | 24 | Tanzania |
| | 25 | Uganda |
| | 26 | Guinea |
| | 27 | Mozambique |
| | 28 | Togo |
| | 29 | Sierra Leone |
| | 30 | Senegal |
| | 31 | Madagascar |
| | 32 | Benin |
| | 33 | Ethiopia |
| | 34 | Guinea-Bissau |
| | 35 | Malawi |
| | 36 | Central African Rep. |
| | 37 | Somalia |
| | 38 | Zimbabwe |
| | 39 | Niger |
| | 40 | Burkina Faso |
| | 41 | Kenya |
| | 42 | Rwanda |
| | 43 | Eritrea |
| | 44 | Comoros |
| | 45 | Burundi |
| | 46 | Congo, Dem. Rep. |
| | 47 | Swaziland |
| smallest | 48 | Liberia |

## Growth of FDI per Person

Primary data: UNCTAD

| | | 1999-2002 |
|---|---|---|
| fastest | 1 | Sierra Leone |
| | 2 | Mauritania |
| | 3 | Mali |
| | 4 | Guinea |
| | 5 | Cameroon |
| | 6 | Congo, Rep. |
| | 7 | Botswana |
| | 8 | Kenya |
| | 9 | Comoros |
| | 10 | Mauritius |
| | 11 | Namibia |
| | 12 | Chad |
| | 13 | South Africa |
| | 14 | Cape Verde |
| | 15 | Guinea-Bissau |
| | 16 | Equatorial Guinea |
| | 17 | Central African Rep. |
| | 18 | Zimbabwe |
| | 19 | Burkina Faso |
| | 20 | Rwanda |
| | 21 | Malawi |
| | 22 | Madagascar |
| | 23 | Zambia |
| | 24 | Tanzania |
| | 25 | Congo, Dem. Rep. |
| | 26 | Senegal |
| | 27 | Niger |
| | 28 | Angola |
| | 29 | Ethiopia |
| | 30 | Togo |
| | 31 | Mozambique |
| | 32 | Swaziland |
| | 33 | Somalia |
| | | SSA average |
| | 34 | Gambia, The |
| | 35 | Seychelles |
| | 36 | Sudan |
| | 37 | Nigeria |
| | 38 | Uganda |
| | 39 | Lesotho |
| | 40 | Djibouti |
| | 41 | São Tomé & Príncipe |
| | 42 | Benin |
| | 43 | Côte d'Ivoire |
| | 44 | Ghana |
| | 45 | Eritrea |
| | 46 | Liberia |
| | 47 | Gabon |
| slowest | 48 | Burundi |

## Growth of FDI per Person

Primary data: UNCTAD

| | | 2003-2006 |
|---|---|---|
| fastest | 1 | Liberia |
| | 2 | Congo, Rep. |
| | 3 | Zimbabwe |
| | 4 | Gabon |
| | 5 | Djibouti |
| | 6 | South Africa |
| | 7 | Sierra Leone |
| | 8 | Niger |
| | 9 | São Tomé & Príncipe |
| | 10 | Guinea-Bissau |
| | 11 | Ghana |
| | 12 | Mauritius |
| | 13 | Somalia |
| | 14 | Rwanda |
| | 15 | Senegal |
| | 16 | Equatorial Guinea |
| | 17 | Mauritania |
| | 18 | Nigeria |
| | 19 | Malawi |
| | 20 | Madagascar |
| | 21 | Benin |
| | 22 | Central African Rep. |
| | 23 | Kenya |
| | 24 | Gambia, The |
| | 25 | Sudan |
| | 26 | Guinea |
| | 27 | Seychelles |
| | 28 | Burkina Faso |
| | 29 | Cape Verde |
| | 30 | Lesotho |
| | 31 | Ethiopia |
| | 32 | Namibia |
| | | SSA average |
| | 33 | Zambia |
| | 34 | Uganda |
| | 35 | Eritrea |
| | 36 | Togo |
| | 37 | Côte d'Ivoire |
| | 38 | Swaziland |
| | 39 | Comoros |
| | 40 | Tanzania |
| | 41 | Botswana |
| | 42 | Burundi |
| | 43 | Mali |
| | 44 | Chad |
| | 45 | Angola |
| | 46 | Mozambique |
| | 47 | Cameroon |
| slowest | 48 | Congo, Dem. Rep. |

## FDI as % of Total Capital Investment

UNCTAD

| | | 1999-2002 |
|---|---|---|
| highest | 1 | Liberia |
| | 2 | Angola |
| | 3 | Sierra Leone |
| | 4 | Chad |
| | 5 | Gambia, The |
| | 6 | Equatorial Guinea |
| | 7 | Nigeria |
| | 8 | Congo, Rep. |
| | 9 | Mozambique |
| | 10 | Swaziland |
| | 11 | Seychelles |
| | 12 | Namibia |
| | 13 | Tanzania |
| | 14 | Sudan |
| | 15 | Zambia |
| | 16 | Togo |
| | 17 | Mauritania |
| | 18 | Cape Verde |
| | 19 | Côte d'Ivoire |
| | | SSA average |
| | 20 | São Tomé & Príncipe |
| | 21 | Mali |
| | 22 | Eritrea |
| | 23 | Malawi |
| | 24 | South Africa |
| | 25 | Uganda |
| | 26 | Congo, Dem. Rep. |
| | 27 | Ethiopia |
| | 28 | Madagascar |
| | 29 | Botswana |
| | 30 | Cameroon |
| | 31 | Ghana |
| | 32 | Benin |
| | 33 | Lesotho |
| | 34 | Mauritius |
| | 35 | Senegal |
| | 36 | Burundi |
| | 37 | Zimbabwe |
| | 38 | Central African Rep. |
| | 39 | Guinea |
| | 40 | Djibouti |
| | 41 | Guinea-Bissau |
| | 42 | Niger |
| | 43 | Rwanda |
| | 44 | Comoros |
| | 45 | Burkina Faso |
| | 46 | Kenya |
| | 47 | Somalia |
| lowest | 48 | Gabon |

## FDI as % of Total Capital Investment

UNCTAD

| | | 2003-2006 |
|---|---|---|
| highest | 1 | Seychelles |
| | 2 | Equatorial Guinea |
| | 3 | Sierra Leone |
| | 4 | Zimbabwe |
| | 5 | Angola |
| | 6 | Mauritania |
| | 7 | Chad |
| | 8 | Djibouti |
| | 9 | Nigeria |
| | 10 | São Tomé & Príncipe |
| | 11 | Sudan |
| | 12 | Gambia, The |
| | 13 | Malawi |
| | 14 | Zambia |
| | 15 | Congo, Rep. |
| | 16 | Central African Rep. |
| | 17 | Ethiopia |
| | 18 | Cape Verde |
| | 19 | Guinea |
| | 20 | Botswana |
| | 21 | Namibia |
| | | SSA average |
| | 22 | Guinea-Bissau |
| | 23 | Côte d'Ivoire |
| | 24 | Tanzania |
| | 25 | Uganda |
| | 26 | Mozambique |
| | 27 | Mali |
| | 28 | Togo |
| | 29 | Madagascar |
| | 30 | Lesotho |
| | 31 | Cameroon |
| | 32 | Gabon |
| | 33 | Ghana |
| | 34 | Benin |
| | 35 | Somalia |
| | 36 | Niger |
| | 37 | South Africa |
| | 38 | Senegal |
| | 39 | Mauritius |
| | 40 | Rwanda |
| | 41 | Burkina Faso |
| | 42 | Comoros |
| | 43 | Eritrea |
| | 44 | Congo, Dem. Rep. |
| | 45 | Kenya |
| | 46 | Burundi |
| | 47 | Swaziland |
| lowest | 48 | Liberia |

# appendix B9: performance tables - investor confidence

## Total Capital Investment as % of GDP

UNCTAD

| | | 1999-2002 |
|---|---|---|
| highest | 1 | Equatorial Guinea |
| | 2 | Lesotho |
| | 3 | São Tomé & Príncipe |
| | 4 | Cape Verde |
| | 5 | Chad |
| | 6 | Seychelles |
| | 7 | Eritrea |
| | 8 | Gabon |
| | 9 | Botswana |
| | 10 | Burkina Faso |
| | 11 | Mauritius |
| | 12 | Senegal |
| | 13 | Mozambique |
| | 14 | Ghana |
| | 15 | Congo, Rep. |
| | 16 | Namibia |
| | 17 | Swaziland |
| | 18 | Mauritania |
| | 19 | Somalia |
| | 20 | Gambia, The |
| | 21 | Ethiopia |
| | 22 | Uganda |
| | 23 | Guinea |
| | 24 | Mali |
| | 25 | Zambia |
| | 26 | Benin |
| | 27 | Sudan |
| | 28 | Cameroon |
| | 29 | Rwanda |
| | 30 | Djibouti |
| | 31 | Tanzania |
| | 32 | Kenya |
| | 33 | Angola |
| | 34 | Togo |
| | 35 | Guinea-Bissau |
| | 36 | Madagascar |
| | | SSA average |
| | 37 | South Africa |
| | 38 | Niger |
| | 39 | Malawi |
| | 40 | Côte d'Ivoire |
| | 41 | Comoros |
| | 42 | Zimbabwe |
| | 43 | Central African Rep. |
| | 44 | Burundi |
| | 45 | Congo, Dem. Rep. |
| | 46 | Nigeria |
| | 47 | Liberia |
| lowest | 48 | Sierra Leone |

## Total Capital Investment as % of GDP

UNCTAD

| | | 2003-2006 |
|---|---|---|
| highest | 1 | Equatorial Guinea |
| | 2 | São Tomé & Príncipe |
| | 3 | Lesotho |
| | 4 | Mauritania |
| | 5 | Cape Verde |
| | 6 | Chad |
| | 7 | Ghana |
| | 8 | Namibia |
| | 9 | Congo, Rep. |
| | 10 | Zambia |
| | 11 | Botswana |
| | 12 | Gambia, The |
| | 13 | Senegal |
| | 14 | Burkina Faso |
| | 15 | Gabon |
| | 16 | Uganda |
| | 17 | Mauritius |
| | 18 | Mozambique |
| | 19 | Sudan |
| | 20 | Eritrea |
| | 21 | Madagascar |
| | 22 | Tanzania |
| | 23 | Ethiopia |
| | 24 | Somalia |
| | 25 | Rwanda |
| | 26 | Seychelles |
| | 27 | Benin |
| | 28 | Djibouti |
| | 29 | Cameroon |
| | 30 | Togo |
| | 31 | Swaziland |
| | 32 | Mali |
| | 33 | Kenya |
| | | SSA average |
| | 34 | Niger |
| | 35 | South Africa |
| | 36 | Guinea-Bissau |
| | 37 | Congo, Dem. Rep. |
| | 38 | Burundi |
| | 39 | Guinea |
| | 40 | Liberia |
| | 41 | Nigeria |
| | 42 | Angola |
| | 43 | Comoros |
| | 44 | Côte d'Ivoire |
| | 45 | Malawi |
| | 46 | Central African Rep. |
| | 47 | Sierra Leone |
| lowest | 48 | Zimbabwe |

## Total Capital Investment as $US per Person

Primary data: UNCTAD

| | | 1999-2002 |
|---|---|---|
| largest | 1 | Seychelles |
| | 2 | Equatorial Guinea |
| | 3 | Gabon |
| | 4 | Mauritius |
| | 5 | Botswana |
| | 6 | Cape Verde |
| | 7 | South Africa |
| | 8 | Namibia |
| | 9 | Swaziland |
| | 10 | Congo, Rep. |
| | 11 | Lesotho |
| | 12 | Djibouti |
| | 13 | São Tomé & Príncipe |
| | 14 | Senegal |
| | 15 | Cameroon |
| | 16 | Angola |
| | 17 | Mauritania |
| | 18 | Côte d'Ivoire |
| | | SSA average |
| | 19 | Guinea |
| | 20 | Kenya |
| | 21 | Ghana |
| | 22 | Sudan |
| | 23 | Benin |
| | 24 | Chad |
| | 25 | Zambia |
| | 26 | Gambia, The |
| | 27 | Somalia |
| | 28 | Burkina Faso |
| | 29 | Mali |
| | 30 | Eritrea |
| | 31 | Mozambique |
| | 32 | Tanzania |
| | 33 | Uganda |
| | 34 | Zimbabwe |
| | 35 | Togo |
| | 36 | Madagascar |
| | 37 | Rwanda |
| | 38 | Comoros |
| | 39 | Nigeria |
| | 40 | Guinea-Bissau |
| | 41 | Central African Rep. |
| | 42 | Niger |
| | 43 | Ethiopia |
| | 44 | Malawi |
| | 45 | Liberia |
| | 46 | Sierra Leone |
| | 47 | Burundi |
| smallest | 48 | Congo, Dem. Rep. |

## Total Capital Investment as $US per Person

Primary data: UNCTAD

| | | 2003-2006 |
|---|---|---|
| largest | 1 | Equatorial Guinea |
| | 2 | Seychelles |
| | 3 | Gabon |
| | 4 | Botswana |
| | 5 | Mauritius |
| | 6 | South Africa |
| | 7 | Namibia |
| | 8 | Cape Verde |
| | 9 | Swaziland |
| | 10 | Congo, Rep. |
| | 11 | Lesotho |
| | 12 | Mauritania |
| | 13 | São Tomé & Príncipe |
| | 14 | Angola |
| | 15 | Cameroon |
| | 16 | Senegal |
| | 17 | Djibouti |
| | 18 | Zambia |
| | 19 | Sudan |
| | | SSA average |
| | 20 | Chad |
| | 21 | Ghana |
| | 22 | Benin |
| | 23 | Kenya |
| | 24 | Burkina Faso |
| | 25 | Côte d'Ivoire |
| | 26 | Nigeria |
| | 27 | Mali |
| | 28 | Uganda |
| | 29 | Mozambique |
| | 30 | Tanzania |
| | 31 | Gambia, The |
| | 32 | Togo |
| | 33 | Madagascar |
| | 34 | Somalia |
| | 35 | Guinea |
| | 36 | Comoros |
| | 37 | Eritrea |
| | 38 | Rwanda |
| | 39 | Niger |
| | 40 | Guinea-Bissau |
| | 41 | Ethiopia |
| | 42 | Liberia |
| | 43 | Congo, Dem. Rep. |
| | 44 | Central African Rep. |
| | 45 | Burundi |
| | 46 | Sierra Leone |
| | 47 | Malawi |
| smallest | 48 | Zimbabwe |

## Growth of Total Capital Investment per Person

Primary data: UNCTAD

| | | 1999-2002 |
|---|---|---|
| fastest | 1 | Sierra Leone |
| | 2 | Chad |
| | 3 | Guinea-Bissau |
| | 4 | Congo, Dem. Rep. |
| | 5 | Equatorial Guinea |
| | 6 | Zambia |
| | 7 | Sudan |
| | 8 | Cameroon |
| | 9 | Cape Verde |
| | 10 | Mozambique |
| | 11 | Tanzania |
| | 12 | Djibouti |
| | 13 | Nigeria |
| | 14 | São Tomé & Príncipe |
| | 15 | Benin |
| | 16 | Madagascar |
| | 17 | Mali |
| | 18 | Mauritania |
| | 19 | Guinea |
| | 20 | Mauritius |
| | 21 | Burundi |
| | 22 | Niger |
| | 23 | Senegal |
| | 24 | Burkina Faso |
| | 25 | Ethiopia |
| | 26 | Togo |
| | 27 | Somalia |
| | 28 | Seychelles |
| | 29 | Botswana |
| | 30 | Uganda |
| | 31 | Kenya |
| | 32 | Gambia, The |
| | 33 | Malawi |
| | 34 | Gabon |
| | | SSA average |
| | 35 | Rwanda |
| | 36 | Eritrea |
| | 37 | Namibia |
| | 38 | Central African Rep. |
| | 39 | Swaziland |
| | 40 | Comoros |
| | 41 | Ghana |
| | 42 | South Africa |
| | 43 | Congo, Rep. |
| | 44 | Lesotho |
| | 45 | Angola |
| | 46 | Côte d'Ivoire |
| | 47 | Liberia |
| slowest | 48 | Zimbabwe |

# appendix B9: performance tables - investor confidence

## Growth of Total Capital Investment per Person

Primary data: UNCTAD

| | 2003-2006 | |
|---|---|---|
| highest | 1 | Equatorial Guinea |
| | 2 | Angola |
| | 3 | Seychelles |
| | 4 | Nigeria |
| | 5 | Burundi |
| | 6 | Mauritania |
| | 7 | Zambia |
| | 8 | São Tomé & Príncipe |
| | 9 | Liberia |
| | 10 | Congo, Dem. Rep. |
| | 11 | Sudan |
| | 12 | Namibia |
| | 13 | Congo, Rep. |
| | 14 | South Africa |
| | 15 | Ghana |
| | | SSA average |
| | 16 | Swaziland |
| | 17 | Lesotho |
| | 18 | Niger |
| | 19 | Botswana |
| | 20 | Mozambique |
| | 21 | Uganda |
| | 22 | Madagascar |
| | 23 | Cape Verde |
| | 24 | Kenya |
| | 25 | Burkina Faso |
| | 26 | Cameroon |
| | 27 | Senegal |
| | 28 | Comoros |
| | 29 | Mali |
| | 30 | Benin |
| | 31 | Gambia, The |
| | 32 | Togo |
| | 33 | Rwanda |
| | 34 | Mauritius |
| | 35 | Côte d'Ivoire |
| | 36 | Ethiopia |
| | 37 | Tanzania |
| | 38 | Gabon |
| | 39 | Chad |
| | 40 | Eritrea |
| | 41 | Djibouti |
| | 42 | Guinea |
| | 43 | Guinea-Bissau |
| | 44 | Somalia |
| | 45 | Central African Rep. |
| | 46 | Sierra Leone |
| | 47 | Malawi |
| lowest | 48 | Zimbabwe |

## Public Investment as % of GDP

AfDB

| | 2000-2002 | |
|---|---|---|
| highest | 1 | Mauritania |
| | 2 | Eritrea |
| | 3 | Ethiopia |
| | 4 | Mozambique |
| | 5 | Seychelles |
| | 6 | Nigeria |
| | 7 | Lesotho |
| | 8 | Malawi |
| | 9 | Zambia |
| | 10 | Chad |
| | 11 | Botswana |
| | 12 | Niger |
| | 13 | Cape Verde |
| | 14 | Guinea-Bissau |
| | 15 | Congo, Rep. |
| | 16 | Ghana |
| | 17 | Swaziland |
| | 18 | Mauritius |
| | 18 | Tanzania |
| | 19 | Madagascar |
| | 19 | Angola |
| | 20 | Namibia |
| | 20 | Benin |
| | 21 | Mali |
| | 22 | Kenya |
| | 23 | Senegal |
| | 24 | Gambia, The |
| | 25 | Uganda |
| | 26 | Rwanda |
| | 27 | Burkina Faso |
| | 28 | Comoros |
| | 29 | Equatorial Guinea |
| | 29 | Sierra Leone |
| | 30 | Central African Rep. |
| | 31 | Guinea |
| | 32 | Gabon |
| | 33 | Burundi |
| | 34 | Djibouti |
| | 35 | Côte d'Ivoire |
| | 36 | Sudan |
| | 37 | South Africa |
| | 38 | Togo |
| | 39 | Cameroon |
| | 40 | Congo, Dem. Rep. |
| | n/a | Liberia |
| | n/a | São Tomé & Príncipe |
| | n/a | Somalia |
| | n/a | Zimbabwe |
| lowest | | |

## Public Investment as % of GDP

AfDB

| | 2003-2006 | |
|---|---|---|
| highest | 1 | Mauritania |
| | 2 | Eritrea |
| | 3 | Lesotho |
| | 4 | Ethiopia |
| | 5 | Ghana |
| | 6 | Tanzania |
| | 7 | Gambia, The |
| | 8 | Equatorial Guinea |
| | 8 | Djibouti |
| | 9 | Nigeria |
| | 10 | Madagascar |
| | 11 | Mauritius |
| | 12 | Zambia |
| | 13 | Guinea-Bissau |
| | 14 | Burundi |
| | 15 | Chad |
| | 16 | Rwanda |
| | 17 | Mali |
| | 18 | Cape Verde |
| | 19 | Swaziland |
| | 20 | Botswana |
| | 21 | Congo, Rep. |
| | 22 | Namibia |
| | 23 | Angola |
| | 24 | Gabon |
| | 25 | Benin |
| | 26 | Niger |
| | 27 | Senegal |
| | 28 | Seychelles |
| | 29 | Sierra Leone |
| | 30 | Uganda |
| | 30 | Mozambique |
| | 31 | Comoros |
| | 32 | Kenya |
| | 33 | Sudan |
| | 34 | Guinea |
| | 35 | Cameroon |
| | 36 | Congo, Dem. Rep. |
| | 37 | Burkina Faso |
| | 37 | Central African Rep. |
| | 38 | Côte d'Ivoire |
| | 39 | Togo |
| | 40 | South Africa |
| | 41 | Malawi |
| | n/a | Liberia |
| | n/a | São Tomé & Príncipe |
| | n/a | Somalia |
| | n/a | Zimbabwe |
| lowest | | |

## Private Investment as % of GDP

AfDB

| | 2000-2002 | |
|---|---|---|
| highest | 1 | Equatorial Guinea |
| | 2 | Lesotho |
| | 3 | Chad |
| | 4 | Botswana |
| | 5 | Cape Verde |
| | 6 | Mozambique |
| | 7 | Gabon |
| | 8 | Cameroon |
| | 9 | Mauritius |
| | 9 | Sudan |
| | 10 | Congo, Rep. |
| | 11 | Seychelles |
| | 12 | Ghana |
| | 13 | Uganda |
| | 14 | Senegal |
| | 15 | Namibia |
| | 16 | Nigeria |
| | 17 | Gambia, The |
| | 17 | South Africa |
| | 18 | Mali |
| | 19 | Togo |
| | 20 | Burkina Faso |
| | 20 | Swaziland |
| | 21 | Guinea |
| | 22 | Benin |
| | 22 | Rwanda |
| | 23 | Tanzania |
| | 24 | Zambia |
| | 25 | Madagascar |
| | 26 | Kenya |
| | 27 | Ethiopia |
| | 28 | Eritrea |
| | 29 | Angola |
| | 29 | Côte d'Ivoire |
| | 30 | Djibouti |
| | 31 | Comoros |
| | 32 | Congo, Dem. Rep. |
| | 33 | Niger |
| | 34 | Mauritania |
| | 35 | Central African Rep. |
| | 36 | Sierra Leone |
| | 37 | Malawi |
| | 38 | Burundi |
| | 39 | Guinea-Bissau |
| | n/a | Liberia |
| | n/a | São Tomé & Príncipe |
| | n/a | Somalia |
| | n/a | Zimbabwe |
| lowest | | |

## Private Investment as % of GDP

AfDB

| | 2003-2006 | |
|---|---|---|
| highest | 1 | Equatorial Guinea |
| | 2 | Cape Verde |
| | 3 | Botswana |
| | 4 | Chad |
| | 5 | Lesotho |
| | 6 | Namibia |
| | 7 | Malawi |
| | 8 | Gabon |
| | 9 | Senegal |
| | 10 | Sudan |
| | 11 | Uganda |
| | 12 | Seychelles |
| | 13 | Congo, Rep. |
| | 14 | Zambia |
| | 15 | Ghana |
| | 16 | South Africa |
| | 17 | Cameroon |
| | 18 | Mauritius |
| | 19 | Burkina Faso |
| | 20 | Gambia, The |
| | 21 | Mozambique |
| | 22 | Mali |
| | 23 | Benin |
| | 24 | Niger |
| | 25 | Tanzania |
| | 26 | Kenya |
| | 27 | Nigeria |
| | 28 | Rwanda |
| | 29 | Djibouti |
| | 30 | Madagascar |
| | 31 | Swaziland |
| | 32 | Congo, Dem. Rep. |
| | 33 | Togo |
| | 34 | Sierra Leone |
| | 35 | Ethiopia |
| | 36 | Guinea |
| | 37 | Côte d'Ivoire |
| | 38 | Mauritania |
| | 39 | Comoros |
| | 40 | Central African Rep. |
| | 41 | Eritrea |
| | 42 | Burundi |
| | 43 | Angola |
| | 44 | Guinea-Bissau |
| | n/a | Liberia |
| | n/a | São Tomé & Príncipe |
| | n/a | Somalia |
| | n/a | Zimbabwe |
| lowest | | |

# appendix B9: performance tables - investor confidence

| Rank | Public Investment as $PPP per Person | Public Investment as $PPP per Person | Private Investment as $PPP per Person | Private Investment as $PPP per Person | Growth of Public Investment per Person |
|---|---|---|---|---|---|
| | AfDB, IMF | AfDB, IMF | AfDB, IMF | AfDB, IMF | AfDB, IMF |
| | 2000-2002 | 2003-2006 | 2000-2002 | 2003-2006 | 2002 |
| | largest | largest | largest | largest | fastest |
| 1 | Seychelles | Equatorial Guinea | Botswana | Botswana | Equatorial Guinea |
| 2 | Botswana | Botswana | Gabon | Equatorial Guinea | Cameroon |
| 3 | Mauritius | Mauritius | Seychelles | Gabon | Burkina Faso |
| 4 | Gabon | Gabon | Equatorial Guinea | Seychelles | Congo, Dem. Rep. |
| 5 | Equatorial Guinea | Seychelles | Mauritius | Mauritius | Zambia |
| 6 | Swaziland | Mauritania | South Africa | South Africa | Botswana |
| 7 | Mauritania | Swaziland | Cape Verde | Namibia | Senegal |
| 8 | Congo, Rep. | Namibia | Namibia | Cape Verde | Gambia, The |
| 9 | Namibia | Angola | Swaziland | Congo, Rep. | Djibouti |
| 10 | Angola | Congo, Rep. | Congo, Rep. | Swaziland | Comoros |
| 11 | South Africa | Cape Verde | Lesotho | Chad | Mali |
| 12 | Cape Verde | Djibouti | Chad | Sudan | Cape Verde |
| 13 | Nigeria | South Africa | Cameroon | Cameroon | Lesotho |
| 14 | Eritrea | Nigeria | Sudan | Senegal | Chad |
| 15 | Lesotho | Lesotho | Angola | Djibouti | Mozambique |
| 16 | Zambia | Ghana | Senegal | Lesotho | Sudan |
| 17 | Chad | Eritrea | Nigeria | Nigeria | Nigeria |
| 18 | Ghana | Chad | Ghana | Ghana | Congo, Rep. |
| 19 | Senegal | Gambia, The | Benin | Benin | Angola |
| 20 | Kenya | Tanzania | Gambia, The | Kenya | Tanzania |
| 21 | Benin | Zambia | Côte d'Ivoire | Zambia | Ethiopia |
| 22 | Djibouti | Madagascar | Guinea | Gambia, The | Sierra Leone |
| 23 | Ethiopia | Benin | Burkina Faso | Burkina Faso | Benin |
| 24 | Mozambique | Senegal | Kenya | Uganda | Guinea-Bissau |
| 25 | Tanzania | Mali | Mozambique | Tanzania | Mauritania |
| 26 | Gambia, The | Ethiopia | Djibouti | Mali | Gabon |
| 27 | Malawi | Sudan | Zambia | Angola | Niger |
| 28 | Burkina Faso | Rwanda | Uganda | Malawi | Côte d'Ivoire |
| 29 | Comoros | Cameroon | Mali | Côte d'Ivoire | Namibia |
| 30 | Côte d'Ivoire | Kenya | Tanzania | Mauritania | Eritrea |
| 31 | Mali | Comoros | Togo | Madagascar | Mauritius |
| 32 | Madagascar | Côte d'Ivoire | Rwanda | Mozambique | Central African Rep. |
| 33 | Niger | Uganda | Mauritania | Rwanda | South Africa |
| 34 | Guinea | Guinea-Bissau | Eritrea | Guinea | Uganda |
| 35 | Uganda | Guinea | Madagascar | Niger | Swaziland |
| 36 | Sudan | Mozambique | Comoros | Togo | Burundi |
| 37 | Guinea-Bissau | Niger | Ethiopia | Sierra Leone | Rwanda |
| 38 | Rwanda | Burkina Faso | Central African Rep. | Ethiopia | Guinea |
| 39 | Central African Rep. | Sierra Leone | Niger | Comoros | Seychelles |
| 40 | Cameroon | Burundi | Malawi | Eritrea | Ghana |
| 41 | Sierra Leone | Central African Rep. | Sierra Leone | Central African Rep. | Malawi |
| 42 | Togo | Togo | Congo, Dem. Rep. | Congo, Dem. Rep. | Kenya |
| 43 | Burundi | Congo, Dem. Rep. | Burundi | Burundi | Madagascar |
| 44 | Congo, Dem. Rep. | Malawi | Guinea-Bissau | Guinea-Bissau | Togo |
| n/a | Liberia | Liberia | Liberia | Liberia | Liberia |
| n/a | São Tomé & Príncipe | São Tomé & Príncipe | São Tomé & Príncipe | São Tomé & Príncipe | São Tomé & Príncipe |
| n/a | Somalia | Somalia | Somalia | Somalia | Somalia |
| n/a | Zimbabwe | Zimbabwe | Zimbabwe | Zimbabwe | Zimbabwe |
| | smallest | smallest | smallest | smallest | slowest |

# appendix B9: performance tables - investor confidence

### Growth of Public Investment per Person

AfDB, IMF

| | | 2003-2006 |
|---|---|---|
| fastest | 1 | Malawi |
| | 2 | Guinea-Bissau |
| | 3 | Djibouti |
| | 4 | Niger |
| | 5 | Burundi |
| | 6 | Sierra Leone |
| | 7 | Seychelles |
| | 8 | Kenya |
| | 9 | Equatorial Guinea |
| | 10 | Zambia |
| | 11 | Madagascar |
| | 12 | Senegal |
| | 13 | Namibia |
| | 14 | Burkina Faso |
| | 15 | South Africa |
| | 16 | Benin |
| | 17 | Ghana |
| | 18 | Tanzania |
| | 19 | Congo, Dem. Rep. |
| | 20 | Mali |
| | 21 | Uganda |
| | 22 | Cape Verde |
| | 23 | Mauritania |
| | 24 | Sudan |
| | 25 | Central African Rep. |
| | 26 | Gambia, The |
| | 27 | Guinea |
| | 28 | Mauritius |
| | 29 | Rwanda |
| | 30 | Mozambique |
| | 31 | Ethiopia |
| | 32 | Congo, Rep. |
| | 33 | Comoros |
| | 34 | Côte d'Ivoire |
| | 35 | Cameroon |
| | 36 | Botswana |
| | 37 | Gabon |
| | 38 | Nigeria |
| | 39 | Swaziland |
| | 40 | Togo |
| | 41 | Lesotho |
| | 42 | Angola |
| | 43 | Chad |
| | 44 | Eritrea |
| | n/a | Liberia |
| | n/a | São Tomé & Príncipe |
| | n/a | Somalia |
| | n/a | Zimbabwe |
| slowest | | |

### Growth of Private Investment per Person

AfDB, IMF

| | | 2002 |
|---|---|---|
| fastest | 1 | Chad |
| | 2 | Sierra Leone |
| | 3 | Congo, Dem. Rep. |
| | 4 | Eritrea |
| | 5 | Nigeria |
| | 6 | Togo |
| | 7 | Mauritania |
| | 8 | Botswana |
| | 9 | Ethiopia |
| | 10 | Tanzania |
| | 11 | Cape Verde |
| | 12 | Burundi |
| | 13 | Seychelles |
| | 14 | Cameroon |
| | 15 | Rwanda |
| | 16 | Sudan |
| | 17 | Niger |
| | 18 | Uganda |
| | 19 | South Africa |
| | 20 | Namibia |
| | 21 | Gabon |
| | 22 | Gambia, The |
| | 23 | Madagascar |
| | 24 | Zambia |
| | 25 | Swaziland |
| | 26 | Congo, Rep. |
| | 27 | Ghana |
| | 28 | Djibouti |
| | 29 | Lesotho |
| | 30 | Mali |
| | 31 | Mozambique |
| | 32 | Comoros |
| | 33 | Central African Rep. |
| | 34 | Benin |
| | 35 | Côte d'Ivoire |
| | 36 | Kenya |
| | 37 | Burkina Faso |
| | 38 | Senegal |
| | 39 | Mauritius |
| | 40 | Equatorial Guinea |
| | 41 | Angola |
| | 42 | Malawi |
| | 43 | Guinea |
| | 44 | Guinea-Bissau |
| | n/a | Liberia |
| | n/a | São Tomé & Príncipe |
| | n/a | Somalia |
| | n/a | Zimbabwe |
| slowest | | |

### Growth of Private Investment per Person

AfDB, IMF

| | | 2003-2006 |
|---|---|---|
| fastest | 1 | Malawi |
| | 2 | Guinea-Bissau |
| | 3 | Djibouti |
| | 4 | Niger |
| | 5 | Burundi |
| | 6 | Sierra Leone |
| | 7 | Seychelles |
| | 8 | Kenya |
| | 9 | Equatorial Guinea |
| | 10 | Zambia |
| | 11 | Madagascar |
| | 12 | Senegal |
| | 13 | Namibia |
| | 14 | Burkina Faso |
| | 15 | South Africa |
| | 16 | Benin |
| | 17 | Ghana |
| | 18 | Tanzania |
| | 19 | Congo, Dem. Rep. |
| | 20 | Mali |
| | 21 | Uganda |
| | 22 | Cape Verde |
| | 23 | Mauritania |
| | 24 | Sudan |
| | 25 | Central African Rep. |
| | 26 | Gambia, The |
| | 27 | Guinea |
| | 28 | Mauritius |
| | 29 | Rwanda |
| | 30 | Mozambique |
| | 31 | Ethiopia |
| | 32 | Congo, Rep. |
| | 33 | Comoros |
| | 34 | Côte d'Ivoire |
| | 35 | Cameroon |
| | 36 | Botswana |
| | 37 | Gabon |
| | 38 | Nigeria |
| | 39 | Swaziland |
| | 40 | Togo |
| | 41 | Lesotho |
| | 42 | Angola |
| | 43 | Chad |
| | 44 | Eritrea |
| | n/a | Liberia |
| | n/a | São Tomé & Príncipe |
| | n/a | Somalia |
| | n/a | Zimbabwe |
| slowest | | |

### Domestic Credit to the Private Sector as % of GDP

IMF, World Bank

| | | 1999-2002 |
|---|---|---|
| largest | 1 | South Africa |
| | | SSA average |
| | 2 | Mauritius |
| | 3 | Namibia |
| | 4 | Eritrea |
| | 5 | Cape Verde |
| | 6 | Zimbabwe |
| | 7 | Ethiopia |
| | 8 | Djibouti |
| | 9 | Mauritania |
| | 10 | Kenya |
| | 11 | Burundi |
| | 12 | Senegal |
| | 13 | Mali |
| | 14 | Seychelles |
| | 15 | Botswana |
| | 16 | Côte d'Ivoire |
| | 17 | Nigeria |
| | 18 | Togo |
| | 19 | Gambia, The |
| | 20 | Lesotho |
| | 21 | Swaziland |
| | 22 | Burkina Faso |
| | 23 | Ghana |
| | 24 | Benin |
| | 25 | Gabon |
| | 26 | Mozambique |
| | 27 | Rwanda |
| | 28 | Cameroon |
| | 29 | Madagascar |
| | 30 | Comoros |
| | 31 | Zambia |
| | 32 | Uganda |
| | 33 | Congo, Rep. |
| | 34 | Malawi |
| | 35 | Guinea-Bissau |
| | 36 | Tanzania |
| | 37 | Central African Rep. |
| | 38 | São Tomé & Príncipe |
| | 39 | Niger |
| | 40 | Guinea |
| | 41 | Chad |
| | 42 | Equatorial Guinea |
| | 43 | Liberia |
| | 44 | Angola |
| | 45 | Sudan |
| | 46 | Sierra Leone |
| | 47 | Congo, Dem. Rep. |
| smallest | n/a | Somalia |

### Domestic Credit to the Private Sector as % of GDP

IMF, World Bank

| | | 2003-2006 |
|---|---|---|
| largest | 1 | South Africa |
| | | SSA average |
| | 2 | Mauritius |
| | 3 | Namibia |
| | 4 | Cape Verde |
| | 5 | Seychelles |
| | 6 | Eritrea |
| | 7 | São Tomé & Príncipe |
| | 8 | Mauritania |
| | 8 | Zimbabwe |
| | 9 | Ethiopia |
| | 10 | Kenya |
| | 11 | Burundi |
| | 12 | Senegal |
| | 13 | Djibouti |
| | 14 | Swaziland |
| | 15 | Botswana |
| | 16 | Mali |
| | 17 | Togo |
| | 18 | Burkina Faso |
| | 19 | Benin |
| | 20 | Nigeria |
| | 21 | Ghana |
| | 22 | Gambia, The |
| | 23 | Côte d'Ivoire |
| | 24 | Rwanda |
| | 25 | Tanzania |
| | 26 | Madagascar |
| | 27 | Cameroon |
| | 28 | Gabon |
| | 29 | Malawi |
| | 30 | Comoros |
| | 31 | Zambia |
| | 32 | Lesotho |
| | 33 | Mozambique |
| | 34 | Uganda |
| | 35 | Niger |
| | 36 | Central African Rep. |
| | 37 | Liberia |
| | 38 | Sudan |
| | 39 | Angola |
| | 40 | Sierra Leone |
| | 41 | Guinea |
| | 42 | Equatorial Guinea |
| | 43 | Chad |
| | 44 | Congo, Rep. |
| | 45 | Guinea-Bissau |
| | 46 | Congo, Dem. Rep. |
| smallest | n/a | Somalia |

# appendix B9: performance tables - investor confidence

## Domestic Credit to the Private Sector as $PPP

IMF, World Bank

| | 1999-2002 |
|---|---|
| 1 | South Africa |
| 2 | Nigeria |
| 3 | Kenya |
| 4 | Ethiopia |
| 5 | Mauritius |
| 6 | Côte d'Ivoire |
| 7 | Namibia |
| 8 | Cameroon |
| 9 | Botswana |
| 10 | Senegal |
| 11 | Ghana |
| 12 | Gabon |
| 13 | Mali |
| 14 | Tanzania |
| 15 | Burkina Faso |
| 16 | Sudan |
| 17 | Angola |
| 18 | Madagascar |
| 19 | Uganda |
| 20 | Eritrea |
| 21 | Mauritania |
| 22 | Benin |
| 23 | Mozambique |
| 24 | Zimbabwe |
| 25 | Zambia |
| 26 | Togo |
| 27 | Congo, Rep. |
| 28 | Rwanda |
| 29 | Burundi |
| 30 | Swaziland |
| 31 | Malawi |
| 32 | Djibouti |
| 33 | Lesotho |
| 34 | Guinea |
| 35 | Cape Verde |
| 36 | Chad |
| 37 | Niger |
| 38 | Seychelles |
| 39 | Gambia, The |
| 40 | Equatorial Guinea |
| 41 | Central African Rep. |
| 42 | Congo, Dem. Rep. |
| 43 | Sierra Leone |
| 44 | Comoros |
| 45 | Liberia |
| 46 | Guinea-Bissau |
| 47 | São Tomé & Príncipe |
| n/a | Somalia |
| | |

*largest* (top) — *smallest* (bottom)

## Domestic Credit to the Private Sector as $PPP

IMF, World Bank

| | 2003-2006 |
|---|---|
| 1 | South Africa |
| 2 | Nigeria |
| 3 | Kenya |
| 4 | Ethiopia |
| 5 | Mauritius |
| 6 | Namibia |
| 7 | Côte d'Ivoire |
| 8 | Botswana |
| 9 | Senegal |
| 10 | Tanzania |
| 11 | Ghana |
| 12 | Sudan |
| 13 | Angola |
| 14 | Cameroon |
| 15 | Burkina Faso |
| 16 | Mali |
| 17 | Uganda |
| 18 | Gabon |
| 19 | Benin |
| 20 | Madagascar |
| 21 | Mauritania |
| 22 | Eritrea |
| 23 | Mozambique |
| 24 | Zambia |
| 25 | Swaziland |
| 26 | Rwanda |
| 27 | Malawi |
| 28 | Togo |
| 29 | Zimbabwe |
| 30 | Burundi |
| 31 | Niger |
| 32 | Equatorial Guinea |
| 33 | Cape Verde |
| 34 | Chad |
| 35 | Guinea |
| 36 | Seychelles |
| 37 | Congo, Rep. |
| 38 | Djibouti |
| 39 | Congo, Dem. Rep. |
| 40 | Gambia, The |
| 41 | Lesotho |
| 42 | Central African Rep. |
| 43 | Sierra Leone |
| 44 | Liberia |
| 45 | São Tomé & Príncipe |
| 46 | Comoros |
| 47 | Guinea-Bissau |
| n/a | Somalia |
| | |

*largest* (top) — *smallest* (bottom)

## Growth of Domestic Credit to the Private Sector

IMF, World Bank

| | 1999-2002 |
|---|---|
| 1 | Sudan |
| 2 | Nigeria |
| 3 | Angola |
| 4 | Sierra Leone |
| 5 | Equatorial Guinea |
| 6 | Benin |
| 7 | Botswana |
| 8 | Gambia, The |
| 9 | Tanzania |
| 10 | Uganda |
| 11 | Mauritania |
| 12 | Burundi |
| 13 | Rwanda |
| 14 | Ghana |
| 15 | Ethiopia |
| 16 | Seychelles |
| 17 | São Tomé & Príncipe |
| 18 | Chad |
| 19 | Cameroon |
| 20 | Cape Verde |
| 21 | Senegal |
| 22 | Burkina Faso |
| 23 | Niger |
| 24 | Central African Rep. |
| 25 | Mali |
| 26 | South Africa |
| 27 | Mauritius |
| 28 | Comoros |
| 29 | Gabon |
| 30 | Zambia |
| | SSA average |
| 31 | Namibia |
| 32 | Swaziland |
| 33 | Madagascar |
| 34 | Guinea |
| 35 | Zimbabwe |
| 36 | Lesotho |
| 37 | Guinea-Bissau |
| 38 | Kenya |
| 39 | Côte d'Ivoire |
| 40 | Malawi |
| 41 | Togo |
| 42 | Mozambique |
| 43 | Congo, Rep. |
| n/a | Congo, Dem. Rep. |
| n/a | Djibouti |
| n/a | Eritrea |
| n/a | Liberia |
| n/a | Somalia |

*fastest* (top) — *slowest* (bottom)

## Growth of Domestic Credit to the Private Sector

IMF, World Bank

| | 2003-2006 |
|---|---|
| 1 | Mozambique |
| 2 | São Tomé & Príncipe |
| 4 | Equatorial Guinea |
| 5 | Malawi |
| 6 | Angola |
| 7 | Tanzania |
| 9 | Seychelles |
| 10 | Guinea-Bissau |
| 11 | Niger |
| 12 | Zambia |
| 13 | Swaziland |
| 14 | Ghana |
| | SSA average |
| 15 | Sierra Leone |
| 16 | Benin |
| 17 | Rwanda |
| 18 | Namibia |
| 19 | Togo |
| 20 | Burkina Faso |
| 21 | Mauritius |
| 22 | Ethiopia |
| 23 | Guinea |
| 24 | Uganda |
| 25 | South Africa |
| 26 | Kenya |
| 27 | Cape Verde |
| 28 | Senegal |
| 29 | Madagascar |
| 30 | Botswana |
| 31 | Gambia, The |
| 32 | Central African Rep. |
| 33 | Mali |
| 34 | Comoros |
| 35 | Nigeria |
| 36 | Chad |
| 37 | Sudan |
| 38 | Mauritania |
| 39 | Lesotho |
| 40 | Congo, Rep. |
| 41 | Cameroon |
| 42 | Côte d'Ivoire |
| 43 | Burundi |
| 45 | Gabon |
| 46 | Zimbabwe |
| n/a | Congo, Dem. Rep. |
| n/a | Eritrea |
| n/a | Liberia |
| n/a | Djibouti |
| n/a | Somalia |

*fastest* (top) — *slowest* (bottom)

# B10 performance tables - regulatory environment

| | Ease of Starting a Business (IFC/ World Bank) | | Ease of Starting a Business (IFC/ World Bank) | | Ease of Dealing with Construction Permits (IFC/World Bank) | |
|---|---|---|---|---|---|---|
| | 2008 | | 2009 | | 2008 | |
| easiest | 1 | Mauritius | 1 | Mauritius | 1 | Kenya |
| | 2 | Seychelles | 2 | South Africa | 2 | Swaziland |
| | 3 | South Africa | 3 | Sierra Leone | 3 | Namibia |
| | 4 | Madagascar | 4 | Madagascar | 4 | Mauritius |
| | 5 | Rwanda | 5 | Rwanda | 5 | Gabon |
| | 6 | Nigeria | 6 | Seychelles | 6 | South Africa |
| | 7 | Zambia | 7 | Zambia | 7 | Seychelles |
| | 8 | Sierra Leone | 8 | Botswana | 8 | Comoros |
| | 9 | Gambia, The | 9 | Liberia | 9 | Ethiopia |
| | 10 | Sudan | 10 | Nigeria | 10 | Senegal |
| | 10 | Tanzania | 11 | Senegal | 11 | Congo, Rep. |
| | 11 | Botswana | 12 | Gambia, The | 12 | Chad |
| | 12 | Namibia | 13 | Sudan | 13 | Gambia, The |
| | 13 | Burkina Faso | 14 | Kenya | 14 | Cape Verde |
| | 14 | Ethiopia | 14 | Tanzania | 15 | Uganda |
| | 15 | Malawi | 15 | Namibia | 16 | Equatorial Guinea |
| | 16 | Kenya | 16 | Burkina Faso | 17 | Djibouti |
| | 17 | Uganda | 17 | Ethiopia | 18 | Mali |
| | 18 | Burundi | 18 | Malawi | 18 | Guinea-Bissau |
| | 19 | Mozambique | 19 | Lesotho | 19 | São Tomé & Príncipe |
| | 20 | Lesotho | 20 | Uganda | 20 | Malawi |
| | 20 | São Tomé & Príncipe | 21 | São Tomé & Príncipe | 21 | Botswana |
| | 21 | Benin | 22 | Ghana | 22 | Benin |
| | 22 | Ghana | 23 | Burundi | 23 | Rwanda |
| | 23 | Central African Rep. | 24 | Mauritania | 24 | Sudan |
| | 24 | Liberia | 25 | Mozambique | 25 | Central African Rep. |
| | 25 | Swaziland | 26 | Gabon | 26 | Angola |
| | 26 | Zimbabwe | 27 | Benin | 27 | Congo, Dem. Rep. |
| | 27 | Comoros | 28 | Central African Rep. | 28 | Madagascar |
| | 28 | Congo, Dem. Rep. | 29 | Swaziland | 29 | Ghana |
| | 29 | Gabon | 30 | Congo, Dem. Rep. | 30 | Mauritania |
| | 30 | Mali | 31 | Angola | 31 | Togo |
| | 31 | Niger | 32 | Congo, Rep. | 32 | Lesotho |
| | 32 | Congo, Rep. | 33 | Niger | 33 | Mozambique |
| | 33 | Côte d'Ivoire | 34 | Comoros | 34 | Zambia |
| | 34 | Cape Verde | 35 | Mali | 35 | Sierra Leone |
| | 35 | Senegal | 36 | Cape Verde | 36 | Cameroon |
| | 36 | Cameroon | 37 | Zimbabwe | 37 | Niger |
| | 37 | Djibouti | 38 | Côte d'Ivoire | 38 | Côte d'Ivoire |
| | 38 | Mauritania | 39 | Cameroon | 39 | Guinea |
| | 39 | Guinea | 40 | Djibouti | 40 | Nigeria |
| | 40 | Equatorial Guinea | 41 | Equatorial Guinea | 41 | Burkina Faso |
| | 41 | Angola | 42 | Guinea | 42 | Tanzania |
| | 42 | Eritrea | 43 | Eritrea | 43 | Burundi |
| | 43 | Togo | 44 | Togo | 44 | Zimbabwe |
| | 44 | Chad | 45 | Chad | 45 | Liberia |
| | 45 | Guinea-Bissau | 46 | Guinea-Bissau | 46 | Eritrea |
| | n/a | Somalia | n/a | Somalia | n/a | Somalia |
| toughest | | | | | | |

### Ease of Dealing with Construction Permits

IFC/World Bank

| | Rank | 2009 |
|---|---|---|
| easiest | 1 | Kenya |
| | 2 | Swaziland |
| | 3 | Mauritius |
| | 4 | Namibia |
| | 5 | South Africa |
| | 6 | Seychelles |
| | 7 | Ethiopia |
| | 8 | Gabon |
| | 9 | Comoros |
| | 10 | Congo, Rep. |
| | 11 | Chad |
| | 12 | Gambia, The |
| | 13 | Cape Verde |
| | 14 | Uganda |
| | 15 | Equatorial Guinea |
| | 16 | Rwanda |
| | 17 | Djibouti |
| | 18 | Madagascar |
| | 19 | Burkina Faso |
| | 19 | Mali |
| | 20 | Guinea-Bissau |
| | 21 | São Tomé & Príncipe |
| | 22 | Senegal |
| | 23 | Botswana |
| | 24 | Angola |
| | 25 | Benin |
| | 26 | Sudan |
| | 27 | Central African Rep. |
| | 28 | Congo, Dem. Rep. |
| | 29 | Ghana |
| | 29 | Mauritania |
| | 30 | Togo |
| | 31 | Zambia |
| | 32 | Lesotho |
| | 33 | Nigeria |
| | 34 | Mozambique |
| | 35 | Cameroon |
| | 36 | Malawi |
| | 37 | Niger |
| | 38 | Côte d'Ivoire |
| | 39 | Guinea |
| | 40 | Sierra Leone |
| | 41 | Tanzania |
| | 42 | Burundi |
| | 43 | Zimbabwe |
| | 44 | Liberia |
| | 45 | Eritrea |
| | n/a | Somalia |
| toughest | | |

### Ease of Employing Workers

IFC/World Bank

| | Rank | 2008 |
|---|---|---|
| easiest | 1 | Uganda |
| | 2 | Gambia, The |
| | 3 | Nigeria |
| | 4 | Namibia |
| | 5 | Swaziland |
| | 6 | Eritrea |
| | 7 | Mauritius |
| | 8 | Kenya |
| | 9 | Lesotho |
| | 10 | Botswana |
| | 11 | Mali |
| | 12 | Ethiopia |
| | 13 | Malawi |
| | 14 | South Africa |
| | 15 | Rwanda |
| | 16 | Seychelles |
| | 17 | Burundi |
| | 17 | Guinea |
| | 18 | Liberia |
| | 19 | Côte d'Ivoire |
| | 20 | Benin |
| | 21 | Mauritania |
| | 22 | Cameroon |
| | 23 | Zambia |
| | 24 | Zimbabwe |
| | 25 | Djibouti |
| | 26 | Chad |
| | 27 | Ghana |
| | 28 | Sudan |
| | 29 | Cape Verde |
| | 30 | Togo |
| | 31 | Central African Rep. |
| | 32 | Madagascar |
| | 33 | Tanzania |
| | 34 | Burkina Faso |
| | 35 | Comoros |
| | 36 | Senegal |
| | 37 | Niger |
| | 38 | Mozambique |
| | 39 | Gabon |
| | 40 | Congo, Rep. |
| | 41 | Sierra Leone |
| | 42 | Congo, Dem. Rep. |
| | 43 | Angola |
| | 44 | Guinea-Bissau |
| | 45 | Equatorial Guinea |
| | 46 | São Tomé & Príncipe |
| | n/a | Somalia |
| toughest | | |

### Ease of Employing Workers

IFC/World Bank

| | Rank | 2009 |
|---|---|---|
| easiest | 1 | Uganda |
| | 2 | Nigeria |
| | 3 | Namibia |
| | 4 | Swaziland |
| | 5 | Gambia, The |
| | 6 | Burkina Faso |
| | 7 | Lesotho |
| | 8 | Mauritius |
| | 9 | Eritrea |
| | 10 | Kenya |
| | 11 | Burundi |
| | 12 | Botswana |
| | 13 | Rwanda |
| | 14 | Mali |
| | 15 | Ethiopia |
| | 16 | Malawi |
| | 17 | South Africa |
| | 18 | Liberia |
| | 19 | Côte d'Ivoire |
| | 20 | Guinea |
| | 21 | Benin |
| | 22 | Seychelles |
| | 23 | Mauritania |
| | 24 | Cameroon |
| | 25 | Zimbabwe |
| | 26 | Zambia |
| | 27 | Djibouti |
| | 28 | Chad |
| | 29 | Tanzania |
| | 30 | Sudan |
| | 31 | Ghana |
| | 32 | Central African Rep. |
| | 33 | Madagascar |
| | 34 | Gabon |
| | 35 | Togo |
| | 36 | Mozambique |
| | 37 | Comoros |
| | 38 | Senegal |
| | 39 | Niger |
| | 40 | Cape Verde |
| | 41 | Congo, Rep. |
| | 42 | Sierra Leone |
| | 43 | Angola |
| | 44 | Congo, Dem. Rep. |
| | 45 | Guinea-Bissau |
| | 46 | Equatorial Guinea |
| | 47 | São Tomé & Príncipe |
| | n/a | Somalia |
| toughest | | |

### Ease of Registering Property

IFC/World Bank

| | Rank | 2008 |
|---|---|---|
| easiest | 1 | Ghana |
| | 2 | Sudan |
| | 3 | Botswana |
| | 4 | Seychelles |
| | 5 | Mauritania |
| | 6 | Equatorial Guinea |
| | 7 | Niger |
| | 8 | South Africa |
| | 9 | Zimbabwe |
| | 10 | Comoros |
| | 11 | Malawi |
| | 12 | Mali |
| | 13 | Central African Rep. |
| | 14 | Benin |
| | 15 | Kenya |
| | 16 | Burundi |
| | 17 | Chad |
| | 18 | Zambia |
| | 19 | Mozambique |
| | 20 | Cape Verde |
| | 21 | Namibia |
| | 22 | Djibouti |
| | 23 | Lesotho |
| | 24 | Gambia, The |
| | 25 | Cameroon |
| | 26 | Rwanda |
| | 27 | Congo, Dem. Rep. |
| | 28 | Swaziland |
| | 29 | São Tomé & Príncipe |
| | 30 | Ethiopia |
| | 31 | Gabon |
| | 32 | Togo |
| | 33 | Guinea |
| | 34 | Mauritius |
| | 34 | Côte d'Ivoire |
| | 35 | Senegal |
| | 36 | Eritrea |
| | 37 | Tanzania |
| | 38 | Uganda |
| | 39 | Guinea-Bissau |
| | 40 | Madagascar |
| | 41 | Angola |
| | 42 | Liberia |
| | 43 | Congo, Rep. |
| | 44 | Burkina Faso |
| | 45 | Sierra Leone |
| | 46 | Nigeria |
| | n/a | Somalia |
| toughest | | |

### Ease of Registering Property

IFC/World Bank

| | Rank | 2009 |
|---|---|---|
| easiest | 1 | Botswana |
| | 2 | Ghana |
| | 3 | Sudan |
| | 4 | Seychelles |
| | 5 | Rwanda |
| | 6 | Mauritania |
| | 7 | Equatorial Guinea |
| | 8 | Niger |
| | 9 | Zimbabwe |
| | 10 | South Africa |
| | 11 | Zambia |
| | 12 | Comoros |
| | 13 | Mali |
| | 14 | Malawi |
| | 15 | Gambia, The |
| | 16 | Kenya |
| | 16 | Benin |
| | 17 | Cape Verde |
| | 18 | Burundi |
| | 19 | Mauritius |
| | 20 | Namibia |
| | 21 | Chad |
| | 22 | Central African Rep. |
| | 23 | Djibouti |
| | 24 | Lesotho |
| | 25 | Cameroon |
| | 26 | Côte d'Ivoire |
| | 27 | Tanzania |
| | 28 | Madagascar |
| | 29 | Burkina Faso |
| | 30 | Mozambique |
| | 31 | São Tomé & Príncipe |
| | 32 | Congo, Dem. Rep. |
| | 33 | Swaziland |
| | 34 | Ethiopia |
| | 35 | Togo |
| | 36 | Guinea |
| | 37 | Gabon |
| | 38 | Senegal |
| | 39 | Sierra Leone |
| | 40 | Eritrea |
| | 41 | Uganda |
| | 42 | Guinea-Bissau |
| | 43 | Congo, Rep. |
| | 44 | Liberia |
| | 45 | Angola |
| | 46 | Nigeria |
| | n/a | Somalia |
| toughest | | |

### Ease of Getting Credit

IFC/World Bank

*easiest*

| Rank | 2008 |
|---|---|
| 1 | Kenya |
| 2 | Botswana |
| 2 | South Africa |
| 3 | Namibia |
| 3 | Swaziland |
| 4 | Cape Verde |
| 5 | Angola |
| 5 | Malawi |
| 5 | Nigeria |
| 6 | Ethiopia |
| 6 | Mauritius |
| 6 | Mozambique |
| 6 | Zambia |
| 6 | Zimbabwe |
| 7 | Benin |
| 7 | Burkina Faso |
| 7 | Cameroon |
| 7 | Central African Rep. |
| 7 | Congo, Rep. |
| 7 | Gabon |
| 7 | Ghana |
| 7 | Lesotho |
| 7 | Mauritania |
| 7 | São Tomé & Príncipe |
| 7 | Sierra Leone |
| 7 | Tanzania |
| 8 | Chad |
| 8 | Côte d'Ivoire |
| 8 | Djibouti |
| 8 | Equatorial Guinea |
| 8 | Gambia, The |
| 8 | Guinea |
| 8 | Guinea-Bissau |
| 8 | Liberia |
| 8 | Mali |
| 8 | Niger |
| 8 | Senegal |
| 8 | Sudan |
| 8 | Togo |
| 9 | Comoros |
| 9 | Congo, Dem. Rep. |
| 9 | Eritrea |
| 9 | Rwanda |
| 9 | Seychelles |
| 9 | Uganda |
| 10 | Burundi |
| 11 | Madagascar |
| n/a | Somalia |

*toughest*

### Ease of Getting Credit

IFC/World Bank

*easiest*

| Rank | 2009 |
|---|---|
| 1 | South Africa |
| 2 | Kenya |
| 3 | Namibia |
| 4 | Botswana |
| 4 | Swaziland |
| 5 | Zambia |
| 6 | Angola |
| 6 | Lesotho |
| 6 | Malawi |
| 6 | Mauritius |
| 6 | Nigeria |
| 6 | Tanzania |
| 6 | Zimbabwe |
| 7 | Ghana |
| 7 | Uganda |
| 8 | Cape Verde |
| 8 | Ethiopia |
| 8 | Mozambique |
| 9 | Cameroon |
| 9 | Central African Rep. |
| 9 | Congo, Rep. |
| 9 | Equatorial Guinea |
| 9 | Gabon |
| 9 | Gambia, The |
| 9 | Liberia |
| 9 | Sudan |
| 10 | Benin |
| 10 | Burkina Faso |
| 10 | Chad |
| 10 | Côte d'Ivoire |
| 10 | Guinea-Bissau |
| 10 | Mali |
| 10 | Mauritania |
| 10 | Niger |
| 10 | Rwanda |
| 10 | Senegal |
| 10 | Sierra Leone |
| 10 | Togo |
| 11 | Burundi |
| 11 | Comoros |
| 11 | Congo, Dem. Rep. |
| 11 | Guinea |
| 11 | São Tomé & Príncipe |
| 11 | Seychelles |
| 12 | Djibouti |
| 12 | Eritrea |
| 12 | Madagascar |
| n/a | Somalia |

*toughest*

### Extent of Investor Protection

IFC/World Bank

*best*

| Rank | 2008 |
|---|---|
| 1 | South Africa |
| 2 | Mauritius |
| 3 | Ghana |
| 3 | Mozambique |
| 4 | Angola |
| 4 | Madagascar |
| 4 | Nigeria |
| 4 | Seychelles |
| 5 | Malawi |
| 5 | Namibia |
| 5 | Zambia |
| 6 | Kenya |
| 6 | Tanzania |
| 7 | Eritrea |
| 7 | Sierra Leone |
| 8 | Botswana |
| 8 | Cameroon |
| 8 | Ethiopia |
| 8 | Zimbabwe |
| 9 | Cape Verde |
| 9 | Central African Rep. |
| 9 | Chad |
| 9 | Comoros |
| 9 | Guinea-Bissau |
| 9 | São Tomé & Príncipe |
| 9 | Uganda |
| 10 | Burkina Faso |
| 10 | Liberia |
| 10 | Togo |
| 11 | Equatorial Guinea |
| 11 | Lesotho |
| 11 | Mauritania |
| 11 | Sudan |
| 12 | Benin |
| 12 | Burundi |
| 12 | Congo, Dem. Rep. |
| 12 | Congo, Rep. |
| 12 | Côte d'Ivoire |
| 12 | Gabon |
| 12 | Mali |
| 12 | Niger |
| 13 | Senegal |
| 14 | Gambia, The |
| 14 | Guinea |
| 14 | Rwanda |
| 15 | Djibouti |
| 16 | Swaziland |
| n/a | Somalia |

*worst*

### Extent of Investor Protection

IFC/World Bank

*best*

| Rank | 2009 |
|---|---|
| 1 | South Africa |
| 2 | Mauritius |
| 3 | Botswana |
| 3 | Ghana |
| 3 | Mozambique |
| 4 | Angola |
| 4 | Madagascar |
| 4 | Nigeria |
| 4 | Seychelles |
| 4 | Sierra Leone |
| 5 | Malawi |
| 5 | Namibia |
| 5 | Zambia |
| 6 | Kenya |
| 6 | Tanzania |
| 7 | Eritrea |
| 8 | Cameroon |
| 8 | Ethiopia |
| 8 | Zimbabwe |
| 9 | Cape Verde |
| 9 | Central African Rep. |
| 9 | Chad |
| 9 | Comoros |
| 9 | Guinea-Bissau |
| 9 | Uganda |
| 10 | Burkina Faso |
| 10 | Equatorial Guinea |
| 10 | Lesotho |
| 10 | Liberia |
| 10 | Mauritania |
| 10 | Togo |
| 11 | Benin |
| 11 | Burundi |
| 11 | Congo, Dem. Rep. |
| 11 | Congo, Rep. |
| 11 | Côte d'Ivoire |
| 11 | Gabon |
| 11 | Mali |
| 11 | Niger |
| 11 | São Tomé & Príncipe |
| 11 | Sudan |
| 12 | Senegal |
| 13 | Gambia, The |
| 13 | Guinea |
| 13 | Rwanda |
| 14 | Djibouti |
| 15 | Swaziland |
| n/a | Somalia |

*worst*

### Ease of Paying Taxes

IFC/World Bank

*easiest*

| Rank | 2008 |
|---|---|
| 1 | Mauritius |
| 2 | Botswana |
| 3 | Ethiopia |
| 4 | Zambia |
| 5 | Seychelles |
| 6 | Swaziland |
| 7 | Comoros |
| 8 | Namibia |
| 9 | Lesotho |
| 10 | Rwanda |
| 11 | Djibouti |
| 12 | Uganda |
| 13 | Sudan |
| 14 | South Africa |
| 15 | Mozambique |
| 16 | Ghana |
| 17 | Malawi |
| 18 | Madagascar |
| 19 | Gabon |
| 20 | Eritrea |
| 21 | Tanzania |
| 22 | Nigeria |
| 23 | Burundi |
| 24 | Guinea-Bissau |
| 25 | Niger |
| 26 | Cape Verde |
| 27 | Liberia |
| 28 | Angola |
| 29 | Chad |
| 30 | Burkina Faso |
| 31 | Equatorial Guinea |
| 32 | Togo |
| 33 | Côte d'Ivoire |
| 34 | Zimbabwe |
| 35 | Sierra Leone |
| 36 | Congo, Dem. Rep. |
| 37 | Mali |
| 38 | São Tomé & Príncipe |
| 39 | Kenya |
| 40 | Benin |
| 41 | Guinea |
| 42 | Senegal |
| 43 | Cameroon |
| 44 | Mauritania |
| 45 | Gambia, The |
| 46 | Central African Rep. |
| 47 | Congo, Rep. |
| n/a | Somalia |

*toughest*

## Ease of Paying Taxes

IFC/World Bank

*easiest*

| | 2009 |
|---|---|
| 1 | Mauritius |
| 2 | Botswana |
| 3 | South Africa |
| 4 | Ethiopia |
| 5 | Zambia |
| 6 | Seychelles |
| 7 | Swaziland |
| 8 | Lesotho |
| 9 | Comoros |
| 10 | Rwanda |
| 11 | Malawi |
| 12 | Liberia |
| 13 | Djibouti |
| 14 | Ghana |
| 15 | Sudan |
| 16 | Uganda |
| 17 | Mozambique |
| 18 | Madagascar |
| 19 | Namibia |
| 20 | Gabon |
| 21 | Eritrea |
| 22 | Tanzania |
| 23 | Burundi |
| 24 | Cape Verde |
| 25 | Guinea-Bissau |
| 26 | Niger |
| 26 | Nigeria |
| 27 | Angola |
| 27 | Chad |
| 28 | Burkina Faso |
| 29 | Togo |
| 30 | Côte d'Ivoire |
| 31 | São Tomé & Príncipe |
| 32 | Congo, Dem. Rep. |
| 33 | Mali |
| 34 | Zimbabwe |
| 35 | Kenya |
| 36 | Sierra Leone |
| 37 | Equatorial Guinea |
| 38 | Benin |
| 39 | Guinea |
| 40 | Senegal |
| 41 | Cameroon |
| 42 | Mauritania |
| 43 | Gambia, The |
| 44 | Central African Rep. |
| 45 | Congo, Rep. |
| n/a | Somalia |

*toughest*

## Ease of External Trade

IFC/World Bank

*easiest*

| | 2008 |
|---|---|
| 1 | Mauritius |
| 2 | Cape Verde |
| 3 | Ghana |
| 4 | Djibouti |
| 5 | Gambia, The |
| 6 | Togo |
| 7 | Seychelles |
| 8 | São Tomé & Príncipe |
| 9 | Liberia |
| 10 | Tanzania |
| 11 | Guinea |
| 12 | Gabon |
| 13 | Guinea-Bissau |
| 14 | Comoros |
| 15 | Benin |
| 16 | Madagascar |
| 17 | Lesotho |
| 18 | Sierra Leone |
| 19 | Cameroon |
| 20 | Equatorial Guinea |
| 21 | South Africa |
| 22 | Senegal |
| 23 | Nigeria |
| 24 | Mozambique |
| 25 | Uganda |
| 26 | Sudan |
| 27 | Namibia |
| 28 | Botswana |
| 29 | Swaziland |
| 30 | Côte d'Ivoire |
| 31 | Kenya |
| 32 | Ethiopia |
| 33 | Mauritania |
| 34 | Congo, Dem. Rep. |
| 35 | Chad |
| 36 | Eritrea |
| 37 | Zambia |
| 38 | Malawi |
| 39 | Mali |
| 40 | Niger |
| 41 | Angola |
| 42 | Rwanda |
| 43 | Burundi |
| 44 | Zimbabwe |
| 45 | Burkina Faso |
| 46 | Congo, Rep. |
| 47 | Central African Rep. |
| n/a | Somalia |

*toughest*

## Ease of External Trade

IFC/World Bank

*easiest*

| | 2009 |
|---|---|
| 1 | Mauritius |
| 2 | Djibouti |
| 3 | Cape Verde |
| 4 | Senegal |
| 5 | Gambia, The |
| 6 | Ghana |
| 7 | Togo |
| 8 | São Tomé & Príncipe |
| 9 | Seychelles |
| 10 | Tanzania |
| 11 | Madagascar |
| 12 | Guinea |
| 13 | Guinea-Bissau |
| 14 | Liberia |
| 15 | Gabon |
| 16 | Benin |
| 16 | Comoros |
| 17 | Sierra Leone |
| 18 | Equatorial Guinea |
| 19 | Cameroon |
| 20 | Sudan |
| 21 | Mozambique |
| 22 | Lesotho |
| 23 | Nigeria |
| 24 | Uganda |
| 25 | South Africa |
| 26 | Kenya |
| 27 | Botswana |
| 28 | Namibia |
| 29 | Ethiopia |
| 30 | Zambia |
| 31 | Swaziland |
| 32 | Côte d'Ivoire |
| 33 | Mauritania |
| 34 | Chad |
| 35 | Congo, Dem. Rep. |
| 36 | Zimbabwe |
| 37 | Eritrea |
| 38 | Mali |
| 39 | Malawi |
| 40 | Rwanda |
| 41 | Niger |
| 42 | Burundi |
| 43 | Angola |
| 44 | Burkina Faso |
| 45 | Central African Rep. |
| 46 | Congo, Rep. |
| n/a | Somalia |

*toughest*

## Ease of Enforcing Contracts

IFC/World Bank

*easiest*

| | 2008 |
|---|---|
| 1 | Namibia |
| 2 | Tanzania |
| 3 | Rwanda |
| 4 | Ghana |
| 5 | Eritrea |
| 6 | Cape Verde |
| 7 | Gambia, The |
| 8 | Seychelles |
| 9 | Equatorial Guinea |
| 10 | Zimbabwe |
| 11 | Ethiopia |
| 12 | Mauritius |
| 13 | South Africa |
| 14 | Zambia |
| 15 | Mauritania |
| 16 | Nigeria |
| 17 | Botswana |
| 18 | Lesotho |
| 19 | Kenya |
| 20 | Burkina Faso |
| 21 | São Tomé & Príncipe |
| 22 | Uganda |
| 23 | Côte d'Ivoire |
| 24 | Guinea |
| 25 | Swaziland |
| 26 | Niger |
| 27 | Malawi |
| 28 | Guinea-Bissau |
| 29 | Mozambique |
| 30 | Sierra Leone |
| 31 | Sudan |
| 32 | Gabon |
| 33 | Burundi |
| 33 | Senegal |
| 34 | Madagascar |
| 35 | Comoros |
| 36 | Togo |
| 37 | Congo, Rep. |
| 38 | Mali |
| 39 | Djibouti |
| 40 | Liberia |
| 41 | Benin |
| 42 | Chad |
| 43 | Central African Rep. |
| 44 | Cameroon |
| 45 | Congo, Dem. Rep. |
| 46 | Angola |
| n/a | Somalia |

*toughest*

## Ease of Enforcing Contracts

IFC/World Bank

*easiest*

| | 2009 |
|---|---|
| 1 | Tanzania |
| 2 | Namibia |
| 3 | Cape Verde |
| 4 | Rwanda |
| 5 | Ghana |
| 6 | Eritrea |
| 7 | Seychelles |
| 8 | Gambia, The |
| 9 | Equatorial Guinea |
| 10 | Mauritius |
| 11 | Zimbabwe |
| 12 | Ethiopia |
| 13 | South Africa |
| 14 | Mauritania |
| 15 | Zambia |
| 16 | Nigeria |
| 17 | Botswana |
| 18 | Lesotho |
| 19 | Kenya |
| 20 | Burkina Faso |
| 21 | Uganda |
| 22 | Côte d'Ivoire |
| 22 | Mozambique |
| 23 | Swaziland |
| 24 | Guinea |
| 25 | Niger |
| 26 | Malawi |
| 27 | Guinea-Bissau |
| 28 | Sierra Leone |
| 29 | Sudan |
| 30 | Senegal |
| 31 | Gabon |
| 32 | Comoros |
| 33 | Togo |
| 34 | Madagascar |
| 35 | Congo, Rep. |
| 36 | Mali |
| 37 | Djibouti |
| 38 | Liberia |
| 39 | Chad |
| 40 | Central African Rep. |
| 41 | Burundi |
| 42 | São Tomé & Príncipe |
| 43 | Cameroon |
| 44 | Congo, Dem. Rep. |
| 45 | Benin |
| 46 | Angola |
| n/a | Somalia |

*toughest*

### Ease of Closing a Business

IFC/World Bank

| | | 2008 |
|---|---|---|
| easiest | 1 | Botswana |
| | 2 | Namibia |
| | 3 | Uganda |
| | 4 | Swaziland |
| | 5 | Lesotho |
| | 6 | Mauritius |
| | 7 | South Africa |
| | 8 | Ethiopia |
| | 9 | Côte d'Ivoire |
| | 10 | Senegal |
| | 11 | Kenya |
| | 12 | Zambia |
| | 13 | Nigeria |
| | 14 | Togo |
| | 15 | Burkina Faso |
| | 16 | Cameroon |
| | 17 | Ghana |
| | 18 | Benin |
| | 19 | Mali |
| | 20 | Tanzania |
| | 21 | Congo, Rep. |
| | 22 | Guinea |
| | 23 | Gambia, The |
| | 24 | Djibouti |
| | 25 | Gabon |
| | 26 | Niger |
| | 27 | Mozambique |
| | 28 | Malawi |
| | 29 | Angola |
| | 30 | Sierra Leone |
| | 31 | Mauritania |
| | 32 | Liberia |
| | 33 | Congo, Dem. Rep. |
| | 34 | Zimbabwe |
| | 35 | Burundi |
| | 35 | Cape Verde |
| | 35 | Central African Rep. |
| | 35 | Chad |
| | 35 | Comoros |
| | 35 | Equatorial Guinea |
| | 35 | Eritrea |
| | 35 | Guinea-Bissau |
| | 35 | Madagascar |
| | 35 | Rwanda |
| | 35 | São Tomé & Príncipe |
| | 35 | Seychelles |
| | 35 | Sudan |
| | n/a | Somalia |
| toughest | | |

### Ease of Closing a Business

IFC/World Bank

| | | 2009 |
|---|---|---|
| easiest | 1 | Botswana |
| | 2 | Uganda |
| | 3 | Namibia |
| | 4 | Swaziland |
| | 5 | Côte d'Ivoire |
| | 6 | Lesotho |
| | 7 | Mauritius |
| | 8 | South Africa |
| | 9 | Ethiopia |
| | 10 | Kenya |
| | 11 | Senegal |
| | 12 | Zambia |
| | 13 | Nigeria |
| | 14 | Togo |
| | 15 | Cameroon |
| | 16 | Ghana |
| | 17 | Guinea |
| | 18 | Burkina Faso |
| | 19 | Tanzania |
| | 20 | Mali |
| | 21 | Congo, Rep. |
| | 22 | Gambia, The |
| | 23 | Benin |
| | 24 | Djibouti |
| | 25 | Mozambique |
| | 26 | Gabon |
| | 27 | Malawi |
| | 28 | Niger |
| | 29 | Angola |
| | 30 | Sierra Leone |
| | 31 | Liberia |
| | 32 | Mauritania |
| | 33 | Congo, Dem. Rep. |
| | 34 | Zimbabwe |
| | 35 | Burundi |
| | 35 | Cape Verde |
| | 35 | Central African Rep. |
| | 35 | Chad |
| | 35 | Comoros |
| | 35 | Equatorial Guinea |
| | 35 | Eritrea |
| | 35 | Guinea-Bissau |
| | 35 | Madagascar |
| | 35 | Rwanda |
| | 35 | São Tomé & Príncipe |
| | 35 | Seychelles |
| | 35 | Sudan |
| | n/a | Somalia |
| toughest | | |

### Overall Ease of Doing Business

IFC/World Bank

| | | 2008 |
|---|---|---|
| easiest | 1 | Mauritius |
| | 2 | South Africa |
| | 3 | Namibia |
| | 4 | Botswana |
| | 5 | Kenya |
| | 6 | Ghana |
| | 7 | Seychelles |
| | 8 | Swaziland |
| | 9 | Ethiopia |
| | 10 | Nigeria |
| | 11 | Zambia |
| | 12 | Uganda |
| | 13 | Lesotho |
| | 14 | Malawi |
| | 15 | Tanzania |
| | 16 | Gambia, The |
| | 17 | Cape Verde |
| | 18 | Mozambique |
| | 19 | Sudan |
| | 20 | Gabon |
| | 21 | Djibouti |
| | 22 | Comoros |
| | 23 | Madagascar |
| | 24 | Rwanda |
| | 25 | Benin |
| | 26 | Zimbabwe |
| | 27 | Cameroon |
| | 28 | Côte d'Ivoire |
| | 29 | Togo |
| | 30 | Mauritania |
| | 31 | Mali |
| | 32 | Sierra Leone |
| | 33 | Burkina Faso |
| | 34 | Senegal |
| | 35 | São Tomé & Príncipe |
| | 36 | Equatorial Guinea |
| | 37 | Guinea |
| | 38 | Angola |
| | 39 | Niger |
| | 40 | Liberia |
| | 41 | Eritrea |
| | 42 | Chad |
| | 43 | Burundi |
| | 44 | Congo, Rep. |
| | 45 | Guinea-Bissau |
| | 46 | Central African Rep. |
| | 47 | Congo, Dem. Rep. |
| | n/a | Somalia |
| toughest | | |

### Overall Ease of Doing Business

IFC/World Bank

| | | 2009 |
|---|---|---|
| easiest | 1 | Mauritius |
| | 2 | South Africa |
| | 3 | Botswana |
| | 4 | Namibia |
| | 5 | Kenya |
| | 6 | Ghana |
| | 7 | Zambia |
| | 8 | Seychelles |
| | 9 | Swaziland |
| | 10 | Uganda |
| | 11 | Ethiopia |
| | 12 | Nigeria |
| | 13 | Lesotho |
| | 14 | Tanzania |
| | 15 | Gambia, The |
| | 16 | Malawi |
| | 17 | Rwanda |
| | 18 | Mozambique |
| | 19 | Cape Verde |
| | 20 | Madagascar |
| | 21 | Sudan |
| | 22 | Burkina Faso |
| | 23 | Senegal |
| | 24 | Gabon |
| | 25 | Djibouti |
| | 26 | Comoros |
| | 27 | Sierra Leone |
| | 28 | Liberia |
| | 29 | Zimbabwe |
| | 30 | Mauritania |
| | 31 | Côte d'Ivoire |
| | 32 | Togo |
| | 33 | Cameroon |
| | 34 | Mali |
| | 35 | Equatorial Guinea |
| | 36 | Angola |
| | 37 | Benin |
| | 38 | Guinea |
| | 39 | Niger |
| | 40 | Eritrea |
| | 41 | Chad |
| | 42 | São Tomé & Príncipe |
| | 43 | Burundi |
| | 44 | Congo, Rep. |
| | 45 | Guinea-Bissau |
| | 46 | Central African Rep. |
| | 47 | Congo, Dem. Rep. |
| | n/a | Somalia |
| toughest | | |

# B11 performance tables - business friendliness

| Index of Economic Freedom<br>The Heritage Foundation & The Wall Street Journal | | Index of Economic Freedom<br>The Heritage Foundation & The Wall Street Journal | | Individual Income Tax Rate<br>The Heritage Foundation & The Wall Street Journal | |
|---|---|---|---|---|---|
| | 2001-2004 | | 2005-2008 | | 2008 |
| best | | best | | lowest | |
| 1 | Botswana | 1 | Botswana | 1 | Angola |
| 2 | Mauritius | 2 | Mauritius | 1 | Mauritius |
| 3 | Namibia | 3 | Uganda | 2 | Guinea-Bissau |
| 4 | South Africa | 4 | South Africa | 3 | Botswana |
| 5 | Uganda | 5 | Madagascar | 3 | Ghana |
| 6 | Swaziland | 6 | Namibia | 3 | Nigeria |
| 7 | Mali | 7 | Swaziland | 4 | Burkina Faso |
| 8 | Senegal | 8 | Kenya | 4 | Djibouti |
| 9 | Burkina Faso | 9 | Cape Verde | 4 | Kenya |
| 10 | Mozambique | 10 | Senegal | 4 | Madagascar |
| 11 | Kenya | 11 | Gambia, The | 4 | Sierra Leone |
| 12 | Tanzania | 12 | Tanzania | 4 | Tanzania |
| 13 | Madagascar | 13 | Ghana | 4 | Uganda |
| 14 | Ghana | 14 | Zambia | 5 | Mozambique |
| 15 | Zambia | 15 | Côte d'Ivoire | 6 | Swaziland |
| 16 | Gabon | 16 | Burkina Faso | 7 | Burundi |
| 17 | Cape Verde | 17 | Mauritania | 7 | Cameroon |
| 18 | Central African Rep. | 18 | Mali | 7 | Equatorial Guinea |
| 19 | Djibouti | 19 | Mozambique | 7 | Ethiopia |
| 20 | Mauritania | 20 | Malawi | 7 | Gambia, The |
| 21 | Côte d'Ivoire | 21 | Guinea | 7 | Lesotho |
| 22 | Benin | 22 | Gabon | 7 | Namibia |
| 23 | Gambia, The | 23 | Cameroon | 7 | Rwanda |
| 24 | Guinea | 24 | Benin | 7 | Zambia |
| 25 | Malawi | 25 | Djibouti | 8 | Benin |
| 26 | Cameroon | 26 | Nigeria | 8 | Guinea |
| 27 | Niger | 27 | Lesotho | 8 | Malawi |
| 28 | Ethiopia | 28 | Equatorial Guinea | 8 | Mali |
| 29 | Nigeria | 29 | Central African Rep. | 8 | Mauritania |
| 30 | Lesotho | 30 | Ethiopia | 8 | South Africa |
| 31 | Equatorial Guinea | 31 | Rwanda | 9 | Cape Verde |
| 32 | Chad | 32 | Niger | 9 | Niger |
| 33 | Rwanda | 33 | Chad | 10 | Zimbabwe |
| 34 | Togo | 34 | Togo | 11 | Central African Rep. |
| 35 | Congo, Rep. | 35 | Sierra Leone | 11 | Congo, Rep. |
| 36 | Guinea-Bissau | 36 | Burundi | 11 | Gabon |
| 37 | Sierra Leone | 37 | Guinea-Bissau | 11 | Senegal |
| 38 | Zimbabwe | 38 | Angola | 12 | Togo |
| 39 | Angola | 39 | Congo, Rep. | 13 | Côte d'Ivoire |
| 39 | Burundi | 40 | Zimbabwe | 14 | Chad |
| n/a | Comoros | n/a | Comoros | n/a | Comoros |
| n/a | Congo, Dem. Rep. | n/a | Congo, Dem. Rep. | n/a | Congo, Dem. Rep. |
| n/a | Eritrea | n/a | Eritrea | n/a | Eritrea |
| n/a | Liberia | n/a | Liberia | n/a | Liberia |
| n/a | São Tomé & Príncipe | n/a | São Tomé & Príncipe | n/a | São Tomé & Príncipe |
| n/a | Seychelles | n/a | Seychelles | n/a | Seychelles |
| n/a | Somalia | n/a | Somalia | n/a | Somalia |
| n/a | Sudan | n/a | Sudan | n/a | Sudan |
| worst | | worst | | highest | |

# appendix B11: performance tables - business friendliness

## Corporate Tax Rate

The Heritage Foundation & The Wall Street Journal

low

| | 2008 |
|---|---|
| 1 | Mauritius |
| 2 | Botswana |
| 2 | Djibouti |
| 2 | Ghana |
| 2 | Guinea-Bissau |
| 2 | Lesotho |
| 2 | Mauritania |
| 2 | Senegal |
| 3 | South Africa |
| 4 | Cape Verde |
| 4 | Central African Rep. |
| 4 | Ethiopia |
| 4 | Kenya |
| 4 | Madagascar |
| 4 | Malawi |
| 4 | Nigeria |
| 4 | Rwanda |
| 4 | Sierra Leone |
| 4 | Swaziland |
| 4 | Tanzania |
| 4 | Uganda |
| 4 | Zimbabwe |
| 5 | Mozambique |
| 6 | Angola |
| 6 | Burkina Faso |
| 6 | Burundi |
| 6 | Côte d'Ivoire |
| 6 | Equatorial Guinea |
| 6 | Gabon |
| 6 | Gambia, The |
| 6 | Guinea |
| 6 | Mali |
| 6 | Namibia |
| 6 | Niger |
| 6 | Zambia |
| 7 | Togo |
| 8 | Benin |
| 8 | Congo, Rep. |
| 9 | Cameroon |
| 10 | Chad |
| n/a | Comoros |
| n/a | Congo, Dem. Rep. |
| n/a | Eritrea |
| n/a | Liberia |
| n/a | São Tomé & Príncipe |
| n/a | Seychelles |
| n/a | Somalia |
| n/a | Sudan |

high

## Voice and Accountability

World Bank

best

| | 1998-2002 |
|---|---|
| 1 | Mauritius |
| 2 | Botswana |
| 3 | Cape Verde |
| 4 | South Africa |
| 5 | Namibia |
| 6 | São Tomé & Príncipe |
| 7 | Benin |
| 8 | Mali |
| 9 | Seychelles |
| 10 | Madagascar |
| 11 | Senegal |
| 12 | Ghana |
| 13 | Mozambique |
| 14 | Malawi |
| 15 | Gabon |
| 16 | Tanzania |
| 17 | Burkina Faso |
| 18 | Lesotho |
| 19 | Zambia |
| 20 | Comoros |
| 21 | Mauritania |
| 22 | Central African Rep. |
| 23 | Niger |
| 24 | Kenya |
| 25 | Gambia, The |
| 26 | Djibouti |
| 27 | Chad |
| 28 | Nigeria |
| 29 | Uganda |
| 30 | Ethiopia |
| 31 | Guinea-Bissau |
| 32 | Cameroon |
| 33 | Côte d'Ivoire |
| 34 | Zimbabwe |
| 35 | Guinea |
| 36 | Togo |
| 37 | Sierra Leone |
| 38 | Swaziland |
| 39 | Angola |
| 40 | Liberia |
| 41 | Congo, Rep. |
| 42 | Eritrea |
| 43 | Rwanda |
| 44 | Burundi |
| 45 | Equatorial Guinea |
| 46 | Sudan |
| 47 | Somalia |
| 48 | Congo, Dem. Rep. |

worst

## Voice and Accountability

World Bank

best

| | 2003-2008 |
|---|---|
| 1 | Mauritius |
| 2 | Botswana |
| 3 | South Africa |
| 4 | Cape Verde |
| 5 | Namibia |
| 6 | Mali |
| 7 | Ghana |
| 8 | São Tomé & Príncipe |
| 9 | Seychelles |
| 10 | Benin |
| 11 | Senegal |
| 12 | Lesotho |
| 13 | Madagascar |
| 14 | Mozambique |
| 15 | Kenya |
| 16 | Niger |
| 17 | Zambia |
| 18 | Comoros |
| 19 | Tanzania |
| 20 | Burkina Faso |
| 21 | Malawi |
| 22 | Sierra Leone |
| 23 | Gambia, The |
| 24 | Guinea-Bissau |
| 25 | Uganda |
| 26 | Gabon |
| 27 | Nigeria |
| 28 | Djibouti |
| 29 | Mauritania |
| 30 | Congo, Rep. |
| 31 | Cameroon |
| 32 | Burundi |
| 33 | Ethiopia |
| 34 | Liberia |
| 35 | Angola |
| 36 | Guinea |
| 37 | Chad |
| 38 | Rwanda |
| 39 | Central African Rep. |
| 40 | Swaziland |
| 41 | Togo |
| 42 | Côte d'Ivoire |
| 43 | Zimbabwe |
| 44 | Equatorial Guinea |
| 45 | Sudan |
| 46 | Congo, Dem. Rep. |
| 47 | Somalia |
| 48 | Eritrea |

worst

## Political Stability

World Bank

best

| | 1998-2002 |
|---|---|
| 1 | Mauritius |
| 2 | Seychelles |
| 3 | Cape Verde |
| 4 | Botswana |
| 5 | São Tomé & Príncipe |
| 6 | Benin |
| 7 | Gambia, The |
| 8 | Mali |
| 9 | Mauritania |
| 10 | Mozambique |
| 11 | Comoros |
| 12 | Gabon |
| 13 | Namibia |
| 14 | Madagascar |
| 15 | Swaziland |
| 16 | Lesotho |
| 17 | Ghana |
| 18 | Burkina Faso |
| 19 | Equatorial Guinea |
| 20 | Tanzania |
| 21 | Togo |
| 22 | Zambia |
| 23 | Niger |
| 24 | Malawi |
| 25 | South Africa |
| 26 | Cameroon |
| 27 | Djibouti |
| 28 | Senegal |
| 29 | Côte d'Ivoire |
| 30 | Ethiopia |
| 31 | Kenya |
| 32 | Guinea |
| 33 | Guinea-Bissau |
| 34 | Eritrea |
| 35 | Congo, Rep. |
| 36 | Nigeria |
| 37 | Zimbabwe |
| 38 | Chad |
| 39 | Central African Rep. |
| 40 | Uganda |
| 41 | Sierra Leone |
| 42 | Rwanda |
| 43 | Angola |
| 44 | Liberia |
| 45 | Sudan |
| 46 | Burundi |
| 47 | Somalia |
| 48 | Congo, Dem. Rep. |

worst

## Political Stability

World Bank

best

| | 2003-2006 |
|---|---|
| 1 | Botswana |
| 2 | Mauritius |
| 3 | Seychelles |
| 4 | Cape Verde |
| 5 | Namibia |
| 6 | São Tomé & Príncipe |
| 7 | Gambia, The |
| 8 | Lesotho |
| 9 | Benin |
| 10 | Ghana |
| 11 | Mozambique |
| 12 | Gabon |
| 13 | Mali |
| 14 | Madagascar |
| 15 | Zambia |
| 16 | Swaziland |
| 17 | Malawi |
| 18 | Burkina Faso |
| 19 | South Africa |
| 20 | Comoros |
| 21 | Equatorial Guinea |
| 22 | Senegal |
| 23 | Mauritania |
| 24 | Tanzania |
| 25 | Niger |
| 26 | Cameroon |
| 27 | Djibouti |
| 28 | Guinea-Bissau |
| 29 | Sierra Leone |
| 30 | Togo |
| 31 | Eritrea |
| 32 | Rwanda |
| 33 | Angola |
| 34 | Guinea |
| 35 | Congo, Rep. |
| 36 | Kenya |
| 37 | Central African Rep. |
| 38 | Chad |
| 39 | Uganda |
| 40 | Ethiopia |
| 41 | Zimbabwe |
| 42 | Liberia |
| 43 | Burundi |
| 44 | Nigeria |
| 45 | Côte d'Ivoire |
| 46 | Sudan |
| 47 | Congo, Dem. Rep. |
| 48 | Somalia |

worst

# appendix B11: performance tables - business friendliness

| | Rank | Govt. Effectiveness<br>World Bank<br>1998-2002 | Govt. Effectiveness<br>World Bank<br>2003-2006 | Regulatory Quality<br>World Bank<br>1998-2002 | Regulatory Quality<br>World Bank<br>2003-2006 | Rule of Law<br>World Bank<br>1998-2002 |
|---|---|---|---|---|---|---|
| best | 1 | South Africa | Botswana | Botswana | Botswana | Mauritius |
| | 2 | Botswana | South Africa | Mauritius | South Africa | Cape Verde |
| | 3 | Mauritius | Mauritius | Namibia | Mauritius | Seychelles |
| | 4 | Namibia | Namibia | South Africa | Namibia | Botswana |
| | 5 | Seychelles | Cape Verde | Uganda | Uganda | Namibia |
| | 6 | Cape Verde | Seychelles | Gabon | Mauritania | South Africa |
| | 7 | Senegal | Senegal | Burkina Faso | Kenya | Lesotho |
| | 8 | Ghana | Ghana | Cape Verde | Cape Verde | Senegal |
| | 9 | Mauritania | Madagascar | Benin | Ghana | Gambia, The |
| | 10 | Lesotho | Lesotho | Senegal | Senegal | Ghana |
| | 11 | Mozambique | Mauritania | Ghana | Madagascar | Benin |
| | 12 | Benin | Mali | Mali | Burkina Faso | Gabon |
| | 13 | Gabon | Mozambique | Zambia | Gabon | São Tomé & Príncipe |
| | 14 | Malawi | Tanzania | Mozambique | Tanzania | Eritrea |
| | 15 | Tanzania | Benin | Gambia, The | Gambia, The | Mauritania |
| | 16 | Madagascar | Uganda | Côte d'Ivoire | Benin | Madagascar |
| | 17 | Uganda | Gambia, The | Malawi | Mali | Mali |
| | 18 | Gambia, The | Gabon | Mauritania | Mozambique | Tanzania |
| | 19 | São Tomé & Príncipe | Burkina Faso | Kenya | Malawi | Malawi |
| | 20 | Swaziland | Kenya | Swaziland | Niger | Zambia |
| | 21 | Burkina Faso | Ethiopia | Lesotho | Lesotho | Swaziland |
| | 22 | Chad | São Tomé & Príncipe | Tanzania | Seychelles | Burkina Faso |
| | 23 | Kenya | Rwanda | Madagascar | Swaziland | Togo |
| | 24 | Mali | Djibouti | Guinea | Zambia | Uganda |
| | 25 | Côte d'Ivoire | Malawi | Cameroon | Rwanda | Mozambique |
| | 26 | Cameroon | Niger | Niger | Cameroon | Djibouti |
| | 27 | Zambia | Swaziland | Togo | São Tomé & Príncipe | Ethiopia |
| | 28 | Zimbabwe | Cameroon | Seychelles | Djibouti | Niger |
| | 29 | Eritrea | Zambia | São Tomé & Príncipe | Togo | Chad |
| | 30 | Djibouti | Nigeria | Eritrea | Côte d'Ivoire | Kenya |
| | 31 | Ethiopia | Eritrea | Djibouti | Ethiopia | Zimbabwe |
| | 32 | Guinea | Angola | Chad | Guinea | Côte d'Ivoire |
| | 33 | Rwanda | Chad | Nigeria | Chad | Cameroon |
| | 34 | Nigeria | Guinea | Rwanda | Nigeria | Guinea |
| | 35 | Togo | Sudan | Central African Rep. | Guinea-Bissau | Comoros |
| | 36 | Niger | Sierra Leone | Ethiopia | Congo, Rep. | Rwanda |
| | 37 | Sudan | Congo, Rep. | Comoros | Sierra Leone | Equatorial Guinea |
| | 38 | Guinea-Bissau | Burundi | Guinea-Bissau | Sudan | Nigeria |
| | 39 | Angola | Côte d'Ivoire | Congo, Rep. | Burundi | Sierra Leone |
| | 40 | Comoros | Equatorial Guinea | Zimbabwe | Angola | Central African Rep. |
| | 41 | Equatorial Guinea | Guinea-Bissau | Sudan | Central African Rep. | Congo, Rep. |
| | 42 | Congo, Rep. | Zimbabwe | Burundi | Equatorial Guinea | Guinea-Bissau |
| | 43 | Burundi | Liberia | Sierra Leone | Comoros | Burundi |
| | 44 | Sierra Leone | Togo | Equatorial Guinea | Eritrea | Sudan |
| | 45 | Central African Rep. | Central African Rep. | Angola | Congo, Dem. Rep. | Angola |
| | 46 | Liberia | Congo, Dem. Rep. | Liberia | Liberia | Liberia |
| | 47 | Congo, Dem. Rep. | Comoros | Congo, Dem. Rep. | Zimbabwe | Congo, Dem. Rep. |
| | 48 | Somalia | Somalia | Somalia | Somalia | Somalia |
| worst | | | | | | |

| | Rule of Law<br>World Bank<br>2003-2006 | Control of Corruption<br>World Bank<br>1998-2002 | Control of Corruption<br>World Bank<br>2003-2006 |
|---|---|---|---|
| best 1 | Mauritius | Botswana | Botswana |
| 2 | Botswana | Eritrea | South Africa |
| 3 | Cape Verde | South Africa | Cape Verde |
| 4 | Seychelles | Mauritius | Mauritius |
| 5 | South Africa | Seychelles | Seychelles |
| 6 | Namibia | Namibia | Namibia |
| 7 | Lesotho | Cape Verde | Madagascar |
| 8 | Mali | Burkina Faso | Burkina Faso |
| 9 | Gambia, The | Mauritania | Lesotho |
| 10 | Madagascar | Swaziland | Eritrea |
| 11 | Ghana | Lesotho | Mauritania |
| 12 | Senegal | Madagascar | Ghana |
| 13 | Malawi | Senegal | Senegal |
| 14 | Tanzania | São Tomé & Príncipe | Mali |
| 15 | Mauritania | Ghana | Rwanda |
| 16 | São Tomé & Príncipe | Gambia, The | Swaziland |
| 17 | Burkina Faso | Ethiopia | Gambia, The |
| 18 | Gabon | Mali | Mozambique |
| 19 | Benin | Côte d'Ivoire | Ethiopia |
| 20 | Zambia | Malawi | Gabon |
| 21 | Eritrea | Gabon | São Tomé & Príncipe |
| 22 | Uganda | Togo | Tanzania |
| 23 | Mozambique | Benin | Djibouti |
| 24 | Ethiopia | Mozambique | Benin |
| 25 | Rwanda | Rwanda | Uganda |
| 26 | Djibouti | Guinea | Malawi |
| 27 | Swaziland | Djibouti | Comoros |
| 28 | Niger | Chad | Togo |
| 29 | Comoros | Sierra Leone | Zambia |
| 30 | Kenya | Zimbabwe | Guinea |
| 31 | Togo | Zambia | Kenya |
| 32 | Cameroon | Guinea-Bissau | Cameroon |
| 33 | Sierra Leone | Uganda | Niger |
| 34 | Burundi | Sudan | Burundi |
| 35 | Guinea-Bissau | Comoros | Congo, Rep. |
| 36 | Chad | Niger | Sierra Leone |
| 37 | Equatorial Guinea | Tanzania | Guinea-Bissau |
| 38 | Guinea | Kenya | Liberia |
| 39 | Congo, Rep. | Congo, Rep. | Côte d'Ivoire |
| 40 | Angola | Burundi | Angola |
| 41 | Nigeria | Cameroon | Central African Rep. |
| 42 | Liberia | Central African Rep. | Chad |
| 43 | Sudan | Nigeria | Sudan |
| 44 | Côte d'Ivoire | Angola | Zimbabwe |
| 45 | Central African Rep. | Somalia | Nigeria |
| 46 | Zimbabwe | Congo, Dem. Rep. | Congo, Dem. Rep. |
| 47 | Congo, Dem. Rep. | Liberia | Equatorial Guinea |
| 48 | Somalia | Equatorial Guinea | Somalia |
| worst | | | |

### General-Size

IMF, World Bank, UNPD

| | 2009 |
|---|---|
| top 1 | Nigeria |
| 2 | South Africa |
| 3 | Ethiopia |
| 4 | Kenya |
| 4 | Tanzania |
| 5 | Angola |
| 5 | Congo, Dem. Rep. |
| 5 | Ghana |
| 6 | Cameroon |
| 6 | Uganda |
| 7 | Cote d'Ivoire |
| 8 | Mozambique |
| 9 | Madagascar |
| 10 | Senegal |
| 11 | Burkina Faso |
| 12 | Zambia |
| 13 | Mali |
| 14 | Chad |
| 14 | Malawi |
| 15 | Niger |
| 16 | Botswana |
| 17 | Guinea |
| 18 | Benin |
| 19 | Gabon |
| 20 | Congo, Rep. |
| 21 | Rwanda |
| 22 | Equatorial Guinea |
| 22 | Togo |
| 23 | Mauritius |
| 23 | Namibia |
| 23 | Sierra Leone |
| 24 | Burundi |
| 24 | Eritrea |
| 25 | Central African Rep. |
| 26 | Lesotho |
| 27 | Swaziland |
| 28 | Gambia, The |
| 29 | Guinea-Bissau |
| 30 | Cape Verde |
| 31 | Comoros |
| 31 | Seychelles |
| n/a | Djibouti |
| n/a | Liberia |
| n/a | Mauritania |
| n/a | São Tomé & Príncipe |
| n/a | Somalia |
| n/a | Sudan |
| n/a | Zimbabwe |
| bottom | |

### Quality of Life

UNDP, UNICEF, AfDB, ITU, UNPD

| | 2003-2007 |
|---|---|
| top 1 | Mauritius |
| 2 | Seychelles |
| 3 | Cape Verde |
| 4 | South Africa |
| 5 | Gambia, The |
| 6 | Namibia |
| 7 | Botswana |
| 8 | Gabon |
| 9 | Comoros |
| 10 | Senegal |
| 11 | Ghana |
| 12 | Togo |
| 13 | Uganda |
| 14 | Kenya |
| 15 | Eritrea |
| 16 | Swaziland |
| 17 | Benin |
| 18 | Tanzania |
| 19 | Lesotho |
| 20 | Cameroon |
| 21 | Nigeria |
| 22 | Equatorial Guinea |
| 23 | Congo, Rep. |
| 24 | Madagascar |
| 25 | Zambia |
| 26 | Cote d'Ivoire |
| 27 | Malawi |
| 28 | Mozambique |
| 29 | Guinea |
| 30 | Rwanda |
| 31 | Burundi |
| 32 | Mali |
| 33 | Ethiopia |
| 34 | Burkina Faso |
| 35 | Guinea-Bissau |
| 36 | Angola |
| 37 | Niger |
| 38 | Congo, Dem. Rep. |
| 39 | Chad |
| 40 | Central African Rep. |
| 41 | Sierra Leone |
| n/a | Djibouti |
| n/a | Liberia |
| n/a | Mauritania |
| n/a | São Tomé & Príncipe |
| n/a | Somalia |
| n/a | Sudan |
| n/a | Zimbabwe |
| bottom | |

### Economic Strength

IMF, World Bank

| | 2003-2006 |
|---|---|
| top 1 | Equatorial Guinea |
| 2 | Cape Verde |
| 3 | Chad |
| 4 | Botswana |
| 5 | South Africa |
| 6 | Senegal |
| 7 | Mauritius |
| 8 | Angola |
| 9 | Namibia |
| 10 | Burkina Faso |
| 11 | Mali |
| 12 | Nigeria |
| 13 | Cameroon |
| 14 | Tanzania |
| 15 | Congo, Rep. |
| 16 | Gabon |
| 17 | Seychelles |
| 18 | Lesotho |
| 19 | Madagascar |
| 20 | Ethiopia |
| 21 | Benin |
| 22 | Swaziland |
| 23 | Gambia, The |
| 24 | Kenya |
| 25 | Ghana |
| 26 | Sierra Leone |
| 27 | Mozambique |
| 28 | Cote d'Ivoire |
| 29 | Niger |
| 30 | Uganda |
| 31 | Togo |
| 32 | Comoros |
| 33 | Zambia |
| 34 | Rwanda |
| 35 | Congo, Dem. Rep. |
| 36 | Malawi |
| 37 | Guinea-Bissau |
| 38 | Central African Rep. |
| 39 | Guinea |
| 40 | Burundi |
| 41 | Eritrea |
| n/a | Djibouti |
| n/a | Liberia |
| n/a | Mauritania |
| n/a | São Tomé & Príncipe |
| n/a | Somalia |
| n/a | Sudan |
| n/a | Zimbabwe |
| bottom | |

# appendix B12: performance tables - the final (end-chapter) ratings

| | Economic Productivity<br>AfDB, IMF, World Bank | | Govt. Earnings & Spending<br>AfDB, IMF, World Bank | | Spending on Health<br>World Bank, WHO | | Purchasing Power<br>IMF, World Bank | | Self-Reliance<br>AfDB, IMF, World Bank, WTO |
|---|---|---|---|---|---|---|---|---|---|
| | 2003-2006 | | 2003-2006 | | 2003-2006 | | 2003-2006 | | 2003-2006 |
| top 1 | Angola | top 1 | Equatorial Guinea | top 1 | Botswana | top 1 | Cape Verde | top 1 | Nigeria |
| 2 | Namibia | 2 | Botswana | 2 | Namibia | 2 | Gabon | 2 | Kenya |
| 3 | Botswana | 3 | Swaziland | 3 | Malawi | 3 | Mauritius | 3 | Equatorial Guinea |
| 4 | Mauritius | 4 | Angola | 4 | Rwanda | 4 | Madagascar | 4 | South Africa |
| 5 | Cape Verde | 4 | Congo, Rep. | 5 | South Africa | 5 | Comoros | 5 | Benin |
| 6 | Swaziland | 4 | Lesotho | 6 | Swaziland | 6 | South Africa | 6 | Tanzania |
| 7 | Gabon | 5 | Seychelles | 7 | Seychelles | 7 | Central African Rep. | 7 | Mauritius |
| 8 | Seychelles | 6 | Namibia | 8 | Uganda | 8 | Ghana | 8 | Niger |
| 9 | South Africa | 7 | Ghana | 9 | Zambia | 9 | Malawi | 9 | Mali |
| 10 | Ghana | 8 | Nigeria | 10 | Lesotho | 10 | Botswana | 10 | Burkina Faso |
| 10 | Tanzania | 8 | South Africa | 11 | Mozambique | 11 | Sierra Leone | 11 | Central African Rep. |
| 11 | Nigeria | 9 | Cape Verde | 12 | Burkina Faso | 12 | Kenya | 12 | Botswana |
| 12 | Kenya | 10 | Burundi | 13 | Gambia, The | 13 | Ethiopia | 13 | Cameroon |
| 12 | Equatorial Guinea | 11 | Gabon | 14 | Cape Verde | 14 | Guinea | 14 | Comoros |
| 13 | Madagascar | 12 | Mauritius | 15 | Gabon | 15 | Senegal | 15 | Ethiopia |
| 14 | Cameroon | 13 | Chad | 16 | Mauritius | 16 | Swaziland | 16 | Angola |
| 15 | Senegal | 13 | Mozambique | 17 | Equatorial Guinea | 17 | Gambia, The | 17 | Cote d'Ivoire |
| 16 | Zambia | 14 | Gambia, The | 18 | Ghana | 18 | Lesotho | 18 | Namibia |
| 17 | Benin | 14 | Malawi | 19 | Tanzania | 19 | Mali | 19 | Congo, Dem. Rep. |
| 18 | Burkina Faso | 15 | Mali | 20 | Mali | 20 | Angola | 20 | Gabon |
| 19 | Cote d'Ivoire | 16 | Eritrea | 21 | Madagascar | 21 | Tanzania | 21 | Togo |
| 20 | Chad | 17 | Cameroon | 22 | Kenya | 22 | Rwanda | 22 | Senegal |
| 21 | Congo, Rep. | 17 | Rwanda | 23 | Guinea-Bissau | 23 | Burkina Faso | 23 | Chad |
| 21 | Gambia, The | 18 | Senegal | 24 | Benin | 24 | Seychelles | 24 | Mozambique |
| 22 | Mali | 19 | Ethiopia | 25 | Ethiopia | 25 | Congo, Dem. Rep. | 25 | Sierra Leone |
| 23 | Mozambique | 20 | Kenya | 26 | Togo | 26 | Benin | 26 | Madagascar |
| 24 | Ethiopia | 20 | Sierra Leone | 27 | Niger | 27 | Congo, Rep. | 27 | Guinea |
| 24 | Rwanda | 21 | Benin | 28 | Senegal | 28 | Togo | 28 | Uganda |
| 25 | Lesotho | 21 | Congo, Dem. Rep. | 29 | Cameroon | 29 | Cameroon | 29 | Rwanda |
| 26 | Sierra Leone | 22 | Uganda | 30 | Central African Rep. | 30 | Cote d'Ivoire | 30 | Ghana |
| 27 | Togo | 23 | Guinea-Bissau | 31 | Chad | 31 | Namibia | 31 | Congo, Rep. |
| 28 | Comoros | 24 | Tanzania | 32 | Eritrea | 32 | Uganda | 32 | Zambia |
| 28 | Malawi | 25 | Zambia | 33 | Guinea | 33 | Niger | 33 | Lesotho |
| 29 | Uganda | 26 | Cote d'Ivoire | 34 | Angola | 34 | Eritrea | 34 | Guinea-Bissau |
| 30 | Guinea | 26 | Madagascar | 35 | Sierra Leone | 35 | Guinea-Bissau | 35 | Seychelles |
| 31 | Eritrea | 27 | Burkina Faso | 36 | Cote d'Ivoire | 36 | Mozambique | 36 | Cape Verde |
| 32 | Congo, Dem. Rep. | 28 | Niger | 37 | Comoros | 37 | Burundi | 37 | Malawi |
| 33 | Niger | 28 | Togo | 38 | Nigeria | 38 | Zambia | 38 | Burundi |
| 34 | Central African Rep. | 29 | Comoros | 39 | Congo, Dem. Rep. | 39 | Chad | 39 | Swaziland |
| 35 | Burundi | 30 | Central African Rep. | 40 | Burundi | 40 | Equatorial Guinea | 40 | Gambia, The |
| 36 | Guinea-Bissau | 31 | Guinea | 41 | Congo, Rep. | 41 | Nigeria | 41 | Eritrea |
| n/a | Djibouti | n/a | Djibouti | n/a | Djibouti | n/a | Djibouti | n/a | Djibouti |
| n/a | Liberia | n/a | Liberia | n/a | Liberia | n/a | Liberia | n/a | Liberia |
| n/a | Mauritania | n/a | Mauritania | n/a | Mauritania | n/a | Mauritania | n/a | Mauritania |
| n/a | São Tomé & Príncipe | n/a | São Tomé & Príncipe | n/a | São Tomé & Príncipe | n/a | São Tomé & Príncipe | n/a | São Tomé & Príncipe |
| n/a | Somalia | n/a | Somalia | n/a | Somalia | n/a | Somalia | n/a | Somalia |
| n/a | Sudan | n/a | Sudan | n/a | Sudan | n/a | Sudan | n/a | Sudan |
| n/a | Zimbabwe | n/a | Zimbabwe | n/a | Zimbabwe | n/a | Zimbabwe | n/a | Zimbabwe |
| bottom | | bottom | | bottom | | bottom | | bottom | |

### Investor Confidence

AfDB, IMF, UNCTAD, World Bank

| | | 2003-2006 |
|---|---|---|
| top | 1 | Equatorial Guinea |
| | 2 | Seychelles |
| | 3 | Namibia |
| | 4 | Cape Verde |
| | 5 | Botswana |
| | 6 | South Africa |
| | 7 | Zambia |
| | 8 | Ghana |
| | 9 | Mauritius |
| | 10 | Congo, Rep. |
| | 11 | Senegal |
| | 12 | Nigeria |
| | 13 | Gabon |
| | 14 | Gambia, The |
| | 15 | Lesotho |
| | 15 | Uganda |
| | 16 | Angola |
| | 17 | Chad |
| | 18 | Tanzania |
| | 19 | Benin |
| | 20 | Burkina Faso |
| | 21 | Kenya |
| | 22 | Malawi |
| | 23 | Mozambique |
| | 24 | Madagascar |
| | 25 | Ethiopia |
| | 26 | Mali |
| | 27 | Cameroon |
| | 28 | Niger |
| | 29 | Swaziland |
| | 30 | Sierra Leone |
| | 31 | Togo |
| | 32 | Cote d'Ivoire |
| | 32 | Rwanda |
| | 33 | Guinea |
| | 33 | Guinea-Bissau |
| | 34 | Burundi |
| | 35 | Congo, Dem. Rep. |
| | 36 | Central African Rep. |
| | 37 | Eritrea |
| | 38 | Comoros |
| | n/a | Djibouti |
| | n/a | Liberia |
| | n/a | Mauritania |
| | n/a | São Tomé & Príncipe |
| | n/a | Somalia |
| | n/a | Sudan |
| | n/a | Zimbabwe |
| bottom | | |

### Regulatory Environment

AfDB, IMF, UNCTAD, World Bank

| | | 2009 |
|---|---|---|
| top | 1 | Mauritius |
| | 2 | South Africa |
| | 3 | Botswana |
| | 4 | Namibia |
| | 5 | Kenya |
| | 6 | Ghana |
| | 7 | Zambia |
| | 8 | Seychelles |
| | 9 | Swaziland |
| | 10 | Uganda |
| | 11 | Ethiopia |
| | 12 | Nigeria |
| | 13 | Lesotho |
| | 14 | Tanzania |
| | 15 | Gambia, The |
| | 16 | Malawi |
| | 17 | Rwanda |
| | 18 | Mozambique |
| | 19 | Cape Verde |
| | 20 | Madagascar |
| | 21 | Burkina Faso |
| | 22 | Senegal |
| | 23 | Gabon |
| | 24 | Comoros |
| | 25 | Sierra Leone |
| | 26 | Côte d'Ivoire |
| | 27 | Togo |
| | 28 | Cameroon |
| | 29 | Mali |
| | 30 | Equatorial Guinea |
| | 31 | Angola |
| | 32 | Benin |
| | 33 | Guinea |
| | 34 | Niger |
| | 35 | Eritrea |
| | 36 | Chad |
| | 37 | Burundi |
| | 38 | Congo, Rep. |
| | 39 | Guinea-Bissau |
| | 40 | Central African Rep. |
| | 41 | Congo, Dem. Rep. |
| | n/a | Djibouti |
| | n/a | Liberia |
| | n/a | Mauritania |
| | n/a | São Tomé & Príncipe |
| | n/a | Somalia |
| | n/a | Sudan |
| | n/a | Zimbabwe |
| bottom | | |

www.ingramcontent.com/pod-product-compliance
Lightning Source LLC
LaVergne TN
LVHW070943210926
848482LV00002B/82
*9780956452603*